MW01170651

BLACK
CAT
PUBLISHING

Editorial, Sales and Customer Service Office

BLACK CAT PUBLISHING INC.
2010 JIMMY DURANTE BLVD. SUITE 100
DEL MAR, CA 92014
USA

http://www.black-cat.pub

Copyright © 2024 by Black Cat Publishing

All rights reserved. No part of the material protected by this copyright notice may be reproduced or utilized in any form, electronic or mechanical, including photocopying, recording, or by any information storage and retrieval system, without written permission from the copyright owner.

Dedication

I would like to dedicate this book to my parents:

Fritz und Elli Engel

I miss them every day. I want to thank especially my family whose support is substantial for all my "little" projects: my wife Katja, our daughters Anna, Emma, and Lena.

—Wolfgang Engel

I would like to dedicate this book to my parents first, whose efforts started it all:

Haitham Bahnassi and Nuha Tahseen. Thanks for everything!

And to my wife Suzy, and to my sons: Omar and Sami.
Love you always, proud of you always!

—Wessam Bahnassi

I would like to dedicate this book to my dad and my husband.

Jeff Wieme, thanks for always encouraging my interest and passion for computers and graphics early on. Mitya Reznikov, thank you for being so supportive of my career and ensuring I have the time and energy to pursue opportunities.

And to Professor Joe Geigel, who saw my potential in computer science and continues to connect the arts and sciences.
Thank you for all you do to guide students to their dream careers.

—Laura Reznikov

I would like to dedicate this book to my family:

My wife Asya Kaplanyan, and my three daughters, Diana, Olivia, and Emily Kaplanyan.

You are my everyday support and the source of inspiration!

—Anton Kaplanyan

I would like to dedicate this book to my grandfather Vladimir, his kindness, brilliant mind and contributions to science were always inspiring me in my life.

—Kirill Bazhenov

I would like to dedicate this book to my wife, my greatest supporter, Wenjia.

And to my son, Leo. I'm so proud of you!

—Nicolas Lopez

Preface

"The reading of all good books is like a conversation with the finest minds of past centuries."

—Rene Descartes (1596–1650)

Like its long line of predecessors, this book is intended to help readers better achieve their goals. It wouldn't have been possible without the help of many people. First and foremost, I would like to thank the following people who helped edit this book:

- Laura Reznikov

- Anton S. Kaplanyan

- Kirill Bazhenov

- Nicolas Lopez

- Peter Sikachev

- Wessam Bahnassi

The cover image depicts a scene from Ubisoft's *Assassin's Creed Mirage*. I would like to thank Nicolas Lugand, Florence Baccard, Marc-Alexis Côté, and Nicolas Lopez for giving us permission to use this image.

I also want to thank Charlotte Byrnes for copy-editing the book.

For the first time, this edition of the book series is sponsored by a company, The Forge Interactive. The Forge covered the Overleaf membership, the cost of designing the cover, the cost of copy-editing, and the cost of sending T-shirts and books to the authors and editors.

My special thanks go out to everyone for supporting this book series and its predecessors since 2001. These books started friendships, careers, companies, and much more over the years. They certainly changed my life in awesome ways!

Love and Peace,

—Wolfgang Engel

Contents

Dedication   3

Preface   5

I   GPU-Driven Rendering   15
Nicolas Lopez and Wolfgang Engel, Editors

1   GPU-Driven Rendering in Assassin's Creed Mirage   17
William Bussière and Nicolas Lopez
   1.1   Introduction 17
   1.2   Database 20
   1.3   CPU Data Management 29
   1.4   GPU Culling 33
   1.5   Bindless Material Management 45
   1.6   Rendering 48
   1.7   Results 51
   1.8   Conclusion and Future Work 53
   1.9   Appendix 55
   Bibliography 59

2   GPU-Driven Curve Generation from Mesh Contour   61
Wangziwei Jiang
   2.1   Introduction 61
   2.2   Overview 61
   2.3   Implementation 66
   2.4   Conclusion and Future Work 82
   Bibliography 84

3   GPU Readback Texture Streaming in Skull and Bones   87
    Malte Bennewitz and Kaori Kato
    3.1   Introduction   87
    3.2   Implementation   87
    3.3   Result   92
    3.4   Conclusion and Future Work   96
    Bibliography   97

4   Triangle Visibility Buffer 2.0   99
    Manas Kulkarni, and Wolfgang Engel
    4.1   Introduction and History   99
    4.2   Overview   101
    4.3   Triangle Filtering 103
    4.4   Bin Rasterization   105
    4.5   Forward++ Shading   106
    4.6   Compute-Driven Triangle Visibility Buffer Benefits 107
    4.7   Performance Results   107
    4.8   Conclusion and Future Development   108
    Bibliography   109

5   Resource Management with Frame Graph in Messiah   111
    Yuwen Wu
    5.1   Introduction   111
    5.2   Overview   111
    5.3   Resource Lifespans   112
    5.4   Transient Resource Allocation 114
    5.5   Ping-Pong Buffers 119
    5.6   Results 121
    5.7   Conclusion   121
    Bibliography   122

6   Multi-mega Particle System   123
    Nicola Palomba and Wolfgang Engel
    6.1   Introduction   123
    6.2   Data Management   125
    6.3   Workflow   130
    6.4   Simulation   130
    6.5   Lighting 137
    6.6   Transparency   139
    6.7   Results 141
    6.8   Conclusions and Future Work   146
    Bibliography   147

II   Rendering and Simulation   149
     Laura Reznikov and Peter Sikachev, Editors

7   The Evolution of the Real-Time Lighting Pipeline in Cyberpunk 2077   151
     Jakub Knapik, Giovanni De Francesco, Dmitrii Zhdan, Edward Liu,
     Evgeny Makarov, Jon Kennedy, Juho Marttila, Michael Murphy,
     Nathan Hoobler, Tim Cheblokov, and Pawel Kozlowski
     7.1   Introduction   152
     7.2   Overview   157
     Part 1. Ray Tracing: Bringing More Realism to Night City   161
     7.3   Ray Tracing Prerequisites   161
     7.4   Directly Sampled Lighting   170
     7.5   Indirectly Sampled Lighting   175
     7.6   Denoising and Supersampling   180
     7.7   Performance   189
     Part 2. Path Tracing: The Unified Lighting Pipeline of the Future .   190
     7.8   Transitioning to Physically Based Lighting   190
     7.9   Increasing Effective Sample Count with ReSTIR   194
     7.10 Improving Sampling Quality with Radiance Caching   203
     7.11 Denoising and Supersampling   213
     7.12 Performance   225
     Part 3. Leveraging AI for Enhanced Performance and Visual Fidelity   226
     7.13 Unified Image Reconstruction   226
     7.14 Frame Generation   233
     7.15 Final Performance   240
     7.16 Future Directions   241
     Bibliography   242

8   Real-Time Ray Tracing of Large Voxel Scenes   247
     Russel Arbore, Jeffrey Liu, Aidan Wefel, Steven Gao, and Eric
     Shaffer
     8.1   Introduction   247
     8.2   History and Related Work   248
     8.3   Voxel Formats   249
     8.4   Voxel Ray Tracing   254
     8.5   Streaming Voxels   258
     8.6   Creating Voxel Models   260
     8.7   Further Extensions   264
     8.8   Conclusions   266
     Bibliography   267

9   Optimizing FSR 2 for Adreno   271
     Randall Rauwendaal
     9.1   Introduction   271
     9.2   Background   271

9.3   Requirements   271
9.4   Mobile vs. Discrete GPU Architecture   272
9.5   Analysis   272
9.6   Optimizations   274
9.7   Conclusion   279
Bibliography   280

10 IBL-BRDF Multiple Importance Sampling for Stochastic Screen-Space
   Indirect Specular   283
   سفيان خياط (Soufiane KHIAT)
   10.1 Introduction   283
   10.2 Approach   285
   10.3 Sampling Theory   287
   10.4 Data Generation   291
   10.5 Runtime Sampling   299
   10.6 Off-Screen Extension   301
   10.7 Limits   302
   10.8 Future Work   304
   10.9 Conclusion   305
   Bibliography   305

11 Practical Clustered Forward Decals   309
   Kirill Bazhenov
   11.1 Introduction   309
   11.2 Forward Decals   309
   11.3 Additional Decal Features   315
   11.4 Conclusion   317
   Bibliography   318

12 Virtual Shadow Maps   319
   Matej Sakmary, Jake Ryan, Justin Hall, and Alessio Lustri
   12.1 Introduction   319
   12.2 Implementation   321
   12.3 Results   333
   12.4 Future Work   334
   12.5 Acknowledgements   335
   Bibliography   336

13 Real-Time Simulation of Massive Crowds   339
   Tomer Weiss
   13.1 Introduction   339
   13.2 Method   340
   13.3 Results   345
   13.4 Implementation   346

13.5 Conclusion 349
Bibliography 349

14 Diffuse Global Illumination 351
Darius Bouma
14.1 Introduction 351
14.2 Clipmap Irradiance Cache 352
14.3 Diffuse ReSTIR GI 363
14.4 Future Work 373
Bibliography 374

III Game Engine Design 377
Wessam Bahnassi, Editor

15 GPU Capability Tracking and Configuration System 379
Thibault Ober and Wolfgang Engel
15.1 Introduction 379
15.2 The Technique 379
15.3 GPU Performance Index 380
15.4 GPU Hardware Configuration 381
15.5 Available Properties 383
15.6 Further Ideas and Improvements 383
15.7 Conclusion 384
Bibliography 385

16 The Forge Shader Language 387
Manas Kulkarni, and Wolfgang Engel
16.1 Introduction 387
16.2 System Overview 388
16.3 FSL Syntax 391
16.4 Example 395
16.5 Further Ideas and Improvements 396
16.6 Conclusion 397
Bibliography 397

17 Simple Automatic Resource Synchronization Method for Vulkan Applications 399
Grigory Javadyan
17.1 Introduction 399
17.2 The Technique 401
17.3 Synchronization State and Synchronization Request 405
17.4 Emitting Barriers 410
17.5 Synchronization in a Single Command Buffer 411

17.6 Synchronization across Command Buffers   413
17.7 Limitations   414
17.8 Results   415
17.9 Future Work   417
17.10 Conclusion   418
Bibliography   418

IV Tools of the Trade   421
   Kirill Bazhenov and Anton Kaplanyan, Editors

18 Differentiable Graphics with Slang.D for Appearance-Based Optimization   423
   Bartlomiej Wronski, Sai Bangaru, Marco Salvi, Yong He, Lifan Wu,
   and Jacob Munkberg
   18.1 Introduction   423
   18.2 What Is Differentiable Programming?   424
   18.3 Differentiable Shader Programming with Slang   433
   18.4 Applications   440
   18.5 Conclusion   450
   Bibliography   451

19 DRToolkit: Boosting Rendering Performance Using Differentiable Rendering   455
   Chen Qiao, Xiang Lan, Yijie Shi, Xueqiang Wang, Xilei Wei, and
   Jiang Qin
   19.1 Introduction   455
   19.2 Overview of Differentiable Rendering   457
   19.3 System Overview   459
   19.4 Renderer Implementation   461
   19.5 Handling Materials   464
   19.6 Processing of Meshes   474
   19.7 Processing of Global Parameters   477
   19.8 Workflow Integration   478
   19.9 Conclusion and Future Work   480
   Bibliography   481

20 Flowmap Baking with LBM-SWE   485
   Wei Li, Haozhe Su, Zherong Pan, Xifeng Gao, Zhenyu Mao, and
   Kui Wu
   20.1 Introduction   485
   20.2 Related Work   486
   20.3 Background   487
   20.4 Our Method   489
   20.5 Results   492
   20.6 Conclusion   495
   Bibliography   495

21 Animating Water Using Profile Buffer   499
Haozhe Su, Wei Li, Zherong Pan, Xifeng Gao, Zhenyu Mao, and
Kui Wu
21.1 Introduction   499
21.2 Background   499
21.3 Our Method   500
21.4 Implementation Details   503
21.5 Results   510
21.6 Conclusion   513
Bibliography   513

22 Advanced Techniques for Radix Sort   515
Atsushi Yoshimura and Chih-Chen Kao
22.1 Introduction   515
22.2 Conventional Radix Sort   516
22.3 Classic Radix Sort on the GPU   516
22.4 Decoupled Look-Back and Onesweep   518
22.5 Optimizations   523
22.6 Performance   525
22.7 Conclusion   527
Bibliography   527

23 Two-Pass HZB Occlusion Culling   529
Miloš Kruškonja
23.1 Introduction   529
23.2 Brief Overview of HZB Culling   529
23.3 Problem   530
23.4 Potential Solutions   531
23.5 Two-Pass Solution   532
23.6 Conclusion   539
Bibliography   540

24 Shader Server System   543
Djordje Pepic
24.1 Introduction   543
24.2 Typical Features of a Shader Compiler   543
24.3 Designing a Dynamic Shader Recompilation System   546
24.4 Considerations when Implementing the Shader Server   551
24.5 Considerations for a Production-Ready Implementation   555
24.6 Conclusion   557
Bibliography   557

About the Editors   559

About the Authors   561

GPU-Driven Rendering

Nicolas Lopez and Wolfgang Engel, Editors

The GPU-driven rendering section represents rendering techniques initiated on the GPU without any or fewer CPU interactions. These techniques require all or most rendering data in GPU memory.

One of the first game teams to present a paper on GPU-driven rendering was the team behind Ubisoft's Anvil engine in 2015. This engine produces games like the *Assassin's Creed* series, *Rainbow Six Siege*, *Ghost Recon Breakpoint*, and *For Honor*. The article "GPU Driven Rendering in *Assassin's Creed Mirage*," by William Bussière and Nicolas Lopez, recaps the last nine years of engine development and explains the architecture behind the impressive visual and performance results in an open-world setting. The authors call their new and improved renderer GPU Instance Renderer (GPUIR). It relies heavily on a database as an efficient way to share the whole scene description between the CPU and GPU. GPUIR utilizes several levels for GPU culling of data (cluster, frustum, and triangle culling on GPU), bindless material management for the vast amount of art assets, and then the actual vertex and pixel shader setup to render large-scale open-world games. If you only have time to read one article in this book, read this one!

The next article, "GPU-Driven Curve Generation from Mesh Contour" by Wangziwei Jiang, introduces the first GPU-driven approach that generates curves from the mesh contour faster than existing approaches with comparable visual results. Additionally, this approach allows vectorizing binary images, leading to broader usage. The article describes a technique that takes in triangulated meshes and outputs a 2D curve, with each curve corresponding to a contiguous portion of the visible contour.

The article "GPU Readback Texture Streaming in *Skull and Bones*," by Malte Bennewitz and Kaori Kato, describes a GPU-driven texture streaming system. It computes the sampled mipmap level in pixels on the screen and reads the computed mipmap level back to the CPU to decide which texture mipmaps to stream in and out. Several options exist for implementing GPU feedback for texture streaming on various gaming platforms. This article describes a cross-platform approach in software that essentially writes the information about required mipmap levels during the G-buffer pass into a UAV texture. This texture has two 16-bit unsigned integer channels: The R channel contains the material ID; the G channel holds the computed mipmap level for up to four UV variables. One material can support up to four unique UV variables for readback texture streaming.

The next article, "Triangle Visibility Buffer 2.0" (TVB 2.0) by Manas Kulkarni and Wolfgang Engel, describes advances in GPU-driven rendering by omitting the whole graphics pipeline to store visibility and depth information into a common 64-bit buffer. Instead of preparing and massaging the triangle data to fit into the indirect draw call workflow, the authors store the triangle visibility and depth values in one buffer with one compute shader, utilizing a simplified rasterizer. TVB 2.0 can render small triangles more efficiently, as it doesn't pay the additional cost of helper lanes and exploits various additional benefits when implementing order-independent transparency, ray tracing, and other graphics techniques. It greatly simplifies code complexity, minimizes memory access to buffers, and exemplifies the trend toward compute-driven rendering without dependency on mesh shaders or other shader types.

The article "Resource Management with Frame Graph in Messiah," by Yuwen Wu, describes a frame graph system with automatic resource management, i.e., automatic resource creation, reuse, and aliasing. It shows their relationship with different problems in computational graph theory. Due to the computational complexity of these problems, optimal solutions may not be feasible. Hence, the author provides greedy algorithms for each scheme. Lastly, this article discusses the management of ping-pong buffers.

The last article, "Multi-mega Particle System" by Nicola Palomba and Wolfgang Engel, describes a GPU-driven particle system architecture that offers particle sets of hundreds of thousands or millions of particles on a mobile phone like the Samsung Galaxy S22. This is achieved by reducing the interactions between GPU and CPU to a minimum by having most of the implementation contained in one compute shader, reducing the number of times that data is accessed in memory. This approach uses a unique way of sorting the particle data on the GPU and consists of three phases: The first phase is used to prepare all the others. It produces the data to sort particles by particle set visibility and computes the bounds of each section of the buffers. The second and most important phase is simulation. This is the only phase that can potentially access the entirety of the particle buffer. The simulation shader initializes particles, kills or respawns them, sorts each section of the buffer, performs part of light culling, rasterizes small particles, and updates each particle's velocity, age, and position. The third phase renders particles too big (in screen space) for the software rasterizer to handle.

We hope you have as much fun reading this section as we had editing it!

—Nicolas Lopez and Wolfgang Engel

GPU-Driven Rendering in Assassin's Creed Mirage

William Bussière and Nicolas Lopez

1.1 Introduction

1.1.1 Anvil Engine

The Anvil game engine is mostly known for being used to produce the *Assassin's Creed* games, but it has also shipped other big franchises such as *Rainbow Six Siege*, *Ghost Recon Breakpoint*, and *For Honor*. It's an engine mostly designed for large systemic worlds with a focus on long-range rendering, massive instance count, and systemic gameplay (Figure 1.1).

Figure 1.1. Large-scale rendering in *Assassin's Creed Mirage*.

1.1.2 Previous Work

Anvil pioneered the use of GPU-driven pipelines in games with *Assassin's Creed Unity* [Haar and Aaltonen 15], released in 2014, and *Rainbow Six Siege*, released in 2015. GPU-driven pipelines have been the cornerstone of all Anvil-based games since then, being improved over time.

Figure 1.2. Clustered culling in *Assassin's Creed Unity*.

In this iteration, all meshes are clustered (Figure 1.2), dynamically batched together (per material), culled on the GPU (per instance, cluster, triangle), and indirectly dispatched via `MultiDrawIndexedInstancedIndirect`. While the concept of clustered meshes is relatively new for video game engines, it has a long-standing history in academic research, as shown in [Kumar et al. 96] or [Cignoni et al. 05]. Also, [Haar and Aaltonen 15] introduced the use of camera depth reprojection, based on [Silvennoinen 12], to remove shadow casters that cannot have any visible shadow receivers and to speed up cascaded shadow map rendering (Figure 1.3).

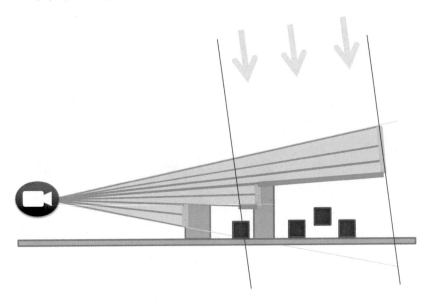

Figure 1.3. Cascaded shadow map rendering optimization with camera depth reprojection. The yellow arrows show the sun direction, and the red lines the extent of the shadow map cascade. The red objects are shadow casters that cannot have a valid receiver as the ground, and the blue objects hide all possible receivers.

Later, [Wihlidal 17] built upon [Haar and Aaltonen 15] and improved triangle culling with a full compute shader-based implementation, while [Haar and Aaltonen 15] precomputed a static per-cluster triangle visibility mask based on a set of fixed angles. Finally, [Karis 21] introduced a virtual geometry pipeline, with cluster level-of-detail (LOD) hierarchies, following the idea of [Cignoni et al. 05], and using mesh shaders and software rasterization for small triangles based on triangle size classification.

1.1.3 Rational

The first iteration of our GPU-driven pipeline was named *BatchRenderer* and designed with DirectX 11 class APIs in mind (Figure 1.4). The main goal of the BatchRenderer was to reduce the cost of very expensive DirectX 11 individual draw calls by leveraging `MultiDrawIndexedInstancedIndirect`. Although, it has several drawbacks:

- **No async:** Culling is done right before rendering.

- **No bindless:** It only supports per-material batching.

- It's either useless or too complex for graphic objects that do not support or require batching.

- It is too inefficient for highly batched graphic objects that are instantiated thousands of times.

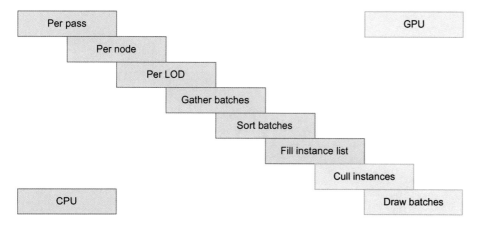

Figure 1.4. The BatchRenderer still had a significant chunk of work performed on the CPU. The GPU side was more complex than indicated here because of cluster expansion and culling.

We worked on a complete rewrite of this system for *Assassin's Creed Valhalla* and *Assassin's Creed Mirage*, designed around DirectX 12 class APIs. We call it the *GPU Instance Renderer* (GPUIR). With the GPUIR, we address the BatchRenderer drawbacks with:

- **Reduced CPU time:** Batch on load, move more steps to the GPU, and more efficient per-shader batching using bindless resources.

- **Reduced GPU time:** Asynchronous per-frame and pass instance culling, and cluster and triangle culling being performed at render time.

- **Limited to opaque static or skinned** mesh instances and their LOD transitions; tightly coupled with mesh LOD selection and texture streaming.

The GPU Instance Renderer is a high-throughput renderer, based on the same core idea of a GPU-driven culling pipeline with a strong emphasis on pre-batching at load/creation time. Through bindless materials and a global geometry buffer, it allows CPU batching "per-shader" instead of "per-material" or "per-geometry." Contrary to the BatchRenderer, it handles stateful LOD transitions on the GPU and takes as input only a list of instance groups (`LeafNodes`) which are then expanded into individual draw calls per pass (e.g., `ZPrepass`, `GBufferPass`) on the GPU (Figure 1.5).

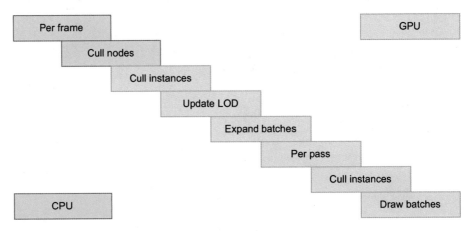

Figure 1.5. With the GPU Instance Renderer, more work was moved to the GPU thanks to the use of Database (Section 1.2) to describe the whole scene on the GPU.

1.2 Database

The GPUIR relies heavily on *Database* as an efficient way to share the full-scene description between the CPU and the GPU. It is one of the backbones of our new GPU-driven pipeline and makes it possible to migrate more CPU work to the GPU.

1.2.1 Rational

Database is not a port of MySQL to the GPU; it is at its heart just a new container for data structures that can be shared between the CPU and the GPU.

We shipped several titles with complex systems such as GPU-driven pipelines that manipulate complex data structures on the GPU, or volumetric baked GI that has persistent trees for sparse volumes. Allocating and maintaining such complex data structures on the GPU can be tedious, as it involves a lot of boilerplate code, updates, etc.

With the Database, we wanted to build a reusable CPU/GPU data container interface that can combine different behaviors of allocation, storage, and replication in a modular fashion and recreate some of the C++ Object-Oriented Programming (OOP) convenience for debugging.

1.2.2 Data Layout

The Shader Input Groups (SIG) Compiler [Rodrigues 17] is our internal compiler for root layouts and shader inputs. It generates binding code for C++ and HLSL. We chose to rely on it to generate all the C++ and HLSL code for the Database, with all the required accessors and optimal data layout (Listing 1.1).

```
databasetable MyObject
{
    float4x4       transform;
    uint           type;
    uint           flags;
    Row<MyObject> parent;
}
```

Listing 1.1. Example of a database table declaration, input for the SIG compiler.

To emphasize the data parallel nature of our approach, we chose to use a database analogy (Figure 1.6) for the data access. A table is an instance of the data container, containing a fixed set of columns of different types and a variable number of rows.

With the help of the code generated by SIG, we can easily declare tables and access their data in C++ and HLSL (Listing 1.2). Note that HLSL is very limited in terms of operator overloading, so the interface has to be similar to the SIG constant buffer interface presented in [Rodrigues 17].

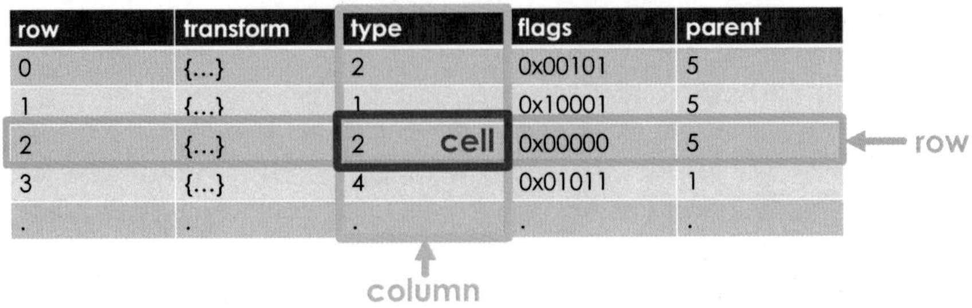

row	transform	type		flags	parent	
0	{...}	2		0x00101	5	
1	{...}	1		0x10001	5	
2	{...}	2	cell	0x00000	5	← row
3	{...}	4		0x01011	1	
.	.	.		.	.	

column

Figure 1.6. Database analogy for Listing 1.1. Each member in the structure would be a column, and each instance within the array of MyObject would be a row in the table (Section 1.2.3).

```
// Table/column/row access in C++
MyObject::Table table;
Matrix44 transform = table.transform[15];
MyObject::Row parent = table.parent[1]

// Table/column/row access in HLSL
MyObjectRO myObjectTable = MyObjectRO::Create(byteAdressBuffer);
float4x4 transform = myObjectTable::GetTransformAt(15);
uint row = myObjectTable.GetParentAt(1);
```

Listing 1.2. Example of how the data declared in Listing 1.1 can be accessed in C++ and HLSL.

Structure of Arrays Through annotations, we can easily switch a table data layout from Array of Structures (AoS) to Structure of Arrays (SoA) (Listing 1.3) without changing the interface to access its data. It is also possible to mix and match AoS and SoA based on data access patterns. There is no difference in the access code, so it's possible to iterate and optimize a table data layout to get the best cache behavior without having to update any code that uses it.

```
databasetable MyObject <DefaultLayout=SoA>
{
    float4x4       transform;
    uint           type;
    uint           flags;
    Row<MyObject> parent;
}
```

Listing 1.3. Example of SoA table declaration, reusing Listing 1.1.

Paged Structure of Arrays   We support another type of data layout called
Paged Structure of Arrays (Paged SoA) (Listing 1.4). Due to the limited way
GPU resources are bound to shaders, it would be inefficient to just use arbitrary
ranges of memory for each column of a table. Instead, it is better to use a single
GPU resource per table, but this becomes very limiting without the use of virtual
memory as one would have to always pre-define the peak memory usage for each
table. Because each column of a table is sequential in memory in the SoA layout,
using virtual memory for large tables would mean that when the table grows, it
would have to grow by at least one page per column. This would be very heavy
for tables with a large number of columns. Instead, we support a data layout
where only chunks of each column are sequential (Figure 1.7). This way a single
page of physical memory can grow all columns simultaneously.

```
databasetable MyObject <RowsPerPage = 16384>
{
    float4x4        transform;
    uint            type;
    uint            flags;
    Row<MyObject> parent;
}
```

Listing 1.4. Example of a paged SoA table declaration in SIG. Note the use of the
RowsPerPage annotation.

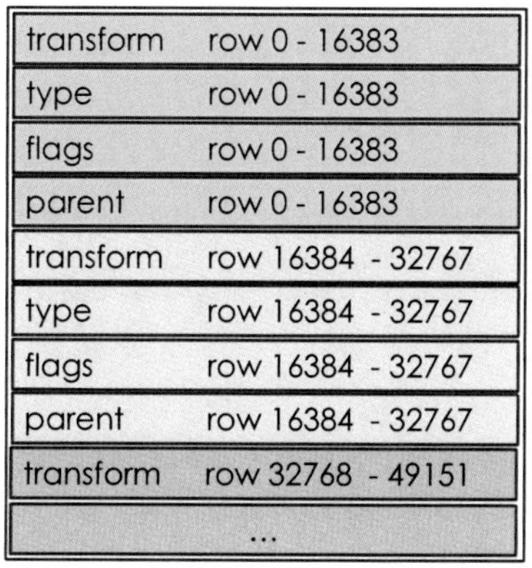

Figure 1.7. Data layout of the paged SoA table in Listing 1.4. Each color represents a
different memory page.

1.2.3 Relations

Relations are links between different table instances.

1 to 1 A simple 1-to-1 relation is the Database version of a pointer (Listing 1.5). Under the hood this is nothing more than a `uint`, but with the convenience of type safety at least in C++. The `row` index that is stored in the `Row` relation becomes a memory location based on a pointer to the destination table stored within the table instance.

```
// Database declaration
databasetable MyObject
{
    Row<MyObject> parent;
    uint          randomProperty;
};
// C++ analogy
struct MyObject
{
    MyObject* parent;
    U32       randomProperty;
};
```

Listing 1.5. A row relation is a simple 1-to-1 relation that is simulating a pointer. Row access is illustrated in Listing 1.2.

1 to n We also support 1-to-n relations, which are just an extension of the previous concept. A `Range` relation is a 1-to-n relation that simulates a pointer with a size (Listing 1.6), while a `PartialRange` is similar to a `Range` but splits the size of a `Range` into a "used size" and a "max size," to emulate `std::vector` behavior of growing and shrinking (Listing 1.7).

```
// Database declaration
databasetable MyObject
{
    Range<MyObject> children;
};
// C++ analogy
struct MyObject
{
    MyObject* children;
    U32       childCount;
};
```

Listing 1.6. A `Range` relation is a 1-to-n relation that simulates a pointer with a size.

```
// Database declaration
databasetable MyObject
{
    PartialRange<MyObjectList> children;
};
// C++ analogy
struct MyObject
{
    Array<MyObject*> children;
};
```

Listing 1.7. A `PartialRange` relation is a 1-to-n relation that is only partially used.

Ownership   We've seen that `Row` and `Range` are just pointers to data stored in
other tables. We can augment these two relations with the concept of ownership,
declared with the `<owner>` attribute. It ensures that owned `rows`, referenced by a
`Row` or a `Range`, are also properly deleted from the corresponding table when an
entry in the owner table is deleted (Listings 1.8 and 1.9).

```
// Database declaration
databasetable TestPOD
{
    int      IntValue;
    float    FloatValue;
};
databasetable TestRange
{
    Range<TestPOD> POD; <owner>
};
```

Listing 1.8. `TestRange` owns the `rows` in the table `TestPOD` referenced by the `Range` POD.

```
// Simple table range
TestPOD::Table tablePOD(G4_KB(1));
TestPOD::Range ranges[16];
S32 intValue[16];
F32 floatValue[16];
for (U32 i = 0; i < 16; i++)
{
    intValue[i] = -S32(i);
    floatValue[i] = i * 0.125f;
}

for (U32 i = 0; i < 16; i++)
    ranges[i] = tablePOD.NewArray(i + 1, intValue, floatValue);

// Adding ranges
TestRange::Table tableRange(G4_KB(1), tablePOD.Ref());
for (U32 i = 0; i < 16; i++)
    tableRange.New(ranges[15 - i]);
```

```
// Do things ...

// delete owned ranges
for (U32 i = 0; i < 16; i += 2)
    tableRange.Delete(i);
```

Listing 1.9. Example of C++ code manipulating the tables declared in Listing 1.8. When an entry in `tableRange` is deleted, all the rows of `tablePOD` referenced by `tableRange::POD` are also deleted, thanks to the `<owner>` attribute.

Index   The most complex relation is an index (Listings 1.10 and 1.11). This annotation automatically generates certain types of indices on the key column. This index allows efficient access of the reverse relation. It works like an index on a secondary key in SQL.

```
// Database declaration
databasetable Component
{
    [index(dense,n)]
    Row<Entity> owner;
    uint        randomProperty;
    ...
};
databasetable Entity
{
    ...
};

// C++ analogy
struct Component
{
    Entity* owner;
    uint    randomProperty;
    ...
};
struct Entity
{
    ...
    Array<Component> components;
};
```

Listing 1.10. Index relation: In this case not only can one retrieve the owner of a `Component` n but also efficiently iterate over all the components with the same owner m.

```
// Let's declare tables of Components and Entities
Entity::Table tableEntity(G4_KB(1));
Component::Table tableComponent(G4_KB(1));

// Some code fills the tables ...

for (U32 i = 0; i < entityCount; i++)
{
    // List holds the index list of all the components
    // referenced by the owner Entity i
    auto list = tableComponent.ownerIndex.Get(i);

    // Iterate over the list of Components and do some stuff ...
    for(tableComponent::Row row : list)
    {
        U32 randomPropertyValue = tableComponent.randomProperty[row];
        // Do some stuff ...
    }
}
```

Listing 1.11. This example iterates over all the components owned by an `Entity i`, on the CPU, using tables declared in Listing 1.10. One can see how powerful and practical this can be to describe a whole scene on the GPU with complex relations between objects.

We wrote a library to operate on these relations as we operate on an array. Some standard functions are also code generated (see Appendix 1.9.1) in C++ and HLSL to easily manipulate the tables on the CPU or the GPU.

1.2.4   Replication

Different table instances handle CPU storage and GPU storage. In some cases, for very large tables, it is not necessary to have a CPU table fully allocated, and we support only allocating and storing dirty rows on the CPU instead until they are flushed to the GPU. We support several modes of data replication to ensure the data is propagated from one instance to another (generally from the CPU to the GPU).

Copy   A copy is the most simple replication available. We support every combination of CPU and GPU table copies, paged or not. If both source and destination are on the GPU, the copy happens directly on the GPU, otherwise, copy works as one would expect when copying data to/from a `ByteAddressBuffer` (mapping buffer to the CPU, etc.), with some extra management related to our database system.

DirtyRows Update   A table built with this policy will update a row dirty mask whenever a row is updated. Continuous dirty row ranges will be replicated into another table on update. Row replication leads to lots of small individual copies, but will produce minimum copy bandwidth.

DirtyPages Update   With this policy, dirty page ranges will be replicated, the same as `DirtyRows` updates, but "dirtyness" happens at a lower granularity (per page instead of per row). The storage to track dirtiness is then smaller, but the required copy bandwidth is higher.

DirtyPageCopy   Both `DirtyRows` and `DirtyPages` require CPU storage. When a value is changed in a row or in a page, it will upload the whole row or page to the GPU. In the case of `DirtyPageCopy`, dirty pages are allocated in a separate data structure in CPU system memory, then copied onto the upload heap on update, and then written into the final GPU storage using a compute shader (Listing 1.12). This replication policy allows table instances to not use any CPU storage for unmodified rows and makes them write only.

```
// Table type declaration with the DirtyPages update policy
databasetable TestUpdatePage <RowsPerPage=64;
    Instance={Persistent;DirtyPages}>
{
    int       IntValue;
    uint      UIntValue;
    float     FloatValue;
    float4    FloatVectorValue;
};

// CPU table creation and data initialization
TestUpdatePage::Table TestUpdatePageCPU(G4_KB(1));
for (U32 i = 0; i < 16; i++)
    TestUpdatePageCPU.New(-S32(i), i, i*0.125f, Vector4(i*-0.5f));

// GPU table creation
TestUpdatePage::TableGPU TestUpdatePageGPU(G4_KB(1));
TestUpdatePageGPU.CreateGPUBuffer(device);

// Copy CPU to GPU
CopyTable(device, TestUpdatePageCPU, TestUpdatePageGPU);

// Update CPU to GPU
UpdateTable(device, TestUpdatePageCPU, TestUpdatePageGPU);
TestUpdatePageCPU.ClearDirtyElements();
```

Listing 1.12. Example of a database table copy and update from the CPU to the GPU. Note the use of the annotation `DirtyPages`.

1.3 CPU Data Management

All inputs to the GPUIR are transformed into database tables for fast consumption and ease of replication to the GPU. The three most important input tables are `CullMeshes`, `CullInstances`, and `LeafNodes`. This section will discuss how these tables are managed, what type of data they hold, and how they are used to kick-start the culling process on GPU.

1.3.1 Render Data

A *LOD selector* in the BatchRenderer represents a set of five geometric levels of detail. The active LOD is selected based on the distance to the camera and transitions between LODs are time based. Each LOD is made up of one or more sub-meshes and each sub-mesh has exactly one material. We decided to keep the concept of LOD selectors in the GPUIR, but only as a way to author data and serialize geometry on disk.

The first thing to set up when creating a collection of instances in the GPUIR is the `CullMeshes` and their render batches. A `CullMesh` is a very close GPU representation of our LOD selectors. In addition to LODs, it holds some information about the passes in which it can be rendered. Each LOD node `CullLODNode` points to a variable number of `CullSubMeshes` where the material and geometry descriptions are stored. See Figure 1.8 for a more complete description of the database tables used to implement `CullMesh`.

To batch as many instances as possible per draw call, we create one batch slot per pipeline state object (PSO). These batch slots contain everything that cannot change during a draw call: a shader template, a specific shader permutation, and various pipeline flags. Since we rely on bindless descriptors to address textures at render time, we don't need to split batches per texture set used on a material. Instead, the association of a geometry with a PSO is made at the `CullSubMesh` level. All the inputs used to create a batch slot are hashed together to create a `BatchHash`. From now on, we will always refer to these batch slots by their hash as they are going to be stored in a hash map. `CullSubMeshes` store one batch hash per pipeline configuration with which they can be rendered (e.g., G-buffer, depth only, transparent).

Render pass masks are dictated by materials; however, some culling operations happen at the `CullMesh` level, so it is necessary to aggregate the information at this level as well. A `MergedBatchHash` stores the combined pass mask of all the `CullSubMeshes` of a `CullMesh`. Additionally, it holds the maximum number of instances and triangle clusters contained in this `CullMesh`. This information will later be used to compute the total number of indirect draw calls to issue for a given world.

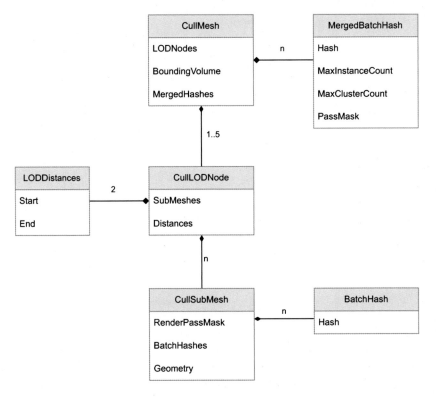

Figure 1.8. Structure of a `CullMesh`. Types are implemented as database tables and linked by row or range properties. Aggregation links use the `<owner>` attribute in their database table declaration (see Section 1.2.3 for more details).

1.3.2 World Data

Once the global render data is ready, we can create the per-world data, namely the `LeafNodes` and their `CullInstances`. A `CullInstance` is made of a transform, a `CullMesh`, LOD states, per-instance material flags, and some per-instance shader constants. As we can define different LOD switch distances for the main view and shadow maps, we store two sets of LOD states per instance.

The GPUIR has been designed to cull and render several millions instances at once. To achieve good culling performances, it relies on a hierarchical structure made of entity groups and `LeafNodes` (see Figure 1.9). An entity group represents a collection of instances of a given type (e.g., trees or buildings) for a given loading cell. These instances are often generated procedurally based on scattering rules or are the result of a process called *optimized instancing* that visits all the entities of a loading cell and selectively merges entities that are compatible with the GPUIR. Inside collections, instances are split into `LeafNodes`. Instances

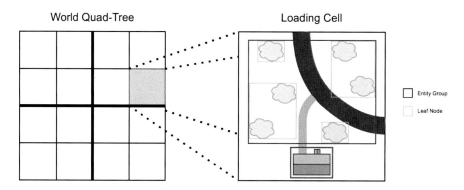

Figure 1.9. Spatial partitioning of the world.

of different `CullMeshes` can be put in the same leaf node, but there are certain constraints to selecting which instances to group. First, each `LeafNode` cannot contain more than 16,384 instances as instance ranges are not allowed to straddle allocation pages in database tables. Second, we try to keep instances that are close together in space in the same leaf node to minimize their bounding volume and make culling more efficient.

`LeafNode` is the lowest level of the hierarchy that is culled on the CPU, so it is also the last opportunity to skip empty draw calls. That's why we compute a pass mask per `LeafNode` and collect all the batch hashes provided by its instances' `CullMesh`. `LeafNode` also leverages the `<owner>` attribute of the SIG compiler to automatically free owned rows in other database tables when one leaf node is removed. So a leaf node owns its instances, their shader constants, and some indirection to `CullMeshes` used for reference counting. Relationships between the world-specific database tables are shown in Figure 1.10.

1.3.3 Coarse CPU Culling

When entity groups are loaded in memory and their world data is created, they are also inserted into a quad-tree culling structure as shown in Figure 1.9. At the beginning of each frame, all entity groups that are visible in at least one render pass are collected. This is done by checking the cells of the quad-tree against the frustum of the render passes. The leaf nodes of these entity groups (Figure 1.11) are tested against each frustum once more, but at this point, we can take advantage of the merged pass mask to skip testing leaf nodes that would not produce any visible instance for the render pass. This leaves us with a list of `PassedLeafNodes` and their corresponding `PassedInstanceRanges`. Instance ranges are sent to the GPU for the next fine-grained culling passes (Figure 1.12).

From the `PassedLeafNodes`, one render batch hash map is built for each pass using batch slot hashes as keys. These hash maps will let the GPU know where

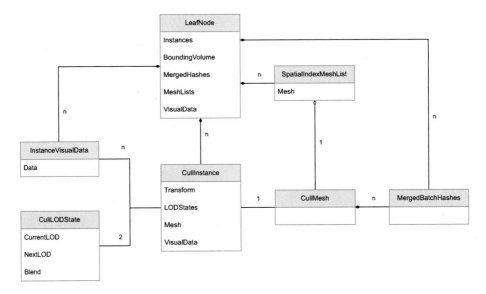

Figure 1.10. World-specific database tables and their relationships. `CullMesh` and `MergedBatchHashes` refer to the same table as in Figure 1.8. Note that `LeafNode` and `CullMesh` own different sets of **MergedBatchHash** rows.

Figure 1.11. `LeafNodes` debug view in *Assassin's Creed Mirage*.

to write the indirect draw call arguments for a render batch of a given pass. To generate these maps, we simply iterate over the `PassedLeafNodes` and allocate one render batch per unique `MergedBatchHash`. The allocated render batches cannot be fully initialized yet as we don't know how many active `CullSubMeshes` are referencing these render batches. This will be determined later on the GPU

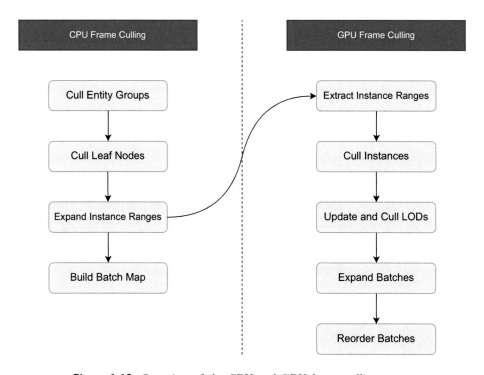

Figure 1.12. Overview of the CPU and GPU frame culling steps.

once culling passes are done (see Section 1.4.2). For now, all we can tell is the maximum number of instances and draw calls that a render batch can contain, which are necessary to prepare indirect draw calls on the CPU.

1.4 GPU Culling

Now that the highest levels of the hierarchy have been culled, we can start processing instances individually. This is where the GPU truly shines since we generally have to process hundreds of thousands of instances at this point. The CPU culling phase produced a series of transient database tables (e.g., `PassedInstanceRanges`, `BatchMap`) ready to be replicated to the GPU alongside the persistent render data and world data tables (e.g., `CullInstances`, `CullMeshes`). To turn all this information into actual draw calls, there are still a few per-frame and per-pass operations that we need to perform on the instances. Note that it is generally possible to execute the GPU culling passes on async queues while other systems are being updated on the graphics queue. In our case, only the triangle and cluster culling operations are done on the graphics queue right before drawing the geometry.

Every shader that will be described in the following sections stores its outputs in transient GPU database tables. Allocations in these tables are performed in two steps by first counting the number of rows requested by a thread group with atomic adds and then making the first thread of the group increment the table size with another atomic add. The return values of the aforementioned operations give us the local offset of each thread and the group write offset, respectively.

1.4.1   Per-Frame GPU Culling

The purpose of the remaining per-frame operations (Figure 1.12) is to update the instance LOD states and produce the sub-mesh instances that will be fed to the per-pass culling operations.

Extract Instance Ranges The list of instances that was sent to the GPU from the CPU culling phase was compressed as `PassedInstanceRanges`. To assign one instance to each GPU thread, we need to extract the individual instance indices from these ranges (Figure 1.13(a)). This is done in two steps by generating tables of search ranges and group ranges so that the instance culling shader can find its instance index by doing a binary search within the group's instance range bounds (Figure 1.13(b)).

Cull Instances and LODs With an instance index at hand, GPU threads can perform one more step of frustum culling. Each instance is tested against every pass frustum and intersected frustums are recorded in a pass mask. If the instance overlaps at least one frustum, its LOD states are output to the LOD update stage. As stated earlier, we keep track of two LOD states per instance, one for the main view and a second one for shadows. Listing 1.13 shows how the LOD state pass masks are computed.

Updating LOD states consists of detecting when LOD transitions start and tracking the ongoing transitions' progress. In our case, we decided to make LOD transitions uninterruptible and always last a fixed amount of time. After the update, each LOD state can export one or two `PassedLODs` to the batch expansion stage depending on if a transition is ongoing or not.

Generate Batches At this point, we have a list of `PassedLODs` and we want to distribute their sub-meshes to the different passes. The pass masks computed up to this point specify in which pass an instance is allowed to be rendered, but we need to choose precisely in which pass it will be rendered. In particular, this is where we decide whether to render a sub-mesh in the z pre-pass or not. To that end, we use a heuristic based on the sub-mesh's average triangle size in screen space. Objects closer to the camera and made of larger triangles are more

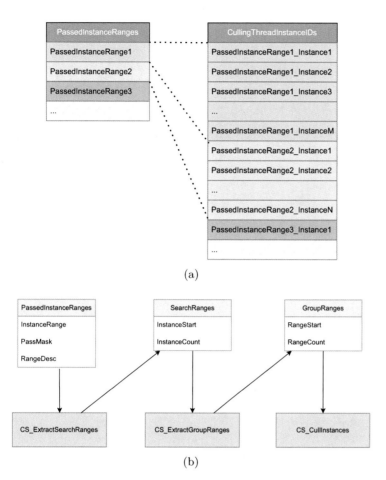

(a)

(b)

Figure 1.13. (a) The goal is to assign one passed instance to each culling thread. (b) First, a single thread group computes a prefix sum of the range instance counts to find the start index of each passed instance group. For each culling thread group, we find the start and end indices of passed instance range by doing binary searches within the search ranges. To finally find the global instance index assigned to a thread, we have one more binary search to do within the start and end passed instance ranges of the group.

likely to be sent to the z pre-pass. Furthermore, we have to choose with what shader permutation to render a sub-mesh. For example, if an object does not require any sort of alpha clip operation (i.e., it is not dithered nor alpha tested), we can select to render the sub-mesh with the *no-clip* optimization.

```
uint CullSphere(in const CullingCommon common, in const float4
    centerRadius, in uint rangePassMask)
{
    uint overlappedMask = 0;
    for(uint i = 0; i < common.GetFrustumCount(); i++)
    {
        uint4 frustumDesc = common.GetFrustumDescAt(i);

        // Check if this frustum needs to be culled against
        uint passMaskOverlap = frustumDesc.z & rangePassMask;
        if (passMaskOverlap == 0)
            continue;

        if (!CullPlanesSphere(common, frustumDesc.x, frustumDesc.y,
    centerRadius))
            overlappedMask |= passMaskOverlap;
    }
    return overlappedMask;
}

void CS_CullInstances(uint3 threadID : SV_DispatchThreadID, uint3
    groupID : SV_GroupID)
{
    // ...
    uint rangePassMask = passedInstanceRanges.GetPassMaskAt(
    instanceRangeRow);
    uint instancePassMask = CullSphere(
        Common, transformedCenterAndRadius, rangePassMask);
    uint mainLODStatePassMask =
        instancePassMask & ~SHADOW_PASS_MASK;
    uint shadowLODStatePassMask =
        instancePassMask & SHADOW_PASS_MASK;
    // ...
}
```

Listing 1.13. The LOD state pass masks are computed from the union of all the passes an instance was not culled from, plus the static shadow pass mask.

Section 1.3.3 describes how the batch map was initialized, associating different render batches to the different render passes based on the MergedBatchHashes of leaf nodes that passed the CPU coarse culling phase. Generating the render batches is a matter of registering the sub-mesh instances to the right render batch given the selected pass and shader permutation. Once all sub-mesh instances have been registered, we reorder them to get the final per-pass sub-mesh instance buffer as illustrated by Figure 1.14.

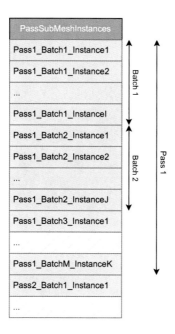

Figure 1.14. This global buffer contains all the passed sub-mesh instances split into their respective passes and render batches. The buffer is compacted to make it easier for pass-culling shaders to quickly find the sub-mesh instance assigned to a thread from the thread ID.

1.4.2 Per-Pass GPU Culling

We are almost ready to generate the individual render batches' draw call arguments, but before we do, there is one last opportunity to cull instances. At the end of this phase, we will have everything necessary to render triangles on screen with the correct material, including the `InstanceInfo` that lets us specify what geometry and material to fetch from the vertex and pixel shaders for each instance. Figure 1.15 shows the remaining culling and draw call preparation steps.

Cull Pass Sub-meshes Here we have the option to execute additional culling tests on the sub-mesh instances. The test we perform depends on the pass and the cost-to-benefit ratio that performing this test gives. For example, we decided to test for occlusion culling using the main view's hierarchical Z-buffer (HZB) for most main view passes (e.g., opaques, emissives) using the sub-mesh's bounding box as the sampling area (see Section 1.4.3). For sun shadows, we opted instead to apply the camera depth reprojection method to cull shadow casters that would not affect any pixel on screen. All sub-mesh instances that pass this last round of tests will necessarily be part of a draw call.

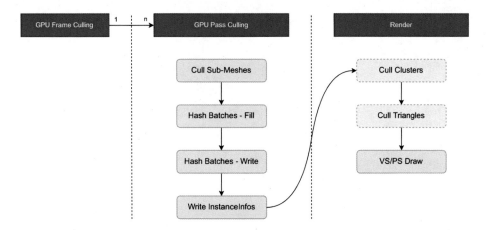

Figure 1.15. Overview of the per-pass culling steps. One culling pipeline is instantiated per pass on the async queue. Once the draw call arguments and `InstanceInfos` are ready, there are optional culling operations (cluster and triangle) that can occur on the graphics queue right before executing the draw calls.

Hash Batches We use a single draw buffer to store the draw call counts per render batch and all the draw call arguments. To find to which draw call an instance belongs, we hash its sub-mesh ID and render batch ID. Technically, the sub-mesh ID would be sufficient to create the draw call hash since it represents a pair of geometry and material, but in our case, we switch between different PSOs when alpha clip is enabled, so we need to register the sub-mesh instance to different draw calls depending on the shader permutation used (Section 1.4.1).

A first pass fills a hash map on the GPU with the draw call hash as the key using a simple closed hashing with linear probing technique to resolve collisions. If an instance is the first to insert its key, it creates an entry in a temporary list of hash map slot descriptors. Otherwise, it increments the instance count for its key in the hash map. In either case, we create a hashed batch to record the hash map location of the draw call and the instance offset within the draw call (Figure 1.16).

A second pass computes the location of each draw call using a single thread group prefix sum. Each thread is assigned a number of hash map slots. It loops over all its slots to count the number of draw calls and `InstanceInfos` it needs to allocate. While doing so, it provides the counts to the prefix sum, which returns the number of draw calls and `InstanceInfos` requested by all the threads with a lower thread ID. Each thread then loops once more over its hash map slots and writes its draw call arguments using the geometry descriptor of the corresponding sub-mesh and the instance count stored in the hash map. It finishes by saving each draw call's first `InstanceInfo` offset in the hash map for the next step.

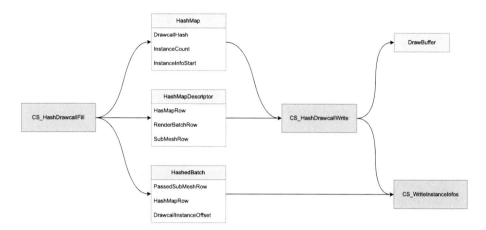

Figure 1.16. Data flow of the two-pass algorithm to compute draw call arguments and `InstanceInfos`. There is one `HashMapDescriptor` per entry in the `HashMap` and as many `HashBatches` as there are sub-mesh instances.

Write InstanceInfos The last step of the per-pass culling phase is to write one `InstanceInfo` per instance in a buffer that will be fed to the vertex and pixel shaders at render time (Listing 1.14). `InstanceInfo` holds a world-view projection matrix, a few packed properties, and some offsets to the unified geometry buffer (Section 1.4.3), unified constant buffer (Section 1.5.3), and bindless material table (Section 1.5.2). The index of an instance's `InstanceInfo` must match the instance ID passed to the vertex shader. We calculate this index by reading the first instance info offset of the draw call from the hash map and adding it to the instance offset within the draw call that was recorded in the hashed batch.

```
// Array of InstanceInfo
ByteAddressBuffer InstanceInfos;

struct InstanceInfo
{
    uint instanceAndLODFade; // LOD and fade flags
    uint vertexInfo; // Vertex data start, format, and stride
    uint instanceMaterialInfo; // Material flags
    uint materialOffsets; // Texture2DOffset and ConstantOffset
    float4x4 worldViewProj; // Transform
}
```

Listing 1.14. `InstanceInfos` format: `vertexInfo` packs the data necessary to fetch vertices in the vertex shader, while `materialOffsets` packs offsets to fetch the bindless material (Section 1.5.2) and constant tables in the pixel shader.

1.4.3   Cluster Culling

In Anvil, all meshes are clustered by default, and each cluster is composed of 64 vertices (Figure 1.17). We store our geometry vertices and indices in unified buffers. All vertex data resides in the same buffer, and we perform the vertex fetch manually based on its vertex ID in the vertex shader. It is no longer a vertex buffer, in the API sense, but a shared byte buffer.

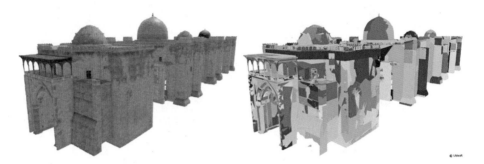

Figure 1.17. Clustered geometry in *Assassin's Creed Mirage*.

Before issuing the actual multi-draw calls, we can perform cluster and triangle culling. These steps are optional and can be enabled per render pass (e.g., `ZPrepass`, `GBufferPass`) if beneficial (depends mainly on data and the type of render pass).

Per-cluster culling is made of two steps—frustum culling and occlusion culling—and runs in a compute shader (Figure 1.18). Each thread handles one cluster. For each of them, we fetch the corresponding `WorldViewProj` matrix in the `InstanceInfos` buffer (Section 1.4.2) and the center and half extents of its bounding box. It is used to compute a projected bounding box for culling.

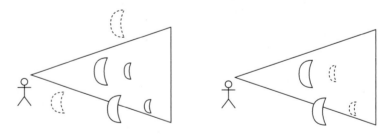

Figure 1.18. Cluster culling: First we perform a per-cluster frustum culling (left) then an occlusion culling (right).

Frustum Culling   For each cluster, we first project its bounding box, then cull it in the normalized device coordinates (NDC) (Listing 1.15).

```
float3 minAABB = float3(1.0f, 1.0f, 1.0f);
float3 maxAABB = float3(-1.0f, -1.0f, 0.0f);
for (float z = -1; z <= 1; z += 2)
  for (float y = -1; y <= 1; y += 2)
    for (float x = -1; x <= 1; x += 2)
    {
        // Projection -> homogeneous space [-w,w][-w,w][0,w]
        float4 posHS = mul(float4(center + halfExtents *
            float3(x, y, z), 1.0f), worldViewProj);
        // Perspective divide -> NDC [-1,1][-1,1][0,1]
        float3 posSS = posHS.w>0? posHS.xyz/posHS.w:float3(0,0,-1);
        // Handle inverted z axis
        posSS.z = posSS.z * ZScaleBias.x + ZScaleBias.y;

        minAABB = min(posSS, minAABB);
        maxAABB = max(posSS, maxAABB);
    }

// Simple frustum culling (inverted z axis)
passed = ((all(minAABB.xy < 1.0f) && all(maxAABB.xy > -1.0f) ||
        minAABB.z <= 0));
```

Listing 1.15. Simple per-cluster frustum culling shader code.

Occlusion Culling   This step is very similar to [Haar and Aaltonen 15] and requires a hierarchical Z-buffer [Hill 10, Greene et al. 93] (Figure 1.19). We first render a partial depth pre-pass with the best nearest occluders, downsample it to 512×256, and combine the result with a reprojection of the last frame's depth. The result is then mipmapped, taking the max of 4 texels to generate the next level, to obtain a depth hierarchy we use for GPU culling.

Figure 1.19. Hierarchical Z-buffer in *Assassin's Creed Mirage*.

During the occlusion pass, we fetch the 2×2 texel neighborhood in the corresponding mip level so the screen area of the cluster bounding box projects to 4 texels, and compare the max Z value of these 4 texels to the min depth value of this bounding box to determine whether it's occluded or not (Listing 1.16).

```
// Viewport rescale -> [0,1][0,1]
float2 minUV = float2(minAABB.x,maxAABB.y)*float2(0.5f,-0.5f)+0.5f;
float2 maxUV = float2(maxAABB.x,minAABB.y)*float2(0.5f,-0.5f)+0.5f;

// Pixel coords in HZB viewport -> [0,HZBWidth][0,HZBHeight]
float2 minHZBPixel = minUV.xy * GetHZBWidthHeightMips().xy;
float2 maxHZBPixel = maxUV.xy * GetHZBWidthHeightMips().xy;

// Compute HZB mipLevel so that the BB projects on 4 texels
float2 texelSize = maxHZBPixel - minHZBPixel;
float mipValue = ceil(log2(max(texelSize.x, texelSize.y)));
float mipScale = rcp(exp2(mipValue));
float2 minMip = minHZBPixel * mipScale;
float2 maxMip = maxHZBPixel * mipScale;

if (all(floor(minMip) == floor(maxMip)))
{
    mipValue -= 1; minMip *= 2; maxMip *= 2;
}
// If the requested mip exists
if (mipValue < GetHZBWidthHeightMips().z)
{
    uint xOffset = floor(minMip.x) == floor(maxMip.x) ? 0 : 1;
    uint yOffset = floor(minMip.y) == floor(maxMip.y) ? 0 : 1;
    float4 maxDepthMask4 =
        float4(1, xOffset, yOffset, xOffset * yOffset);

    // Fetch the corresponding 2x2 neightborhood pixels
    float4 maxDepth4 = float4(
        GetHZBTexture().SampleLevel(s_PointClamp,
          minUV.xy, mipValue, float2(0, 0)),
        GetHZBTexture().SampleLevel(s_PointClamp,
          minUV.xy, mipValue, float2(1, 0)),
        GetHZBTexture().SampleLevel(s_PointClamp,
          minUV.xy, mipValue, float2(0, 1)),
        GetHZBTexture().SampleLevel(s_PointClamp,
          minUV.xy, mipValue, float2(1, 1)) );

    maxDepth4 = max(1 - maxDepthMask4, maxDepth4);

    // Take the max depth value
    float maxDepth = max(
        max(maxDepth4.x,maxDepth4.y),max(maxDepth4.z,maxDepth4.w));

    // Conservative depth test to determine if occluded or not
    passed = minAABB.z < maxDepth;
}
```

Listing 1.16. Per-cluster occlusion culling shader code using a HZB.

1.4.4 Triangle Culling

Per-triangle culling is made of three steps—zero area and backface culling, frustum culling, and small triangle culling—and runs in a compute shader (Figure 1.20). Each thread handles one triangle. For each of them, again, we fetch the corresponding `WorldViewProj` matrix in the `InstanceInfos` buffer (Section 1.4.2) and transform vertices before doing any culling (Listing 1.17).

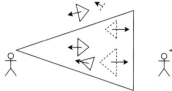 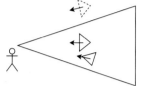

Figure 1.20. Triangle culling: First we perform per-triangle zero area and backface culling (left), followed by frustum culling (center), and, finally, small triangle culling (right).

```
float4 vtx[3];
for (uint i = 0; i < 3; i++)
{
    float3 posOS = FetchVertexPosition(index[i],
      vertexStart, vertexStride);
    vtx[i] = mul(float4(posOS, 1), worldViewProj);
}
```

Listing 1.17. Fetch vertices in the unified geometry buffer and transform them to the homogeneous space. Note that we don't do the perspective divide yet.

Zero Area and Backface Culling   We check the determinant of the 2D homogeneous matrix as described in [Wihlidal 17] and [Olano and Greer 97] (Listing 1.18). (`det > 0`) means a frontfacing triangle, while (`det = 0`) means a zero area triangle. A triangle with collinear vertices is degenerate and has an area of zero.

```
float det = determinant(float3x3(
    vtx[0].xyw, vtx[1].xyw, vtx[2].xyw) );
passed = (det > 0) || (twoSided && det != 0);
```

Listing 1.18.   Zero area and backface triangle culling shader code testing the determinant of the 2DH Matrix. Note the special case for double-sided geometry.

Frustum Culling   This step (Listing 1.19) is very similar to the per-cluster frustum culling step (Listing 1.15), except it is 2D.

```
float2 minAABB = 1.0f;
float2 maxAABB = 0.0f;
for (uint i = 0; i < 3; i++)
{
    // Perspective divide and viewport rescale
    float2 posSS = (vtx[i].xy / vtx[i].w) * 0.5f + 0.5f;
    minAABB = min(minAABB, posSS);
    maxAABB = max(maxAABB, posSS);
}
// Simple frustum culling
passed = all(minAABB < 1.0f) && all(maxAABB > 0.0f);
```

Listing 1.19. Per-triangle frustum culling shader code.

Small Triangle Culling   To cull small triangles, we use the same approach as [Wihlidal 17] and snap the triangle bounding box min and max to the nearest pixel corner (Figure 1.21). We then test the snapped coordinates to determine if they cover the center of a pixel or not (Listing 1.20).

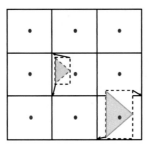

Figure 1.21. Small triangle culling: The triangle bounding box corners are snapped to the closest pixel corners and then compared to each other to determine whether it crosses a pixel center or not.

```
minAABB *= GetScreenWidthHeight();
maxAABB *= GetScreenWidthHeight();
passed = !any(round(minAABB) == round(maxAABB));
```

Listing 1.20. Small triangle culling shader code.

Instancing and Index Buffer Compaction   When cluster and triangle culling are enabled, they impact what geometry can be rendered at the instance level. We can no longer use the original index buffer because these culling steps break instancing. Instead, we output a new compacted index buffer containing per-instance visible triangle indices, following a similar approach as described in [Haar and Aaltonen 15]. It is the final step of the triangle culling compute job, where each thread calculates the output write position into this new index buffer, and writes its triangle indices when it passes culling.

For the same reason, it is also necessary to update the `DrawBuffer` (Section 1.6) that provides the arguments to `ExecuteIndirect` with additional draw entries to account for the fact that instances of the same batch can now have a different visible geometry and have to be split into different `DrawIndexedInstanced` calls. The indices of these new draw entries are augmented with the instance ID necessary to fetch the original `InstanceInfo` parameters (Section 1.4.2) to correctly access its geometry and resources during rendering.

1.5 Bindless Material Management

1.5.1 General Design

Our materials rely on a data-driven node-based shader system (Figure 1.22). To output the final shader code, the shader graph is parsed and resolved, and then the graph code is inserted into a common material shader template. This template is made of a vertex shader and a pixel shader. They both include mandatory header and footer code that are not part of the graph but depend on material and mesh properties (e.g., deferred, forward, TAA dither, vertex format).

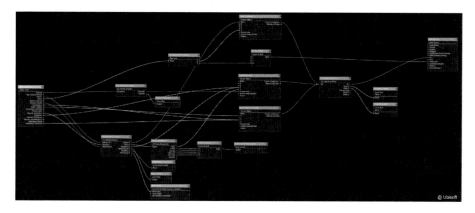

Figure 1.22. Shader graph editor in Anvil.

1.5.2 Bindless Descriptor Table

As described in Section 1.3, we represent the scene in our GPU-driven pipeline using database tables (Figure 1.23).

A material bindless table represents all the textures—2D, 3D, or cube—necessary to render a frame. This table is a unified array of resource descriptors

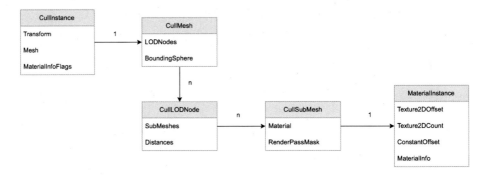

Figure 1.23. Database tables (Section 1.2) used to describe the scene and their relations. `Texture2DOffset` and `Texture2DCount` are used to access bindless resources in the bindless material table on the CPU or the GPU.

with 32K entries. All three resource types are aliased and stored in the same array, but a smaller range is reserved for 3D and cube textures as we need just a few of them (Listing 1.21).

```
ShaderInputGroup MaterialBindless
<Bindless; ForceAliasingOfTextures>
{
    Texture2D<float4> textures; <BindlessMaxCount = 32768>
    Texture3D<float4> textures3D; <BindlessMaxCount = 32>
    TextureCube<float4> texturesCube; <BindlessMaxCount = 32>
};
```

Listing 1.21. Declaration of bindless ressource arrays in SIG. Note that `Texture2D`, `Texture3D`, and `TextureCube` entries are aliased.

When a mesh is loaded and added to the scene, it triggers the allocation or update of its material descriptors in the bindless material table (Figure 1.24). All the necessary descriptors are then copied to the table. The descriptor range is then referenced by `Texture2DOffset` and `Texture2DCount` in the corresponding `MaterialInstance` table entry so it can properly be accessed on the GPU at render time.

1.5.3 Constants Management

Constant buffers are not ideal to hold a large amount of instance parameter data. Because we perform most of our culling steps on the GPU, we need to upload all the instance parameter data for entities within the view frustum, which can be substantial. To do so, we use a single-byte buffer shared for all passes that hold all instance shader parameters (Figure 1.25). Its allocation and update mechanism are almost identical to the bindless material descriptor table described in Section 1.5.2.

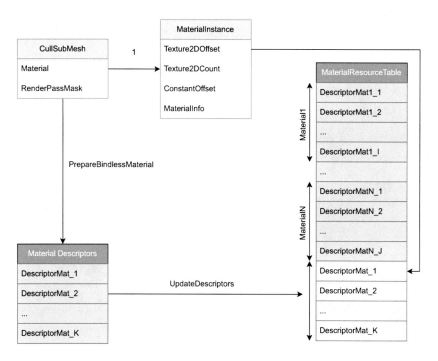

Figure 1.24. Allocation and copy of a new descriptor range in the material resource table. `Texture2DOffset` points to the first descriptor in this table, and `Texture2DCount` stores the number of descriptors relative to this instance material entry.

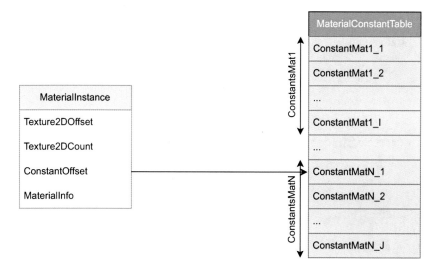

Figure 1.25. A `MaterialInstance` references a range of constants in the global `MaterialConstantTable`.

Before rendering, `Texture2DOffset` and `ConstantOffset` are fetched for all visible instances from the corresponding `MaterialInstance` and packed together as a `uint materialOffsets` in `InstanceInfos` (Section 1.4.2).

1.6 Rendering

At render time, for each render batch that passed culling (Section 1.3.1), we set the correct PSO; bind the unified geometry and index buffers (Section 1.4.3), the bindless and constant tables (Section 1.5), etc.; and issue an `ExecuteIndirect` to render a batch of draws with a series of `DrawIndexedInstanced` commands. All the necessary draw arguments are in a `DrawBuffer`, populated during the GPU culling steps (Section 1.4). The same buffer stores both the draw counts and the draw arguments (Figure 1.26).

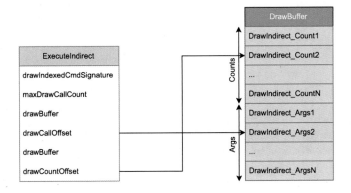

Figure 1.26. On PC DirectX 12, we issue an `ExecuteIndirect`. `maxDrawCallCount` is the maximum number of visible batches (`drawcall`) after CPU culling, while `DrawIndirect_Count` values in `DrawBuffer` represent the number of batches that passed the GPU culling. The minimum of these two values determines the number of `DrawIndexedInstanced` commands to execute.

1.6.1 Vertex Shader

At render time, we use the instance ID in the vertex shader to fetch the matching `InstanceInfos` entry (more details in Section 1.4.2). We then unpack the required properties (vertex data start, format, and stride) to manually fetch the corresponding vertex from the unified geometry buffer based on its vertex ID (Listing 1.22).

`Texture2DOffset` and `ConstantOffset` are also fetched from `InstanceInfos` in the vertex shader, then passed together as a single non-interpolable `uint` value to the pixel shader (Figure 1.27)). They are used in the pixel shader to access respectively the bindless `MaterialResourceTable` and the `MaterialConstantTable`.

```
VS_INPUT FetchVertices(in uint vertexStart, in uint vertexFormat, in
    uint vertexStride, in uint vertexID)
{
    uint vertexOffset = vertexStart + vertexStride * vertexID;

    VS_INPUT output = (VS_INPUT)0;
    output.m_Position = ToSHORT4(FETCH2(getClusterVertexDataStatic(),
    vertexOffset));
    output.m_Normal = ToUBYTE4(FETCH1(getClusterVertexDataStatic(),
    vertexOffset));
    ...
    return output;
}
```

Listing 1.22. Vertex fetch from the unified geometry buffer using vertex ID, start, and stride. Vertex fetch macros are available for all common types (e.g., `FETCH1`, `FETCH2`, `ToUBYTE4`, `ToSHORT4`).

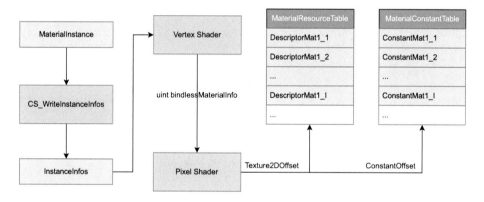

Figure 1.27. Bindless resource access flow on the GPU. `Texture2DOffset` and `ConstantOffset` are packed together in `bindlessMaterialInfo`.

1.6.2 Pixel Shader

`Texture2DOffset` and `ConstantOffset` are unpacked in the pixel shader. We make use of macros to hide all the complexity related to bindless resource management. Under the hood, these macros take a texture slot index as an input, and sum it to `Texture2DOffset` to properly access the corresponding texture descriptor in the `bindlessMaterialInfo` (Listings 1.23 and 1.24).

```
static uint g_BindlessTex2DOffset = 0;
static uint g_BindlessConstantOffset = 0;

// Global macros used to access textures
#define MATERIAL_TEX2DALIAS(INDEX, NAME, SAMPLER)   Tex2DAndSampler Get
    ##NAME() { return
    GetTexture2DTypeAndSamplerStateType(
    Get_MaterialBindless_textures(
    g_BindlessTex2DOffset + INDEX), s_##SAMPLER); }
// ...

// Global macros used to access a single float constant
#define MATERIAL_CONSTLOADSCALAR(OFFSET, CONVERSION)
    CONVERSION(gpuCullingInstanceParams.
    GetBindlessMaterialConstants().Load(
    g_BindlessConstantDOffset + (OFFSET) * 4) )
#define MATERIAL_CONSTALIASFLOAT(TYPE, ALIASNAME, OFFSET)
    TYPE Get##ALIASNAME() {
    return (TYPE)(MATERIAL_CONSTLOADSCALAR(OFFSET, asfloat)); }
#define MATERIAL_FLOAT(OFFSET, NAME)
    MATERIAL_CONSTALIASFLOAT(float, NAME, OFFSET);
// ...
```

Listing 1.23. HLSL macros used to access bindless textures and constants. They rely on accessors generated by the SIG compiler, such as `Get_MaterialBindless_textures`. `g_BindlessTex2DOffset` represents the offset to the start of the texture descriptor range of the current material in the bindless material table (Section 1.5.2), and `INDEX` the relative index of the texture being accessed by the pixel shader. `g_BindlessConstantOffset` points to the start of the constant range of the same material in the material constant table (Section 1.5.3).

```
MATERIAL_TEX2DALIAS(0, Layer0Diffuse_0, StandardSampler);
MATERIAL_TEX2DALIAS(1, Layer0Normal_1, StandardSampler);

MATERIAL_FLOAT(4, _1Layer0ScaleU_1);
MATERIAL_FLOAT(5, _1Layer0ScaleV_2);

#define Layer0Diffuse_0 GetLayer0Diffuse_0()
#define Layer0Normal_1 GetLayer0Normal_1()

#define _1Layer0ScaleU_1 Get_1Layer0ScaleU_1()
#define _1Layer0ScaleV_2 Get_1Layer0ScaleV_2()

// Some code ...

float2 uvScaled = uvDiffuse *
    float2(_1Layer0ScaleU_1, _1Layer0ScaleV_2);
float4 Layer0Diffuse_0_sample =
    Sample2D(Layer0Diffuse_0, uvScaled);
```

Listing 1.24. Pixel shader code generated from a shader graph. Texture and constant indices are generated by the shader graph HLSL code generation step.

1.7 Results

Even though we called it a GPU pipeline, a significant chunk of the BatchRenderer is still on the CPU (Figure 1.4). A lot of batching happens at the per-pass level on the CPU and only the final culling of instances happened on the GPU.

The GPU Instance Renderer, on the other hand, performs all batching at load time and combines per-frame and per-pass culling. The culling also happens per instance before instances are split up into different LODs, sub-meshes, and passes (Figure 1.5). We also use bindless materials and, on the GPU, map all meshes with the same PSO and geometry onto the same draw call to improve vertex shading performance and eliminate empty draw calls.

The decision was made early on to split culling into per-frame and per-pass, both dispatched on the async queue, mainly because of GPU LOD management and temporal blending logic. It also means that there is some culling that happens multiple times. On one hand, it's good because we operate on much tighter bounding volumes in the per-pass culling (sub-meshes), but on the other hand we'd like to investigate the possibility of reducing the per-frame culling steps to a strict minimum, although it's not a bottleneck.

1.7.1 BatchRenderer versus GPU Instance Renderer

In terms of performance, we achieved a significant speed-up for all our geometry passes, both on the GPU and the CPU (Table 1.1). For distant geometry, which is heavily instanced, we even observed in some cases a speed up of 50× between the BatchRenderer and the GPU Instance Renderer on the CPU, going from 6.8 ms down to 0.14 ms for a particular scene.

Pass	BatchRenderer	GPUIR	Speed-up
GBuffer CPU	1.43 ms	0.708 ms	2x
GBuffer GPU	3.72 ms	0.605 ms	6x
SunShadows CPU	1.89 ms	0.834 ms	2.26x
SunShadows GPU	1.42 ms	0.673 ms	2.1x

Table 1.1. Cost of our main geometry render passes on PlayStation 5 at 4K. We rendered the scene shown in Figure 1.28, where we compare the BatchRenderer and the GPU Instance Renderer as the main rendering pipelines. The CPU time is expressed in thread time.

Table 1.2 shows that culling jobs are not always faster with the GPUIR, but they can now be dispatched on the async queue early in the frame. In our test scene, 98% of the 435K instances within the camera frustum were culled on the GPU (Table 1.3).

Figure 1.28. Synthetic test map designed for comparing the BatchRenderer and the GPU Instance Renderer. The entire frame is rendered using either one of these pipelines on the PlayStation 5 at 4K.

Pass	BatchRenderer	GPUIR
GPUCulling	0.525 ms	
GPUCullingFrame		0.328 ms
GPUCullingPass(es)		0.28 ms
Total	0.525 ms	0.608 ms

Table 1.2. GPU culling cost when running our test map on PlayStation 5 (Figure 1.28). The BatchRenderer culling passes have to run on the graphics queue right before render, while the GPU Instance Renderer culling can be run on the async queue.

	Draw Calls	Instances
Pre culling	27197	435133
Post culling	2445	8673
Culled	91%	98%

Table 1.3. Draw calls are the total number of `DrawIndexedInstanced` across all `ExecuteIndirect`, and instances are the total number of instances across all draw calls. In this particular case, only 2% of instances within the camera frustum passed all GPU culling steps.

1.7.2 GPU Instance Renderer in Assassin's Creed Mirage

In *Assassin's Creed Mirage*, it's not uncommon to encounter frames where over 1 million instances are dispatched to the GPU for culling, while tens of thousands of instances are actually rendered (Tables 1.4 and 1.5). In this section, we show the results of the GPU Instance Renderer on a typical frame of the game (Figure 1.29).

	Geometry Pass(es)	CullingFrame	CullingPass(es)
CPU	2.19 ms		
GPU	1.47 ms	0.22 ms	0.43 ms

Table 1.4. GPU Instance Renderer cost in *Assassin's Creed Mirage* on a typical frame when running on PlayStation 5 (Figure 1.29). These numbers aggregate all geometry passes in the frame (e.g., opaque, shadows).

Figure 1.29. Typical *Assassin's Creed Mirage* scene rendered at 1527p (dynamic resolution Sscaling) at 60 FPS on PlayStation 5, then upscaled to 4K.

	Draw Calls	Instances
Pre culling	147813	1299517
Post culling	2982	17539
Culled	98%	98.5%

Table 1.5. Culling efficiency in *Assassin's Creed Mirage* when rendering the scene shown in Figure 1.29. To interpret these values, refer to Table 1.3.

1.8   Conclusion and Future Work

The CPU has always been the main bottleneck in the *Assassin's Creed* games. This article described our effort to reduce this bottleneck by implementing a new GPU-driven pipeline: the GPU Instance Renderer.

Our main goal was to reduce the CPU cost of our previous pipeline, the BatchRenderer. We achieved this by batching instances at load time, introducing bindless resources (Section 1.5) for better batching, and moving more work to the GPU, thanks to our new utility library Database (Section 1.2) that allows for complex scene description and data replication between the CPU and the GPU. While our primary objective wasn't specifically focused on GPU execution time, we achieved significant improvements through better batching, culling optimizations, and leveraging async computes. Our findings, as demonstrated in Section 1.7, highlight substantial benefits for both the CPU and GPU resulting from this new pipeline.

When it comes to cluster and triangle culling, we've made it optional in this iteration because the benefits could vary across different scenes and render passes. This feature was introduced relatively late in the development of the GPUIR, and we think it could be greatly improved by moving it to mesh shaders. By doing so, we could eliminate the need for additional buffers (Section 1.4.4), handle instancing better, and streamline the whole process. The main reason we didn't implement this for *Assassin's Creed Mirage* is because it's a cross-gen game, and mesh shaders were not supported across all target platforms, including PlayStation 4 and Xbox One.

In the future, we aim to expand the GPU Instance Renderer to support continuous levels of detail made of cluster hierarchies, akin to the virtual geometry presented in [Karis 21]. We also intend to explore work graphs to assess if they could help us improve and streamline our pipeline. However, it's important to note this API is not yet available across all the main platforms we develop on.

Acknowledgements

We would like to thank Ulrich Haar, who helped us implement the GPU Instance Renderer, and Francis Boivin, Michel Gaudreault, Alexandre Blaquière, Daryl Teo, Mykola Naichuck, Lionel Berenguier, Jack Minnetian, Frederic Matz, Sylvain Marleau, Kaori Kato, Luc Poirier, Christian Desautels, Robert Foriel, Danny Oros, and the whole *Assassin's Creed Mirage* and Anvil teams for their contribution and support. We would also like to thank Sebastian Aaltonen, Tiago Rodrigues, Graham Wihlidal, and Brian Karis for their work on, respectively, [Haar and Aaltonen 15], [Rodrigues 17], [Wihlidal 17], and [Karis 21]; Michel Bouchard for all the nice discussions; Wolfgang Engel for his editorial work; and Manon Gomes, Joel Morange, Marc-Alexis Côté, and Florence Baccard.

1.9   Appendix

1.9.1   Database "Hello World" Code Generation

```
struct TestStructure
{
    int       IntValue;
    // SSEAlign will force alignment of FloatVectorValue on 16 bytes
    float4   FloatVectorValue; <SSEAlign>
};


databasetable TestStructureTable
{
    int              IntValue;
    TestStructure    Structure;
};
```

Listing 1.25. Simple database table declaration, input for the SIG Compiler.

```
struct TestStructureTableRO
{
    ByteAddressBuffer Table;
    uint               Size;
    uint               ReservedSize;

    static TestStructureTableRO
    Create(const ByteAddressBuffer table)
    {
        TestStructureTableRO newTable;
      uint2 header = table.Load2(0);
        newTable.Table = table;
        newTable.Size = header.x;
        newTable.ReservedSize = header.y;
        return newTable;
    }
    bool IsValid(in const uint row)
    {
      if(row >= Size) return false;
        uint offsetInBytes = GetTableOffsetSoA(row, 0, 0, 0, 4, ReservedSize);
        return Table.Load(offsetInBytes) != uint(-1);
    }
    int GetIntValueAt(in const uint row)
    {
        uint offsetInBytes = GetTableOffsetSoA(row, 0, 0, 0, 4, ReservedSize);
        int value = asint(Table.Load(offsetInBytes + 0));
        return value;
    }

    // IntValue is located at offset 0 in struct TestStructure
    // FloatVectorValue is located at offset 16 in struct TestStructure
    // (because of the use of <SSEAlign> in TestStructure declaration)
    //
    // Note the use of asint and Load for reading the int value,
    // and Load4 and asfloat for reading the float4 values
    TestStructure GetStructureAt(in const uint row)
    {
        uint offsetInBytes = GetTableOffsetSoA(row, 0, 4, 0, 32, ReservedSize);
        TestStructure value;
        value.IntValue = asint(Table.Load(offsetInBytes + 0));
        value.FloatVectorValue = asfloat(Table.Load4(offsetInBytes + 16));
        return value;
    }
};
```

```
struct TestStructureTableRW
{
    RWByteAddressBuffer Table;
    uint                Size;
    uint                ReservedSize;

    static TestStructureTableRW Create(const RWByteAddressBuffer table)
    {
        TestStructureTableRW newTable;
      uint2 header = table.Load2(0);
        newTable.Table = table;
        newTable.Size = header.x;
        newTable.ReservedSize = header.y;
        return newTable;
    }
    bool IsValid(in const uint row)
    {
      if(row >= Size) return false;
        uint offsetInBytes = GetTableOffsetSoA(row, 0, 0, 0, 4, ReservedSize);
        return Table.Load(offsetInBytes) != uint(-1);
    }
    int GetIntValueAt(in const uint row)
    {
        uint offsetInBytes = GetTableOffsetSoA(row, 0, 0, 0, 4, ReservedSize);
        int value = asint(Table.Load(offsetInBytes + 0));
        return value;
    }
    TestStructure GetStructureAt(in const uint row)
    {
        uint offsetInBytes = GetTableOffsetSoA(row, 0, 4, 0, 32, ReservedSize);
        TestStructure value;
        value.IntValue = asint(Table.Load(offsetInBytes + 0));
        value.FloatVectorValue = asfloat(Table.Load4(offsetInBytes + 16));
        return value;
    }
    void SetIntValueAt(in const uint row, in const int value)
    {
        uint offsetInBytes = GetTableOffsetSoA(row, 0, 0, 0, 4, ReservedSize);
        Table.Store(offsetInBytes + 0, asuint(value));
    }

    // Similarly to GetStructureAt, we use the same offsets for storing data
    // Note the use of asuint as we store everyting in a ByteAddressBuffer
    void SetStructureAt(in const uint row, in const TestStructure value)
    {
        uint offsetInBytes = GetTableOffsetSoA(row, 0, 4, 0, 32, ReservedSize);
        Table.Store(offsetInBytes + 0, asuint(value.IntValue));
        Table.Store4(offsetInBytes + 16, asuint(value.FloatVectorValue));
    }
    void SetAt(const in uint row, in const int IntValue, in const TestStructure Structure)
    {
        SetIntValueAt(row, IntValue);
        SetStructureAt(row, Structure);
    }
};
```

Listing 1.26. Example of generated HLSL code and accessors for Listing 1.25.

```
namespace TestStructureTable {
struct Type
{
    static const U32 Hash = 0x1089437D; // Hash of TestStructureTable
```

```
        static database::TableTypeDesc GetDesc(database::TableColumnDesc columns[2], database
        ::TableStreamDesc streams[2])
        {
            database::TableColumnAttribute<CBInt>(
                columns[0],"IntValue", "CBInt", 0, 0, 0, 4);
            database::TableColumnAttribute<TestStructure>(
                columns[1],"Structure", "TestStructure", 0, 4, 0, 32);

            TableStreamSoA(streams[0], 0, 4);
            TableStreamSoA(streams[1], 4, 32);

            return {"TestStructureTable", columns, 2, streams, 2, Hash, 0, (U32)-1};
        }
};

typedef database::TableRow<Type> Row;
typedef database::TableRange<Type> Range;
typedef database::TablePartialRange<Type> PartialRange;
typedef database::TableRef<Type> Ref;

struct Table : database::TableBase<Table, database::TableStorageCPU<Table>, database::
        TableRowAllocatorPersistent<Table>, database::TableWriterSimple<Table>>
{
    typedef Table TableT;
    typedef TestStructureTable::Row RowT;
    typedef TestStructureTable::Range RangeT;
    typedef TestStructureTable::PartialRange PartialRangeT;
    typedef TestStructureTable::Ref RefT;

    Table(U32 maxRows)
        : database::TableBase<Table, database::TableStorageCPU<Table>, database::
        TableRowAllocatorPersistent<Table>, database::TableWriterSimple<Table>>(maxRows, Type
        ::GetDesc(Columns, Streams))
        , Index{ *this }
        , IntValue{ *this, 0, 0 }
        , Structure{ *this, 0, 1 }
    { }

    void SetReferences() { }

    database::TypedTable<TableT> Index;
    database::TypedTableColumnRW<TableT, CBInt, database::RowAccess<0, 0, 4>> IntValue;
    database::TypedTableColumnRW<TableT, TestStructure, database::RowAccess<0, 4, 32>>
        Structure;

    RowT New(const CBInt& IntValue_, const TestStructure& Structure_)
    {
        RowT row = RowT::ToDerived(Alloc());
        if(row.IsValid())
        {
            IntValue.Set(row, IntValue_);
            Structure.Set(row, Structure_);
        }
        return row;
    }
    RangeT NewArray(U32 count, const CBInt* IntValue_, const TestStructure* Structure_)
    {
        RangeT row = RangeT::ToDerived(Alloc(count, 1));
        if(row.IsValid())
        {
            if(IntValue_) IntValue.Set(row, IntValue_);
            if(Structure_) Structure.Set(row, Structure_);
        }
        return row;
    }
```

```
    database::TableColumnDesc Columns[2];
    database::TableStreamDesc Streams[2];

    Table::RefT Ref() { return {this, 0x1089437D /* TestStructureTable */}; }
};
} // namespace TestStructureTable
```

Listing 1.27. Example of generated C++ code and for Listing 1.25. It is more engine-specific than its HLSL counterpart and relies heavily on the SIG Compiler and some engine utility code. This is shared as a reference so the reader can start writing their own database compiler with a clear target in mind.

1.9.2   Database Dirty Page Update Code

```
template<typename TT0, typename TT1>
void TypedTableUpdate::UpdateTableDirtyRangeCPUToGPU(GfxComputeDevice& device, const TT0&
    Source, TT1& Dest, const Range& range)
{
    Assert(((range.Row + range.Count - 1) / C_DIRTY_TABLE_PAGE_SIZE) <=
        (Source.Size() / C_DIRTY_TABLE_PAGE_SIZE));
    Assert(((range.Row + range.Count - 1) / C_DIRTY_TABLE_PAGE_SIZE) <=
        (Dest.Size() / C_DIRTY_TABLE_PAGE_SIZE));

    // Update dirty page range
    U32 startOffset = range.Row * C_DIRTY_PAGE_SIZE;
    U32 countInBytes = range.Count *  C_DIRTY_PAGE_SIZE;
    U32 destOffset = startOffset + Dest.StreamData(0).OffsetInBytes + TableColumnDesc::
    C_GPU_TABLE_HEADER;

    ScopedWriteableBufferMap bufferMap(device, *Dest.GetGPUBuffer(),
        destOffset, countInBytes);
    MemCopy(bufferMap.GetDataPtr(), Source.DataPtr() + Source.StreamData(0).OffsetInBytes
    + startOffset, countInBytes);
}

template<typename TT0, typename TT1>
void TypedTableUpdate::UpdateRangesCPUToGPUInternal(GfxComputeDevice& device, const TT0&
    Source, TT1& Dest)
{
    U32 maxElements;
    const G4::BitArray<>& dirtyElements = Source.GetDirtyElements(maxElements);
    U32 dirtyElementCount = Source.GetDirtyElementCount();

    // Find dirty Element range for update
    U32 currentElement = 0;
    U32 startElement = C_INVALID_ROW;
    Bool currentDirty = false;
    while ((dirtyElementCount > 0) &&
        (currentElement < maxElements))
    {
        Bool dirty = dirtyElements.get_element(currentElement) > 0;
        startElement = !currentDirty && dirty ? currentElement : startElement;
        if (currentDirty && !dirty)
        {
            // End of dirty range
            UpdateTableDirtyRangeCPUToGPU(device, Source, Dest,
                { startElement, currentElement - startElement });
            dirtyElementCount -= currentElement - startElement;
        }
        currentDirty = dirty;
```

```
        currentElement++;
    }

    if (currentDirty)
        UpdateTableDirtyRangeCPUToGPU(device, Source, Dest, { startElement, currentElement
        - startElement });
}
```

Listing 1.28. C++ code that handles a dirty page update. This is the code that `UpdateTable` in Listing 1.12 ends up calling when a table uses the `DirtyPages` update policy.

Bibliography

[Cignoni et al. 05] P. Cignoni, F. Ganovelli, E. Gobbetti, F. Marton, F. Ponchio, and R. Scopigno. "Batched Multi Triangulation." In *VIS 05: IEEE Visualization 2005*, pp. 207–214. IEEE Press, 2005. https://vcg.isti.cnr.it/Publications/2005/CGGMPS05/BatchedMT_Vis05.pdf.

[Greene et al. 93] Ned Greene, Michael Kass, and Gavin Miller. "Hierarchical Z-Buffer Visibility." In *Proceedings of the 20th Annual Conference on Computer Graphics and Interactive Techniques, SIGGRAPH '93*, p. 231–238. Association for Computing Machinery, 1993. https://doi.org/10.1145/166117.166147.

[Haar and Aaltonen 15] Ulrich Haar and Sebastian Aaltonen. "GPU Driven Rendering Pipelines." Presented at SIGGRAPH, 2015. https://advances.realtimerendering.com/s2015/aaltonenhaar_siggraph2015_combined_final_footer_220dpi.pdf.

[Hill 10] Stephen Hill. "Rendering with Conviction." Presented at Game Developers Conference, 2010. https://www.selfshadow.com/talks/rwc_gdc2010_v1.pdf.

[Karis 21] Brian Karis. "Nanite: A Deep Dive." Presented at SIGGRAPH, 2021. https://advances.realtimerendering.com/s2021/Karis_Nanite_SIGGRAPH_Advances_2021_final.pdf.

[Kumar et al. 96] Subodh Kumar, Dinesh Manocha, Bill Garrett, and Ming Lin. "Hierarchical Back-Face Culling." Technical report, 1996. https://wwwx.cs.unc.edu/~geom/papers/documents/technicalreports/tr96014.pdf.

[Olano and Greer 97] Marc Olano and Trey Greer. "Triangle Scan Conversion Using 2D Homogeneous Coordinates." In *Proceedings of the ACM SIGGRAPH/EUROGRAPHICS Workshop on Graphics Hardware, HWWS '97*, p. 89–95. Association for Computing Machinery, 1997. https://doi.org/10.1145/258694.258723.

[Rodrigues 17] Tiago Rodrigues. "Advanced Graphics Tech: Moving to DirectX 12: Lessons Learned." Presented at Game Developers Conference, 2017. https://www.gdcvault.com/play/1024386/Advanced-Graphics-Tech-Moving-to.

[Silvennoinen 12] Ari Silvennoinen. "Chasing Shadows." *Game Developer Magazine* 19:2 (2012), 49–53. https://arisilvennoinen.github.io/Publications/Chasing_Shadows.pdf.

[Wihlidal 17] Graham Wihlidal. "Optimizing the Graphics Pipeline with Compute." In *GPU Zen: Advanced Rendering Techniques*, edited by Wolfgang Engel, pp. 277–320. Black Cat Publishing, 2017.

GPU-Driven Curve Generation from Mesh Contour

Wangziwei Jiang

2.1 Introduction

The contour or silhouette lines are crucial in art forms such as movies, animation, and games. In real-time graphics, two methods are being used: Games such as *Borderlands* render thick outlines using an edge detection image filter; For outlining characters, games like *Guilty Gear Xrd* [Motomura 15] and *Genshin Impact* use the "inverted hull" method, which draws an extruded mesh with frontface culling. Both methods are limited to plain black lines; this is because sophisticated stylization (Figure 2.1) requires explicit curve topology: the contours are extracted as curves in 2D or 3D, represented as polylines or splines, which can be stylized with textured strokes or other procedural stylization [Bénard and Hertzmann 19].

To address this limitation, we introduced the first real-time approach that generates curves from the mesh contour [Jiang et al. 22]. Compared to existing methods in games, it generates explicit curve topology, allowing for sophisticated stylizations that have never been achieved in real-time. Additionally, our method includes the ability to vectorize binary images, leading to broader usage. It generates curves comparable to offline line art renderers [PSOFT 17, Grabli 13], but also shares their common weakness—curves flicker when they are heavily stylized; this will be discussed in Section 2.4.1.

This article discusses the technical facets of our method, followed by a discussion of its limitations.

2.2 Overview

Any contour rendering method has to answer two fundamental questions.

How Can We Define the Mesh Contour? Contour curves separate the surface into front- and backfacing regions. In triangular meshes, it is discretized as any edge between a frontface and a backface. Subsequently, these edges or their pixels can be used to construct the curves (Figure 2.3).

61

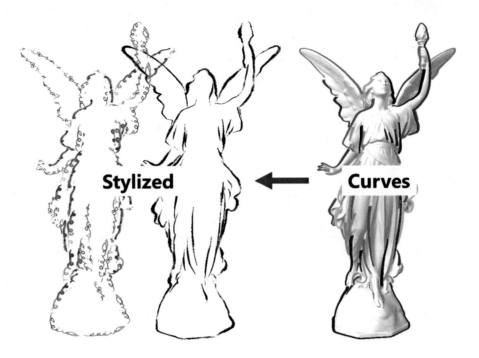

Figure 2.1. Sophisticated stylization of contour curves. Extracted curves can be stylized with different brush simulations [DiVerdi 13], which is commonly implemented in digital painting applications such as Adobe Photoshop and Adobe Illustrator.

2D or 3D Curves? Ideally, contour edges could be connected into 3D polylines. However, in reality, these edges often exhibit tiny zigzags, kinks, loops, and other undesirable topological complexity, regardless of how finely the surface was sampled—neither traditional smoothing nor remeshing helps. Cleaning up such a mess is computationally expensive [Bénard et al. 14]. However, there is a silver lining: once the contour edges are rasterized, the resulting 2D lines exhibit a clean topology (Figure 2.4). Furthermore, pixel grids are better suited for parallelization.

The above observation leads to an image-space solution, which takes in triangulated meshes and outputs 2D curves; each curve corresponds to a contiguous portion of the visible contour (Figure 2.2). In the upcoming sections, we will provide a conceptual overview of the method. Subsequently, we will elaborate on the implementation details.

2.2.1 Contour Rasterization

The simplest solution for collecting contour pixels is to apply an image filter to G-buffers or screen texture and collect feature pixels. However, the image

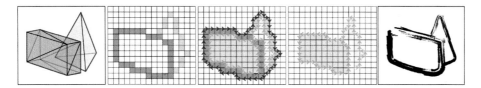

Figure 2.2. Overview of our method. From left to right: contour as mesh edges (marked as red), contour pixels, traced borders, contour curves, and stylized strokes.

filter usually generates noise pixels, which can significantly damaging the curve topology.

To ensure accuracy, our method follows the geometric definition to select contour edges and render them to a texture (contour image). The resulting pixels from the contour edges are referred to as the contour pixels. When the screen resolution is sufficient, these pixels are noise-free and accurately correspond to the mesh contour.

Specifically, we first identify and gather the contour edges by selecting edges between front- and backfaces. Then, contour edges are rendered as 2-pixel-wide lines. The outcome is referred to as a contour image, which resembles a line drawing made up of thin strips of contour pixels (Figure 2.3).

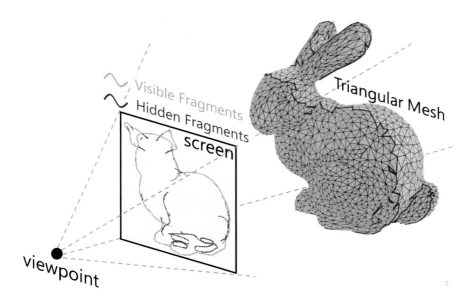

Figure 2.3. Rasterizing contour from edges (marked as red on the bunny mesh) to screen, with an occlusion test to discard hidden contour.

After obtaining the contour image, an evident approach would be to take the contour image, extract a skeleton that is one pixel wide, and then connect the skeleton pixels to create curves. Unfortunately, intricate procedures are required for line junction resolution, which makes a real-time GPU implementation unfeasible (Figure 2.4). Instead, we present a novel algorithm based on image tracing.

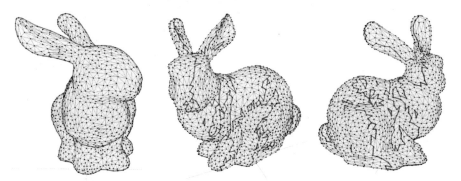

Figure 2.4. From left to right: camera view and two side views of the contour edges. Contour curves appear to be smooth on screen, but have very irregular topology on the mesh.

2.2.2   Generate 2D Curves

Based on the rasterized lines, pixel borders are traced and then segmented to produce curves.

Image Tracing We parallelize Potrace [Selinger 03], a standard image tracing method used in image processing applications, to trace the borders around the contour pixels. Potrace works on binary images consisting of foreground and background pixels. It traces the boundaries around the foreground pixels, creating closed sequences of pixel edges. In our case, where the contour image consists of contour pixels and empty pixels, the Potrace algorithm is an ideal choice, and its simplicity allows for easy parallelization.

The tracing process consists of two stages (Figure 2.5).

In the first stage, the algorithm identifies the contour pixels and extracts the border loops surrounding them. Borders are created by connecting the edges between the contour pixels and the empty pixels. To establish connections, Potrace employs a straightforward approach that involves examining a 2×2 neighborhood of each pixel.

In the second stage, the algorithm reorganizes the image borders stored in linked lists by converting them into linear arrays. In the original Potrace algorithm, this is done by selecting a starting edge and following its linked list,

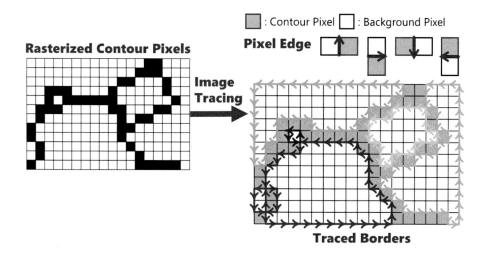

Figure 2.5. Applying image tracing to the contour image.

transforming each list into an array. Subsequently, pixel edges along traced borders are stored in circular arrays, where the chosen starting edge becomes the first element.

The iterative traversal in the second phase poses a big challenge for parallelization. To overcome this, we employ a technique called parallel list ranking to convert the linked lists into arrays.

To wrap up, after image tracing, pixel edges are generated and connected, surrounding the borders of contour pixels. These pixel edges are then stored in a pool of circular arrays, where each array corresponds to a traced border.

Border Segmentation   Finally, we take portions from traced borders to create contour curves (Figure 2.6), which resemble the image lines generated from contour rasterization (Section 2.2.1). The intuition is that these image lines are very thin, usually 1 to 2 pixels wide, hence their shape can be closely resembled by the surrounding borders.

To accurately depict a contour curve, a suitable segment from the surrounding border(s) is chosen. This selection should ensure that there is a unique correlation between the curve and border segment, and each segment should align with the visibility transitions. To achieve this, we developed a simple yet effective heuristic (Figure 2.7).

The heuristic works by the fact that each contour curve divides the surrounding image into "inside" and "outside" sections. This division occurs because each projected contour edge separates the nearby screen into two parts: either inside or outside the mesh surface. Since a contour curve consists of pixel samples from these contour edges, it exhibits the same characteristic.

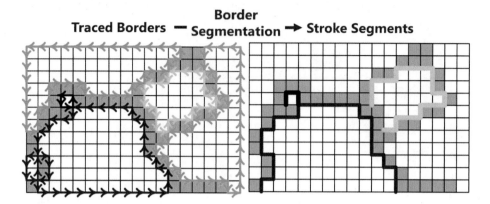

Figure 2.6. Segmenting the traced borders to generate curves. Take the head of the Stanford bunny as an example.

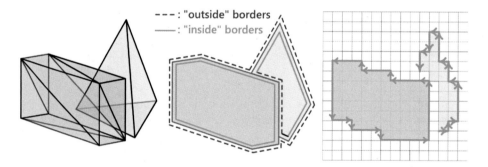

Figure 2.7. Heuristic to extract contour curves. From left to right: a box partially occludes a tetrahedron, image borders are traced, and only "inside" borders are preserved. Note that visibility changes when the contour switches between inside and outside.

While both the inside and outside of a curve are covered by traced borders, we only consider the "inside" part to represent the contour curve. This ensures that the curve maintains proper topology since visibility transitions occur when the border shifts between the "inside" and "outside" regions. We will describe how to identify inside- or outside-borders in Section 2.3.4.

2.3   Implementation

This section presents the technical aspects of our method. We start by introducing several parallel computing primitives. Equipped with these tools, we then explain the actual implementation of the method.

2.3.1 Parallel Computing Primitives

In parallel programming, efficient algorithm primitives are encapsulated for frequently encountered patterns. This subsection aims to describe the ones used in our approach and provide guidelines for efficient implementation.

Scan To efficiently calculate the prefix sum of array elements, a technique called parallel scan can be employed [Mark Harris 07]. This involves dividing the input array into smaller blocks that fit within a thread group or SIMD wave. Then, partial prefix sums are calculated for each block on group shared memory or vector registers. These partial sums are combined with the sums of preceding blocks, which can be computed from the prefix sum of per-block total sums. This method is used in tasks such as integration. In a more generic case, the operator is not limited to adding—you can do multiplication, maximum, minimum, etc.

A parallel scan requires three passes [Blelloch 90]: computing partial sums within each block ("upsweep"), scanning on block aggregates to compute per-block offsets ("reduce"), and adding those offsets back to each block ("downsweep"). When the data scale is large, each thread can sequentially scan on a chunk of items and use the partial sum for the global scan. When wave/warp intrinsics are supported on the GPU, the upsweep phase can be recursively split into three phases. A recent work provides a single-pass scan, using a "look-back" window buffer to sync partial sums between different thread groups [Merrill and Garland 16]. This idea is not limited to parallel scans but can also apply to other algorithms that have sequential dependency between thread groups, for example, Radix Sort or Jacobi solvers. (See Listing 2.1.)

```
// Data type, can be int, float, etc.
#define T uint
// Scan operator, can be mul, max, min, etc.
#define SCAN_OP(a, b) (a + b)

// For intra-wave scan,
// there are two special cases for optimization:
// (1) For summation, one can just use WavePrefixSum.
T AddScanWave(T val, bool inclusive = false)
{
  T scanResWarp = WavePrefixSum(val);
  return (!inclusive) ? scanResWarp : (scanResWarp + val);
}
// (2) For bit counting, just use WavePrefixCountBits.
T BitScanWave_(bool val, bool inclusive = false)
{
  uint scanResWarp = WavePrefixCountBits(val);
  return (!inclusive) ? scanResWarp : (scanResWarp + val);
}
// (3) Otherwise, Generic Intra-Wave Scan is needed:
#define WARP_SCAN_PASS(i)
prev = WaveReadLaneAt(scanResWarp, laneId - i);
scanResWarp =
```

```
  ((i <= laneId) ? (SCAN_OP(prev, scanResWarp)) : scanResWarp);

T GenericScanWave(T val, bool inclusive = false)
{
  uint laneId = WaveGetLaneIndex();

  T scanResWarp = val;
  T prev;
  /* Inclusive generic warp scan */
  WARP_SCAN_PASS(1u)
  WARP_SCAN_PASS(2u)
  WARP_SCAN_PASS(4u)
  WARP_SCAN_PASS(8u)
  WARP_SCAN_PASS(16u)

  T prevIncSum = WaveReadLaneAt(scanResWarp, max(laneId, 1) - 1);
  return inclusive ? scanResWarp :
  (laneId > 0 ? prevIncSum : T_IDENTITY);
}



// ----------------------------------------------------------
// Scan operator within a thread group

// Group shared memory to cache the scan result of each wave
groupshared T SCAN_CACHE[THREAD_GROUP_SIZE / 32u];

T ScanBlock(T value, uint groupIdx : SV_GroupIndex, bool inclusive =
  false)
{
  T sum = WavePrefixSumFunc(value, inclusive);

  /* Get wave size and wave index */
  const uint waveSize = WaveGetLaneCount();
  const uint waveIdx = groupIdx / waveSize;

  if (WaveGetLaneIndex() == waveSize - 1){
    SCAN_CACHE[waveIdx] = inclusive ? sum : SCAN_OP(sum, value)
  }
  GroupMemoryBarrierWithGroupSync();

  const uint numWaves = TG_SIZE / waveSize;
  if (groupIdx < numWaves)
  {
    const T laneSum = SCAN_CACHE[groupIdx];
    const T waveSum = WavePrefixSumFunc(laneSum, false);
    SCAN_CACHE[groupIdx] = waveSum;
  }
  GroupMemoryBarrierWithGroupSync();

  sum = SCAN_OP(SCAN_CACHE[waveIdx], sum);
  return sum;
}
```

Listing 2.1. Block-level parallel scan using wave intrinsics.

Compaction Stream compaction, a.k.a. stream filtering or selection, takes an array and outputs the desired elements to another array. This new array is then used for further processing. A good example is cluster culling, where only visible meshlets are retained to reduce the workload.

Parallel scan operator can be employed for a compaction, where preserved elements have values of 1 and deleted elements 0. The output addresses of preserved ones are their prefix sums.

Out-of-order compaction can be optimized with a single-pass approach using atomic counters. In this approach, each thread group counts for its compacted elements, uses that count to increment-fetch a global atomic counter, and adds the fetched value back to its partial sums.

Segmented Scan Sometimes, we need to scan separately on arbitrary contiguous segments within the input array. Such an operation can be implemented as an extension of the scan primitive. With a "head flag" array to distinguish segment headers and a few minor adjustments, the parallel scan algorithm can be modified to implement a segmented scan (Listing 2.2).

```
// Intra-Wave SegScan
#define WARP_SEGSCAN_PASS(i)
prev = WaveReadLaneAt(scanResWarp, laneId - i);
scanResWarp =
((i <= distToSeghead) ? (SCAN_OP(prev, scanResWarp)) : scanResWarp);


T CAT(SegScanIncWave_, tag)(
bool inclusive,
uint laneId, T val, bool hf,
out uint hfBitMaskWholeWave,
out uint hfBitMaskPrevLanes,
out T scanResWarpInc
){
  T scanResWarp = val;

  uint laneMaskRt = /* Inclusive lane mask */
  ((~(0u)) >> (WaveGetLaneCount() - 1 - laneId));
  hfBitMaskWholeWave = WaveActiveBallot(hf);
  hfBitMaskPrevLanes = (hfBitMaskWholeWave & laneMaskRt);

  uint distToSeghead =
  hfBitMaskPrevLanes != 0 ?
  laneId - firstbithigh(hfBitMaskPrevLanes) : laneId;
  T prev;

  WARP_SEGSCAN_PASS(1u)
  WARP_SEGSCAN_PASS(2u)
  WARP_SEGSCAN_PASS(4u)
  WARP_SEGSCAN_PASS(8u)
  WARP_SEGSCAN_PASS(16u)

  scanResWarpInc = scanResWarp;/* Output inclusive sum */
```

```
    T prevIncSum = WaveReadLaneAt(scanResWarp, max(laneId, 1) - 1);
    return inclusive ? scanResWarp :
    ((laneId > 0 && distToSeghead != 0) ? prevIncSum : T_IDENTITY);
}


// ----------------------------------------------------------
// Intra-Block SegScan
groupshared T SCAN_CACHE[SCAN_CACHE_SIZE];
// ==1 if element is the head of a segment
groupshared uint SCAN_CACHE_HF[SCAN_CACHE_SIZE];

T SegScanIncBlock(
bool inclusive,
uint groupIdx : SV_GroupIndex,
T val, bool hf, out bool hfScanBlock
) {
  const uint waveSize = WaveGetLaneCount();
  uint laneId = WaveGetLaneIndex();
  uint waveId = groupIdx.x / waveSize;

  T valScanWaveInc;
  uint hfBitMaskWholeWave, hfBitMaskPrevLanes;
  T valScanWave = WaveSegScanInc(
  inclusive,
  laneId, val, hf,
  /* Out */
  hfBitMaskWholeWave, hfBitMaskPrevLanes,
  valScanWaveInc
  );
  /* OR-reduction of self&prev lanes' flags in this wave */
  bool hfScanWave = hfBitMaskPrevLanes != 0;

  T valWaveTotal = WaveReadLaneAt(
  valScanWaveInc, waveSize - 1
  );
  bool hfWaveTotal = /* OR-reduction of ALL flags in this wave */
  (hfBitMaskWholeWave != 0);

  GroupMemoryBarrierWithGroupSync();
  if (laneId == waveSize - 1)
  {
    SCAN_CACHE[waveId] = valWaveTotal;
    SCAN_CACHE_HF[waveId] = hfWaveTotal;
  }
  GroupMemoryBarrierWithGroupSync();

  if (waveId == 0)
  {
    T valWave = SCAN_CACHE[laneId];
    uint hfWave = SCAN_CACHE_HF[laneId];
    T dummy;
    T prevWaveSum = WaveSegScanInc(
    true, /* Always inclusive scan */
    laneId, valWave, hfWave,
```

```
    /* Out */
    hfBitMaskWholeWave, hfBitMaskPrevLanes,
    dummy
    );

    if (laneId < SCAN_CACHE_SIZE)
    {
      SCAN_CACHE[laneId] = prevWaveSum;
      SCAN_CACHE_HF[laneId] = hfBitMaskPrevLanes;
    }
  }

  GroupMemoryBarrierWithGroupSync();

  T valScanBlock = valScanWave;
  if (waveId != 0 && (!hfScanWave))
  {
    T prevWaveAcc = SCAN_CACHE[waveId - 1];
    valScanBlock = SCAN_OP(prevWaveAcc, valScanBlock);
  }

  hfScanBlock = hfScanWave;
  if (waveId != 0)
  hfScanBlock = (hfScanBlock || (SCAN_CACHE_HF[waveId - 1] != 0));

  return valScanBlock;
}
```

Listing 2.2. Block-level parallel segmented scan using wave intrinsics.

Allocation   In the process of stream allocation, an array is provided as input.
For each element of the array, a varying number of items are generated and
then stored in a new array. This concept can be seen in rasterization, where
every triangle is converted into a varying number of pixels. A segmented scan
operator is employed to carry out an order-preserving allocation. Similar to
parallel compaction, out-of-order allocation can be optimized into a single pass
using incrementing atomic counters.

The four primitives mentioned above are crucial for manipulating one-dimen-
sional arrays, which is the main format to store contour curves, generated from
pixel edges stored as linked lists. The conversion from linked lists to arrays is
parallelized with the list ranking algorithm.

List Ranking   List ranking computes the position, or rank, of each node in a linked
list. That is, the ith item in the list should be assigned the number i. This can
be implemented with a simple pointer-jumping process called Wyllie's algorithm
(Listing 2.3).

List ranking can be equivalently viewed as performing a prefix sum on the
linked list, where the accumulated values on each node are all equal to one.
Wyllie's algorithm also applies when the values are arbitrary on each node.

```
struct JumpPointer
{
  uint prevItemID;
  uint prefixSum;
};

void ListRanking_WyllieScheme(
uint itemId,
RWStructuredBuffer<JumpPointer> linkBufIn,
RWStructuredBuffer<JumpPointer> linkBufOut
){
  JumpPointer link = linkBufIn[itemId];
  JumpPointer linkPrev = linkBufIn[link.prevItemID];

  bool isListHead = link.prevItemID == itemId;
  // Accumulate prefix sum
  link.prefixSum = isListHead ? link.prefixSum : (linkPrev.prefixSum +
    link.prefixSum);
  // Pointer jumping
  link.prevItemID = isListHead ? link.prevItemID : linkPrev.prevItemID
  ;

  linkBufOut[itemId] = link;
}
```

Listing 2.3. Simple implementation of Wyllie's list ranking.

Ranking lists up to length n requires $\log(n)$ iterations, but this poses no issue as the pixel edges we are ranking are very sparse on the screen—from our experience, contour pixels only occupy 1% to 5% of the mesh's screen bounding box. For 2K image resolution, 18 iterations are adequate. To optimize, we spliced the list nodes into independent sets and applied pointer jumping to a small subset. This strategy reduced the time by 50%; however, it significantly raised the code complexity, making maintenance very challenging. Another simpler optimization would be to insert a compaction pass to remove the lists that already finished ranking, but that brings the overhead of reading indirect indices for later ranking passes.

2.3.2 Contour Rasterization

In this section, we'll cover detecting contour edges and the challenges of rendering them into an image.

To begin with, a compute kernel is dispatched on every face to determine its orientation, followed by another kernel to identify contour edges with two opposing faces or only one adjacent face (boundary edge). Concave edges are discarded since concave contours are always occluded. To utilize the sparsity of mesh contour (which usually make up 3% to 10% of the total mesh edges), we employ a parallel compaction kernel to collect the contour edges.

```
float4 LineAntiStipping(
  float4 posHClip, // Homogeneous Clip Space position of the vertex
  bool isBegVtxOnEdge, // The start vertex on the oriented edge?
  float2 screenSizeInv,
  float2 edgeScreenDir, // Screen direction of the edge
  float2 edgeScreenNormal // Screen normal of the edge
){
  float4 posHClipOpti = posHClip;
  // Depth bias
  posHClipOpti.z -= 1.0e-7 * posHClip.w;
  // Extrude out line on screen
  posHClipOpti.xy +=
  edgeScreenNormal * posHClip.w * screenSizeInv * 1.0f;
  // Extend line on screen
  float2 extendVec = (isBegVtxOnEdge) ? edgeScreenDir : -edgeScreenDir
  ;
  posHClipOpti.xy +=
  extendVec * posHClip.w * screenSizeInv * 1.5f;

  return posHClipOpti;
}
```

Listing 2.4. Vertex shader code to reduce line stipping.

Then, contour edges are drawn as line primitives onto the frame buffer. This process creates narrow pixel strips resembling 2D contour curves. These pixel strips have two necessary conditions for successful curve generation: they should be (1) thin enough to be approximated by their boundary curves and (2) consistently visible to avoid breaks caused by the "stippling" artifact.

Line stipping occurs when a thin line is mistakenly occluded by polygon fragments, due to different rasterization rules and depth aliasing. Contour features are particularly susceptible to this problem as the surrounding surface visibility is unstable. Hence, it is challenging to draw thin wireframe lines while avoiding stipping.

To overcome this, when drawing contour edges, we move them outward along their screen normals and slightly elongate them to fill any potential gaps (Listing 2.4). This approach is simpler and gives similar results compared to our original software rasterization scheme in [Jiang et al. 22].

One thing to note is that the four sides of the image should be bound with dummy contour pixels to ensure a valid input for image tracing.

2.3.3 Image Tracing

This section discusses implementation of the image tracing algorithm.

First, we detect pixel edges between contour and empty pixels, orienting each edge such that the contour pixel is on its right side. Then we use the allocation primitive (Section 2.3.1) to index the detected pixel edges.

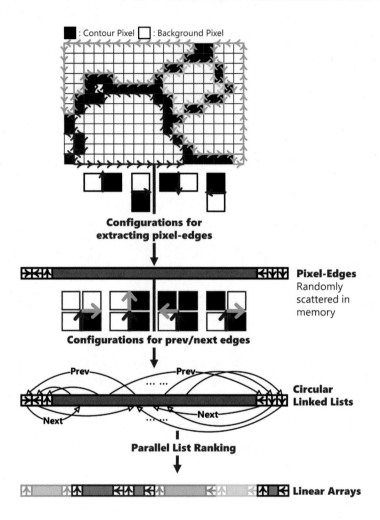

Figure 2.8. Process of the image tracing algorithm.

Next, we establish bidirectional pointers to connect these oriented edges. This entire process is carried out in a single pass based on a 2×2 window of each edge (see the configurations in Figure 2.8).

Finally, we utilize two list ranking passes to rearrange pixel edges into circular arrays. Recall that list ranking applies a prefix sum on a linked list by pointer jumping, thus the summing operator can be arbitrary (Section 2.3.1). During the first pass, we identify the head of each list using a integer-max prefix sum to locate the edge with the highest ID, then set the previous pointer of the header to itself. The second pass calculates the offsets from edges to their list header with an integer-add prefix sum.

Ranking pixel edges into circular arrays allows for two efficient operations.

Segmentation The first operation segments each circular array, given keys assigned to each item (Listing 2.5). To do this, we first identify the head and tail items by detecting the difference in keys compared to the predecessor and successor. Then, we calculate the offset from each item to its segment head/tail by two segmented scans; since the array is circular, we need to merge the two parts of the segment that extend between two ends of the array (Figure 2.9).

```
// Total number of elements in all arrays
uint GetNumAllElems();

// Circular array topology
struct CircularArrayInfo
{
  uint headItemID; // Beginning item
  uint tailItemID; // Ending item
  uint length;     // Array length
};
CircularArrayInfo GetCircularArrayInfo(uint itemID);

uint PrevItemID(uint itemID, CircularArrayInfo circArr)
{
  return itemID == circArr.headItemID ?
  circArr.tailItemID : itemID - 1;
}
uint NextItemID(uint itemID, CircularArrayInfo circArr)
{
  return itemID == circArr.tailItemID ?
  circArr.headItemID : itemID + 1;
}
void IsSegHeadOrTail(
uint itemID, out bool headFlag, out bool tailFlag
){ // Detect two ends of key segments
  CircularArrayInfo circArr = GetCircularArrayInfo(itemID);
  headFlag = (keyBuf[itemID] != keyBuf[PrevItemID(itemID)]);
  tailFlag = (keyBuf[itemID] != keyBuf[NextItemID(itemID)]);
}

// Segment topology, stored for each element
// --------------------------------------------------
// Index distance from each element to its segment head
RWStructuredBuffer<uint> RWBufSegRank;
// Length of each segment
RWStructuredBuffer<uint> RWBufSegLen;


[numthreads(GROUP_SIZE_SETUP, 1, 1)]
void CircularArraySegmentation_Main(
uint3 id : SV_DispatchThreadID,
uint groupIdx : SV_GroupIndex,
uint3 gIdx : SV_GroupID)
{
  ...
```

```
    uint segscanVal = 1;

    // 1st seg-scan pass -------------
    uint itemID = SV_DispatchThreadID.x;
    bool headFlag, tailFlag;
    IsSegHeadOrTail(itemID, /* Out */ headFlag, tailFlag);
    bool segScanHeadFlag_1 =
      headFlag || itemID == circularArray.headItemID;
    uint offsetToSegHead = SegmentedScan(
      itemID, segScanHeadFlag_1, segscanVal
    );
    RWBufSegRank[itemID] = offsetToSegHead;
    RWBufSegLen[itemID] = itemID - offsetToSegHead;
    ...

    // 2nd seg-scan pass -------------
    // Scan in a reversed order
    itemID = GetNumAllElems() - 1 - SV_DispatchThreadID.x;
    bool headFlag, tailFlag;
    IsSegHeadOrTail(itemID, /* Out */ headFlag, tailFlag);
    bool segScanHeadFlag_2 =
      tailFlag || itemID == circularArray.tailItemID;
    uint offsetToSegTail = SegmentedScan(
      itemID, segScanHeadFlag_2, segscanVal
    );
    uint segmentLen = offsetToSegHead + offsetToSegTail + 1;

    bufSegLen[itemID] = segmentLen;

    ...
}


// Fix circular jumps in the segmentations
// --------------------------------------------------
RWStructuredBuffer<uint> RWBufSegRank_fixed;
RWStructuredBuffer<uint> RWBufSegLen_fixed;

[numthreads(GROUP_SIZE_SETUP, 1, 1)]
void CircularArraySegmentation_FixCircularJumps(
  uint3 id : SV_DispatchThreadID,
  uint groupIdx : SV_GroupIndex,
  uint3 gIdx : SV_GroupID)
{
  uint itemID = SV_DispatchThreadID.x;

  uint segRank = RWBufSegRank[itemID];
  uint segHeadID = itemID - segRank;

  uint segLen = bufSegLen[itemID];
  uint segTailID = segHeadID + segLen - 1;

  CircularArrayInfo circArr = GetCircularArrayInfo(itemID);
  bool firstSegInLoop = (segHeadID == circArr.headItemID);
  bool lastSegInLoop  = (segTailID == circArr.tailItemID);
```

```
bool segmentIsTheWholeArray = (segLen == circArr.length);

bool needFix = // A segment is crossing the circular boundary?
(keyBuf[circArr.headItemID] == keyBuf[circArr.tailItemID])
&& (!segmentIsTheWholeArray);

// Merge the two segments,
// one at the start and the other at the end of the array
[branch] if (firstSegInLoop && needFix)
{
  uint prevSegLen = bufSegLen[edgeloop.tailEdgeID];
  RWBufSegRank_fixed[itemID] = segRank + prevSegLen;
  RWBufSegLen_fixed[itemID] = segLen + prevSegLen;
}
[branch] if (lastSegInLoop && needFix)
{
  uint nextSegLen = bufSegLen[edgeloop.headEdgeID];
  RWBufSegLen_fixed[itemID] = segLen + nextSegLen;
}

...

}
```

Listing 2.5. Parallel segmentation of circular arrays.

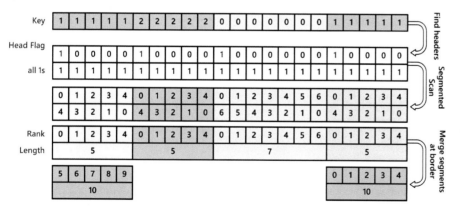

Figure 2.9. An example of segmenting a circular array into four segments. First, the segment head/tails are detected. Then, two segmented-scan passes are applied to compute the distance from each item to its segment head/tail. Finally, we correct the segmentation by merging the first and last segmented sequences.

Filtering The second operation enables efficient traversal of neighboring items (Figure 2.10). It can be seen as extending 1D convolution for multiple circular arrays. To accelerate neighboring queries, item attributes are cached in the group shared memory. We also cache extra items to account for jumps when the traversal crosses the head and tail of the circular array.

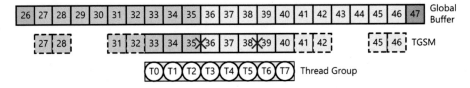

Figure 2.10. An example of filtering circular arrays. Arrays are colored differently. Let the thread group size be 8, and it's processing from item 33 to 40. Suppose the filtering radius is 2. We cache item data in group shared memory to accelerate neighboring queries. Except for caching items 31 to 42, we also cache extra items 27, 28, 45, and 46 to account for circular jumps at 35 and 39.

2.3.4 Curve Generation

In this section, we explain how to generate contour curves from the traced image. We provided an overview of the solution in Section 2.2.2, where we performed a test on traced borders to determine if their pixel edges are located inside or outside their enclosed surface.

To conduct such a test, we compare the orientations of pixel edges against their surrounding contour pixels. The pixel edges with consistent orientation are considered inside the mesh surface and part of the contour curves. This simple heuristic works surprisingly well for all types of topology. Now we explain how to estimate the orientation of pixel edges and contour pixels.

Orientation of Pixel Edges A pixel edge is oriented such that the enclosed contour pixel is always on its right-hand side. However, its four discrete directions are insufficient for our needs.

Instead, we fit a quadratic curve to the local shape around each pixel edge (Figure 2.11). The fitting scheme is based on the work of Lewiner et al. [Lewiner et al. 05]. We consider a pixel edge as a 2D sample point p_0. To estimate the tangent on p_0, the algorithm takes in a window of sample points (pixel edges): $\{p_{-q}, \ldots p_0, \ldots p_q\}$. Let the curve $r(s)$ be parameterized with arclength s, and set p_0 as the origin ($p_0 = r(0)$). We approximate $r(s)$ as a second order curve using Taylor expansion:

$$r(s) = r^{'}(0)s + \tfrac{1}{2}\, r''(0)s^2 + g(s)s^3. \qquad (2.1)$$

Next, we discretize the curve parameter s as the arclength distance from point p_k to p_0:

$$s_{\pm k} = \begin{cases} \pm\sum_{d=e}^{e\pm k} \|p_{d\pm 1}p_d\|, & k = 1, \ldots n \\ 0, & k = 0 \end{cases} \qquad (2.2)$$

Figure 2.11. Estimated tangent on traced borders.

Then, we substitute s_k into Equation (2.1) and try to minimize the squared difference $\sum_{k=-n}^{n} w_k (p_k - r(s_k))^2$, which can be separated for the x- and y-axes: Equations (2.3) and (2.4) provide the formula for the x-axis, and the computation on the y-axis can be carried out similarly:

$$E\left(x_0', x_0''\right) = \sum_{k=-n}^{n} w_k \left(x_k - r(s_k)\right)^2 \qquad (2.3)$$

We minimize Equation (2.3) by solving a simple linear system:

$$\begin{bmatrix} a_1 & a_2 \\ a_3 & a_4 \end{bmatrix} \cdot \begin{bmatrix} x_0' \\ x_0'' \end{bmatrix} = \begin{bmatrix} b_{x,1} \\ b_{x,2} \end{bmatrix},$$
$$a_m = \sum_{k=-n}^{n} w_k s_k^m, \quad m = 1, 2, 3, \qquad (2.4)$$
$$b_{x,l} = \sum_{k=-n}^{n} w_k s_k^l x_k, \quad l = 1, 2.$$

By definition, the tangent at the central sample p_0 is the normalized first-order derivative $r'(0)/\|r'(0)\|$, where $r'(0) = (x_0', y_0')$, which can be easily calculated after solving Equation (2.4). The second-order feature (curvature) can also be estimated using x_0'', but we omit that for simplicity.

Curve fitting can be efficiently parallelized with the filtering operator defined in Section 2.3.3. Two filtering passes are involved. The first pass samples the midpoint of each edge and then applies the Laplacian operator to smooth the midpoints. To estimate the tangent, the second kernel (Listing 2.6) applies the curve fitting to these points: it accumulates parameters $w_k s_k^m$ and $w_k s_k^l x_k$ from neighboring points and then solves the system in Equation (2.4). We take 25 taps, which means visiting 25 neighboring pixel edges. This is still efficient since the contour pixels are very sparse on the screen, and we are caching the samples into group shared memory using our filtering operator.

```
// Visit each neighboring pixel edge in the local window
// and accumulate weighted least squares parameters
void AccumulateWLSFittingParams(
  uint windowSize,
  float l, float2 dl,
  inout float3 a_123,
  inout float4 b_x1y1_x2y2
){
  float wi = abs(l) / (float)windowSize;

  float val = wi * l * l;
  a_123[0] += val; // a1 <- a1 + wi * li^2
  val *= (0.5 * l);
  a_123[1] += val; // a2 <- a2 + wi/2 * li^3
  val *= (0.5 * l);
  a_123[2] += val; // a3 <- a3 + wi/4 * li^4

  dl = (wi * l) * dl;
  b_x1y1_x2y2.xyzw += float4(dl.xy, 0.5 * l * dl.xy); // bx1, by1, bx2
  , by2
}

// Info for each traced image border
struct CircularArrayInfo
{
  uint headItemID; // Beginning pixel edge ID
  uint tailItemID; // Ending pixel edge ID
  uint length;      // # pixel edges in this border
};

// Operator defined in Section 2.3.3
// Here we use it to get the neighboring pixel edge position
float2 SegmentedFiltering(int offset, CircularArrayInfo border);

// Fit locally to a quadratic curve
void CurveFitting(
  float2 ptclCoord,
  CircularArrayTopology borderLoop,
  out float2 tangent
){
  // WLS Params -------------------------------------------
  float3 a_123 = 0;   // .xyz: [a1, a2, a3]
  float4 b_x1y1_x2y2 = 0; // .xyzw: [bx1, by1, bx2, by2]

  float l_1 = 0; // Current arc len (left)
  float l_r = 0; // Current arc len (right)

  // Accumulate Params -----------------------------------
  #define FITTING_RADIUS 8u
  uint windowSize = FITTING_RADIUS*2u + 1u;
  [unroll]
  for (uint d = 1; d <= FITTING_RADIUS; ++d)
  { // Traverse backward
```

```
    float2 neighCoord = SegmentedFiltering(-d, borderLoop);
    float2 dl = neighCoord - ptclCoord;
    l_l -= length(dl); // Negative arc-length

    AccumulateWLSFittingParams(windowSize, l_l, dl, a_123, b_x1y1_x2y2
);
  }
  [unroll]
  for (uint d = 1; d <= FITTING_RADIUS; ++d)
  { // Traverse forward
    float2 neighCoord = SegmentedFiltering(+d, borderLoop);

    float2 dl = neighCoord - ptclCoord;
    l_r += length(dl);
    AccumulateWLSFittingParams(windowSize, l_r, dl, a_123, b_x1y1_x2y2
);
  }

  #define A1 a_123[0]
  #define A2 a_123[1]
  #define A3 a_123[2]
  #define BX1 b_x1y1_x2y2.x
  #define BY1 b_x1y1_x2y2.y
  #define BX2 b_x1y1_x2y2.z
  #define BY2 b_x1y1_x2y2.w
  float dInv = rcp((A1 * A3) - (A2 * A2));
  float2 dr = float2(    // (dr/dx, dr/dy)
  (A3 * BX1) - (A2 * BX2),
  (A3 * BY1) - (A2 * BY2)
  );
  dr *= dInv;
  tangent = normalize(dr);
}
```

Listing 2.6. Parallel segmentation of circular arrays.

Orientation of Contour Pixels Seen from the viewpoint, vertices at a frontface (respectively backface) have a counterclockwise (respectively clockwise) winding order. Let each contour edge share the same vertex winding with its adjacent frontface, then the contour curves can be consistently oriented. Then, we obtain the 2D orientation for each contour edge by subtracting the screen positions of the end and start vertices. The orientation is encoded as color and rendered to the contour pixels.

2.3.5 Generating Curve Geometry

Now that each curve is extracted as a sequence of pixel edges, we convert them into polylines for rendering. We simply use the center point of the pixel edges as polyline vertices.

For stylization, curves are expanded along their normal direction to obtain a strip mesh, which can be used for texture mapping or other styles.

2.4 Conclusion and Future Work

2.4.1 Performance and Limitations

We mainly compare to CPU-based lineart renderers since these were the only ones able to extract mesh contour as curves or polylines, and our goal is to bring these features to realtime rendering using the power of GPU.

Our image-space method, when compared to those renderers, produces curves that have better topology and smoother shape, with a superior performance. Some rendering results are provided in Figures 2.12 and 2.13.

For a detailed comparison to existing CPU-based alternatives such as Lineart, Freestyle, and Pencil+4, we'd refer readers to Section 7.3 in our paper [Jiang et al. 22]. Here we provide the performance comparison to Pencil+4 [PSOFT 17], which is the best CPU-based renderer in terms of both speed and curve quality. All experiments were performed on a GTX 1070 GPU, under a screen resolution of 1920×1080. As the data shows (Table 2.1), our image-space method has superior performance and is stable despite of the increasing mesh complexity.

Aliasing Due to image-space algorithms' common limitations, our method encounters aliasing issues, especially at inefficient image resolutions. To avoid image aliasing, we have developed a GPU-based approach to extract 3D curves by connecting half edges on the triangular mesh, but again, the polygonal mesh,

Figure 2.12. An example of stylized contour curves from our method. From left to right: curve segmentation, stylized curves, and curves combined with toon shading.

Figure 2.13. Another example: curves are stylized with a water-ink style.

Mesh (tris)	Bunny (5K)	Cow (6K)	Teapot (6K)
Ours	0.76	0.78	0.7
Pencil+4	7.93	8.43	9.32
Mesh (tris)	Fandisk (13K)	Rocker. (20K)	Horse (97K)
Ours	0.75	0.63	0.86
Pencil+4	8.21	9.22	14.84
Mesh (tris)	David (100K)	Dragon (249K)	Lucy (300K)
Ours	1.02	1.42	0.96
Pencil+4	67.00	208.00	183.60

Table 2.1. Comparison of timings (ms) of our approach to Pencil+4.

which itself is an aliased sample from a smooth surface, also brings jaggy curves with a messy topology. In general, generating smooth 3D curves with a clean topology remains challenging for polygonal meshes (Figure 2.4). It is reported that the contour is greatly smoother on analytical surfaces such as subdivision surfaces [Hertzmann and Zorin 00], but the contour visibility poses a challenge [Bénard et al. 14].

Flickers in Curve Topology Another limitation is the temporal coherence, a problem that still plagues all existing line-art solutions. Animated curves pose a significant challenge when it comes to maintaining temporal coherence. Even the slightest motion can cause contour curves to vanish, split, merge, or slide abruptly. These rapid changes in contour topology often result in undesirable flickering. To be honest, achieving such a goal can be hard even for experienced animation artists.

The difficulty of maintaining temporal coherence depends on the artistic style applied to the curves. For instance, if we only slightly vary the brush width along the curves, we can employ techniques similar to temporal antialiasing (TAA) on the width parameter. However, when we apply texture to each curve, it becomes difficult to ensure the spatial-temporal coherence of the texture mapping.

In general, an ideal temporal optimizer should have the ability to recognize and anticipate long-term changes in the curve structure, while disregarding abrupt changes due to geometry or image aliasing. It should then adjust the stylized appearance of the curves accordingly.

We have developed a GPU-driven algorithm to reduce the flickers. Inspired by 3D reconstruction algorithms, where the reconstructs new geometry from sensors and tracks old geometry to fit into the new geometry, except for generating curves from scratch in each frame, we also maintain a persistent set of curves. Each curve consists of a sequence of particles, which adapt their position and topology to the newly generated curves. Stylization parameters are stored in each particle and hence can be explicitly controlled for temporal coherence. The solution greatly reduces the flickers under rigid motion, but is still questionable for non-rigid deformations and heavy image aliasing. It also requires a high frame rate for a stable solution. We believe that 3D contour curves are required in order to make this optimizer robust.

2.4.2 Conclusion

In summary, in this article we introduced the first GPU-driven algorithm that generates curves from visible mesh contours. It is a good replacement for CPU-based line-art renderers [Grabli 13, PSOFT 17], both for better quality and faster speed. The method contains a parallel image tracing algorithm, providing real-time vectorized image data for rendering applications such as denoising. However, it is not ready for massive use in games, which have a limited budget for rendering resolution and require a coherent curve topology for animated scenes. However, it is feasible for specific scenes when the camera and scene are nearly static, such as the background scene in a fighting game. This method provides a start for a more powerful line-art renderer, which can generate both 2D and 3D curves from mesh features with a temporal coherent topology.

Bibliography

[Blelloch 90] Guy Blelloch. "Prefix Sums and Their Applications." Technical report, Carnegie Mellon University, 1990. https://www.cs.cmu.edu/~guyb/papers/Ble93.pdf.

[Bénard and Hertzmann 19] Pierre Bénard and Aaron Hertzmann. "Line Drawings from 3D Models: A Tutorial." *Foundations and Trends in Computer Graphics and Vision* 11:1-2 (2019), 1–159.

[Bénard et al. 14] Pierre Bénard, Aaron Hertzmann, and Michael Kass. "Computing Smooth Surface Contours with Accurate Topology." *ACM Transactions on Graphics* 33:2 (2014), 1–21.

[DiVerdi 13] Stephen DiVerdi. "A Brush Stroke Synthesis Toolbox." In *Image and Video-Based Artistic Stylisation*, edited by Paul Rosin and John Collomosse, pp. 23–44. Springer, 2013.

[Grabli 13] Stéphane Grabli. "Freestyle: A Software for Non-Photorealistic Line Drawing Rendering from 3D Scenes." https://freestyle.sourceforge.io, 2013.

[Hertzmann and Zorin 00] Aaron Hertzmann and Denis Zorin. "Illustrating Smooth Surfaces." In *Proceedings of the 27th Annual Conference on Computer Graphics and Interactive Techniques*, *SIGGRAPH '00*, p. 517–526. ACM Press/Addison-Wesley Publishing Co., 2000. https://doi.org/10.1145/344779.345074.

[Jiang et al. 22] Wangziwei Jiang, Guiqing Li, Yongwei Nie, and Chuhua Xian. "GPU-Driven Real-Time Mesh Contour Vectorization." In *Eurographics Symposium on Rendering*, edited by Abhijeet Ghosh and Li-Yi Wei, pp. 93–105. The Eurographics Association, 2022.

[Lewiner et al. 05] Thomas Lewiner, João D. Gomes Jr, Hélio Lopes, and Marcos Craizer. "Curvature and Torsion Estimators Based on Parametric Curve Fitting." *Computers & Graphics* 29:5 (2005), 641–655.

[Mark Harris 07] John D. Owens Mark Harris, Shubhabrata Sengupta. "Parallel Prefix Sum (Scan) with CUDA." Technical report, Nvidia, University of California, Davis, 2007.

[Merrill and Garland 16] Duane Merrill and Michael Garland. "Single-Pass Parallel Prefix Scan with Decoupled Look-Back." Technical Report NVR-2016-002, NVIDIA, 2016.

[Motomura 15] Junya Christopher Motomura. "GuiltyGear Xrd's Art Style: The X Factor Between 2D and 3D." Presented at Game Developers Conference, 2015. https://gdcvault.com/play/1022031/GuiltyGearXrd-s-Art-Style-The.

[PSOFT 17] PSOFT. "Pencil+ 4 Software, Version 4.0.7." https://www.psoft.co.jp/en/product/pencil, 2017.

[Selinger 03] Peter Selinger. "Potrace: A Polygon-Based Tracing Algorithm." Potrace (online), http://potrace.sourceforge.net/potrace.pdf, 2003.

GPU Readback Texture Streaming in Skull and Bones

Malte Bennewitz and Kaori Kato

3.1 Introduction

Skull and Bones is an open-world naval combat multiplayer game, which was developed with Anvil, one of Ubisoft's in-house engines. The game supports up to 20 players playing at the same time and each player may have a gigantic customizable ship. With highly customizable assets and the maximum number of players, it was expected that the game would not be able to avoid going over the streaming budget in the worst case. Keeping visual quality at the best within the limited memory budget was a big challenge for the tech team.

Texture streaming is one of the essential techniques to utilize memory on modern video games as asset texture resolution has been increasing with increasing output resolution. In order to achieve the best visual quality, scalability is crucial. Classic texture streaming techniques use a reference position, usually the camera or player position, to calculate a priority per texture in order to decide on the CPU which mipmap levels to load or unload. This is only a rough estimation, an educated guess on what texture data the GPU is actually going to read during draw calls.

In order to improve the efficiency of the game's texture memory usage, we needed a texture streaming technique that is closer to the GPU to ideally only keep texture data in memory that is being used for the draw calls of the current frame. We implemented GPU-driven texture streaming, which computes the sampled mipmap level in pixels on the screen and reads the computed mipmap level back to the CPU to decide which texture mipmaps to stream in or out.

3.2 Implementation

3.2.1 Overview

There are multiple options to use GPU feedback for texture streaming. Some platforms have hardware features to help compute the mipmap level required by the GPU, e.g., DirectX 12's Sampler Feedback Streaming [Microsoft 21]. Due to big differences between the graphics APIs on different platforms, we took a software approach in *Skull and Bones* to have the same behavior and one implementation everywhere.

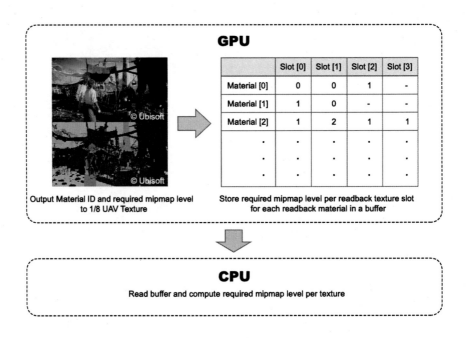

Figure 3.1. Overview of runtime steps of GPU readback texture streaming.

Figure 3.1 shows an overview of our system. We write information about required mipmap levels from pixel shaders during the G-buffer pass into a UAV texture, which has two channels of type 16-bit unsigned integer. The R channel contains the material ID; the G channel holds the computed mipmap level for up to four UV variables. This means that one material can support up to four unique UV variables for readback texture streaming. We call those four slots readback texture slots. This information is processed and then read back to the CPU to inform the texture streamer about which textures and mipmap levels have been used by the last frame. The following sections will go into detail on each step involved.

3.2.2 Offline Preparation

Since we needed material pixel shaders to write to that UAV texture explicitly, the first challenge was to inject the shader code for that into the material shaders. Materials in Anvil are created with a node graph editor. We modified the shader builder that generates shader code from node graphs. It parses a node graph, detects UV variables that are used to sample textures, and assigns readback texture slots for each unique variable. At the same time, a shader code block for computing the required mipmap level for each readback texture slot is also injected into the pixel shader. The information of readback texture slots, which is pairs of a readback texture slot index and a texture register index, is stored in shader meta data and used as a table at runtime. Note that multiple texture register indices can be associated with one readback texture slot, depending on how they are sampled: e.g., albedo, normal, roughness, and metalness maps as used in physically based rendering are usually sampled with the same UV variable and therefore only require a single readback texture slot.

3.2.3 Runtime UAV Output

At runtime, during the G-buffer pass, all opaque material shaders fill out the readback UAV texture with feedback information about the textures they sampled. Since we wanted the new streaming technique to not have a negative performance impact, we needed it to be as fast as possible. Writing the readback information for each pixel was deemed too expensive and redundant since neighboring pixels usually require the same mipmap level of a texture. Therefore, we decided to have the UAV texture use 1/8th of the G-buffer width and height and only have every 64th pixel write that sample information. That means one pixel in the UAV texture represents a 8×8 tile of the G-buffer. To avoid missing information about the 63 pixels of a tile that do not write to the UAV in one frame, we apply jittering guaranteeing that every pixel in a tile will write sampling information eventually, spread over multiple frames.

A downside of writing to a UAV texture in a pixel shader is that the UAV write is not affected by late depth testing, which is performed in the raster operations (ROP) stage if early depth tests are disabled. UAV operations in pixel shaders disable early depth testing automatically, but for normal opaque shaders, early depth testing can be forced with a shader attribute; see [Microsoft 19]. However, shaders that discard pixels (e.g., alpha-testing) or modify depth have to use late depth tests. As a result, there can be unexpected overwrites in the UAV from materials that do not actually end up in the G-buffer. This could be prevented by rendering all objects in a depth pre-pass, which is not the case in *Skull and Bones*. However, this turned out not to be an issue for us due to a high-frequency filter applied to the readback information on the CPU, which absorbs the noise.

The mipmap level for trilinear filtering can be calculated as in Listing 3.1; see [Segal and Akeley 12].

```
float2 xy = uv * textureSize;
float2 dx_xy = ddx_fine(xy);
float2 dy_xy = ddy_fine(xy);
float mipLevel = 0.5 * log2(max(dot(dx_xy, dx_xy),
                                dot(dy_xy, dy_xy)));
```

Listing 3.1. Mipmap level calculation for trilinear filtering.

```
float2 dx_uv = ddx_fine(uv);
dx_uv.y *= aspectRatio;
float2 dy_uv = ddy_fine(uv);
dy_uv.y *= aspectRatio;
float normalizedMipLevel = 0.5 * log2(max(dot(dx_uv, dx_uv),
                                          dot(dy_uv, dy_uv)));

// Calculation is independent of texture size until here:
float mipLevel = normalizedMipLevel + log2(textureWidth);
```

Listing 3.2. Mipmap level calculation for trilinear filtering independent of texture size.

This formula requires the texture size. However, our asset pipeline allows artists to use sets of textures such as albedo, normal, specular map, etc., and all of them are usually sampled using the same UV variable. The textures could have different sizes, so the mipmap level could be different per texture even though they are sampled with the same UV variable. That means we would need to use one readback slot per texture if we would store the mipmap level in the UAV. To avoid that limitation, the calculation can be rearranged to make it independent of the texture size and calculate a "normalized" mipmap level instead.

Listing 3.2 is equivalent to Listing 3.1. Note that the factor 0.5 does not have to be applied to textureWidth because it is cancelled out:

$$\frac{\log_2(\texttt{textureWidth}^2)}{2} = \frac{2\log_2(\texttt{textureWidth})}{2} = \log_2(\texttt{textureWidth}).$$

The calculation in Listing 3.2 allows to keep the calculation on the GPU independent of the texture sizes and to store a single "normalized" mipmap level per UV variable (i.e., per readback slot). The last line of calculating the actual mipmap level can be moved to the CPU where it is calculated for all textures associated with one readback slot.

For anisotropic filtering, the formula is slightly different, but follows the same approach; see [Segal and Akeley 22].

To reduce bandwidth for the UAV texture, the normalized mipmap value is cast to an unsigned integer and stored in four bits (value range 0–15), which allows four normalized mipmap values to be stored in the 16-bit G channel of the UAV texture. This value range is enough for textures up to a size of 32768 pixels.

3.2.4 Runtime Post-Processing

Once we obtain the image that stores readback material information for all tiles of the frame, we need to summarize the information to get the highest desired normalized mipmap levels per material. In order to reduce bandwidth for the CPU readback and evaluation, we do that in two passes to produce a tightly

packed buffer with a size of 128 KiB (16 bits per readback material), indexed
by material ID. It contains the values of the most-detailed required normalized
mipmap level for four readback texture slots per material. The first compute
shader essentially calculates the per-frame maximum for each readback slot using
global atomics. Pseudocode for this step is listed in Listing 3.3. It can be
optimized using group-shared memory, which we will skip here for simplicity.
Since atomics do not work with packed data, the second compute shader is run
to pack the readback data with per-frame maximum normalized mipmap values
tightly in 16 bits per material. This whole post-processing can be run on the
async compute queue to be almost for free.

```
Texture2D<uint2> materialFeedback;
RWByteAddressBuffer readback;

// Execute for each pixel of the feedback texture.
void collectMaximum(uint2 pixelPos)
{
    uint2 rawFeedback = materialFeedback[pixelPos];
    uint materialId = rawFeedback.x;
    uint rbSlots = rawFeedback.y;

    for (uint i = 0; i < 4; ++i)
    {
        // Unpack feedback value from readback slot.
        // Each slot covers 4 bit.
        uint normalizedMip = (rbSlots >> (4 * i)) & 0xF;
        uint oldValue;
        // Atomics work on 4 bytes, so we need 4 bytes per slot.
        uint byteAddress = materialId * 4 * 4 + i;
        readback.InterlockedMax(byteAddress, normalizedMip, oldValue);
    }
}
```

Listing 3.3. Pseudocode to generate readback buffer.

3.2.5   CPU Readback

The buffer produced in Section 3.2.4 is read back to the CPU, or at least a portion
of it, depending on the number of materials registered in the system. For each
material, the desired mipmap levels are calculated for all textures associated
with each readback texture slot, as in Listing 3.4.

Note that the texture height is irrelevant because the `normalizedMipLevel` has
the texture aspect ratio already factored in (see Listing 3.2).

This is where the table mentioned in Section 3.2.2 gets used to know which
textures are associated with each readback texture slot for a given material.

After the most-detailed mipmap level per texture is calculated on the CPU,
the system compares the GPU feedback with the currently loaded mipmap level.
If there is a difference, the feedback request is scheduled and starts being tracked.

```
// For each material with readback information,
// calculate the desired mipmap level for each readback slot:
for (uint slot = 0; slot < 4; ++slot)
{
    char rawSlotData = readbackMaterial.rawSlotData[slot];
    int normalizedMipLevel = unpack(rawSlotData);
    for (Texture& t : readbackMaterial.texturesPerSlot[slot])
    {
        int idealMipLevel = normalizedMipLevel + log2(t.width);
        if (idealMipLevel != t.currentMipLevel)
        {
            addPendingRequest(t, idealMipLevel);
        }
    }
}
```

Listing 3.4. Processing of readback data on CPU.

If the difference is persistent for a few frames, the feedback is considered valid and a streaming request is issued to load or unload mipmap data. Currently, we wait for 30 frames before unloading a mipmap level. This high-frequency filter is needed as the readback data is rather noisy due to the nature of sparse feedback (only one pixel in an 8×8 tile writing to the readback UAV texture) and UAV write order artifacts. It helps to avoid frequent loading and unloading of the same mipmap level that can cause a noticeable popping issue.

3.3   Result

We measured the number of streamable textures in an actual game scene. In a pirate den, where resource density is quite high, there are around 2400 textures registered in the GPU readback texture streaming system.

When we have enough streaming memory budget (typically at lower screen sizes), enabling the GPU readback streaming system releases 50 to 240 MiB of unused texture mipmap data, depending on the scene. The more objects there are in front of the camera, occluding many objects in the background, the more streamed texture data is released. The quality is maintained as shown in Figure 3.2.

When the screen size is 4K, insufficient quality was observed in some cases with the default loading distance for texture mipmaps. GPU readback texture streaming helps detect those cases and loads missing texture mipmaps. In Figure 3.3, the green color shows where pixel shaders sampled the most-detailed mipmap level that is currently loaded. That is the ideal case, since we do not waste memory for unused texture data. Red and magenta show where pixel shaders tried to sample a mipmap level that is not loaded. This means a loss of quality, seen as blurred textures, because the texture streaming caused the desired mipmap level to not be available.

■	< Most-detailed mipmap level available - 1
■	= Most-detailed mipmap level available - 1
▨	= Most-detailed mipmap level available
□	= Most-detailed mipmap level available + 1
■	> Most-detailed mipmap level available + 1

Figure 3.2. Game scene in *Skull and Bones* with streaming debug mode in 1080p. Top: GPU readback streaming is disabled, 727 MiB used for texture streaming. Bottom: GPU readback streaming is enabled, 650 MiB used for texture streaming.

Figure 3.3. Game scene in *Skull and Bones* with streaming debug mode in 4K on PlayStation 5 in Quality Mode. Top: GPU readback streaming is disabled. Bottom: GPU readback streaming is enabled.

We also compared visual quality under a condition with very insufficient streaming memory. Figure 3.4 shows the same scene as Figure 3.2 but with a much smaller streaming memory budget. The visual quality is preserved when GPU readback streaming is enabled. However, when the camera moves around, some texture streaming delay, seen as texture popping, could be observed when the amount of insufficient memory is extreme. This case is normally avoided by

Figure 3.4. Same scene as Figure 3.2 but with a streaming memory budget of 300 MiB. Top: GPU readback streaming is disabled. Bottom: GPU readback streaming is enabled.

applying a mipmap bias when computing the required mipmap level for low-end platforms.

3.3.1 Performance

Table 3.1 shows the additional cost when GPU readback texture streaming is enabled on PlayStation 5 in quality mode and 4K resolution. Given the benefits of more efficient memory usage, this technique provides a fairly low-cost solution.

Pass Cost	CPU	GPU
G-buffer (added cost for writing to UAV)		136 μs
Readback buffer generation in async compute		67 μs
Buffer readback, evaluation, and mipmap calculations	157 μs	
Misc. (registering materials, applying feedback, etc.)	24 μs	

Table 3.1. CPU and GPU runtime cost for GPU readback texture streaming at 4K on PlayStation 5.

3.3.2 Limitations

As mentioned in Section 3.2, there are some limitations such as that the system only supports four unique UV variables used for sampling textures in G-buffer materials. Depending on the shader complexity, that might not be enough for all use cases. The system also does not yet support custom shader operators, which allows artists to write their own shader code in a node of a shader graph. In *Skull and Bones*, around 87 percent of textures used in opaque materials are tracked by GPU readback texture streaming.

Using GPU readback streaming means that the loaded textures depend on the view, and loading may be triggered by just rotating the camera while the player stays at the same position. *Skull and Bones* was going to be released only on the current generation consoles and PC, which allowed us to take advantage of having fast SSDs on all platforms. Therefore, HDD loading latency was not a concern.

3.4   Conclusion and Future Work

GPU readback texture streaming helped reduce the pressure on streaming memory usage in *Skull and Bones* as it allows to use the texture memory budget more efficiently. The system also improves scalability compared to the old system, which required technical artists to set a streaming budget per resource category per game mode per platform.

With increasingly complex shaders that require more unique UV variables, the limitation of only four readback texture slots per material will have to be addressed. This could be solved with more than one 16-bit texture channel or dynamic slot counts and improved packing, while closely monitoring performance impact.

Another approach to explore is combining GPU readback texture streaming with a rendering pipeline in which UV derivative computation is required. Recently, there were many examples of visibility buffer rendering [Burns and Hunt 13] to address small triangles [Karis et al. 21] or quad unfriendly assets [McLaren 22]. These techniques compute UV derivatives in the shaders, and potentially we could support GPU readback texture streaming for them easily with lower additional costs.

Bibliography

[Burns and Hunt 13] Christopher A. Burns and Warren A. Hunt. "The Visibility Buffer: A Cache-Friendly Approach to Deferred Shading." *Journal of Computer Graphics Techniques* 2:2 (2013), 55–69. http://jcgt.org/published/ 0002/02/04/.

[Karis et al. 21] Brian Karis, Rune Stubbe, and Graham Wihlidal. "A Deep Dive into Nanite Virtualized Geometry." Presented at SIG-GRAPH, 2021. https://advances.realtimerendering.com/s2021/Karis_ Nanite_SIGGRAPH_Advances_2021_final.pdf.

[McLaren 22] James McLaren. "Adventures with Deferred Texturing in Horizon Forbidden West." Guerrilla, 2022. https://www.guerrilla-games.com/read/ adventures-with-deferred-texturing-in-horizon-forbidden-west.

[Microsoft 19] Microsoft. "earlydepthstencil." Windows App Development, Direct3D Reference for HLSL, 2019. https://learn.microsoft.com/en-us/ windows/win32/direct3dhlsl/sm5-attributes-earlydepthstencil.

[Microsoft 21] Microsoft. "Sampler Feedback." DirectX-Specs, 2021. https:// microsoft.github.io/DirectX-Specs/d3d/SamplerFeedback.html.

[Segal and Akeley 12] Mark Segal and Kurt Akeley. "The OpenGL Graphics System: A Specification, Version 4.2." Khronos, 2012. https://registry. khronos.org/OpenGL/specs/gl/glspec42.core.pdf.

[Segal and Akeley 22] Mark Segal and Kurt Akeley. "The OpenGL Graphics System: A Specification, Version 4.6." Khronos, 2022. https://registry. khronos.org/OpenGL/specs/gl/glspec46.core.pdf.

Triangle Visibility Buffer 2.0

Manas Kulkarni, and Wolfgang Engel

Figure 4.1. Triangle Visibility Buffer 2.0.

4.1 Introduction and History

This article describes improvements to a rendering architecture called *Triangle Visibility Buffer* (Figure 4.1). The main idea is to track triangles throughout the whole rendering pipeline and store their visibility in a buffer in the current scene.

Historically, what is described here was not a straightforward process of implementing one paper or one consistent vision. The original idea of the Triangle Visibility Buffer is based on an article by Burns and Hunt [Burns and Hunt 13]. Schied and Dachsbacher extended what was described in the original article [Schied and Dachsbacher 15, Schied and Dachsbacher 16]. Christoph Schied implemented a modern version with an early version of OpenGL (supporting `MultiDrawIndirect`) into The Forge rendering framework in September 2015. We ported this code to all platforms and simplified and extended it in the following years by adding a triangle filtering stage following [Chajdas 16] and [Wihlidal 17] and a new way of shading. Our ongoing improvements simplified the approach incrementally, and the architecture started to resemble what was described in the original article [Burns and Hunt 13] again, leveraging the modern tools of the newer graphics APIs.

In contrast to [Burns and Hunt 13], the actual storage of triangles in our implementation of a visibility buffer happens due to the triangle removal and draw compaction step with an optimal "massaged" data set. By removing overdraw in the visibility buffer and depth buffer, we run a shading approach that shades everything with one regular draw call. We called the shading stage *Forward++* due to its resemblance to forward shading and its usage of a tiled light list for applying many lights. It was a step up from Forward+, which requires numerous draw calls. We described all this in several talks at game industry conferences, for example, Game Developers Conference Europe 2016 [Engel 16] and XFest 2018, showing considerable performance gains due to reduced memory bandwidth compared to traditional G-buffer–based rendering architectures. A blog post has been updated over the years for what we now call *Triangle Visibility Buffer 1.0* (TVB 1.0) [Engel 18].

An open-source implementation of the approach is available on GitHub [The Forge 24].

Today our approach is well adopted in many game engines, sometimes adjusted to the needs of the type of game that uses it.

This article outlines our work between 2018 and today and features new major developments in the realm of the Triangle Visibility Buffer architecture. With GPUs' ever-improving performance, we found it worth investigating an approach that completely bypasses the traditional drawing APIs and pipeline stages. Instead of preparing and massaging the data to fit into the indirect draw call workflow, we "draw" the triangle IDs with one compute shader into the visibility buffer. In other words, draw calls are not necessary anymore to fill the visibility buffer or the depth buffer. Our method does not depend on mesh shaders and can, therefore, run on hardware that does not support them. Additionally, we eliminate the need for a graphics pipeline, render small triangles more efficiently, as we do not pay the additional cost for helper lanes, and exploit various other benefits.

This simplification reduces code complexity, minimizes memory access to buffers, and opens up new opportunities, such as a native implementation of order-independent transparency and ray tracing. It follows the trend toward GPU-driven rendering with compute shaders. This approach is *Triangle Visibility Buffer 2.0* (TVB 2.0).

After an overview of the main concepts in the next section, the implementation description in later sections follows the data flow through the Triangle Visibility Buffer rendering pipeline.

4.2 Overview

At its core, the TVB 2.0 pipeline aims to successively transform the unordered triangle data into smaller spatially related work items to the shading of single pixels. We assign triangles to screen-space bins and rasterize them separately during the *Bin Rasterization* stage, described in Section 4.4. Additionally, triangles classified as small based on their screen-space area are directly rasterized (Section 4.3). The overall memory costs for our demo are shown in Table 4.1.

All input data is stored in a single set of vertex buffers (non-interleaved) and one index buffer. We store all data (static geometry and animated geometry) in world space to reduce the number of memory indirections and transformations. Unlike the earlier versions of the Triangle Visibility Buffer [Engel 16, Engel 18], the latest TVB 1.0 version, available on GitHub, also supports animation in the form of skinning. To make skinning an integral part of the triangle pipeline, we store the skinned data in the same buffers as the static geometry. This part of the buffer is being updated asynchronously for animation. With the skinning data in the same set of buffers with the same layout, all TVB 2.0 processing stages handle animation transparently.

The algorithm imposes almost no restrictions on the input data besides a uniform vertex format. In our demo, we use 3×32 bit floats for positions and 2×16-bit half-precision floats for texture coordinates and normals. We declare an array of mesh entries referencing material data and vertex offsets to associate material data with triangles.

Surface appearance is determined by a material index, which references a set of diffuse, normal, and specular maps to use and whether the geometry is two-sided. The TVB 2.0 demo supports opaque and alpha-tested geometry. We do not impose ordering restrictions or omit antialiasing.

We now outline the purpose and structure of the two main buffers used in our approach—the *visibility buffer* and *bin buffer*—as well as the general flow of data throughout a frame.

Buffer	Size
UV Data	11.7 MB
Normal Data	11.7 MB
Vertex Positions	35 MB
Index Buffer	31 MB
Bin Buffer	52 MB
Visibility Buffer	25 MB
Total	~166 MB

Table 4.1. TVB 2.0 memory costs overview (San Miguel).

4.2.1 Visibility Buffer

The visibility buffer stores depth and triangle IDs for every screen pixel. By deferring shading or texturing and all surface property lookups, we eliminate overdraw while minimizing memory access. We use a large unified visibility buffer for multiple views. A `uint64_t` format is used, which packs two 32-bit values and allows us to use 64-bit atomic operations. We implement depth testing by storing the depth in the most significant bits. The visibility buffer is filled during the Filtering and Bin Rasterization stages and read during the Forward++ shading stage.

4.2.2 Bin Buffer

To transform the linear array of triangles into a set of spatially coherent work units, we use the bin buffer as intermediate storage. During triangle filtering, triangle indices are written to the buffer and consumed in the Bin Rasterization stage. This contrasts to TVB 1.0 where full vertex indices must be written to memory. The size is configured to match the expected amount of triangles in the scene. The maximum number of bins in the x and y directions is fixed at compile time, and a bin always maps to the same number of pixels. Since mapping screen-space coordinates to bin indices is handled dynamically, the implementation supports variable resolutions with a single set of bins. For example, the shadow map in the TVB 2.0 demo uses a fixed resolution of 1024×1024 pixels while the main render target size is dynamically configurable. The bin nuffer is organized into two sections. The first $x \times y$ elements contain counters for the amount of triangles assigned to each bin. After the counters, the memory is divided into equally sized bin ranges. This fixed assignment simplifies memory access and lets us avoid dependent memory lookups necessary for any linked data structure. We pack additional information into the triangle indices stored in the bins to improve memory use. A single bit controls the geometry set, 8 bits are used for the material ID, and the remaining 23 bits are used for the triangle index.

4.2.3 Operation

By only using compute shaders, using the hardware efficiently is simpler than with a traditional rasterization pipeline. Since the bin buffer and visibility buffer are just regions of memory that do not get accessed concurrently, we can overlap the rasterization of multiple views and can bypass pipeline state changes and render target setup. For small triangles, it is more efficient to bypass the bin buffer and directly rasterize triangles. We refer to the processing of such triangles as *small-scale rasterization*. The only synchronization point in a frame that requires a barrier is between the Filtering and Bin Rasterization stages. The implementation further supports a single-queue mode and an async compute variant. In the case of async compute, filtering overlaps with the main rasteri-

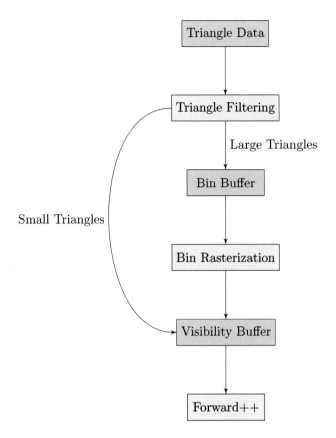

Figure 4.2. TVB 2.0 pipeline.

zation by a frame. The different buffers, stages, and data flow are illustrated in Figure 4.2.

4.3 Triangle Filtering

The first stage of the TVB 2.0 pipeline is the `triangle_filtering.comp.fsl` shader. We kept the name from TVB 1.0, but this stage is now responsible for a range of additional work. The main common aspect is that this stage loads every triangle in the scene, performs culling tests, and potentially emits some data. It is launched as a single dispatch, sized to match the total amount of scene triangles. Each thread is responsible for processing a single triangle and performs filtering tests (Section 4.3.1) and either binning (Section 4.3.2) or small-scale rasterization (Section 4.3.3).

4.3.1   Triangle Culling

Compared to TVB 1.0, the actual algorithms to filter out triangles didn't change much. This logic removes degenerate and backfacing triangles that clip through the near clipping plane of the view frustum and/or are outside of the view frustum. It also removes triangles too small to cover a pixel center or sampling point, considering multisample antialiasing. For most of the shader source code for the triangle filtering, we would like to refer to [Engel 16, Engel 18] and [Chajdas 16, Wihlidal 17] on whose initial work our approach was based.

Multi-view Triangle Filtering   Our first addition to the original algorithms mentioned above was to filter out triangles for multiple views simultaneously (like main camera view, shadow map, reflection maps, etc.). This way, the majority of triangles are culled, and the following passes only have to deal with a smaller number of triangles. Triangle removal comes at the cost of loading the index and vertex data of every triangle, potentially transforming vertices, and skipping triangles that should be removed. The cost of accessing (reading and writing) the triangle data on the typical GPUs game players use (low-end GPUs: mostly mobile device GPUs and console GPUs) is higher than the cost of running the visibility tests. One way to amortize the memory read/write cost even more is to remove invisible triangles for several views—such as a main camera view, a shadow map view, a reflective shadow map view, etc.—at the same time. Essentially, we load the triangle data once and loop over all views.

Multi-view triangle removal proved highly beneficial in stereoscopic rendering when only the remaining triangle set visible through both eyes was sent to the graphics pipeline for drawing.

4.3.2   Triangle Binning

For large triangles, we compute a fast, coarse rasterization over the screen bins. We choose bins of size 128×128, at a resolution of 1920×1080 on our target hardware. This size yields the best trade-off between binning efficiency and memory accesses. We compute the extent of the screen-space vertex coordinates for each triangle and view. The resulting axis-aligned bounding box (AABB) is used to loop over the intersected bins. For each bin, we atomically increase a shared per-bin counter. To reduce the number of atomic memory transactions with main memory, we let a single thread reserve a range of triangle indices for each bin based on the accumulated triangle counters. Finally, we repeat the loop over the AABB and write the triangle index back to the bin buffer counters.

4.3.3   Small Triangle Rasterization

For triangles with an area below the pixel threshold δ, we avoid main memory altogether and directly rasterize them to the visibility buffer. We chose a δ of 1024 pixels, which was optimal by benchmarking different values. This direct data path reduces the memory pressure on the bins and reuses the triangle data, which is already in memory. Since we filter triangles for multiple views at once, we also extend that idea to apply small-scale rasterization. The unified visibility buffer allows us to offset the writes to send triangles to different views. The rasterization loop and depth testing using a single atomic operation are largely identical to the Bin Rasterization stage (Section 4.4).

4.4   Bin Rasterization

In TVB 1.0, we stored triangle ID data in the visibility buffer by running indirect draw calls. Triangles needed to be tracked and compacted to prepare those calls so that no empty draw calls would be executed. In TVB 2.0, we replace these draw calls by a single indirect compute dispatch, the Bin Rasterization stage. This stage is implemented in the shader `raster_depth.comp.fsl`. The goal is to transform a linear array of triangle indices for each bin into a rasterized screen tile. We use a single dispatch, launching n groups for each bin, where n is the maximum bin triangle capacity divided by the group size. Thus, each thread linearly maps to a triangle in the bin. Similarly to the previous stage, we aim to reduce the amount of atomic transactions with main memory. To achieve this, we use a shared buffer representing a tiny section of the visibility buffer, called a *sub-bin*. We choose a `uint64_t` array of 64×64 elements, which equals 32 Kb and fits into the Local Data Share (LDS). Each thread is responsible for rasterizing a triangle over the sub-bin. The execution is highly coherent since all threads use the same fixed loop. After rasterization into the shared buffer, we must flush the data back to the visibility buffer. These writes to main memory are distributed among all threads of the group.

Since the 64×64 region does not match the 128×128 bin extents, we must repeat the Bin Rasterization stage for each sub-bin. Using separate threads is much more efficient than letting the threads loop over four sub-bin regions.

The contents of the visibility buffer after the current stage are shown in Figure 4.3. The small-scale triangles are shown in blue, while the remaining triangles are green.

4.4.1   Depth Blit

After Bin Rasterization we use a compute pass to extract the packed depth values and write these to depth buffers. This is advantageous for later effects in the pipeline such as god rays, ambient occlusion, and shadow mapping. Using this pass, we can avoid loading and decoding 8-byte values and can only fetch the required depth.

Figure 4.3. Visibility buffer contents.

4.5   Forward++ Shading

Once the depth buffer and visibility buffer are filled, we can run the Forward++
shading stage. We dispatch one draw call with a single triangle covering the
viewport. The visibility buffer entry for the current pixel is retrieved and de-
coded. Using the resulting triangle index, we retrieve triangle indices and index
into the vertex buffer to retrieve world-space positions. The following computations regarding shading and derivatives computation are largely identical to
TVB 1.0, and we omit the details. In brief, we efficiently compute derivatives,
sample the textures referenced by the material ID, and apply tiled lighting. The
source code can be found in the file `visibilityBuffer_shade.frag.fsl`.

Platform	RX 7600	PS5	PS5	Macbook M2	iPhone 15 Pro
Resolution	1080p	1080p	4K	1080p	1704 × 786
Filter Triangles	3.5 ms	3.4 ms	15.5 ms	11.3 ms	19.3 ms
Bin Rasterization	1.1 ms	1.4 ms	8.0 ms	10.9 ms	10.2 ms
Shading	0.7 ms	1.3 ms	3.8 ms	1.8 ms	6.4 ms
Total	3.8 ms	5.2 ms	15.6 ms	13.7 ms	19.3 ms

Table 4.2. Performance measurements (San Miguel, view from Figure 4.1).

4.6 Compute-Driven Triangle Visibility Buffer Benefits

The outlined algorithm significantly reduces CPU-GPU dependencies and eliminates the challenging need to fit the data into fixed-function interfaces. With TVB 1.0, a range of triangle filtering dispatches had to be followed by a batch compaction pass whose output was fed into a range of indirect draws. Preparing the indirect draw calls was complex, error-prone, and difficult to debug. With TVB 2.0, the first stages of the pipeline can be reduced to two compute dispatches: filtering and rasterization. Only two buffers get written and read during these stages. The unified representation of scene and visibility data enables efficient implementations of various effects with low overhead.

4.6.1 Order-Independent Transparency with a Triangle Visibility Buffer

With older G-buffer–based rendering architectures, one had to store per-pixel data layers to implement order-independent transparency (OIT). This required large amounts of memory bandwidth and memory. With a Triangle Visibility Buffer, only triangle IDs need to be layered. This is a substantial gain in memory access performance and storage requirements.

4.7 Performance Results

We benchmark our algorithm on PC, PlayStation 5, Macbook M2, and iPhone 15 Pro (Table 4.2). The San Miguel scene contains 8M indexed vertices and a significant amount of alpha-tested geometry. The results are promising on higher-end devices. We observe total frame GPU times ranging from 1.2× to 1.7× across devices compared to the rasterization-based pipeline.

On AMD RDNA hardware, we generally achieve good occupancy and overlap. The most expensive stages are Triangle Filtering and Bin Rasterization. On Metal devices, no 64-bit atomic operations to LDS are exposed, which forces us to write directly to the main memory.

4.8   Conclusion and Future Development

We have a range of improvements and extensions we want to explore for the future. Compared to a fully shaded frame or a G-buffer, a visibility buffer holds significantly more information about the scene. We can interpret the buffer as a discrete sampling of the scene geometry.

4.8.1   Work Graphs

The next step in the development of our solution is the integration of GPU work graphs. A single GPU work graph dispatch can transform the input triangle data into a visibility buffer that is ready for shading. We plan to avoid the intermediate bin memory and instantaneously dispatch the finer work items. This further reduces global synchronization and memory round trips and should allow for a more granular grouping of triangles. Instead of using a fixed triangle area threshold, multiple grids of different sizes can be used to assign triangles to threads for rasterization optimally. We have already experimented with integrating purely compute-based shader graphs into the visibility buffer algorithm, but we expect the imminent availability of draw nodes that give access to the hardware rasterizer to be more efficient.

4.8.2   Upscaling

Current upscaling methods rely on dense per-pixel motion vectors and temporal accumulation. The operation is, in essence, a heuristic and will inevitably fall short in certain situations or require expensive modeling of priors to achieve high-quality results. An interesting approach is to rasterize the scene at full resolution and shade at reduced resolution. During the upscaling operation, we can use the triangle IDs to correctly map and expand pixels to the initial full resolution.

4.8.3   TAA

The fundamental issue of temporal antialiasing (TAA) is the heuristic used to determine whether a sample originates from the current surface point. A wrong choice results in artifacts such as ghosting. With triangle IDs the identities of samples can be accurately tracked between frames.

4.8.4   Ray Tracing with a Triangle Visibility Buffer

Extending the previous idea of visibility buffer–based order-independent transparency, we can just as well store "2.5D" lists of triangles and access these spatially. This would enable ray tracing implementations that do not depend on dedicated hardware and driver support or any duplicated representation of scene data.

Acknowledgements

Since 2015, many people have worked on this ongoing research project. We mentioned many in [Engel 18]. Over the last couple of years, the following people have been contributing to and improving the architecture: Berk Emre Saribas, Borja Portugal, Olaf Schalk, David Erler, and Manas Kulkarni. It is always a team effort at The Forge Interactive to sustain and push these projects forward. Thanks to everyone who contributed.

Bibliography

[Burns and Hunt 13] Christopher A. Burns and Warren A. Hunt. "The Visibility Buffer: A Cache-Friendly Approach to Deferred Shading." *Journal of Computer Graphics Techniques* 2:2 (2013), 55–69. http://jcgt.org/published/0002/02/04.

[Chajdas 16] Matthaeus Chajdas. "GeometryFX." AMD Developer Website, 2016. http://gpuopen.com/gaming-product/geometryfx/.

[Engel 16] Wolfgang Engel. "4K Rendering Breakthrough: The Filtered and Culled Visibility Buffer." GDC Vault, 2016. https://www.gdcvault.com/play/1023792/4K-Rendering-Breakthrough-The-Filtered.

[Engel 18] Wolfgang Engel. "Triangle Visibility Buffer." Wolfgang Engel's Diary of a Graphics Programmer Blog, 2018. http://diaryofagraphicsprogrammer.blogspot.com/2018/03/triangle-visibility-buffer.html.

[Schied and Dachsbacher 15] Christoph Schied and Carsten Dachsbacher. "Deferred Attribute Interpolation for Memory-Efficient Deferred Shading." Kit Publication, 2015. http://cg.ivd.kit.edu/publications/2015/dais/DAIS.pdf.

[Schied and Dachsbacher 16] Christoph Schied and Carsten Dachsbacher. "Deferred Attribute Interpolation Shading." In *GPU Pro 7*, edited by Wolfgang Engel, pp. 83–96. A K Peters/CRC Press, 2016.

[The Forge 24] The Forge. "Triangle Visibility Buffer." The Forge Interactive GitHub repository, 2024. https://github.com/ConfettiFX/The-Forge.

[Wihlidal 17] Graham Wihlidal. "Optimizing the Graphics Pipeline with Compute." In *GPU Zen: Advanced Rendering Techniques*, edited by Wolfgang Engel, pp. 277–320. Black Cat Publishing, 2017.

Resource Management with Frame Graph in Messiah

Yuwen Wu

5.1 Introduction

Modern game engines commonly utilize a graph structure (a.k.a. Frame Graph or Render Graph) to manage their render pipelines, and so does the Messiah Engine, an in-house cross-platform game engine widely used in NetEase Games.[1] One key feature of Frame Graph is automatic resource management, i.e., automatic resource creation and automatic resource reuse and aliasing, which not only simplifies pipeline authoring but also saves a significant amount of memory.

Although it is not deeply discussed in the original Frame Graph lecture [O'Donnell 17], resource management is not as trivial as it sounds, especially when multiple queues are involved. A frame graph with async compute or async copy may not be an interval order [Trotter 18], which makes the representation of resource lifetimes a little bit tricky. In this article, we will explore a simple and systematic representation of resource lifespans, as well as the resource aliasing algorithm and the management of ping-pong buffers, among other related topics.

5.2 Overview

Although Frame Graph has many different and interesting aspects compared to traditional rendering pipeline organization, this article only limits the discussion to resource management. In the Messiah Engine, render resources can be categorized into the following three types:

1. **Persistent:** This type of resource has a long-term existence and can be used across multiple frames.

2. **Transient:** Transient resources have very short lifespans and will not last beyond the current frame. These resources are typically used for intermediate results or temporary storage.

3. **Ping-pong:** Used only for ping-pong buffers, we can ignore this type for now until it is discussed in detail in Section 5.5.

---

[1] Games built on the Messiah Engine include *Diablo Immortal*, *Knives Out*, and *Where Winds Meet*, etc.

The resource management system is responsible for allocating and freeing resources properly and should also keep the memory footprint small. For persistent resources, we can't optimize them any further because their storage is persistent and hence exclusive. However, for transient resources, a frame graph can come into play. We can analyze the lifespan of each resource from the graph, and place resources with non-overlapping lifespans onto the same memory location, through resource reuse/aliasing.

5.3   Resource Lifespans

To determine the lifespan of each resource, we can first linearize the frame graph through topological sorting, then assign each pass a `passId` according to the linearized order. Now the lifespan of a resource can be simply represented as a closed interval [`first, last`], where `first` is the minimum `passId` of all passes that use the resource and `last` is the maximum. This approach works great, until we need to account for scenarios involving multiple queues, e.g., async compute/copy [Hodes and Dunn 17].

Since render passes from different queues can be executed simultaneously, the linearized order doesn't match the execution order anymore, which makes the previous lifespan representation no longer valid. For example, in Figure 5.1 the resource c (lifespan: $[3, 4]$) and resource d (lifespan: $[5, 6]$) can overlap although their intervals are disjoint. Some engines solve this by forcibly extending the interval to some sync point [O'Donnell 17], but doing so could hinder potential memory sharing. Actually as we will see next, it is impossible for a single interval to represent the order correctly.

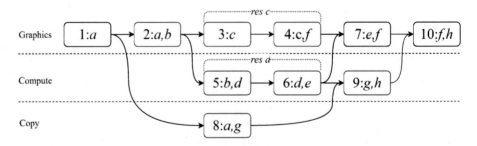

Figure 5.1. A frame graph that has multiple queues, where each node is labeled in the form of `passId`:*resources*: e.g., "2:*a,b*" means its `passId` is 2, and it touches resources a and b in the rendering.

5.3.1 Interval Order

If a partially ordered set P can be mapped to some set of intervals with order preserved, we say it is an *interval order*. According to Fishburn's theorem [Trotter 18], P is an interval order if and only if it does not contain any $(2 + 2)$ sub-poset. However, in a frame graph, this kind of $(2+2)$ structure is very likely to appear.

In Figure 5.2, the four nodes a, b, c, and d form a so-called $(2 + 2)$ sub-poset. Upon examination of this structure, we can easily recognize that it is impossible to assign an interval to each node to represent their dependencies without imposing additional, unnecessary orders.

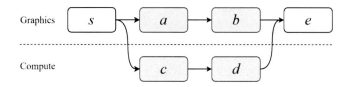

Figure 5.2. An example of a $(2 + 2)$ structure (colored in grey).

5.3.2 Lifespan Representation

While a single interval is inadequate to represent the order, we can use multiple intervals instead, i.e., maintain an interval for each queue. (There seems to be no research on this type of multiple-interval order). Furthermore, since each resource can only be initialized once in one queue, this multiple-interval representation can be simplified by using a single-start and multiple-ends structure, as in Listing 5.1.

```
namespace HardwareQueue {
    enum EHardwareQueue { Graphics, Compute, Copy, Count };
}
using HardwareQueue::EHardwareQueue;

struct ResourceLifespan {
    uint16  First{ 0xFFFF };
    uint16  Last[HardwareQueue::Count]{ 0 };

    // Extend the lifespan to include a specified pass.
    void Extend(uint16 pass, EHardwareQueue queue) {
        First = std::min(First, pass);
        Last[queue] = std::max(Last[queue], pass);
    }
};
```

Listing 5.1. The structure to represent the lifespan.

Dependency	1	2	3	4	5	6	7	8	9	10
Graphics	0	1	2	3	2	2	4	1	2	7
Compute	0	0	0	0	0	5	6	0	6	9
Copy	0	0	0	0	0	0	0	0	8	8

Table 5.1. The cross-queue dependencies corresponding to Figure 5.1.

To determine the order of two multiple-interval lifespans, first we build an auxiliary table `CrossQueueDeps` to store the cross-queue pass dependencies, in which `CrossQueueDeps[p][q]` stores pass p's predecessor in queue q, or 0 if no predecessor; e.g., for the graph shown in Figure 5.1 we should set `CrossQueueDeps[6][0]` to 2 because pass 2 is the last one in queue 0 (Graphics) in the dependency chain $1 \rightarrow 2 \rightarrow 5 \rightarrow 6$. Table 5.1 lists the full cross-queue dependencies.

With the `CrossQueueDeps` table, it is very straightforward to determine the relationship between two lifespans: just check the dependency in each queue separately, and then combine the results (see Listing 5.2).

```
// Returns -1 if lhs is before rhs, 1 if after,
//         or 0 if they overlap.
int OverlapTest(ResourceLifespan lhs, ResourceLifespan rhs) {
    bool before = true, after = true;
    for (uint8 i = 0; i != HardwareQueue::Count; ++i) {
        before &= CrossQueueDeps[rhs.First][i] >= lhs.Last[i];
        after  &= CrossQueueDeps[lhs.First][i] >= rhs.Last[i];
    }
    return before ? -1 : (after ? 1 : 0);
}
```

Listing 5.2. Function to determine the order of two lifespans.

Till now we finally obtained an accurate and efficient way of determining whether resource lifespans overlap, which provides a solid foundation for resource allocation.

5.4   Transient Resource Allocation

This section will discuss how we allocate resources, but before delving into specifics, let us first provide an overview of our frame graph compilation process. We have a pass compiler and a resource compiler. The pass compiler performs operations such as unused pass elimination and pass merging. For tile-based architectures, it also transforms render passes to sub-passes if possible to utilize the on-chip memory and reduce bandwidth. The resource compiler runs after the pass compiler because it relies on its output, e.g., whether a resource can be marked as `memoryless` (or lazily allocated in Vulkan terminology) depends on whether it is only alive among a sub-pass chain, which cannot be determined until the sub-pass analysis is completed.

Our pass compiler and resource compiler have different implementations on different platforms. Regarding the resource compiler, we have three different allocation schemes due to differences in device capabilities:

1. **Reuse:** The most basic scheme, where resources with the same descriptions (format, dimension, etc.) can be redirected to the same device resource if their lifespans don't overlap.

2. **Aliasing:** This scheme further allows resources with different descriptions to share the device memory; not all platforms support it, though.

3. **Restricted aliasing:** Similar to aliasing but does not allow offsetting. See details in Section 5.4.2.

For ease of maintenance, we implemented a unified algorithm for the second and third schemes, which will be described in Section 5.4.2. For now, let's start with the basic reuse scheme.

5.4.1   Resource Reuse

This scheme is mainly for legacy APIs like Direct3D 11 (Desktop) and OpenGL, which don't provide interfaces for manual resource placement. For these APIs, we can only optimize resources exactly like an old-style resource pool does, though the latter lacks the convenience of a frame graph and requires manual retrieval and return of resources.

The resource reuse algorithm is quite simple, and its implementation is provided in Listing 5.3. Note that to maximize resource reuse, we merge resource usages here. For instance, if one resource is required for both RTV and SRV usage, and another resource is needed for UAV and SRV, we can create an underlying resource that supports RTV, SRV, and UAV together.

It can be proven that this greedy algorithm is optimal if all resources with the same description are only accessed in a single queue (the problem is called *interval partitioning* [Kartik 13] in this simple case). However, obtaining the optimal solution becomes challenging in general cases, as it can be formalized as *graph coloring* on a graph $G_r = (V, E)$, where V represents all resources with description r and E connects resources with overlapping lifespans. The interval partitioning problem corresponds to the case when G_r is an *interval graph*. But generally G_r is rather an *incomparability graph*, which is much harder to color (theoretically solvable in polynomial time since incomparability graphs are *perfect* [Wikipedia 24], but the algorithm is obscure [Nickel 05]). Fortunately, the greedy algorithm as an approximate solution also performs well in practice.

5.4.2   Resource Aliasing

Modern graphics APIs, such as Direct3D 12 and Vulkan, enable more flexible resource management. They divide resource creation into two distinct steps:

```cpp
struct CachedResource {
    ResourceDesc                    Desc;
    std::vector<ResourceLifespan>   Lifespans;
};

void Compile(const std::vector<TransientResource>& resources) {
    std::multimap<ResourceDesc, CachedResource> cache;
    for (const TransientResource& res : resources) {
        ResourceDesc key = res.Desc;
        // Clear usage to allow reuse on different usages.
        key.Usages = 0;

        auto [it, end] = cache.equal_range(key);
        for (; it != end; ++it) {
            CachedResource& cached = it->second;
            bool overlapped = false;
            for (ResourceLifespan life : cached.Lifespans) {
                if (OverlapTest(life, res.Lifespan) == 0) {
                    overlapped = true;
                    break;
                }
            }
            if (!overlapped) {
                // Reuse cached resource.
                cached.Desc.Usages |= res.Desc.Usages;
                cached.Lifespans.emplace_back(res.Lifespan);
                break;
            }
        }
        if (it == end) {
            // Add to cache if can't reuse existing resources.
            cache.emplace(key,
                CachedResource{ res.Desc, { res.Lifespan }});
        }
    }

    // Commit all resources that will be actually created.
    for (auto it = cache.begin(); it != cache.end(); ++it) {
        CommitResource(it->second.Desc);
    }
}
```

Listing 5.3. The resource reuse algorithm.

memory allocation and resource placement, each with its own separate interface. Based on this flexibility, you can freely place different resources on the same memory location, provided that each resource is properly accessed and synchronized. This technique is known as *resource aliasing*, and it typically saves more memory compared to resource reuse.

It is worth mentioning that prior to iOS 13, the Metal API from Apple only provided a very high-level resource placement interface, where you could not specify the exact offset in the MTLHeap where the resource is allocated, but rather

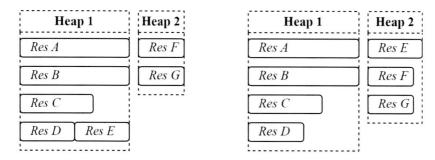

Figure 5.3. Illustrations of aliasing (left) and restricted aliasing (right).

left it up to the API to decide. We believe Apple intended to simplify memory management, but it made fine resource aliasing more difficult to implement in practice. Due to this inconvenience, we choose to completely disable offsetting below iOS 13 and only allocate resources at the beginning of the heap. This approach, which we call *restricted aliasing*, affects the design of the aliasing algorithm. With no offsetting, we cannot create a big heap and sub-allocate all resources from it, instead we should create a bunch of small heaps and make them tight to avoid memory waste. To reduce code divergence, we also use this small-heap policy in the regular offset aliasing; see Figure 5.3.

Before starting resource aliasing, we first need to query the memory requirement of each resource from the device, as shown in Listing 5.4. The function's return value indicates the type of memory required, and resources with different memory types will not be allocated in the same heap. Additionally, you can return −1 to exclude this resource from aliasing at all.

Let's focus on the algorithm. We begin by categorizing the resources based on their required memory type and process each category separately. This allows us to focus on one memory type, without loss of generality. The problem at hand is to arrange resources properly to minimize the total memory footprint, which varies depending on the scenario. In the restricted scenario with no offsetting, it becomes a *max coloring problem*. When offsetting is allowed, it has only been well studied for the single-queue case (where the resources form an interval graph), known as *interval coloring* or *dynamic storage allocation*. However, regardless

```
struct MemoryRequirement {
    uint32    Size{ 0 };
    uint32    Alignment{ 0 };
};
virtual int GetMemoryRequirement(
    const ResourceDesc& desc, MemoryRequirement* req) = 0;
```

Listing 5.4. The interface to query the memory requirement.

of the scenario, this problem remains NP-hard [Gupta et al. 97]. Therefore, we don't aim for an optimal solution but employ a simple greedy algorithm instead, which can be coarsely described as follows:

1. Sort the resources (stably) in descending order according to their required memory size.

2. For each resource r, iterate through the resources before it and identify a set of resources S whose lifespans do not overlap with it. If there exists a resource in S whose description is identical to r, reuse it directly.

3. Otherwise, attempt to create an aliased resource by sharing the memory of one `AliasSrc` in S. If successful, set r as an `AliasDst`.

4. If both reuse and aliasing fail, allocate a new block of memory for r and set it as an `AliasSrc`.

Steps 1, 2, and 4 remain the same regardless of whether offsetting is enabled or not, with the only difference occurring in step 3. The code for step 3 can be found in Listings 5.5 and 5.6, which correspond to the cases of offsetting being enabled and disabled, respectively. Keep in mind that while the algorithm presented here works well for our needs, alternative algorithms might yield superior results under varying requirements. We also plan to explore different algorithms in the future for more efficient allocation.

```cpp
bool Alias(TransientResource& r,
        std::vector<TransientResource>& S) {
    TransientResource* aliasSource = nullptr;
    uint32 aliasOffset = 0;
    for (TransientResource& src : S) {
        if (!src.IsAliasSrc)
            continue;
        // Get occupied ranges.
        std::vector<std::pair<uint32, uint32>> ranges;
        for (TransientResource* dst=src.Dst; dst; dst=dst->Dst) {
            if (OverlapTest(dst->Lifespan, r.Lifespan) == 0) {
                uint32 offset = dst->AliasOffset;
                ranges.emplace_back(offset,
                    offset + dst->Requirement.Size);
            }
        }
        std::sort(ranges.begin(), ranges.end());
        ranges.emplace_back(src.Requirement.Size,
            src.Requirement.Size);
        // Calculate free ranges.
        std::vector<std::pair<uint32, uint32>> freeRanges;
        freeRanges.emplace_back(0, 0);
        for (const auto& it : ranges) {
            auto& last = freeRanges.back();
            if (last.second >= it.first)
```

```
                    last.second = std::max(last.second, it.second);
                else
                    freeRanges.emplace_back(it);
            }
            // Best-fit policy
            uint32 bestFit = 0xFFFFFFFF;
            for (uint32 k = 1; k < freeRanges.size(); ++k) {
                uint32 begin = freeRanges[k - 1].second;
                uint32 end = freeRanges[k].first;
                uint32 alignedBegin = ALIGNOF(begin,
                    r.Requirement.Alignment);
                if (alignedBegin + r.Requirement.Size <= end) {
                    uint32 fit = end - begin - r.Requirement.Size;
                    if (fit < bestFit) {
                        aliasOffset = alignedBegin;
                        bestFit = fit;
                    }
                }
            }
            if (bestFit != 0xFFFFFFFF) {
                aliasSource = &src;
                break;
            }
        }
    }
    // Create an aliased resource.
    if (aliasSource != nullptr) {
        CreateAliasedResource(r, aliasSource, aliasOffset);
        return true;
    }
    return false;
}
```

Listing 5.5. Creating an aliased resource (offsetting enabled).

5.5   Ping-Pong Buffers

Ping-pong buffers are becoming more prevalent in rendering due to the frequent use of temporal accumulation in rendering effects. These double-buffers are switched back and forth for read and write, typically occurring in two consecutive frames. The lifetime of a ping-pong buffer is delicate, while not transient due to its crossing of frame boundaries, it should not be considered persistent because it only lives for exactly one frame plus a little bit (Figure 5.4). Therefore, we classify ping-pong buffers into a separate ping-pong category.

The resource management system handles ping-pong buffers similarly to transient resources, but with a few special treatments. When writing to a ping-pong resource, mark it as `BringToNextFrame` and move the underlying device resource to an external cache. When reading from a ping-pong resource, mark it as `TakenFromLastFrame` and retrieve the corresponding device resource from the external cache. The lifespans are also extended based on these marks (Listing 5.7).

```
bool AliasN(TransientResource& r,
            std::vector<TransientResource>& S) {
    TransientResource* aliasSource = nullptr;
    for (TransientResource& src : S) {
        if (!src.IsAliasSrc)
            continue;

        // Check whether it is free for sharing.
        bool free = true;
        for (TransientResource* dst=src.Dst; dst; dst=dst->Dst) {
            if (OverlapTest(dst->Lifespan, r.Lifespan) == 0) {
                free = false;
                break;
            }
        }
        if (free) {
            aliasSource = &src;
            break;
        }
    }
    // Create an aliased resource.
    if (aliasSource != nullptr) {
        CreateAliasedResource(r, aliasSource, 0);
        return true;
    }
    return false;
}
```

Listing 5.6. Creating an aliased resource (no offsetting).

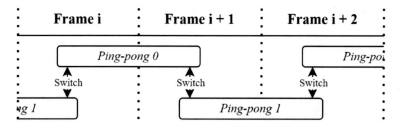

Figure 5.4. The lifetime of a ping-pong buffer.

```
void Extend(ResourceLifespan& life, uint8 flags) {
    if (flags & TakenFromLastFrame)
        life.First = 1;
    if (flags & BringToNextFrame)
        life.Last[0] = 0xFFFF;
}
```

Listing 5.7. Extending the lifespan of a ping-pong resource.

The treatments above enable ping-pong buffers to share memory with other resources outside of their lifespans. There remain many subtle details to consider, especially in the case that ping-pong resources are involved in aliasing, which is error-prone and needs careful handling. Since these details are specific to the engine, further discussion will not be pursued here. Note that all treatments and details above are transparent to pipeline authors; they only need to create resources with a `PingPong` flag, and the resource management system will handle everything else automatically.

5.6 Results

Table 5.2 shows a result of resource management. The "Ping-Pong Opt" column indicates whether the ping-pong buffer optimization is enabled. If it is "Off," all ping-pong resources are treated as persistent. Please note that the numbers only count the resources created in the pipeline, mostly render targets. External resources such as vertex buffers and textures are not included.

Ping-Pong Opt	Reuse	Aliasing	Restricted Aliasing
Off	865	728	738
On	669	630	636

Table 5.2. The total memory footprint (in megabytes) under different configurations.

5.7 Conclusion

Proper representation of lifespan is crucial for effective resource management. In this article, we first explained the limitation of commonly used interval-based representation and proposed a systematic approach that is more accurate. We then introduced two resource allocation schemes, resource reuse and resource aliasing, and showed their relationship with different problems in computational graph theory. Due to the computational complexity of these problems, optimal solutions may not be feasible. Hence, we provided greedy algorithms for each scheme. Lastly, we discussed the management of ping-pong buffers.

Despite the popularity of the Frame Graph in game engines, there is a lack of detailed discussion on its resource management. This article aims to fill that gap by providing an in-depth description of the resource management system in the Messiah Engine. Hope it gives you some insights.

Bibliography

[Gupta et al. 97] Amitabh Gupta, Amit Kumar, and Rajeev Rastogi. "Max-Coloring and Online Coloring with Bandwidths on Interval Graphs." *SIAM Journal on Computing* 26:2 (1997), 306–325.

[Hodes and Dunn 17] Stephan Hodes and Alex Dunn. "Deep Dive: Asynchronous Compute." Presented at Game Developers Conference, 2017. https://www.gdcvault.com/play/1024365/Deep-Dive-Asynchronous-Compute.

[Kartik 13] Kukreja Kartik. "Interval Partitioning Problem." Everything Under the Sun, September 26, 2013. https://kartikkukreja.wordpress.com/2013/09/26/interval-partitioning-problem/.

[Nickel 05] Robert Nickel. "Graph Coloring: Application of the Ellipsoid Method in Combinatorial Optimization." Citeseer, 2005. https://www.fernuni-hagen.de/MATHEMATIK/DMO/mitarbeiter/nickel/talk_seminarellipsoid/ausarb_seminarellipsoid.pdf.

[O'Donnell 17] Yuriy O'Donnell. "FrameGraph: Extensible Rendering Architecture in Frostbite." Presented at Game Developers Conference, 2017. https://www.gdcvault.com/play/1024612/FrameGraph-Extensible-Rendering-Architecture-in.

[Trotter 18] William T. Trotter. "Interval Order & Interval Graph Algorithms." Lecture 16, Math 3012 Open Resources, Georgia Tech, 2018. https://sites.gatech.edu/math3012openresources/lecture-videos/lecture-16/.

[Wikipedia 24] Wikipedia. "Perfect Graph: Comparability Graphs." Accessed June, 2024. https://en.wikipedia.org/wiki/Perfect_graph#Comparability_graphs.

Multi-mega Particle System
Nicola Palomba and Wolfgang Engel

Figure 6.1. Final demo of our particle system.

6.1 Introduction

Not much has changed in particle system architecture since the 2010s: most systems deal with relatively small amounts of particles (a few hundred), except for occasional outlier effects, such as rain, that run on the GPU. Most existing systems are CPU-based or require CPU interaction before submitting work to the GPU, substantially reducing their performance. Therefore, artists were trained to work around these restrictions and design particle effects that could suit the rigid architecture of CPU-based systems.

With GPUs allowing for way more arithmetic power than years ago, it is possible to relax these limitations and have particle systems made of hundreds of thousands, if not millions, of particles. This article presents a GPU-driven particle system in which interaction with the CPU is reduced to a minimum, and most of the implementation is contained in a single compute shader, reducing the times data travels through memory.

We built a demo using The Forge rendering engine to implement the particle system. On an AMD RX 6400, 10,000 light-emitting firefly particles, 4 million transparent particles, and 8 dynamic shadow-casting particles can be handled at around 25 ms per frame. On a European Samsung Galaxy S22, we can simulate up to 4 million transparent particles (while having 2 million of them visible simultaneously) and 10,000 lights running at around 30 FPS.

6.1.1   Visibility Buffer

To support many lights and reduce the overhead for shadows, we use the Triangle Visibility Buffer rendering architecture [Engel 18], developed by our company, The Forge, and now used by most modern rendering engines. It is a GPU-driven rendering technique consisting of multiple phases, each contributing to greatly reducing the amount of drawn triangles and shaded pixels.

- **Triangle filtering:** Triangle vertices and indices are processed by a compute shader to cull as many of them as possible, using the current camera matrices to evaluate whether a triangle is visible or not and, in case it's visible, apply additional metrics to attempt culling. The indices of the triangles that cannot be culled become part of a set of indirect arguments: it is possible to use a set of arguments for the main camera view and one for the shadow map view so that the vertex and index buffers are accessed only once for all the views. Alpha-masked geometry is handled separately, using a similar approach and using the diffuse textures to know which parts of a triangle should be discarded.

- **Batch compaction:** Since triangle filtering runs on batches (of 256 triangles in our case), it can produce empty draw calls, so a shader is used to remove them and avoid overhead in the following phases.

- **Visibility buffer pass:** An `ExecuteIndirect` call is issued to store the data needed to shade the scene in an R8G8B8A8 render target: 1 bit is used to represent whether the triangle is alpha masked or not, 8 bits are used to store the draw call ID, and the last 23 bits are used to store the triangle ID, relative to the draw ID.

- **Visibility buffer shading:** The previously mentioned render target is shaded appropriately. The IDs are used to access the vertex buffer and reconstruct the barycentric coordinates of each triangle, which are used to retrieve any other information (normals, texture coordinates, etc.) needed to shade it. Similar to the case of deferred shading, the amount of shaded pixels is minimal compared to forward shading. Still, the whole process has a much lower impact on memory since it does not need as many render targets.

6.2 Data Management

We define a *particle system* as a collection of particle sets. A *particle set* is a
set of particles that share the same properties, such as texture, particle size,
maximum speed, or AI behavior. Each particle set is made of single *particles*,
which keep track of their current position, age, and velocity. Multiple particle
sets can achieve a certain, more complex effect. For example, a particle set that
emulates fire and one that implements smoke can simulate a bonfire particle
effect. Listing 6.1 shows the declaration of the structures used to represent
particles and particle sets.

```
STRUCT(ParticleData)
{
  DATA(uint2, VelocityAndAge, None);
  DATA(uint2, Position, None);
};
STRUCT(ParticleSet)
{
  // X,Y,Z: volume of the particle set, W: scale of its particles
  DATA(float4, Size, None);
  // Position of the particle set
  DATA(float3, Position, None);
  // Amount of particles to be spawned per second
  DATA(float, ParticlesPerSecond, None);
  // Color of all particles in the set
  DATA(float3, Color, None);
    // Radius of the emitted light
  DATA(float, LightRadius, None);
  // AI type of the particle
  DATA(uint, ParticleType, None);
  // Describes whether particles should cast shadows or emit lights
  DATA(uint, LightBitfield, None);
  // Maximum amount of particles to allocate
  DATA(uint, MaxParticles, None);
  // Lifetime of the particle
  DATA(float, InitialAge, None);
  // Forces for the flocking algorithm
  DATA(uint, BoidsAvoidSeekStrength, None);
  DATA(uint, BoidsSeparationFleeStrength, None);
  DATA(uint, BoidsCohesionAlignmentStrength, None);
  DATA(uint, SteeringStrengthMaxSpeed, None);
};
```

Listing 6.1.   Particle and particle set structures, from shader header
`particle_defs.h.fsl`.

All the particles are stored in the same buffer. Particle properties (such as
the particle set to which they belong or whether they emit light) are described by
a 32-bit bitfield, which is stored in a different buffer. The fact that bitfields are
stored separately allows us to avoid accessing a whole particle in certain cases.
For example, the light clustering shader can detect if a particle is dead just by

looking at the bitfield without retrieving and unpacking the particle to which it belongs. Of course, buffers need to be mirrored: If a particle is located at index i of the particle buffer, its bitfield must be at the same index of the bitfield buffer. Listing 6.2 shows a few notable examples of bitfield values.

```
// Each bitfield type has a mask that allows us to isolate a
// certain property, in this case the allocation state.
#define BITFIELD_ALLOCATION_BITS_MASK 0x1FFFFU
#define BITFIELD_SET_INDEX_MASK 0xFFFFU
#define BITFIELD_IS_ALLOCATED 0x10000U
// State of the particle
#define BITFIELD_STATE_BITS_MASK 0xE0000U
#define BITFIELD_IS_ALIVE 0x20000U
#define BITFIELD_IS_MOVING 0x40000U
// AI behaviour of particles
#define BITFIELD_TYPE_BITS_MASK        0x300000U
#define BITFIELD_TYPE_RAIN             0x0U
#define BITFIELD_TYPE_FIREFLIES        0x100000U
#define BITFIELD_TYPE_FIREFLIES_BOIDS 0x200000U
// Used to render particles with different orientations
#define BITFIELD_BILLBOARD_MODE_BITS_MASK 0x1800000U
#define BITFIELD_BILLBOARD_MODE_SCREEN_ALIGNED 0x0U
#define BITFIELD_BILLBOARD_MODE_VELOCITY_ORIENTED 0x800000U
// Lighting flags: A particle can emit light, cast shadows,
// or not affect the lighting of the scene.
#define BITFIELD_LIGHTING_MODE_BITS_MASK   0x6000000U
#define BITFIELD_LIGHTING_MODE_NONE        0x0U
#define BITFIELD_LIGHTING_MODE_LIGHT       0x2000000U
#define BITFIELD_LIGHTING_MODE_LIGHTNSHADOW 0x4000000U
#define BITFIELD_COLLIDE_WITH_DEPTH_BUFFER  0x400000U
#define BITFIELD_LIGHT_CULLED              0x8000000U
```

Listing 6.2. Examples of bitfield values, from shader header `particle_defs.h.fsl`.

The bitfield and the particle buffers are divided into three main sections: Section 1 contains particles that emit light and cast shadows, and section 2 contains particles that only emit light. The rest is stored in section 3. Each of those sections is divided into two subsections, one for particles that belong to an active (visible) particle set and one for inactive particles. The bounds of each section are stored in a small read/write buffer, computed by the preparation shader. A simple representation of the structure of the particle buffer is shown in Table 6.1.

Light + shadow		Light		Standard	
Active	Inactive	Active	Inactive	Active	Inactive

Table 6.1. Layout of the particle buffer.

6.2.1 Packing

To reduce the amount of memory read by the shaders as much as possible, we had to apply aggressive data-packing techniques. Packing is mostly applied to particles, while particle sets store 32-bit precision data that can be used to unpack particles.

In addition, particle sets are not stored anywhere. Instead, they are created and returned by the `GetParticleSet` function every time it is called: Creating a particle set is not an intensive operation since it mostly consists of assignments, and we found that it performs better than accessing a buffer containing particle sets. A theoretical particle system editor would let users set parameters on the CPU and generate the appropriate `GetParticleSet` function once editing is finished and the system can be exported. The data would then be settled, and it would be impossible to change it at runtime from the CPU side of the application. Listing 6.3 reports a simplified version of the `GetParticleSet` function.

```
ParticleSet GetParticleSet(uint idx) {
  const float steering = 0.02f;
  ParticleSet swarm;
      swarm.Size = float4(3,3,3,0.003);
  swarm.Position = float3(8,6,11);
  swarm.ParticleType = BITFIELD_TYPE_FIREFLIES_BOIDS;
  swarm.Color = float3(1.0, 0.9, 0.0);
  swarm.LightBitfield = BITFIELD_LIGHTING_MODE_NONE;
  swarm.MaxParticles = 1000000;
  swarm.ParticlesPerSecond = 100000;
  swarm.SteeringStrengthMaxSpeed = pack2Floats(steering, 2.0f);
  swarm.InitialAge = 10.0;
  swarm.LightRadius = LIGHT_SIZE;
  swarm.Size = float4(float3(1,1,1), 0.003);

  ParticleSet lightSet = swarm;
  lightSet.ParticleType = BITFIELD_TYPE_FIREFLIES;
  lightSet.LightBitfield = BITFIELD_LIGHTING_MODE_LIGHT;
  lightSet.MaxParticles = 10000;
  lightSet.ParticlesPerSecond = 1000;
  lightSet.SteeringStrengthMaxSpeed = pack2Floats(steering, 0.05);
  lightSet.LightRadius = LIGHT_SIZE;

      ParticleSet shadow = lightSet;

  switch (idx) {
    case 0:
        swarm.Position = float3(6,6,10);
        return swarm;
    case 1:
        swarm.Position = float3(-6, 6, 10);
        return swarm;
    case 2:
        lightSet.Position = float3(2, 8, 5);
        lightSet.Size = float4(10, 6, 8, 0.02);
```

```
            return lightSet;
        default:
            shadow.Color = float3(0.8, 1.0, 0.1);
            shadow.LightBitfield = BITFIELD_LIGHTING_MODE_LIGHTNSHADOW;
            shadow.MaxParticles = 8;
            shadow.ParticlesPerSecond = 0.8;
            shadow.InitialAge = 10.0;
            shadow.Size = float4(10, 6, 8, 0.1);
            shadow.SteeringStrengthMaxSpeed = pack2Floats(steering, 1.0f);
            return shadow;
    }
}
```

Listing 6.3. Simplified version of the `GetParticleSet` function, from shader header `particle_sets.h.fsl`.

The first step in packing consists of normalizing the values to be in the $[0, 1)$ range and having a guaranteed minimum precision. The current age of a particle is divided by its initial age, and the velocity is divided by the maximum speed stored in the particle set. The position of particles is expressed relative to the position of the particle set, so before normalizing the position of the particle, dividing it by the size of the particle set, the position of the particle set is subtracted. The opposite process is applied to unpack a particle. Since particles can move around the scene, in certain cases, it might be appropriate to multiply the particle set size by a certain factor, depending on the behavior of the particle set, so that it includes particles outside its bounds. This is shown in Listing 6.4.

```
ParticleData PackParticle(ParticleSet particleSet, float3 position,
    float4 velocityAndAge)
{
  ParticleData ret;
  position.xyz -= particleSet.Position;
  position.xyz /= PARTICLE_PACKING_SCALE;
  velocityAndAge.xyz /= particleSet.MaxSpeed;

  ret.Position = packFloat3FixedPoint(position);
  ret.VelocityAndAge = uint2(pack2Floats(velocityAndAge.x,
    velocityAndAge.y),
 pack2Floats(velocityAndAge.z, velocityAndAge.w / particleSet.InitialAge
    ));

  return ret;
}
```

Listing 6.4. Packing function, from shader header `particle_packing.h.fsl`.

Age and velocity are then converted to `float16` and packed into two unsigned integers, resulting in 8 bytes of final space. Sixteen bits of precision allow for a guaranteed difference between a representable floating point number and the next one of around ± 0.0005 if numbers are kept in the $[0, 1)$ range like in our case. In the worst-case scenario of the particle system running at 60 FPS, this allows for a minimum acceleration of $0.0005/\frac{1}{60} = 0.03$ m/s^2.

We have 32 bits left for the position that we can use to pack three `float32` values in the $[0, 1]$ range. Packing them into three `float16` would allow for the same amount of precision as the velocity, with a minimum supported velocity of 0.03 m/s: that would leave us with 16 extra bits that could be used to store additional per-particle data. Since we do not need those extra bits, we pack the position into three fixed-point values of 21 bits each: 1 bit for the sign and 20 for the fractional part. This allows for a minimum epsilon of around $\frac{1}{2^{20}} = 0.0000009537$, which is more than enough to support low velocities. If a particle set is too big and normalization causes aliasing or loss of precision, it can be split into multiple sets with the same settings. This process also improves performance since those particle sets can be culled more easily. Listing 6.5 shows code to pack and unpack a `float3` into a `uint2`.

```
uint2 packFloat3FixedPoint(float3 v)
{
  const float maxVal = (1 << 20)-1;
  uint3 vUint = uint3(0,0,0);

  for (uint i=0; i<3; i++)
  {
    // Absolute number after the point
    vUint[i] = uint(round(abs(v[i] * maxVal)));
    // Sign
    vUint[i] |= (v[i] > 0 ? (1 << 20) : 0);
  }

  // Layout of the output: [(21 bits of X - 11 bits of Y), (unused bit,
    remaining 10 bits of Y, 21 bits of Z)]
  return uint2((vUint.x << 11) | (vUint.y >> 10), ((vUint.y & ((1 << 10)
    -1)) << 21) | vUint.z);
}

float3 unpackFloat3FixedPoint(uint2 v)
{
  const float maxVal = (1 << 20)-1;
  uint3 vUint = uint3(0,0,0);
  vUint[0] = v.x >> 11;
  vUint[1] = ((v.x & (1 << 11)-1) << 10) | (v.y >> 21);
  vUint[2] = (v.y & (1 << 21)-1);

  // Rebuild the number: value * sign
  float3 ret;
  for (uint i=0; i<3; i++)
    ret[i] = (float(vUint[i] & ((1 << 20)-1)) / maxVal) * ((vUint[i] >>
    20) > 0 ? 1 : -1);

  return ret;
}
```

Listing 6.5. Pack/unpack `float3`, from shader header `particle_packing.h.fsl`.

6.3 Workflow

We built every part of the demo, remembering that memory bandwidth is the biggest bottleneck in modern rendering approaches. The simplest way to reduce memory usage is to process data in one run to reduce the time needed for subsequent phases to complete. This means the buffers containing particle data are only accessed completely in the simulation shader. In contrast, other shaders (such as the light clustering or the visibility buffer shading shaders) only access a small portion. Triangle filtering follows a similar principle, running over the index and vertex buffers only once per frame to reduce overhead for the following phases.

The particle system goes through three different steps to complete a frame.

- The first one is used to prepare all the other ones: it only accesses the particle sets. It produces the data needed to sort particles by particle set visibility and to compute the bounds of each section of the buffers.

- The second and most important step is simulation, which is the only one that can potentially access the entirety of the particle buffer. The simulation shader initializes particles, kills or respawns them, sorts each section of the buffer, performs part of light culling, rasterizes small particles, and updates each particle's velocity, age, and position.

- The third phase consists of rendering particles that are too big (in screen space) to be handled by the software rasterizer.

6.4 Simulation

6.4.1 Preliminary Step

Before starting the simulation, a preliminary step is necessary to compute the index separating active and inactive particles for each buffer section. To do this, the shader iterates over all the particle sets, each belonging to a section. A simple frustum-bounding box test is used to determine whether or not a set is visible: if it is, then the end index of the active section is increased by the number of particles it contains. The previous bounds are saved so that the simulation shader can detect a status change and move particles out of the wrong section of the buffer. During the first frame, the shader also computes the amount of particles to be instantiated for each section.

6.4.2 Particle Initialization

Starting from this point, the simulation shader will handle everything. During the first frame, all particles must be instantiated. Given an index i, we first check in which part of the buffer the particle is (light + shadow, light, standard) using the bounds provided by the preparation shader, then we select the right particle set iterating through all of them, accumulating the number of particles a of the previous sets: if $i > a \wedge a + \texttt{currParticleCount} < i$, then particle i belongs to the current particle set. We assign the particle to it, setting the BITFIELD_SET_INDEX_MASK (Listing 6.2) part of its bitfield to the index of the set. The age of the particle is set to a negative value ranging from 0 to $-$InitialAge that depends on the index of the particle, relative to the particle set start index: since at every frame, the age field is increased by the time delta, in that way, particles are gradually spawned over time. This is demonstrated in Listing 6.6.

```
uint Bitfield = 0;
// Find the particle range to which this particle belongs.
uint3 startIndices = uint3(0, lightNShadowCount, lightNShadowCount +
    lightCount);

uint3 endIndices = uint3(lightNShadowCount, lightNShadowCount +
    lightCount, lightNShadowCount + lightCount + standardCount);
uint3 bitfields = uint3(BITFIELD_LIGHTING_MODE_LIGHTNSHADOW,
    BITFIELD_LIGHTING_MODE_LIGHT, BITFIELD_LIGHTING_MODE_NONE);

// For each lighting type
for (uint i=0; i<3; i++)
{
    // Find the beginning of the current buffer section.
    particleBufferOffset = startIndices[i];
    // Allocate all particle sets that are of that type.
    for (uint j=0; j<MAX_PARTICLE_SET_COUNT; j++)
    {
        particleSet = GetParticleSet(j);
        particleCount = particleSet.MaxParticles;
        particlesPerSecond = particleSet.ParticlesPerSecond;

        if (particleSet.LightBitfield == bitfields[i])
        {
            // If the particle that we are allocating sits in the
current area of the buffer, allocate it.
            if (particleIdx >= particleBufferOffset && particleIdx <
particleBufferOffset + particleCount)
            {
                // Initialize the bitfield.
                Bitfield |= BITFIELD_IS_ALLOCATED | j | bitfields[i] |
particleSet.ParticleType;
                // Light isn't visible at the beginning.
                Bitfield |= BITFIELD_LIGHT_CULLED;

                setIndex = j;
                particleTypeIndex = i;
                Age = float(particleIdx - particleBufferOffset) / -
particlesPerSecond;

                SaveParticle(particleSet, particleIdx, Bitfield, float3
    (0,0,0), Age, float3(0,0,0));
```

```
                RETURN();
        }

        particleBufferOffset += particleCount;
    }
  }
}
```

Listing 6.6. Allocation of a single particle, from shader `particle_` `simulate.comp.fsl`.

When the age of a particle becomes a positive value, it can be initialized, and its initial bitfield, position, and velocity are set according to the particle set to which it belongs. The age is set to the initial age specified in the particle set: in each frame, it will decrease by the time delta until it reaches a negative value. At that point, the state change will be reflected in the bitfield (using the BITFIELD_IS_ALIVE bit in Listing 6.2), and the particle will be considered dead. Similarly to how it was instantiated, the age will be set to a negative number ranging from 0 to −InitialAge. It will increase each frame by the time delta until it is positive, starting the cycle again. Code in Listing 6.7 implements this process.

```
if (!isAlive)
{
    // Particle is dead, but age is positive: must spawn.
    if (Age >= 0.0f) {
        isAlive = true;

        switch (particleSet.ParticleType) {
        case PARTICLE_BITFIELD_TYPE_FIREFLIES:
            InitialAge = particleSet.InitialAge;
            Age = InitialAge;
            LightRadius = particleSet.LightRadius;
            Position = particleSet.Position ;
            Velocity.xyz = randFloat3Normalized() * steeringSpeed.y;
            Bitfield |= BITFIELD_IS_MOVING;
            break;

        case PARTICLE_BITFIELD_TYPE_FIREFLIES_BOIDS:
            InitialAge = particleSet.InitialAge;
            Age = InitialAge;
            LightRadius = particleSet.LightRadius;
            Velocity.xyz = randFloat3Normalized() * steeringSpeed.y;
            Position = particleSet.Position ;
            Bitfield |= BITFIELD_IS_MOVING;
            break;

        case PARTICLE_BITFIELD_TYPE_RAIN:
            InitialAge = particleSet.InitialAge;
            Age = InitialAge;
            Position = particleSet.Position.x;
            Bitfield |= BITFIELD_IS_MOVING
```

```
                        | BITFIELD_IS_ACCELERATING
                        | BITFIELD_COLLIDE_WITH_DEPTH_BUFFER
                        | BITFIELD_BILLBOARD_MODE_VELOCITY_ORIENTED;
                Velocity.xyz = float3(5.0f, -10.0f, 0.0f);
                break;
        }

        Bitfield |= BITFIELD_IS_ALIVE | particleSet.ParticleType |
    particleSet.LightBitfield;
        SaveParticle(particleSet, particleIdx, Bitfield, Position, Age,
    Velocity);
        }
        else  {
            // Wait for the right time to respawn.
            Age -= Get(TimeDelta);
            SaveParticle(particleSet, particleIdx, Bitfield, Position, Age,
    Velocity);
        }
}
else if (Age < 0) {
    // Kill particle.
    Bitfield &= ~BITFIELD_IS_ALIVE;
    // Set negative age; particle will respawn when Age > 0.
    Age = -max(0.0, float(particleCount) / float(particlesPerSecond) -
    InitialAge);

    SaveParticle(particleSet, particleIdx, Bitfield, Position, Age,
    Velocity);
}
```

Listing 6.7. Instantiation and death of a particle, from shader `particle_simulate.comp.fsl`.

6.4.3 Sorting

Before simulating particles, the shader checks whether or not a particle set changed its visibility state. If it did, particles belonging to that set are sorted according to the new state, moving them to the right subsection of the particle buffer. Inactive particles are not simulated, which means that threads that handle particles whose index is located in the inactive bounds of the buffers return immediately without accessing any memory. Even though dead particles don't contribute to the final scene, they must still be accessed to increase their age and make them respawn later, so there is no point in sorting them. Shaders like the one used for culling lights can ignore dead particles just by accessing their bitfield, saving a full particle access.

Due to the way GPUs work, there are a few constraints that a potential sorting algorithm must follow:

- Each visit to a buffer element should translate to a single thread in the compute shader. While a thread can access a small number of other elements, the concept is that it can sort and simulate a single particle. Otherwise, performance starts degrading.

- There should be no assumptions regarding the order in which each thread finishes sorting or simulating. Synchronization is only available for small buffer chunks via group memory barriers.

- Sorting must be done in place to avoid increasing the memory requirements for the application. Small support buffers could be used. This constraint suggests that swap-based algorithms are the best candidates for the problem.

- Sorting must be done in the same pass as a simulation to avoid unnecessary memory round trips. This constraint greatly restricts the number of solutions since, when swapping particles, the shader could retrieve a particle being simulated by an interrupted thread, which could then resume its execution with incoherent data, effectively replacing a particle with a duplicate of another.

Since sorting has a theoretical lower limit of $O(n * \log(n))$ and each thread of the simulation shader, for performance reasons, handles only a single particle at once, we trace back our problem to a different one to reduce the limit to $O(n)$, noticing that we can take advantage of a few additional properties that are unique to our case:

- The preliminary shader lets us know exactly how many particles changed their state during a certain frame by computing the new bounds of the particle buffer and by storing the previous bounds: the difference between them is the number of particles that changed state.

- We only need to sort two types of elements: active and inactive. This means that the problem is similar to sorting a binary array.

- If we assume that our buffer was correctly sorted in the previous frame, we only need to find outlier elements in the wrong subsections.

The final algorithm consists of a simple, swap-based, in-place technique. We define the *swap area* as the buffer area between the previous and new bounds of a certain section of the buffer; the swap area is not simulated, and all threads assigned to a particle located in it return immediately.

Let's first examine the case in which a particle set, for example, the one with index 1, became invisible. Its particles could be anywhere around the buffer; some might already be in the correct subsection. First of all, the simulation shader checks if its index is located in the inactive section, outside of the active area: if so, the thread returns since it is guaranteed that no particles belonging to particle set 1 are there (the buffer was correctly sorted in the previous frame,

Figure 6.2. Representation of a buffer section where a particle set changed its visibility state. Yellow indicates a simulated buffer area. The arrows represent the direction along which the inactive particles bound moves.

so no active particles are in the inactive section). If the thread is assigned to a particle belonging to particle set 1, it must sort it. The thread can return if the particle is already in the swap area to avoid simulating an inactive particle. If the particle is outside the swap area (so it is in the active section), the previous bound is used as an index to search for active particles to swap with. Once a suitable index is found, particles are swapped, and the new one is simulated: the swap area is not simulated, so the procedure is thread-safe.

Let's also examine the case in which Particle Set 1 became active again. This time, the simulation shader cannot return if assigned to a particle in the inactive area; in fact, any particle in that area could have become active again. Everything works the same as in the previous case (increasing the previous bound instead of decreasing it), but this time, particles are simulated before being moved to the swap area. Figure 6.2 shows a visual representation of this process.

A problem might occur if there are many contiguous inactive particles in the swap area. In that case, the thread attempting to swap particles has to perform many accesses to the buffer, clogging the simulation. The issue is mitigated by the fact that the previous bound is decreased concurrently, which, for a single thread, reduces the number of attempts for a successful swap. We found that, on PC, more than four threads can handle this edge case efficiently, while on the S22, at least eight threads are needed: below those thresholds, searching for an empty spot to swap the particle can make the simulation lag noticeably. After a configurable amount of failed attempts, a help system for the threads that are not advancing is triggered; when this happens, the other threads in the current wave start searching for a swap index. When a suitable index is found, it is written in the group shared memory so that the threads having trouble sorting their particles can just read it as soon as it's available: we take advantage of the whole wave when necessary. We ported our demo to all platforms (PC, consoles, mobile) without noticing any stuttering, even at high camera speeds, which should trigger sorting more often.

6.4.4   Boids

Boids are a model introduced by Craig Reynolds to represent the behavior of groups of animals such as flocks of birds, schools of fish, or even herds [Reynolds 87]. We implemented this algorithm to show how our particle system can support programmable AI behaviors. The model uses steering behaviors to simulate how individual agents (called boids) interact. In particular, three forces are applied:

- Separation, which is used to keep a certain distance between one boid and another.

- Alignment, the tendency of boids to steer toward the average velocity of their neighbors.

- Cohesion, the tendency of boids to move toward the center of their neighborhood.

In addition, to have a more interesting scene, we implement the seek behavior, which consists of making all boids steer toward a target. In our demo, one particle set follows a target that moves in circles around the scene, while the other swarms have the position of the particle set to which they belong as the target. Depending on the strength of each force, it is possible to tune the behavior of a particle set.

The original algorithm compares each boid with all the other ones, resulting in an $O(n^2)$ algorithm. Given the very high number of particles, this is unfeasible, so we resorted to a few compromises that still provide a good final result. Since particles are processed in batches of 32 elements, we use thread group shared memory to store particles' positions and velocities in the same batch. After issuing a memory barrier, each particle in the same batch has data regarding the particles in the same batch. While this does not guarantee that particles contiguous in the particle buffer are also close in world space, it provides a good approximation of the actual state of the particle set. Depending on the target platform, it might be necessary to use less shared memory in favor of directly accessing the particle buffer. On an AMD RX 6400, occupancy for the simulation shader is 100%.

6.4.5   Rasterization

The last phase of the simulation shader consists of rasterization. To avoid having a hardware rasterizer go through all the particles again, we implemented a simple software rasterizer. The hardware rasterizer handles particles whose screen-space bounding box is bigger than a certain threshold, accessing a small buffer containing the indices of said particles.

The bounding box is obtained by adding the half size of the particle to its position and multiplying the resulting points by the view-projection matrix. Particles outside the view frustum are prematurely culled, while the visible ones are rasterized by filling the screen-space bounding box, sampling from the texture specified in the particle set. Since the particle's position is already being projected in screen space, particles that emit light can also be culled during this step by checking whether or not their radius intersects the frustum, saving processing time for later clustering.

6.5   Lighting

Lighting is the biggest challenge of the particle system, besides simulating millions of particles. The visibility buffer approach provides a solid base to build upon: the number of pixels to be shaded is reduced, and the amount of memory necessary to draw a frame is lower than with other techniques, such as deferred shading.

In our demo, particles can emit light and cast shadows. Multiple steps are needed to support as many of them as possible to perform aggressive culling and reduce shading overhead.

6.5.1   Light Culling

We have already explained how lights are roughly culled during the rasterization step of the simulation shader if they are outside the screen's bounds. Particles that survive that process are passed to the light cluster.

We divide the screen horizontally into 32 sections and vertically into 16 sections, producing 512 rectangular tiles. Each tile corresponds to a thread of the compute shader used to cull lights, and each thread group processes a particle. This is more efficient than having a thread group process more lights for the same tile. Since this approach tends to create big tiles, we trade some computing time in the light-culling shader to save more when shading using sub-clusters. Each tile is divided into sections, and each thread group culls the same lights for multiple sub-clusters.

Finally, we use the depth buffer (automatically generated during the first visibility buffer pass, with no need for a depth pre-pass) to obtain additional information regarding the scene, as described more thoroughly in [Harada 12]. For each tile, we compute the minimum and maximum depth ($\mathtt{depthMin}, \mathtt{depthMax}$) in the area they cover, and we build a 32-bit mask in which bit N is set to 1 if the tile overlaps depth buffer samples located between $((\mathtt{depthMax}-\mathtt{depthMin})/32)*N$ and $((\mathtt{depthMax}-\mathtt{depthMin})/32)*(N+1)$.

When a light is processed, the `depthMin` and `depthMax` values for the tile it is located in are retrieved and used to compute the bitmask for that light. Similarly to the depth bitmask, it represents which areas of the z-axis are influenced by the light: if there is no intersection between the two bitmasks, then no depth samples are affected by the light. Therefore, it can be safely culled.

After culling lights, the shader that produces the final frame must retrieve the ones that should be used for a certain fragment. Its screen-space coordinates are used to understand in which tile it is located and to retrieve the number of lights that affect it. Then, for each light, the particle it corresponds to is read to get additional data needed for shading, such as the color and position of the light. To save time, the shader does not compute the whole PBR pipeline if the world-space distance between the fragment and the light is bigger than its radius or if `dot(normal, lightDir)` ≤ 0, cases in which the light does not affect the scene.

6.5.2   Point Light Shadows

Point light shadows are expensive to compute, given the need to render the scene six times to draw a depth cube map that can later be used to shade the scene. With the number of triangles in video games increasing every year, it is extremely important to reduce the number of primitives to be rasterized by the shadow pass shader as much as possible. To do that, we again take advantage of the visibility buffer workflow, particularly triangle filtering.

6.5.3   Triangle Filtering for Shadow Generation

The visibility buffer lets programmers cull triangles for multiple views in a single compute dispatch [Engel 18], hiding memory operations behind culling calculations. We use triangle filtering to build additional sets of indirect arguments, one per omnidirectional shadow, which only includes the triangles visible from one or more cube map views. In addition to applying the usual culling metrics, we also cull triangles when all their vertices are more distant from the center of the view than the radius of the light cast by the particle. Shadows are visible only inside the volume of the light that produces them; for this reason, when triangles are rasterized during the shadow pass, the camera's far plane is set to the radius of the point light that casts the shadows.

Another optimization consists of culling only triangles for the cube map faces visible from the main camera: this is implemented by checking whether or not the frustum of a certain face intersects the one of the main camera.

6.5.4   Omnidirectional Shadows

After all the indirect arguments are generated by the triangle filtering pass, we render the depth cube maps for each shadow. Since we, unfortunately, have to rely on the hardware rasterizer, the demo sometimes performs unnecessary state changes, for example, when binding the resources for drawing to a face that is not visible. Another limitation on performance is that a single face might only contain a portion of the triangles drawn for the entire cube map, which means that the shader has to go through data that does not contribute to the rendering of a certain face. Creating a set of indirect arguments per face would increase the overhead of triangle filtering too much; ideally, a software rasterizer would have access to the triangles for a certain cube map and decide exactly which ones should be rasterized and to which faces.

Finally, the shadow test is performed in the shading shader, which stores its results in a separate texture composed along with transparency data to create the final frame. This setup helps improve the performance of shadow filtering since a potential shader would only have to blur the pixels visible on screen and not the whole cube map.

6.6 Transparency

In the case of our particle system, sorting particles and drawing them in the correct order is unfeasible for two reasons: The first is that we use a software rasterizer while also simulating particles, and we cannot assume anything about the order in which a particle is processed. The second reason is that no modern sorting algorithm can efficiently handle millions of particles: both bitonic sort [Batcher 68] and radix sort [Harada and Howes 11], known to be highly parallelizable algorithms suited for GPU usage, fail to provide an acceptable execution time. Knowing this, an order-independent transparency (OIT) algorithm is needed to handle alpha blending. We considered different algorithms:

- Moment-based OIT [Münstermann et al. 18] provides accurate results but requires two geometry passes to work. We cannot afford to go through the particle buffer more than once.

- Weighted blended OIT [McGuire and Bavoil 13] and its variations only provide an approximation of the actual blended color: besides this point, it could be adopted for devices that do not have very efficient hardware, such as low-tier mobile phones or laptops with integrated GPUs.

- Linked list–based OIT seemed the best candidate for the task. As the amount of memory needed to store lists is considerable, we explored multilayer alpha blending (MLAB) [Salvi and Vaidyanathan 14] to reduce the number of elements of lists by using tail blending. Still, this approach produces artifacts in particles (as shown in Figure 6.3 and reported in [Münstermann et al. 18]) and cannot be implemented in a compute shader. The only way MLAB can work is either by using fragment shader interlocks or rasterizer order views. Both of these approaches only work with a hardware rasterizer and are only available on certain platforms.

Figure 6.3. Artifacts produced by MLAB when rendering particles. Notice the sharp edges of the textures in the points where transparency transitions to a value higher than 0.

We use bounded arrays instead of lists since particles can take up a considerable portion of the screen with many overlapping layers; otherwise we cannot know the amount of space the lists will take in advance. Using arrays also removes the need to store the index of the next element, saving space and improving performance in the resolve pass.

6.6.1 Linked-List OIT

The basic idea of using linked lists for OIT consists of storing transparency samples in a list instead of directly drawing them while keeping track of the number of samples in the lists. In a later composition pass, lists are sorted by depth to retrieve the correct order for each pixel, and finally, samples are blended. To do this, samples must be stored with premultiplied alpha.

When a semitransparent fragment must be rendered, its coordinates are used to compute the position of the list to which it belongs. An integer value is atomically increased to reserve a location in the list; then the sample is assigned. To reduce the algorithm's overhead, we pack transparency samples into two **uints**: the first is used to store the premultiplied color, and the second one keeps track of the depth of the sample. Once the application needs to sort samples, it can store them using the packed format to save registers (the depth value is already represented in its unpacked form and can be used by casting it to a float) and later unpack the colors of the samples to compute the final result.

Figure 6.4. Multiple overlapping semitransparent surfaces rendering correctly without requiring any sorting.

This approach is suitable for both software and hardware rasterization. It requires a single geometry pass and is thread-safe. (See Figure 6.4.)

6.7   Results

Timings have been taken on a European Samsung Galaxy S22, which ships with the RDNA-based Xclipse 920 GPU, and on an AMD RX 6400. The screenshots in Figures 6.5–6.12 report the approximate timings for both platforms. It is important to note that performance may vary depending on the state of the scene, which is practically unpredictable: depending on the point of view, more lights, shadows, or semitransparent surfaces could be visible. We stressed the application by choosing camera angles with as many elements as possible.

The screenshots in Figures 6.5–6.8 were obtained by running the demo on an AMD RX 6400 GPU with a rendering resolution of 1920×1080.

The screenshots in Figures 6.9–6.12 were obtained by running the demo on a European Samsung Galaxy S22, which uses the Xclipse 920 GPU based on RDNA architecture with a rendering resolution of 1170×540.

Overall time	24.92 ms		Light clustering	2.21 ms
GPU time	24.88 ms		Shading	4.54 ms
Triangle filtering	4.69 ms		Render particles	1.51 ms
Point shadows	0.81 ms		Simulate particles	7.50 ms
VB filling	0.96 ms		Resolve transparency	1.60 ms

Figure 6.5. Performance for a view with all particle sets active.

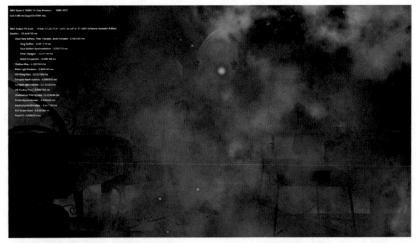

Overall time	23.62 ms		Light clustering	1.39 ms
GPU time	23.65 ms		Shading	2.99 ms
Triangle filtering	3.48 ms		Render particles	6.69 ms
Point shadows	0.56 ms		Simulate particles	3.86 ms
VB filling	0.32 ms		Resolve transparency	3.33 ms

Figure 6.6. Performance for a view with many transparent surfaces.

Overall time	23.94 ms		Light clustering	1.99 ms
GPU time	23.96 ms		Shading	5.37 ms
Triangle filtering	4.57 ms		Render particles	0.19 ms
Point shadows	1.26 ms		Simulate particles	7.49 ms
VB filling	1.15 ms		Resolve transparency	0.92 ms

Figure 6.7. Performance for a view with many surfaces affected by lights.

Overall time	23.66 ms		Light clustering	2.71 ms
GPU time	23.64 ms		Shading	4.05 ms
Triangle filtering	5.57 ms		Render particles	0.19 ms
Point shadows	1.00 ms		Simulate particles	7.11 ms
VB filling	1.18 ms		Resolve transparency	0.61 ms

Figure 6.8. Performance for an intensive top-down view.

Overall time	31.37 ms
GPU time	31.34 ms
Triangle filtering	2.63 ms
VB filling	1.32 ms
Light clustering	3.27 ms

Shading	6.16 ms
Render particles	0.51 ms
Simulate particles	12.65 ms
Resolve transparency	3.83 ms

Figure 6.9. Performance for a view with all particle sets active.

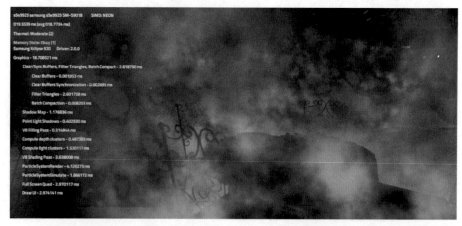

Overall time	18.77 ms
GPU time	18.71 ms
Triangle filtering	2.62 ms
VB filling	0.51 ms
Light clustering	2.00 ms

Shading	3.64 ms
Render particles	4.12 ms
Simulate particles	1.87 ms
Resolve transparency	2.97 ms

Figure 6.10. Performance for a view with many transparent surfaces.

Overall time	32.10 ms
GPU time	32.09 ms
Triangle filtering	2.78 ms
VB filling	2.06 ms
Light clustering	3.50 ms

Shading	8.13 ms
Render particles	0.03 ms
Simulate particles	12.56 ms
Resolve transparency	2.06 ms

Figure 6.11. Performance for a view with many surfaces affected by lights.

Overall time	32.59 ms
GPU time	32.59 ms
Triangle filtering	2.98 ms
VB filling	2.28 ms
Light clustering	4.54 ms

Shading	6.03 ms
Render particles	0.34 ms
Simulate particles	13.25 ms
Resolve transparency	2.17 ms

Figure 6.12. Performance for an intensive top-down view.

6.8   Conclusions and Future Work

In this article, we have presented the foundations for a GPU-driven particle system that can handle millions of particles by using aggressive data packing strategies, simulating only the visible effects at a certain time, and minimizing the number of times that the buffer containing the particles is accessed. There are three main routes that we can explore to improve the current state of the particle system.

6.8.1   Feature Additions

The system lacks functionality to let artists approximate real-life effects, such as modifying properties over time. In addition, it does not support meshes yet, a feature that would probably require a more advanced rasterizer. It would probably improve the rendering times of particles close to the camera. Another feature that could be implemented consists of collisions. At the moment, particles can collide with the depth buffer but cannot do anything more; implementing collision resolution would provide an additional tool to approximate certain particle effects. This could be done by using a simplified version of the scene geometry to reduce the time needed to process collisions. The system could also include animations and particles that can receive lighting from the environment or cast their shadows onto the scene.

6.8.2   Optimizations

Despite the demo running on a Samsung Galaxy S22 at 30 FPS with a high number of lights and particles, it is always good to work on improving performance. One of the bottlenecks is caused by shadows. As mentioned previously, a more advanced software rasterizer would allow us to increase the triangle throughput when rendering and reduce the number of state changes needed for a single cube map face while allowing for a higher level of tuning. Regarding triangle filtering, right now, we create a set of indices to be drawn per shadow; this is not feasible for higher amounts of shadows (filtering for 20 point-light shadows takes around 17 ms on an AMD RX 6400). A high number of sets means that more triangles will be filtered, which also translates to higher costs in triangle filtering since each set must go through the whole triangle list. A compromise must be found, and merging sets of indices of close shadows could be a good first step. Metrics to do so should be simple and require very few computations to produce an effective improvement. Culling triangles in a top-down fashion, starting with a radius that encapsulates more than one shadow and gradually reducing it to iterate over fewer triangles for the bottom levels, could also be a good way to proceed, even though a lot of care must be implemented.

6.8.3 Particle Editor

The last way we could proceed with our particle system is by implementing a particle editor. The main challenge would probably be granting a sufficient degree of artistic freedom. When millions of particles are involved, certain AI behaviors could require a very specific implementation that would be hard to achieve without directly modifying the simulation shader. We have already started working on the foundations to build an editor.

Bibliography

[Batcher 68] Kenneth E Batcher. "Sorting Networks and Their Applications." In *Proceedings of the April 30–May 2, 1968, Spring Joint Computer Conference*, pp. 307–314. Association for Computing Machinery, 1968.

[Engel 18] Wolfgang Engel. "Triangle Visibility Buffer." Wolfgang Engel's Diary of a Graphics Programmer Blog, 2018. http://diaryofagraphicsprogrammer. blogspot.com/2018/03/triangle-visibility-buffer.html.

[Harada and Howes 11] Takahiro Harada and Lee Howes. "Introduction to GPU Radix Sort." In *Heterogeneous Computing with OpenCL*. Morgan Kaufman, 2011.

[Harada 12] Takahiro Harada. "A 2.5D Culling for Forward+." In *SIGGRAPH Asia 2012 Technical Briefs*, pp. 18:1–18:4. Association for Computing Machinery, 2012.

[McGuire and Bavoil 13] Morgan McGuire and Louis Bavoil. "Weighted Blended Order-Independent Transparency." *Journal of Computer Graphics Techniques* 2:4 (2013), 122–141.

[Münstermann et al. 18] Cedrick Münstermann, Stefan Krumpen, Reinhard Klein, and Christoph Peters. "Moment-Based Order-Independent Transparency." *Proceedings of the ACM on Computer Graphics and Interactive Techniques* 1:1 (2018), 7:1–7:20.

[Reynolds 87] Craig W Reynolds. "Flocks, Herds and Schools: A Distributed Behavioral Model." In *Proceedings of the 14th Annual Conference on Computer Graphics and Interactive Techniques*, pp. 25–34. Association for Computing Machinery, 1987.

[Salvi and Vaidyanathan 14] Marco Salvi and Karthik Vaidyanathan. "Multilayer Alpha Blending." In *Proceedings of the 18th Meeting of the ACM SIGGRAPH Symposium on Interactive 3D Graphics and Games*, pp. 151–158. Association for Computing Machinery, 2014.

Rendering and Simulation

Laura Reznikov and Peter Sikachev, Editors

The Rendering and Simulation section presents a deep dive into the latest advancements in real-time graphics and simulation techniques. In this section, we explore the innovative methods and groundbreaking technologies that are shaping the future of digital rendering and interactive experiences. From optimizing real-time lighting pipelines in blockbuster video games to achieving realistic global illumination and real-time massive crowd simulation, these articles collectively highlight the challenges and solutions at the forefront of the industry.

Our first article, "The Evolution of the Real-Time Lighting Pipeline in *Cyberpunk 2077*" by Jakub Knapik, Giovanni De Francesco, Dmitrii Zhdan, Edward Liu, Evgeny Makarov, Jon Kennedy, Juho Marttila, Michael Murphy, Nathan Hoobler, Tim Cheblokov, and Pawel Kozlowski, delves into the sophisticated lighting techniques employed in one of the most visually stunning games of our time, highlighting challenges and solutions for achieving realism. The authors take us through the evolution from ray tracing to path tracing and the approaches taken to achieve real-time performance. The coverage of current techniques such as ReSTIR GI, Spatially Hashed Radiance Caching, ReLAX denoising, DLSS Ray Reconstruction, and Frame Generation make this article a great read.

Next, "Real-Time Ray Tracing of Large Voxel Scenes," by Russel Arbore, Jeffrey Liu, Aidan Wefel, Steven Gao, and Eric Shaffer, explores optimizing ray tracing for expansive voxel environments, focusing on maintaining real-time performance while handling large-scale scenes. This article delves into voxel representations, their interaction with real-time ray tracing advancements, and strategies for managing the substantial memory demands of large voxel scenes, with a focus on the Illinois Voxel Sandbox (IVS).

Following this, "Optimizing FSR 2 for Adreno" by Randall Rauwendaal discusses the optimization of AMD's FidelityFX Super Resolution 2 for Adreno GPUs, essential for enhancing visual quality on mobile platforms. By analyzing and refining FSR's performance on Adreno GPUs, this article aims to maintain the algorithm's quality while improving efficiency for high-quality gaming on mobile devices.

"IBL-BRDF Multiple Importance Sampling for Stochastic Screen-Space Indirect Specular" by Soufiane KHIAT presents a novel approach for improving the quality of indirect specular reflections using multiple importance sampling. It combines BRDF and light sampling to optimize screen-space reflection (SSIS) for dynamic environments, focusing on practical implementation in Unity's High Definition Render Pipeline (HDRP).

"Practical Clustered Forward Decals" by Kirill Bazhenov introduces a technique for decals that doesn't rely on the depth buffer and instead works by projecting decal textures in the main pass pixel shader. This method, similar to clustered forward lighting, optimizes performance and offers advanced features like animated decals, height-based blending, and parallax effects.

"Virtual Shadow Maps," by Matej Sakmary, Jake Ryan, Justin Hall, and Alessio Lustri, details the implementation of virtual shadow maps, an application of virtual textures, to enhance the realism of dynamic shadows and offers a comprehensive guide for integration into modern rendering engines. The authors' example implementation of VSMs provides an efficient solution by using a system of 16 overlapping cascades, each with sparse pages dynamically allocated based on visibility, optimizing memory usage and providing high-quality shadows.

"Real-Time Simulation of Massive Crowds" by Tomer Weiss provides techniques for simulating and rendering large crowds in real time, crucial for creating immersive and believable environments. This article details a GPU-accelerated framework using position-based dynamics (PBD) and constraints-based methods to ensure physical realism and efficient performance.

Finally, "Diffuse Global Illumination" by Darius Bouma explores methods for achieving realistic global illumination in real time, discussing the challenges and solutions in simulating diffuse light interactions. This article introduces the ReSTIR-based clipmap irradiance cache to efficiently manage indirect lighting queries, enhancing responsiveness and detail in dynamic and complex scenes.

–Laura Reznikov

The Evolution of the Real-Time Lighting Pipeline in Cyberpunk 2077

Jakub Knapik, Giovanni De Francesco, Dmitrii Zhdan, Edward Liu, Evgeny Makarov, Jon Kennedy, Juho Marttila, Michael Murphy, Nathan Hoobler, Tim Cheblokov, and Pawel Kozlowski

Figure 7.1. Screenshot from *Cyberpunk 2077*.

7.1 Introduction

When we embarked on the *Cyberpunk 2077* project at CD PROJEKT RED, we aimed to push the boundaries and create a more expansive, immersive, and visually stunning game than anything we had ever attempted. Fueled by our massive ambition, we started almost from scratch. We explored uncharted territory by developing a first-person perspective game, a new concept at the studio, constructing a gigantic vertical city at the heart of it, depicting a fully dynamic living world with a complete day-night cycle and variable weather conditions, and trying to deliver all that in an engine still in early development. This daring approach enabled us to break free from the tunnel vision we would naturally carry from the past and open our minds to new possibilities we had never attempted.

From the beginning, we knew that the lighting and rendering of that multidimensional sculpture we called Night City would be challenging. We moved from a relatively simple lighting scenario in *The Witcher* game, with its trees and not very tall building occlusions, into the vertical greeble created by the futuristic metropolis of *Cyberpunk 2077*. Considering any large arbitrary city and imagining ourselves standing there, we notice that the view around us divides into multiple spaces. The variety of lighting scenarios brought by those random scenes is staggering, as are the technical challenges that come with them. (See Figure 7.2.) However, we think the environment's verticality and dynamic nature of light are, by far, the most challenging.

Figure 7.2. Various lighting scenarios in *Cyberpunk 2077*.

Figure 7.3. The same scene at night (left) versus during the day (right).

Let us look at the low-architecture city scenario, with small buildings, sparse placement, trees, and small objects as the leading light occluders. We can rely on sunlight and relatively simple skylight. Those provide the primary energy gradient that draws shapes around us. It helps us properly read the space. With this balanced light, our brain can understand the scale of the environment and see the distances around us.

On top of that, from a rendering point of view, we have computationally simple sky lighting and shadow maps to generate. However, the situation dramatically turns if we surround ourselves with complex tall buildings instead. Instantly, it becomes rare to see the sun reaching street level. We can only rely on the sun at noon or when it randomly finds space between all the dense city structures throughout the day. Most light comes from high above us through complex environmental occlusion, like in a well. In this scenario, simple ambient occlusions and shadows will not work. We need to create gradients that would explain to our brain the interplay of light, often coming from many directions. That way, we will feel the organic, smooth transitions between immensely different spaces and gain the context of scale and perception of vast dimensions. We will feel immersed. However, the already challenging lighting increases complexity due to constantly changing light throughout the day (Figure 7.3). It means we can't rely on existing pre-baked solutions to provide an excellent global illumination solution.

Lighting the Night City also presents enormous challenges to art and production. *Cyberpunk 2077* has many interior locations that are visually stable due to their enclosed nature. However, it also contains many open ones with light sources of mixed types, along with open-world locations where the constantly changing day, night, and weather cycles impact their lighting (Figure 7.4). It is a massive production scope to deliver. To solve that problem, we reached for a real-world reference. If we create a rendering and lighting solution that relies on realistic parameters and a decent approximation of lighting, we could assume coherent and, very importantly, predictable results. This mechanism could give us a good starting point for artists to pick up and do the visual magic. We assumed that even a basic setup would provide us with an immersive world representa-

Figure 7.4. A complex, open-world lighting situation.

tion in any spot in the city. It would not be artistically polished, but at least a believable baseline. That predictability of the solution was a key component of all the work we did throughout developing the rendering solution for *Cyberpunk 2077*, which always aimed to create a proper lighting sandbox for the Night City.

Creating an efficient solution capable of providing dynamic global illumination (GI) for a vast number of light sources that can light an open-world city is complex and requires many intelligent solutions. If we break down the rendering pipeline into layers of separate systems, each works independently, providing a piece of the puzzle but working within its internal approximation of the solution. In that case, the outcome can sometimes be inconsistent and not predictable. That brings a tricky dilemma of performance versus accuracy, occasionally displayed as visual glitches and luminance inconsistencies in the city's most geometrically complex areas. We used a probe-based GI system per sector with a variable density scattering system capable of delivering indirect diffuse information for all the lights and the sky within ca. 120 meters from the player to provide dynamic indirect illumination. Every probe with its six vectors includes information about the light in those directions, considering geometry occlusion and converting it into luminance information. While fast and responsive, it is susceptible to less-than-perfect mesh geometry, such as thin walls or kitbash models, which often lead to visual artifacts or energy leaks (Figure 7.5).

Traditional reflection probes deliver reflections with extra support from the screen-space reflections. The obvious drawback is that the probes are calculated with an artificial ambiance value, as they cannot see the outcome of the GI system. Both systems contribute to indirect illumination with their respec-

Figure 7.5. Examples of energy leaks (left) and visual artifacts (right).

tive simplifications and, in reality, represent slightly different perceptions of the world. Those deviations often manifest in edge cases and bring inconsistencies that require manual tweaking by artists to bring back the visual consistency and the expected look, especially with mixed lighting and open-world locations where the light energy dynamic range is the greatest. However, not taking anything from the sheer beauty and speed of the rasterizer solution we used in the game, there is another way.

Two years before the release, we started an ambitious process of bringing ray tracing to *Cyberpunk 2077* as an additional quality rendering mode. Preparing our proprietary Red Engine 4 to work in this new way was a complex process, picking the most quality-compromised rendering subsystems and replacing them with new subsystems that produce higher-accuracy results. We have yet to make the lighting entirely predictable, as specific layers still rely on rasterizing solutions. Nevertheless, this move allowed us to fix the game's overall visual consistency and quality dramatically, bringing much higher image realism and adding new visual features. We released *Cyberpunk 2077* with two quality trims during the game's launch, but the chase of the ultimate goal, the creation of the lighting sandbox, is not yet finished. The revolution started after the 2020 release when we began a new chapter of ray tracing development, bringing path tracing to *Cyberpunk 2077*.

Our initial goal was to provide the engine with a reference rendering mode (or a photo mode) that would ignore all the subsystems and their approximations and replace them with a unified ray tracing solution for direct and indirect illumination. This technology's fundamental gain is the overall spatial predictability of unified rendering. The fact that we render whole indirect illumination with one system that delivers both indirect diffuse and specular is a massive revolution. Super-accurate occlusion in its unbiased form guarantees that regardless of how complicated or kitbashed the environment is, we will get a very stable, coherent, and balanced image if there are enough samples: precisely the area in which the previous approach was struggling the most. In a massive open world, that is the revolution that the whole rendering and lighting team working on Red Engine 4 always aimed to achieve. (See Figure 7.6 and 7.7.)

Figure 7.6. Interior lighting example in *Cyberpunk 2077*.

Figure 7.7. A scene with complex lighting in *Cyberpunk 2077*.

However, that is just half of the story. One of the challenges in lighting the massive futuristic city is the sheer number of lights and the rendering budget required to generate shadows. We are bound to 10 shadow maps in the game, with just a tiny subset capable of rendering dynamic objects. That is a significant number in the "world of rasterizing engines," yet realistic rendering of a futuristic street with all the lamps, neon lights, and moving cars becomes challenging. With ReSTIR DI, we are practically unbounded in the budget, and every light we render can cast a very accurate shadow at almost no cost. That provides an effortless approach to lighting even the most complex in-game scenarios, putting a seal on our ultimate sandbox lighting solution for Night City.

At the same time, with rapid technological software progress, hardware was making massive performance leaps forward, bringing something new every year. That quickly changed our ambition from a screenshot tool to something we had not considered: a real-time, playable at 60+ FPS UHD path tracing solution for *Cyberpunk 2077* called Ray Tracing: Overdrive. Its release created a shock wave in the whole gaming world. Even the most skeptical players who naturally gravitate toward less cutting-edge focused platforms asked when they would get that on their screens. For some time, it became the ultimate benchmark of what computer games could finally deliver. After some time, the outcome still amazes the author, just like the unforgettable cooperation of a beautifully talented team that led to this.

—Jakub Knapik

7.2 Overview

In its initial release in December 2020, *Cyberpunk 2077* supported two different approaches to lighting: a traditional rasterization pipeline and a more novel ray tracing pipeline. Rasterization is the rendering technique that games have been using for real-time graphics for over 20 years, and the technique has achieved stellar visuals throughout this time frame. However, we are at the point where we have reached the limits of image fidelity that rasterization can deliver. To better understand the motivation behind the ray tracing pipeline, we are going to describe a typical real-time lighting pipeline and point out some of the shortcomings of rasterization.

7.2.1 The Limitations of Rasterization

The lighting in a rasterization pipeline is typically split into direct lighting, where the surface is illuminated directly by a light source, and indirect lighting, where the surface is illuminated indirectly from a light source that has bounced off, potentially multiple times, other surfaces before reaching it. Each of these lighting components is further split into diffuse and specular components. Figure 7.8 presents the direct and indirect diffuse lighting of a scene from *Cyberpunk 2077*.

One of the primary limitations of rasterization when performing lighting is that any geometry that is either occluded or outside the view frustum is inaccessible. The lighting must rely on either screen-space techniques that make use of what geometry is available in the G-buffer, world-space data structures that approximate global interactions between light and geometry, or pre-baked lighting data. Techniques based on pre-baking typically lack precision due to memory constraints, and they are cumbersome to work with during production since baking can be extremely time-consuming. Furthermore, in a typical rasterization pipeline, all of the light components are calculated by algorithms designed to

Figure 7.8. Direct (left) and indirect (right) diffuse lighting in *Cyberpunk 2077*.

produce almost noise-free results. Nevertheless, deterministic techniques pose a dual challenge. Though they circumvent the need for sophisticated and costly denoisers, they fall short in achieving the quality attainable through probabilistic methods.

In the case of direct lighting, assuming there are no shadows, many techniques exist to calculate the final color of the surface lit by a specific light, even an area light, in a noise-free manner. However, to produce a noise-free final lighting buffer, we have to evaluate all lights affecting a specific part of the scene at all times. Hence, common guidance is to not overlap more than four lights or so at any given time. Furthermore, real scenes *do* contain shadows, many of which are necessary for even basic levels of realism. The most popular way of delivering shadows in a rasterization pipeline is with shadow maps. Unfortunately, to generate a shadow map from a light, all of the geometry in the scene must be reprojected from the perspective of that light, which is computationally expensive. This is feasible to do for a small number of lights, but the associated cost limits the number of shadow maps that can be produced in real time for each frame.

Calculating indirect lighting is typically more expensive than calculating direct lighting since it involves solving the direct lighting problem on secondary surfaces in addition to solving the problem of finding which secondary surfaces are visible from primary surfaces in the first place. The standard solution is to calculate these indirect lighting effects offline and then bake them into the game for runtime use. However, this approach only works for static lighting and geometry, and it can impact development time due to the slow offline processing. Artists have to either wait for the assets to bake or work with approximations that may not faithfully approximate the baked result, both of which can slow down production.

Screen-space techniques, like screen-space ambient occlusion and screen-space reflections, make use of what geometry is available in the G-buffer. These techniques can help with recovering global lighting phenomena in dynamic settings, but still visibly suffer from their lack of access to the geometry of the entire scene.

These global lighting limitations are not the only problems inherent in rasterization pipelines. Each phenomenon, such as shadows or reflections, is calculated by an independent system, and there is no inherent connection between any two of them, much less any broader unifying technical foundation on which they all build (Figure 7.9). Interactions between these systems must be hand-crafted at a technical level and manually tuned by artists and engineers for specific locations in the game world.

7.2.2   The Power of Ray Tracing

A rasterization pipeline starts with triangles and determines which pixels they cover, whereas a ray tracing pipeline starts with each pixel and determines which triangle it sees. However, while generations of graphics processing units (GPUs) were designed to accelerate rasterization pipelines, it was not until 2018 that NVIDIA introduced the Turing architecture of GPUs specifically designed to accelerate ray tracing. This architecture added hardware to efficiently calculate ray-triangle intersections.

Unlike rasterization, ray tracing need not treat every visibility calculation as a projection of all the triangles in the scene. Instead, rays can be traced from arbitrary points in space to determine visibility along one line at a time. With this operation accelerated in hardware, graphics pipelines are no longer limited by what geometry may be available in the G-buffer and instead have access to all of the geometry in the scene. This functionality allows for physically correct shadows, reflections of objects outside of the primary visibility region, ambient occlusion calculations at arbitrary scales, and more accurate diffuse global illumination that includes emissive geometry.

Updating a modern rendering engine from a rasterization pipeline to a ray tracing pipeline cannot be done in a single step. Ray tracing support was added to Red Engine 4 in piecemeal fashion. Prior to the addition of any ray tracing effects, the engine must first support the creation and updating of the ray tracing acceleration data structure. The first stage of this functionality means sorting

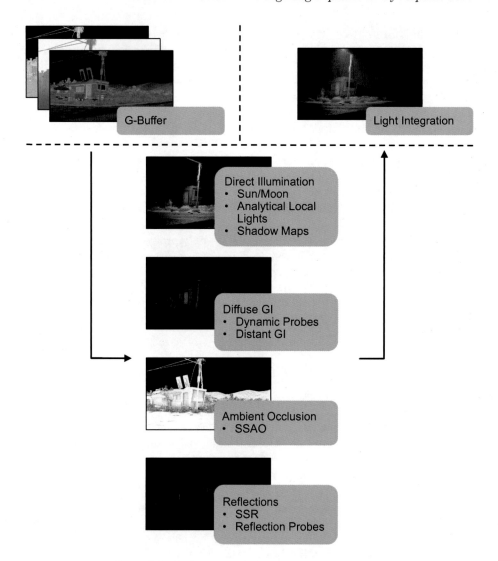

Figure 7.9. Lighting pipeline based on rasterization.

static from dynamic scene geometry. But geometry alone is not sufficient for computer graphics, and so the second stage involves connecting the geometry to its material properties. Along the way, building debug visualization features is critical to diagnosing and fixing errors.

Once the basic requirements for ray tracing are implemented, rasterization techniques can be replaced by ray tracing ones. But the entire pipeline cannot be replaced at once. The complexity of a rendering pipeline demands that the transition be made one effect at a time in order to ensure both technical and artistic continuity between the two paths. Additionally, a game must not only run ray tracing effects on cutting-edge hardware, but also maintain rasterization fallbacks for older hardware.

An important difference between rasterization and ray tracing techniques is that the former are largely deterministic while the latter are largely stochastic. As a result, ray tracing features require denoising passes to smooth out the final image. The denoising passes are developed in tandem with the ray tracing techniques they are paired with as they rely on specific information from the ray tracing passes to be available.

The next sections in Part 1 focus on how the ray tracing infrastructure and first ray tracing and denoising techniques were implemented in Red Engine 4. Part 2 covers the transition from a hybrid ray tracing and rasterization pipeline to a unified path tracing pipeline that was made possible by significant increases in GPU performance and fundamental breakthroughs in path tracing algorithms. Part 3 focuses on the additional techniques developed along the way that are applicable beyond ray tracing or path tracing technology, such as unified image reconstruction and frame generation.

Part 1   Ray Tracing: Bringing More Realism to Night City

7.3   Ray Tracing Prerequisites

7.3.1   Ray Tracing Acceleration Structure

The main engineering marvel that allows us to efficiently incorporate ray tracing into lighting pipelines is the bounding volume hierarchy (BVH), also called the acceleration structure. The acceleration structure holds the data about most of the scene geometry and materials and, unlike the G-buffer in rasterization pipelines, is not limited to the geometry visible in the camera's view frustum. Furthermore, the acceleration structure allows for extremely efficient traversal while searching for the closest piece of geometry from an arbitrary position and direction.

Instance Processing *Cyberpunk 2077* is set in a densely populated city environment filled with lots of objects, representing not only architectural structures but also various details and characters that bring the game world to life. While static objects dominate across the world, dynamic objects require more effort to ensure no visible glitches occur when integrating their data into the top-level acceleration structure (TLAS) for rendering. Static objects, including rigid bodies, greatly benefit from multi-threaded processing (Figure 7.10); their acceleration structures do not need updates, but monitoring their lifetimes, updating

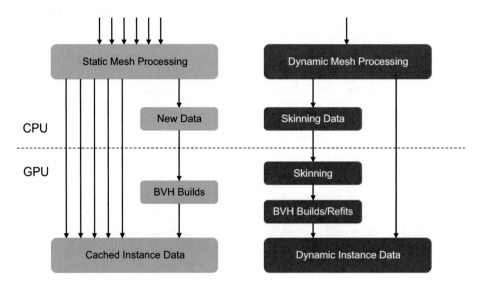

Figure 7.10. Parallel mesh processing for instance data generation.

matrices (we always positioned the camera at the origin for the TLAS), and performing compaction are still necessary to increase tracing efficiency and reduce GPU memory consumption. Instance batching, similar to the rasterization pipeline, proves beneficial by using a single bottom-level acceleration structure (BLAS) for all meshes of the same level of detail (LOD), requiring only updates to matrix and material data. Maximizing caching and data reuse is crucial, with all material-specific data stored on the GPU and individual instances holding references to this data. If no new data is streamed within a frame, only new matrix data is updated for the instance during TLAS build call.

When new static objects appear in a frame, consistent performance is achieved by limiting the number of updates per frame. Dynamic objects, however, are a different challenge, necessitating continuous updates and potentially introducing significant overhead each frame. This also requires limiting the number of updates in scenarios involving a large number of dynamic objects. Initial strategies, such as sorting objects by distance and assigning weights based on size and type, were found to be ineffective in certain scenarios. A more successful approach has been to track the number of ray hits per dynamic object and then transfer this data back to the CPU with minimal latency, prioritizing objects with higher ray hits for updates (Figure 7.11). This method significantly improves the set of objects that need to be updated within a given budget. However, care should be taken to ensure that cached representations of objects still represent their valid topology, otherwise, we may never give them a chance to be updated. To address this, approximately 20 percent of the dynamic update budget is allocated for the meshes that have not been recently processed. Additionally, meshes nearby are

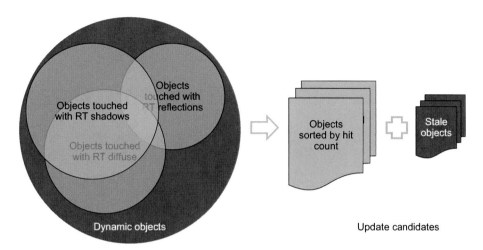

Figure 7.11. Optimized object selection based on the active set of ray-traced effects.

given the highest priority to ensure there are no visible inconsistencies between screen pixels and their geometrical mesh representations used in ray tracing as we were not shooting primary rays; otherwise, this may not be needed.

Dynamic Mesh Updates Before updating the bottom-level acceleration structures, we need to perform updates for underlying dynamic meshes. These typically include characters, foliage, and objects used with destruction or deformation. Each mesh may consist of multiple chunks, each with its own set of input data parameters and corresponding API state changes. Utilizing naive mesh skinning through compute shaders resulted in significant overhead on both the CPU and GPU. Our method involved batching several meshes and their chunks for processing with a single `Dispatch()` call. This approach heavily relied on a "bindless" resource access model to minimize additional state changes and enable direct access to vertex buffers from the shader. Each batch consisted of up to 256 vertices and was mapped to a separate thread block, which utilized a unified set of constants for processing. This allowed the use of a single compute `Dispatch()` call to process all the meshes sharing the same shader code (Figure 7.12).

7.3.2 Adapting Materials for the Ray Tracing Pipeline

For applications such as simple shadowing or ambient occlusion, ray tracing is only used to establish visibility between two points and so only basic mesh geometry data is required (provided we are not relying on alpha-masked transparency). However, for applications that use the rays to sample irradiance (such as those sampling glossy reflections or emissive area light sources), some version of the BRDF must be evaluated and so must tie into the engine's material

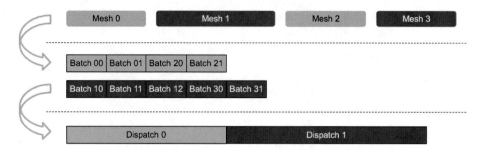

Figure 7.12. Dynamic mesh updates with batching.

shading system. Since *Cyberpunk 2077* uses a physically based material system, the material system produces a standardized output structure defining physical properties that are then fed into a shared lighting evaluation system (Listing 7.1).

```
class RTSurfaceData
{
  float3 BaseColor;          // Diffuse albedo, but also influences emissive
    light color depending on context
  float3 Normal;             // Normalized surface normal direction
  float Metalness;           // [0-1] GGX Metalicity data
  float Roughness;           // [0-1] GGX Roughness data
  float EmissiveEV;          // Exposure value relative to camera to adjust
    the Base Color for emissive contribution
  float MaterialEmissiveEV;  // Separate exposure not adapted to camera used
    for GI
};
```

Listing 7.1. Standardized output produced by the material system and provided to the common lighting code.

The required mesh data includes conventional components such as normals, tangents, and various texture coordinates, as well as some more exotic triangle-level helper data such as vertex coloring and instance information used for certain material types. These were provided as separate arrays in video memory allowing for per-vertex and per-instance data, permitting them to be fetched and interpolated on demand if needed by the mesh being evaluated. Meanwhile, the material parameters can take on a number of different layouts given the variety of base materials and variations thereof employed by the artists. More importantly, these different materials are implemented in the base renderer as a set of largely independent procedural shaders, and each code path would have to be present in the ray hit evaluation code. This presents not only a logistical challenge but a performance one as well, as evaluating divergent shading paths within a SIMD wavefront can dramatically reduce efficiency.

Given all these concerns, the ray tracing material system uses a condensed set of modified materials, with material constant buffers computed at runtime, textures sampled using a "bindless" approach, and simplified shader paths evaluated in a hybrid "übershader" architecture that condenses logically similar material together into a smaller set of distinct shading paths and then implements these distinct shaders as branches within the ray hit evaluation code.

Shading Performance and Material Unification Conventional wisdom for material/pixel shaders in a rasterization context is to create many distinct shaders with only the functionality necessary to render the exact object being drawn. This produces shaders with minimal complexity, divergence, and register footprint, and is generally a good strategy for rasterization where the shader wavefronts evaluating pixels are by their nature evaluating the same material type, usually with the same material parameters guiding which branches do occur within. These workloads are usually coherent and with high occupancy, and so are generally limited by either compute instruction throughput or memory bandwidth. Unfortunately, we usually do not have the luxury of such coherent workloads when evaluating ray hits as adjacent threads in a wavefront will likely be evaluating hits against entirely different meshes with their own parameters and code paths. As a result, there is a strong incentive to minimize divergence between threads by combining logically similar code paths where possible, even if it results in some degree of "wasted" cycles. In practice this unification mainly takes the form of turning static permutations in the rasterization shader into dynamic branches in the ray tracing implementation, hoisting common code out of the branches where possible, and finding opportunities where ostensibly distinct materials can be combined into a single shader by adding new branches. Using these approaches, we were able to reduce a set of 30 separate material types into 17 different ray shader evaluation paths (3 of which cover the majority of common objects in most environments).

It should be noted that there are some limits to how much combining of the materials is advisable. While execution divergence is probably the primary concern in a ray hit evaluation system, occupancy (the number of parallel wavefronts in flight relative to the theoretical maximum supported by the hardware) is a close competitor. This occupancy can be limited by several factors, but the most relevant here is likely to be shader register count. Since the shading units have limited total register file size to share among all executing wavefronts, as the simultaneous register count of a shader increases, the number of wavefronts executing that shader that can run in parallel decreases. With rasterization this is only of limited concern as the cost of a single material only affects the rendering of objects using that material. However, with ray tracing the entire workload can be affected merely by the existence of a particularly expensive material type. This is because the shaders register footprint is determined as the max of any possible path through the code, meaning that with an übershader architecture the occupancy is effectively limited by the most complex single material being modeled (regardless of whether any rays corresponding to that material are being evaluated). In *Cyberpunk 2077*, this occupancy was limited by parallax window material, which used a parallax ray casting technique and a randomized atlas of procedural room data to generate plausible building interiors without modeling them individually. This was by far the most expensive branch of the hit shading code, but it was determined to be too important to visual quality to omit.

Simplification and Image Quality In addition to the desire to simplify shaders for performance reasons, there are also image quality motivations for not simply using the direct rasterization shaders when evaluating the materials. Many high-impact material classes (such as the large, bright, emissive billboards scattered across the environment) have procedural shading elements that produce features such as simulated scanlines or subpixel elements. While adding to the desired aesthetic in the directly rendered view, these elements are subtle enough that they do not impact the converged signal when sampled with rays for area lighting, yet high enough frequency that they introduce noise due to aliasing. Technically speaking, the procedural features are smaller than the Nyquist limit implied by the aggregate sampling density of rays. Furthermore, the problem extends beyond spatial aliasing and occurs with temporal features as well. For example, certain emissive objects are given a brief randomized "flicker" that alters their rendered luminance during direct rendering. Since denoising of the ray-traced signal is reliant upon temporal accumulation of samples, this brief flicker essentially presents the same problem in time: a feature too small to be accurately reproduced with the available sample rate, but dramatic enough to noticeably impact the output. To mitigate these problems, these procedural elements were omitted from the ray tracing versions of the materials in favor of providing a more spatially and temporally stable signal.

Material Caching and Proxies Early on it was realized that a certain class of multilayer materials would present a challenge to fully reproduce in ray tracing effects as they would be too expensive to evaluate using the shaders from primary rasterization but also could not be trivially simplified by omitting components. This is due to these multilayer materials being defined by combining multiple high-detail texture layers together using a set of alpha masks as weights. While this approach could be expensive due to the need to sample from potentially dozens of textures in the pixel shader (and was in theory unbounded in the number of layers that could be composited), it was not a major issue for the rasterization implementation as these objects would tend to be distant background elements and occupy a small portion of the total frame. However, with ray tracing this became a more substantial problem: it was not possible to use the same multipass approach used during rasterization to blend multiple layers together, and rays hitting these potentially expensive objects could take dramatically longer to evaluate than those hitting other materials and could therefore end up slowing down the execution of the entire wavefront.

To address this, a special *multilayer proxy* system was created. Whenever a mesh with a multilayer material was loaded, this proxy system would perform the compositing normally done in the rasterization shader and store it into a pool of textures that would then be provided to the ray tracing system for shading. On a hit, the material evaluation code would simply sample these textures and return the physical surface contents cached therein. As a result, the previously expensive shading cost was translated into more manageable load-time and memory footprint demands. These costs were easier to accommodate within the given performance budget; however, to minimize the risk of transient frame rate spikes, some additional measures were taken.

Load-time performance impact was limited by placing a limit on the number of proxies that could be generated per frame. Additional requests beyond this cap were queued, and the corresponding materials were given minimally noticeable default texture values until the request could be handled and the proxies could be rendered. In practice this was not a common occurrence; however, it allowed for an extra degree of control and ensured consistent frame times.

The video memory budget, conversely, was something that had to be carefully attended to. The first method of addressing this was by allowing for the size of these cached tiles to vary, as it was realized that they would likely not need to be anywhere near the full fidelity of the rasterization passes. Thus, the multi-layer proxy size could be adjusted anywhere from 128×128 texels to $2K \times 2K$ texels depending on the hardware configuration. In practice it was found that 512×512 would suffice as indistinguishable for most circumstances in glossy reflections. Further reduction in memory footprint was achieved by transcoding the composited textures to a block compressed format using a GPU compute shader after the compositor pass. This resulted in a set of three textures per tile: base color (BC1), surface roughness (BC4), and metalicity (BC4).

Unfortunately, this approach does have some negative impact on image quality. One of the benefits of the multilayer material approach, motivating its original use, is the ability for artists to combine many different texture layers with dramatically different texel densities over large areas. This facilitates things like decal rendering and the use of high-frequency tiled textures layered over one another across large meshes. However, this usage makes it hard to faithfully bake the composited texture into a proxy, as the effective texel density with UV tiling is far higher than practical for a cached version. As a result, some of the multilayer proxies demonstrate far less detail than their source materials depending on the area the UV space is stretched over and how aggressively the artists have used tiling to provide high-resolution detail (Figure 7.13). The overall tone and texture of the materials are preserved, however clear differences can be seen for objects using multilayer materials that employ detail textures repeated over a large surface area. This issue could be improved by either using higher resolution proxies (or adaptively setting the proxy resolution based on source material tiling rate), tessellating the meshes to allow for multiple smaller proxies to cover the same area, or some combination of the two. However, in practice it was felt that this loss of detail was not generally noticeable except when shading perfectly glossy reflections on flat surfaces, and further mitigation was deemed to be not worthwhile.

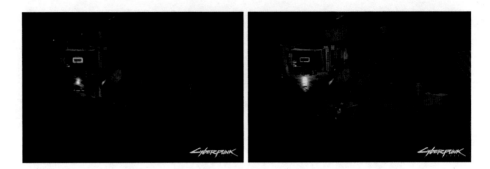

Figure 7.13. Materials as seen using the normal rasterization shading path (left) and direct visualization of the ray tracing material evaluation output (right).

Special Case Material Evaluation As mentioned previously, material evaluation cannot be avoided even for rays that are only used for visibility tests (such as for shadowing or ambient occlusion) since computing visibility correctly in the presence of objects that use alpha masking to define opacity requires at least a partial evaluation of the material (involving, at a minimum, texture coordinate interpolation and transformation and texture sampling). These materials are even more performance-sensitive than the full shading case since this evaluation is invoked for every potential hit. In the case of dense foliage, for example, alpha-tested materials could be evaluated dozens of times per ray. To reduce the impact of visibility tracing for alpha-tested materials, a separate code path was added for use whenever only opacity information was needed (such as for "any hit" ray shaders). Applying the same approach used to condense the varied material shader permutations into more unified code paths, the opacity-only evaluation path requires a small subset of the full material constants (reducing memory bandwidth cost) and is able to combine evaluation of multiple source materials into a single path with minimal branching (reducing divergence). A similar optimization was subsequently added for cases where only material emissive output was required, allowing for similar gains when sampling direct irradiance (such as when integrating area lighting).

7.3.3 Debug Visualization

Debug visualization plays a crucial role in understanding the processes happening within a ray-traced scene, especially in hybrid approaches where primary rays are not traced during normal rendering. To optimize performance and render quality, several aspects require monitoring. It's essential to identify which objects are included in the top-level acceleration structure, as sometimes there might be more or fewer objects than necessary. For dynamic objects, tracking their updates is vital to maintain optimal performance, which may necessitate additional data tracking within the ray tracing component. For instance, updates to car

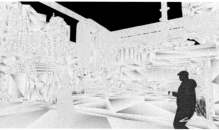

Figure 7.14. Debug visualization of the BVH, where green indicates static meshes, yellow dynamic meshes, and red updated meshes.

deformation should only occur upon impact. Once the deformation is applied, the mesh can remain permanently altered without incurring extra overhead for BLAS updates. Monitoring the geometrical complexity of the BVH is another critical factor. A high number of overlapping meshes can drastically reduce tracing performance. Splitting complex meshes into individual non-overlapping parts or merging overlapping parts into a single BLAS can enhance performance. The update method for dynamic objects also matters; bottom-level acceleration structures can be entirely rebuilt or just refitted. Refitting maintains the previous BVH structure but updates the boundaries to cover a new set of vertices. While refit operations are generally faster, they are not suitable for objects that undergo significant changes to their bounding volumes between frames, as this can lead to a substantial decrease in tracing speed.

In *Cyberpunk 2077*, we implemented several visualization modes for debugging purposes. These modes feature color-coded geometry instances to distinguish various types of static and dynamic objects, as well as to monitor their updates (Figure 7.14). Additionally, a performance mode is used for the identification of hot spots during the tracing of primary rays (Figure 7.15) using a shader with timer instrumentation [MacArthur and Stich 20]. Lastly, a fully shaded mode was available for primary rays, allowing to check shading accuracy and material correctness.

Figure 7.15. BVH tracing complexity visualization using a shader with timer instrumentation.

7.4   Directly Sampled Lighting

Direct lighting refers to light that leaves a light source and travels directly to a surface without first bouncing off (reflection) or passing through (refraction) another surface. Every mesh that is able to see a light source directly will be exposed to direct lighting.

The lighting contribution from analytical lights is categorized as direct lighting and rendered in the direct lighting G-buffer pass. In a traditional rasterization-based real-time renderer, the direct lighting component is separated from the indirect lighting component, as they are rendered using very different technologies, and the latter is usually much more complex to generate.

In the ray tracing domain though, the separation is less strict, as light is treated as a ray, and therefore the first and the secondary bounce are often handled by similar algorithms. As a result, we introduce alternate concepts of directly sampled lighting and indirectly sampled lighting. *Directly sampled lighting* refers to lighting from rays that are intentionally aimed at light sources. In *Cyberpunk 2077*, directly sampled lighting covers all of the analytical lights in the scene. In contrast, *indirectly sampled lighting* refers to lighting from rays that are *not* intentionally aimed at light sources. Light coming from rays randomly generated according to the BRDF that end up hitting emissive surfaces or the environment map fall into the category of indirectly sampled lighting. Note that directly and indirectly sampled lighting describe the way in which light rays are generated, whereas direct and indirect lighting describe whether light travels uninterrupted from a light source to a surface or if it first bounces off another surface. As a result, indirectly sampled lighting coming from emissive surfaces, and the environment map may in fact be part of the direct lighting for a surface.

One of the most important benefits of ray tracing technology is its ability to calculate shadows more accurately and efficiently for direct lighting compared to traditional rasterization techniques such as shadow maps. The use of shadow maps in the classic rasterization renderer has always been a weak spot, as it has many drawbacks, both visually and on a performance level. As a technique, it's one of the oldest tricks of real-time graphics, and the ability to replace it with a more correct and physically based method brings many benefits.

The first ray tracing implementation in the Red Engine allowed us to have pixel-perfect shadows coming from analytical point, spot, and area lights, plus analytical directional lights like the sun and moon. Another significant benefit brought by ray tracing has been the ability to render correct soft shadows created by light sources with a surface area. You may know that all light sources in the real world possess a specific size. A point light with zero area size can exist only in computer graphics, and it is still a necessary optimization today. But recent years have seen a growing adoption of area light sources in video games. While these area lights improve the shading fidelity, they also reduce the accuracy of the shadows, because area light only generates a soft shadow, and this can't be rendered by shadow maps. At most, shadow maps can emulate the softness

Figure 7.16. Rasterized (left) and ray-traced (right) character shadows. Panam Palmer, *Cyberpunk 2077*.

and the transition between light and shadow by blurring the whole shadow, but this is very far from being correct or reliable. Ray tracing makes up for these shortcomings.

Night City, especially during the evening, is mainly lit by long neon tubes, neon signs, and big billboards rather than small light bulbs. These light sources introduced soft shadows into the scene and significantly improved visual fidelity and believability. Characters in particular greatly benefit from soft shadows since the penumbra effect enhances their facial features and helps with their expressions' readability (Figure 7.16).

Furthermore, the artist working with such tech has a much easier job during the lighting phase, as shadow maps have always been tedious due to their limited resolution, shadow-leaking artifacts, constraints on the number of polygons rendered, etc.

It must be said, though, that if a game uses both shadow technologies like in *Cyberpunk 2077*, the work for the artist is still greater as it has to ensure that both work properly in every condition. This will be a common drawback until the rendering engine will be able to finally rely solely on ray-traced shadows.

Directly sampled lighting makes another big jump with the introduction of path tracing, and specifically ReSTIR DI, as we will discuss in the Part 2 of this article, bringing the astonishing ability to completely remove the shadow budget and give every light in the scene the ability to cast shadows. A true milestone in real-time rendering.

Figure 7.17. Original sun rendering with shadow mapping (left) and ray-traced sun shadows (right).

7.4.1 Sun Shadows

Sun shadows are among the most commonly used lighting effects present in games. In *Cyberpunk 2077*, the initial sunlight simulation utilized cascaded shadow maps alongside screen-space tracing. Although rasterization techniques have evolved to create a realistic representation of sunlight, certain lighting conditions still require manual adjustments and specific treatments. In contrast, a ray-traced implementation delivers precise results across all scales, providing soft shadows from distant obstacles and per-pixel accurate self-shadows for nearby objects and characters (Figure 7.17). The process involves stochastically casting rays from the main depth buffer toward the sun disk using a uniform sample distribution. When utilizing a single ray per pixel, the resulting shadow mask image can exhibit considerable noise. To mitigate this issue, we use a fixed noise pattern in the screen space. This helps to reduce pixels simmering on the frames with static camera. The need for stochastic ray distribution introduced an additional denoising phase, utilizing a custom SIGMA denoiser designed for stochastic shadows processing. The geometry in the top-level acceleration structure is parameterized with the camera positioned at the coordinate origin, ensuring consistent and stable ray-traced effects throughout camera movement. An initial ray offset was still applied along the view vector to minimize any potential inconsistency with rasterized geometry.

At first glance, ray tracing outperforms rasterization methods in nearly every aspect, offering pixel-perfect accuracy, physically accurate contact shadows, and efficient bypassing of backfacing pixels that don't require tracing. However, the challenge arises with semitransparent objects, including particles, which are effortlessly managed by shadow map cascades in a pipeline designed for opaque surfaces. A potential workaround involves a hybrid approach, combining ray casting for opaque shadows with shadow map cascades for everything else. This solution can feel inefficient, as it requires maintaining the cascades at full resolution and quality without knowing which parts of them will be needed.

We proposed an alternative solution that maintained original shadow map cascades for transparent-only surfaces at a reduced resolution. Shadow maps were incorporated into the pipeline as before, but we used ray casting to update specific areas as needed. A preliminary rasterization pass marked potential areas for transparent objects within the shadow map, guiding targeted ray casting updates. This method demonstrated effectiveness in quality and performance across various game scenarios. Further optimizations, such as visibility tests for transparent objects from the camera's perspective, could improve efficiency. With multi-resolution conservative depth buffer, we could determine the occlusion status for entire objects with a few texture look-ups, avoiding unnecessary shadow map texels updates. Transitioning from rasterization to ray tracing also had additional CPU-side performance savings as there was no longer a need to perform per-mesh visibility tests, batching, and rendering to update shadow map cascades on each frame. The only thing to keep in mind was that all shadow map fallbacks used in other ray tracing-based effects, including reflections, should also be replaced. Every effect now should have had a dedicated visibility test for the sun. Partial replacement of rasterized shadow maps with ray tracing might have been a good initial step for ray tracing adoption. However, a comprehensive pipeline redesign simultaneously improved both quality and performance without compromises.

7.4.2   Local Lights Shadows

Local lighting with physically based shadows significantly enhances visual fidelity. From the very beginning, we made the decision to support area lights with specific physical properties to control shadow softness as well as accurate lighting through analytically defined light shapes. Initially, the approach utilized variance shadow maps within a rasterization-based framework. These maps, by incorporating an extra pre-filter step beyond traditional shadow mapping techniques, enable the generation of soft shadows more efficiently than screen-space filtering. However, this method is prone to light-leaking artifacts in scenes with complex depth variations, and managing controllable penumbra sizes poses additional challenges. Ray tracing emerged as an ideal solution, similar to ray-traced shadows used for the sun. It accurately models penumbras for various light shapes and seamlessly supports omnidirectional lighting, which is typically difficult to achieve (Figure 7.18).

For each light source, we calculated the potential screen coverage to identify a conservative rectangular region to be used for tracing. The output from the ray-casting pass was a single-channel texture, capturing the distance to the nearest occluder, if any, and storing that in a 16-bit floating-point format texture. Subsequent denoising stages utilized the same screen boundaries, incorporating shortcuts for entirely illuminated or shadowed areas. We didn't use any temporal passes in the shadow mask filtering; this helped a lot in optimizing our tracing and denoising tasks for peak efficiency with limited memory consumption. This way, any number of lights could be processed per frame using fixed memory footprint. The filtering technique involved two sequential specialized

Figure 7.18. Original shading with shadow mapping (left) and ray-traced local shadows from rectangular area light (right).

Figure 7.19. Original shading with shadow mapping (left) and ray-traced local shadows (right).

stages. The initial stage pre-filtered shadows and estimated the average distance to occluders. Utilizing this data, the second stage performed a sparse spatial filtering pass using the average distance to the occluder and light shape to evaluate the filtering footprint in screen space (Figure 7.19).

One unexpected issue with computing lighting contributions directly from emissive objects was the resulting mismatch between where emissive objects occurred and where analytic lights had been placed. In *Cyberpunk 2077*, the lighting design of the environments was usually done very early in the development of a given area, using a simple rough-in "white room" environment that lacked things like surface textures/material definitions and decorative assets. Artists would create the rough shape of the structures and place and adjust analytic lights as needed to get the look they wanted, then hand the area over to other teams to fill with texture and detail. In most cases these lights were placed with an eye toward what physical features would be present; however, this was not always the case. Additionally, while many of the objects placed during the detailing pass included analytic lights in their scene graph that would be checked and approved by the lighting artists when the object was an explicit light source (like billboards, computer screens, and ceiling or floor lamps), this was not universally true of all objects that included emissive materials. The combination of these factors resulted in several issues.

First, it meant that there would be some emissive objects that were previously approximated by an analytic light that was now redundant, effectively doubling the lighting contribution of that object. For cases where the light was included in the object scene graph, this could be handled automatically; however, as the lighting artists placed some lights in the unpopulated "white-room" scene, there was not always an explicit tie between an emissive surface and an approximating light. These "untethered" lights could also not be disabled universally, as there were some cases where they were used to tweak the ambient lighting of the scene in a non-physical but aesthetically desirable way.

Second, there was the problem of emissive details and objects brightening a scene where no additional lighting was desired. Without ray-traced lighting, marking texels as emissive was often used as a localized effect to add detail and visual pop to objects in an often otherwise dark environment. If those surfaces suddenly began illuminating their environment too much, then it would produce a very different aesthetic effect.

Ultimately, the solution to both these issues was to facilitate the need for non-physical lighting behavior by adding per-asset and per-light overrides. Manually placed analytic lights were given a separate "ray tracing" weight so that their contribution could be reduced or removed entirely on an individual basis when the emissive lighting system was enabled. Lights included in object scene graphs were given a similar weight that was applied to all instances of the asset as well as a per-instance override to allow for fine-tuning special cases. Meshes were then given a separate "ray tracing emissive intensity" parameter for adjusting the contributions of those emissive texels to match their desired visual impact, as well as a per-instance override of this property. Using these new tools, the lighting team was able to comb through the content once more and adjust the lighting to match their aesthetic goals for both analytic and ray-traced lighting modes, though the process was labor intensive.

7.5 Indirectly Sampled Lighting

In contrast to direct lighting, which travels uninterrupted from a light source to a surface, indirect lighting first bounces off of one or several other surfaces before hitting a surface. Effects like diffuse global illumination, ambient occlusion, and reflection all fall into this category.

In a deferred renderer, these effects can have their own G-buffer pass. The indirect lighting of the G-buffer usually consists of the ambient light component coming from environment reflection maps and/or data from the global illumination system.

As mentioned before, the separation between direct and indirect lighting can be less strict in the ray tracing domain. Similarly to the concept of the directly

Figure 7.20. Johnny Silverhand, *Cyberpunk 2077.*

sampled lighting, we introduce a concept of indirectly sampled lighting, where the sampling of a light source happens randomly following rays that were generated based on material properties of a surface. In the context of *Cyberpunk 2077,* even direct lighting from emissive geometry and skylight is indirectly sampled.

In *Cyberpunk 2077,* ray tracing brings enormous visual benefits to direct lighting from these types of light sources, but also effects like diffuse global illumination and reflections (Figure 7.20). They are no longer a mere approximation of reality. Reflections behave realistically, substituting the old reflection probes or screen-space reflections methods. Ambient occlusion is no longer a cheap screen-space effect, and the sky illuminates the environment in a realistic and precise way, substituting the low-quality irradiance probes-based system. On top of that, ray tracing enabled us to cast diffuse lighting from emissive meshes such as neon signs, screens, and billboards.

While most of these changes required little to no additional work from the artists' side to work properly, some of them did. For instance, implementing diffuse lighting from emissive meshes turned out to be quite a tedious process because most of these meshes had an analytical light associated with them to represent the lighting that would come out from such a surface. To avoid having a double light contribution when ray tracing is enabled, we had to develop different systems and tactics. Some would work automatically, but some would require the artist to tweak them on a case-by-case basis. The final result was worth the additional work from developers and artists. However, this could have been avoided if ray tracing had been present at the first stages of development by creating a more elegant solution to deal with this issue from the beginning.

Figure 7.21. Sky lighting with original rendering (left) and ray-traced diffuse illumination (right).

7.5.1 Diffuse Indirect Illumination and Ambient Occlusion

Diffuse indirect illumination was intended to be a foundational element for ray tracing, and it required consideration of several factors during its implementation. The existing global illumination solution provided multi-bounce global illumination using dynamic irradiance probes, although this approach required extensive tuning. Despite the best efforts of developers, the quality still varied too much between scenes. The ray-traced approach aimed to complement, rather than completely replace, the existing solution. An initial variant calculated diffuse illumination from the sky (Figure 7.21) at a rate of one ray per pixel (RPP) using hemisphere sampling with a cosine-weighted distribution; later we switched to 0.5 RPP for the sky sampling.

For our hybrid pipeline, we also introduced an additional set of irradiance probes that excluded direct sky contributions but maintained the propagation of further indirect bounces to preserve energy. We saw immediate improvements with all these changes, yielding more accurate and detailed sky signals. Indirect contact shadows became feasible.

The existing ambient occlusion effect was also enhanced by ray tracing. By acquiring the closest hit distance from hemisphere tracing, we simply required different ray length normalization compared to the original ambient occlusion effect implementation. The ray-traced ambient occlusion effect used four additional variables to adjust the effective normalization radius based on ray origin distance to the camera (Figure 7.22). This method enabled the capture of occlusion data from objects of varying scales.

With four ambient occlusion parameters defined (near and far distances with corresponding AO radiuses), the final AO radius for each scene point is calculated as:

$$\texttt{lerp}\left(\texttt{AoRNear}, \texttt{AoRFar}, \texttt{saturate}\left(\frac{\texttt{pointDistance} - \texttt{AoDNear}}{\texttt{AoDFar} - \texttt{AoDNear}}\right)\right)$$

A crucial component for diffuse illumination was the support for the emissive surfaces (Figure 7.23). Numerous dynamic billboards were placed throughout

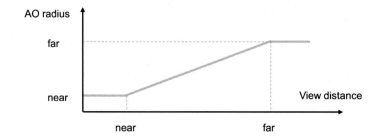

Figure 7.22. Ray-traced ambient occlusion effect parameterization.

Figure 7.23. Emissive surfaces with original rendering (left) and ray-traced diffuse Illumination (right).

the city, some with local proxies to simulate their lighting effect, although many lacked an analytical fallback, limiting their impact on the scene to the emissives in the primary view. Emissive mesh parts were categorized as oriented bounding boxes with dynamic directional flux values, calculated based on emissive variables defined per frame.

The sampling of emissive objects was performed in two phases. The first phase, similar to tiled lighting, involved compiling a list of potentially visible objects (lights) per tile, selecting one based on the probability density function (PDF), and encoding the selected object and triangle along with the sampling PDF into a 32-bit screen-sized target for subsequent sampling in the ray tracing pass. During the ray tracing phase, we evaluated the ray direction for selected triangle sampling and compared the emissive object ID returned by the `TraceRay()` call with the currently selected one. If they matched, we used the radiance associated with the ray hit and previously evaluated scales to compute the final radiance value for the emissive object's contribution. To maximize efficiency with a single ray per pixel, we divided our ray budget, allocating half to diffuse lighting and AO calculations and the other half to emissive object sampling via checkerboarding. Following both passes, a separate resolve phase was conducted to blend both signals, providing a unified output to the denoiser.

The next major milestone involved incorporating full lighting into the first bounce. It required support for engine materials in the ray tracing pipeline. Lighting consisted of direct contributions from the sun and local lights, alongside indirect components from the global illumination system. Direct sun lighting utilized ray casting for visibility evaluation, while local lights employed a world-space grid acceleration structure to compile a list of lights, sampling a fixed number of candidates using resampled importance sampling (RIS).

7.5.2   Reflections

Ray-traced reflections (Figure 7.24) require comprehensive material support, which was developed concurrently with the reflections themselves. However, creating a fully operational pipeline entails much more, including the integration of mesh decals, volumetric effects, particle systems, additional geometry, and so forth. While each component contributes to the overall effect, it is not essential to support every feature comprehensively. Given that everything comes at costs, it is crucial to be reasonable about what is desirable from what is necessary for production. Priority was given to materials and analytical shading for volumetric effects wherever feasible, with certain effects relying on screen-space data as a fallback. This approach is similar to screen-space reflections, which shade pixels by utilizing on-screen data with a gentle signal fade-off at the edges.

The redesign required for reflections also extended to geometry management, as now every out-of-frustum object around the camera is potentially visible. Consequently, in-game systems managing vehicles and characters were adapted as well. Additional geometry support was implemented by adding an extra sphere around the camera for geometry collection along with an enlarged camera frustum and volumes required to support diffuse illumination and sun shadows. The sphere radius was empirically determined to be 2 kilometers. For off-screen objects, mesh proxies were employed for efficiency. These proxies represent simplified chunks of geometry merged into clusters, reducing the total number of

Figure 7.24. Reflections rendered with original technique (left) and ray-traced reflections (right).

Figure 7.25. Reflections rendered with original technique (left) and ray-traced transparent reflections (right).

instances to ensure predictable performance. This strategy enabled a modest increase in the total instance budget by only 10–15 percent with the activation of ray-traced reflections, compared to the baseline performance featuring only diffuse illumination and shadows. We also adjusted the game logic to ensure the loading and updating of all nearby characters, including their animations.

In addition to opaque surfaces, support was extended to semi-transparent objects. Transparent reflections were implemented for materials such as glass, clear coats, water surfaces, and other types (Figure 7.25). Initially, objects made from these materials utilized forward shading, requiring extra processing for ray tracing compatibility. To address this, we developed a lightweight rasterization pass that populated a minimal G-buffer with depth and normal attributes of the nearest transparent surface to the camera. Subsequently, a full-screen ray tracing pass was executed on designated pixels, evaluating mirror reflections on the identified surfaces. We opted not to consider surface roughness in the tracing process, as stochastic sampling would necessitate an additional denoiser pass for a noise-free result. Instead, during the standard rasterization phase for transparent surfaces, we combined the evaluated material with an environment map and the ray-traced output based on roughness levels to simulate glossy reflections.

With ray-traced reflections in place we had laid the groundwork for supporting path-traced rendering, which includes the addition of extra bounces for each ray, enhancing the visual fidelity and realism.

7.6   Denoising and Supersampling

Adding ray-traced diffuse and specular sampling adds noise into the final image. Since the corresponding BRDF lobes can't be covered with just a single ray, they must be sampled stochastically using Monte Carlo integration. To eliminate noise from the final signal, the results must be accumulated temporally and processed spatially by sending them through an algorithm called a *denoiser*.

NVIDIA Real-Time Denoisers (NRD) is a spatiotemporal API agnostic denoising library. The library has been designed to work with low ray-per-pixel signals. NRD is a fast solution that depends on input signals and environment conditions. The following subsections briefly describe the NRD denoisers used in the game in all ray tracing modes of *Cyberpunk 2077* apart from Ray Tracing: Overdrive. The goal is to provide an overview of how they work, highlighting their most important and interesting characteristics without delving into their low-level implementation details. NRD denoisers used in Ray Tracing: Overdrive mode of *Cyberpunk 2077* are described in Part 2. The NRD source code is publicly available [NRD 22].

7.6.1 Shadow Denoising

SIGMA (from the Greek $\sigma\kappa\iota\alpha$, meaning shadow) is a specialized shadow denoiser that comes with the NRD library. The denoiser makes use of a shadow's penumbra properties, so it requires closest hit distances rather than a boolean state "in shadow" or "not in shadow." SIGMA doesn't use the popular À-trous filtering method [Dammertz et al. 10], because it requires many iterations. Instead, SIGMA spatially redistributes the incoming shadow mask (assuming 1 RPP input), following the penumbra size for the currently processed pixel in only two spatial passes and skipping processing in fully lit and fully shadowed regions for performance. To stabilize the final output in areas with wide penumbras, a temporal stabilization pass is applied in the end of the denoising pipeline. SIGMA is very lightweight, so despite the fact that it was initially designed for sun shadows, it can be used for per-light shadow denoising. For example, SIGMA takes only 0.3 ms on a GeForce RTX 4080 at native 1440p resolution per light.

SIGMA inputs and outputs are listed in Table 7.1.

Inputs	Description
Penumbra size	*(noisy)* Distance from the pixel to the occluder multiplied by either tan(LightAngularRadius) when $N \cdot L \geq 0$, or 0 when $N \cdot L < 0$, or ∞ if the ray in unoccluded. Needed to estimate the kernel radius and also implicitly used as the binary shadow mask
ViewZ	*(guide)* Linearized depth, needed for the world-space position reconstruction
Normal	*(guide)* World-space normal, needed to define the kernel basis
Motion vector	*(guide)* Motion vector for the primary hit, needed only for the temporal stabilization pass (if enabled)

Outputs	Description
Denoised shadow	Smooth shadow, i.e., the percentage by which a pixel is lit by a given light. This buffer also serves as the history buffer for the temporal stabilization pass in the next frame (if enabled)

Table 7.1. SIGMA inputs and outputs.

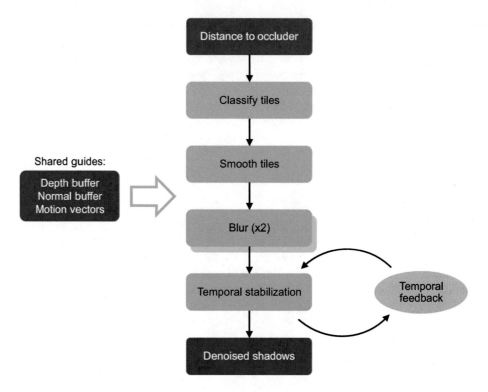

Figure 7.26. SIGMA denoising pipeline.

Here is a brief overview of the passes (see Figure 7.26):

- **Classify tiles:** This pass splits the screen into 16×16 tiles, assigning 0 if all pixels are either lit, shadowed, or outside of the denoising range or 1 otherwise. Also, it computes coarse estimation of a blur radius for the entire tile based on penumbra size across all pixels.

- **Smooth tiles:** The next pass blurs out low-resolution tile texture, respecting blur radius.

- **Blur passes:** There are two blur passes; each pass can be split into the following phases:

    - **Early out if** (preferring tile-based checks):
        * The tile/pixel is outside of the denoising range.
        * The tile is fully lit or shadowed.
        * The tile/pixel $N \cdot L < 0$.

– **Blur radius computation:** The next pass finds an average distance to an occluder and projects it to the shadow receiver. This is done for a 5×5 kernel in the group shared memory. The final sum is bilaterally weighted.

– **Spatial processing:** This pass applies a randomly rotated 8-tap Poisson disk kernel of the radius, computed in the previous phase. Plane distance is used to cut off taps, located outside of the surface. The filter doesn't mix samples with different signs in the $N \cdot L$ term to avoid shadow bleeding.

• **Temporal stabilization:** The last pass stabilizes output in regions with wide penumbra. Behavior is similar to TAA, but variance is computed for 5×5 area. The accumulation factor depends on the penumbra size, and accumulation is disabled in regions with hard shadows. Also, there is a simple anti-lag logic, accelerating accumulation if a shadow in the history buffer doesn't fit in the local variance.

To achieve better image quality, it is recommended to use SIGMA in conjunction with a low-discrepancy sampling. It can be a static-on-screen blue noise or a short sequence of animated blue noise frames.

7.6.2 Indirect Diffuse and Specular Radiance Denoising

Denoising processes noisy inputs spatially and temporally, implying potential data reuse in a large radius around a pixel. It makes using irradiance (lighting information with applied materials) almost impossible because it introduces a large amount of blurriness. In order to make noisy inputs more friendly for denoising and for preserving material details, we apply *material demodulation* to the diffuse and specular signals produced by the tracer. The goal of demodulation is to extract the incoming radiance (without materials) from the irradiance (with materials):

$$\frac{1}{N} \cdot \sum_{i=1}^{N} (\texttt{diffR}(i) \cdot \texttt{albedo}) \approx \texttt{Denoising}\left(\frac{\texttt{diffR}}{\texttt{albedo}}\right) \cdot \texttt{albedo},$$

$$\frac{1}{N} \cdot \sum_{i=1}^{N} (\texttt{specR}(i) \cdot \texttt{specBrdf}) \approx \texttt{Denoising}\left(\frac{\texttt{specR} \cdot \texttt{specBrdf}}{\texttt{envBrdf}}\right) \cdot \texttt{envBrdf},$$

where

• N is the number of diffuse or specular paths;

• $\texttt{diffR}(i)$ and $\texttt{specR}(i)$ are the radiance for diffuse and specular paths, respectively, for the ith sample in Monte Carlo integration;

- `diffR` and `specR` are the radiance for diffuse and specular paths, respectively, for the selected sample (assuming one path per pixel input);

- `albedo` is the diffuse albedo;

- `specBrdf` is the specular BRDF $= F$(micro parameters), where F is a function depending on the sampling model;

- `envBrdf` is the pre-integrated specular (or environment) BRDF depending on macro parameters (reflectivity at normal incidence, roughness, $N \cdot V$) [Hirvonen et al. 19], sometimes referenced as the "specular albedo."

ReBLUR [Zhdan 21] is a specialized spatiotemporal radiance denoiser capable of working with separated diffuse and specular signals. A diffuse-specular variant merges diffuse and specular denoising into a single entity, sharing computations where possible for performance. The denoiser is acceptably fast: it takes ca. 2.5 ms on a GeForce RTX 4080 at native 1440p resolution. Instead of using À-trous filtering, ReBLUR blurs out the accumulated history again and again trying to reach a converged state or suppresses very bright input samples (outliers), if a heuristic predicts "boiling" or "sparkly" behavior (sampling with low rays per pixel by the definition assumes not only noise in the denoiser input but also various kinds of temporal instabilities in the denoiser output). ReBLUR's approach has many pitfalls and it's hard to control (for example, suboptimal spatial weights can lead to massive over-blurring due to the positive feedback loop), but at the same time it allows a reduction of spatial passes. ReBLUR has only two spatial passes with 9-tap kernels, while À-trous filtering usually requires five passes with 3×3 kernels. The other difference from À-trous is that spatial filtering is performed in the world (actually lobe) space instead of the screen space. There are no luminance stoppers in spatial processing, so the denoising is driven by hit distances instead along with geometry- and material-based weights. Applying a temporal stabilization pass on top is a good option, which ReBLUR can optionally perform at the very end of the denoising pipeline.

ReBLUR inputs and outputs are listed in Table 7.2

The denoiser produces denoised diffuse and specular radiance, which are stored separately.

Here is a brief overview of the passes (see Figure 7.27):

- **Classify tiles:** The first pass accelerates the processing of "sky" regions (outside of denoising range) by splitting the screen into 16×16 tiles and assigning 0 to a tile if all of its pixels are outside of the denoising range.

- **Pre-pass:** This pass improves the input signal quality by spatially reusing the noisy signal in the area, defined by the BRDF lobe. It performs poorly when the sparsity of the input signal is higher than the search radius of the Pre-pass. In this case, a rare bright pixel can be spread across neighbors, transforming the entire dark region with the outlier into just a bright blob. Pre-pass search radius must be carefully tuned to avoid such situations.

Inputs	Description
Diffuse and specular radiance	*(noisy)* HDR radiance separated into diffuse and specular components
Hit distance	*(noisy)* Separated diffuse and specular hit distances for the first bounce, needed for the spatial weights and specular virtual motion tracking
ViewZ	*(guide)* Linearized depth, needed for the world-space position reconstruction
Normal and roughness	*(guide)* World-space normal and linear roughness, needed to define the lobe and the spatial weights
Motion vector	*(guide)* Motion vector for the primary hit, essential for the temporal accumulation pass
Outputs	**Description**
Denoised diffuse and specular	Denoised HDR radiance separated into diffuse and specular components, denoised normalized hit distances provided in *alpha* channels (ambient and specular occlusion respectively)

Table 7.2. ReBLUR inputs and outputs.

Another goal of this pass is to estimate specular lobe virtual motion, which is the key to successful specular reprojection.

- **Temporal accumulation:** The next pass accumulates new data with the reprojected history. Several confidence factors control the accumulation speed, and geometry-based plane distance is used for disocclusion tracking. While diffuse reprojection is based only on surface motion, specular reprojection additionally uses virtual motion, i.e., motion of the reflected world. The embedded firefly suppressor tries to limit the intensity of sporadic high energy pixels to ease the burden on the spatial passes and reduce the "boiling" effect.

- **History fix:** This pass is selectively applied to pixels with a short history, i.e., in disoccluded regions and immediately after a disocclusion. The main goal is to reconstruct any missing history in such regions by applying an ultra-wide bilateral blur. A big stride between pixels helps to break repetitive patterns and blobbing.

- **Fast history clamping:** The slower main history is clamped, based on variance, to the faster history produced by the temporal accumulation pass. This helps to minimize lags and mitigate potential reprojection inefficiencies, but works only if local variance is low.

- **Anti-firefly:** To avoid biasing ReBLUR, this pass uses very wide variance-based color clamping to remove fireflies. The kernel is 9×9 with the excluded 3×3 center region. The latter potentially contains a firefly that we need to get rid of. Additionally, the checkerboard resolve and up to 4×4 reprojection kernel can transform a single pixel-outlier into a small blob (which fits into the excluded 3×3 region).

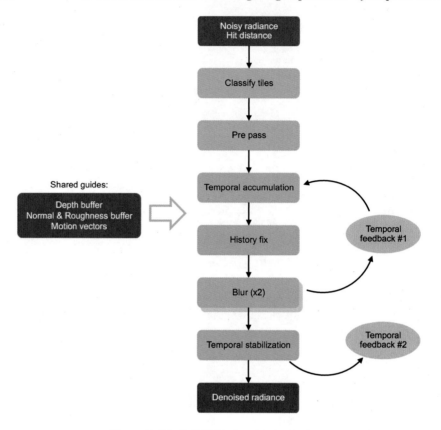

Figure 7.27. ReBLUR denoising pipeline.

- **Blur passes:** These passes perform spatial filtering. They are based on bi-lateral filtering driven by geometry and material-based weights. It's worth noting that strictness of the blur radius and all weights depends on the history length (that's the simplest convergence measure). For example, the normal weight is determined by the following [Lagarde 14]:

$$\texttt{normalWeight} = \texttt{linearRoughness} \cdot \sqrt{\frac{\texttt{percentOfVolume}}{1 - \texttt{percentOfVolume}}},$$

where

  - $\texttt{linearRoughness} = \sqrt{m}$, the perceptually linear roughness,
  - $\texttt{percentOfVolume} = \texttt{lerp}\left(C, 1, \frac{1}{1+\texttt{historyLength}}\right)$, the amount of BRDF lobe volume, approaching some user-provided constant value C if accumulation goes well.

Unfortunately, the reality of spatial filtering is that convergence confidence based only on history length is often inadequate. For example, we can easily find a valid situation where an outlier is passed through firefly suppression and anti-firefly filtering because we want to minimize bias and darkening. However, strict spatial filtering produces suboptimal results. To mitigate this negative effect the temporal accumulation pass additionally produces *estimated error* (the luminance difference between the accumulated history and the noisy input), which doesn't affect weights but preserves blur radius in areas with high errors.

- **Temporal stabilization:** On each frame we work simultaneously with clean and noisy signals: the clean signal accumulated and processed for several frames and a new noisy signal from the current frame added on top of the history. Unfortunately, two passes of spatial filtering is not enough to eliminate "boiling" in this case, so a temporal stabilization pass is used to suppress it. This pass is logically closer to TAA than to the temporal accumulation pass, but the reprojection scheme fully matches the main accumulation pass. Since we have clean "slow main" history and "even slower temporally stabilized" history, we can estimate an anti-lag factor. This is logically very close to the math used for prediction in the stock market.

NRD has evolved a lot due to work on *Cyberpunk 2077* affecting all aspects of denoising: temporal reprojection, normal and roughness weight calculations, fast history clamping, firefly suppression, history reconstruction in disoccluded regions, curvature estimation, 0-roughness reflection tracking, and others. Interestingly, in earlier versions, ReBLUR used mip-based signal reconstruction in disocclusions, which worked well but only for diffuse. Later, a hierarchical mip-based reconstruction approach was introduced to handle low-mid roughness specular, but it never worked well. Nowadays, ReBLUR uses a sparse 5×5 filter with a large 10-pixel stride for disocclusions.

7.6.3 Antialiasing and Supersampling

After the denoising and lighting composition are done, upscaling and antialiasing (AA) still need to be applied. The lighting composition stage uses albedo buffers that are aliased and temporally jittered. In the case of rendering with temporal upscaling techniques, which become more and more mainstream, the albedo buffers will be at input resolution. Temporal upscaling and temporal antialiasing will resolve to the input resolution, and the aliased albedo buffer and lighting buffer will resolve to the full upscaled resolution and will temporally stabilize the output further.

Cyberpunk 2077 supports the following list of AA/upscaling techniques:

- Temporal antialiasing (TAA) [Yang et al. 20],

- NVIDIA Deep Learning Supersampling Super Resolution (DLSS-SR) [Liu 20],

- NVIDIA Deep Learning Supersampling Antialiasing (DLSS-AA),

- AMD FidelityFX Super Resolution (FSR) [AMD 22],

- Intel Arc Xe Super Sampling (XeSS) [Kawiak et al. 22].

Temporal AA has been extensively used in gaming over the past several decades and has subsequently been adapted to perform temporal upscaling. This adaptation incorporates the subpixel jitter offset from each low-resolution input sample. FidelityFX Super Resolution is one notable example of such an adaptation. Nevertheless, a significant challenge associated with these temporal reprojection-based techniques lies in effectively discerning when to reuse accumulated samples from prior frames and when it is preferable to discard them. Numerous heuristics have been devised over the years to solve this problem with varying degrees of success and different sets of trade-offs—certain heuristics work really well in limited scenarios that are common for certain games, but might not be generally well suited for all engines and games. Like hand-crafted denoisers, numerous hyper-parameters were often tweaked based on to what content the technique applies. Heuristics aim to strike a balance between the Pareto curve of lack of ghosting and temporal stability where improving one usually implies hurting the other, forming a Pareto curve of those two traits.

In recent years, DLSS started to leverage the power of AI to solve this problem and to great success. Hand-crafted heuristics are replaced by a neural network, which is trained from huge quantities of real data. This led to superior image quality, reducing ghosting drastically while improving stability at the same time (Figure 7.28), especially when at large upscaling ratios. XeSS followed the trend and also utilises DL techniques to provide a temporal upscaler.

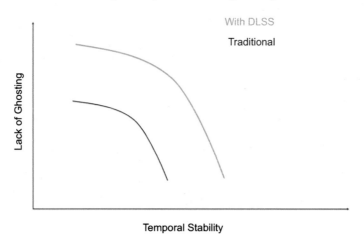

Figure 7.28. AI-based reconstruction like DLSS is ahead of traditional heuristics-based ones.

However, even with AI-driven temporal AA and upscaling, yet another challenge remains with titles like *Cyberpunk 2077* that require denoisers. Denoisers are essentially temporal reconstructions for shading signals, while TAA is temporal reconstructions for visibility and geometries. When upscaling is required, subpixel jitter offset is required to reconstruct the signal at upscaled resolutions. While DLSS and temporal upscaling can properly reconstruct visibility at upscaled resolution, they cannot do so for shading, because the denoisers running at input resolutions have removed all the subpixel jitter after the temporal accumulation step. This is one of the motivations for AI-based unified reconstruction like DLSS Ray Reconstruction (DLSS-RR), which is a unified algorithm that reconstructs shading, visibility, and geometry all at high resolution. In Section 7.13 about DLSS-RR, we provide comparisons to demonstrate the benefits of higher-resolution shading from such a unified reconstruction technique.

7.7   Performance

Table 7.3 presents the configurations of resolution and DLSS-SR mode across a few GPUs that we used for testing, and Table 7.4 shows the performance of all ray tracing–related passes on these configurations in Ray Tracing: Ultra mode of *Cyberpunk 2077*.

GPU	Resolution	DLSS-SR Mode
GeForce RTX 4060	1080p	Quality
GeForce RTX 4070	1440p	Balanced
GeForce RTX 4080	2160p	Performance
GeForce RTX 4090	2160p	Performance

Table 7.3. Default resolutions and DLSS-SR modes per GPU.

Render Passes	GeForce RTX 4060	GeForce RTX 4070	GeForce RTX 4080	GeForce RTX 4090
BLAS Static	0.09	0.08	0.08	0.07
BLAS Dynamic	0.61	0.43	0.37	0.38
TLAS	0.53	0.42	0.37	0.35
RT Sun Shadows	0.74	0.52	0.50	0.36
RT Local Shadows	0.45	0.34	0.34	0.23
RT Diffuse GI & RTAO	1.38	1.15	1.05	0.77
RT Opaque Reflections	1.01	0.75	0.74	0.48
RT Transparent Reflections	0.13	0.10	0.11	0.08
NRD	2.93	2.32	2.24	1.55
DLSS-SR	0.64	0.61	0.81	0.58
Other Render Passes	6.78	5.48	6.07	4.46
Total Frame Time	**15.29**	**12.20**	**12.68**	**9.31**

Table 7.4. *Cyberpunk 2077* in-game benchmark times (in ms) for Ray Tracing: Ultra.

Part 2   Path Tracing: The Unified Lighting Pipeline of the Future

7.8   Transitioning to Physically Based Lighting

After decades of research and development, traditional rasterization graphics are able to produce compelling visuals. However, the projection algorithm suffers from a fatal flaw: the G-buffer only contains information for geometry visible to the camera, but the light seen at each pixel is a function of the geometry in the entire scene. In order to model light interactions that rely on this geometry, such as shadows or indirect light, rasterization pipelines had to either rely on screen-space techniques, which rely on what little information *is* in the G-buffer, pre-bake the lighting into the assets ahead of time, which is costly during production and only works for static phenomena, or construct world-space data structures to approximate global lighting phenomena. Unfortunately, all of these approaches are designed independently, and most scale poorly.

The common requirement for computing global lighting phenomena is determining visibility. Shadows require each pixel to calculate whether the light is visible from the surface at that pixel. Indirect lighting requires the same calculation be performed for the indirect surface, then for the primary surface to the indirect. However, the key flaw in the projection algorithm is that it is extremely inefficient for calculating anything but primary visibility for a large film plane. The projection algorithm requires that all the potentially visible triangles be projected in every visibility test. This cost is efficiently amortized in the camera's primary visibility calculation, since each triangle projection can potentially cover many pixels, every triangle undergoes the same projection, and every final pixel is of course visible to the user. However, this algorithm loses its effectiveness when scaled down to the pixel level. For example, using projection to calculate light visibility for each pixel would multiply the cost of the depth buffer computation by the number of pixels and then again by the number of lights! This is not practical for a toy scene that has one light, let alone a real scene with dozens or hundreds. Even shadow maps, which instead calculate approximate visibility from the light's point of view, still require projecting all the triangles in the scene.

Another quirk of the projection algorithm is that it does not conceptually match the way light actually moves around in reality. A more physically based approach would involve casting a ray out from each pixel and finding the closest triangle it intersects, mimicking the behavior of a photon. While this approach still technically involves testing every triangle in the scene, space-partitioning data structures enable the ray-triangle intersection algorithm to consider only a roughly logarithmic number of triangles. This approach, called ray tracing, is much more efficient for calculating visibility in general, and it forms the backbone of many physically based rendering algorithms. One such algorithm called path tracing is implemented in *Cyberpunk 2077*. To understand path tracing, we first need a primer on the rendering equation, which formally describes the problem we are trying to solve.

7.8.1 Background: The Rendering Equation

In a 1986 paper, James Kajiya introduced the rendering equation to accurately model the quantity of light emanating from a surface in a particular direction [Kajiya 86]. The equation considers the light being emitted by the surface itself, plus all the light hitting the surface and the surface's material properties that dictate how that light is reflected. Formally, the outgoing light L_o from a point $\mathbf{x}$ in a particular direction ω_o is given by the following equation:

$$L_o(\mathbf{x}, \omega_o) = L_e(\mathbf{x}, \omega_o) + \int_\Omega f_r(\mathbf{x}, \omega_i, \omega_o) L_i(\mathbf{x}, \omega_i)(\omega_i \cdot n) \, d\omega_i,$$

where L_e is the light emitted from $\mathbf{x}$ in the direction ω_o, f_r is the bidirectional reflectance distribution function (BRDF) that describes how much light incoming from direction ω_i is reflected in direction ω_o at the point $\mathbf{x}$, L_i is the amount of light hitting the point $\mathbf{x}$ from the direction ω_i, and $\omega_i \cdot n$ is the angle between the incoming direction and the surface normal n. The integral's domain Ω represents the hemisphere of all possible incoming directions above the point, and the integral itself sums up all the light coming in from each incoming angle ω_i in Ω.

Of particular interest is the L_i term. This incoming light is a function of the lights in the scene, as well as other geometry in the scene that may occlude or reflect light toward the surface. Light that travels directly from a light source to the point is called *direct light* (Figure 7.29), and light that is first reflected off another object before hitting the point is called *indirect light* (Figure 7.30). The possibility of indirect light in the L_i term means that the rendering equation is implicitly recursive. For example, to solve for the light being reflected by a mirror, the rendering equation must be solved at the surface reflected by the mirror. Thus, solving the rendering equation at one point implies solving the rendering equation at many other points, which quickly makes the task of computing it quite complicated.

The task becomes more complicated yet, as solving the rendering equation at other points begs the question: which points? The answer is infinitely many. There are an infinite number of directions from which light may hit a point and reflect back toward the camera. If the surface is not fully opaque, light may come from inside the surface as well, "doubling" the already infinite number of possible directions to consider. And each of the points in the scene hit by these directions must in turn recursively have its rendering equation computed in identical fashion, and so on.

Closed-form solutions to the rendering equation were, and remain, computationally intractable for all but the simplest scenes. However, Kajiya introduced

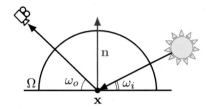

Figure 7.29. Direct lighting at a point **x**. Light leaves the source, hits a surface point **x** at the incoming angle ω_i, then bounces toward the camera at the outgoing angle ω_o.

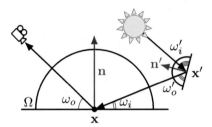

Figure 7.30. Indirect lighting at a point **x**. Light first bounces off an indirect surface point **x**′ before hitting the primary surface **x**. Light can bounce off many indirect surfaces before hitting the primary surface.

a probabilistic approach to solving the equation. That approach is called *path tracing*.

7.8.2 What Is Path Tracing?

Path tracing models light geometrically as a ray that bounces around the scene. Each ray originates in a pixel of the camera's film plane and extends out into the scene until it intersects the first visible surface. Surfaces are typically modeled as triangles, so finding this intersection is a matter of efficiently computing ray-triangle intersections. In turn, this efficiency comes from organizing triangles into a space-partitioning data structure so that a ray is only tested against those triangles that lie relatively close to its path.

Once a surface has been intersected, the path tracer must then engage in the real task of calculating the light the surface is reflecting back into the pixel. Rather than try to somehow exhaustively send rays out in every direction, the path tracer instead shoots a single ray out from the surface in a new randomly generated direction. It approximates the rendering equation at whatever surface is hit by this new ray by shooting yet another ray in a random direction, proceeding recursively in this manner until some termination condition is met, such as hitting a light or leaving the scene entirely. The end result is a calculation of how much light is reflected back into a pixel along a single path through the scene, hence the name *path tracing*.

The path tracer does not end with a lighting value from a single randomly generated path. This path is instead treated as a sample drawn from the probability space of all possible paths that could contribute to the final outgoing light value. The path tracer then generates many such paths and averages them together to compute an estimate of the true value of the lighting equation.

In mathematical terms, the path tracing algorithm creates an estimator of the true value of the lighting equation. If this estimator is unbiased, then it will be correct on average. If it is correct on average, then even if any particular sample is incorrect in isolation, when averaged with many other such samples, the end result will in fact be correct. The first goal in building a good path tracer is to ensure that it is unbiased so that it actually produces the correct image. However, the much harder goal is to design a path tracer that converges to the correct image quickly, as path tracing is naturally very slow.

7.8.3 Why Path Tracing Is Naturally Slow

Path tracing is costly for several reasons. The first is that while tracing a ray through the scene using a space-partitioning data structure is far more efficient than rasterizing the entire scene, it still requires substantial computation and memory traffic. The ray-triangle intersection math cannot be avoided, and the data for the triangles and the data structure must all be read from memory. Material properties and textures must also be read in from memory in order to evaluate the BRDF and do alpha testing. These memory requests are likely to have high spatial coherence for the primary surface—since neighboring pixels are likely to be shading the same surface—but have very poor coherence for secondary surfaces—since the randomly generated outgoing rays of any two neighboring pixels are unlikely to point toward the same surface.

A second source of inefficiency is the relatively small size of most lights in most scenes. Consider the average room you find yourself in: the lights are likely very small compared to the walls, floor, ceiling, and furniture. The chance that a ray shot in a random direction from a surface will hit a light is therefore very small. As a result, many paths need to be traced in order to have a good chance of finding those paths that actually hit a light source. In technical terms, this means that path tracing converges very slowly.

The two main ways to accelerate convergence are to improve the effective sample count per unit of computation time or to improve the quality of the samples taken in the first place. The good news is that, unlike the ray tracing operation itself, both of these approaches are fertile grounds for optimization. The next section focuses on increasing effective sample count and maximizing the usage of the most valuable samples through an algorithm called *Reservoir-based Spatio-Temporal Importance Resampling* (ReSTIR), and Section 7.10 focuses on improving the quality of initial samples by using radiance caching. Both techniques derive from the observation that rather than shooting rays at random, it would be better to shoot rays in directions most likely to actually contribute light.

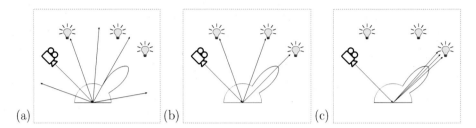

Figure 7.31. (a) Uniform sampling is fast and simple, but each ray has a very low chance of hitting a light. (b) Importance sampling according to light directions gives each ray a good chance of actually hitting a light source. (c) Importance sampling according to the BRDF gives each ray a good chance that whatever it hits will be maximally reflected back to the camera.

7.9   Increasing Effective Sample Count with ReSTIR

Selecting the outgoing ray direction with uniform probability has two major advantages: it is easy to implement and it is unbiased. However, its big flaw is that it is very unlikely to select a direction from which light is actually coming (Figure 7.31(a)). The statistical technique of importance sampling can be used to dramatically improve these odds.

Importance sampling strays from uniform sampling and instead samples from a probability distribution that places more probability density in regions that are expected to contribute larger values (Figure 7.31(b)). For example, one distribution might heavily favor directions that point directly toward lights. Another might favor directions more likely to contribute most of their light based on the material properties of the surface, such as those in the direction of the mirror reflection for glossy surfaces.

However, skewing the probability distribution away from the uniform one introduces bias into the estimator. After all, directions that are picked much more frequently will weight the average of the samples more heavily toward them. In order to correct for this added bias, importance sampling techniques scale the results down by the probability by which they were picked. Thus, if an importance sampling technique favors picking directions pointing at lights 10× more than it does any other direction, the resulting light values from those directions is scaled down by a factor of 10×.

Importance sampling techniques are easier to create when many specific details about the scene are known ahead of time and incorporated into the algorithm. However, creating importance sampling techniques that work for *general* scenes is much harder. The two main general approaches involve favoring directions pointing at lights, from which all light by definition must come at some point, and favoring directions most likely to contribute reflected light based on the surface material properties, such as the mirror reflection direction when dealing with mirrors or glossy surfaces. For example, one importance sampling technique may pick a light direction with 40% probability, a direction around the specular lobe of the surface with 40% probability, and any other direction with 20% probability, scaling each one appropriately in the final averaging estimate.

A partitioning of the sampling space by importance sampling strategy remains unbiased, assuming each individual strategy is unbiased. However, in order to benefit from each one, the path tracer still must select multiple samples. Given n strategies, the path tracer must take at least n samples to have any chance of deploying each routine. While this technique does significantly improve sampling quality, and thus convergence time, it still requires many samples to produce a quality image. The next step is to implement a technique for combining multiple importance sampling strategies into a single sampling process.

7.9.1 Resampled Importance Sampling (RIS)

The question of what information to include in an importance sampling distribution is not trivial. For example, we might decide to favor sampling not only from directions pointing at lights, but also from directions based on the power (i.e., brightness) of each light. This distribution can be calculated once per frame, and sampling from this distribution is not too expensive. However, if the algorithm were to favor sampling visible lights, it would be much more expensive, as it would have to calculate the set of visible lights that is unique for each primary hit point by casting as many visibility rays from each point to the light as there are lights. Likewise, sampling lights based on the amount they reflect off the surface would also require constructing the distribution afresh for each primary hit point by evaluating the BRDF for each light. The cost of including certain pieces of information in the sampling distribution can thus easily come close to solving the rendering equation in the first place, thereby negating any practical efficiency improvements.

To mitigate this problem, a technique called *resampled importance sampling* (RIS) samples from a sequence of distributions, factoring in the relative cost of evaluating each distribution. First, RIS draws a large number of samples from a distribution that is cheap to sample from. Next, RIS calculates more expensive information for each of the initial samples in order to build a second distribution. RIS then draws a final sample from this second distribution. The final sample is of meaningfully higher quality than one drawn from the initial cheap distribution but does not incur the cost of fully computing the second, more expensive distribution.

For example, an initial first batch of 10 samples may be drawn from the distribution of lights arranged by power (Figure 7.32(a)). Then, the amount of light reflected in the outgoing direction may be calculated by evaluating the BRDF for these initial samples, thus constructing a second distribution (Figure 7.32(b)). From this second distribution, a final sample may be drawn as the

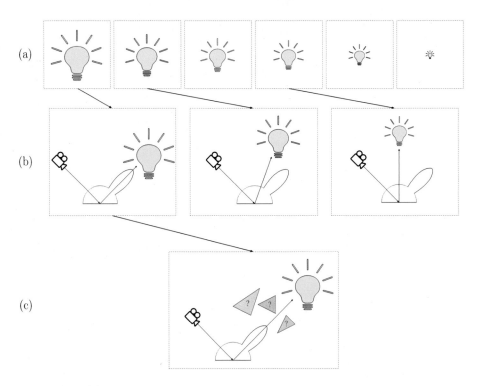

Figure 7.32. (a) RIS draws the most samples from the cheapest distribution, such as one where a light's probability is proportional to its power. (b) RIS then incorporates more expensive information, such as the BRDF contribution of each of the sampled lights. (c) The last sample incorporates the most expensive information, such as the visibility term.

direction to send the next incoming ray (Figure 7.32(c)). This sample will be of higher quality than one drawn from the light power distribution alone, and it will have been cheaper than constructing the full distribution that considers the BRDF contribution of all lights in the scene.

However, there is a drawback to RIS: the samples drawn from the cheap distribution need to be stored somewhere, and storage is at a premium on GPUs. If they are stored in registers, then they will decrease the number of warps, or shader threads, that can run simultaneously. If they are stored in GPU memory, then they will incur memory traffic costs. And if they are stored in some intermediate form of storage, such as group shared memory, then they may incur a combination of such costs. The success of an RIS implementation for GPU path tracing thus rests on an optimization to significantly reduce these memory costs. The weighted reservoir sampling algorithm does just that.

7.9.2 Weighted Reservoir Sampling (WRS)

Weighted reservoir sampling (WRS) is a technique for selecting a single sample from a sequence of weighted samples without needing to have access to the entire sequence. WRS accomplishes this task by keeping track of a small data structure called a *reservoir* that contains, among a few other things, the selected sample, a weight value that is proportional to the sample's probability of being chosen, and a running total of all the weights of all samples considered so far. For each new sample, WRS adds its weight to the running total and then divides the sample's weight by the running total to form its chance of replacing the existing sample in the reservoir. The end result is a sample that is chosen with the probability of its weight over the total weight of all samples.

WRS provides the desired ability to sample from a distribution as it is constructed while using very little memory overhead. The combination of WRS with RIS forms the basis of the initial sampling routine in *Cyberpunk 2077*'s path tracer.

7.9.3 Combining RIS and WRS

WRS is combined with RIS as follows: For each pixel, a sample is first chosen from a simple distribution that is cheap to evaluate, such as directions toward lights as weighted by light power. Then, the BRDF is evaluated for this lighting direction to determine the light actually reflected back along the incident ray. This contribution forms the weight for that sample, which is then stored with the light direction in the pixel's reservoir. This process of first cheaply choosing a random light direction and then evaluating the more expensive BRDF is then repeated, with each successive sample streamed into the pixel's reservoir. After considering a set number of initial samples, the reservoir contains a sample that was drawn from a distribution that approximately considers the combination of the light power and BRDF terms.

The combination of RIS and WRS is quite powerful in this context, as the number of samples can be scaled up or down to tune for performance or image quality. Likewise, the individual distributions can be changed without affecting the overall structure of the algorithm. For example, light power might turn out to be a poor heuristic for sampling lights, and a uniform sampling method could be used instead. Meanwhile, the BRDF calculations could remain unchanged. Alternatively, perhaps the initial sampling distribution could both consider light power and distance from the camera instead of just light power. Shadow rays could be cast from the surface to the light to determine the actual visibility for some or all of the samples. A cheap approximation of the BRDF may be used instead of a full computation. Outgoing directions may be sampled with probability proportional to the BRDF to begin with, abandoning preselected light directions entirely. The possibilities are many.

Another key strength of WRS is that it allows reservoirs to be combined to produce a new reservoir whose sample is selected with a probability equal to its weight over the new total weight from both reservoirs. This allows for algorithms to consider different lighting sources in sequence, combining them all together in the end. For example, one pass might consider point lights, another area lights, a third the environment light, a fourth infinite lights, and a fifth directions determined by the BRDF, and each pass could be calculated independently and then streamed into a single reservoir.

In practice, *Cyberpunk 2077*'s path tracer originally took its initial samples from the distribution of lights weighted by power and distance from the camera. However, this sampling strategy did not improve over uniform sampling in practice, as neither power nor camera proximity was a good proxy for final light contribution. As a result, the path tracer took its initial samples uniformly from the light list. For the second stage, it evaluated the BRDF contribution of the light to form the weight for the reservoir.

7.9.4 ReSTIR DI

The combination of RIS and WRS provides a powerful way to efficiently sample direct lighting directions. Unfortunately, it is not enough to produce compelling results on its own, at least not for modern games running at 60 FPS or even 30 FPS. The complexity of modern game scenes simply requires path tracers to use a larger number of samples, even if those samples are selected from well-crafted distributions. While it may be tempting to simply increase the number of samples taken each frame until the image looks good, this approach is very expensive and still not viable for modern scenes on modern hardware. In fact, path-traced image quality converges proportional to the square root of the number of samples, so raw sample count would need to quadruple for image quality to double.

The discussion so far has focused on generating new samples with increasing degrees of cleverness. Of all these samples, some will be high value for the final image. But given the spatiotemporal coherence of real-time rendering, these high-value samples are likely to be valuable for both future pixels and neighboring pixels. A technique that shares samples with other pixels over space and time would allow the path tracer to increase its *effective* sample count per pixel without needing to further increase the number of genuine initial samples it generates per pixel. The technique implemented in *Cyberpunk 2077*'s path tracer that does this is called *ReSTIR DI*.

Reservoir-based Spatio-Temporal Importance Resampling for Direct Illumination, or ReSTIR DI [Bitterli et al. 20], probabilistically resamples reservoirs over time and space with two additional render passes. The temporal resampling pass (Figure 7.33) reprojects each pixel back into the previous frame and determines whether the surface at that pixel is similar enough to the surface in the pixel in the original frame. If so, the reservoir from the previous frame is com-

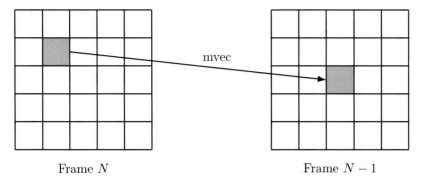

Frame N Frame $N - 1$

Figure 7.33. During the temporal resampling pass, each pixel inspects the pixel at its surface's reprojected position in the previous frame to see if it contains viable a reservoir. If so, it gets resampled back into the original pixel.

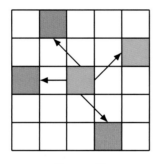

Frame N

Figure 7.34. During the spatial resampling pass, each pixel inspects several of its neighbors to see if they contain viable reservoirs. If so, they are resampled back into the original pixel.

bined with the reservoir in the current frame, with the light from the previous reservoir being taken with probability proportional to its quality. This temporal resampling leads to an accumulation of sample quality and sample count over time. The spatial resampling pass (Figure 7.34) inspects the neighbors of each pixel, and if the surface at a neighbor is similar enough to the surface at the original pixel, the two reservoirs are combined as in the temporal resampling pass. This spatial resampling leads to a multiplicative increase in the effective sample count per pixel. The combination of temporal and spatial resampling leads to an exponential increase in the effective number of samples taken each frame, leading to a significant reduction in convergence time.

ReSTIR DI is able to deliver compelling results for direct illumination, but leaves open the problem of indirect illumination. Indirect illumination is much harder to solve for in general, since the set of light sources is not known in advance like it is for direct illumination.

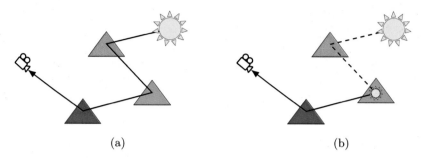

(a)   (b)

Figure 7.35. (a) Indirect light paths bounce off at least one other surface before hitting the primary surface and reflecting back into the camera. (b) ReSTIR GI collapses the path from the light to the secondary surface down to a single point estimate, which it then treats like a light source.

7.9.5   ReSTIR GI

All of the effort that goes into sampling lights helps with computing the direct lighting for a point. But the rendering equation requires the calculation of indirect lighting as well, or light that has bounced off at least one other surface first before hitting the point whose lighting is currently being calculated (Figure 7.35(a)). In order to tackle this problem, researchers developed ReSTIR for Global Illumination, or *ReSTIR GI* [Ouyang et al. 21].

The key insight of ReSTIR GI is to calculate the outgoing light at an indirect point and then treat that point as though it were itself a light source (Figure 7.35(b)). From each primary surface, the path tracer traces a ray, not aiming at lights as in ReSTIR DI, but aiming uniformly or according to the BRDF so as to hit some other surface. The secondary surface hit by this ray then becomes a sample point. The path tracer then estimates the incoming light for this secondary point. In the simplest case, this amounts to estimating the direct lighting for the secondary point, but can also include estimates for further multi-bounce indirect lighting. The sample point, the radiance emitted toward the primary point, and a small number of additional variables are then stored in a reservoir, just as with ReSTIR DI.

After the path tracer has generated the reservoir for the indirect sample point, ReSTIR GI takes over. As with ReSTIR DI, it resamples from the previous frame's reservoirs to accumulate sampling quality over time, then resamples from neighboring pixels to increase the effective sample count per frame. At each stage, care must be taken to identify sources of bias and, depending on the expense, correct for them. For example, one source of bias comes from the fact that the set of light paths that illuminate one surface is not guaranteed to be the same as the set of light paths that illuminate its neighbor, so a sample from one domain may not be valid in the other. ReSTIR corrects for this bias by shooting a visibility ray from the surface to the secondary surface resampled from its neighbor. Likewise, ReSTIR can also use cheaper but less accurate bias correction methods to trade off accuracy for performance. The final result of this resampling and bias correction is a significant improvement in image quality over standard indirect path tracing.

7.9.6   Practical ReSTIR GI

Because ReSTIR DI focuses only on direct lighting, its shader implementation only needs access to primary surfaces to illuminate, light sources to sample from, and scene geometry (plus materials for alpha) to test against. This makes ReSTIR DI a good initial first step in a transition from a rasterizer to a path tracing implementation. However, ReSTIR GI additionally requires a path tracer in order to generate its indirect samples. The natural progression, and the one developers followed for *Cyberpunk 2077*, is to next build a path tracer for indirect light and then finally integrate ReSTIR GI on top of it.

The need for a path tracing pass makes ReSTIR GI more computationally expensive than ReSTIR DI. *Cyberpunk 2077*'s initial implementation was made twice as expensive by its separation of diffuse and specular indirect light into their own path tracing and ReSTIR GI passes. As an optimization, the individual diffuse and specular path tracing passes were combined into a single path tracing pass that randomly selected one of the two lobes to sample. This initial sample was then sent to both the diffuse and specular ReSTIR GI pipelines, which, with some adjustment of the probability math to account for the different source distributions (Listings 7.2 and 7.3), still produced a significant improvement over the baseline path tracer.

```
// The general idea of this function is to estimate diffuse probability
    but also clamp it to 1/20 pixels (unless full metal).
float EstimateDiffuseProbability(SurfaceData baseSurface, float3 viewDir
    )
{
  float roughness = baseSurface.Roughness;
  float NoV = abs(dot(baseSurface.Normal, viewDir));

  // [Hirvonen et al. 19]
  float3 Fenv = EnvBRDFApprox(baseSurface.Specular, roughness *
    roughness, NoV);

  float lumSpec = RGBToLuminance(Fenv);
  float lumDiff = RGBToLuminance(baseSurface.Albedo * (1.0 - Fenv));
  float lumSum = lumDiff + lumSpec;

  float diffProb = lumSum > 0.f ? lumDiff / lumSum : 1.f;

  if ((0.f < diffProb) && (diffProb < 1.f))
  {
      diffProb = clamp(diffProb, 0.05f, 0.95f);
  }

  return diffProb;
}
```

Listing 7.2. Helper functions for probability adjustment of ReSTIR GI samples.

```
float3 N = primarySurf.normal;
float3 L = normalize( initReservoir.position - primarySurf.worldPos );
float3 V = primarySurf.viewDir;
float3 H = normalize( V + L );
float NoV = saturate( dot( N, V ) );
float NoH = saturate( dot( N, H ) );

float roughness = primarySurf.surface.Roughness;
float alpha = roughness * roughness;
float alphaSquared = alpha * alpha;

float diffProbability = EstimateDiffuseProbability( primarySurf.surface,
    V );
float diffPdf = EvalCosHemispherePdf( N, L );
float specProbability = 1.f - diffProbability;
// See [Heitz 18]
float specPdf = SampleGGXVNDFReflectionPdf( alpha, alphaSquared, NoH,
    NoV );
float pdf = diffuseProbability * diffPdf + specProbability * specPdf;

inputReservoir = RTXDI_MakeGIReservoir( initReservoir.position,
    initReservoir.normal, sampleRadianceHitDist.rgb, pdf );
```

Listing 7.3. Probability adjustment for ReSTIR GI samples. The initial sample is stored in the `initReservoir` during the path tracing pass, and then its probability parameter is adjusted in the first ReSTIR GI pass as shown here.

The *Cyberpunk 2077* engine made two significant changes to the original ReSTIR GI implementation. The first addressed the issue of sample age. As time elapses, the scene and perspective change more, and samples are more likely to go out of date. The presence of outdated indirect samples manifests as lagging indirect lighting phenomena. The original ReSTIR GI implementation added a validation pass to address this problem, although simply capping the sample history length to eight frames produced a comparable result without the added overhead of an additional pass.

The second change addressed the fact that ReSTIR GI was originally designed for resampling of diffuse light. Pixels close to one another in space and time are likely to only have small differences in the diffuse contribution from the same secondary light source. However, as a material becomes glossier, its specular lobe narrows, and in turn the region of indirect surfaces that can potentially reflect or emit light narrows as well. In the limit, mirror reflections allow a single indirect source of light for one point that is not reflected at all by any of its neighboring points. To address this issue in its spatial resampling of specular light paths, ReSTIR GI reduces the radius of the circle around the pixel in which it performs resampling in proportion to the surface roughness value, disabling spatial resampling entirely for roughness values below 0.1. The need for enhanced sampling techniques goes down as the range of possible indirect light sources goes down, and at a certain point even becomes counterproductive. By using ReSTIR GI to the extent necessary, *Cyberpunk 2077*'s path tracer saw a significant improvement in indirect lighting quality where possible without incurring quality degradation where it wasn't.

7.10 Improving Sampling Quality with Radiance Caching

A *radiance cache* is a system that can be queried about radiance at an arbitrary position, going into an arbitrary direction, and at an arbitrary time. At least that's what a perfect radiance cache would be. In reality, however, a typical radiance cache approximates radiance distribution in a scene with a limited spatial, directional, and temporal resolution.

Since real-time path tracing has become feasible only very recently, many forms of radiance cache were developed to directly estimate indirect lighting in real-time applications. For example, pre-baked uniform 3D grids of probes that quickly became somewhat dynamic [Hooker 16] are still very popular. These probe grids were further improved with hardware ray tracing to enable even more dynamism and reduce the occlusion and light leaking issues [Majercik et al. 19]. To avoid some of the probe placement issues around arbitrary geometry, the probes can also be associated with a specific position on a particular surface [Brinck et al. 21]. Unreal Engine 5's lighting system, Lumen, employs a radiance cache based on screen-space probes that decouples the tracing resolution from the rendering resolution [Wright 21]. Building on this solution, a two-level radiance cache combining screen-space probes with a hash grid was also introduced [Boisse 23]. While all these solutions typically require only a fraction of the runtime performance cost needed for path tracing, none of them are capable of reaching the image quality that path tracing can deliver.

On the other side of the spectrum, there are radiance caches that were designed to coexist with and augment path tracing. Neural Radiance Cache (NRC) [Muller et al. 21] first utilizes path tracing to train a neural network about radiance distribution in a scene, and then this neural network is available to the main path tracer for inference. Spatially Hashed Radiance Cache (SHaRC) [Gameworks 24] works similarly, but instead of training a neural network, it accumulates radiance in a hash grid stored in the GPU memory. Figure 7.36 depicts how path tracing and this kind of radiance cache can be used

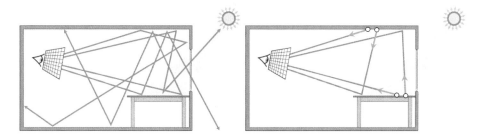

Figure 7.36. The result of path tracing without radiance cache (left) is typically much more noisy than the result of path tracing with radiance cache (right) that approximates reflected light.

(a) An indirectly lit location in *Cyberpunk 2077*.

(b) The indirect diffuse lighting generated by a path tracer that doesn't utilize a
radiance cache (left) and the one that does (right).

Figure 7.37. Importance of radiance cache in *Cyberpunk 2077*.

together to improve the overall signal quality. In a nutshell, instead of tracing
long paths that might ultimately struggle with finding important light sources,
it's possible to utilize the radiance cache after fewer bounces. Assuming the radiance cache is high quality, a combination of path tracing and radiance cache can
result in higher image quality overall. Figure 7.37 presents a mostly indirectly
lit location in *Cyberpunk 2077* and compares the signal quality generated by an
indirect light path tracer that doesn't utilize a radiance cache with the one that
does. Since NRC was not yet available during the development, SHaRC became

the radiance cache of choice for path tracing in Ray Tracing: Overdrive mode of *Cyberpunk 2077*.

7.10.1 Spatially Hashed Radiance Cache

Spatially Hashed Radiance Cache (SHaRC) is a world-space radiance cache that stores radiance in a GPU hash grid. Each point in space gets discretized with a logarithmic scale based on the distance to the camera (Figure 7.38) and produces a set of coordinates and a level of detail within a uniform world-space grid. When

(a) An underpass location in *Cyberpunk 2077*.

(b) SHaRC's accumulated radiance at the primary surface in *Cyberpunk 2077*.

Figure 7.38. Debug visualization of SHaRC.

deployed in a path tracer, SHaRC improves the quality of every path and can deliver more light bounces. Although SHaRC can cause additional temporal lag, like any other cache, it is highly adjustable with respect to performance, image quality, resolution, and temporal lag itself. In addition, SHaRC doesn't require substantial modifications to the existing path tracer code and the rendering loop needs to only accommodate two additional passes to update the radiance cache prior to the final path tracing that utilizes it.

Hash Key At the core of any hash-based solution is a hash key. To generate a hash key, SHaRC uses a position within the grid, a level of detail based on the distance from the camera, and a (geometry) normal that helps with avoiding artifacts on thin geometry. Listing 7.4 presents the bit allocation for each component that we used in *Cyberpunk 2077*. It also shows global grid parameters that include the camera position, logarithm base that controls levels of detail distribution and voxel size ratio change between neighboring levels, and scene scale that directly controls voxel size.

Listing 7.5 shows how to calculate the level of detail, voxel size, and grid position from a world-space sample position.

Finally, Listing 7.6 computes the 64-bit spatial hash key.

Hash Grid Data Structure Another core element of a hash-based solution is a hash grid data structure. SHaRC consists of only a couple of resources allocated in video memory:

- **Hash entries buffer:** This structured buffer with 64-bit entries stores the hash keys.

- **Voxel data buffer:** This raw buffer with 128-bit entries stores the accumulated radiance, sample count, and frame count since the last update. Two instances are used to store the previous and current frame data.

```
#define POS_BIT_NUM        18
#define POS_BIT_MASK       ((1u << POS_BIT_NUM) - 1)
#define LEVEL_BIT_NUM      7
#define LEVEL_BIT_MASK     ((1u << LEVEL_BIT_NUM) - 1)
#define NORMAL_BIT_NUM     3
#define NORMAL_BIT_MASK    ((1u << NORMAL_BIT_NUM) - 1)

struct GridParams
{
    float3 cameraPos;
    float   logBase;
    float   sceneScale;
};
```

Listing 7.4. SHaRC hash key bit allocation and grid parameters.

```
float LogBase(float x, float base)
{
    return log(x) / log(base);
}

uint GetGridLevel(float3 samplePos, GridParams gridParams)
{
    float d = length(gridParams.cameraPos - samplePos);
    float logBase = floor(LogBase(d, gridParams.logBase));
    return clamp(logBase, 1, LEVEL_BIT_MASK);
}

float GetVoxelSize(uint gridLevel, GridParams gridParams)
{
    return pow(gridParams.logBase, gridLevel) / gridParams.sceneScale;
}

// Based on logarithmic caching by Johannes Jendersie
int4 GetGridPositionLog(float3 samplePos, GridParams gridParams)
{
    uint  gridLevel = GetGridLevel(samplePos, gridParams);
    float voxelSize = GetVoxelSize(gridLevel, gridParams);
    int3  gridPos   = floor(samplePos / voxelSize);

    return int4(gridPos.xyz, gridLevel);
}
```

Listing 7.5. SHaRC level of detail, voxel size, and grid position computation.

```
uint64_t ComputeSpatialHash(float3 samplePos, float3 sampleNormal,
    GridParams gridParams)
{
    // gridPos.xyz - position; gridPos.w - level
    uint4 gridPos = asuint(GetGridPositionLog(samplePos, gridParams));

    uint64_t hashKey =
      (((uint64_t)gridPos.x & POS_BIT_MASK)     << (POS_BIT_NUM * 0))
    | (((uint64_t)gridPos.y & POS_BIT_MASK)     << (POS_BIT_NUM * 1))
    | (((uint64_t)gridPos.z & POS_BIT_MASK)     << (POS_BIT_NUM * 2))
    | (((uint64_t)gridPos.w & LEVEL_BIT_MASK) << (POS_BIT_NUM * 3));

    uint normalBits =
      (sampleNormal.x >= 0 ? 1 : 0)
    + (sampleNormal.y >= 0 ? 2 : 0)
    + (sampleNormal.z >= 0 ? 4 : 0);

    hashKey |=
      ((uint64_t)normalBits << (POS_BIT_NUM * 3 + LEVEL_BIT_NUM));

    return hashKey;
}
```

Listing 7.6. SHaRC hash key computation.

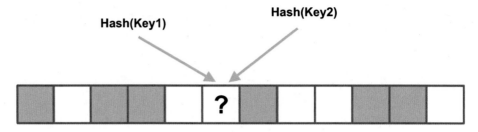

Figure 7.39. Two distinct keys have the same hash value, resulting in a hash collision.

The number of entries in each buffer is the same and represents the number of scene voxels used for radiance caching. In *Cyberpunk 2077*, we used 2^{22} elements, which made SHaRC consume around 167 MB of video memory. The hash entries buffer is necessary for hash collision resolution.

Hash Collisions Hash collisions happen when two distinct keys map to identical hash values (Figure 7.39). The hash function should aim to minimize the likelihood of these collisions, but ultimately, they are unavoidable.

SHaRC uses open addressing with linear probing to resolve hash collisions. Open addressing means using a contiguous array of cells in memory and linear probing is a strategy that helps with mitigating collisions by scanning the cells in the hash grid sequentially (Figure 7.40).

Listing 7.7 presents how the hash entries buffer is utilized to enable open addressing with linear probing in SHaRC.

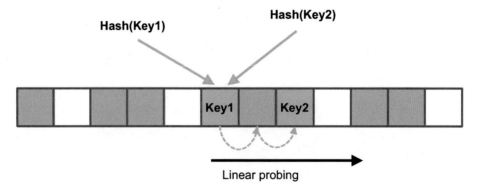

Figure 7.40. Open addressing with linear probing stores colliding entries in distinct locations by traversing a sequence of alternative cells in a deterministic order.

```
#define BUCKET_SIZE 32
#define CAPACITY      2 * 1024 * 1024 // 2^22

bool HashMapInsert(const uint64_t hashKey, out uint cacheEntry)
{
    uint     hash          = Hash(hashKey);
    uint     slot          = hash % CAPACITY;
    uint64_t prevHashKey = INVALID_HASH_KEY;

    for (uint offset = 0; offset < BUCKET_SIZE; ++offset)
    {
        AtomicCompareExchange(
            slot + offset, INVALID_HASH_KEY, hashKey, prevHashKey);

        if (prevHashKey == INVALID_HASH_KEY ||
            prevHashKey == hashKey)
        {
            cacheEntry = slot + offset;
            return true;
        }
    }

    return false;
}

bool HashMapFind(const uint64_t hashKey, inout uint cacheEntry)
{
    uint     hash          = Hash(hashKey);
    uint     slot          = hash % CAPACITY;
    uint64_t prevHashKey = INVALID_HASH_KEY;

    for (uint offset = 0; offset < BUCKET_SIZE; ++offset)
    {
        uint64_t storedHashKey = hashEntriesBuffer[slot + offset];

        if (storedHashKey == hashKey)
        {
            cacheEntry = slot + offset;
            return true;
        }
    }

    return false;
}
```

Listing 7.7. SHaRC conflict resolution.

Updating and Resolving the Cache Updating the cache consists of two stages: a
path tracer that updates the current frame cache (Figure 7.41) and a resolve
pass that mainly combines previous and current frame data whilst also evicting
stale data (Listing 7.8).

Since we are not generating an image, but rather trying to update random
voxels of the cache with the most up-to-date information, there is no need to
execute path tracing on every single pixel. Instead, we can trace only a fraction
of paths, but potentially with more bounces. In fact, in *Cyberpunk 2077* we are
tracing paths only from a random 4% of pixels but we are tracing them for up
to four bounces, instead of just two. SHaRC also supports backpropagation and
is capable of querying the previous frame's cache at the end of the path.

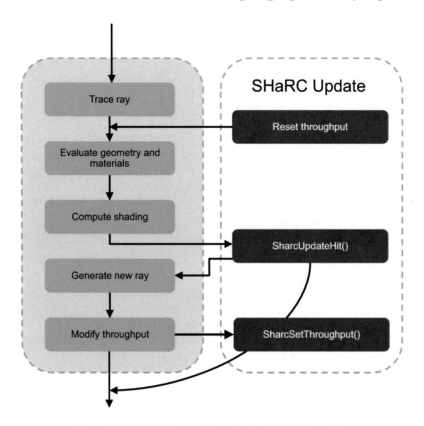

Figure 7.41. Path tracer loop during SHaRC update.

```
#define RADIANCE_SCALE          1e4f
#define LINEAR_BLOCK_SIZE        256
#define SAMPLE_NUM_MAX           64
#define STALE_FRAME_NUM_MAX      64
#define SAMPLE_BIT_NUM           20
#define SAMPLE_BIT_MASK          ((1u << SAMPLE_BIT_NUM) - 1)
#define FRAME_BIT_NUM            (32 - SAMPLE_BIT_NUM)
#define FRAME_BIT_MASK           ((1u << FRAME_BIT_NUM) - 1)

struct SharcVoxelData
{
    float3 radiance;
    uint sampleNum;
    uint frameNum;
};

SharcVoxelData SharcUnpackVoxelData(uint4 dataPacked)
{
    SharcVoxelData data = (SharcVoxelData)0;
    data.radiance = dataPacked.xyz / RADIANCE_SCALE;
    data.sampleNum = (dataPacked.w >> 0) & SAMPLE_BIT_MASK;
    data.frameNum = (dataPacked.w >> SAMPLE_BIT_NUM) & FRAME_BIT_MASK;

    return data;
}
```

```
[NUMTHREADS(LINEAR_BLOCK_SIZE, 1, 1)]
CS_MAIN(in uint2 did : SYS_DISPATCH_THREAD_ID)
{
    HashKey hashKey = u_SharcHashEntries[did.x];
    if (hashKey == INVALID_HASH_KEY) return;

    uint4 dataPackedPrev = u_SharcVoxelDataPrev.Load4(did.x * 16);
    uint4 dataPacked = u_SharcVoxelData.Load4(did.x * 16);
    uint4 packedData = dataPacked + dataPackedPrev;
    uint sampleNum = packedData.w & SAMPLE_BIT_MASK;

    if (sampleNum > SAMPLE_NUM_MAX)
    {
        packedData.xyz *= (float)SAMPLE_NUM_MAX / sampleNum;
        packedData.w = sampleNum = SAMPLE_NUM_MAX;
    }

    uint frame = (dataPackedPrev.w >> SAMPLE_BIT_NUM) & FRAME_BIT_MASK;
    packedData.w = sampleNum;

    // Increment frame counter for stale samples
    if ((dataPacked.w & SAMPLE_BIT_MASK) == 0)
    {
        ++frame;
        packedData.w |= ((frame & FRAME_BIT_MASK) << SAMPLE_BIT_NUM);
    }

    // Evict stale samples
    if (frame > STALE_FRAME_NUM_MAX)
    {
        packedData = 0;
        u_SharcHashEntries[did.x] = INVALID_HASH_KEY;
    }

    u_SharcVoxelData.Store4(did.x * 16, packedData);
}
```

Listing 7.8. SHaRC resolve.

Querying the Cache The only things necessary to query radiance data from SHaRC are world-space positions and geometry normals; it's not necessary to evaluate material data. The main data structure is a GPU buffer that is queryable from any shader. Figure 7.42 depicts an interaction between the path tracer and SHaRC during rendering.

Knowing when to fetch the data from the cache, versus tracing another bounce, becomes the more difficult element to solve. To avoid some rendering artifacts, we should continue tracing until the path segment length is bigger than the voxel size. What's more, specular lobes should be treated with care. For the glossy specular lobe, we can estimate its effective cone spread (Figure 7.43), and if it exceeds the spatial resolution of the voxel grid, then the cache can be used. Cone spread can be estimated as

$$2.0 * \texttt{ray.length} * \sqrt{\frac{0.5 * a^2}{1 - a^2}},$$

where a is the material roughness squared [Akenine-Möller et al. 21].

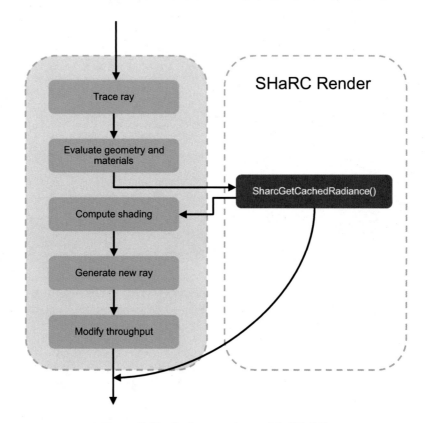

Figure 7.42. Path tracer loop with SHaRC.

Figure 7.43. SHaRC cone spread.

Figure 7.44 presents the impact of using SHaRC in a path tracer after the previously mentioned conditions were met.

(a) Path-traced reference.

(b) Reference path depth (left) and path depth with SHaRC (right)
(blue = 1 bounce, green = 2 bounces, red = 3+ bounces).

Figure 7.44. Optimized path depth with SHaRC in Bistro. (©Amazon Lumberyard.)

7.11   Denoising and Supersampling

Implementing full path tracing in Ray Tracing: Overdrive mode of *Cyberpunk 2077* added lifelike realism to the scenes, but also made denoising significantly more complicated. In Ray Tracing: Overdrive, we still use the SIGMA denoiser described in Part 1 to denoise ray-traced sun shadows, but we switched from ReBLUR to ReLAX, another denoiser available in the NRD library, to process the indirect radiance and the entirety of the remaining direct radiance. ReLAX was designed specifically to handle signals produced by algorithms like ReSTIR DI and ReSTIR GI described in Sections 7.9.4–7.9.6. Figure 7.45 presents an example scene from *Cyberpunk 2077* that shows how both direct and indirect illumination contribute to realistic lighting in the game. We will use this scene to discuss the denoising solution implemented for path tracing in *Cyberpunk 2077*.

Figure 7.45. Dogtown, *Cyberpunk 2077*.

7.11.1   Differences in Direct and Indirect Radiance Noise Profiles

The direct and indirect radiance signals have significantly different noise properties in Ray Tracing: Overdrive mode of *Cyberpunk 2077*, which led us to make
certain decisions in the chosen denoising architecture. The direct radiance comes
from the ReSTIR DI pass, which provides very dense signal with relatively low
noise thanks to its temporal and spatial reuse mechanisms. The indirect radiance
comes from indirect light path tracing pass. Even with significant improvements
from SHaRC and ReSTIR GI, indirect light path tracer cannot provide a signal
that is as dense and clean as the one we get from ReSTIR DI. Figures 7.46 and
7.47 show direct and indirect noisy lighting from Ray Tracing: Overdrive mode
of *Cyberpunk 2077*.

7.11.2   Direct and Indirect Radiance Denoising

ReLAX is a drastic evolution of the classic Spatiotemporal Variance-Guided
Filtering (SVGF) denoiser [Schied et al. 17]. It introduces multiple heuristics,
intermediate buffers, and denoising stages that improve image quality, stability,
and responsiveness. Figure 7.48 shows a comparison of the classic SVGF and
ReLAX denoising pipelines and the following list contains a brief overview of the
ReLAX passes:

- **Classify tiles:** The first pass accelerates the processing of "sky" regions
  (outside of denoising range) by splitting the screen into 16×16 tiles and
  assigning 0 to a tile if all of its pixels are outside of the denoising range.

Figure 7.46. Direct diffuse (top) and specular (bottom) lighting signal in Ray Tracing: Overdrive mode of *Cyberpunk 2077*.

- **Hit distance reconstruction:** This pass fills the gaps in hit distance values based on surface similarity heuristics if probability-based diffuse/specular sampling is used.

- **Pre-pass:** The next pass improves the input signal quality by spatially reusing the noisy signal in the area, defined by the BRDF lobe. It performs poorly when the sparsity of the input signal is higher than the search radius

Figure 7.47. Indirect diffuse (top) and specular (bottom) lighting signal in Ray Tracing: Overdrive mode of *Cyberpunk 2077*.

of the pre-pass. In this case, a rare bright pixel can be spread across neighbors, transforming the entire dark region with the outlier into just a bright blob. The pre-pass search radius must be carefully tuned to avoid such situations. Another goal of this pass is to estimate specular lobe virtual motion, which is the key to successful specular reprojection.

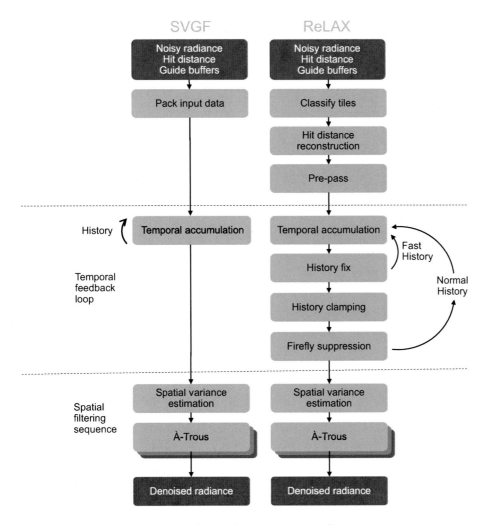

Figure 7.48. ReLAX denoising pipeline.

- **Temporal accumulation:** This pass accumulates new data with the reprojected history. Several confidence factors control the accumulation speed, and geometry-based plane distance is used for disocclusion tracking. While diffuse reprojection is based only on surface motion, specular reprojection additionally uses virtual motion, i.e., motion of the reflected world.

- **History fix:** Selectively applied on pixels with short history, i.e., in disoccluded regions and right after a disocclusion, this pass's main goal is to reconstruct missing history in such regions by applying an ultra-wide bilateral blur. A big stride between pixels helps to break repetitive patterns and blobbing.

- **History clamping:** The slow regular history is clamped, based on variance, to the fast history produced by the temporal accumulation pass. It helps to minimize lag and mitigate potential reprojection inefficiencies, but works only if local variance is low.

- **Firefly suppression:** The cross-bilateral Rank-Conditioned Rank Selection (RCRS) filter is run in a 3×3 region surrounding the current pixel to suppress single-pixel outliers.

- **Spatial variance estimation:** The next pass estimates the spatial variance of the signal based on a 5×5 region surrounding the current pixel in areas right after disocclusion, where temporal variance, required for À-Trous spatial passes, is not valid.

- **À-Trous:** This sequence of cross-bilateral wavelet-based spatial filters is guided by the variance of the signal and the content of the guide buffers.

ReLAX requires two sets of inputs: buffers containing the noisy radiance values themselves, as well as additional pieces of relevant data stored in *guide buffers* that aid in the denoising process. The noisy radiance values are stored in full-screen buffers and are broken down into direct and indirect components, and then again into diffuse and specular components. ReLAX inputs and outputs are listed in Table 7.5. These buffer requirements are standard in most of the state-of-the-art denoisers.

From a performance standpoint, it is intuitive to combine direct/indirect diffuse signals and direct/indirect specular signals and run those combined diffuse and specular signals through a denoiser. Unfortunately, since ReLAX is based

Inputs	Description
Diffuse and specular radiance and hit distance	*(noisy)* HDR radiance separated into diffuse and specular components, with hit distance provided in *alpha* channels
ViewZ	*(guide)* Linearized depth, needed for the world-space position reconstruction
Normal and Roughness	*(guide)* World-space normal and linear roughness, needed to define the lobe and the spatial weights
Motion vectors	*(guide)* Motion vectors for the primary hit, essential for the temporal accumulation pass
Outputs	**Description**
Denoised diffuse and specular	Denoised HDR radiance separated into diffuse and specular components

Table 7.5. ReLAX inputs and outputs.

on tracking the signal variance, tuning the parameters that would deal with combined signals led to inevitable degradation of the denoising quality. For instance, if we tweak the settings to maintain high spatial fidelity and responsiveness of the direct illumination contribution, the denoised output loses stability because the indirect signal contribution adds too much temporal and spatial variance at the input. And vice versa, if we tweak ReLAX's settings to maintain stability, we lose spatial details, sharp shadows, and the responsiveness of the direct illumination contribution.

What are the statistical properties of the input signals? Let's start with direct radiance. Since we use a variance guided denoiser, low variance of the radiance signal at the input of ReLAX allows us to be aggressive with the variance-based rejection in the spatial filtering part of the denoiser. As a result, we are able to conserve as many spatial details in ReLAX output as possible. In other words, shadows are sharp and lighting details are crisp.

Low variance of the direct illumination signal at the input helps us to improve ReLAX's responsiveness as well. The previous denoiser diagrams in Figure 7.48 showed that in addition to temporally accumulated signal, which we call *regular history*, ReLAX also uses a so-called *fast history*. Fast history follows the same logic as the regular history, although it uses more aggressive temporal accumulation weights that can make it potentially unstable, albeit very responsive, to changing lighting conditions.

One of the most notable enhancements in ReLAX is the addition of responsive history buffers. In conjunction with a history clamping stage, these improve the responsiveness of ReLAX in scenes with highly dynamic lighting.

We accelerate the regular history toward following the fast history without introducing much noise and instability by using the well-known technique of *color clamping*: based on the signal variance of the fast history within the neighborhood of a pixel, we clamp the color of the regular history in YCoCg color space to the bounding box defined by fast history color and the variance multiplied by a clamping aggressiveness factor.

ReSTIR DI produces input for the denoiser with low signal variance, so we can make the fast history temporal accumulation very responsive, essentially limiting the fast history length to one to two frames, and make color clamping very aggressive. These combined settings improve the responsiveness of the regular history leading to a very responsive denoiser.

The scene in Figure 7.49 shows light streaming into a dark room through rotating fan blades, which is a prime example of how the fast history helps to make ReLAX more responsive to such dynamic lighting conditions.

The images in Figure 7.50 show denoised direct radiance with and without using fast history. Using the fast history and color clamping logic described above makes ReLAX responsive to the changing lighting conditions. The moving shadows cast by rotating fan blades are clearly defined with the fast history, while the regular history is accumulated over many frames, which makeS it impossible for the denoiser to react to moving shadows.

Figure 7.49. Dynamic scene from *Cyberpunk 2077.*

The indirect radiance input signal has higher spatial and temporal variance compared to the direct radiance input signal. This means the indirect illumination has more variation in its spatial distribution and changes more over time than the direct illumination. Fortunately, indirect illumination is more subtle and in most cases does not require shadows that are as sharp and as high in spatial fidelity as do shadows from direct illumination. We can adjust ReLAX's settings for the indirect signal in a way that prioritizes stability over preserving fine spatial details and fast temporal responsiveness.

Relaxing the spatial filtering heuristics can help ReLAX adapt to the high spatial variance of the indirect signal. Increasing the number of accumulated frames in the temporal loop can improve the stability of the denoised indirect signal, which has lower inherent stability compared to the direct signal.

As the result, we implemented two instances of the same denoiser with different settings. One instance processes the direct diffuse and specular signals and is tuned for maintaining spatial details and responsiveness. The other instance processes the indirect diffuse and specular signals and is tuned to prioritize stability in order to handle the higher spatial and temporal variance of the indirect illumination. Figures 7.51 and 7.52 show direct and indirect denoised lighting from Ray Tracing: Overdrive mode of *Cyberpunk 2077.*

7.11.3   BRDF Demodulation

ReLAX has been designed to work best with pure radiance coming from a particular direction. This doesn't mean that denoising won't work, but for the best

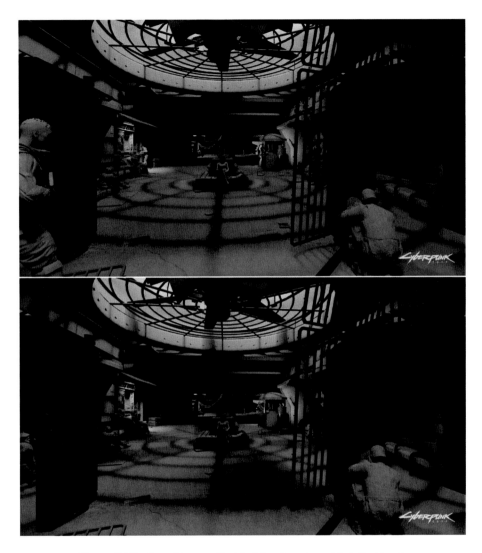

Figure 7.50. Fast history disabled (top) and enabled (bottom).

result, this means that materials should be decoupled from the input signal. In other words, *irradiance*, typically produced by a ray tracer, needs to be transformed into *radiance*. Using the standard technique of albedo demodulation greatly improved the surface albedo details, since the surface albedo didn't go through the denoising pipeline anymore. However, this led to a loss of fidelity on materials with highly detailed normal maps. One of the reasons for this loss of detail is that, with any movement or jitter, the tiny subpixel-sized specular

Figure 7.51. Direct diffuse (top) and specular (bottom) lighting signal in Ray Tracing: Overdrive mode of *Cyberpunk 2077*, after denoising.

highlights and diffuse details change significantly from frame to frame, but the temporal accumulation stage in ReLAX accumulates those over multiple frames, essentially removing those tiny details.

To improve this, we came up with a *BRDF ratio demodulation* technique (Listing 7.9). The idea is to calculate and store the BRDF's returned ratios of reflected radiance in the current pixel over the average in the surrounding area.

Figure 7.52. Indirect diffuse (top) and specular (bottom) lighting signal in Ray Tracing: Overdrive mode of *Cyberpunk 2077*, after denoising.

The ratios are calculated per pixel, separately for diffuse and specular radiance, and stored in a two-channel FP16 buffer. After the denoising is done, the calculated ratios are applied to denoised diffuse and specular signals. Since indirect lighting is much more subtle than direct lighting, in order to save performance, we decided to apply this technique to direct lighting only.

```
// BRDF demodulation for denoiser
Surface centerSurface = GetGBufferSurface(pixelPos);
float3 N = centerSurface.normal;
float3 V = centerSurface.viewDir;
float3 L = normalize(lightWorldPos - centerSurface.worldPos);
float NdotL = dot(N, L);
float centerDepth = centerSurface.depth;
float2 factor = float2(1.0f, 1.0f);
if (RTXDI_IsValidReservoir(centerSample) && (NdotL > 0))
{
    // Calculate center BRDF
    LightingComponents centerBRDF = BRDF(L, N, V, centerSurface.params);
    float2 centerBRDFf =
        calcLuminances(centerBRDF.Diffuse, centerBRDF.Specular);
    centerBRDFf = clampFloat2(centerBRDFf, 0.001f, 1000.0f);

    // Average BRDF for surrounding pixels in "+" pattern
    float2 sumBRDFf = float2(0, 0);
    float neighborCount = 0;
    for (int i = 0; i <= 3; ++i)
    {
        int2 offset;
        switch (i)
        {
            case 0: offset = int2(1, 0); break;
            case 1: offset = int2(-1, 0); break;
            case 2: offset = int2(0, 1); break;
            case 3: offset = int2(0, -1); break;
        }

        // Sample neighbor surface
        Surface sampleSurface = GetGBufferSurface(pixelPos + offset);
        float sampleDepth = sampleSurface.depth;
        N = sampleSurface.normal;

        // Ignore neighbors with very different depth
        if (abs(centerDepth - sampleDepth) > centerDepth * 0.02f) continue;

        // Calculate neighbor BRDF
        LightingComponents sampleBRDF = BRDF(L, N, V, centerSurface.params);
        float2 sampleBRDFf =
            calcLuminances(sampleBRDF.Diffuse, sampleBRDF.Specular);
        sampleBRDFf = clampFloat2(sampleBRDFf, 0.001f, 1000.0f);

        // Accumulate BRDF for the sample
        sumBRDFf += sampleBRDFf;
        neighborCount += 1.0f;
    }

    if (neighborCount > 0)
    {
        sumBRDFf /= neighborCount;
        factor.x = (sumBRDFf.x > 0.0f) ? centerBRDFf.x / sumBRDFf.x : 1.0f;
        factor.y = (sumBRDFf.y > 0.0f) ? centerBRDFf.y / sumBRDFf.y : 1.0f;
        factor = pow(factor, 0.7f);
        factor = clamp(factor, float2(0, 0), float2(15.0f, 15.0f));
    }
}
// Write out BRDF denodulation factor
brdfFactor[pixelPos] = factor;
```

Listing 7.9. BRDF demodulation.

When calculating the final lighting result after denoising, the direct radiance is multiplied by the previously calculated ratio (Listing 7.10).

```
// BRDF modulation
float2 brdfFactor = brdfFactor[pixelPos];
directDiffuseRadiance *= brdfFactor.x;
directSpecularRadiance *= brdfFactor.y;
```

Listing 7.10. BRDF Modulation.

7.11.4 Antialiasing and Supersampling

The original approach to antialiasing and supersampling in Ray Tracing: Over-drive mode of *Cyberpunk 2077* was the same as for other modes described in Section 7.6.3. Ultimately, however, the unified image reconstruction described in Section 7.13 has become the better approach.

7.12 Performance

Table 7.6 presents the configurations of resolution and DLSS-SR mode across a few GPUs that we used for testing, and Table 7.7 shows the performance of all path tracing–related passes on these configurations in Ray Tracing: Overdrive mode of *Cyberpunk 2077*.

GPU	Resolution	DLSS-SR Mode
GeForce RTX 4060	1080p	Quality
GeForce RTX 4070	1440p	Balanced
GeForce RTX 4080	2160p	Performance
GeForce RTX 4090	2160p	Performance

Table 7.6. Default resolutions and DLSS-SR modes per GPU.

Render Passes	GeForce RTX 4060	GeForce RTX 4070	GeForce RTX 4080	GeForce RTX 4090
BLAS Static	0.12	0.10	0.09	0.09
BLAS Dynamic	0.62	0.42	0.37	0.38
TLAS	0.73	0.43	0.38	0.36
RT Sun Shadows	0.75	0.52	0.49	0.36
ReSTIR DI	4.20	3.02	2.95	1.79
Indirect Light Path Tracer	6.05	4.29	3.81	2.66
RT Transparent Reflections	0.14	0.11	0.11	0.09
ReSTIR GI	2.09	1.75	1.69	1.33
NRD	5.02	3.85	3.77	2.60
DLSS-SR	0.63	0.61	0.80	0.57
Other Render Passes	7.29	5.54	5.51	4.43
Total Frame Time	**27.64**	**20.64**	**19.97**	**14.66**

Table 7.7. *Cyberpunk 2077* in-game benchmark times (in ms) for Ray Tracing: Overdrive.

Part 3   Leveraging AI for Enhanced Performance and Visual Fidelity

The previous parts of this article focused on the rendering pipeline and the various techniques and algorithms required to implement real-time path-tracing in *Cyberpunk 2077*. While this resulted in amazing visual fidelity, it wasn't the end of the story. The release of the Ray Tracing: Overdrive mode of *Cyberpunk 2077* was perfectly aligned to coincide with the release of NVIDIA's AI-based frame generation technology (DLSS 3.0 Frame Generation) and, later, the denoising/upscaling technology known as DLSS 3.5 Ray Reconstruction.

This part will cover how these techniques improved the performance and image quality of the game while also touching upon the latency improvements made. Finally, we will wrap up the article by discussing possible future work to further improve the Ray Tracing: Overdrive mode.

7.13   Unified Image Reconstruction

DLSS Ray Reconstruction (DLSS-RR) is an alternative way, available in *Cyberpunk 2077*, to perform image denoising and upscaling with a single unified method. When DLSS-RR is active, all others denoisers are disabled. Instead of having different denoisers for different signals, the "full" noisy input signal combined from stochastic sampling is passed onto a single post-process denoiser. This allows all effects to be handled in a unified manner and allows for denoised effects to be reconstructed with the upscaled output resolution (Figure 7.53). This results in higher-resolution lighting effects, such as high-resolution reflections, and improving the general information about the entire signal leads to higher-quality denoising with more detail.

Ray Reconstruction relies on getting information (radiance and metadata) about the individual pixels to perform denoising. This data is referred to as *guide buffers*, which are listed in Table 7.8.

These buffers are a superset of the data needed for DLSS Super Resolution, with the addition of information on primary-hit material parameters and information helping to determine specular motion. Using these guide buffers, the image reconstruction network is able to pick up spatial and temporal dependencies between guide buffers and the input radiance, utilizing them to reconstruct a higher-resolution, denoised image.

Specular albedo is the only guide buffer here that is not commonly used in games. This buffer is based on a specular environment BRDF approximation from [Hirvonen et al. 19].

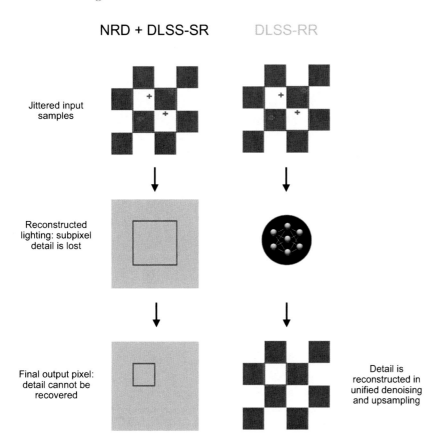

Figure 7.53. Unified denoising and upscaling is able to preserve output resolution subpixel detail.

7.13.1 Image Quality

Ray Reconstruction increases the image quality in many ways. Figure 7.54 shows the difference in a more diffuse scenario. Ray Reconstruction is especially good at keeping high-frequency AO and shadow detail, making, for example, objects more grounded.

The network is also able to smooth reflections with more detail than traditional methods, and at higher output resolution when upscaling is used. An example of this is shown in Figure 7.55. This especially shows why the unified approach is important for keeping high-resolution detail (see Figure 7.53).

Ray Reconstruction also significantly improves the responsiveness to changes in lighting, with a significant reduction in lighting lag. This is most noticeable in scenes with changing lights.

Input buffers	Description
Noisy color	Radiance in HDR
Albedo	Diffuse reflectivity of material
Specular albedo	Pre-integrated specular BRDF, depending on roughness, reflectivity at normal incidence, and $N \cdot V$ [Hirvonen et al. 19]
Roughness	Linear roughness (GGX normal distribution function)
Shading normal vectors	World-space normal
First bounce ray distance	In world space
Depth	HW depth or linear depth
Motion vectors	Pixel-space 2D motion vectors

Input parameters	Description
Projection jitter	Vector from sample to pixel center, in pixels
View matrix	Using D3D convention
Projection matrix	Using D3D convention

Output buffers	Description
Denoised and upscaled color	Radiance in HDR

Table 7.8. Input buffers, parameters, and output buffers of DLSS-RR.

Figure 7.54. NRD + DLSS-SR (left) and DLSS-RR (right). Ray Reconstruction is able to reproduce small-scale lighting detail better than handcrafted denoisers, including contact shadows and diffuse lighting.

Figure 7.55. NRD + DLSS-SR (left) and DLSS-RR (right). Ray Reconstruction can reconstruct sharp reflection due to unified denoising and upscaling giving more context to the denoiser.

7.13.2 Performance

Although the main objective of Ray Reconstruction is image quality, and not performance, using Ray Reconstruction can give performance benefits. This benefit is achieved by replacing many handcrafted denoising algorithms with a single unified denoiser. The speed benefit depends on how many handcrafted denoising algorithms are used and how expensive they are. The runtime of Ray Reconstruction is fixed regardless of the number of lighting effects in the game.

Table 7.9 presents the configurations we used for testing, and Table 7.10 shows the FPS difference with Ray Reconstruction enabled and disabled in Ray Tracing: Overdrive mode. In general, using unified reconstruction has a slight performance benefit of 0–4%. Lower-end graphics cards can however benefit more, especially when DLSS Frame Generation (FG), discussed further in Section 7.14.1, is used. This is due to the lower video memory cost of unified denoising, versus DLSS-SR and NRD combined.

GPU	Resolution	DLSS-SR Mode
GeForce RTX 4060	1080p	Quality
GeForce RTX 4070	1440p	Balanced
GeForce RTX 4080	2160p	Performance
GeForce RTX 4090	2160p	Performance

Table 7.9. Default resolutions and DLSS-RR modes per GPU.

FPS	GeForce RTX 4060	GeForce RTX 4070	GeForce RTX 4080	GeForce RTX 4090
Without DLSS-FG				
DLSS-SR + NRD	34	48	50	58
DLSS-RR	37	49	51	60
Speedup	1.09	1.02	1.02	1.03
With DLSS-FG				
DLSS-SR + NRD	59	78	77	94
DLSS-RR	71	78	80	94
Speedup	1.20	1.00	1.04	1.00

Table 7.10. Ray Reconstruction FPS in *Cyberpunk 2077*'s Ray Tracing: Overdrive mode compared to traditional denoising and upscaling (DLSS-SR + NRD), with DLSS Frame Generation enabled or disabled. Ray Reconstruction is a slight speed improvement in most cases.

In other ray tracing modes, the performance benefit is smaller. This depends on how many denoisers are active, lowering the cost of traditional denoising.

7.13.3 Challenges

As we discussed earlier, Ray Reconstruction is able to utilize the patterns of noise and correlations within guide buffers to figure out signal from the noise, providing a high-quality denoised image. However, as the denoiser utilizes these correlations between the guide buffers in a very efficient way, it is very easy for bad inputs to cause unintended denoiser behavior. These kinds of bad inputs can be roughly put into two categories: correlated sampling and screen-space filtered effects. Most of the issues are caused by post-processing passes that operate on noisy data.

Correlated Sampling In the context of denoising and image reconstruction, *correlated sampling* means noise patterns that are either biased in some way or significantly different from white noise. This kind of correlated sampling can be caused by many different effects or methods used in a renderer.

In *Cyberpunk 2077*, blue noise sampling, with pre-generated blue noise, is used for many different effects in both ray tracing and path tracing modes. Although this is good practice in general, this can cause issues with Ray Reconstruction. Typically, blue noise textures have a limited period, and Ray Reconstruction can detect this, resulting in the sampling pattern becoming visible in the output. This was fixed by replacing blue noise with a xxHash32-based hash function, which has excellent statistical properties [Jarzynski and Olano 20], when Ray Reconstruction is enabled. The hash function is shown in Listing 7.11.

```
uint xxhash32(uint4 p)
{
    const uint PRIME32_2 = 2246822519U, PRIME32_3 = 3266489917U;
    const uint PRIME32_4 = 668265263U, PRIME32_5 = 374761393U;
    uint h32 = p.w + PRIME32_5 + p.x*PRIME32_3;
    h32 = PRIME32_4*((h32 << 17) | (h32 >> (32 - 17)));
    h32 += p.y * PRIME32_3;
    h32 = PRIME32_4*((h32 << 17) | (h32 >> (32 - 17)));
    h32 += p.z * PRIME32_3;
    h32 = PRIME32_4*((h32 << 17) | (h32 >> (32 - 17)));
    h32 = PRIME32_2*(h32^(h32 >> 15));
    h32 = PRIME32_3*(h32^(h32 >> 13));
    return h32^(h32 >> 16);
}
```

Listing 7.11. xxHash32 hash function used for random sampling [Jarzynski and Olano 20].

Using GPU hash functions is done in such a way that spatial and temporal correlations are minimized between pixels and between lighting effects (including different ray bounces). This can be done when using a $4 \rightarrow 1$ hash function (as above), by assigning the frame index as input x, pixel coordinates as inputs y and z, and a unique ID for each effect as input w.

Additional sampling-related challenges also needed to be solved for normal ray tracing modes. The light sampling used in ray-traced lighting (in non–path tracing modes) uses a shared-memory tile-based culling method. This method introduces a slight bias to the output, visible when accumulating the output over many frames. Though this is significantly blurred with the traditional denoising pipeline, Ray Reconstruction detects this correlation, resulting in the bias being visible in the output. The solution was to remove this shared-memory tile optimization and perform per-pixel light sampling when Ray Reconstruction is on. The trade-off is having a somewhat more noisy image for Ray Reconstruction to denoise.

The game also utilizes checkerboarded lighting in ray tracing modes. To the denoiser, this checkerboarded lighting looks like a heavy sample correlation, resulting in artifacts. The solution when Ray Reconstruction was enabled was to change the rendering method to stochastically sample half-resolution lighting, operating like Russian roulette in path tracing. Each frame, every pixel has an independent 50% chance of being sampled, and if sampled, the radiance of the sample is boosted by the inverse sampling probability.

When doing stochastic random sampling of the pixels, we want to avoid the inefficient warp utilization caused by fully random sampling. Statistically, each warp would only be half-full on average when the sampling ratio is 0.5. To avoid this inefficiency, the random sampling is done in a separate compute shader. Sampled pixels are compacted to a single argument buffer. Listing 7.12 shows how this sampling and compaction is done. Arguments are first compacted using group-shared memory atomics and finally using global memory atomics. This two-step compaction is done to avoid global memory atomic contention.

```
RW_STRUCTBUFFER(uint) PixelIndexBuffer : register(u11);
RW_STRUCTBUFFER(AdaptiveSamplingData) AdaptiveSamplingDataBuffer :
    register(u12);

TEXTURE2D<float> depthTexture : register(t1);

GROUPSHARED uint s_Idx;
GROUPSHARED uint s_GroupOutputBase;

[NUMTHREADS(32, 32, 1)]
CS_MAIN(uint3 DTid: SYS_DISPATCH_THREAD_ID, uint2 groupThreadIndex:
    SYS_GROUP_THREAD_ID)
{
    const uint2 pixelPos = DTid.xy;
    const bool isFirstInGroup = (groupThreadIndex.x == 0) && (
    groupThreadIndex.y == 0);
    if (isFirstInGroup)
    {
        s_Idx = 0;
    }

    GROUP_BARRIER_GROUP_SYNC;

    uint idxInGroup = 0;
    bool addToOutput = false;

    const int2 screenSize = int2(gCommonConstants.ScreenSize.xy);
    if (pixelPos.x < screenSize.x && pixelPos.y < screenSize.y)
    {
        const float depth = depthTexture[pixelPos];
        if (!IsSky(depth))
        {
            const uint deterministicRand = xxhash32(uint4(
    gCommonConstants.FrameData.x, pixelPos.x, pixelPos.y, 59));
            const float rand = Between01(deterministicRand);

            if (rand < gCommonConstants.diffuseSamplingRatio.x)
            {
                InterlockedAdd(s_Idx, 1, idxInGroup);
                addToOutput = true;
            }
        }
    }

    GROUP_BARRIER_GROUP_SYNC;

    if (isFirstInGroup)
    {
        const uint numToAddInGroup = s_Idx;
        uint groupOutputBase;
        InterlockedAdd(AdaptiveSamplingDataBuffer[0].numRays,
    numToAddInGroup, groupOutputBase);
        s_GroupOutputBase = groupOutputBase;
    }

    GROUP_BARRIER_GROUP_SYNC;

    if (addToOutput)
    {
        const uint idx = s_GroupOutputBase + idxInGroup;
        PixelIndexBuffer[idx] = (pixelPos.y << 16) | (pixelPos.x);
    }
}
```

Listing 7.12. Random sampling and compaction for stochastic half-resolution sampling.

Screen-Space Filtered Effects Because the denoiser needs individual input samples with associated metadata, all kinds of image-level warping, reprojection, or blurring easily cause issues with denoising, with the failure mode being the denoiser letting through the noise. These kinds of effects are very common in modern post-processing pipelines, with these effects often being applied before upscaling. *Cyberpunk 2077* has an extensive post-processing pipeline, where many different effects are done. The most important warping effect in the game is weapon scopes: the scope of each weapon has its own lens characteristics, with lens distortion and chromatic aberration.

When rendering scope lenses as a post-process effect, the guide buffers are not warped according to the lens characteristics. If Ray Reconstruction is called after this effect, the guide information for each sample will be incorrect, resulting in ineffective denoising with noise pass-through. In addition, warping the noisy input with most filter kernels will spread noise across multiple pixels, resulting in correlated noise, which is difficult for the denoiser to effectively remove. The solution for this was to render certain warping effects, including weapon scopes and underwater effect, in output resolution after Ray Reconstruction. The performance effect of this is minimal, as these passes are very light compared to ray tracing and path tracing rendering.

7.14   Frame Generation

Integrating path tracing into *Cyberpunk 2077* brought huge improvements to the image quality and realism of lighting within the game, but this came with an associated performance cost that needed further help to achieve our performance target of path-traced rendering at 2160p resolution at 60 FPS on a GeForce RTX 4080. For the final push, we moved away from the rendering pipeline and looked at the final display pipeline and frame generation.

The concept of *frame generation*, or motion interpolation, is nothing new and has been a staple technology in televisions for several years. While motion interpolation in TVs does improve the perceived frame rate and hence smoothness, it is not without issues such as digital artifacts and the Soap Opera Effect [Wright 22]. To achieve the TV's native refresh rate (e.g., 120 Hz) from the original (e.g., 24/30 Hz) content, the display hardware needs to add several interpolated frames to each original frame of content, but this significantly increases input lag, or latency. Though this does not impact most users, the general fix for gamers is to disable motion interpolation while in Game Mode, which, clearly, is not ideal.

To avoid these issues, we knew frame generation needed to be integrated directly into *Cyberpunk 2077*'s game engine rather than relying on the display hardware or even the GPU to perform in isolation. NVIDIA had been developing its Deep Learning Supersampling technology for some time, and the natural evolution of the upscaling AI networks was to target frame interpolation through its AI-based convolutional autoencoder found in DLSS 3.

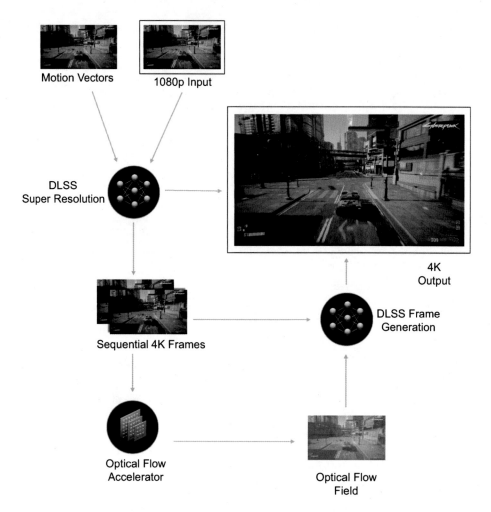

Figure 7.56. The full DLSS 3 pipeline.

7.14.1   DLSS 3 Frame Generation

DLSS 3 Frame Generation (DLSS-FG), in its most basic form, takes a pair of consecutive frames at display resolution and generates a new intermediate frame, via its deep learning network, for display by the hardware, thus increasing the frame rate by up to 2×. Figure 7.56 shows the DLSS 3 pipeline and demonstrates that AI can generate 7/8ths of the displayed pixels by transforming a 1080p input image into a pair of 2160p output images.

To combat the various artifacts often present in TV-based frame generation, the deep learning network is provided with contextual guide buffers, such as

Figure 7.57. DLSS-FG guide buffers showing the final image (top left), the HUD-less buffer (top right), motion vectors (bottom left), and depth buffer (bottom right).

depth and motion vectors as well as a HUD-less buffer (without UI components) and various camera matrices, some of which can be seen in Figure 7.57. These are used to better reconstruct the generated frame and reduce artifacts in a way that TVs are not able to.

Game engine motion vectors are geometry-based and will not encode the motion of details such as lighting and shadow detail, particles, and reflections. The game engine motion vectors are augmented by a hardware unit called the *Optical Flow Accelerator* (OFA), described in [Lin and Burnes 22]. This takes the pair of input frames and generates an optical flow field describing the direction and speed of the pixels as they move between the two frames to capture these missing details.

In Figure 7.58, the optical flow field has correctly detected that the shadow of the motor bike (in green) is in roughly the same location on the screen between the two frames, whereas the game engine motion vectors tracked the motion of the road geometry (red). Combining the two sets of motion vectors results in correctly reconstructed shadows. Frame generation without the optical flow field would cause artifacts and visible stutters in the shadow reconstruction, as shown in Figure 7.59.

Games don't always create motion vectors for all geometry, which can cause artifacts that the OFA cannot resolve. One such scenario in *Cyberpunk 2077* was found while rendering the glass lens of rifle scopes when the rifle was carried in hand, as shown in the first image in Figure 7.60. The glass lens was transparent and, as such, was not present in the G-buffer, so it had no motion vectors.

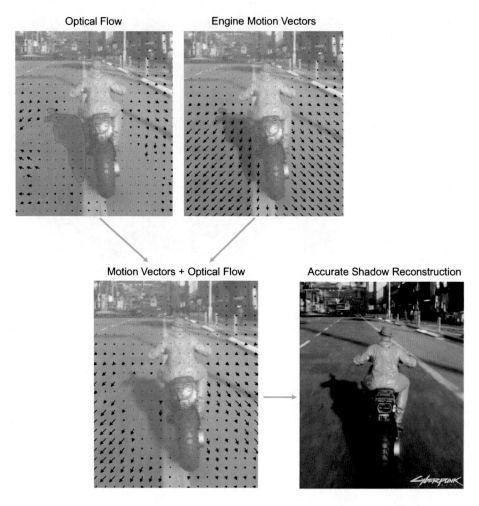

Figure 7.58. Combining motion vectors with the optical flow field for accurate motion estimation.

However, the rest of the rifle scope geometry used single-sided nontransparent materials and did have motion vectors. As a result, the motion vectors at the location of the scope did not match the glass lens, as shown in the middle image. This was further complicated when the scope was brought up to aim through. It used the same shader and material, but this time it rendered correctly as frame generation needed the motion vectors to match the geometry visible through the lens rather than the lens itself. The solution, as shown in the final image, was to generate the motion vectors for the glass lens when the gun was in hand, and to not generate the motion vectors for the lens when the scope was aimed through.

Engine Motion Vectors Miss RT Effects   Inaccurate Shadow Reconstruction

Figure 7.59. DLSS-FG without an optical flow field.

Figure 7.60. Fully rendered rifle scope (left), rifle scope with missing motion vectors (middle), and rifle scope with fixed motion vectors (right).

The final critical part of frame generation is the ability to display both the real and generated frames in a timely manner. Some solutions rely on the vertical synchronization (vsync) signal from the display to pace the displayed frames, but this can be restrictive in certain scenarios. DLSS 3 takes a more flexible approach and integrates a software pacer thread to ensure the generated frames are presented to the display at regular intervals and are independent of any vsync framerate limitations.

It is important to appreciate that frame generation is not for free so the 2× frames generated may not always result in a 2× increase in FPS. There is an associated cost for doing the work including the frame interpolation GPU time, any extra buffer copies required, creation of the guide buffers and workarounds for issues such as the missing motion vectors mentioned previously etc. These can all change from game to game. To realize an FPS gain, it should be cheaper

FPS	GeForce RTX 4060 1080p	GeForce RTX 4070 1440p	GeForce RTX 4080 2160p	GeForce RTX 4090 2160p
DLSS-FG Disabled	38	49	51	60
DLSS-FG Enabled	71	78	80	94
Speedup	1.87	1.59	1.57	1.57

Table 7.11. Performance gains from DLSS-FG in *Cyberpunk 2077* Overdrive mode.

to generate an interpolated frame than it is to fully render a real frame. The ratio between the two will influence the performance impact. In scenarios where your game is CPU-bound, the extra GPU cost of frame generation may be fully hidden by CPU work allowing the game to achieve the full 2× performance gain. In GPU-bound situations, however, the gains will be lower, and in some situations, especially with short frame times, frame generation may provide no benefit and could slow the game down.

Table 7.11 shows the final performance gain from enabling DLSS-FG, with a 1.57× performance increase on a GeForce RTX 4080 at 2160p. A speedup of 1.87× on a GeForce RTX 4060 demonstrates a greater-than-expected gain due to *Cyberpunk 2077* been partially CPU-bound at 1080p. All of the data was captured with DLSS Super Resolution and DLSS Ray Reconstruction enabled.

For more information about DLSS 3 Frame Generation, including integration guides, visit the official GitHub repository for the NVIDIA Streamline SDK [NVIDIA Gameworks 22].

7.14.2 Latency

Latency in this context is the measure of time between an input action and the time a frame is displayed in response to this input action, i.e., the time between clicking the mouse to fire a gun and the display of the muzzle flash on the screen showing the gun has been fired. The importance of low latency in competitive gaming and how aim accuracy and techniques such as "peeker's advantage" can make a competitive difference are discussed in [Schneider 20]. Outside the world of competitive e-sports, poor latency can make the game lag and feel unresponsive, breaking the immersion and impacting the gaming experience. Therefore, it is important to ensure latency is reduced as much as possible.

The different phases the input action travels to reach the display can be seen in Figure 7.61. The changes caused by the input action are first handled in the simulation phase of the engine (animation, physics, camera movements, etc.), then the render phase generates the command lists that will draw the new world state before the framebuffer is finally presented, via the graphics API, to the driver. At this point, the driver will prepare the command lists and send them

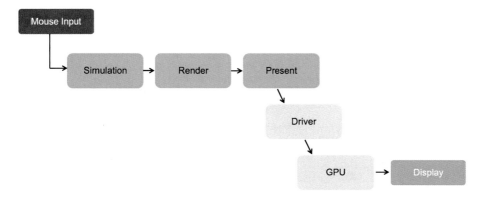

Figure 7.61. The different phases of work that contribute to system latency.

to the GPU to be executed before the framebuffer is finally presented to the display.

Increasing the time taken for any of these phases (e.g., increasing the time of the render phase by enabling path tracing) or adding extra phases to this pipeline (as required for frame generation) will increase the input latency. The latency is further complicated by bubbles in either the CPU or GPU timeline as either the GPU is the bottleneck, causing the CPU to stall, or the CPU is the bottleneck, causing the GPU to wait for work, or a combination of the two.

In the GPU-bound case, the CPU may be working ahead of the GPU by two to three frames as it queues up work on the render queue before it is blocked waiting for a new framebuffer to write to. These extra frames equate to additional latency.

In the CPU-bound case, the render submit phase is typically the bottleneck and will block the forward progress of the next simulation phase as the render submit phase of frame N is typically overlapped with the simulation phase for frame $N + 1$. At the start of a frame, the simulation phase typically processes the current input and then stalls waiting for the previous frames render phase to complete before the renderer can consume the new input from the simulation. This stall will equate to additional latency.

There are various solutions to these issues, such as frame limiters and using vsync to control the flow of frames through the engine, but GPU vendors often provide better solutions, such as NVIDIA's Reflex SDK and AMD's Anti-Lag SDK. These are tightly integrated with the GPU, the drivers, and the game to ensure the best latency reduction is achieved.

A good integration of the Reflex SDK will see the CPU and GPU well paced with each other, reducing the render queue to zero, thereby reducing the latency from multiple frames in flight. When CPU-bound, the Reflex SDK will ensure

Latency (ms)	GeForce RTX 4060 1080p	GeForce RTX 4070 1440p	GeForce RTX 4080 2160p	GeForce RTX 4090 2160p
DLSS-FG and Reflex Disabled	93	70	67	58
DLSS-FG and Reflex Enabled	67	63	61	56

Table 7.12. Latency reduction impact of enabling DLSS-FG with Reflex.

the input is consumed and processed as late as possible by the simulation phase just before the render phase needs it. Reflex also has the ability to boost the GPU frequency, which could otherwise be reduced with light GPU workloads, to further reduce the time taken to get the input through the engine and to the display.

A core concept in a Reflex integration is the *frame ID*, which is used to track the progress of the input through all of the phases shown in Figure 7.61. This caused issues in *Cyberpunk 2077* as many of the different systems within the engine had different, disconnected frame IDs and passing the wrong or inconsistent frame ID to the SDK would cause problems. In fact, using incorrect frame IDs is one of the most common integration issues seen.

As previously mentioned, frame generation introduces extra latency as two sequential frames are required before an intermediate frame can be generated. Table 7.12 shows how Reflex was used not only to remove the extra latency cost incurred, but also to improve the latency from the baseline measurement taken without frame generation enabled.

7.15   Final Performance

The goal for the Ray Tracing: Overdrive mode was to deliver a path-traced rendering experience at 2160p resolution while maintaining a smooth 60 FPS on the GeForce RTX 4080 GPU. As Table 7.14 shows, the development team not only met this target, but exceeded it. The end result is a *Cyberpunk 2077* experience that not only looks stunning with its path-traced graphics, but also delivers a silky smooth 80 FPS performance on the GeForce RTX 4080 at 2160p resolution. This was a huge achievement that was only made possible through the hard work of many people implementing the optimizations and techniques discussed throughout this article.

GPU	Resolution	DLSS-SR Mode
GeForce RTX 4060	1080p	Quality
GeForce RTX 4070	1440p	Balanced
GeForce RTX 4080	2160p	Performance
GeForce RTX 4090	2160p	Performance

Table 7.13. Display resolutions and DLSS-SR modes used to capture the final performance data.

Final Performance (FPS)	GeForce RTX 4060 1080p	GeForce RTX 4070 1440p	GeForce RTX 4080 2160p	GeForce RTX 4090 2160p
RT Overdrive	71	78	80	94

Table 7.14. Final performance figures, with DLSS-FG enabled, in *Cyberpunk 2077* Overdrive mode.

7.16   Future Directions

With all the effort, we managed to transition the fundamental part of the rendering pipeline into a modern, unified solution. While doing so, we focused on the most critical part of the equation, the opaque layers, which opened the door to more challenges. Real-time graphics will always differ from other visual media as their performance is more budget-bound. Still, at the same time, games will always push for fidelity previously only available in linear media. To continue this progress, we must address the bottleneck of bounding volume hierarchy tree updates for growingly complex and animated deformable geometry, enabling the creation of expansive, realistic environments with lifelike animations. This resolution will allow us to create even bigger worlds with true-to-life characters. However, the chase will continue, as we must also tackle the rendering of transparent materials and volumetric effects to integrate those seamlessly into our cohesive images. By decoupling these render layers from legacy techniques like reflection probes, we can unlock the potential to render particle effects and even intricate hair details in real time. This comprehensive approach will unify all crucial render layers into a harmonious solution, consistently delivering predictable and breathtaking results. As we navigate these challenges and push the boundaries of what is possible in real-time rendering, we should remain persistent in our commitment to innovation and excellence. The road ahead may be daunting, but even considering the authors' bias, we can say that determination has proved to be enough to feel encouraged in our path. With determination and ingenuity, we can continue to elevate visual fidelity standards in real-time graphics and create truly immersive experiences for audiences worldwide.

—Jakub Knapik

Acknowledgements

NRD RTXDI Peter Sikachev Nathan Hoobler Natalia Komovich Giovanni De Francesco
Przemyslaw Gontkowski Path-traced RTXDI DaJuan McDaniel NVIDIA Marcin Gollent Johannes Deligiannis NRD Natalia Komovich
Ivan Zinkevich George Santo Oleg Arutiunian Cyberpunk 2077 Jon Kennedy Tim Cheblokov
Seth Williams NVIDIA Rasmus Barringer Jakub Knapik Tim Green Jakub Boksansky DLSS RTXGI Pawel Kozlowski
Juho Marttila Matt Rusiniak Rasmus Barringer Marcin Kulikowski Bartosz Cetlinski
Shaveen Kumar Cezary Bella Michael Songy Vitaly Kurin DLSS Mikolaj Mik
Vladimir Mulabaev Giovanni De Francesco NVIDIA NVIDIA Juha Sjoholm
Vignesh Gunasekaran Benjamin Hirsch Mikolaj Mik Edward Liu NVIDIA Bartlomiej Dybisz
Dane Johnston Alexey Mastov DLSS Piotr Gutaker Dmitrii Zhdan Dmitry Pekunev
Michael Murphy DLSS Michael Songy NVIDIA
Cezary Bella Tim Cheblokov NRD Dean Bent Path-traced
George Scotto NRD Matt Rusiniak DLSS Juho Marttila Lukasz Iwanski RTXGI
Tim Green Nikolay Shadrin Michal Witanowski Martin Stich RTXGI Cezary Bella Juha Sjoholm
Mateusz Gajdzik Kirill Artyomin Shaveen Kumar Jaakko Haapasalo RTXGI Tim Green Edward Liu DLSS
Fedor Gatov Khariton Kantiev Alexey Panteleev RTXDI Charles Tremblay-Corbeil Pawel Kozlowski Marcin Gollent Leroy Sikkes Michael Murphy
Dmitrii Zhdan Piotr Gutaker Jon Kennedy Juha Sjoholm Jan Hernanowicz Michael Murphy Seth Williams Martin Stich
CD Projekt RED Cyberpunk 2077 Rafal Nowakowski Tim Green RTXGI RTXGI NRD Path-traced
CD Projekt RED Jon Story Kacper Kosciennik Nathan Hoobler Fedor Gatov Johnny Costello Alexey Barkovoy
Ray-traced Ray-traced Benjamin Hirsch Nikolay Shadrin NRD Seth Williams Evgeny Makarov Kamil Nowakowski Alexey Mastov
Jakub Knapik Dean Bent Oleg Arutiunian Ray-traced Dean Bent NVIDIA
Evgeny Makarov Cyberpunk 2077

Bibliography

[Akenine-Möller et al. 21] Tomas Akenine-Möller, Cyril Crassin, Jakub Boksansky, Laurent Belcour, Alexey Panteleev, and Oli Wright. "Improved Shader and Texture Level of Detail Using Ray Cones." *Journal of Computer Graphics Techniques* 10:1 (2021), 1–24. http://jcgt.org/published/0010/01/01/.

[AMD 22] AMD. "AMD FidelityFX Super Resolution 2.0." GPUOpen, 2022. https://gpuopen.com/fsr2/.

[Bitterli et al. 20] Benedikt Bitterli, Chris Wyman, Matt Pharr, Peter Shirley, Aaron Lefohn, and Wojciech Jarosz. "Spatiotemporal Reservoir Resampling for Real-Time Ray Tracing with Dynamic Direct Lighting." *ACM Transactions on Graphics (SIGGRAPH 2020)* 39:4 (2020), 148:1–148:17.

[Boisse 23] Guillaume Boisse. "Two-Level Radiance Caching." Presented at Game Developers Conference, 2023. https://gpuopen.com/gdc-presentations/2023/GDC-2023-Two-Level-Radiance-Caching-GI.pdf.

[Brinck et al. 21] Andreas Brinck, Xiangshun Bei, Henrik Halen, and Kyle Hayward. "Global Illumination Based on Surfels." Presented at SIGGRAPH, 2021. https://www.ea.com/seed/news/siggraph21-global-illumination-surfels.

[Dammertz et al. 10] Holger Dammertz, Daniel Sewtz, Johannes Hanika, and Hendrik P.A. Lensch. "Edge-Avoiding À-Trous Wavelet Transform for Fast Global Illumination Filtering." In *Proceedings of the Conference on High*

Performance Graphics, p. 67–75. Eurographics Association, 2010. https://jo.dreggn.org/home/2010_atrous.pdf.

[Gameworks 24] NVIDIA Gameworks. "RTXGI 2.0 SDK." GitHub, 2024. https://github.com/NVIDIAGameWorks/RTXGI.

[Heitz 18] Eric Heitz. "Sampling the GGX Distribution of Visible Normals." *Journal of Computer Graphics Techniques* 7:3 (2018), 1–13. https://jcgt.org/published/0007/04/01/.

[Hirvonen et al. 19] Antti Hirvonen, Atte Seppälä, Maksim Aizenshtein, and Niklas Smal. "Accurate Real-Time Specular Reflections with Radiance Caching." In *Ray Tracing Gems: High-Quality and Real-Time Rendering with DXR and Other APIs*, edited by Eric Haines and Tomas Akenine-Moller, p. 571–607. Apress, 2019.

[Hooker 16] JT Hooker. "Volumetric Global Illumination at Treyarch." Presented at SIGGRAPH, 2016. https://research.activision.com/publications/archives/volumetric-global-illumination-at-treyarch.

[Jarzynski and Olano 20] Mark Jarzynski and Marc Olano. "Hash Functions for GPU Rendering." *Journal of Computer Graphics Techniques* 9:3 (2020), 21–38. http://jcgt.org/published/0009/03/02/.

[Kajiya 86] James Kajiya. "The Rendering Equation." *ACM SIGGRAPH Computer Graphics* 20:4 (1986), 143–150. https://dl.acm.org/doi/10.1145/15886.15902.

[Kawiak et al. 22] Robert Kawiak, Hisham Chowdhury, Rense de Boer, Gabriel Neves Ferreira, and Lucas Xavier. "Intel Xe Super Sampling (XeSS): An AI-Based Upscaling for Real-Time Rendering." Presented at Game Developers Conference, 2022. https://www.intel.com/content/www/us/en/content-details/726651/intel-xe-super-sampling-xess-an-ai-based-upscaling-for-real-time-rendering.html.

[Lagarde 14] Sebastien Lagarde. "Moving Frostbite to Physically Based Rendering 3.0." Presented at SIGGRAPH, 2014. https://seblagarde.files.wordpress.com/2015/07/course_notes_moving_frostbite_to_pbr_v32.pdf.

[Lin and Burnes 22] Henry C. Lin and Andrew Burnes. "NVIDIA DLSS 3: AI-Powered Performance Multiplier Boosts Frame Rates by up to 4X." NVIDIA GeForce, 2022. https://www.nvidia.com/en-us/geforce/news/dlss3-ai-powered-neural-graphics-innovations/.

[Liu 20] Edward Liu. "DLSS: Image Reconstruction for Real-Time Rendering with Deep Learning (Presented by NVIDIA)." Presented at Game Developers Conference, 2020. https://www.gdcvault.com/play/1026697/DLSS-Image-Reconstruction-for-Real.

[MacArthur and Stich 20] Jim MacArthur and Martin Stich. "Profiling DXR Shaders with Timer Instrumentation." NVIDIA Technical Blog, 2020. https://developer.nvidia.com/blog/profiling-dxr-shaders-with-timer-instrumentation/.

[Majercik et al. 19] Zander Majercik, Jean-Philippe Guertin, Derek Nowrouzezahrai, and Morgan McGuire. "Dynamic Diffuse Global Illumination with Ray-Traced Irradiance Fields." *Journal of Computer Graphics Techniques* 8:2 (2019), 1–30. http://jcgt.org/published/0008/02/01/.

[Muller et al. 21] Thomas Muller, Fabrice Rousselle, Jan Novak, and Alexander Keller. "Real-Time Neural Radiance Caching for Path Tracing." *ACM Transactions on Graphics* 40:4 (2021), 36:1–36:16. https://doi.org/10.1145/3450626.3459812.

[NRD 22] NRD. "NVIDIA Gameworks/NRD SDK." GitHub, 2022. https://github.com/NVIDIAGameWorks/RayTracingDenoiser.

[NVIDIA Gameworks 22] NVIDIA Gameworks. "Streamline SDK." GitHub, 2022. https://github.com/NVIDIAGameWorks/Streamline.

[Ouyang et al. 21] Yaobin Ouyang, Shiqiu Liu, Markus Kettunen, Matt Pharr, and Jacopo Pantaleoni. "ReSTIR GI: Path Resampling for Real-Time Path Tracing." *Computer Graphics Forum (Proceedings of High Performance Graphics)* 40:8 (2021), 17–29.

[Schied et al. 17] Christoph Schied, Anton Kaplanyan, Chris Wyman, Anjul Patney, Chakravarty R. Alla Chaitanya, John Burgess, Shiqiu Liu, Carsten Dachsbacher, Aaron Lefohn, and Marco Salvi. "Spatiotemporal Variance-Guided Filtering: Real-Time Reconstruction for Path-Traced Global Illumination." In *Proceedings of High Performance Graphics*, pp. 2:1–2:12. Association for Computing Machinery, 2017. https://research.nvidia.com/publication/2017-07_spatiotemporal-variance-guided-filtering-real-time-reconstruction-path-traced.

[Schneider 20] Seth Schneider. "Introducing NVIDIA Reflex: Optimise and Measure Latency in Competitive Games." NVIDIA GeForce, 2020. https://www.nvidia.com/en-gb/geforce/news/reflex-low-latency-platform/.

[Wright 21] Daniel Wright. "Radiance Caching for Real-Time Global Illumination." Presented at SIGGRAPH, 2021. https://advances.realtimerendering.com/s2021/Radiance%20Caching%20for%20real-time%20Global%20Illumination%20(SIGGRAPH%202021).pptx.

[Wright 22] Gavin Wright. "Soap Opera Effect (Motion Interpolation)." TechTarget, 2022. https://www.techtarget.com/whatis/definition/soap-opera-effect-motion-interpolation.

[Yang et al. 20] Lei Yang, Shiqiu Liu, and Marco Salvi. "A Survey of Temporal Antialiasing Techniques." *Computer Graphics Forum* 39:2 (2020), 607–621.

[Zhdan 21] Dmitry Zhdan. "ReBLUR: A Hierarchical Recurrent Denoiser." In *Ray Tracing Gems II: Next Generation Real-Time Rendering with DXR, Vulkan, and Optix*, edited by Adam Marrs, Peter Shirley, and Ingo Wald, pp. 823–844. Apress, 2021.

Real-Time Ray Tracing of Large Voxel Scenes

Russel Arbore, Jeffrey Liu, Aidan Wefel,
Steven Gao, and Eric Shaffer

Figure 8.1. A sample render from the Illinois Voxel Sandbox.

8.1 Introduction

Geometry representation is a fundamental concern of almost all computer graphics applications. In modern rendering engines, triangles are the most common geometry representation because they compactly represent an explicit surface and are computationally efficient to rasterize. Additionally, triangles have proven to be effective for decades, enabling techniques such as skeletal animation and compute-driven rendering. However, triangles fundamentally represent volumes implicitly. This is a limiting factor when an application demands volumetric rendering and simulation.

Voxels (short for volumetric elements) are an alternative geometric representation that explicitly represents volumetric data. A voxel can be thought of as a 3D pixel. It represents a unit-cube volume with associated data. Similar to triangles, this data can be customized. However, unlike triangles, where this data only exists at the surface of an object, a voxel representation stores data at regular intervals covering a 3D volume. These properties have made voxels popular for volumetric rendering, medical visualization, fluid simulation, and highly interactive worlds. A well-known use of voxels is in the extremely popular game *Minecraft*, where the world consists of modifiable "blocks."

Despite their advantages, voxels have historically been less popular in real-time 3D graphics than triangles. Voxel representations often have hefty memory requirements as they represent data across a volume rather than across a surface. Furthermore, surface rasterization is a major component of most computer graphics applications, so explicitly surfaced geometries, like triangles, are preferred over implicitly surfaced geometries, like voxels. Finally, computed animation techniques, such as skeletal animation, work best for nonuniform model representations, such as triangle meshes and signed distance fields.

Recent advances in real-time ray tracing provide a new opportunity to explore the potential of using voxels as a primary geometry representation. Unlike rasterization, ray tracing has proven to be efficient at rendering both surface and volume geometries. Throughout this article, we will explore how voxel representations work, how they interact with recent advances in real-time ray tracing, how to manage the memory required for massive scenes, and how to create voxel geometries. We will discuss these topics in the context of the Illinois Voxel Sandbox (IVS), a voxel engine built to interactively render large voxel scenes. In this engine, we use the Vulkan API to build a framework that can flexibly support different voxel representations.

8.2   History and Related Work

Voxels have a long history of use in computer graphics. One of the first publications relevant to IVS described a *DDA* (Digital Differential Analyzer) algorithm for ray marching against voxels [Amanatides and Woo 87]. The key contribution of the paper was to adapt an algorithm traditionally used for rasterizing lines to instead march a ray with no preferred axis. A more thorough discussion of this algorithm can be found in Section 8.4.

A seminal work in voxel storage formats was introduced in 2010 [Laine and Karras 10]. This paper developed a practical implementation of sparse voxel octrees (SVOs) for use on the GPU and detailed a storage format with a packed node representation and a ray tracing algorithm for rendering SVOs. The original motivation for this paper was rendering complex, originally triangle-based, geometry—to avoid the blockiness of voxels, the authors included "contour" information in voxels. This allows storing a "slab" around a complex geometry inside a voxel, which is used during ray tracing to represent a more refined shape. The authors also introduced a scheme where internal nodes in the octree can store a single child pointer, rather than eight—all children nodes of an internal node must be stored sequentially, where the child pointer of the internal node points to the first child. More details on SVOs can be found in Section 8.3.

The GigaVoxels system [Crassin et al. 09] is another important voxel rendering system, which supports dynamic rendering of voxel objects stored as SVOs. It also generalizes SVOs in one sense by enabling N^3 children per node, where $N = 2$ would represent a standard SVO. Another key contribution of the GigaVoxels system is to upload voxels to the GPU only when needed for rendering. Nodes in an SVO are organized in an LRU (least recently used) cache, so nodes that have not been referenced recently will have their memory recycled for newly uploaded nodes. As a result, GigaVoxels is capable of rendering scenes containing billions of voxels, which may not fit entirely on the GPU at once. For more details on how IVS handles voxel uploading and unloading, see Section 8.5.

The voxel systems described above are just a sample of the ever-growing number of projects found in professional, academic, and hobbyist settings. Voxels have arguably been most popularized by the game *Minecraft*, where voxels are primarily used for their simulation capabilities and are the basis of an interactive sandbox world. Voxels in the world, called blocks, are rendered by assembling and rasterizing a triangle mesh. Other objects in the world are rasterized models in the "style" of voxels. More recently, the game *Teardown* builds worlds out of smaller voxels. Individual objects are fracturable and obey rigid body physics, leading to a highly interactive environment. Each object is rendered by rasterizing their associated bounding box—the fragment shader then performs DDA ray marching against voxels in a 3D texture per object. The increase in the number of voxels between these applications necessitates different approaches to rendering: rasterization scales more poorly than ray tracing for rendering large amounts of voxels, so as scenes represent more detailed geometries, it is unsurprising that ray tracing-based methods are introduced. Voxels are also used for certain medical visualizations. Certain medical imaging technologies produce large spatial datasets, such as CT and MRI scans. These scans take multiple 2D image slices that are spatially adjacent. When concatenated, a volumetric dataset is formed, which needs to be rendered and displayed for analysis by medical professionals. A comprehensive study of 3D visualization techniques for medical applications can be found in [Zhou et al. 22].

8.3 Voxel Formats

A principal concern when using voxels is storage. Unlike triangular models, where the explicit surface representation grows roughly quadratically with respect to the model's detail in one dimension, voxel models explicitly represent a volume that grows cubically. Additionally, for rendering, a large voxel resolution is needed in practice to avoid an overly "blocky" look. This has motivated a large body of work in representing voxel volumes as efficiently as possible.

While storage size is a chief concern of any voxel format, we'd also like to render voxel models stored in these formats at interactive frame rates. Thus, another concern for all of the formats we discuss is how quickly they are ray-marched. There is sometimes a trade-off between memory compression and rendering performance, which we illustrate below.

8.3.1 Regular Grids

The most naive voxel storage format is a regular grid. This is stored simply as a 3D array, where each voxel in the volume is stored sequentially in memory. In GPU memory, this can also be stored as a 3D texture. This may change the voxel storage order in memory, but this is not usually visible to the programmer. This format has several advantages: Most importantly, it is very simple. It is also quite fast to ray-march small- to medium-sized models in this format—for a more in-depth discussion of how to ray-march all of the formats described, see Section 8.4. Additionally, it is the most straightforward representation to edit. However, because its memory usage scales cubically with the level of detail of the model, it quickly becomes impractical to store larger volumes as a regular grid. Figure 8.2 shows a slice of a raw grid.

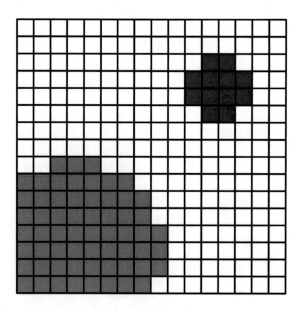

Figure 8.2. Voxels stored in a raw grid. Each grid cell is uniformly sized, and contains a single homogeneous voxel value. Only a 2D slice of the volume is shown.

8.3.2   N-Level Grids

The first compressed format we will discuss is the *two-level grid*. This format is similar to a regular grid, except that there is an additional layer of indirection applied. The regular grid of voxels is divided into larger, equally sized regions, often called *chunks*. Each chunk either points to a small grid of voxels inside the chunk or is empty and points to nothing. Each nonempty chunk points to a grid with uniform size. If the represented volume is highly sparse, and loosely the size of chunks is smaller than the average size of sparse regions, then significant storage savings can be realized. There is a trade-off in chunk size. Forming smaller chunks means that more empty voxels will fall inside of empty chunks, and thus will incur no storage cost. However, more chunks will then be needed to cover the same resolution, and chunks themselves incur a storage overhead. Additionally, during ray marching, we can skip over empty chunks: if we shrink chunks, rays will skip over smaller distances when encountering empty chunks. This format is surprisingly effective at reducing both storage and ray marching costs for certain volumes. There are two common extensions made to this format. First, it can be extended into an N-level grid—instead of one upper-level grid, we can create multiple nesting levels. Second, we can compress chunks that contain uniform voxel values as well as empty chunks. By storing just the one voxel value inside the chunk, we include empty chunks in the same scheme by setting their value to the "empty" value. However, N-level grids suffer from the same trade-offs as two-level grids. Bumping resolution either increases chunk sizes, which means fewer chunks will be uniform, or increases the number of chunks, increasing the overhead of chunking. A popular N-level grid implementation can be found in the OpenVDB library. Figure 8.3 shows a slice of a two-level grid.

8.3.3   Sparse Voxel Formats

Although N-level grids can compress uniform chunks, those uniform chunks must be of a certain size. Voxel volumes often have fine detail that is far smaller than the size of a chunk. This results in missed compression opportunities near heterogeneities in the volume. However, we cannot globally shrink the size of chunks arbitrarily. The core idea behind the sparse voxel octree is to flexibly size uniform chunks. A voxel volume is represented as a tree, where leaf nodes store voxel values. Based on the distance to the root, a leaf node may represent a single voxel or a uniform chunk of voxels. The height of the tree is the log of the maximum resolution. Internal nodes in the tree represent a subregion of the volume and have eight children, representing the octants that evenly divide the subregion along three dimensions. In practice, many SVO implementations don't explicitly store "empty" child nodes, so internal nodes can have less than eight children. In implementations based on [Laine and Karras 10], an internal node stores a single pointer to a slice of child nodes. The amount and spatial position of the child nodes are determined by a valid mask of 8 bits stored in

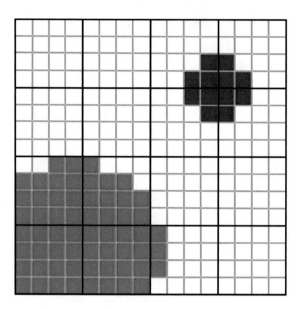

Figure 8.3. Voxels stored in a two-level grid. The black grid is the upper-level grid, and the cyan grid is the lower-level grid. In the bottom-level grid, the grid cells are individual voxels, just like in the raw grid case. Only a 2D slice of the volume is shown.

the parent node. Leaf nodes are identified by a leaf mask. A nice property of SVOs is that subregions in the tree are divided exactly when there is detail in the volume that needs to be further represented. In the worst case, SVOs can incur more storage overhead than N-level grids if a volume has no uniformity to exploit, due to needing many internal nodes to represent detailed subregions. In practice, SVOs are much better than N-level grids at compression. SVOs can benefit ray marching, as they can more precisely cull empty regions of voxels. In practice, the octree traversal and management of internal nodes can be expensive in a ray march, so grid formats can perform surprisingly well compared to SVOs for medium-sized models.

A common extension made on top of SVOs is to deduplicate nodes. SVO nodes are often redundant, such as leaf nodes representing different parts of a volume holding identical data. As described by [Kämpe et al. 13], we can convert our octree into a directed acyclic graph (SVDAG) during construction by removing all but one of these nodes and changing all references to deleted nodes to the one remaining node: see Section 8.6 for a more detailed discussion of voxel format conversion. Traversing an SVDAG is conceptually identical to traversing an SVO, but they can differ slightly in implementation. An internal SVDAG node must store multiple distinct pointers to its children, since there is no guarantee that an internal node's children in an SVDAG can be stored sequentially, unlike

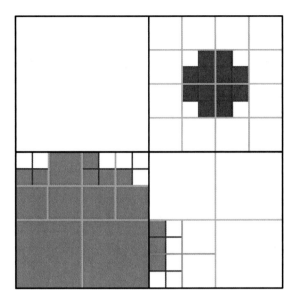

Figure 8.4. Voxels stored in a sparse voxel octree. Grid cells, representing volumes containing heterogeneous data, are various powers of two in size. Grid cells are subdivided exactly where the underlying voxel data is heterogeneous. Only a 2D slice of the volume is shown.

in SVOs. SVDAGs present a large improvement in compression over SVOs but exhibit similar ray marching performance. Figure 8.4 shows a slice of a sparse voxel structure. The visualization is identical for SVOs and SVDAGs.

8.3.4 Distance Fields

The formats discussed above are presented in ascending order of compression performance. Given that we also care about rendering performance, this begs the question of whether we can increase ray marching performance by adding information to a voxel format. A format that does this is called *distance fields* (DF). A distance field voxel volume is quite similar to a regular grid voxel volume, except each empty voxel stores a distance to the nearest nonempty voxel. Conceptually, it is clear how this accelerates ray marching; explicitly storing the distance to the nearest nonempty voxel allows rays to take fewer, larger steps during ray marching. A more detailed discussion of ray marching distance fields can be found in Section 8.4. The immediate question is how poorly this impacts model storage size. Given that a distance must be stored per empty voxel, a naive implementation of distance fields would demand adding a small number of bytes per voxel. In practice, we can often reduce or eliminate this extra storage cost depending on the exact application. Firstly, we can in practice clamp distances to integers in the range 1 to 255, so distance can be stored in a single byte. In IVS, distance fields actually take the same amount of space as regular grids, since distance fields are encoded in the otherwise scarcely used alpha channel of each voxel's color. The encoding we've chosen is that an alpha value of 0 corresponds to a solid voxel, while an alpha value of at least 1 corresponds to an empty voxel that is at least alpha distance units away from another voxel. A second question is how to measure distance: the two most common answers are Hamming distance and Euclidean distance, depending on the application. We've chosen to store Hamming distance in IVS, as this corresponds to the number of DDA steps that can be taken before potentially hitting a solid voxel.

When using different voxel representations in IVS, we observed that no single voxel format was suitable for representing all voxel models at all times: regular grids are easily editable, distance fields boast impressive ray marching performance, and SVDAGs are excellent at compression. To remain as flexible as possible, IVS supports the simultaneous use of several voxel formats.

8.4   Voxel Ray Tracing

A natural approach to rendering voxels is ray marching. As voxels represent a volume explicitly, it is conceptually simple to march a ray through space and record a hit when the volume at a certain point is nonempty. However, the answers to more specific questions are less obvious. How large should ray marching steps be? How does the choice of voxel format affect the ray marching process? How do we cast rays against many non-axis-aligned voxel volumes simultaneously? IVS demonstrates one answer to all of these questions using the Vulkan ray tracing API.

8.4.1   Broad-Phase Scanning

The Vulkan ray tracing API represents scenes as a two-level tree structure consisting of a top-level acceleration structure (TLAS) and bottom-level acceleration structures (BLAS). The TLAS contains instance references to each BLAS, which in turn contain geometric data. IVS structures a scene as a single TLAS where each voxel model corresponds to a single BLAS. Additionally, each BLAS instance inside the TLAS may contain an associated affine transformation, so objects do not have to be aligned to a global grid. We note that while nonuniform scaling is technically permissible under this setup, this may result in undesired nonlinear ray marching. We rely on hardware-accelerated ray tracing to perform intersection testing with each BLAS instance's bounding box. This is a broad-phase scan to identify which voxel objects are potential intersection candidates—at this point, we know that the ray has entered a space where there may be voxels, although it may end up passing through the space without intersecting any at all.

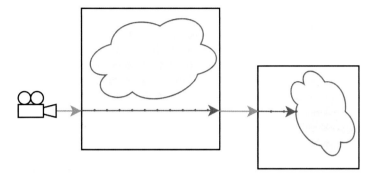

Figure 8.5. Broad-phase and narrow-phase intersection in a scene. The blue portions of the ray are the broad-phase portion of the intersection, and the red portions are the narrow-phase portion. Red ticks correspond to individual steps during ray marching.

8.4.2 Narrow-Phase Testing

Another key component of modern ray tracing execution models is the programmability of different shaders throughout a complex pipeline. More specifically, Vulkan provides programmability for ray generation, intersection tests, hit behavior, and miss behavior. We are primarily interested in the intersection and closest hit shaders, which allows us to override the default behavior of ray-triangle intersection testing and instead write software implementations to test for voxel intersections. When a potential intersection candidate is identified through the broad-phase scanning, the intersection shader is executed as a narrow-phase test to determine whether an actual voxel is hit or not. For all formats implemented in IVS, this is where voxel ray marching occurs. Figure 8.5 visualizes the difference between broad-phase and narrow-phase ray intersection.

The intersection test and hit behavior are programmable on a per-object basis. This enables the coexistence of different voxel formats with different attributes within the same scene. The format of a voxel model controls how the voxels are structured in memory, which is the chief concern of the intersection shader. The attributes of a voxel model describe what information is stored on a per-voxel basis, which is a chief concern of the closest hit shader.

8.4.3 Intersecting Regular Grids

As there are several voxel formats described in Section 8.3, there is a corresponding amount of ray marching routines implemented in intersection shaders in IVS. The simplest routine is for ray marching a regular voxel grid. It is very easy to access a voxel at any given point inside a regular grid, so the main implementation detail is how far to march the ray each step. It is simple to see that a regular step size will result in incorrect rendering: a ray intersecting the corner of a voxel may step completely over the voxel, resulting in an incorrect miss. The standard solution to this problem presents a variable step size, where a ray steps exactly the distance until it hits the face of a voxel [Amanatides and Woo 87]. After one step, the routine checks if the hit voxel is empty or not. If it's nonempty, an intersection is reported immediately. If it's empty, then the minimum distance to another voxel face is calculated, and the ray steps by that amount. This process repeats until a nonempty voxel is hit, or until the ray steps outside the bounds of the regular grid. The distance to only three voxel faces is calculated per step: the three faces on the "other side" of the voxel the ray has intersected last. This routine is quite fast in practice, as spatially local accesses to a voxel grid texture realize high cache efficiency on modern GPUs. However, this approach doesn't take advantage of large regions of empty space in a voxel model. Thus, high-resolution regular grids can be slow to ray-march. Listing 8.1 shows a pseudo-GLSL implementation of this algorithm.

```
// ray_pos should be on the border of the raw voxel volume.
bool intersect_raw(vec3 ray_pos, vec3 ray_dir) {
    ivec3 ray_voxel = ivec3(min(ray_pos, ivec3(CHUNK_WIDTH - 1,
    CHUNK_HEIGHT - 1, CHUNK_DEPTH - 1)));
    ivec3 ray_step = ivec3(sign(ray_dir));

    // Keep track of the distance to each of the three nearest
    // voxel faces.
    vec3 ray_delta = abs(vec3(length(ray_dir)) / ray_dir);
    vec3 side_dist = (sign(ray_dir) * (vec3(ray_voxel) - ray_pos) + (
    sign(ray_dir) * 0.5) + 0.5) * ray_delta;

    while (all(greaterThanEqual(ray_voxel, ivec3(0))) && all(lessThan(
    ray_voxel, ivec3(CHUNK_WIDTH, CHUNK_HEIGHT, CHUNK_DEPTH)))) {
        uint32_t data = lookup_voxel(ray_voxel);

        if (data != 0) {
            return true;
        }

        // Instead of subtracting from the side distances, add
        // to them.
        bvec3 mask = lessThanEqual(side_dist.xyz, min(side_dist.yzx,
    side_dist.zxy));
        side_dist += vec3(mask) * ray_delta;
        ray_voxel += ivec3(mask) * ray_step;
    }
    return false;
}
```

Listing 8.1. Algorithm for intersecting a ray with a raw grid of voxels.

8.4.4   Intersecting N-Level Grids

An advantage of N-level grids in terms of compression is the ability to represent large uniform regions of space compactly. We can also use this representation to more efficiently ray-march empty regions of space. Ray marching an N-level grid is conceptually similar to ray marching a regular grid. However, N-level grids have an explicit grid hierarchy that must be traversed. One can imagine ray marching an N-level grid as a recursive process: marching starts at the highest level grid, and whenever a ray hits a nonempty grid cell, the ray is marched against the next level grid inside that grid cell. A hit is recorded when the ray hits a nonempty voxel in the lowest level of the hierarchy. If no hit is found, ray marching continues at the highest level grid. In practice, N is usually fixed, so a fixed nesting of loops is programmatically sufficient for implementation.

8.4.5   Intersecting Sparse Voxel Structures

Ray marching against SVOs and SVDAGs is conceptually identical, so we will discuss them simultaneously. Unlike N-level grids, the depth of sparse voxel structures is not fixed, so actual recursion is needed. Otherwise, the ray marching process is similar: ray-march against the octants at the highest level of the structure, and on hitting a nonempty octant, recursively ray-march against that octant. On hitting a leaf node, report an intersection. A benefit of ray marching sparse voxel structures is that we can more aggressively step over large empty spaces in a voxel model. While conceptually simple, implementing ray marching for sparse voxel structures can be tricky. Recursion is forbidden in most shading languages, so an explicit stack must be maintained—this results in a larger number of memory accesses. Additionally, the control flow for ray marching against sparse voxel structures is more complex than that of the previously discussed formats. Combined, these factors mean that ray marching sparse voxel structures can be slower than expected in practice. Listing 8.2 shows a pseudo-GLSL implementation of this algorithm. Although we show the algorithm in recursive form here, the IVS implementation uses a while loop and a manually managed stack. Additionally, much of the information about a node acquired via helper functions is actually stored or derived from their parent node.

8.4.6   Intersecting Distance Fields

Unlike the other formats, distance fields are specifically designed to accelerate ray marching performance. In IVS, distance fields store a Hamming distance to the nearest nonempty voxel. We use this Hamming distance to elide voxel occupancy checks that would otherwise require dispatching texture loads. In other words, we ray-march distance fields in a similar manner as regular grids, but we unconditionally repeat the single-step procedure several times rather than a single time in between voxel occupancy checks. The number of steps taken in between checks is the Hamming distance from the last empty voxel to the nearest nonempty voxel.

```
// Helper function to iterate over the sub-volumes of a node.
vec3 subpositions(uint child) {
    return vec3(
    bool(child % 2) ? 1.0 : 0.0,
    bool((child / 2) % 2) ? 1.0 : 0.0,
    bool((child / 4) % 2) ? 1.0 : 0.0
    );
}

bool intersect_sv(vec3 ray_pos, vec3 ray_dir, uint node_id) {
    if (is_leaf_node(node_id)) {
        return true;
    }
    int direction_kind = int(ray_dir.x < 0.0) + 2 * int(ray_dir.y < 0.0)
     + 4 * int(ray_dir.z < 0.0);
    vec3 low = get_node_position(node_id);
    float diff = get_node_size(node_id) / 2.0;
    for (uint idx = 0; idx < 8; ++idx) {
        // direction_kind controls the iteration order over
        // each node's children.
        uint child = direction_kind ^ idx;
        uint child_node_id = lookup_node(stack_frame.node_id).children[
child];
        if (node_valid(child_node_id)) {
            vec3 sub_low = low + subpositions(child) * diff;
            vec3 sub_high = sub_low + diff;
            if (ray_hits_box(ray_pos, ray_dir, sub_low, sub_high) &&
    intersect_sv(ray_pos, ray_dir, child_node_id) {
                return true;
            }
        }
    }
    return false;
}
```

Listing 8.2. Algorithm for intersecting a ray with a sparse voxel volume.

8.5   Streaming Voxels

A key part of a modern rendering engine is dynamically managing which objects in a scene consume memory on the GPU, which is a scarce resource. This is usually accomplished by uploading geometry to the GPU dynamically as it becomes visible and deallocating the memory occupied by geometry that becomes obscured. Given the high memory requirements of voxel volumes, this is imperative for IVS to get right. We adopt a two-pronged approach: IVS immediately performs uploading of visible voxel models and periodically deallocates memory for obscured voxel models.

8.5.1   Chunk Loading

The first concern is how to lazily load voxel models onto the GPU, with as little overhead as possible. Based on the dynamic world the camera is in, a voxel model may first become visible on any given frame. However, a key assumption of IVS is that on the vast majority of frames, new voxel models are not revealed. Thus, we'd like to incur zero overhead on frames where no new models appear.

As described in Section 8.4, modern graphics APIs expose functionality in their ray tracing API for dynamically dispatching to different shaders based on which geometry gets hit. IVS takes advantage of this by creating bounding boxes in the ray tracing acceleration structure for unloaded models. The intersection shader for this geometry will record hits in a small structure called the *chunk request buffer* (CRB) and always fails to report an intersection. In effect, unloaded models are invisible to the camera, but report back to the engine whenever a ray hits them. IVS will then scan the CRB every frame for new chunks to load. This approach has several advantages. First, on the majority of frames where no ray hits an unloaded model, little overhead is incurred. Second, this approach integrates cleanly with IVS's ray tracing pipeline for rendering—effects such as reflection and global illumination are accounted for, and if enough indirect rays intersect with an unloaded model, that model will be requested as well.

However, there are some caveats to this approach. First, when path tracing, rays can bounce in random directions and may load more models than fit in GPU memory. This of course depends on the geometry of the scene, but is a problem in any scene that's not a confined space. The contribution of one or two rays is usually not worth loading a whole voxel model. Thus, IVS will record the number of rays that hit an unloaded model in the CRB: only unloaded models that record a number past some threshold will be loaded.

Second, accesses to the CRB must be atomic—there are potentially many intersection shader instances that will be modifying a given CRB entry. This is especially true if a new voxel model appears on screen close to the camera: depending on the screen resolution, there may be thousands of intersection shader instances contending for one CRB entry. Fortunately, this contention only occurs on frames where a model is visible on screen that wasn't visible before—for most interactive applications, these frames constitute a drastic minority. Thus, the contention bottleneck doesn't constitute a fatal blow to overall responsiveness.

Third, there is the question of how exactly to structure the CRB. The approach IVS takes is to have a small CRB (32 entries), where each entry stores a model ID and a hit count. On a hit to an unloaded model, the model ID is taken modulo the size of the CRB, and that CRB entry has its model ID updated and its hit count incremented. This means the CRB in IVS is approximate—a model hit with one ray may get loaded if it "hijacks" the CRB entry of a model with many ray hits. In practice, this is tolerable because IVS scans the CRB every frame, so the model with many ray hits would be loaded one frame later. Furthermore, the size of the CRB can be increased to reduce the probability of unwanted "hijacks," but regardless, these unwanted models are likely to be quickly deallocated.

8.5.2 Chunk Unloading

Another concern is how to deallocate the memory of models that have become non-visible. Unlike loading unloaded models, there is less urgency here as non-visible models do not affect the resultant render. Checking for non-visible loaded models is significantly more expensive than detecting now-visible unloaded models. IVS creates a much larger *chunk deallocation buffer* (CDB), since we need an exact count of how many rays hit every model—every ray hit must atomically increment a CDB entry, causing contention. To address these challenges, IVS performs deallocation in a separate pipeline from rendering, where all closest hit shaders are swapped out for a shader that updates the CDB. This pipeline only executes periodically. Similarly to chunk loading, there is a threshold for the number of rays, below which chunks will be unloaded. To prevent excessive back-and-forth loading and deallocating, this threshold is significantly smaller than the threshold to load chunks.

Together, these mechanisms maintain relevant models in GPU memory, while preventing wasted usage by non-visible models. There are a couple of tweakable parameters that control the behavior of this system. On the loading side, the primary parameter is the hit threshold for loading chunks. IVS implements a simple path tracer, meaning this threshold needs to be fairly high - it is currently set to 128 hits. For deallocation, the two main parameters are the hit threshold and the period of the pipeline. In IVS, the hit threshold is 4, and the period is every 128 frames. Although unexplored in IVS, it may make sense to dynamically adjust these parameters. For example, if GPU memory usage is approaching peak capacity, it may make sense to run deallocation more frequently or to raise both thresholds. Figure 8.6 visualizes the voxel streaming process at a high level.

8.6   Creating Voxel Models

In order to render a scene composed of voxel models, one needs to first acquire voxel models. Depending on the application, voxel volume data can be easily acquired. For medical applications, data recorded by multi-slice scanning technologies, such as MRI and CT scans, is already resident in a volumetric form, so little conversion is necessary. In some applications, volumetric data is generated procedurally, such as in games like *Minecraft*. Generating terrain is a well-studied problem that we won't discuss much here, except to make clear that voxels are a natural fit for this task. There also exist tools for creating voxel models from scratch, such as MagicaVoxel.

8.6.1   Voxelization

For IVS, one of our goals was to render popular models in 3D graphics literature in a voxelized format. This necessitated implementing a conversion process from triangle models to voxel models. In IVS, this process is quite simple: we loop over every triangle in a model and fill in every voxel the triangle intersects on some regular voxel grid. We handle vertex attributes by determining which point on the triangle is closest to the center of a voxel and interpolating the three vertex

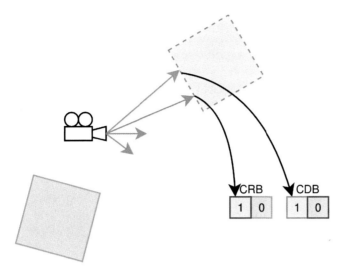

Figure 8.6. Chunk loading and unloading process. Blue rays are dispatched every frame for rendering; on hitting an unloaded chunk, such as the blue chunk, they record the hit in the chunk request buffer. Orange rays are dispatched periodically; on hitting a chunk, they record the hit in the chunk deallocation buffer. The CRB is approximate and handled on the host every frame, whereas the CDB is exact and handled periodically. The slots highlighted in red correspond to chunks that need to be requested or deallocated.

values of the triangle to calculate the voxel's data. This approach is simple to implement, but has two major drawbacks: it is slow, and it creates a thicker "shell" of voxels.

Alternatively, triangle models can be voxelized very quickly using rasterization on the GPU. The main insight needed to understand this algorithm is that rasterization solves a similar problem as voxelization: instead of converting a 3D triangle mesh into a 3D voxel grid, rasterization converts a 3D triangle mesh into a 2D pixel grid. The gist of the algorithm is to rasterize the triangle mesh in two dimensions and to determine the third by interpolating vertex coordinates in the fragment shader. The coordinate in three dimensions is then used to write the fragment attributes into the voxel buffer. More details can be found in [NVIDIA 24].

In IVS, raw voxel volumes are but one format—there also exist N-level grids, SVOs, SVDAGs, and DFs. We discuss converting from a raw voxel volume to each of these formats below.

8.6.2 Constructing N-Level Grids

Converting a raw volume to an N-level grid is fairly straightforward. The basic idea is to visit the voxels in the raw volume in the same order that a post-order traversal through the N-level grid tree would visit. For a two-level grid, this would mean traversing all of the voxels in one sub-grid before moving on to another sub-grid. When all of the voxels in a sub-grid hold the same data, the current sub-grid can be compressed to represent that voxel data directly.

8.6.3   Constructing Sparse Voxel Structures

Converting a raw volume to an SVO is a similar process, but slightly trickier. Unlike N-level grids, where the N is known to the programmer who can construct N nesting levels of loops, an SVO has variable height across the volume. Thus, the routine to construct an SVO is naturally recursive. The routine takes as argument a sub-volume of a voxel volume and returns an SVO node. Additionally, a mutable list of SVO nodes is accessible and is where the completed SVO resides. In the base case, where the sub-volume is a single voxel, the routine returns a leaf SVO node containing the voxel data. When the sub-volume is larger than a single voxel, recursively call the routine on the subdivided octants of the subregion. If all of the nodes are leaf nodes with the same voxel data, then return a leaf node with that voxel data. Otherwise, push the nonempty leaf nodes to the SVO node list, and return an internal node containing a pointer to the first nonempty leaf nodes pushed to the SVO node list. After calling this routine, push the returned root node to the end of the list. This is a more general form of the N-level grid construction algorithm, where looping over the octants corresponds to looping over the grid cells in one sub-grid. Constructing SVDAGs is extremely similar, with one main difference. In the recursive case, before pushing a node to the SVDAG node list, check if it's already somewhere in the list; if so, don't insert the node onto the list, and set the corresponding child pointer of the current internal node to the node already in the list. Since the children nodes are not necessarily sequential in memory, this means SVDAG nodes must store eight child pointers, rather than just one. IVS maintains a hash table from seen nodes to indices in the node list for deduplication.

One concern when building SVOs and SVDAGs is the memory consumption of the source raw voxel volume. It is common when constructing larger sparse voxel volumes that the corresponding raw voxel volume doesn't fix in memory. There is an algorithm for constructing sparse voxel columns from a stream of voxels rather than an entirely resident raw voxel volume [Baert et al. 14]. The trick is to stream voxels in the order visited by the recursive construction procedure. The authors identify this order as *Morton order*, which is a particular linearization of an N-dimensional grid. It happens that the Morton order is the same order as individual voxels would be visited in a post-order traversal of an SVO. The actual construction algorithm is conceptually identical, but instead of indexing into a raw voxel volume to get the next individual voxel, a Morton order iterator over voxels is iteratively consumed. The algorithm as presented in the paper also transforms the recursive routine described above into an explicit stack and loop. Listing 8.3 shows a pseudo-C++ implementation of this algorithm, adapted to constructing SVDAGs. Note that the algorithm presented in the paper also takes care to optimize the case of inserting, and then compressing, empty voxels into the SVO. Our implementation in IVS doesn't perform this optimization.

```
vector<Node> construct_svdag() {
    uint32_t power_of_two = log2(CHUNK_WIDTH);
    uint32_t bounded_edge_length = 1 << power_of_two;
    vector<vector<Node>> queues(power_of_two + 1);
    const uint64_t num_voxels = bounded_edge_length *
    bounded_edge_length * bounded_edge_length;
    vector<Node> svdag;
    map<Node, uint32_t> deduplication_map;

    for (uint64_t morton = 0; morton < num_voxels; ++morton) {
        auto [x, y, z] = morton_decode(morton);

        Node leaf_node;
        // If outside the model, set the leaf node to the empty value.
        leaf_node.leaf = lookup_voxel(x, y, z);
        queues.at(power_of_two).emplace_back(leaf_node);
        uint32_t d = power_of_two;
        while (d > 0 && queues.at(d).size() == 8) {
            Node node;
            bool identical = true;
            for (uint32_t i = 1; i < 8; ++i) {
                identical = identical && queues.at(d).at(i) == queues.at
(d).at(0);
            }

            if (identical) {
                node = queues.at(d).at(0);
            } else {
                for (uint32_t i = 0; i < 8; ++i) {
                    Node child = queues.at(d).at(i);
                    // This deduplication is the only necessary
                    // addition to construct a SVDAG instead of
                    // a SVO.
                    if (!ichild.is_empty() && deduplication_map.contains
(child)) {
                        node.children[i] = deduplication_map[child];
                    } else if (!ichild.is_empty()) {
                        uint32_t child_idx = svdag.size();
                        svdag.push_back(child);
                        node.children[i] = child_idx;
                        deduplication_map.insert({child, child_idx});
                    }
                }
            }

            queues.at(d - 1).emplace_back(node);
            queues.at(d).clear();
            --d;
        }
    }

    svdag.push_back(queues.at(0).at(0));
    return svdag;
}
```

Listing 8.3. Algorithm for constructing a sparse voxel directed acyclic graph.

8.6.4 Constructing Distance Fields

Converting a raw voxel volume to a DF is quite simple since the process just involves adding extra data to the raw voxel volume. This conversion is parameterized by a number k, which represents the maximum distance that can be stored in a voxel. The larger the k, the more aggressively we can ray-march, but the longer it will take to construct the DF. To calculate the DF, we need to calculate the distance from each voxel to the nearest nonempty voxel. This can be done in parallel for each voxel individually. For each voxel, loop over all of the voxels that are at most k voxels away, and find the closest voxel that is nonempty. That distance is the DF value for that voxel. This algorithm scales cubically both in the size of the voxel volume and in k.

8.7 Further Extensions

The techniques discussed in this article are not exhaustive. In this section, we attempt to briefly survey some recent literature related to voxel rendering and simulation.

8.7.1 Neural Representations

Scene representation not only dictates the procedures and performance of rendering, as we have discussed in Sections 8.3 and 8.4, but also presents opportunities, if aptly chosen, in inverse rendering and the optimization problems that arise therefrom. With recent developments in neural-based methods for scene reconstruction and generation, volumetric rendering and voxel-based scene representation have gained a new application.

Formulating rendering as the mapping from a parameter space to the image space enables the exploration of an array of optimization problems insofar as the mapping is differentiable. Such mappings are called differentiable image parameterizations (DIP) and pertain to many of the recent neural and point-based volumetric rendering techniques, e.g., neural radiance fields (NeRF) [Mildenhall et al. 21] and Gaussian splatting [Kerbl et al. 23]. Fundamentally, both of these methods are built on top of radiance fields, which take a position and direction as input to return a color value (also known as the plenoptic function).

Although the original NeRF technique doesn't model the scene representation as a voxel grid, subsequent works have shown that radiance fields could have better convergence and rendering performance with a voxel representation. Voxel embeddings are more effective than positional encoding, and using SVOs to create a hierarchy of multilayer perceptions (MLP) improves both rendering and training time compared to NeRFs [Liu et al. 20]. Abandoning the MLP that models the plenoptic function in NeRF, a sparse voxel grid has been proposed that stores the opacity and spherical harmonics (SH) coefficients at vertices of the voxel [Fridovich-Keil et al. 22]. When ray tracing, trilinear interpolation from the vertex data can be used to calculate the corresponding color and opacity at ray intersection. PlenOctrees, an extension in representing radiance fields as voxels, utilizes an SVO that stores the SH coefficients and the opacity [Yu et al. 21]. Each ray traverses the SVO and accumulates the color computed from the SH coefficients and the ray direction. Each voxel effectively represents a discretized sample of the plenoptic function. With support for custom vertex attributes, IVS could be extended to render PlenOctrees scenes with a modified intersection shader.

Since voxels can store arbitrary volumetric data, they could also be used to store inputs for neural networks. These neural networks could be trained for a variety of tasks. For example, MLPs can be trained to perform intersection tests with better GPU occupancy [Fujieda et al. 23].

8.7.2 Animated Voxel Models

Animation is a challenge when representing models with voxel volumes. While triangle vertices may easily stretch to match deformable geometry, the rigidity of voxels is less conducive to this approach. To our knowledge, two projects attempt to address this problem.

The first [Engmark Espe et al. 19] tackles rigid-body animation. It decomposes voxel volumes into several SVO components, such that each can be animated separately via translations and rotations. The equivalent granularity in IVS is at the level of BLAS instances: an object can be broken into separate voxel volumes, each with an associated BLAS and transformation matrix.

The second [Bautembach 11] attempts a more skeletal approach to animated SVOs such that they appear deformable. This involves physically moving voxels and scaling them to avoid inter-voxel gaps. This was implemented in a rasterization-based pipeline, and it's unclear how conducive this method is for ray tracing, so we note that this work may be more difficult to implement in IVS.

An alternative form of animation that could be easily implemented on top of IVS is a "flipbook" animation. To accomplish this, an array of "voxel frames" could be provided to the engine, and the renderer could then index into the array to decide which "voxel frame" should be tested for intersection at a given timestamp. One drawback of this approach is the high memory cost: naively, the size of the animated voxel volume would scale linearly with the number of animation frames. Although unexplored in IVS, it's possible that certain voxel formats could perform "temporal" compression, in addition to spatial compression.

8.7.3 Format Extensions

All of the formats we discussed in IVS involve lossless compression. In other words, formats such as SVOs and SVDAGs will represent the exact same geometry as a raw voxel model. However, further compression can be achieved by allowing for lossy compression. SVDAGs can be extended such that similar nodes are deduplicated, even if they aren't identical [van der Laan et al. 20]. Each level creates a subtree similarity graph based on Hamming distance, and clusters of nodes are merged into the node with the highest similarity sum. Parameters can be adjusted to control compression ratio and error rate.

Compression generally makes it more difficult to interactively edit voxel scenes, because the data structures are less conducive for modification. This challenge has been addressed by introducing a hash map corresponding to the SVDAG structure [Careil et al. 20]. When a part of the voxel model is modified, the hash map can help determine whether the new geometry should create new nodes or if child pointers can be reassigned to existing geometry.

A method to fracture a single SVO into multiple SVOs uses the octree data structure to identify boundaries and separate disjoint voxel sets [Domaradzki and Martyn 18]. Furthermore, the authors also introduced a new method to detect collisions between SVOs.

8.8 Conclusions

In this article, we presented Illinois Voxel Sandbox, an extensible system for voxel rendering research (Figure 8.7 shows an example render using IVS). We described the most-used formats for storing voxel data and their trade-offs between ray marching performance and storage size. We discussed the early works that made voxel ray tracing feasible, such as [Amanatides and Woo 87] and [Laine and Karras 10]. We described several different voxel storage formats with var-

Figure 8.7. Another sample render from the Illinois Voxel Sandbox.

ious trade-offs. Regular grids are simple to implement, but memory inefficient. N-level grids allow for modest compression and intersection performance improvements. Sparse voxel formats such as SVOs and SVDAGs provide the best memory compression, but their recursive nature can lead to slower ray tracing. Meanwhile, distance fields forgo compression to maximize intersection performance. We addressed the implementation of ray marching against each of these voxel formats and ray tracing against scenes containing multiple voxel volumes. We described how to manage loading and unloading voxel data to the GPU. Finally, we discussed the methods for creating voxel data, either using domain specific techniques or by conversion from triangle data.

Voxels are an unconventional primitive for modern graphics, but their volumetric nature means they can be particularly useful in some applications. As game designers strive to build more interactive worlds, we foresee voxels playing a bigger role in simulation. Volumetric data will continue to be an important target of visualization, especially in medicine. With the growth of neural representations in graphics, it is likely that voxels will continue to play an enabling role in novel rendering techniques.

We'd like to thank Morgan McGuire for supplying various models in their computer graphics archive [McGuire 17] that we've used throughout development.

Bibliography

[Amanatides and Woo 87] John Amanatides and Andrew Woo. "A Fast Voxel Traversal Algorithm for Ray Tracing." Eurographics Technical Paper, 1987. https://api.semanticscholar.org/CorpusID:60696902.

[Baert et al. 14] J. Baert, A. Lagae, and Ph. Dutré. "Out-of-Core Construction of Sparse Voxel Octrees." *Computer Graphics Forum* 33:6 (2014), 220–227. https://onlinelibrary.wiley.com/doi/abs/10.1111/cgf.12345.

[Bautembach 11] Dennis Bautembach. "Animated Sparse Voxel Octrees." Personal website, 2011. https://bautembach.de/#asvo.

[Careil et al. 20] V. Careil, M. Billeter, and E. Eisemann. "Interactively Modifying Compressed Sparse Voxel Representations." *Computer Graphics Forum* 39:2 (2020), 111–119. https://onlinelibrary.wiley.com/doi/abs/10.1111/cgf.13916.

[Crassin et al. 09] Cyril Crassin, Fabrice Neyret, Sylvain Lefebvre, and Elmar Eisemann. "GigaVoxels: Ray-Guided Streaming for Efficient and Detailed Voxel Rendering." In *Proceedings of the 2009 Symposium on Interactive 3D Graphics and Games*, pp. 15–22. Association for Computing Machinery, 2009. http://maverick.inria.fr/Publications/2009/CNLE09.

[Domaradzki and Martyn 18] Jakub Domaradzki and Tomasz Martyn. "Procedural Fracture of Shell Objects." *Computer Science Research Notes* 2801 (2018), 1–9.

[Engmark Espe et al. 19] Asbjørn Engmark Espe, Øystein Gjermundnes, and Sverre Hendseth. "Efficient Animation of Sparse Voxel Octrees for Real-Time Ray Tracing." Preprint, arXiv.1911.06001, 2019. https://arxiv.org/abs/1911.06001.

[Fridovich-Keil et al. 22] Sara Fridovich-Keil, Alex Yu, Matthew Tancik, Qinhong Chen, Benjamin Recht, and Angjoo Kanazawa. "Plenoxels: Radiance Fields without Neural Networks." In *2022 IEEE/CVF Conference on Computer Vision and Pattern Recognition (CVPR)*, pp. 5491–5500. IEEE, 2022.

[Fujieda et al. 23] Shin Fujieda, Chih-Chen Kao, and Takahiro Harada. "Neural Intersection Function." Preprint, arXiv.2306.07191, 2023. https://arxiv.org/abs/2306.07191.

[Kämpe et al. 13] Viktor Kämpe, Erik Sintorn, and Ulf Assarsson. "High resolution sparse voxel DAGs." *ACM Transactions on Graphics* 32:4 (2013), 101:1–101:13. https://doi.org/10.1145/2461912.2462024.

[Kerbl et al. 23] Bernhard Kerbl, Georgios Kopanas, Thomas Leimkühler, and George Drettakis. "3D Gaussian Splatting for Real-Time Radiance Field Rendering." *ACM Transactions on Graphics* 42:4 (2023), 139:1–139:14. https://repo-sam.inria.fr/fungraph/3d-gaussian-splatting/.

[Laine and Karras 10] Samuli Laine and Tero Karras. "Efficient Sparse Voxel Octrees." In *Proceedings of the 2010 ACM SIGGRAPH Symposium on Interactive 3D Graphics and Games, I3D '10*, p. 55–63. Association for Computing Machinery, 2010. https://doi.org/10.1145/1730804.1730814.

[Liu et al. 20] Lingjie Liu, Jiatao Gu, Kyaw Zaw Lin, Tat-Seng Chua, and Christian Theobalt. "Neural Sparse Voxel Fields." Preprint, arXiv.2007.11571, 2020. https://arxiv.org/abs/2007.11571.

[McGuire 17] Morgan McGuire. "Computer Graphics Archive." Casual Effects, 2017. https://casual-effects.com/data.

[Mildenhall et al. 21] Ben Mildenhall, Pratul P. Srinivasan, Matthew Tancik, Jonathan T. Barron, Ravi Ramamoorthi, and Ren Ng. "NeRF: Representing Scenes as Neural Radiance Fields for View Synthesis." *Communications of the ACM (ECCV 2020)* 65:1 (2021), 99–106.

[NVIDIA 24] NVIDIA. "The Basics of GPU Voxelization." NVIDIA Developer, 2024. https://developer.nvidia.com/content/basics-gpu-voxelization.

[van der Laan et al. 20] Remi van der Laan, Leonardo Scandolo, and Elmar Eisemann. "Lossy Geometry Compression for High Resolution Voxel Scenes." *Proceedings of the ACM on Computer Graphics and Interactive Techniques* 3:1 (2020), 2:1–2:13. https://doi.org/10.1145/3384541.

[Yu et al. 21] Alex Yu, Ruilong Li, Matthew Tancik, Hao Li, Ren Ng, and Angjoo Kanazawa. "PlenOctrees for Real-Time Rendering of Neural Radiance Fields." In *2021 IEEE/CVF International Conference on Computer Vision (ICCV)*, pp. 5732–5741. IEEE, 2021.

[Zhou et al. 22] Liang Zhou, Mengjie Fan, Charles Hansen, Chris R. Johnson, and Daniel Weiskopf. "A Review of Three-Dimensional Medical Image Visualization." *Health Data Science* 2022 (2022), 9840519. https://spj.science.org/doi/abs/10.34133/2022/9840519.

Optimizing FSR 2 for Adreno

Randall Rauwendaal

9.1 Introduction

Temporal super-resolution techniques have become ubiquitous in modern AAA titles, offering both performance and fidelity improvements. While major independent hardware vendors have showcased proprietary machine learning–based super-resolution techniques such as NVIDIA Deep Learning Super Sampling (DLSS) [Liu 20] and Intel Xe Super Sampling (XeSS) [Kawiak et al. 22], only AMD FidelityFX Super Resolution (FSR) has been designed in such a manner as to work across competing hardware. Despite this, it is still designed overwhelmingly for "desktop" class discrete GPUs with high bandwidth and power requirements. In this article we analyze FSR and explore optimizations that will accelerate the FSR approach on Qualcomm® Adreno™ class mobile GPUs while retaining its general level of quality.[1]

9.2 Background

At the time of this publication, the FSR algorithm has reached version 3 with the addition of Frame Generation, adding interpolated frames between rendered frames. Though the shaders themselves do not significantly differ between FSR 2.2 and FSR 3. More notably, FSR 3 deprecated two of the optional stages of the algorithm intended to automatically generate the Reactive mask and Texture-and-Composition mask. This leaves five remaining essential stages and one optional sharpening stage based on the spatial upscaling of FSR 1 [Lottes and Garcia 21].

Our objective is to improve performance of FSR 2.2 on commonly available Adreno class mobile GPUs without significantly modifying the quality or behavior of the FSR algorithm.

9.3 Requirements

Temporal reprojection methods have strict performance requirements. They must upscale fast enough to avoid objectionable perceptual artifacts. In the case

---

[1]Snapdragon and Qualcomm branded products are products of Qualcomm Technologies, Inc. and/or its subsidiaries.

of temporal upscaling techniques, the performance cost of the algorithm must be budgeted within the savings of reducing the render resolution.

To be practical, the full cost of the upscale must be significantly less than the time saved by rendering at lower resolution. Given that at 60 FPS a frame must render in 16 ms, this represents a hard upper bound for frame execution time. Assuming half the frame time can be saved by reducing render resolution, we have at most 8 ms to work with; thus we target execution times for the full FSR 2.2 workload well less than this to complete a $2\times$ upscale from 960×540 to 1920×1080 resolution. We target devices with the Snapdragon® 8 Gen 2 GPU and newer.

9.4   Mobile vs. Discrete GPU Architecture

Despite exposing the same APIs, mobile and discrete GPU architectures face radically different design constraints. Discrete GPU architectures can draw hundreds of watts and operate at temperatures exceeding $80°$C, while mobile GPUs must operate in the single-digit watt range and keep temperatures comfortable to hold in the hand *without* the benefit of active cooling. These considerations manifest themselves in different evolutionary paths for mobile and discrete GPUs. Whereas discrete GPUs have been able to increase their compute resources and their bandwidth dramatically, the power and thermal demands of these increases are untenable in the mobile domain. Mobile GPUs must maintain their low power envelope and therefore face greater incentive to pursue less general purpose but more efficient solutions, often relying less on moving data toward compute and more on moving compute toward data.

9.5   Analysis

We took several strategies to investigating FSR: we ported the public code base to Android frameworks and captured preliminary data from a device with a Snapdragon 8 Gen 2 GPU.

In order to simplify analysis and facilitate experimentation, we post-processed the FSR shaders and generated simplified versions eliminating macro expansions and pre-processor permutations.

We captured the FSR 2.2 sample using RenderDoc [Karlsson 24] and saved the inputs and outputs of every stage as .dds files. This allowed us to validate our implementation against a known reference and determine if our modifications changed the output. These RenderDoc outputs combined with the post-processed shaders allowed us to experiment much more productively without modifying the original code base.

We also spent a good bit of time simply looking for patterns in the code that could be optimized.

9.5.1 Neighborhood Operations

One common pattern is neighborhood operations; every stage has at least one neighborhood operation:

- **Compute Luminance:** There is a reduction operation over the entire image to compute the luminance value.

- **Reconstruct & Dilate:** There is a 3×3 neighborhood search for the nearest depth value.

- **Depth Clip:** There are several 3×3 neighborhood operations computing motion divergence, depth divergence, and the reactive factor.

- **Create Locks:** This stage computes thin feature confidence over a 3×3 neighborhood.

- **Reproject & Accumulate:** Finally, this stage computes a Lanczos filter over a 4×4 region.

9.5.2 Texture Gather

A typical pattern seen in FSR is an array gather followed by array processing. That is, FSR gathers a neighborhood region into an array and then processes that array. However, this is done somewhat naively, and we have several avenues to further optimize these paths. For instance, many of these "gather" operations only operate on a single channel. In this case it can be more efficient to use a `textureGather` operation to return the results from four texels at once, rather than using the `texelFetch` function four times. Note that this works best for single-channel fetches; the more channels, the less likely this optimization will provide a benefit as the `textureGather` operations must be repeated per channel.

9.5.3 Beyond Texture Gather

The `textureGather` optimization is available on pretty much all hardware, and while it should be more efficient, it may not provide a significant benefit on platforms that are not bandwidth bound. On Qualcomm Adreno GPUs we have access to functionality that can potentially provide an even greater benefit, the `vk_qcom_image_processing` extension [Leger and Zhang 22]. This extension allows us to do much more than thin out our texture fetches; it allows us to move our texture processing to where our data is, into the texture processor itself. We refer to this as the Texture-Processor-as-Image-Processor, or TPIP for short.

Support for the Vulkan extension is relatively recent (see [Lutgen 24] for necessary SDK and driver versions); however, this functionality has been exposed since 2019 on OpenCL as `cl_qcom_accelerated_image_ops` [Le et al. 19].

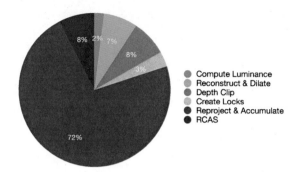

Figure 9.1. Distribution of execution time of the FSR 2.2 stages.

Effectively, the TPIP allows us to perform a convolution entirely with the texture processor, so instead of just decreasing the bandwidth between the texture processor and shader processor by a small amount, we can almost entirely eliminate it and just get the desired result back.

Unfortunately, we cannot use this method for everything; there are some critical caveats to using the TPIP. The operations performed on the texture data must be associative, meaning that you must be able to factor them out and apply them to the result of the convolution. In practice, if you are applying complex operations in the inner loop of your neighborhood processing that you cannot factor out, you probably cannot easily leverage the TPIP without changing the behavior of your algorithm.

9.6   Optimizations

Following Amdahl's law [Amdahl 67], we focus the majority of our efforts where they will do the most good, and as made evident by Figure 9.1, that is on the Reproject & Accumulate stage. Though where we find optimizations applicable to the other stages, we apply them there as well. Most of our optimization focused on reducing texture operations and texture bandwidth, though we did also attempt some simplifications to reduce ALU utilization, and performed some mathematical range analysis in order to remove unnecessary bounds checking with confidence. We examine optimizations as they apply to each required stage of the FSR algorithm.

9.6.1   Compute Luminance Pyramid

Though early testing exhibited poor performance in the Compute Luminance stage, driver and compiler improvements to the `GL_KHR_shader_subgroup_quad` extension improved performance to the point that it was the fastest stage in the entire algorithm.

9.6.2 Reconstruct & Dilate

The Reconstruct & Dilate kernel dilates both the depth buffer and the motion vectors, and it does this by searching the 3×3 neighborhood around each depth value to find the "nearest" depth, and stores that in an output buffer. To dilate the motion vectors, FSR relies on the coordinate where the nearest depth value was found and uses that to select the corresponding dilated motion vector. The depth dilation is an excellent candidate for the TPIP: we can simply configure a "nearest" sampler with the appropriate reduction mode, then in our shader call `textureBoxFilterQCOM`, as in Listing 9.1.

```
float nearestDepth = textureBoxFilterQCOM(sampler2D(r_input_depth,
    nearestSampler), iPxLrPos, vec2(3,3)).r;
```

Listing 9.1. Finding the nearest depth with `textureBoxFilterQCOM`.

And we would have nearest depth value. This results in an approximately 4–5% improvement for the stage. Unfortunately, since we have the requirement to dilate the motion vectors and the `vk_qcom_image_processing` extension does not allow us to configure a mode that provides coordinates, we must try something else. There is, however, `vk_qcom_image_processing2` [Leger 23], which provides the `textureBlockMatchWindowSAD` and `textureBlockMatchWindowSSD` functions that do provide coordinates, and we could potentially abuse these functions to achieve the desired result, but this would restrict us to Snapdragon 8 Gen 3 hardware.

9.6.3 Depth Clip

Depth Clip has a number of neighborhood operations. Note that `Compute-DepthClip` is 2×2, while `ComputeDepthDivergence`, `ComputeMotionDivergence`, and `PreProcessReactiveMasks` all have 3×3 neighborhood operations.

Compute Depth Clip The `computeDepthClip` function is a good example of a function that has too much inner-loop complexity for `vk_qcom_image_processing`, but is an ideal candidate for `textureGather`. As a 2×2 operation, we can hoist the loads out the loop and replace them with a single call to `textureGather`; see Listing 9.2.

```
ivec2 offsets[4] = { ivec2(0,1), ivec2(1,1), ivec2(1,0), ivec2(0,0) };
uvec4 uvPrevDepthVals = textureGather(usampler2D(
    r_reconstructed_previous_nearest_depth, s_PointClamp), bilinearInfo.
    iBasePos, 0);
```

Listing 9.2. We reorder the `offsets` to match the gather order in the Vulkan spec, and reorder the `fWeights` array in `GetBilinearSamplingData` to match.

Then, inside the loop, we can substitute texture loads for array accesses, as in Listing 9.3.

```
const float fPrevDepthSample = uintBitsToFloat(uvPrevDepthVals[
    iSampleIndex]);
```

Listing 9.3. Array access instead of texture load.

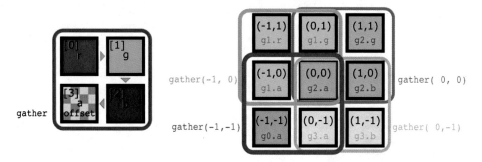

Figure 9.2. Pattern of four `textureGather`s over a 3×3 neighborhood.

3×3 Neighborhood Operations This stage also has four 3×3 neighborhood operations, all of which are unsuitable for `vk_qcom_image_processing`. These appear in `ComputeMotionDivergence`, `ComputeDepthDivergence`, and `PreProcessReactiveMasks`, though they are all handled in a near identical manner.

By replacing 3×3 texture fetches with `textureGather`s, we can reduce the gathering step of these neighborhood operations from nine operations to four. This incurs some unfortunate overhead as this fetches 16 values when we only need nine, but we generally find it is still a win, and until there is a 3×3 gather function, it is the best we can do. The overlap of the `textureGather` operations is visualized in Figure 9.2, and a mapping between the gathered quads and the array of values is shown in Listing 9.4. The performance gains for the 3×3 neighborhood operations are more variable; we see a gain in the `PreProcessReactiveMasks` function only when both the reactive samples and the transparency and composi-

```
float sampleArray[9];

// s_PointClamp uses unnormalizedCoordinate=VK_TRUE
vec4 s0 = textureGatherOffset(sampler2D(texture, s_PointClamp), pos+0.5f
    , ivec2(-1,-1), 0);
vec4 s1 = textureGatherOffset(sampler2D(texture, s_PointClamp), pos+0.5f
    , ivec2(-1, 0), 0);
vec4 s2 = textureGatherOffset(sampler2D(texture, s_PointClamp), pos+0.5f
    , ivec2( 0, 0), 0);
vec4 s3 = textureGatherOffset(sampler2D(texture, s_PointClamp), pos+0.5f
    , ivec2( 0,-1), 0);

sampleArray[6] = s1.r; sampleArray[7] = s1.g; sampleArray[8] = s2.g;
sampleArray[3] = s1.a; sampleArray[4] = s2.a; sampleArray[5] = s2.b;
sampleArray[0] = s0.a; sampleArray[1] = s3.a; sampleArray[2] = s3.b;
```

Listing 9.4. The 3×3 `textureGather` code for Figure 9.2.

Optimizations	% Improvement
Gather Depth Clip	8.52
Gather Depth Divergence	−3.68
Gather Reactive + T & C	2.42
Gather Reactive + T & C + Depth Clip	10.60
Gather Reactive + T & C + Depth Clip + Depth Divergence	9.70

Table 9.1. `textureGather` optimizations for the **Depth Clip** stage.

tion samples are gathered, while we see a small regression when depth divergence is gathered. We recommend profiling 3×3 gathers to ensure a benefit; our results are shown in Table 9.1.

9.6.4   Create Locks

Create Locks is the smallest shader, and there is only one 3×3 neighborhood operation in `ComputeThinFeatureConfidence`. We can apply our standard `textureGather` to optimize this, but it only improves performance a bit under 1%. The `ComputeThinFeatureConfidence` function looks for thin features in the 3×3 neighborhood; it accomplishes this by looking for "similarity" in each of the 2×2 corners of the 3×3 neighborhood. This could potentially be accomplished as a sophisticated example of `vk_qcom_image_processing`. Similarity could be computed with `textureBlockMatchSADQCOM` or `textureBlockMatchSSDQCOM`, while the minimum and maximum luma values of the neighborhood could be computed with two `textureBoxFilterQCOM` operations with minimum and maximum filters, respectively. However, this would change the behavior of the `ComputeThinFeatureConfidence` function as it's "similarity" calculation does not match the behavior of `textureBlockMatchSADQCOM` or `textureBlockMatchSSDQCOM`.

9.6.5   Reproject & Accumulate

As seen in Figure 9.1, the Reproject & Accumulate stage takes the lion share of execution time. This is unsurprising as it operates at the full presentation resolution (as opposed to fractional render resolution) and incurs the most memory bandwidth. Optimizing Reproject & Accumulate gives us the most bang for our buck.

ALU Optimization   One notable area of code optimization is found in the Reproject & Accumulate kernel: the `Lanczos2Ref_row` functions are used to compute the Lanczos weights as offset by motion vectors and apply these weights to the previously gathered 4×4 neighborhood.

Each invocation of `Lanczos2Ref_row` computes weights based on the last parameter, and then applies them to the color values passed in the first four parameters. Given the input `fpxFrac.x` is the same in the first four invocations, this means that the Lanczos weights are computed redundantly three out of four times; see Listing 9.5. Correcting this provides a nearly 13% improvement for the stage; see Table 9.2.

```
vec4 fColorX0 = Lanczos2Ref_row(Samples.fColor00, Samples.fColor10,
    Samples.fColor20, Samples.fColor30, fPxFrac.x);
vec4 fColorX1 = Lanczos2Ref_row(Samples.fColor01, Samples.fColor11,
    Samples.fColor21, Samples.fColor31, fPxFrac.x);
vec4 fColorX2 = Lanczos2Ref_row(Samples.fColor02, Samples.fColor12,
    Samples.fColor22, Samples.fColor32, fPxFrac.x);
vec4 fColorX3 = Lanczos2Ref_row(Samples.fColor03, Samples.fColor13,
    Samples.fColor23, Samples.fColor33, fPxFrac.x);
vec4 fColorXY = Lanczos2Ref_row(fColorX0, fColorX1, fColorX2, fColorX3,
    fPxFrac.y);
```

Listing 9.5. Redundant Lanczos invocations.

Optimization	% Improvement
Weight Factorization	12.93
Range Analysis Optimization	17.75
Range & Weight Optimizations	16.32
vk_qcom_image_processing lanczos	32.92

Table 9.2. Optimizations for the Reproject & Accumulate stage.

Range Analysis From the kernel's main to the innermost Lanczos evaluation, the code descends through six functions (see Listing 9.6), which does not itself necessarily represent a problem. What does become problematic is that many of these innermost functions are called many times, and many of them have various forms of range and bound checks. These checks are prudent given unknown inputs, but costly when innermost functions are called $20\times$; see Listing 9.6.

However, we do know the inputs, and by tracking the valid ranges for function parameters as we traverse the call stack, we can reach conclusions about the ranges of parameters passed to the innermost functions.

For instance, we discover `Lanczos2Ref_samples` parameter `fPxFrac` can only have inputs $x, y \in [0, 1], [0, 1]$, which propagates to the t parameter for `Lanczos2Ref_row`, and when `Lanczos2Ref_element` is called, the x parameter is expanded to values $\in [-2, 2]$ before the `Lanczos2RefNoClamp` input is restricted back down to values $\in [0, 2]$.

Immediately, it is obvious the `abs` function in `Lanczos2RefNoClamp` serves no purpose because the inputs are guaranteed to already be positive. In `Lanczos2Ref_element` the `min` comparison versus 2 is also redundant as its inputs are already restricted $\in [-2, 2]$. In fact, removing all range checks in `Lanczos2Ref_element` and `Lanczos2RefNoClamp` results in no change to the mean squared error of the output and improves performance substantially.

```
Reproject_and_Accumulate ()
  Accumulate ( uDispatchThreadId );
    InitParams ();
      ReprojectHistoryColor ( params , fHistoryColor ,
    fTemporalReactiveFactor , bInMotionLastFrame );
    HistorySample ( params.fReprojectedHrUv , iDisplaySize );
      16 x WrapHistory ( ClampCoord ( iPxSample , iPxOffset , iTextureSize ));
    Lanczos2Ref_samples ( samples [16] , fPxFrac );
      5 x Lanczos2Ref_row ( samples [4] , fPxFrac );
        4 x Lanczos2Ref_element (x);
          Lanczos2RefNoClamp (x);
```

Listing 9.6. Full call-stack to Lanczos evaluation. Note: Lanczos functions have been renamed to be more verbose.

QCOM Image Processing Luckily for us, the costly 4×4 Lanczos evaluation in the Reproject & Accumulate stage is one of the features of FSR to which vk_qcom_image_processing *can* be applied. At first glance, it may seem that this is unsuitable as the original algorithm dynamically computes weights for the Lanczos kernel as offset by motion vectors and vk_qcom_image_processing relies on precomputed weights.

Fortunately, vk_qcom_image_processing has a mechanism to address this well. The extension has the concept of *phases*, which allow us to compute multiple sets of weights corresponding to different sub-pixel offsets. By leveraging phases, we can compute up to 1024 unique sets of weights to apply for different pixel offsets [Lutgen 24]. The only downside is that this replaces all of our other Reproject & Accumulate optimizations, but it gives us nearly double the benefit; see Table 9.2.

9.6.6   Robust Contrast Adaptive Sharpening

We elected not to focus on the Robust Contrast Adaptive Sharpening (RCAS) stage for several reasons. First, it is not an essential stage of algorithm. Second, it is already quite well optimized. Lastly, Qualcomm has already developed a spatial upscale solution in Snapdragon Game Super Resolution (SGSR) [Li et al. 23], which is ideally suited to its hardware; SGSR is more analogous to FSR 1, though we expect it could be readily adapted to a sharpening pass competitive with RCAS.

9.7   Conclusion

We have shown there are several ways to further optimize the FSR algorithm for Adreno GPUs, though we suspect we have only scratched the surface. We have not applied our range analysis method to all stages of the algorithm, and we expect there are more opportunities to leverage vk_qcom_image_processing with further analysis. Though, at a certain point, the overhead of investigating

FSR likely exceeds the benefit of simply constructing a new super-resolution implementation designed from the ground up utilizing the capabilities of Adreno GPUs. For instance, it is questionable whether a heavyweight operation like a 4×4 Lanczos filter is even necessary Jorge Jimenez managed to reduce their filter to nine samples, then five, and finally only one [Jimenez 17].

Finally, we have not yet leveraged one of the greatest strengths of Adreno GPUs, tiled execution. Most tiling implementations are unsuitable to perform the type of neighborhood processing found in FSR due to the need to access data from neighboring tiles. Unique amongst these, Adreno architecture introduces the concept of a tile "apron," allowing tiles to store a copy of data that would otherwise be restricted to a neighboring tiles local memory. While this is a capability of the hardware, implementation will have to wait on its exposure.

Acknowledgements

Thanks to my colleagues Alex Bourd, Shangqing Gu, Mike Currington, Matt Hoffman, Wade Lutgen, and Qian Shen for their invaluable feedback and review.

Bibliography

[Amdahl 67] Gene M. Amdahl. "Validity of the Single Processor Approach to Achieving Large Scale Computing Capabilities." In *Proceedings of the April 18–20, 1967, Spring Joint Computer Conference—AFIPS '67 (Spring)*, pp. 483–485. ACM Press, 1967. https://dl.acm.org/doi/10.1145/1465482.1465560.

[Jimenez 17] Jorge Jimenez. "Dynamic Temporal Antialiasing and Upsampling in Call of Duty." Activision Research, 2017. https://research.activision.com/publications/2020-03/dynamic-temporal-antialiasing-and-upsampling-in-call-of-duty.

[Karlsson 24] Baldur Karlsson. "RenderDoc." Homepage, 2024. https://renderdoc.org.

[Kawiak et al. 22] Robert Kawiak, Hisham Chowdury, Rense de Boer, Gabriel Neves Ferreira, and Lucas Xavier. "Intel Xe Super Sampling (XeSS)—An AI-Based Super Sampling for Real-Time Rendering." Intel, 2022. https://www.intel.com/content/www/us/en/content-details/726651/intel-xe-super-sampling-xess-an-ai-based-upscaling-for-real-time-rendering.html.

[Le et al. 19] Roto Le, Balaji Calidas, Jay Yun, Vijay Ganugapati, and Peng Zhou. "cl_qcom_accelerated_image_ops." Qualcomm OpenCL SDK Note,

GitHub, 2019. https://github.com/willhua/QualcommOpenCLSDKNote/blob/master/docs/extensions/cl_qcom_accelerated_image_ops.txt.

[Leger and Zhang 22] Jeff Leger and Ruihao Zhang. "VK_QCOM_image_processing(3) Manual Page." Khronos Registry, 2022. https://registry.khronos.org/vulkan/specs/1.3-extensions/man/html/VK_QCOM_image_processing.html.

[Leger 23] Jeff Leger. "VK_QCOM_image_processing2(3) Manual Page." Khronos Registry, 2023. https://registry.khronos.org/vulkan/specs/1.3-extensions/man/html/VK_QCOM_image_processing2.html.

[Li et al. 23] Siqi Li, Yunzhen Li, and Dave Durnil. "Introducing Snapdragon Game Super Resolution." Qualcomm, 2023. https://www.qualcomm.com/news/onq/2023/04/introducing-snapdragon-game-super-resolution.

[Liu 20] Edward Liu. "DLSS 2.0—Image Reconstruction for Real-Time Rendering with Deep Learning." NVIDIA On-Demand, 2020. https://www.nvidia.com/en-us/on-demand/session/gtcsj20-s22698/.

[Lottes and Garcia 21] Timothy Lottes and Kleber Garcia. "Improved Spatial Upscaling through FidelityFX Super Resolution for Real-Time Game Engines." Presented at SIGGRAPH, 2021.

[Lutgen 24] Wade Lutgen. "High-Order Filtering and Block Matching: New Image Processing Extension for Vulkan Optimizes Performance and Power Usage." Qualcomm Developer Blog, 2024. https://developer.qualcomm.com/blog/high-order-filtering-and-block-matching-new-image-processing-extension-vulkan-optimizes.

IBL-BRDF Multiple Importance Sampling for Stochastic Screen-Space Indirect Specular

سفيان خياط (Soufiane KHIAT)

Figure 10.1. Importance sampling using a reflection probe.

10.1 Introduction

When dealing with the intricate subject of indirect specular (IS) reflection and specifically image-based lighting (IBL), one may find that the task of identifying an appropriate sample can be quite daunting. It is a technical challenge that requires a thorough understanding of sampling techniques, such as the bidirectional reflectance distribution function (BRDF), the Trowbridge–Reitz function [Trowbridge and Reitz 75], GGX (ground glass unknown) [Walter et al. 07], and the visible normal distribution function (VNDF). These techniques, as detailed in [Heitz 18], are vitally important for sampling and require a properly thought-out and executed strategy. Alternatively, one could also consider the method of environment importance sampling, as explained in [Shirley et al. 19].

Despite these available techniques, it is essential to note that the effectiveness of each strategy varies significantly. It is highly dependent on the roughness of the surface in question, as illuminated by the research published in [Veach 98]. Therefore, a comprehensive understanding of the surface's nature and characteristics is a prerequisite for selecting the most effective strategy.

In the context of path tracing, this issue can be solved by using a multiple importance strategy with BRDF and light samplings [Veach 98]. However, in rasterized real-time rendering (RRTR), we usually have only one sample per pixel (spp), or even less, and a limited amount of GPU memory. In this article, our primary focus will be on screen-space reflection (preferring screen-space indirect specular (SSIS)). However, the strategy explained here can also be applied to real-time ray tracing (RTRT) or other rendering contexts.

Ray marching on Hi-Z screen-space cone-traced reflections [Uludag 14] involves many samples on the depth buffer; coupled with stochastic screen-space reflection [Stachowiak and Uludag 15], we have to generate the best sample as possible, each time we generate a direction to reduce the noise and fireflies. For that we have to sample either the BRDF or the environment based on the roughness of the surface, which needs extra data, like the conditional marginals and marginals of the reflection probes. Proper algorithms to generate this data will be explain in Section 10.4.

In the context of a game, we can bake the data on disk and compute it in real time to allow us to support destruction and dynamic environments, or for large scale games, the data can be streamed during the exploration of the open environment. This decision has to be made by each game depending on their reflection probe resolution, maximum camera speed, and budget available at each frame. In our context, we propose runtime and time-sliced baking on demand with a garbage collector to release and allocate memory dynamically.

Many rendering engines now incorporate a per-pixel lights list (such as Forward+, Tiled, Clustered, Froxel, etc.) that can enhance the quality of SSIS results. These rendering engines provide access to more pixel-level information compared to the initial implementation of SSIS. As a result, we can now determine on a per-pixel basis which reflection probes influence which pixels, as shown in Figure 10.2.

In this article, we will share a reference implementation based on Unity, specifically using the High Definition Render Pipeline (HDRP). HDRP provides a publicly available modern rendering engine for our algorithms.

Finally, we will discuss an extension of the algorithm to have "off-screen" information in Section 10.6 and the limits of this approach in Section 10.7.

We would like to emphasize that the application of this technique on SSIS is just one possibility. It can be used for indirect diffuse lighting,[1] path tracing, or any rendering step that needs lighting of the environment.

---

[1]Sometimes wrongly named global illumination (GI).

Figure 10.2. Unity HDRP debug view displays the reflection probe count per tile, accessible per pixel at runtime.

10.2 Approach

With Unity HDRP, 2D octaheral atlases are created to store reflection probes, IES profiles, and cookies[2] in order to manage memory. See Figure 10.3. For this article, we will base our memory management of marginals on the same data structure.

Reflection probes are stored using octahedral projection, which comes in various flavors as shown in [Lambers 16]. Since this operation will be performed multiple times per frame (and per pixel), we will prioritize fast octahedral encoding/decoding, optimized from the reference implementation in [Cigolle et al. 14] (see Listings 10.1 and 10.2), over conformal or equal-area methods [Lambers 16].

```
float2 PackNormalOctQuadEncode(float3 n)
{
    n *= rcp(max(dot(abs(n), 1.0), 1e-6));
    float t = saturate(-n.z);
    return n.xy + float2(n.x >= 0.0 ? t : -t,
                         n.y >= 0.0 ? t : -t);
}
```

Listing 10.1. Encoding from a spherical normalized vector to an octahedral projection $[-1, 1]$, performed by HDRP.

---

[2]RGBA16_Float or R11G11B10 based on user settings.

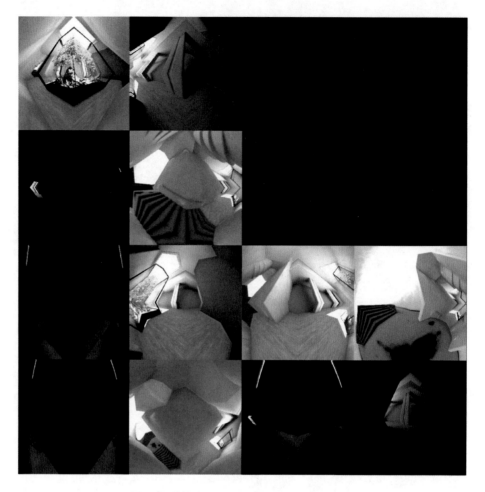

Figure 10.3. HDRP atlas reflection probe.

```
float3 UnpackNormalOctQuadEncode(float2 f)
{
    float3 n = float3(f.x, f.y, 1.0 - abs(f.x) - abs(f.y));

    float t = max(-n.z, 0.0);
    n.xy += float2(n.x >= 0.0 ? -t : t,
                   n.y >= 0.0 ? -t : t);

    return normalize(n);
}
```

Listing 10.2. Decoding from an octahedral projection $[-1, 1]$ to a spherical normalized vector, performed by HDRP.

10.3   Sampling Theory

A detailed dissertation on multiple importance sampling, heuristics, and weighting has been presented [Veach 98, Pharr et al. 16]. In the context of SSIS, we are only limited to 1 spp. Specifically, with RRTR, it is challenging to achieve proper blue noise, especially in high dimensions. Although it is not the main focus of this article, it may be important to refer to [Turquin 20] for better insights.

The importance sampling is defined as follow, to integrate F:

$$F = \int_D f(x)d\mu$$
$$F \approx \frac{1}{N} \sum_{i=1}^{N} \frac{f(X_i)}{p(X_i)}, \tag{10.1}$$

where F is the integral of f, the function over the domain D, N is the number of samples we take, p is the probability distribution function (PDF), X_i is a random variable over the domain p,[3] and μ is the differential of integration. The speed of convergence depends on the similarity between f and p. It's important to note that we don't allow the PDF to be zero, as it will generate a division by zero, which can be catastrophic for all of us.

In the case of multiple PDFs, a multiple importance sampling is needed:

$$F = \sum_{i=1}^{n} \frac{1}{n_i} \sum_{j=1}^{n_i} w_i(X_{i,j}) \frac{f(X_{i,j})}{p_i(X_{i,j})}, \tag{10.2}$$

where n is the number of PDFs, n_i the number of samples for the PDF i, $X_{i,j}$ the sample for the ith PDF and the jth sample, and $w_i(X_{i,j})$ the weight applied for the $X_{i,j}$ sample, with the function f and the PDF p_i.

In our case, we have two PDFs[4] ($n = 2$), so we can simplify Equation (10.2):

$$F = \frac{1}{N_1} \sum_{i=1}^{N_1} w_1(X_i) \frac{f(X_i)}{p_1(X_i)} + \frac{1}{N_2} \sum_{i=1}^{N_2} w_2(X_i) \frac{f(X_i)}{p_2(X_i)}. \tag{10.3}$$

Indeed, this formula relies on a sum; nevertheless, in our case this sum will be performed by the temporal accumulation system. In practice we will produce $w_1(X_i)f(X_i)/p_1(X_i)$ or $w_2(X_i)f(X_i)/p_2(X_i)$ each frame per pixel. It's not the main focus of this article, but numerous strategies are used to accumulate, such as exponential blending with sample rejection based on the speed of the pixel that reflects and the pixel that is reflected. The user can chose the HDRP settings of the screen-space reflection (SSR) to consider screen-space speed, world-space speed, or both. That means, based on user settings, we can sample the motion

---

[3]In our case a blue noise generator will be used.
[4]Light and BRDF detailed later.

 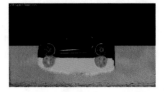

Figure 10.4. Screen-space motion vector (left) and a speed rejection (right), where red indicates rejected, orange partially accumulated, and green accumulated. A side-traveling camera tracks a car moving centered. The system of rejection keeps the car sample, which is fixed relative to the camera, and rejects (partially) the other; note that the car rims are spinning so they are also rejected.

vector twice from the current pixel and/or the pixel hit after ray marching, and with two units: screen-space unit or world-space unit; see Figure 10.4. This approach has been chosen to be light on memory, and we can improve the accumulation algorithm by allowing a variance buffer or any recent improvement shown in the literature [He et al. 13, Schied et al. 17, Dundr 18].

10.3.1 Cumulative Distribution Function and Its Inverse

To have a random sample respecting a given PDF $p(t)$, we need to compute the inverse of the cumulative distribution function (CDF), noted $CDF^{-1}(t)$.

To produce a desired CDF, we make sure to have a proper PDF that always generates a strictly increasing CDF. This allows us to have a bijective[5] CDF and $CDF^{-1}(t)$. So, intuitively,

$$CDF(t) = \int_{min}^{t} f(x)dx,$$
$$y = CDF(t),$$
$$CDF^{-1}(y) = t. \tag{10.4}$$

A standard implementation for importance sampling is to perform a dichotomic search with the CDF to find the proper value by normalizing the input and output on $[0, 1]$. We decided to use a texture to store the inverse CDF. The reason for this choice will be discussed later in this section.

As an example, let's consider the PDF illustrated in Figure 10.5(a), with the mean[6] of each Gaussian marked in dashed orange. The CDF and its inverse are shown in Figures 10.5(b) and (c). Intuitively, we can observe in the inverse CDF

---

[5] For a function $y = f(x)$, we have for each x a unique y and for each y a unique x.

[6] A Gaussian is defined by two values, a mean μ that is its center and the covariance matrix Σ (the standard deviation in 1D) that contains the parameter describing how and where the Gaussian is spread, noted $X \sim \mathcal{N}(\mu, \Sigma)$.

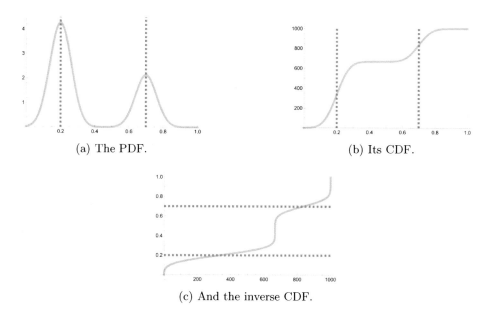

(a) The PDF.   (b) Its CDF.

(c) And the inverse CDF.

Figure 10.5. An example of a bimodal PDF, its CDF, and the inverse of this CDF. The dashed orange lines represent the mean of the PDF.

that there is a footprint on the abscissa (x-axis) proportional to the mode[7] of the PDF. Additionally, we can notice that the high slope on the inverse CDF, which corresponds to a very low probability, is equivalent to the low value on the PDF. If we randomly sample a number on the abscissa and read its equivalent ordinate (y-coordinate), we will obtain a histogram of the data set that respects the PDF, as shown in Figure 10.6.

We should emphasize that the integral of a PDF is always equal to one. In our specific case, the PDF should never be zero,[8] as division by zero can occur in Equation (10.1). Hence, when generating data, it is crucial to ensure that our buffers are never zero. By taking this never-zero consideration into account, we guarantee that the inverse CDF is always bijective, eliminating the need for a dichotomic search as demonstrated in various implementations.

We understand that some readers may consider our approach unorthodox or "wrong," especially when dealing with discontinuities or zero values in the PDF. However, in the context of RRTR, it's crucial to bypass the dichotomic

---

[7]In the case of a distribution with a sum of multiple Gaussians, we call that a multimodal Gaussian and sometimes we commonly name a mode, mean, or center of each Gaussian.

[8]With the exception of a Dirac BRDF ("perfect mirror"), but in RRTR, perfect mirrors are modeled with low roughness and never with zero roughness. Therefore, we don't need a special case here; we just need to be careful about numerical stability.

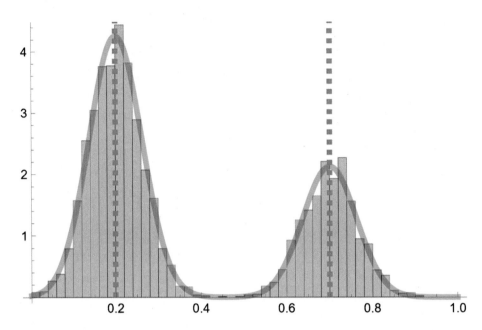

Figure 10.6. Histogram with 4096 samples using the inverse CDF with 32× buckets compared to the PDF.

search. This method could severely impact performance, resulting in incoherent performance per pixel, depending on our random (or blue noise) generator.

Such inconsistencies are unacceptable in real-time applications, particularly in game production where elements like camera angles, gameplay events, decals, or visual effects are unpredictable. If these arguments are not convincing, consider the use of the original PDF with a bilinear sampler, which can address conceptually the issue of "discontinuities."

As for zero values on the PDF, we opt for a very low probability, like FLT16_MIN.[9] Given the dynamic nature of games, with constantly moving cameras and frame rates of 30/60/120 FPS, coupled with temporal algorithms for accumulation and rejection, we believe this approach can provide a practical solution, without offending any mathematicians.

In the case of 2D octahedral projection, we need two inverse of CDFs, one to select which row of the image to sample and the other which row of the octahedral projection.

---

[9]In practice, the choice of this ϵ number can be tricky, for instance $x + \epsilon$ can be equal to x depending on the value of x on IEEE-754. So careful consideration about numerical stability must be taken here.

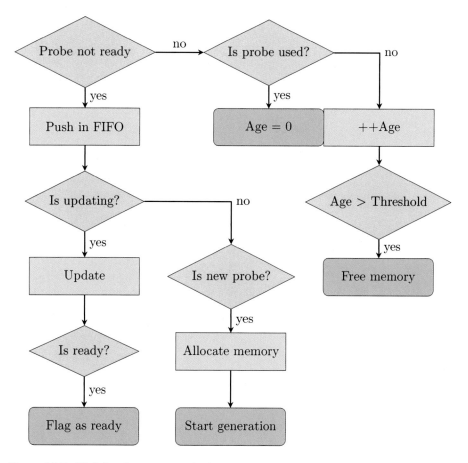

Figure 10.7. High-level process applied for each probe at each frame on the CPU side.

10.4 Data Generation

In Unity HDRP, there are various scheduling strategies available for generating the rendering of the cube map reflection probe. These strategies include real-time, baked, or on demand. Once the reflection probe is ready, which includes the convolution for a proper BRDF (Trowbridge–Reitz [Trowbridge and Reitz 75], GGX [Walter et al. 07]), Velvet, etc.), it can be sent to our importance sampling manager. The reference implementation [Khiat 24] processes one mipmap per frame. However, in real production code, it is necessary to profile each platform to determine how many mipmaps per frame can fit within a given budget, especially for lower-resolution mipmaps.

Figure 10.7 illustrates the scheduling strategy for a given frame, applied per reflection probe.

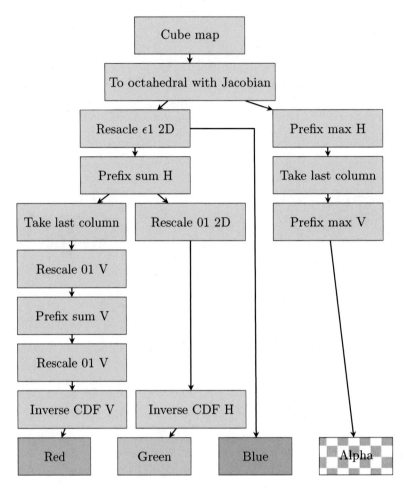

Figure 10.8. Data generation flow chart, done per mipmap. We store on each channel a different value: Red: The inverse CDF of the sum of rows that our marginal, Green: The inverse CDF of each rouws, that our conditional marginal, Blue: The rescale PDF, Alpha: The maximum of the original pre-scale PDF for later reconstruction.

We have a FIFO (first in, first out) pool of reflections that requires data generation for importance sampling. If a probe is already being processed for generation, it is marked as "Update" in Figure 10.7 and no action is taken for this probe. Otherwise, we begin the process of generating the data by allocating memory and initializing the process. In this context, "Update" refers to generating one mipmap of the required marginals. The update process is illustrated in Figure 10.8.

To manage memory, we utilize a simple counter to track the age of the probe. If the probe becomes too old, we release the memory of the marginals. The age

```
// 1. CDF of rows (density where each row is a CDF)
cdfFull = GPUScan.ComputeOperation
                    (density, Add, Horizontal, format1);
// 2. CDF L (L: CDF of {sum of rows})
sumRows = Alloc(1, height, colorFormat: format1);
// Last column contains the data we want
CopyTexture(cdfFull, 0, 0, width - 1, 0, 1, height,
                sumRows, 0, 0, 0, 0);
// Pre-normalize to avoid overflow
minMaxSumRows = GPUScan.ComputeOperation
                            (sumRows, MinMax, Vertical, format2);
Rescale01(sumRows, minMaxSumRows, Vertical, true);
cdfL = GPUScan.ComputeOperation(sumRows, Add, Vertical);
// 3. Min max of each row
minMaxRows = GPUScan.ComputeOperation
                        (cdfFull, MinMax, Horizontal);
// 4. Min max of L
minMaxCDFL = GPUScan.ComputeOperation(cdfL, MinMax, Vertical);
// 5. Rescale CDF rows (for precision and reducing banding)
Rescale01(cdfFull, minMaxRows, Horizontal);
// 6. Rescale CDF L (for precision and reducing banding)
Rescale01(cdfL, minMaxCDFL, Vertical, true);
// 7. Inverse CDF rows
conditionalMarginal = InverseCDF1D.ComputeInverseCDF
                            (cdfFull, density, Horizontal, format4);
// 8. Inverse CDF L
marginal            = InverseCDF1D.ComputeInverseCDF
                            (cdfL, density, Vertical, format1);
```

Listing 10.3. Code used to generate the marginal on Unity.

indicates how many frames have passed since the probe was used in the atlas (see Figure 10.3).

Finally we have a simple flag to mark this probe as ready for importance sampling; without this flag enabled, only the BRDF importance sampling is available.

The data generation, such as the marginal (Listing 10.3), conditional marginal, PDF, and integral, may differ from other available sources. The presented approach aims to be more numerically stable. It includes multiple extra steps to avoid numerical overflow,[10] even if they may not be mathematically necessary. These extra steps, like multiple "Rescale 01" operations, are repeated to limit overflow and maximize numerical precision in subsequent calculations. For example, without a "Rescale01," it is easy to overflow a prefix sum, especially with our data stored in float16 or encoded with 11 or 10 bits. Even if we don't overflow, it's easy to underflow, too: for instance, a reflection probe stored in the octahedral projection after normalization by dividing by its integral and multiplying it by the Jacobian, can easily have values below the smallest number that can be represented. That's why we store the PDF rescale between ϵ and 1 to be reconstructed later.

---

[10]Which is easy to overflow, particularly with R11G11B10, R10G10B10A2, or even with R16G16B16A16.

All GPU parallel prefix sums and prefix min max are computed using a modified version of the Hillis and Steele algorithm [Hillis and Steele 86] detailed in [Harris et al. 07].[11]

In Figure 10.8, we use V and H to denote vertical and horizontal operations, respectively. For comprehensiveness, it's important to note that "Rescale 01 V," "Rescale 01 H," and "Rescale ϵ1 2D" require an additional internal step. This involves the need of "Prefix Max H" or "V" to identify the maximum values in each row or column, which allows us to remap all values between 0 and 1.

For "Rescale 01 2D" or "Rescale ϵ1 2D," we first need a "Prefix MinMax H," followed by "Take last column," and then "Prefix MinMax V." This ensures the 2D min max is stored on the last cell, allowing us to remap between 0 and 1 (or between ϵ and 1).[12]

10.4.1   Octahedral and Jacobian

Storing a reflection probe can be done in numerous ways, as `TextureCubeArray` or `Texture2DArray` if all our reflection probes have the same resolution. However Unity allow us to override the default size per probe, so we need a solution supporting variable size probes. Unity HDRP solves this by saving all reflection probes in a 2D atlas with an octahedral projection. An equirectangular projection (Figure 10.9, top) could be used, but a non-square projection with transcendental functions will disqualify this projection. Unity HDRP decided to have a fast octahedral projection, as in the bottom of Figure 10.9 (see Listings 10.1 and 10.2).

If we transform spherical data to an equirectangular[13] projection, we need to take into consideration the absolute value of the determinant of the Jacobian, shortened as "the Jacobian," as opposed to the Jacobian matrix.

It can be computed by taking the determinant of the Jacobian of the frame changing from one to another one. Transitioning from a spherical coordinate to a Cartesian coordinate, use the transformation z:

$$z = \{r\sin(\theta)\cos(\phi), r\sin(\theta)\sin(\phi), r\cos(\theta)\}.$$

The Jacobian matrix is

$$\begin{pmatrix} \sin(\theta)\cos(\phi) & r\cos(\theta)\cos(\phi) & -r\sin(\theta)\sin(\phi) \\ \sin(\theta)\sin(\phi) & r\cos(\theta)\sin(\phi) & r\sin(\theta)\cos(\phi) \\ \cos(\theta) & -r\sin(\theta) & 0 \end{pmatrix}.$$

By taking the determinant of this Jacobian matrix, we get after simplification $|r^2\sin(\theta)|$, which can be simplified to $|\sin(\theta)|$ as we work with the unit sphere.

---

[11]More recent implementations can give much better results, by using local memory or/and wave intrinsics. See [Liani 24] for an effective implementation.

[12]The value of ϵ will be `FLT16_MIN` or a small number representable for a given `RenderTarget` format.

[13]Sometime called lat-long.

Figure 10.9. Equirectangular (top) and fast octahedral (bottom) projections. ("Rostock–Laage Airport" HDRI from [Zaal 24].)

To underline the importance of the Jacobian, see Figure 10.10. We took the exact same points from a uniform sphere sampling and projected them onto an octahedral 2D projection. It is obvious that the density is different and the "uniformity" is not preserved. This is what the Jacobian describes.

For octahedral projection the derivation will be a bit more complex; it will be delegated to Mathematica [Khiat 24]. We need the Jacobian matrix:

$$J_F(M) = \begin{pmatrix} \dfrac{\partial f_1}{\partial x_1} & \cdots & \dfrac{\partial f_1}{\partial x_n} \\ \vdots & \ddots & \vdots \\ \dfrac{\partial f_m}{\partial x_1} & \cdots & \dfrac{\partial f_m}{\partial x_n} \end{pmatrix}.$$

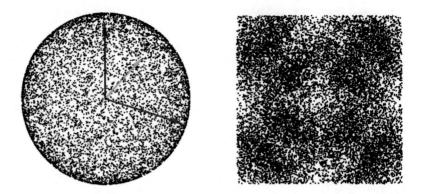

Figure 10.10. A spherical uniform sampling projected onto an octahedral map.

With F is `UnpackNormalOctQuadEncode` (see Listings 10.1 and 10.2), which contains the `max`, `abs`, and `sqrt` functions and branches, which complexify our Jacobian. The function projects a Cartesian vector from a unit sphere to a $[-1, 1]^2$ plane. To simplify the calculation, we note that an octahedron is symmetrical, so we can compute the Jacobian only for one of the eight faces and a change of variables to remap the coordinates. With the projection $\{x, y\} \in [-1, 1]^2$, we can be constrained to the positive section of the plane. The colored region in Figure 10.11 is $\{x, y\} \in [0, 1]^2$. To consider the green triangle, we add the constraint $x + y < 1$ (or $x + y > 1$ for the blue one).[14]

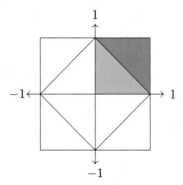

Figure 10.11. A 2D plane of the octahedral projection; the colored region is the zone considered for the Jacobian.

---

[14] The case where $x + y = 1$ is the same for the blue and the green region.

As the Jacobian matrix is too large to display (see [Khiat 24] for the full derivation), we will only show the determinant:

$$J_{\text{upper}}(u, v) = \frac{u + v - 1}{\left(2u^2 + 2u(v - 2) + 2(v - 2)v + 3\right)^2},$$

$$J_{\text{lower}}(u, v) = -\frac{u + v - 1}{\left(2u^2 + 2u(v - 1) + 2(v - 1)v + 1\right)^2}.$$

These expressions are plotted in Figure 10.12; note that the plot is similar to the densities shown in Figure 10.10.

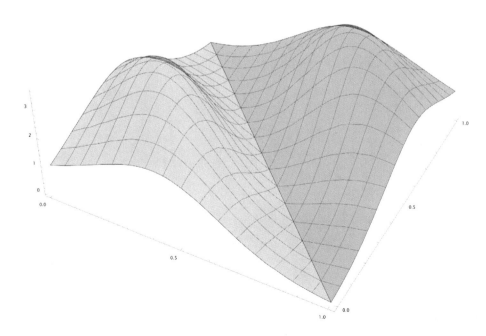

Figure 10.12. The two parts of the Jacobian: J_{lower} in green and J_{upper} in blue.

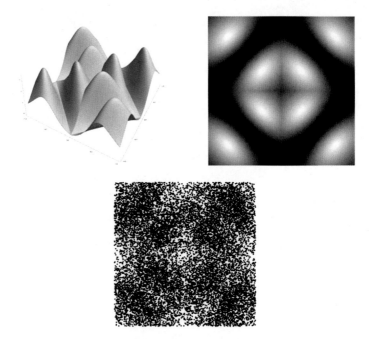

Figure 10.13. The Jacobian of an octahedral projection (top), compared to a uniform sphere sampling projected onto an octahedron (bottom).

To obtain our full Jacobian, we provide a change of variable as follow:

$$\tilde{u}(u,v) = \frac{1}{2}((1-2|u|)\mathrm{sgn}(|u|+|v|-1)+1),$$

$$\tilde{v}(u,v) = \frac{1}{2}((1-2|v|)\mathrm{sgn}(|u|+|v|-1)+1),$$

$$J_{\mathrm{full}}(u,v) = J_{\mathrm{lower}}(\tilde{u}(u,v),\tilde{v}(u,v)),$$

$$J_{\mathrm{full}}(u,v) = \frac{||u|+|v|-1|}{\left(|u|(3-2|v|)+||u|+|v|-1|+3|v|-2\left(u^2+v^2+1\right)\right)^2},$$

(10.5)

which give us Figure 10.13. Note that J_{full} is given after the changing of variable and simplification; the change of variable is illustrated in Figure 10.14 (see [Khiat 24] for details).

10.4.2   Conditional Marginal and Row Marginal

Conditional Marginal As illustrated in [Shirley et al. 19], sampling 2D data can be easily achieved in two steps. First, select which row to sample, with the inverse CDF of the sum of each rows. Once the row is selected, use the inverse CDF of the selected row to select the proper column.

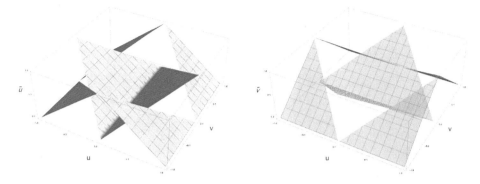

Figure 10.14. Change of variable for u (left) and v (right).

As shown in Figure 10.15, each row is treated independently at this stage. There is a small caveat: after performing the CDF of each row, we copy the last column into a separate buffer for use in the row marginal, detailed in the next section. After backing up this column, we normalize all rows between 0 and 1 based on their min max from a "Prefix Min-Max Vertical."

Row Marginal Once we have the CDF of each rows, before normalizing each rows and having them independent we copy the last column, and this copy is normalized between 0 and 1. As the other steps that is done with a Prefix Min-Max and rescaling. After as the previous step we do our prefix sum and inverse CDF.

10.5 Runtime Sampling

At runtime we can collect the list of reflection probes per pixel. As shown in Listing 10.4. The two integers `envLightStart` and `envLightCount` are used to read a binded buffer containing all the relevant structs such as `capturePosition`, `weight`, `influenceShapeType`, etc.

To blend between reflection probes, we have a weight per pixel. All the weights are summed to 1. These have to be computed differently if the `influenceShapeType` is a `ENVSHAPETYPE_SPHERE` or a `ENVSHAPETYPE_BOX`. Because we can't

```
uint envLightStart , envLightCount;
GetCountAndStart(localInput , LIGHTCATEGORY_ENV,
      /*out*/ envLightStart , /*out*/ envLightCount);
```

Listing 10.4. Helper used by Unity HDRP to grab the light list per pixel, here the reflection probe.

(a) The input PDF.

(b) The CDF.

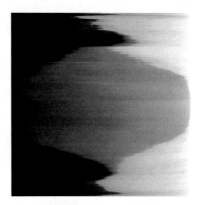

(c) The inverse CDF.

Figure 10.15. (a) Luminance of the octahedral projection multiplied with the Jacobian. (A histogram transform was performed to make the data visible in print; the image shown is not the raw data used by the CDF.) (b) The CDF per row. (c) The inverse CDF per row.

precompute the CDF per pixel, with the weights used for the blending, we need to compute the CDF at runtime. By doing a simple scan of all reflection probes, we can importance-sample properly which reflection probe to sample.

Once the reflection probe is selected, we can directly sample the data we described in Section 10.4.2, with the proper weight. As shown in Listing 10.5, all the data is stored in an atlas.

```
float3 Xi;
// Blue noise from: [1] https://eheitzresearch.wordpress.com/762-2/
Xi.x = BlueNoise(positionSS, _FrameCount, 0);
Xi.y = BlueNoise(positionSS, _FrameCount, 1);
Xi.z = BlueNoise(positionSS, _FrameCount, 2);
```

```
float3 wi; // Light Direction
float weight;
bool sampleEnv;
if (Xi.z >= roughness)
{
  // VNDF brdf sampling from: [2] https://inria.hal.science/hal
     -00996995/en
  wi = ImportanceSamplingGGXVNDF(weight /*[out]*/,
                             Xi.xy, n, wo, roughness);
  sampleEnv = false;
}
else
{
  float2 atlasCoords0 =
    GetAtlasCoords(index, float2(0.5f, Xi.x));
  float row = SampleTex2DArray(_MISInfosAtlas, atlasCoords0).x;

  float2 octSample = float2(Xi.y, row);
  float2 atlasCoords1 = GetAtlasCoords(index, octSample);
  float4 sampleInfos =
    SampleTex2DArray(_MISInfosAtlas, atlasCoords1);

  Lwo = SampleTex2DArray(_ReflectionAtlas, atlasCoords1);
  float2 oct01 = octSample;
  float2 oct = oct01 * 2.0f - 1.0f;
  outgoingDir = UnpackNormalOctQuadEncode(oct);

  float3x3 worldToIS = /* ... */; // IS: Influence space
  float3 positionIS = /* ... */;
  float3 dirIS = normalize(mul(outgoingDir, worldToIS));

  float3x3 worldToPS = /* ... */; // PS: Proxy space
  float3 positionPS = /* ... */;
  float3 dirPS = mul(outgoingDir, worldToPS);
  float projectionDistance;
  if (envLightData.influenceShapeType == ENVSHAPETYPE_SPHERE)
  {
    projectionDistance =
      IntersectSphereProxy(envLightData, dirPS, positionPS);
  }
  else if (envLightData.influenceShapeType == ENVSHAPETYPE_BOX)
  {
    projectionDistance =
      IntersectBoxProxy(envLightData, dirPS, positionPS);
  }
  outgoingDir =
    (envLightData.capturePositionRWS +
      projectionDistance * outgoingDir) - positionWS;
  outgoingDir = normalize(outgoingDir);
  sampleEnv = true;
}
```

Listing 10.5. Code to importance-sample the reflection probe.

10.6   Off-Screen Extension

Like all screen-space algorithms, we face common limitations [Wronski 14] such
as missing off-screen information and thin-wall issues. In our case, when there's
a miss, we can fall back on the appropriate local reflection probe with the correct

parallax projection using importance sampling. Although this approach doesn't solve all problems, it can mitigate inconsistencies or gaps in our indirect specular plate. This solution yields good results for static scenes, such as architectural rendering. However, its use should be evaluated based on specific needs. For instance, a typical night scene with corridors and numerous dynamic emissive bouncing balls may pose a challenge to our approach and should be considered carefully. Despite this, it remains a problem for all screen-space indirect specular algorithms. With an adequate temporal algorithm, it is still a viable approach given the current state of screen-space algorithms.

Without designing carefully a failure case, the fallback can be quite interesting, especially given the cost of ray marching. In this section, we'll explore two ideas. First, if we have a direction from the environment, we trace in that direction, though this doesn't improve performance. Alternatively, we could consider directly sampling the reflection probe and bypassing the entire Hi-Z ray marching process. This method could save us substantial depth sampling, as the ray marching step can be highly incoherent per wave. The latter concept is still valid in terms of importance sampling, as the second method aims to sample the lighting when we encounter high roughness, rather than necessarily generating a direction for the SSIS. Ray marching is a means of achieving light sampling, but we already store the lighting in the reflection probe. This approach saves us a lot of performance at the cost of losing intersection with dynamic objects. We expose the two methods as options for our user to evaluate what's appropriate for different scenes.

10.7   Limits

When we generate a direction from environment importance sampling, the sample is created based on a given capture position. We need to reproject the direction for a specific world position, considering the shape of the reprojection,[15] as shown in Figure 10.16(a).

However, in some cases, most of the samples are generated in a specific direction. For instance, a scene with a single emissive light source, like the slice of the Cornell box illustrated in Figure 10.16(b), will generate a direction orthogonal to the normal for all ceiling pixels. This is a clear failure case.

To mitigate this situation, we can generate N new directions with a new random number until we obtain a non-orthogonal direction. Alternatively, we can fall back on BRDF sampling, which will give us the same result as before any change on the SSIS.

Another challenge is to consider only the hemisphere on the 2D octahedral projection based on the normal on the pixel surface considered. It can be challenging to find the proper region on the $[-1, 1]^2$ plane that correspond to a given normal hemisphere n. Intuitively, we want to compute the bounding box of the

---

[15]Unity HDRP allows rectangular (variable size) and spherical reprojection.

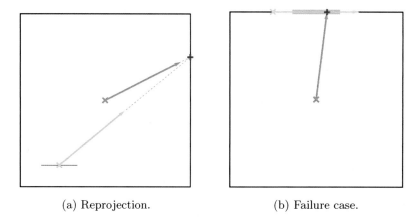

(a) Reprojection.   (b) Failure case.

Figure 10.16. Parallax reprojection of the reflection probe importance sampling: the red × is the capture position of the reflection probe, the blue × is the current considered pixel, and the red + is the reprojected position on the reflection probe.

useful region and remap ξ_1 and ξ_2 from our random (blue noise) generator, as shown in Figure 10.17.

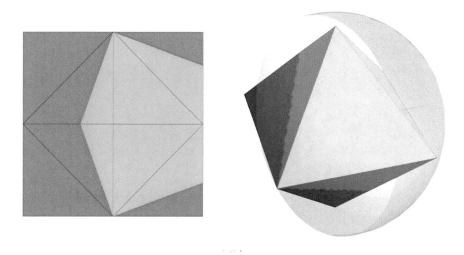

Figure 10.17. The blue region represents the upper hemisphere projection and is the interesting region for sampling.

But if we are exhaustive, we can see how complex a projected hemisphere can be, Which made the idea of having a bounding box obsolete, as shown in Figure 10.18.

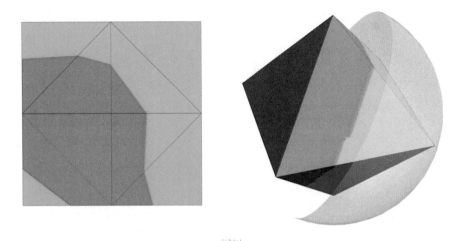

Figure 10.18. A more complicated region for sampling; the blue region represents the upper hemisphere projection.

A working solution would be to triangulate the blue region (Figure 10.18) and important-sample it, which is too expensive for a real-time application. For now, sampling a hemisphere in a 2D octahedral projection efficiently is still an open problem.[16]

10.8   Future Work

The work presented in [Wang et al. 19] allowed us to have indirect specular outside screen with irregular probe placement. This works well for a surface with low roughness and can support off-screen reflections. By adding this IBL-BRDF importance sampling to the pipeline, we can have a "ray-guiding" strategy for better convergence, which could solve complex scenarios such the famous Veach scene.

A further area for enhancement could be to conduct a comprehensive analysis to leverage different mipmap levels of marginals. This is critical in order to effectively handle multi-scale rendering. The goal here is to use the roughness of the surface as a guiding factor in importance sampling the reflection probe, which has already been convolved with the appropriate BRDF. This would allow for a more efficient rendering as it will reduce the bandwidth used.

---

[16]Left as an exercise to the reader.

10.9   Conclusion

In this article, we introduced RRTR to the concept of MIS, typically reserved for path tracers and offline rendering. While our focus was on image-based lighting and BRDFs, the ability to access light lists per pixel opens doors for extension to any light source, with the caveat of associated costs.

We deliver the derivation of the Jacobian for an octahedral projection that mitigates the gaps in correctness in our algorithms.

These techniques offer promising solutions for addressing limitations inherent in screen-space techniques, enhancing the quality of SSIS algorithms across a wide range of scenes and lighting scenarios.

The discourse presented here unveils a realm of possibilities for future research and development in SSIS algorithms. And we still think that rasterizer rendering in contemporary rendering methodologies is not dead.

Bibliography

[Cigolle et al. 14] Zina H. Cigolle, Sam Donow, Daniel Evangelakos, Michael Mara, Morgan McGuire, and Quirin Meyer. "A Survey of Efficient Representations for Independent Unit Vectors." *Journal of Computer Graphics Techniques* 3:2 (2014), 1–30. http://jcgt.org/published/0003/02/01/.

[Dundr 18] J. Dundr. "Progressive Spatiotemporal Variance-Guided Filtering." Presented at Central European Seminar on Computer Graphics, 2018. https://api.semanticscholar.org/CorpusID:210183307.

[Harris et al. 07] Mark Harris, Shubhabrata Sengupta, and John D. Owens. "Parallel Prefix Sum (Scan) with CUDA." In *GPU Gems 3*, edited by Hubert Nguyen, Chapter 39, pp. 851–876. Addison-Wesley, 2007.

[He et al. 13] K. He, J. Sun, and X. Tang. "Guided Image Filtering." *IEEE Transactions on Pattern Analysis and Machine Intelligence* 35:06 (2013), 1397–1409.

[Heitz 18] Eric Heitz. "Sampling the GGX Distribution of Visible Normals." *Journal of Computer Graphics Techniques* 7:4 (2018), 1–13. http://jcgt.org/published/0007/04/01/.

[Hillis and Steele 86] W. Daniel Hillis and Guy L. Steele. "Data Parallel Algorithms." *Communications of the ACM* 29:12 (1986), 1170–1183. https://doi.org/10.1145/7902.7903.

[Khiat 24] Soufiane Khiat. "gpuzen3-ibl-brdf-mis-ssis." GitHub, 2024. https://github.com/soufianekhiat/gpuzen3-ibl-brdf-mis-ssis.

[Lambers 16] Martin Lambers. "Mappings between Sphere, Disc, and Square." *Journal of Computer Graphics Techniques* 5:2 (2016), 1–21. http://jcgt.org/published/0005/02/01/.

[Liani 24] Max Liani. "About Fast 2D CDF Construction." Art, Tech and Other Nonsense, 2024. https://maxliani.wordpress.com/2024/03/09/about-fast-2d-cdf-construction/.

[Pharr et al. 16] Matt Pharr, Wenzel Jakob, and Greg Humphreys. *Physically Based Rendering: From Theory to Implementation*, Third edition. Morgan Kaufmann Publishers Inc., 2016.

[Schied et al. 17] Christoph Schied, Anton Kaplanyan, Chris Wyman, Anjul Patney, Chakravarty R. Alla Chaitanya, John Burgess, Shiqiu Liu, Carsten Dachsbacher, Aaron Lefohn, and Marco Salvi. "Spatiotemporal Variance-Guided Filtering: Real-Time Reconstruction for Path-Traced Global Illumination." In *Proceedings of High Performance Graphics, HPG '17*, pp. 2:1–2:12. Association for Computing Machinery, 2017. https://doi.org/10.1145/3105762.3105770.

[Shirley et al. 19] Peter Shirley, Samuli Laine, David Hart, Matt Pharr, Petrik Clarberg, Eric Haines, Matthias Raab, and David Cline. "Sampling Transformations Zoo." In *Ray Tracing Gems: High-Quality and Real-Time Rendering with DXR and Other APIs*, edited by Eric Haines and Tomas Akenine-Möller, pp. 223–246. Apress, 2019. https://doi.org/10.1007/978-1-4842-4427-2_16.

[Stachowiak and Uludag 15] Tomasz Stachowiak and Yasin Uludag. "Stochastic Screen-Space Reflections." ACM SIGGRAPH Course: Advances in Real-Time Rendering, 2015.

[Trowbridge and Reitz 75] T. S. Trowbridge and K. P. Reitz. "Average Irregularity Representation of a Rough Surface for Ray Reflection." *Journal of the Optical Society of America* 65:5 (1975), 531–536. https://opg.optica.org/abstract.cfm?URI=josa-65-5-531.

[Turquin 20] Emmanuel Turquin. "From Ray to Path Tracing: Navigating through Dimensions." ACM SIGGRAPH Course: Advances in Real-Time Rendering, 2020.

[Uludag 14] Yasin Uludag. "Hi-Z Screen-Space Cone-Traced Reflections." In *GPU Pro 5*, edited by Wolfgang Engel, pp. 149–192. CRC Press, 2014.

[Veach 98] Eric Veach. "Robust Monte Carlo Methods for Light Transport Simulation." Ph.D. thesis, Stanford University, Stanford, CA, USA, 1998.

[Walter et al. 07] Bruce Walter, Stephen Marschner, Hongsong Li, and Kenneth Torrance. "Microfacet Models for Refraction through Rough Surfaces." In *EGSR07: 18th Eurographics Symposium on Rendering*, pp. 195–206. Eurographics Association, 2007.

[Wang et al. 19] Yue Wang, Soufiane Khiat, Paul G. Kry, and Derek Nowrouzezahrai. "Fast Non-uniform Radiance Probe Placement and Tracing." In *Proceedings of the ACM SIGGRAPH Symposium on Interactive 3D Graphics and Games*, pp. 5:1–5:9. Association for Computing Machinery, 2019.

[Wronski 14] Bart Wronski. "The Future of Screenspace Reflections." Personal website, 2014. https://bartwronski.com/2014/01/25/the-future-of-screenspace-reflections/.

[Zaal 24] Greg Zaal. "HDRIs." Poly Haven. Accessed February 14, 2024. https://polyhaven.com/hdris.

Practical Clustered Forward Decals

Kirill Bazhenov

11.1 Introduction

A decal is a texture (or a set of textures) with transform information that is projected onto an arbitrary surface in the world. It is an invaluable tool in the game engine toolbox.

Decals are commonly used to communicate the gameplay state and make it react to player actions—for instance, a player character can leave footprints on the ground, spilled liquids can create reflective ponds of water, and various other dynamic effects. Animated decals further enhance the presentation quality of the game.

Decals are also useful for art production. They allow the artists to quickly add details to arbitrary surfaces in the world or break texture repetition without going through the costly UV unwrapping step or changing the underlying assets. The art team can also save the valuable texture budget by reusing the same decal with different orientation and scale and reducing the need to create lots of unique individual textures.

11.2 Forward Decals

In the past decals were often implemented with a so-called D-buffer (also called decal buffer or deferred decals) approach, for example as described in [Hammer 19]. This was typically implemented by rendering decals into a separate render target using instanced cubes and projecting decal textures onto the depth buffer behind the cube geometry.

In this article we present an alternative approach that doesn't rely on the depth buffer and instead works by projecting decal textures in the main pass pixel shader. We call this *Clustered Forward Decals* because of how similar it is to the clustered forward lighting solution [Persson 13, Gneiting 20].

11.2.1 Decal GPU Representation

In the GPU memory we represent each decal with the following 64-byte structure:

```
struct Decal
{
    Transform transform;
    uint packedTextureHandles;
    float tileScaleXY;
    uint flags;
    float data;
    float normalizedTime;
    uint packedSortData;
};
```

There are two fields in this structure that require a detailed explanation: `flags` and `data`.

Decal `flags` is a 32-bit bitfield that we use to encode various decal features and behavior (for instance, the presence of the height map texture or how the decal alpha channel is computed).

Decal `data` is arbitrary context-dependent data that contains different values based on decal flags. We will demonstrate how it is used in Section 11.3.

The size and alignment of this structure is performance critical, and we recommend to avoid making it larger than 64 bytes.

11.2.2 Decal Transform and Projection on Arbitrary Surface

A decal transform can be represented with three components: position, rotation quaternion, and scale. This is more compact than using a 4×4 matrix and still supports everything that a decal needs.

```
struct Transform
{
    float3 translation;
    float4 rotation;
    float3 scale;
};
```

From the game engine perspective, it is convenient to represent a decal as a unit-cube game object. Then, by moving and rotating this cube, we can position the decal in the world, and by scaling the cube, we can control the decal size. A decal transform can then be obtained by inverting the game object transform.

In order to "apply" the decal to the surface, first we need to project the surface position into the decal space. This is done by transforming the world-space position using the decal transform we just mentioned:

```
float3 TransformPoint(Transform transform, float3 position)
{
    position += transform.translation;
    position = RotatePoint(position, transform.rotation);
    position *= transform.scale;
    return position;
}
```

This operation will give us a point in decal space. If any component is outside of the range $[-0.5, 0.5]$, this means that it's outside of the decal and should be skipped. We recommend using a dynamic branch for this.

The 2D texture coordinate UV is obtained using the following operation: UV = (P.xy + 0.5) * 2; assuming the z-axis is "up," the z-coordinate is ignored.

```
float3 decalPos = TransformPoint(decal.transform, worldPos);
[branch]
if (all(decalPos.xz >= -0.5.xx) && all(decalPos.xz <= 0.5.xx))
{
    float2 decalUV = decalPos.xz + 0.5.xx;
    // Proceed to sample the decal
}
```

11.2.3 Lossless Quaternion Compression

A normalized rotation quaternion can be compressed to further reduce the memory footprint or make space for additional data in the decal structure.

This compression relies on the fact that quaternion $Q(x, y, z, w)$ represents the same rotation as $Q(-x, -y, -z, -w)$.

First, we check if w is negative and negate the quaternion if that's the case. This allows us to assume w is always positive and only store the XYZ components as `float3`.

Then, W is reconstructed as $w = \sqrt{1 - x^2 - y^2 - z^2}$.

Quaternion data can be compressed even further by storing individual components in `unorm16` format. This is no longer lossless, but has good enough precision in case there is a need to free more space in the decal structure.

11.2.4 Sampling the Decal

After obtaining the decal UV, there is one more step before we can sample it. We need to calculate the correct UV derivatives. We cannot use automatic UV gradients because they will break on the decal boundary. We used a dynamic branch to skip pixels outside of the decal, and this branch will diverge in regions where multiple decals intersect, leading to incorrect UV gradients computed by the GPU.

Instead, we can derive the UV gradients from world position like this:

```
const float2 worldUV = worldPos.xz * DecalTexelDensity;
const float4 gradUV = float4(ddx(worldUV), ddy(worldUV));
```

We introduce a new parameter called *decal texel density*, and adjusting it will control the target texel density for decals. This is a workaround that helps make sure that decals have the same amount of pixels as the surface they are applied to (assuming that underlying assets are authored with consistent texel density in the first place).

Before sampling the decal texture, we multiply `gradUV` by the decal scale and use `SampleGrad` to get the correct decal color for this pixel:

```
float4 decalGradUV = gradUV * decal.transform.scale.xyxy;
float4 color = decalColorTexture.SampleGrad(
    decalSamplerState,
    decalUV,
    decalGradUV.xy, decalGradUV.zw);
```

11.2.5 Decal Culling Strategies

Oriented Bounding Box Since decals are represented as unit cubes, we can derive the oriented bounding box (OBB) of the decal from its game object transform. For example, to test if the point is inside the decal OBB, we transform that point into the local decal space and test it against a unit sized axis aligned box. The OBB is then used for culling the decals.

Having a proper oriented bounding box is very important. Elongated decals like long road segments will produce a large axis-aligned bounding box (AABB) when rotated, which will result in a lot of false positives when culling the clusters and wasted memory bandwidth on processing the decals that are never going to hit the pixel.

Clustered Decals Decal culling is practically identical to the light culling described in [Persson 13, Gneiting 20]. The only difference is that instead of light bounding spheres and cones, we are using decal OBBs to assign decals to clusters.

11.2.6 Blending Decals

There are at least two different strategies for decal blending that can used simultaneously.

Sorted Blending For sorting decals we will be using one 32-bit sorting key, which will be composed from two parameters. We will call them *sort key* and *sort layer*. We pack them into the high and low bits of the 32-bit sorting key.

The sort key is initialized to the ID of the decal game object such that the decals lower in the game object tree will get a numerically higher ID. The sort layer is an arbitrary user-defined value that further controls the ordering of the decal.

Decal sorting is then performed in the culling compute shader. In our case, it was a single threaded insertion sort using the packed 32-bit key. The cost of this sorting is not significant because the amount of decals per tile is small.

Alternatively, it is possible to use a bitonic sort that runs in a single thread group as described in [Thomas 14, Turánszki 19].

Height-Based Blending Physically based rendering materials often come with the height map texture; in the case of decals, this can be used to implement order-independent blending.

The implementation finds the maximum blending height between the current height and the next decal height and then blends the decal color using two height values as blending weights. This approach does not require decal sorting, but requires each participating decal to define a height map.

```
float3 HeightBlendColor(float3 color0, float height0, float3 color1,
    float height1) {
    float heightBase = max(height0, height1) - HeightBlendBias;
    float heightWeight0 = max(height0 - heightBase, 0);
    float heightWeight1 = max(height1 - heightBase, 0);
    return ((color0 * heightWeight10) + (color1 * heightWeight1)) / (
    heightWeight0 + heightWeight1);
}
```

11.2.7 Skinned Decals

Projecting decals on the skinned mesh result in swimming artifacts because decals are not following the bone animation correctly. This can be solved by applying the corresponding bone transforms to the decal transform before computing the decal UV. This additional decal transform can be computed in the vertex shader and passed to the pixel shader for resolving.

Using the bone transform on the decal will make it correctly follow the animation and avoid the swimming issue. The bone needs to be transformed to world space before applying the decal transformation. Any procedural vertex animation can be implemented in the same way by applying the animation transform to the decal transform before resolving.

An alternative approach [Gneiting 20, "Geometry Decals" section] stores decal transforms together with the geometry and blends the decal directly without culling. This works well with animated geometry, but such decals cannot be applied to arbitrary world-space geometry.

11.2.8 Static Decal Baking

Most static decals can be optimized offline. Instead of resolving multiple decals every frame, we can resolve them into a texture and reuse the result every frame.

At a high level this works by creating a *virtual decal* that references a virtual texture page, then resolving several decals into that virtual texture page as part of streaming or level loading. To maintain reasonable decal quality, we need to make sure that all decals that get baked into the virtual decal have similar sizes and orientations. Orientation is particularly important because it has a big impact on projected texture stretching.

One way to approach this problem is to quantize decal rotation and use it to bin decals based on their rotation. We recommend using Euler angles and quantizing them to 8-bit `unorm` format (24 bits in total, packed into a 32-bit integer). This leaves us with a finite set of unique orientations for virtual decals. Then, decals in each bin are grouped spatially, and a heuristic is used to determine good candidates for baking.

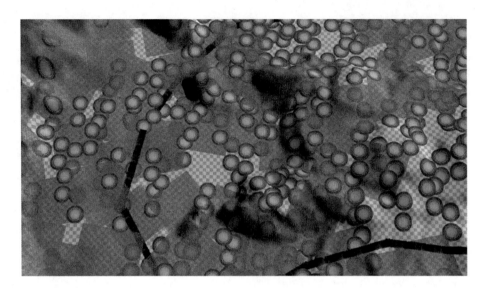

Figure 11.1. Baked static decals.

Alternatively, K-means clustering can be used to group spatially close decals with similar orientations together. K-means clustering can theoretically yield better results with less stretching, however we didn't find any meaningful difference in practice.

Baking itself is very similar to the decal resolving in the pixel shader, but instead of the world geometry we are going to use a virtual plane that is oriented according to its orientation bin and placed in the world where the static decals are. The virtual decal is then appended to the list of other decals and is otherwise treated as a regular decal itself. (See Figure 11.1.)

Runtime Texture Compression An obvious improvement to virtual textures is runtime compression. An efficient way to compress a texture to BC3 or BC5 on the GPU uses a compute shader [Walbourn 18].

BC7 and ASTC compression are more complicated because they support a lot of additional block modes and the search space for encoding options is exponentially larger.

How BC7 compression works is described in [Reed 12]. In order to be practical, we need to reduce the compression search space. We recommend limiting it to BC7 Mode 4 and Mode 5 only. These modes are good candidates for decals because they have 6- and 8-bit alpha endpoints and the alpha is separate from the color. Limiting the search space to these two modes allows brute-forcing the compression in async compute in a reasonable time.

Runtime ASTC compression can be implemented in a similar fashion. With available endpoint modes [ARM 24] and by limiting the endpoint modes to 6- or 8-bit separate alpha, we can reasonably compress ASTC at runtime. ASTC also supports varying the block size. It is possible to vary the block size and trade off texture quality for compression speed based on the hardware performance.

11.3 Additional Decal Features

Parallax Decals Parallax occlusion mapping [Tatarchuk 06] is often used to improve surface details in many games. Parallax mapping techniques rely on modifying the UV channel based on the input height map before the texture is sampled.

With forward decals, it is possible to resolve a decal and apply a parallax map effect to the surface before the actual shading calculations. This can be used to create a variety of different effects that are not possible with deferred decals.

11.3.1 Animated and Custom Gameplay Decals

Dynamic decals can be animated. The most common approach to animating the decals are flip books. Technical artists often bake the result of a frame-by-frame complex simulations into the texture and use the game time to drive the animation and interpolation of these keyframes.

Because each decal structure contains it's own time stamp since the decal was spawned, we can use it to drive a flip book animation.

11.3.2 SDF Shapes

The alpha channel of the decal can be multiplied by a 2D signed distance function to create complex and interesting decal shapes. The shape type is encoded into the 32-bit decal flags discussed in Section 11.2.1, and the shape radius or size is stored in the context-dependent decal data.

We are going to use a few examples from [Quilez 24] to show how to achieve different shapes by using the decal UV to compute a distance to several analytical shapes. These shapes can be combined using signed distance field (SDF) boolean operators from the same article.

Let us start with a regular square decals with no additional SDF shaping functions applied, as in Figure 11.2.

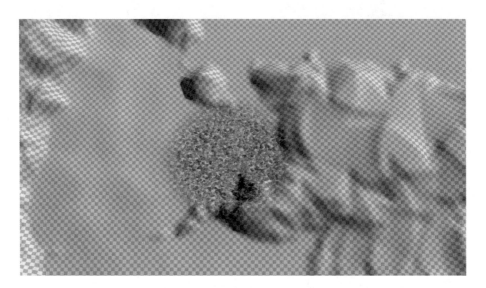

Figure 11.3. Circular shaped decal.

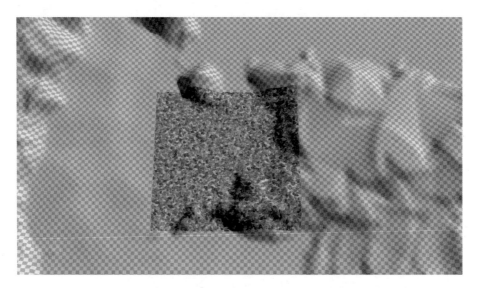

Figure 11.2. Base decal with no features enabled.

A circular shaped decal as in Figure 11.3 can be achieved with the following:

```
float sdfCircle = 1.0 - dot(decalPosition.xz, decalPosition.xz);
sdfCircle = smoothstep(0.75, 0.95, sdfCircle);
color.a *= sdfCircle;
```

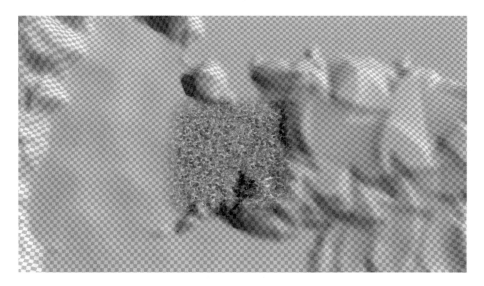

Figure 11.4. Rounded box shaped decal.

A rounded box shaped decal as in Figure 11.4 can be achieved with the following:

```
float2 boxPosition = float2(0.5, 0.5);
float2 boxExtent = float2(0.25, 0.25);
float boxRadius = 0.01;

float sdfBox = 1.0 - length(max(abs(decalUV - boxPosition) - boxExtent,
    0.0)) - boxRadius;
sdfBox = smoothstep(0.75, 0.95, sdfBox);
color.a *= sdfBox;
```

11.3.3 Text Decals with Localization

A commonly overlooked use case for decals is various text objects that often need localization. These can be implemented by pre-rendering the localized text into the decal texture once and then using these as regular decals in the game world. These are static decals that could be baked into the virtual texture, however we don't recommend doing that because block compression will ruin the text quality.

11.4 Conclusion

We presented a practical approach to implement decals in a forward renderer and described the flexibility and other advantages over deferred decals.

Bibliography

[ARM 24] ARM. "Adaptive Scalable Texture Compression Developer Guide." ARM Developer. Accessed June, 2024. https://developer.arm.com/documentation/102162/0430/The-ASTC-format.

[Gneiting 20] Axel Gneiting. "Rendering the Hellscape of Doom Eternal." ACM SIGGRAPH Course: Advances in Real-Time Rendering, 2020. https://advances.realtimerendering.com/s2020/RenderingDoomEternal.pdf.

[Hammer 19] Philip Hammer. "Bindless Deferred Decals in The Surge 2." Presented at Digital Dragons, 2019. https://www.slideshare.net/philiphammer/bindless-deferred-decals-in-the-surge-2.

[Persson 13] Emil Persson. "Practical Clustered Shading." Presented at SIGGRAPH, 2013. https://www.humus.name/Articles/PracticalClusteredShading.pdf.

[Quilez 24] Inigo Quilez. "Distance Functions." Personal website. Accessed June, 2024. https://iquilezles.org/articles/distfunctions/.

[Reed 12] Nathan Reed. "Understanding BCn Texture Compression Formats." Personal blog, 2012. https://www.reedbeta.com/blog/understanding-bcn-texture-compression-formats/.

[Tatarchuk 06] Natalya Tatarchuk. "Practical Parallax Occlusion Mapping for Highly Detailed Surface Rendering." Presented at SIGGRAPH, 2006. https://advances.realtimerendering.com/s2006/Tatarchuk-POM.pdf.

[Thomas 14] Gareth Thomas. "Holy smoke! Faster Particle Rendering Using Direct Compute." Presented at AMD and Microsoft Developer Day, 2014. https://www.slideshare.net/slideshow/holy-smoke-faster-particle-rendering-using-direct-compute-by-gareth-thomas/35656271.

[Turánszki 19] János Turánszki. "Thoughts on Light Culling: Stream Compaction vs Flat Bit Arrays." Wicked Engine Devblog, 2019. https://wickedengine.net/2019/02/24/thoughts-on-light-culling-stream-compaction-vs-flat-bit-arrays/.

[Walbourn 18] Chuck Walbourn. "Fast BC3 Block Compression." Microsoft Xbox-ATG-Sample, GitHub, 2018. https://github.com/microsoft/Xbox-ATG-Samples/blob/main/XDKSamples/Graphics/FastBlockCompress/Shaders/BC3Compress.hlsl.

Virtual Shadow Maps

Matej Sakmary, Jake Ryan, Justin Hall,
and Alessio Lustri

12.1 Introduction

Shadow mapping is ubiquitous in real-time applications due to its good performance and compatibility with existing rasterization pipelines. However, the growing demands for graphical fidelity and performance continue to increase the complexity of shadow mapping techniques. The simplest way to increase the quality of a shadow map—increasing its resolution—scales its memory cost quadratically and increases the likelihood of cache misses when sampling, leading to worse performance. This makes it an impractical way to achieve acceptable quality in diverse scenes. Moreover, shadow maps suffer from two major forms of aliasing: perspective aliasing and projective aliasing, shown in Figure 12.1.

Perspective aliasing occurs when screen pixels do not map to shadow texels in a one-to-one manner. In a basic shadow map implementation, this can be observed by simply moving the viewer closer to or farther from the edge of a shadow. When close, the edge has a jagged appearance due to individual

Figure 12.1. Left: Shadows exhibiting perspective aliasing from insufficient shadow map resolution. Right: Projective aliasing can be seen by the jagged shadow edges on the wall.

shadow texels mapping to many screen pixels. Even when filtered, a slight shift in occluding geometry or the casting light will appear jittery. When far from the shadow, the shadow map over-samples the scene and consumes more memory than necessary.

When the direction of incident light is almost parallel to the surface, projective aliasing occurs. In this case, the projection of a texel onto that surface will cover a large area, making the depth sample an inaccurate representation of the blocker. For an observer, this gives the edges of shadows a jagged appearance, even when there is otherwise no visible perspective aliasing.

12.1.1   Previous Work

Cascaded Shadow Maps (CSMs) is a popular algorithm used to alleviate both types of aliasing in directional lights [Dimitrov 07]. In CSMs, the viewer's frustum is partitioned into smaller frusta, each fit with its own light space matrix and assigned a shadow map. The scene is then rendered to each shadow map using the cascade's frustum. The result is an improved distribution of shadow texels. A denser shadow map is placed near the viewer where detail is most needed, while distant regions receive coarser shadows. *Sample Distribution Shadow Maps* (SDSMs) improve CSMs by using a per-frame analysis of the rendered scene to calculate tight-fitting frusta, maximizing the efficiency of the shadow sample distribution regardless of scene content [Lauritzen et al. 11].

Although these techniques reduce aliasing, the fundamental compromise between shadow quality and memory cost remains. It is thus common for rendering engines to provide several options for shadows, each with their own set of trade-offs. For example, screen-space ray tracing is often used for sharper and more detailed contact shadows in contrast to those provided by shadow mapping implementations.

With the release of Unreal Engine 5 (UE5), Epic Games added *Virtual Shadow Maps* that scale to support the detailed geometry enabled by Nanite [Epic Games 22, Karis 21].

12.1.2   Virtual Memory Overview

Virtual Shadow Maps (VSMs), as the name might suggest, are an application of *virtual textures* [van Waveren 09, Barrett 08] for shadow mapping. Virtual texturing itself is essentially a generalization of *virtual memory*.

By separating the logical address space (seen by the user) from its physical backing, the appearance of a very large contiguous memory space can be achieved without the need to reserve physical memory for it. This is done by dividing the logical address space into pages that are dynamically backed by physical memory.

Virtual memory provides numerous benefits in operating systems. For virtual texturing and thus also VSMs, its primary purpose is to provide an abstraction allowing for a highly reduced memory footprint. That is, only the pages of a VSM that are visible need to be allocated.

As mentioned above, it is common to combine multiple shadowing algorithms to achieve the best visual result. The efficient distribution of shadow texels that VSMs offer makes them viable as a standalone technique. Thus, VSMs also serve to unify multiple shadowing paths, making it easier to author scenes without having to consider how each path may be affected.

Inspired by UE5, we re-derive and implement Virtual Shadow Maps in our renderer. This article and the accompanying demo application serve as pedagogical tools to understand this technique. This is mainly motivated by the lack of resources that describe this technique in detail at the time of writing. We could find only one resource [Haar 15] that mentioned VSMs, and it only does so in passing.

12.2 Implementation

Our implementation supports a VSM for a directional light, consisting of 16 overlapping 4096×4096 cascades arranged in a concentric manner. Every cascade consists of a sparsely allocated set of pages, with each page spanning 128×128 texels. Each cascade's frustum is twice the size of the previous cascade's. The size of the first cascade, specified in world-space units, thus determines the resolution and quality of the entire VSM. In our implementation, we chose to make our first cascade 2×2 meters wide, with the last cascade covering a diameter of 65 km. The virtual resolution of cascades, their number, and the resolution of pages can vary.

A *virtual page table* (VPT) is used to map virtual addresses to physical addresses when we sample the shadow map. The VPT also contains metadata: page allocation status, visibility status, and a dirty flag. The allocation status flag marks pages that are backed by a physical page. The visibility status flag indicates whether the page is visible to the viewer in this frame. The dirty status flag indicates that the physical page contents are no longer valid and should be redrawn. We further define a *physical page table* (PPT) that provides the mapping of physical pages to virtual pages (the inverse of the VPT).

Sparse (or tiled) resources in graphics APIs initially seem like an obvious choice for VSMs. However, the API for sparse resources does not allow for an indirect GPU-driven approach. To know which VSM pages need to be backed by physical memory would require GPU readback. This adds unacceptable latency and leads to shadow pop-in. Our implementation opts for a manual allocation scheme that allows for execution of every part of the algorithm on the GPU and avoids this round trip latency.

Page Caching Caching is a common and important optimization for shadow mapping in the semi-static scenes frequently found in real-time applications. We implement a per-page caching scheme for VSMs. After a page is drawn and sampled, it is not discarded. Instead, its contents are preserved, and the allocation is left untouched, continuing its lifetime into the next frame. By doing this, we minimize the number of required draws and allow for more efficient culling.

To support caching, individual cascade frustums are snapped to the page grid. Further, the light position is constrained so that, when modified, it slides along a plane parallel to the near-plane of the respective light matrix. This constraint is necessary for the depth stored in cached pages to remain valid even after translating the light matrix.

As the cascade frustum moves to follow the main camera, new pages, previously located on the edge just outside of the cascade frustum, might need to be drawn. In order to preserve previously cached pages, we utilize a sliding window, also called *2D wraparound addressing* in [Asirvatham and Hoppe 05]. As new pages enter the frustum when it moves, old pages exit, as illustrated by Figure 12.2. With a sliding window, the newly entered pages are mapped to the location in the VPT previously occupied by old, exiting pages. This requires us

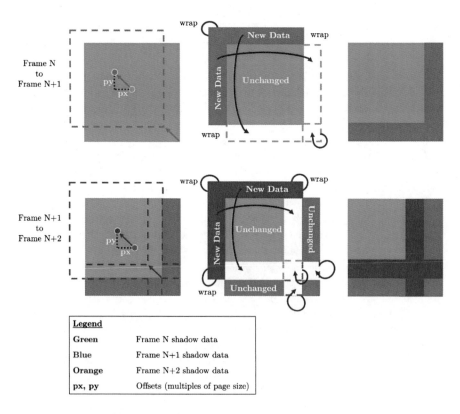

Figure 12.2. Sliding window and caching.

```
ivec3 virtual_page_coords_to_wrapped_coords(ivec3 page_coords, ivec2
    cascade_offset)
{
    // Make sure that the virtual page coordinates are in page
    // table bounds to prevent erroneous wrapping
    if( any(lessThan(page_coords.xy, ivec2(0))) ||
        any(greaterThan(page_coords.xy, ivec2(VSM_PAGE_TABLE_RESOLUTION
    - 1))))
    {
        return ivec3(-1, -1, page_coords.z);
    }
    const ivec2 offset_page_coords = page_coords.xy + cascade_offset.xy;

    const ivec2 wrapped_page_coords = ivec2(mod(offset_page_coords.xy,
    vec2(VSM_PAGE_TABLE_RESOLUTION)));
    // Third coordinate specifies the VSM cascade level
    return ivec3(wrapped_page_coords, page_coords.z);
}
```

Listing 12.1. Function used to convert from coordinates obtained by projecting by cascades light matrix into wrapped coordinates.

to store a per-cascade offset of the respective light matrix position from the origin. Therefore, a translation function projecting from virtual page coordinates into wrapped coordinates is given by Listing 12.1. The wrapped coordinates are then used to look up VPT entries.

In dynamic scenes, it is sometimes necessary to invalidate cached pages. For example, changing the direction of a directional light will invalidate all its pages. A mechanism to invalidate cached pages overlapped by moving objects is also necessary.

We will now explain in further detail each step of our approach to implementing Virtual Shadow Maps. Figure 12.3 gives an overview of our implementation of VSMs.

12.2.1 Bookkeeping

The bookkeeping phase comprises a set of smaller tasks that prepare the data to draw the shadow map. This consists of five steps, which will be described in detail in this section. The execution flow diagram, along with all the resources used, can be seen in Figure 12.4.

Freeing Invalidated Pages The first step in bookkeeping is to free cached pages that have been invalidated by a change in the position of the light matrix or by the page intersecting a moving object. From the CPU, we receive a per-cascade input containing the number of pages the light matrix moved compared to the previous frame and a bitmask representing the set of pages invalidated by dynamic objects. We then simply free the appropriate entries in the VPT by resetting their allocation status to 0. The code to free invalidated pages is then given by Listing 12.2.

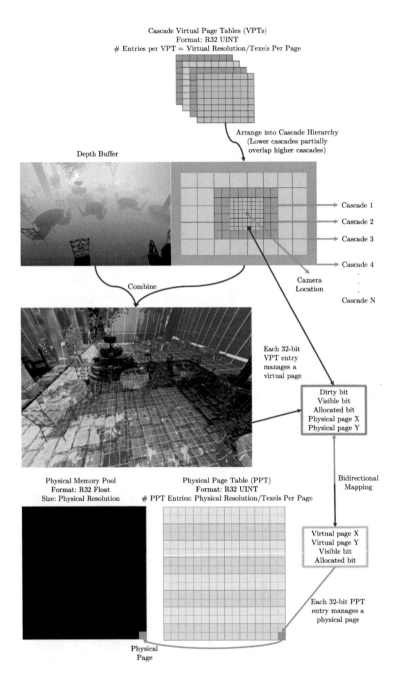

Figure 12.3. Virtual memory system overview.

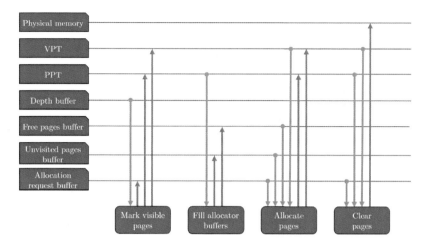

Figure 12.4. Setup flowchart.

```
// Cascade shift gives the offset in pages relative to the cascade
// position previous frame cascade offset is the offset used
// for the sliding window
void free_wrapped_pages(ivec2 cascade_shift, ivec2 cascade_offset)
{
    const ivec3 page_coords = ivec3(gl_LocalInvocationID.xyz);

    const bool should_clear_wrap =
        (clear_offset.x > 0 && page_coords.x <  cascade_shift.x) ||
        (clear_offset.x < 0 && page_coords.x >
    VSM_PAGE_TABLE_RESOLUTION + (cascade_shift.x - 1)) ||
        (clear_offset.y > 0 && page_coords.y <  cascade_shift.y) ||
        (clear_offset.y < 0 && page_coords.y >
    VSM_PAGE_TABLE_RESOLUTION + (cascade_shift.y - 1));
    const bool should_clear_dynamic = extract_page_bit_from_mask(
    page_coords, bitmask);
    const ivec3 wrapped_page_coords =
    virtual_page_coords_to_wrapped_coords(page_coords, cascade_offset);

    if(should_clear_wrap || should_clear_dynamic)
    {
        const uint page_entry = imageLoad(virtual_page_table,
    wrapped_page_coords).r;
        if(get_is_allocated(page_entry))
        {
            imageStore(virtual_page_table, wrapped_page_coords, uvec4(0)
    );
        }
    }
}
```

Listing 12.2. Function used to free invalidated pages. First, we determine if the virtual page needs to be freed from the data sent from the CPU. If the page does need freeing, we translate into wrapped corrdinates and reset its state.

Mark Visible Pages Each screen pixel is assigned a shadow cascade index based on a heuristic. A heuristic is used because simply choosing the most detailed possible cascade does not provide adequate control over shadow detail and memory consumption.

We describe two different heuristics, each of which has its own advantages and disadvantages.

The first heuristic prioritizes achieving pixel-perfect shadows—a one-to-one mapping of screen pixels to shadow map texels. This heuristic is similar to how mipmap levels are selected when sampling textures. To achieve this, we obtain the world-space size of each texel by unprojecting its opposing sides into world space and finding their distance. The clip level is then decided by the following formula:

$$\text{level} = \max\left(\left\lceil \log_2\left(\frac{T_w}{T_{c_0}}\right)\right\rceil, 0\right), \tag{12.1}$$

where T_w and T_{c_0} are the screen-space texel world size and cascade 0 texel world size, respectively. Although this heuristic has a theoretically optimal cascade selection, it does not take into account the available resolution of each cascade. This may cause a pixel to fall into a cascade outside of the cascade frustum itself. This happens when the resolution of the shadow map is close to or higher than the resolution of the screen. In practice, a biasing term can be introduced, offsetting the cascade selection to favor higher cascades.

The second heuristic is simpler and does not achieve as tight of a screen pixel to shadow texel mapping as the first. In contrast to the first heuristic, the issue of mapping texels outside of each cascade frustum is not present. The formula of the second heuristic is given by the following equation:

$$\text{level} = \max\left(\left\lceil \log_2\left(\frac{d}{s_{c_0}}\right)\right\rceil, 0\right), \tag{12.2}$$

where d is the world-space distance of the texel from the camera and s_{c_0} is the side length of the 0th cascade's frustum. An advantage of this heuristic is that the chosen level for a given location in world space is rotationally invariant; that is, if the viewer rotates their camera, no virtual page that remains in view will be invalidated.

To know which pages need to be drawn, we first need to find the set of pages that are visible in this frame. This consists of a pass over the current frame depth buffer. Similarly to SDSM, VSM requires a full-resolution depth buffer drawn from the viewer's perspective. For each depth texel, one of the previously described heuristics is used to select the corresponding cascade. Using the selected cascade matrices, the fragment is reprojected into the cascade UV coordinates and the corresponding entry from the VPT is read. Then one of three actions is taken, depending on the state of the page stored in the page table. If the page has not yet been allocated, its coordinates are added to the

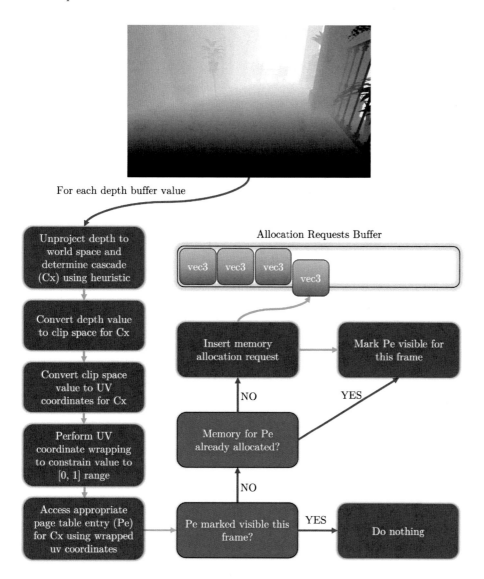

Figure 12.5. Overview of the depth analysis used to select a suitable cascade for each pixel.

buffer storing allocation requests for this frame. If the page is already allocated but not yet marked as visible, we mark it as visible this frame. Lastly, if the page is allocated *and* marked as visible, we do nothing (Figure 12.5).

Figure 12.6 shows how we visualized cascade selection and page states for debugging.

Figure 12.6. Left: Visualization showing the cascade levels and visible pages. The pink pages are those invalidated by the motion of a moving sphere whose shadow is visible. Right: The status of each page in first VSM cascade is shown. Currently visible pages are denoted by bright red. Pages that are cached, but not visible are denoted by dark red. Black pages consume no physical memory.

Filling Allocator Buffers In preparation for allocation, we distribute the physical pages into two buffers. The first buffer contains the coordinates of all pages that have not yet been allocated to a VSM page. The second buffer holds the coordinates of all physical pages that have been allocated but are backing virtual pages that were not marked as visible in this frame. If a physical page is both allocated and backs a shadow map page that is visible in this frame, it is not inserted into either buffer since it will not be freed.

Allocating Pages The allocation pass maps the shadow map pages stored in the allocation requests buffer to physical pages stored in the two buffers prepared in the last step. The allocator attempts to use physical pages from the first buffer, holding unallocated pages. Only when there are insufficient free pages are the pages in the second buffer used (Figure 12.7). In this case, the page must first be freed before it is reused. Since the physical page entry stores the coordinates of the virtual page that it backs, freeing the physical page and assigning it to a virtual page can both be done in the same pass. Before proceeding with the allocation, we look up the virtual page entry currently backed by the physical page and reset it to the not allocated state. To complete the allocation, both the physical page and new virtual page are marked as allocated, and each stores the others' coordinates for future reference.

Clear Pages Before drawing the VSM, we need to clear the physical memory of the dirty pages. We cannot simply clear all physical pages, as we wish to preserve

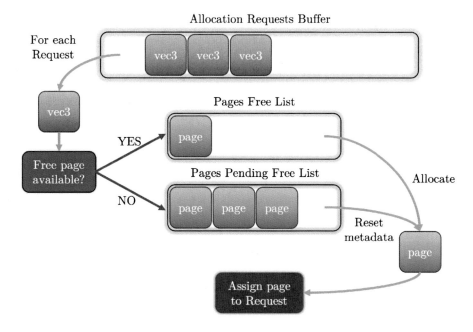

Figure 12.7. Overview of the page allocation system.

cached pages. Therefore, we use the allocation requests buffer to determine pages that have just been allocated and need to be cleared. Then, an indirect dispatch clears the corresponding physical pages.

12.2.2   Drawing Phase

Hierarchical Page Culling   After determining which virtual pages are visible to the viewer and allocating physical pages to back them, the scene is rendered to each cascade. Due to the VSM having many cascades, it is critical to have effective and granular scene culling. In a typical frame, only a fraction of the pages in each cascade will be marked as dirty at any time. With this knowledge, we define a structure called the hierarchical page buffer (HPB) (Figure 12.8). Similarly to how a hierarchical Z-buffer (Hi-Z) [Greene et al. 93] is built from the depth buffer for the purpose of occlusion culling, we build the HPB from each cascade VPT for the purpose of culling geometry that does not overlap any dirty page. Thus, each HPB level is constructed as a 2×2 reduction of the lower level, with the lowest level reducing the VPT itself. Contrary to Hi-Z, we do not reduce the depth. Instead, we do a max reduction of the dirty status flag marking the page as being drawn into this frame. Figure 12.9 illustrates this culling scheme.

To achieve granular culling, our drawing was implemented with meshlets combined with mesh shaders. One meshlet is mapped to a single task shader

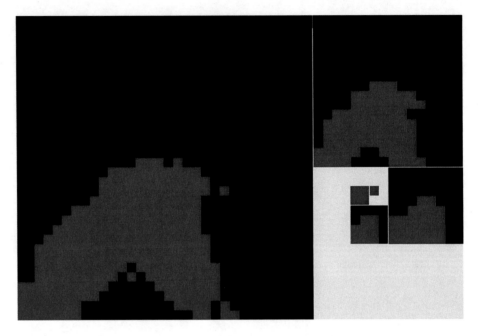

Figure 12.8. Mipmap chain for the hierarchical page buffer. Red: dirty page. Black: cached or unused page.

invocation. The task (or amplification) shader performs frustum culling followed by culling against the HPB.

When culling geometry against the HPB, we follow a process almost identical to culling against a Hi-Z. First, the meshlet bounding box is projected by the cascade light matrix. The minimum and maximum bounds of the projected bounding box are then calculated and the appropriate level of the HPB is selected. The selection is done in the same way as when using Hi-Z: we select the level in which the bounding-box bounds intersect exactly four texels. Lastly, if any of the four intersected texels is marked as dirty, the meshlet survives culling; otherwise, it is discarded.

After culling, a group of 32 mesh shader threads is dispatched for each of the surviving meshlets. The fragment shader calculates the page entry coordinates, translates them into wrapped coordinates, and looks up the corresponding VPT entry. Fragments that are mapped to page entries that are not marked both allocated and dirty do nothing. Fragments that map onto a valid VPT page read the physical page coordinates from the virtual page entry. Following this, the fragment offset inside the physical page is calculated, and an atomic min operation is used to store the new depth. The fragment shader code is presented in Listing 12.3.

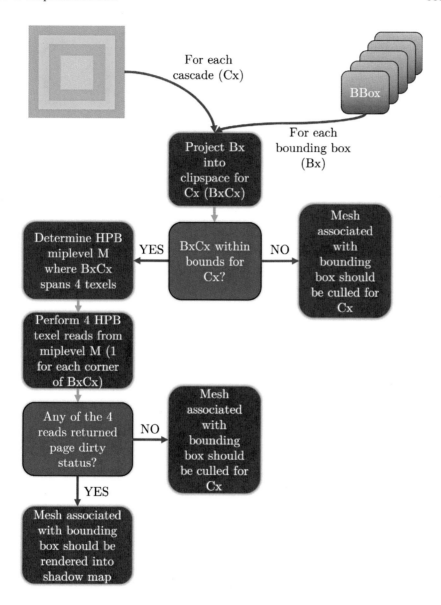

Figure 12.9. HPB culling scheme overview.

While this culling system is used for our implementation of VSMs, it can be applied more generally to any shadow mapping algorithm. To build an HPB for culling, the only input needed is the set of visible shadow pages, which is derived from the *Mark Visible Pages* pass.

```
layout (location = 0) in flat uint cascade_index;
layout (location = 1) in flat ivec2 cascade_offset;
void main()
{
    const vec2 virtual_uv = gl_FragCoord.xy / VSM_TEXTURE_RESOLUTION;
    const ivec3 page_coords = ivec3(floor(virtual_uv *
    VSM_PAGE_TABLE_RESOLUTION), cascade_index);
    const ivec3 wrapped_page_coords =
    virtual_page_coords_to_wrapped_coords(page_coords, cascade_offset);

    const uint page_entry = imageLoad(virtual_page_table,
    wrapped_page_coords).r;

    if(get_is_allocated(page_entry) && get_is_dirty(page_entry))
    {
        const ivec2 physical_page_coords = unpack_physical_page_coords(
    page_entry);
        const ivec2 virtual_texel_coords = ivec2(gl_FragCoord.xy);
        const ivec2 in_page_texel_coords = ivec2(mod(virtual_texel_coord
    , VSM_PAGE_SIZE));
        const ivec2 in_memory_offset = physical_page_coords *
    VSM_PAGE_SIZE;
        const ivec2 memory_texel_coords = in_memory_offset +
    in_page_texel_coord;

        imageAtomicMin(vsm_memory, memory_texel_coords, floatBitsToUint(
    gl_FragCoord.z));
    }
}
```

Listing 12.3. The fragment shader used to draw the shadow maps into pages in memory. First, we check if the fragment maps to a page that should be drawn into. Following is a translation process from the unwrapped VPT coordinates into the location of the texel in the memory block assigned to the virtual page. Lastly, image atomic min is performed storing the new fragment depth.

12.2.3 Sampling Phase

When sampling the VSM, the cascade of the shaded pixel needs to be determined. For this purpose, we reuse the heuristic that was used to mark the visible pages. The receiver's position is transformed into the light space of the sampled cascade. This is then translated into VPT texture coordinates and wrapped to obtain the final VPT entry location. From the VPT entry, the coordinates of the physical texel in the physical page are calculated following the same process utilized when drawing VSM pages.

Although the VSM is detailed, a single shadow sample per shaded texel is insufficient for compelling soft shadows. For this purpose, further filtering of the VSM needs to be used. Common shadow filtering algorithms, such as PCF and PCSS [Fernando 05], can be used together with VSMs.

Although this approach works for most shaded pixels, an issue arises when the sampling region crosses the physical page boundary. The pass marking the visible pages assumes that we will perform a shadow test only for the texels visible in this frame. When filtering, this assumption is broken. One or more samples from the filtering region may fall into parts of the world that are not visible from the main camera. The guarantee of at least one physical page backing each sampled texel thus no longer holds.

This can cause artifacts when the edge of a shadow is near the edge of a page. To mitigate the issue and restore the guarantee when shadow filtering is desired, the Mark Visible Pages pass must be modified. Instead of marking only the page directly corresponding to the visible texel, we mark all pages lying in a region around it. This region must be greater than or equal to the size of the filtering region.

12.3   Results

All performance data was collected with an RTX 3070 GPU and R9 5950X CPU. Performance was tested by moving the camera along a predetermined path in the Bistro scene containing $\sim 4,000,000$ triangles. (See Tables 12.1 and 12.2.)

Figure 12.10 shows a scene containing millimeter-scale and kilometer-scale geometry, which poses a significant problem for traditional solutions. VSMs overcome the issues by allocating memory to near and distant pages as necessary.

We show how VSMs allow us to achieve nearly pixel-perfect shadows in diverse scenes for the price of just one 4096×4096 backing texture. For example, if a density of one shadow texel per screen texel is desired, the upper bound of memory usage will be approximately equal to the number of screen pixels in well-behaved scenes.

	Bookkeeping	Cull and draw	Total
4096×4096 VSM, 128×128 pages			
Uncached	245 µs	2128 µs	2373 µs
Cached	103 µs	285 µs	388 µs
4096×4096 VSM, 64×64 pages			
Uncached	216 µs	1,858 µs	2074 µs
Cached	109 µs	350 µs	459 µs
2048×2048 VSM, 128×128 pages			
Uncached	150 µs	985 µs	1135 µs
Cached	99 µs	238 µs	337 µs
2048×2048 VSM, 64×64 pages			
Uncached	137 µs	811 µs	948 µs
Cached	103 µs	217 µs	320 µs

Table 12.1. Mean GPU times for the primary passes in various configurations. Cached: the previously described scheme for caching pages is used. Uncached: every visible page is redrawn every frame.

4096 × 4096 VSM, 128 × 128 pages	
Samples	**Time**
0 (base)	314µs
1	375µs
4	509µs
8	635µs
16	886µs

Table 12.2. Mean GPU times for our shading pass at 1920 × 1080 with various VSM sample counts. We found no correlation between the VSM or page size and the shading time.

Figure 12.10. Hard shadows from three perspectives in a scene containing 5km-wide terrain and Bistro. The VSM parameters remained the same for each image. A single 4096 × 4096 texture provided sufficient physical memory in each case.

Additional cascades that are not visible incur the trivial cost of maintaining bookkeeping structures (the VPT and PPT). Only if any page in a cascade becomes dirty does the scene need to be culled and rendered to the cascade.

12.4 Future Work

12.4.1 Translucency and Participating Media

Some shadow-receiving effects do not contribute to the depth buffer, subverting our depth-based analysis in Mark Visible Pages. Translucent objects and ray-marched participating media are common examples of such effects. Because they have no correlation with the depth buffer, the VSM may lack depth information where it samples, producing errors in the resulting shadows.

One way to solve this issue is to ensure that every location in the viewer frustum has at least one valid page that could be sampled. To minimize memory usage, pages from coarser cascades that intersect the frustum should be marked visible. This ensures that low-resolution shadows are available everywhere. This strategy is used by UE5.

A different strategy is to mark the page as visible when a page fault occurs. With this, the page will become backed by physical memory the next time the allocator is executed. Although simpler, this approach leads to shadows "popping in" as there is one frame of latency between the page fault and the allocation. To mitigate this, the non-depth-writing passes can be executed one more time each frame, recording page faults before the allocation pass.

12.4.2 Local Lights

While UE5 has proven that using VSMs for local lights is feasible, we elected to simplify our implementation by focusing on directional lights only, where VSMs offer the greatest benefit.

12.4.3 Dynamic Time of Day

As previously described, a change in the light source's position or direction requires all pages in its VSM to be invalidated. With a dynamic time-of-day system, all pages would be invalidated every frame.

To maintain cached pages, the Sun's rotation can be quantized such that invalidation only occurs every N frames. A reprojection scheme like the one described in [Pavlo 19] can be used to eliminate the artifacts that result.

12.4.4 Optimizations

Optimizing the drawing phase of VSMs remains an open problem for us. Profiling and empirical testing revealed reducing fragment shader invocations (particularly those that do not map to dirty pages) to yield the largest performance gains. Our current optimizations (HPB culling and caching) focus on this. Figure 12.11 shows our utilities for detecting overdraw.

The most granular way to avoid fragment shader invocations on non-dirty pages is to use compute shader rasterization. With this, fixed-function costs and helper invocations on the edges of triangles would be avoided. We suspect a substantial benefit for coarser VSM cascades, due to the triangles becoming proportionately smaller.

12.5   Acknowledgements

Matej Sakmary was supported by the Grant Agency of the Czech Technical University in Prague, project no. SGS22/173/OHK3/3T/13.

Figure 12.11. Left: Because our shadow rendering is bound by fragment shader invocations, having a visualization of shadow overdraw was important. Right: A texture showing the status of pages in the PPT. Hotter colors correspond with lower (near) cascades, with red being the nearest. Darker colors denote cached pages, as in Figure 12.6.

Bibliography

[Asirvatham and Hoppe 05] Arul Asirvatham and Hugues Hoppe. "Terrain Rendering Using GPU-Based Geometry Clipmaps." In *GPU Gems 2*, edited by Matt Pharr, Chapter 2, pp. 27–46. Addison-Wesley, 2005.

[Barrett 08] Sean Barrett. "Sparse Virtual Texture Memory." Presented at Game Developers Conference, 2008. https://www.gdcvault.com/play/417/Sparse-Virtual-Texture.

[Dimitrov 07] Rouslan Dimitrov. "Cascaded Shadow Maps." NVIDIA Developer Documentation, 2007. https://developer.download.nvidia.com/SDK/10.5/opengl/src/cascaded_shadow_maps/doc/cascaded_shadow_maps.pdf.

[Epic Games 22] Epic Games. "Virtual Shadow Maps." Unreal Engine Documentation, 2022. https://dev.epicgames.com/documentation/en-us/unreal-engine/virtual-shadow-maps-in-unreal-engine.

[Fernando 05] Randima Fernando. "Percentage-Closer Soft Shadows." In *ACM SIGGRAPH 2005 Sketches*, pp. 35–es. Association for Computing Machinery, 2005.

[Greene et al. 93] Ned Greene, Michael Kass, and Gavin Miller. "Hierarchical Z-Buffer Visibility." In *Proceedings of the 20th Annual Conference on Com-*

puter Graphics and Interactive Techniques, pp. 231–238. Association for Computing Machinery, 1993.

[Haar 15] Ulrich Haar. "GPU-Driven Rendering Pipelines." Presented at SIGGRAPH, 2015. https://advances.realtimerendering.com/s2015/ aaltonenhaar_siggraph2015_combined_final_footer_220dpi.pdf.

[Karis 21] Brian Karis. "Nanite: A Deep Dive." Presented at SIG-GRAPH, 2021. https://advances.realtimerendering.com/s2021/Karis_ Nanite_SIGGRAPH_Advances_2021_final.pdf.

[Lauritzen et al. 11] Andrew Lauritzen, Marco Salvi, and Aaron Lefohn. "Sample Distribution Shadow Maps." In *Symposium on Interactive 3D Graphics and Games*, pp. 97–102. Association for Computing Machinery, 2011.

[Pavlo 19] Turchyn Pavlo. "Parallax-Corrected Cached Shadow Maps." In *GPU Zen 2*, edited by Wolfgang Engel, pp. 143–152. Black Cat Publishing, 2019.

[van Waveren 09] J.M.P. van Waveren. "id Tech 5 Challenges." Presented at SIGGRAPH, 2009. https://web.archive.org/web/20091007031619/http: //s09.idav.ucdavis.edu/talks/05-JP_id_Tech_5_Challenges.pdf.

Real-Time Simulation of Massive Crowds

Tomer Weiss

13.1 Introduction

Crowds are common in games, movies, and other entertainment media. In such media, crowds vary greatly, ranging from pedestrians to animals to swarms to robots. When recreating crowds virtually, there are many technical details involved including rendering, animation, and simulation. In this article, we focus on simulating crowd behavior dynamics.

Crowd behaviors include anticipation of future states and potential navigation conflicts, movement to a navigational goal, movement in groups, and moving in a smooth manner by avoiding sudden turns or accelerations. Other crowd aspects include maintaining physical realism, as in we do not want situations where crowd agents take up the same space.

In the following sections, we first lay the groundwork by detailing core simulation principles, followed by a step-by-step explanation of our algorithm tailored for simulating crowds on a GPU. We also discuss how to control the behavior of crowds with real-time parallel computation, easily supporting thousands or more agents on screen, along with examples and implementation strategy. This article is based on existing work [Weiss et al. 19, Weiss 19, Weiss 23].

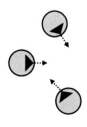

Figure 13.1. Left: Agent. Middle: Multi-agent crowds. Right: Our simulation abstracts crowd agents as moving discs, to simplify computation of agent motion. This article focuses on computing the position and velocity of such discs. After such computation, the discs are rendered as crowd agents (middle).

13.2   Method

Our framework is grounded in methods for simulating physical phenomena with particle-based constraints [Macklin et al. 14]. Constraint-based dynamics have been used for applications such as fluid dynamics, deformable materials such as cloth, and rigid bodies. However, in our case, crowd agents are not mere objects, but rather self-actuated. That is, each crowd member behaves in an independent manner where if there is a physical barrier, agents navigate around it rather than collide with it as a particle would. Thus, we develop several innovations that allow the simulation of crowds with such constraints.

Below we detail how we define crowds in terms of data, followed by an overview of our algorithm. Then, we focus on the specific constraints we use to emulate crowd behaviors.

In terms of data, to simplify the computation of crowd dynamics, we abstract crowd agents as discs moving on a plane. Assuming that we have N crowd agents, each agent i, where $i = 1, 2, \ldots, N$, is associated with the following data:

- a disc of radius $r_i \in \mathbb{R}$,

- a group affiliation $n \in \mathbb{N}$,

- a position $\boldsymbol{x}_i \in \mathbb{R}^2$,

- a navigation goal position $\mathbf{g}_i \in \mathbb{R}^2$,

- a velocity $\boldsymbol{v}_i \in \mathbb{R}^2$,

- a preferred speed $v_{\mathrm{pref}} \in \mathbb{R}$

- a predicted position $\boldsymbol{x}^* \in \mathbb{R}^2$,

- a mass $m_i \in \mathbb{R}$,

- an inverse mass $w_i = 1/m_i \in \mathbb{R}$,

where additional parameters can be added as needed by the user. Static entities such as walls or impassable areas need to be defined separately (See Section 13.2.4).

In our algorithm, agents make independent navigational decisions by selecting a velocity vector $\boldsymbol{v}_i$ (Algorithm 13.1, line 3). Each agent calculates its velocity independently. Then, given such velocity, each agent calculates its initial predicted position $\boldsymbol{x}_i^*$. These predicted positions are used for resolving emergent environment dynamics, such as agent-agent collisions, agent spatial relationships, and obstacle avoidance.

Computations are done via functions called *constraints* (line 7). Constraints check if agents follow certain conditions that we expect crowd agents to follow. If the conditions are not met, constraints calculate what positional corrections are needed to satisfy the constraints. Such corrections are an adjustment to the

---

Algorithm 13.1: Crowd simulation loop.

---

1 foreach *agent i* do
2   Resolve existing overlaps and update position $\boldsymbol{x}_i$
3   Plan velocity $\boldsymbol{v}_i$
4   Calculate predicted position $\boldsymbol{x}_i^* \leftarrow \boldsymbol{x}_i + \Delta t \boldsymbol{v}_i$
5 end
6 while *iter < solver iterations* do
7   foreach *active constraint group G* do
8         $\Delta \boldsymbol{x} \longleftarrow 0, n \longleftarrow 0$
9   solve all constraints in G for $\Delta \boldsymbol{x}, n$
10   update $\boldsymbol{x}^* \longleftarrow \boldsymbol{x}^* + \Delta \boldsymbol{x}/n$
11   end
12 end
13 foreach *agent i* do
14     $\boldsymbol{v}_i \longleftarrow \text{clamp}(v_{\max}, (\boldsymbol{x}^* - \boldsymbol{x})/\Delta t)$
15   Update position $\boldsymbol{x}_i \leftarrow \boldsymbol{x}_i^*$
16 end

---

agent's predicted position to satisfy the constraint. In the case of n corrections affecting a single agent, we calculate the average correction to get the updated predicted position (line 10). After all constraints are projected, we update the agent's velocity based on its predicted position. If the velocity is higher than a user-defined threshold, we restrict it to the maximum allowed (line 14). Note that this does not affect the predicted position. Finally, we update the position of each agent (line 15), and the cycle begins anew for the subsequent time step.

13.2.1 Velocity Planning

In the beginning of each time step, agents choose a velocity that leads them toward their navigational goal position **g**. Changes to the agent's velocity direction and magnitude may result in sudden turning or acceleration that may appear visually unnatural. To simulate a smoother navigation, we interpolate between the current and desired velocities:

$$\boldsymbol{v}_i = \kappa \boldsymbol{v}_i + (1 - \kappa) v_{\text{pref}} * (\mathbf{g}_i - \boldsymbol{x}_i),$$

where $\kappa \in (0, 1)$ is the interpolation weight. Thus, agents select a velocity that leads them straight toward their current locomotion goal, irrespective of the current agents or obstacles. Though this is a simple strategy, it is effective in many cases. Regardless, other velocity planning strategies are possible [van Toll and Pettré 21].

13.2.2 Dynamics Constraints

Constraints measure whether an agent is obeying certain conditions that we define for simulating crowds dynamics. One important condition is for agents to not overlap. Often, this condition may not be satisfied due to emergent dynamics, such as a high density crowd moving in a small space. In such cases, we use *position-based dynamics* (PBD) to modify agents positions in each time step [Macklin et al. 14].

PBD defines constraints as

$$\text{equality } C(\boldsymbol{x}) = 0 \quad \text{or} \quad \text{inequality } C(\boldsymbol{x}) \geq 0,$$

where $\boldsymbol{x} = [\boldsymbol{x}_1, \dots, \boldsymbol{x}_n]^T$ represents positional and other data of agents involved in the constraint. If the constraint conditions are not held, PBD modifies the positions of each agent involved in the constraint with positional corrections $\Delta \boldsymbol{x}_i$. The positional corrections are vectors in the direction that follows the constraint gradient:

$$\Delta \boldsymbol{x}_i = -s \nabla_{\boldsymbol{x}_i} C(\boldsymbol{x}), \quad s = \frac{k w_i C(\boldsymbol{x})}{\sum_{i=1}^{n} w_i \| \nabla_{\boldsymbol{x}_i} C(\boldsymbol{x}) \|^2}, \tag{13.1}$$

where the stiffness parameter $k \in [0, 1]$ signals the strength of the correction. Each correction is then added to the agent's current predicted position. In the following subsections, we detail the constraints we use and how they are integrated in our simulator.

13.2.3 Constraints: Agent Overlap

Agents may overlap with each other during the course of the navigation, for example in case they choose a velocity the leads them to close proximity. This may occur when agents' paths cross. (See Figure 13.2.)

To resolve such conflict, we abstract agents i and j as overlapping discs. We then calculate the amount of overlap with

$$C(\boldsymbol{x}_i^*, \boldsymbol{x}_j^*) = \| \boldsymbol{x}_{ij}^* \| - (r_i + r_j) \geq 0, \tag{13.2}$$

where i and j are agents, $\boldsymbol{x}_{ij} = \boldsymbol{x}_i^* - \boldsymbol{x}_j^*$, and r_i and r_j are the agents i and j corresponding disc radii.

Figure 13.2. Crossing crowd flows. From four different corners of a rectangle, crowd flows meet at the center.

In case the constraint above is not satisfied, we use Equation (13.1) to calculate positional corrections:

$$\Delta\boldsymbol{x}_i = -\frac{w_i}{w_i+w_j}C(\boldsymbol{x}_i^*,\boldsymbol{x}_j^*)\frac{\boldsymbol{x}_{ij}^*}{\|\boldsymbol{x}_{ij}^*\|}, \quad \Delta\boldsymbol{x}_j = +\frac{w_j}{w_i+w_j}C(\boldsymbol{x}_i^*,\boldsymbol{x}_j^*)\frac{\boldsymbol{x}_{ij}^*}{\|\boldsymbol{x}_{ij}^*\|}, \qquad (13.3)$$

where $w_i = 1/m_i$ is the inverse mass of the i-th agent, and similarly for w_j. Note that if one agent is much heavier compared to the other, i.e., bear versus rabbit, then the heavier agent will barley move to correct and overlap. Rather, the lighter agent will do most of the positional correction.

13.2.4 Constraints: Static Obstacles

Virtual environments may contain impassible terrain, e.g., walls or mountains. To prevent agents from crossing such areas, we detect the closest overlapping obstacle point $\boldsymbol{x}_j^*$ and use a modified overlap constraint (Section 13.2.3) with $r_j = 0$. The positional correction follows Equation (13.3), but with $w_j = 0$ to model the obstacle being unmovable. Thus, the collision resolve action is taken only by agent i.

13.2.5 Constraints: Long-Range Interaction

In a crowd, pedestrians anticipate collisions with others, preforming changes to their navigation to avoid a collision. In the crowds literature, this anticipation correlates with a perceived *time to collision* (TTC). Assuming agent paths are linear (see Figure 13.3), and given the agents current positions $\boldsymbol{x}_{ij} = \boldsymbol{x}_i - \boldsymbol{x}_j$ and predicted position $\boldsymbol{x}_{ij}^* = \boldsymbol{x}_i^* - \boldsymbol{x}_j^*$ differences, we calculate

$$\text{TTC} = \frac{b - \sqrt{b^2 - ac}}{a}, \quad \text{where}$$

$$a = \frac{\|\boldsymbol{x}_{ij}^*\|}{\Delta t^2}, \quad b = -\frac{\boldsymbol{x}_{ij} \cdot \boldsymbol{x}_{ij}^*}{\Delta t}, \quad c = \|\boldsymbol{x}_{ij}\|^2 - (r_i + r_j)^2. \qquad (13.4)$$

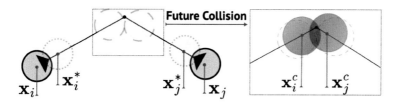

Figure 13.3. Long range interaction. Agents paths may cross in a crowd. We detect such situations by calculating the time to collision (Equation (13.4)) assuming the agents are discs continuing in the same speed and direction.

There are several solutions to this quadratic equation: If $TTC < 0$, the agents' paths have intersected in the past, and the constraint is satisfied. Otherwise, agents are predicted to collide.

In case of a predicted collision, we first check whether the collision will occur in a nearby time window $TTC < \tau$, where τ is a constant threshold for agent reaction. If TTC is above such a threshold, no action is needed as agents do not typically plan their motion far in advance. If TTC is below the threshold and is positive, we use a modified version of the agent overlap constraint to modify the agents' positions to avoid the impending collision (Section 13.2), albeit with two main differences.

First, instead of the predicted position $\boldsymbol{x}_i^*$, we use the positions

$$\boldsymbol{x}_i^c = \boldsymbol{x}_i + \frac{\tau_c(\boldsymbol{x}_i^* - \boldsymbol{x}_i)}{\Delta t}, \quad \tau_c = \Delta t \left(1 + \left\lfloor \frac{TTC}{\Delta t} \right\rfloor \right),$$

where $\boldsymbol{x}_i^c$ is the expected position of agent i assuming the current trajectory and speed, and τ_c is rounded to discrete time steps. To remind the reader, at time TTC the agents' discs are only touching (Figure 13.3), not overlapping. Therefore, we select a future time τ_c where the agents will overlap, which will trigger a positional correction similar to Section 13.2.3.

Second, instead of fully applying the correction in Equation (13.3), we use

$$\Delta \boldsymbol{x} = k e^{-\tau_c^2/\tau} \Delta \boldsymbol{x},$$

where we replace $\Delta \boldsymbol{x}$ with the corresponding correction for agents i and j. The parameter $e^{-\tau_c^2/\tau}$ ties the correction strength to TTC. Thus, the closer the agents are time-wise to colliding, the stronger the avoidance behavior will be. Such scaling is necessary to avoid excessive avoidance behavior when agents are far away from each other.

13.2.6 Constraints: Groups

Agents may elect to locomote in groups. We propose a constraint for simulating pairs of agents locomoting together:

$$C(\boldsymbol{x}_i^*, \boldsymbol{x}_j^*) = ||\boldsymbol{x}_{ij}^*|| - d = 0, \tag{13.5}$$

where d is the desired distance for this pair. The correction for this constraint is similar to the agent overlap constraint (Section 13.2.3):

$$\Delta \boldsymbol{x}_i = -k \frac{w_i}{w_i + w_j} \left(||\boldsymbol{x}_{ij}^*|| - d \right) \frac{\boldsymbol{x}_{ij}^*}{||\boldsymbol{x}_{ij}^*||}, \quad \Delta \boldsymbol{x}_j = +k \frac{w_j}{w_i + w_j} \left(||\boldsymbol{x}_{ij}^*|| - d \right) \frac{\boldsymbol{x}_{ij}^*}{||\boldsymbol{x}_{ij}^*||}. \tag{13.6}$$

Larger groups can be formed using this constraint by linking pairs of agents in a group (Figure 13.4).

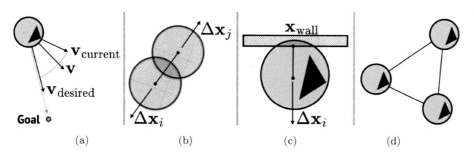

Figure 13.4. Constraints. All our constraints are defined geometrically, and their satisfaction modifies the agent's behavior. (a) During agent navigation, we interpolate between the current and desired velocity to get smoother locomotion. (b) Overlaps between agent pairs are resolved by modifying their predicted positions along the vector that connects their centers. (c) To resolve overlaps with obstacles, we find the nearest wall point and correct the agent's position along the vector between the agent and that point. (d) Groups of two or more agents can be defined by using pair connections between agents.

13.2.7   Maximum Agent Speed

At the end of the simulation loop, an agent's velocity is determined by the final predicted position (Algorithm 13.1, line 14). To model physical limitations on how fast an agent can accelerate, we use a maximum speed limit. In case the velocity is greater than a predefined limit, we clamp the agent's velocity vector to a maximum length that matches a user-defined maximum speed for that agent.

13.3   Results

Our method easily supports thousands of agents in real time with all the above constraints. Supporting more agents in interactive runtimes is possible; see our discussion in the next section. We demonstrate our method in the following scenarios:

- **Group locomoting through a crowd:** A small triangle-shaped group passes through a dense group. The challenge here is that the group needs to stay together while locomoting (Figure 13.1).

- **Crossing flow:** Starting from four different corners of a rectangular plane, agents in long column-shaped groups are tasked with locomoting to the other opposing corner. The difficulty in this case is that agents face a constant stream of opposing agents that obstruct them from reaching their goal (Figure 13.2).

Figure 13.5. Armies. Our method enables the simulation of high-density armies organized in formations (left). Here, the two opposing armies are tasked with locomoting
past each other, which causes tension when the armies meet (right). This interaction
triggers our collision agent overlap resolve constraint (Section 13.2.3).

- **Armies:** Two opposing armies, which are further subdivided to rectangular formations, are tasked to pass each other. Unlike a battlefield situation,
  the challenge here is to locomote through the opposing army group to the
  other side (Figure 13.5).

13.4   Implementation

Our algorithm supports massive crowds by parallelization constraint computation with GPUs. We implemented our algorithm in both CUDA and Taichi-Dev,
which is a Python-based library for parallel computing of VFX simulations [Hu
et al. 19]. We ran our implementation on both an Apple MacBook Pro with
2.5 GHz Intel Core i7 CPU and an NVIDIA GeForce GT 750M GPU, and an
Apple MacBook Pro M1. On both machines, we achieved real-time performance.

Below we give more details on the data structures we used for nearest neighbor search and our parallel computing code in CUDA. Full implementation details of other constraints will be available in our publicly linked repository. Implementing our method in other GPU frameworks such as WebGPU, Metal, and
similar should yield similar performance results.

13.4.1   Data Structures

A main computational bottleneck in our method is finding nearest neighbors,
since how close agents are to each other influences their interactions, such as
collision avoidance maneuvers. A naive implementation of nearest neighbors is
via two for loops, which results in $O(n^2)$. That means, if we are simulating 1000
agents, we will need to compute 1 million operations, which quickly becomes
non-interactive. To address such issues, we use a uniform hash grid.

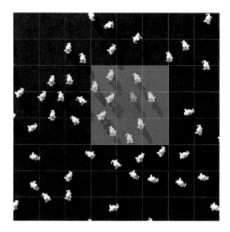

Parameter	Value
Simulation	
Time step Δt	0.01
# Iterations	3
κ velocity interpolation	0.01
Grid cell size	4 agents
Grid radius expansion	5%
Agents	
Agent radius r	0.1
Preferred speed v_{pref}	0.01
Max speed	0.1
Constraints	
Time-to-collision threshold	20
$k_{\mathrm{long\ range}}$	0.01
k_{group}	0.01

Figure 13.6. Left: Spatial hash grid for detecting nearest neighbors. For an agent in the purple shaded cell, we are searching for neighboring agents in a 3×3 cell window, visualized in green. Right: Algorithm parameters used by our method.

Our uniform-cell-size hash grid is constructed at the beginning of each simulation time step (Algorithm 13.1), which is when we compute the cell index to which an agent belongs. Each grid cell includes a buffer list for storing the indexes of agents associated to the cell. Then, to find the nearest neighbor for an agent during the simulation time step, we query all grid cells in a 3×3 window that is centered on such an agent cell. Since a major concern is computation time, we construct the grid using a fast GPU implementation [Green 08].

Agents' predicted positions may change during a time-step due to constraint solving. To avoid missing a potential colliding pair, during grid construction and detection phase we expand the agent's disc radius by a small fraction (see the table in Figure 13.6).

We found uniform hash grids to be most efficient for our demonstrations, which mainly involve high-density crowds. However, using other specialized data structures for nearest neighbor detection is also possible, such as KD-trees and similar.

13.4.2 Constraints

Constraints act on one or more agents at the time, and are either always or conditionally active. To implement "always active" equality constraints (such as grouping in Section 13.2.6), for each constraint type we create a list with all the indices of agents that participate in the constraint. During the simulation time step, we then iterate over the array to find the relevant positional corrections.

To implement inequality conditional constraints, such as ones that depend on agent distances, we first compute distances using the nearest neighbor grid and then iterate over each conditional constraint group. For each constraint, we

```
__device__ void agentOverlapConstraint(
int        i,           // Agent identifiers
int        j,
float      margin,      // Minimum distance allowed
float      wi,          // Typically wi = wj = 0.5
float      wj,
float2 *   pos,         // Agent positions
float2 *   deltaX,      // Positional correction buffer
int    *   deltaXCtr    // Positional correction counter
)
{
    float contact_distance = distance(x[i], x[j]) - margin;
    if(f<0)
    {
        float2 contact_vec=(pos[i]-pos[j])/d;
        atomicAdd(&deltaX[i],-wi*contact_distance*contact_vec);
        atomicAdd(&deltaXCtr[i],1);
        atomicAdd(&deltaX[j],-wj*contact_distance*contact_vec);
        atomicAdd(&deltaXCtr[j],1);
    }
}
```

Listing 13.1. Resolving agent collisions. Each constraint independently affects the agents dynamics by contributing positional corrections.

then check whether the constraint condition is active and, if so, calculate the positional corrections for agents associated with the constraint (Listing 13.1).

Our crowd dynamics engine is blind to the internals of each constraint and only knows about the number of constraint iterations per time step, stiffness, and constraint ordering. These factors affect overall constraint strength and the visual results:

- **Iteration number:** Users can vary the number of times in which constraints are solved. While a single iteration is sufficient in scenarios with limited numbers of agents, more iterations may be required in complex scenarios, such as ones with large or dense crowds. This is because our algorithm solves each constraint independently without solution convergence guarantees. Regardless, visual errors are typically not noticeable, and are usually alleviated with more iterations or a smaller simulation time step.

- **Stiffness:** This determines how much of the positional correction we are using when satisfying the constraint. It allows simulating behaviors that are slow to affect the agent's behavior, such as long-range collision avoidance and grouping.

- **Ordering:** We solve the constraints in the same order each time step, where the equality constraints are solved first, followed by the inequality constraints. Note that the order of evaluation is important, since each constraint adjusts the predicted position independently, unaware of other constraints. For example, if we evaluate agent overlaps after grouping, we may end with colliding agents. Thus, constraints that are solved later during the loop are effectively more influential on the agents final position.

13.4.3 Rendering Setup

We rendered our results in Unity, after running the simulation offline where we saved the agents' positions in each time step. When animating, we used online assets of agents walking and standing from Mixamo, and tuned the walk to match the agent's speed. Other animations, such as running or side stepping, are possible depending on the type and desired level of detail of the target crowds.

All scenario entities, including crowds dimensions, positions, preferred velocities, and locomotion goals, were configured manually for each scenario. However, such data can be changed dynamically during the simulation as needed via additional scripting.

13.5 Conclusion

We presented a method for simulating massive crowds. Our method is fully parallelized with a GPU-ready implementation. We implemented our method in CUDA, but we have also experimented with other GPU frameworks and achieved similar computational cost [Hu et al. 19].

While our work focused on specific pedestrian-style crowds, it can be expended to other moving objects in 2D and 3D spaces, such as robots, cars, and spaceships. Such domains may use the similar or modified constraints with parameter changes.

Note that our framework is influenced by parameter variations, which should be carefully tuned for each application. For example, an application that allows more dramatic agent motions may require larger agent sizes, with no acceleration clamping. Data structures may also require additional tuning—for example, a long-range agent-agent interaction may require a grid with larger cell sizes, or enlarging the search window during nearest neighbor search.

Our work can be easily combined with existing game engines and VFX software, some of which already utilize position-based dynamics for simulating physical phenomena [Macklin et al. 14]. Readers who want to know more details on constraints-based crowd simulation, please refer to [Weiss 19, Weiss et al. 19, Weiss 23].

Bibliography

[Green 08] Simon Green. "Cuda Particles." *NVIDIA Whitepaper* 2:3.2 (2008), 1.

[Hu et al. 19] Yuanming Hu, Tzu-Mao Li, Luke Anderson, Jonathan Ragan-Kelley, and Frédo Durand. "Taichi: A Language for High-Performance Computation on Spatially Sparse Data Structures." *ACM Transactions on Graphics* 38:6 (2019), 201:1–201:16.

[Macklin et al. 14] Miles Macklin, Matthias Müller, Nuttapong Chentanez, and Tae-Yong Kim. "Unified Particle Physics for Real-Time Applications." *ACM Transactions on Graphics* 33:4 (2014), 153:1–153:12.

[van Toll and Pettré 21] W. van Toll and J. Pettré. "Algorithms for Microscopic Crowd Simulation: Advancements in the 2010s." *Computer Graphics Forum: State of the Art Reports* 40:2 (2021), 731–754.

[Weiss et al. 19] Tomer Weiss, Alan Litteneker, Chenfanfu Jiang, and Demetri Terzopoulos. "Position-Based Real-Time Simulation of Large Crowds." *Computers & Graphics* 78 (2019), 12–22.

[Weiss 19] Tomer Weiss. "Implementing Position-Based Real-Time Simulation of Large Crowds." In *2019 IEEE International Conference on Artificial Intelligence and Virtual Reality (AIVR)*, pp. 306–3061. IEEE, 2019.

[Weiss 23] Tomer Weiss. "Fast Position-Based Multi-Agent Group Dynamics." *Proceedings of the ACM on Computer Graphics and Interactive Techniques* 6:1 (2023), 14:1–14:15.

Diffuse Global Illumination
Darius Bouma

Figure 14.1. Example of diffuse global illumination.

14.1 Introduction

Global illumination is a key component in creating a realistic and immersive gaming experience. The techniques described in this article are directly used in our in-house rendering framework called Breda, which we use in our upcoming benchmark called *Evolve*, as well as the recent demo for Samsung on their latest XClipse 940 GPU, powering the S24. Trying to accurately capture all of the scene's bounce light from numerous light sources in real time is a difficult task. Typically the frame budget only allows a very limited amount of rays to be traced, which would require heavy denoising in order to somewhat reliably estimate indirect lighting in a scene. Conserving micro detail while keeping a stable and responsive image has proven to be particularly challenging. In order to address these challenges, ReSTIR [Bitterli et al. 20, Ouyang et al. 21, Wyman and Panteleev 22] is used for both the secondary rays and irradiance cache, amortizing the workload both spatially and temporally. Some trade-offs are made that sacrifice correctness, however in return we get highly responsive and detailed indirect diffuse lighting. To cache indirect lighting in world space, we chose to go for a ReSTIR-based clipmap irradiance cache [Stachowiak 22].

14.2   Clipmap Irradiance Cache

The main purpose of an irradiance cache is to answer queries that require indirect lighting information at a given intersection. These contributions are cached, saving a lot of computation time for any system that needs to sample indirect lighting. Clipmap cascades are used to keep the entry cell size roughly constant in screen space regardless of the distance to the camera. The cache is not temporally stable and lacks resolution for an accurate direct representation of irradiance in the scene, however it performs very well when sampled indirectly from paths at a relatively low cost. Entries are allocated on demand and trace four candidate paths along with four additional validation paths every frame. (See Table 14.1.) With an upper bound of 65,535 entries, this would net a total of 524,280 rays in the worst-case scenario. In reality, the cache barely reaches this upper bound, typically running around 20,000 active allocations.

	Timings	Bounce Rays	Shadow Rays
Update Lifetimes	14 μs		
Reproject Cascades	110 μs		
Trace Candidates	232 μs	4	4
Trace Validate	315 μs	4	4
Build SH	46 μs		
Total	717 μs	8 per entry	8 per entry

Table 14.1. Clipmap irradiance cache running in Breda on an RTX 3060.

14.2.1   Initialization

The clipmap consists of 12 cascades, each containing $32 \times 32 \times 32$ cells that represent an indirection to an irradiance cache allocation. Each cell utilizes a 16-bit index to the underlying irradiance cache entry along with an additional 2 bits for flagging the cell as occupied and available for sampling. The remaining 12 bits are unused, allowing for a potential increase in the number of irradiance cache allocations if so desired. The underlying irradiance cache can hold up to 65,535 entries, where each entry has a lifetime, trace origin, ReSTIR sample data, and L1 spherical harmonics (SH) to store the total irradiance contribution. (See Listing 14.1.)

- **Clipmap cells:** This is the only buffer that needs double buffering. The clipmap relies on history data that's potentially indexed with different positional data.

- **Entry pool:** Available allocation entries are stored in the form of a FIFO queue. The pool is initialized by setting the value to the index. An atomic counter is used to fetch and recycle allocation indices.

```
struct IrradianceCacheSample {
    Reservoir reservoir;
    float3 incomingRadiance;
    float hitT;
    float3 sampleDirection;
};

struct IrradianceCacheEntryData {
    // Samples for 4 x 4 octahedron mapping
    IrradianceCacheSample samples[16];
};
```

Listing 14.1. Irradiance cache data per entry.

- **Entry lifetimes:** Each entry has a lifetime that is used to recycle the entries back to the entry pool. A special value is assigned here to mark entries as deallocated, which is also used to initialize the entire buffer.

- **Entry origins:** Each irradiance cache entry traces rays from a probe origin; to avoid self-intersection, the origin is moved back along the ray direction from which it was allocated. The surface normal is used here in order to later scale down samples that would result self-lighting.

- **Irradiance samples:** Entries are represented in a 4×4 octahedral mapping, where all of the samples hold a ReSTIR reservoir, incoming radiance, hit distance, and sample direction.

- **Spherical Harmonics:** A single L1 SH is stored per entry.

To address the memory footprint, the data is compressed from 640 bytes to 256 bytes. This is done using octahedron encoding [Cigolle et al. 14] for the sample directions and *R9G9B9E5* is used for the incoming radiance. Finally the reservoir is compressed to 32 bits: 16 bits for the sample count (M) and 16 bits for the contribution weight (W). The lighting contribution and sample direction are already known, thus the full reservoir can be reconstructed using the reservoir M and W. (See Listing 14.2.)

```
Reservoir reconstructReservoir(float selectedWeight, uint
packedReservoir) {
    Reservoir result;
    result.M = f16tof32(packedReservoir & 0xffff);
    result.W = f16tof32(packedReservoir >> 16u);
    // W was initially constructed from
    // wSum / (M * selectedWeight), so the logic can be
    // reversed to reconstruct wSum. This assumes
    // `W` is > 0.
    result.wSum = selectedWeight * M / W;
    return result;
}
```

Listing 14.2. Reservoir reconstruction from 32 bits.

```
uint computeCascadeIndex(float3 cameraPositionWs, float baseCellSize
, uint cascadeResolution, float3 samplePositionWs) {
    float3 relativePosition = samplePositionWs - cameraPositionWs;
    float greatestDistance = max(max(abs(relativePosition.x),
        abs(relativePosition.y)), abs(relativePosition.z));

    float cascadeCenterToEdgeDistance = (baseCellSize * (float)(
cascadeResolution - 1)) * .5;
    uint cascadeIndex = 0;
    if (greatestDistance >= cascadeCenterToEdgeDistance) {
        cascadeIndex = (uint)log2(greatestDistance /
cascadeCenterToEdgeDistance) + 1;
    }

    return clamp(cascadeIndex, 0, kMaxNumberOfClipmapCascades - 1);
}
```

Listing 14.3. Cascade index.

14.2.2   Cache Lookup

When querying the clipmap, the associated cell needs to be loaded in order to determine if the indirection points to a valid allocation. This is done by converting the query position in world space to a local coordinate within the clipmap. First off, the relative distance to the clipmap cell is measured, which is used to calculate the cascade index (Listing 14.3). The resolution of the clipmap cascade is reduced by 1 during sampling for a very specific reason: the origins of the cascades are based on the cell size, but don't always align properly. By conservatively sampling from a higher cascade, sampling outside of the cascade is prevented.

Since all of the clipmap cells are located linearly in a buffer, a 3D index within the current cascade needs to be converted to a linear buffer index. We know that all of the cascades are centered around the camera, however to find the cell index within the cascade, the cascade origin needs to be known, as well as the cascade bounds (Listing 14.4).

```
float3 calculateCascadeOrigin(float3 cameraPositionWs, float
baseCellSize, uint cascadeIndex) {
    float cascadeCellSize = (float)(1U << cascadeIndex) *
baseCellSize;
    return floor(cameraPositionWs / cascadeCellSize) *
cascadeCellSize;
}

Aabb calculateCascadeBounds(float3 cameraPositionWs, float
baseCellSize, uint cascadeResolution, uint cascadeIndex) {
    float3 cascadeOrigin = calculateCascadeOrigin(cameraPositionWs,
baseCellSize, cascadeIndex);
    float cascadeSize = baseCellSize * (float)cascadeResolution * (
float)(1U << cascadeIndex);

    Aabb result;
    result.minBounds = -cascadeSize * 0.5 + cascadeOrigin;
    result.maxBounds = cascadeSize * 0.5 + cascadeOrigin;

    return result;
}
```

Listing 14.4. Cascade origin and bounds.

The sampling position can then be converted to a relative index within the cascade. After this, all that's left to do is to linearize the relative index and account for the size of all cascades that come before the current cascade, which gives the global index. (See Listing 14.5.)

```
uint computeBufferLocation(float3 cameraPositionWs, float
    baseCellSize, uint cascadeResolution, float3 samplePositionWs) {
    uint cascadeIndex = computeCascadeIndex(cameraPositionWs,
    baseCellSize, cascadeResolution, samplePositionWs);
    // Note that the bounds are in world space.
    Aabb bounds = calculateCascadeBounds(cameraPositionWs,
        baseCellSize, cascadeResolution, cascadeIndex);

    if (any(samplePositionWs < bounds.minBounds) || any(
    samplePositionWs > bounds.maxBounds)) {
        return ~0u; // Position is out of bounds.
    }

    float3 cascadeSize = bounds.maxBounds - bounds.minBounds;
    uint3 relativeIndex =
        uint3(((samplePositionWs - bounds.minBounds) / cascadeSize)
    * cascadeResolution);

    // Linearize to global buffer index.
    uint location = cascadeIndex * cascadeResolution *
    cascadeResolution * cascadeResolution;
    location += relativeIndex.x;
    location += relativeIndex.y * cascadeResolution;
    location += relativeIndex.z * cascadeResolution *
    cascadeResolution;
    return location;
}
```

Listing 14.5. Calculating buffer location.

With the clipmap cell index known, the metadata is loaded to determine if the cell is free or occupied. If the cell is free, an `InterlockedOr` is performed to see if the query is the first one to touch the cell. This is extremely important as multiple sources might be trying to allocate an irradiance cache entry; not being careful here can result in oversubscribing the irradiance cache. If the result is not yet flagged as occupied, the query can safely proceed with allocating an entry. If the allocation has succeeded, a new probe origin and hit normal is stored. (See Listing 14.6.)

In a scenario where most of the queries are trying to sample/allocate the same clipmap cell, contention may become a very big problem. This is especially true when the irradiance cache has a low resolution, increasing the odds that queries are performed on the same cell. To mitigate this problem, the cell metadata is loaded up front. If the cell is marked as occupied, the atomic will be skipped, which will drastically reduce contention. This does however come at a slight cost when cells are unoccupied, as both a memory load and dependent atomic are performed.

When the cell both is occupied and contains valid sampling data, the entry SH is resolved based on the hit normal [Hazel et al. 15]. Additionally, a new probe origin is also stored for the cell, which serves as a way to prevent

```
uint clipmapCellLocation = computeBufferLocation(cameraPositionWs,
baseCellSize, cascadeResolution, samplePositionWs);
uint metadata = clipmapCellBuffer.Load<uint>(clipmapCellLocation *
sizeof(uint));

bool isOccupied = (metadata & kAllocatedBit) == kAllocatedBit;
// Only perform the InterlockedOr if the cell is free to reduce
// contention.
if(!isOccupied) {
    clipmapCellBuffer.InterlockedOr(clipmapCellLocation * sizeof(
uint), kAllocatedBit | kJustAllocatedBit, metadata);
    bool wasFirstToAllocate = (metadata & kAllocatedBit) !=
kAllocatedBit;
    if(wasFirstToAllocate) {
        const uint counterOffsetInBytes = 0u;
        const uint dataOffsetInBytes = sizeof(uint);
        // First request an available pool entry.
        uint freeIndex;
        entryPool.InterlockedAdd(counterOffsetInBytes, 1u, freeIndex
);
        // Retrieve the actual allocation index.
        uint allocationIndex = entryPool.Load<uint>(
dataOffsetInBytes + freeIndex * sizeof(uint));

        // Pack the new allocation index and update the cell
        // metadata.
        metadata |= allocationIndex << 16u;
        clipmapCellBuffer.Store<uint>(clipmapCellLocation * sizeof(
uint), metadata);
        .. // Store associated data using the allocationIndex.
    }
}

bool justAllocated = (metadata & kJustAllocatedBit) ==
kJustAllocatedBit;
// Early out if no sampling data is available.
if(justAllocated) {
    return 0;
}

uint allocationIndex = metadata >> 16u;
// Proceed to sample SH data at allocationIndex.
..
```

Listing 14.6. Cache lookup and allocation.

potentially bad probe origins from persisting throughout many frames. Note that atomically allocating probe origins using a "first come first served" principle is *not* deterministic. If determinism is desired, an alternative probe origin allocation scheme is needed.

Lifetimes are updated for allocation indices each frame, ensuring no stale allocations survive longer than necessary. During this process we proceed to deallocate any entries that no longer have a valid lifetime. All associated data related to the allocation is cleared upon deallocating an entry, which includes all ReSTIR reservoir data, tracing origins, and spherical harmonics. For simplicity we avoid directly updating the clipmap references here, as the reprojection pass will already take care of invalid references by validating the associated lifetimes.

14.2.3 Reprojecting Cascades

In order to use history lighting information, we need to reproject the clipmap cascades. Each frame we calculate how many cells each cascade has moved, which is then used to scroll each cascade individually. If a clipmap entry in the cascade is about to go out of the cascade bounds, the underlying allocation needs to be flagged for recycling, which is done by setting the lifetime to 0. It's important that this happens during the reprojection, as letting the cells decay on their own will cause massive spikes in allocation counts when moving the camera around. Additionally, if a reprojected cell originates from a different cascade, it's discarded as the tracing origin may not fall within the bounds of the new cascade.

14.2.4 Updating the Cache

Candidate Paths Due to the dynamic nature of the irradiance cache, the assumption can be made that these entries will never fully converge as they are frequently updated with a new tracing origin. For that reason it's very important to gather lighting contributions uniformly, especially when an irradiance cache entry was just allocated. To ensure a uniform distribution, each frame four candidate paths are traced from the entry's origin, which update the octahedron faces using checkerboard indexing. Doing so prevents only a single side of the octahedron receiving new samples in a single frame by chance. Additionally, an R2 sequence [Roberts 18] is used per octahedron face to further improve a uniform distribution.

Paths originating from an entry query the irradiance cache recursively, which over time results in "infinite" light bounces. This is also where the probe's associated normal is used to scale down contributions that point toward this specific normal. The resulting data is used to create a ReSTIR reservoir, which is then merged with the history reservoir.

Validation Paths In order to keep the cache responsive to lighting changes, four additional previous paths are validated each frame [Stachowiak 22]. A total of four frames (Figure 14.2) is needed to provide all the samples with data. The validation is performed on the last frame to receive new candidates, which would be two frames ahead of/behind the current frame. Using this validation scheme, we ensure that no set of samples will be stale for longer than one frame. In the scenario of no history data being present, canonical paths are traced instead.

The paths are replayed using the random number of that given frame, which is then validated based on the difference in hit distance or incoming radiance compared to the previously stored data. (See Listing 14.7.) If the difference is large enough, we will need to inform the reservoir of the new lighting conditions. The strategy here is to determine the maximum distance between the history contribution and the newly measured contribution, and use this delta to scale the reservoir's sample count down.

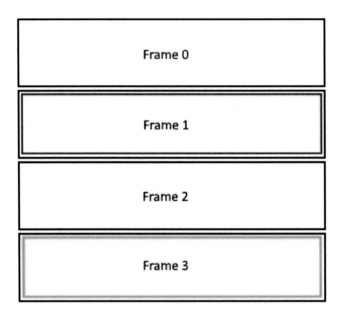

Figure 14.2. Validation is performed on samples that originate two frames ago, marked with red. Canonical paths are traced for the current frame, marked with green.

```
float dist = max3(abs(validationContribution - previousContribution)
  / (validationContribution + previousContribution));
const float minDist = 0.1;
const float maxDist = 0.6;
float validity = 1.0 - smoothstep(minDist, maxDist, dist);
```

Listing 14.7. Generating a validity factor.

The validity could then be used to linearly scale down the reservoir sample count (Listing 14.8); this improves responsiveness to changes to lighting conditions greatly, but does not respond quite well to smaller changes. Instead, a nonlinear curve can be used to respond well to both small and large changes, while still preserving temporal stability.

```
const float reservoirClamp = 20;
float suggestedSampleCount = exp2(log2(reservoirClamp) * invalidity)
  ;
```

Listing 14.8. Determining validation sample count.

Additionally, when validating history samples, the stored sample is directly updated with the re-evaluated lighting contribution. Ideally, the contribution weight is adjusted as well to reflect the change of the selected sample, however in practice this makes close to no difference as the reservoir quickly picks up newer samples during subsequent resampling stages.

14.2.5 Resolving Data

To reduce the memory footprint for cache entries, spherical harmonics are used, which nicely avoids having to resolve 16 path results each time the irradiance cache is queried. The SH coefficients can be compressed using FP16; optionally, this can be compressed even further using YCoCg spherical harmonics [Shyshkovtsov et al. 19], which can be compressed to 12 bytes at acceptable quality levels. Packing the coefficients using R11G11B10 or R9G9B9E5 turned out to differ too much visually from the expected result.

Only valid samples are considered when building the SH; if only one frame's worth of samples is traced for an entry, only those samples should be added to the SH. Furthermore, to increase temporal stability, the spherical harmonics coefficients are interpolated each frame.

14.2.6 Modifying Lookup

Clipmap cells are essentially axis-aligned bounding boxes (AABBs), as seen in Figure 14.3, which is problematic when axis-aligned geometry is located exactly on the boundary of two cells. Due to floating point imprecision, artifacts similar to Z-fighting start to appear. To mitigate the issue, we can modify the lookup

Figure 14.3. Clipmap visualized.

Figure 14.4. Applying periodic shift on clipmap lookup [Gautron 22].

function by applying a periodic shift [Gautron 22]; this increases the quantity of intersections with geometry but nearly always prevents full overlap with geometry. (See Figure 14.4.)

14.2.7   Ranking System

With a clipmap recursively allocating new entries, we run into potential query collisions when geometry is small enough to fit within the bounds of one of the axes of a clipmap cell. In such a scenario, we need a way to avoid light leaking through the geometry. (See Figure 14.5.)

A way to improve this is to use a ranking system [Stachowiak 22]. Rays that originate from the camera will have a rank of 1, entries that were allocated from this ray will trace their rays with their allocated rank + 1, and so on. A clipmap tracing the origin will only be considered if the query rank is less than or equal to the rank it currently has. (See Figure 14.6.)

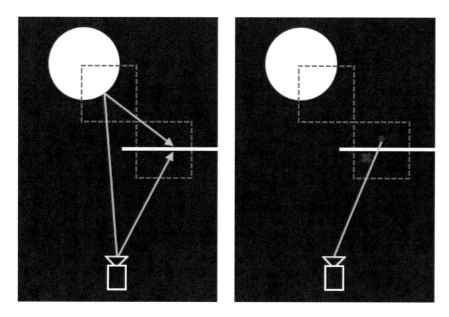

Figure 14.5. Light leak caused by tracing the origin, potentially originating from either side of the geometry.

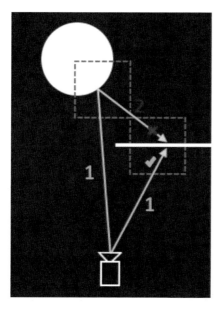

Figure 14.6. Rejecting trace origin candidates that have a greater rank compared to the entry rank.

Figure 14.7. Self-lighting showing the irradiance cache in dense geometry in Amazon Lumberyard Bistro [Amazon Lumberyard 17].

14.2.8 Rejecting Queries from the Same Cell

In the scenario where a query that starts within a clipmap cell, hits the geometry within that same cell, invalid lighting is potentially sampled. (See Figure 14.7.) Optionally, queries that have a hit distance smaller than the size of a cell can be rejected. This preserves occlusion detail, at the cost of some darkening. However, it does prevent "boiling" artifacts from the temporally unstable irradiance cache from showing in such scenarios.

14.2.9 Sampling Cache from Mirror Reflections

Sampling the irradiance cache from mirror or almost mirror-like reflections will show the individual clipmap cells. There are two workarounds to this problem;

- **Add a jitter:** Adding a jitter to the cell indexing based on the tangent plane of the sampling location drastically helps here, but is prone to some initial light leaks. The ranking system should automatically take care of these situations, however it may produce unwanted results in more complex geometry situations.

- **Modify periodic shift:** Modifying the lookup periodic shift in a way that it'll cover the entire cell, along with a tiny bit of jitter, hides these artifacts. However, just like jittering the cell by a larger number, this is prone to initial light leaks.

Both of these workarounds heavily rely on the ranking system as stochastically sampling neighbor cells may cause indices that leak through geometry. In

	Timings	Bounce Rays	Shadow Rays
Trace candidates	823 µs	0.25 rpp	0.25 rpp
Temporal resampling	143 µs		
First spatial resampling	210 µs		
Second spatial resampling	200 µs		
Validate sample visibility	110 µs		0.25 rpp
Patch reservoirs	55 µs		
Resolve	1103 µs		
Total	2.64 ms	0.25 rpp	0.5 rpp

Table 14.2. ReSTIR GI running at half-resolution (native 1440p) on an RTX 3060, showing resulting rays per pixel (rpp).

these cases the neighbor cells will be assigned with origins that fall outside their cell position, essentially acting as additional cells to sample from in areas that matter the most.

14.3 Diffuse ReSTIR GI

All of the tracing and resampling kernels are run at half-resolution, where each candidate traces a single bounce path. (See Table 14.2.) In the case of a path not hitting a light source, the irradiance cache described in Section 14.2 is queried to measure the irradiance at the hit point. Once every three frames, the temporal reservoirs are re-evaluated by replaying the chosen paths [Stachowiak 22]. The temporal reservoir M is scaled down based on the difference in lighting contribution and hit distance. During spatial resampling, we trade correctness for speed by not testing visibility. Instead, the visibility is tested after two spatial resampling steps, which recovers detail at the cost of some bias. Finally, a resolve pass shades the final contribution and upscales it to the native resolution. A denoiser is still needed after the resolve pass, however relatively basic temporal reprojection in combination with a bilateral filter is already nearly enough.

14.3.1 Candidate Paths

Candidate paths are traced using a uniform hemisphere distribution [Ouyang et al. 21]. When using a cosine weighted direction, the likelihood that grazing angles are sampled is low, even if they provide the biggest lighting contribution. It's important to use a low-discrepancy sequence here such as blue noise; the higher quality the initial candidates are, the better ReSTIR performs in subsequent passes. These paths do not require many bounces as we are just trying to connect a single bounce diffuse path to one of the irradiance cache entries, which will inform the path of how much indirect lighting contributes to the hit

Figure 14.8. Candidate diffuse paths.

point. Since the irradiance cache only gives information for any indirect lighting, an explicit light sample needs to be traced as well from the hit point. (See Figure 14.8.)

The BRDF and sampling PDF are not applied during the candidate generation as we would need to demodulate the samples every time when trying to resample reservoirs. Instead, we need to store all the information needed to resample and shade the final chosen reservoir:

- sample direction,

- hit distance,

- hit normal,

- lighting contribution.

In order to reduce the memory footprint, this data is compressed to a total of 16 bytes using octahedron encoding [Cigolle et al. 14] for both the sample direction and hit normals, along with R9G9B9E5 for the lighting contribution.

The sample direction and hit distance can be reused to construct ray-traced ambient occlusion. Though this is not directly used during resampling, it may prove very useful during denoising passes.

14.3.2 Temporal Resampling

Applying the BRDF weight here would make the temporal samples cosine distributed, resulting in small or complex geometry to potentially have low-quality samples available. To ensure these objects have high-quality samples, only the incoming lighting is used as the target function during temporal resampling, resulting in a uniform distribution. Some care is needed with reprojecting history data into the current frame, as artifacts produced by invalid reprojection are very difficult to filter. To avoid bad samples from propagating throughout multiple frames, depth and geometric normal rejection heuristics are used. The depth rejection needs to be very tight, however being too strict with normal rejection may decrease temporal stability with a moving camera. (See Listing 14.9.)

```
float relativeDepthDiff = abs(historyDepth / currentDepth - 1.0f);
bool rejectDepth = relativeDepthDiff > 0.03;

float normalSimilarity = dot(historyNormal, centerNormal);
// ReSTIR GI suggests rejecting angles outside of 25 degrees,
// which would be 0.86. Using a rejection value of 0.3 trades
// some accuracy for temporal stability.
bool rejectNormal = normalSimilarity < 0.3;
```

Listing 14.9. Rejection heuristics.

A Jacobian needs to be applied here to account for geometric differences [Ouyang et al. 21], as the resampling origin in world space does not stay the same throughout frames. A form of permutation sampling [Panteleev 21] is applied, which improves the temporal characteristics when sampling the history samples. The idea behind permutation sampling is to avoid correlations between pixels by using a per-frame jitter and afterward performing an ordered spatial exchange for each history pixel. Randomly sampling the history may by chance cause a sample to be reused between multiple pixels simultaneously. It's suggested to use an XOR value of 3, however this does not seem to perform very well on lower-resolution passes. Since the entire ReSTIR pipeline is ran at half-resolution, a slightly more complex sequence is needed to avoid block artifacts. (See Listing 14.10.)

```
int2 permutationSample(int2 samplePos, int2 jitter, uint sampleIndex
, uint frameIndex) {
    int2 result = samplePos;
    const uint sampleSeed = (frameIndex + sampleIndex) & 3u;
    const uint2 sequenceA = uint2(3u - sampleSeed, 1u + sampleSeed);
    const uint2 sequenceB = uint2(sequenceA.x ^ sampleSeed,
sequenceA.y ^ sampleSeed) & 3u;
    if (sampleIndex > 0) {
        result = (result + jitter) ^ sequenceA;
        result = (result + jitter) ^ sequenceB;
        result -= jitter;
    }
    return result;
}
```

Listing 14.10. Permutation sampling sequence.

To boost convergence, the temporal reuse pass also gathers additional reservoirs using permutation sampling in the scenario that a reservoir has a low sample

Figure 14.9. Permutation sampling.

count. (See Figure 14.9.) This is done until either the upper bound of permutations has been reached (5) or the reservoir M has reached or exceeded the M clamp value. Allowing a high M clamp during temporal reuse will reduce the workload for a denoiser, however this comes at the increased risk of temporal artifacts and responsiveness. Even when validating the temporal reservoirs, a higher M clamp tends to still be significantly less responsive and prone to correlation artifacts. ReSTIR GI suggests an M clamp of 20, however we found that an M clamp of 12 seems to be the sweet spot for responsiveness and convergence, bringing the best of both worlds.

With permutation sampling and gathering additional reservoirs, it's unknown if the spatial sample is actually visible from the origin of the pixel into which we are trying to merge. Ignoring this visibility term will result in loss of contact shadows along with blurry indirect shadows, both of which are unacceptable. Testing visibility for all of these samples is too expensive for a real-time implementation. As a workaround, a visibility guiding factor generated by the previous frame (covered in Section 14.3.5) is used as an additional rejection heuristic, which follows a fitted curve. (See Listing 14.11.)

```
    float validityDiff = exp2(-20 * abs(centerValidity - historyValidity
    ));
    // Only apply this validity rejection when gathering spatial
    // reservoirs (permutation sampling).
    if (validityDiff < 0.3 && sampleIndex > 0) {
        continue;
    }
```

Listing 14.11. Rejecting validity.

Figure 14.10. Permutation sampling with guiding.

If the guiding factor differs too much, the sample is rejected. This essentially creates a split between indirectly shadowed and non-shadowed pixels, which recovers contact shadows and preserves indirect shadows. (See Figure 14.10.)

14.3.3 Validating Reservoirs

Samples chosen by temporal reservoirs may change due to changes in the scene or in lighting conditions. If we don't update these reservoirs that potentially have stale data, we end up with very unresponsive indirect lighting. A good way to increase responsiveness is to re-trace the selected samples from the temporal reservoirs, however shooting an additional path per pixel just for the purpose of making the reservoirs responsive is very costly. Ideally, the validation work would be spread out over multiple frames; however, due to the nature of permutation sampling, this may not be possible as stale samples may survive validation if they are shared spatiotemporally. Instead, the reservoir validation is performed once every three frames. It's important to only validate history reservoirs that actually end up being reprojected into the new frame. (See Figure 14.11.)

For the pixels on screen that don't have a history available due to disocclusion etc., canonical paths are traced instead. This way all of the pixels during a validation frame will either have a history or candidates available, preventing any gaps in samples.

When the light sample is re-measured, the sample count is adjusted based on the lighting contribution and hit distance; if any of these factors show a big difference, we clamp the sample count of the reservoir down and update the

Figure 14.11. Tracing selection with a moving camera: green indicates that validation logic should be executed, and red indicates candidates generation.

stored selected contribution with the validated contribution value. This will make the temporal reservoirs very responsive to changes.

14.3.4   Spatial Resampling

Two spatial reuse passes are used in order to share as many unique reservoirs between pixels as possible. The first pass is aimed at less-complex geometry and resamples six neighbor reservoirs in a radius up to 42 pixels. The second pass is aimed toward scenarios where geometry is slightly more complex, such as vegetation or thin objects, and resamples up to five neighbor reservoirs in a radius up to 20 pixels. This second pass relies on the results of the first spatial reuse pass, effectively extending the search radius from the first pass while taking care of smaller details. The sampling radius is based on a fitted curve for each of the spatial reuse passes:

$$\text{first pass radius} = \left(\frac{\texttt{sampleIndex}}{\texttt{numSamples}}\right)^{0.5} \cdot \texttt{maxRadius},$$

$$\text{second pass radius} = \left(\frac{\texttt{sampleIndex}}{\texttt{numSamples}}\right)^{1.5} \cdot \texttt{maxRadius}.$$

Figure 14.12. Spatial reuse without visibility testing.

The sampling angle starts with a random offset and is incremented by the golden ratio for every iteration. Rejection heuristics are mostly identical to temporal resampling, with the exception of the validity factor. Additionally, unlike temporal reuse, the BRDF weight is used here in the target function when resampling, making the distribution cosine weighted again. It's very important to reconnect spatial samples to the target reservoir's origin rather than directly reusing the reservoir's sample direction. The use of a Jacobian is needed as well to account for geometric differences.

We chose to not test visibility in any of the spatial reuse passes (as in Figure 14.12), and instead we test the visibility of the final surviving sample. The contribution weight (W) of the reservoir is set to 0 if the visibility test failed. Applying a single deferred visibility test (as in Figure 14.13) is biased, as the sum of weights gathered in spatial resampling may contain contributions of samples that were not visible. That being said, in practice this provides a very nice trade-off as all contact shadows and indirect shadows have been recovered.

Alternatively, there are several different ways to approach visibility testing, such as ray-marching visibility in screen space [Stachowiak 22] or actually tracing visibility every time a reservoir is considered for reuse. Ray-marching the visibility is relatively cheap, but primarily suffers from screen-space limitations and lack of accuracy. Tracing a ray for each reuse is accurate but currently way too expensive for a real-time implementation.

The biggest performance win with resampling lies in coherent memory access and reducing the memory footprint. Since spatial resampling can only resample with information that originated from the temporal reuse pass, only a pixel

Figure 14.13. Spatial reuse with deferred visibility testing.

reference is stored for the selected reservoir sample data, which greatly reduces the memory footprint.

14.3.5   Visibility Guiding

The deferred spatial reservoir visibility test does provide some information that will be useful during the resolve and filtering passes. We know that in general samples with a very high contribution will be prioritized during resampling, meaning that most visible indirect shadows are likely going to be caused by these selected high-contribution samples. Treating the visibility result as a shadow factor gives us a result similar to ray-traced ambient occlusion, however this takes light contribution directionality into account, highlighting most of the contact shadow and indirect shadowing regions of the scene. (See Figure 14.14.)

Scenarios where indirect shadows and contact shadows are the sharpest/most visible mainly occur when the validated hit distance is substantially smaller compared to the target distance, while thin objects primarily have shadows when the light source has a relatively shallow angle with respect to the object. Based on these two observations, the Boolean hit value is modified to be a scalar by increasing the weight for shallow angles and very large hit differences. Since the guiding factor is exclusively used to reject resampling, we primarily care about the contrast between contact/indirect shadow regions and regularly indirectly lit surfaces; the factor does not need to be perfectly denoised to be effective. (See Figure 14.15.)

Figure 14.14. Accumulated visibility tests.

Figure 14.15. Visibility guiding factor.

14.3.6 Post-Validation Cleanup

After validating the spatial reuse reservoirs, the invalidated reservoirs will have zero contribution as we have no way to accurately represent these reservoirs, resulting in an increase of variance before the final resolve. Falling back to candidate or temporal reservoirs for these invalidated reservoirs is not a great idea either as this adds even more variance and potential outliers. Instead, a

(a) Validated output.   (b) Patched reservoirs.

Figure 14.16. (a) Validated output showing excessive darkening due to invalidated reservoirs. (b) Patching invalidated reservoirs results in an overall higher-quality result.

tiny 2×2 pixel search is performed with very strict depth and normal rejection in order to find the closest valid reservoir (as in Figure 14.16). If a reservoir is found, its merged into the center pixel's reservoir. No additional rays are traced here to test visibility. If the reservoir survived the rejection heuristics, the neighbor sample is assumed to be visible as the origin is close enough to the target pixel.

14.3.7 Resolve

A final resolve pass is performed to upscale the half-resolution reservoirs to full resolution. (See Figure 14.17.) The history visibility guiding factor described in Section 14.3.5 is reprojected and updated with the new factor that was generated from the current frame. In order to reduce the workload for the denoising steps, multiple samples are gathered in a radius of up to 10 pixels, which are weighed based on visibility, normal, and depth similarity. In order to get away with aggressive neighbor sampling without losing too much detail, each sample is scaled by its weight and added to the L1 SH. After gathering all samples, the L1 SH is scaled by one over the weight sum and resolved to the shading normal of the pixel.

Resolving multiple pixels in a bigger area greatly improves temporal stability for the subsequent denoising passes, almost enough to remove all noise with temporal reprojection (Figure 14.18). Even though basic temporal reprojection already gets us very far, a more specialized denoiser is needed to get a completely artifact-free image under very fast camera movement.

Additionally, the guiding factor is used here to reject samples that differ too much in visibility, preventing the loss of contact/indirect shadows (Figure 14.19).

Figure 14.17. Resolving reservoirs to full resolution.

Figure 14.18. Temporal reprojection.

14.4 Future Work

A clipmap irradiance cache in combination with ReSTIR GI provides a good foundation for dynamic diffuse GI, however in highly dynamic and complex scenes there is still room for improvement. Temporal resampling tends to introduce pixel correlations that are very difficult to filter. Removing the temporal

Figure 14.19. Preserving indirect and contact shadows with a visibility guiding factor in Amazon Lumberyard Bistro [Amazon Lumberyard 17].

part may solve these correlations, however this would greatly increase the workload for the denoiser. Additionally, there is still room for optimization. We chose to have a relatively expensive resolve pass in order to have the spatiotemporal denoiser do much less work, however this may not be necessary with a more involved denoising algorithm.

Finally, performing deferred ReSTIR visibility checks is biased, but works well enough for a believable GI solution. Tracing a visibility ray each time a reservoir is resampled is not practical for a game workload (yet). Alternatively, a better way to cache/reuse visibility could be explored, which would replace the visibility tests during the resampling of reservoirs.

Bibliography

[Amazon Lumberyard 17] Amazon Lumberyard. "Amazon Lumberyard Bistro." Open Research Content Archive (ORCA), 2017. http://developer.nvidia.com/orca/amazon-lumberyard-bistro.

[Bitterli et al. 20] Benedikt Bitterli, Chris Wyman, Matt Pharr, Peter Shirley, Aaron Lefohn, and Wojciech Jarosz. "Spatiotemporal Reservoir Resampling for Real-Time Ray Tracing with Dynamic Direct Lighting." *ACM Transactions on Graphics* 39:4 (2020), 148:1–148:17. https://cs.dartmouth.edu/wjarosz/publications/bitterli20spatiotemporal.html.

[Cigolle et al. 14] Zina H. Cigolle, Sam Donow, Daniel Evangelakos, Michael Mara, Morgan McGuire, and Quirin Meyer. "A Survey of Efficient Representations for Independent Unit Vectors." *Journal of Computer Graphics Techniques* 3:2 (2014), 1–30. https://jcgt.org/published/0003/02/01/.

[Gautron 22] Pascal Gautron. "Advances in Spatial Hashing: A Pragmatic Approach towards Robust, Real-Time Light Transport Simulation." In *SIGGRAPH '22: ACM SIGGRAPH 2022 Talks*, pp. 6:1–6:2. Association for Computing Machinery, 2022. https://doi.org/10.1145/3532836.3536239.

[Hazel et al. 15] Graham Hazel, Chris Doran, and William Joseph. "Geomerics Reconstructing Diffuse Lighting." Presented at Computer Entertainment Developers Conference, 2015. https://web.archive.org/web/20160313132301if_/http://www.geomerics.com/wp-content/uploads/2015/08/CEDEC_Geomerics_ReconstructingDiffuseLighting1.pdf.

[Ouyang et al. 21] Y. Ouyang, S. Liu, M. Kettunen, M. Pharr, and J. Pantaleoni. "ReSTIR GI: Path Resampling for Real-Time Path Tracing." *Compututer Graphics Forum* 40:8 (2021), 17–29. http://dx.doi.org/10.1111/cgf.14378.

[Panteleev 21] Alexey Panteleev. "Permutation Sampling." X (formerly Twitter), November 8, 2021. https://twitter.com/more_fps/status/1457749362025459715.

[Roberts 18] Martin Roberts. "The Unreasonable Effectiveness of Quasirandom Sequences." Extreme Learning, April 25, 2018. https://extremelearning.com.au/unreasonable-effectiveness-of-quasirandom-sequences/.

[Shyshkovtsov et al. 19] Oles Shyshkovtsov, Sergei Karmalsky, Benjamin Archard, and Dmitry Zhdan. "Exploring Raytraced Future in Metro Exodus." Presented at Game Developers Conference, 2019. https://developer.download.nvidia.com/video/gputechconf/gtc/2019/presentation/s9985-exploring-ray-traced-future-in-metro-exodus.pdf.

[Stachowiak 22] Tomasz Stachowiak. "Global Illumination Overview." GitHub, 2022. https://github.com/EmbarkStudios/kajiya/blob/main/docs/gi-overview.md.

[Wyman and Panteleev 22] Chris Wyman and Alexey Panteleev. "Rearchitecting Spatiotemporal Resampling for Production." In *High-Performance Graphics 2021—Symposium Papers*, pp. 23–41. Eurographics Association, 2022. https://doi.org/10.2312/hpg.20211281.

Game Engine Design
Wessam Bahnassi, Editor

Welcome to the Game Engine Design section, where the focus is on enriching your knowledge with solutions to problems that arise with the latest GPU hardware capabilities, the wide range of platforms to target, and the verbosity of graphics APIs.

The first article in the section, "GPU Capability Tracking and Configuration System" by Thibault Ober and Wolfgang Engel, demonstrates The Forge engine's cross-platform GPU tracking and configuration system, which aids in the setup of graphical user settings in games and ranking GPUs available in the machine. The system takes key information into account (e.g., driver version, VRAM, and GPU type) and has it go through validation logic that can be customized for each game via text files.

Next, "Forge Shader Language" by Manas Kulkarni covers another aspect of The Forge engine. This article shows the approach taken to streamline the development of shaders. It enables a single shader source file to compile and run on all target platforms, without losing the optimizations and capabilities exposed by each of the target platforms' native shader compilers. Additionally, adding support for new targets is simple and does not require expert knowledge in writing compilers.

Last, but far from the least, is Grigory Javadyan's article "Simple Automatic Resource Synchronization Method for Vulkan Applications." Vulkan requires its users to manually manage the insertion of synchronization barriers at the right times. The author presents a simple approach to enable an engine to automatically handle this task. This approach trades off some of the parallelism achievable with render graphs for simplicity in implementation, maintenance, and usage.

I hope you find these ideas inspiring to how you drive decisions for your game engine's architecture, and I would like to extend a big thank you to each of the contributors in this section for their time, dedication, and effort.

GPU Capability Tracking and Configuration System

Thibault Ober and Wolfgang Engel

15.1 Introduction

Keeping track of all the hardware and features that a cross-platform application must support has become quite a challenging task. In this article, we present a cross-platform GPU tracking and configuration system. Our system enables us to assign a performance index to each video card or console, reject some incompatible drivers, and also define rules for choosing a specific GPU on the current machine or even enabling or disabling certain hardware features. This system is used to pre-fill the user settings for what is commonly called graphics or display settings. These are the settings the game player can pick like Ultra, High, Medium, and Low, different pre-filled resolutions, screen-space ambient occlusion (SSAO) quality, higher or lower quality shadow maps, more or less lights, ray tracing on or off, etc. Let's assume there are at least two different flavors of an NVIDIA RTX 3080 GPU. One comes with 10 GB and the other one with 12 GB. The 12-GB version is able to run the game at a higher resolution, so the user dialog will be pre-filled—depending on how much memory the game requires—with let's say 1080p for the 10-GB version but 1440p for the 12-GB version. In case the user wants to see the game ray-traced, the 10-GB version might not be able to provide enough memory, so ray tracing is not an option that the user can select.

15.2 The Technique

This GPU capability tracking system is designed to build a full-featured user panel and to automate the whole process in the rendering backend. So, the user only gets offered what is available.

At launch, two files are loaded that hold all the necessary information. They allow to data-drive the system and can be updated without needing to recompile the full application. In case new GPUs are released, those *.txt files can be updated. As a fallback, there is also a system that evaluates GPUs that do not have an entry in those files based on their properties. It also allows to disable specific GPU functionalities based on some editable rules: for example, you can disable raster order views on a specific GPU or disable ray tracing if there is not enough memory available. These options can be employed to establish development constraints, such as limiting the number of textures that can be bound, or to evaluate your program across various configurations.

15.3 GPU Performance Index

The first file loaded is responsible for listing all available hardware. This data is organized in multiple files depending on the targeted platform: android_gpu.data, pc_gpu.data, xbox_gpu.data, etc. (See Listing 15.1.) Along with each hardware, it stores the model ID, the vendor ID, and a performance index that can be updated later on. The top of the file lists all of the currently defined GPU vendors and their names, which will be used for advanced logging information and turning on specific formats when parsing the driver version. For GPUs whose model IDs are not in the list, we provide access to some default settings. This can

```
BEGIN_VENDOR_LIST;
intel; 0x163C, 0x8086, 0x8087;
nvidia; 0x10DE
amd; 0x1002, 0x1022;
qualcomm; 0x5143;
imagination technologies; 0x1010;
samsung; 0x144D;
arm; 0x13b5;
apple; 0x106b;
END_VENDOR_LIST;

BEGIN_DEFAULT_CONFIGURATION;
DefaultPresetLevel; Low;
END_DEFAULT_CONFIGURATION;

#VendorId; DeviceId; Performance; Name
BEGIN_GPU_LIST;
# --- PC & Linux ---
0x10de; 0x0045; Low; NVIDIA GeForce 6800 GT
0x10de; 0x0040; Low; NVIDIA GeForce 6800 Ultra
...
0x10de; 0x2860; Ultra; GeForce RTX 4070 Max-Q / Mobile;
0x10de; 0x2704; Ultra; GeForce RTX 4080;
...
0x8086; 0xA780; Medium; Intel(R) Xe Graphics
...
# --- Mobile ---
0x5143 ; 0x6060001 ; Medium; Adreno 660;
0x5143 ; 0x6050002 ; Low; Adreno 650;
0x5143 ; 0x6060201 ; Low; Adreno 644;
# --- XBOX ---
0x7a0d; 0x2; Low; Xbox One;
0x7a0d; 0x3; Low; Xbox One S;
0x7a0d; 0x4; Medium; Xbox One X;
...
END_GPU_LIST;
```

Listing 15.1. Content of gpu.data.

be used as a fallback, but also for testing purposes. You can, for example, set all graphics cards to the highest setting and see if any errors arise on a benchmark.

15.4 GPU Hardware Configuration

The next file is named gpu.cfg, which contains the following:

- the rules for selecting a GPU against another,

- the information regarding discarding specific driver version,

- the rules for enabling or disabling some hardware features,

- the rules for turning off and on some application specific settings.

During framework initialization, we iterate over all available devices and collect all the relevant information about them. All this information is then stored in a `GPUSetting` structure. This structure contains all the supported extensions and features (wave ops, ray tracing, HDR, etc.). It lists all the capabilities of the device (maximum number of textures, amount of VRAM, etc.) along with the `GPUPerformance` index assigned in the previous step. All its attributes can be accessed programmatically. They can be used to pre-fill a user-setting panel, to set memory usage limits, or to display an error message if some features are not supported. This system also comes with a feature configuration system inside the gpu.cfg file. Most of the previous properties are available along with the hardware vendor and device ID, allowing application developers to come up with custom rules to configure their renderer.

15.4.1 GPU Selection Rules

For selecting a specific GPU, we compare them against one another in their discovery order. Once one is rejected, it will no longer be used as a potential candidate. We define a priority list of properties, each of them to be evaluated in ascending order. Once one GPU returns a higher value than its counterpart, it will be picked as the selected one. Note that the GPU discovery order can affect the final outcome. If a given property does not exist on the current platform (for example, `DirectXFeatureLevel` on macOS), it is just ignored and we move to the next one.

As shown in Listing 15.2, the last rule concerning the hardware vendor can be used to prioritize a discrete GPU over an integrated one. The `PreferredGPU` property is a special variable that can hold the model or device ID of a specific GPU. Usually empty, it can hold the user's selection; it is currently used to switch the active device while the program is running after re-triggering a renderer initialization.

```
BEGIN_GPU_SELECTION;
GraphicQueueSupported == 1;
deviceid == PreferredGPU;
GpuPerformanceIndex;
DirectXFeatureLevel;
# Intel vendor 0x8086 && 0x8087 && 0x163C
VRAM;
VendorID != 0x8086, VendorID != 0x8087, VendorID != 0x163C;
END_GPU_SELECTION;
```

Listing 15.2. GPU selection, gpu.cfg.

```
BEGIN_DRIVER_REJECTION;
# amd: 0x1002, 0x1022
0x1002; DriverVersion <= 23.10.23.03; 09a pixelated;
0x1022; DriverVersion <= 23.10.23.03; 15a flickers;
END_GPU_SETTINGS;
```

Listing 15.3. Driver rejection, gpu.cfg.

15.4.2 Driver Rejection Rules

The syntax is pretty self-explanatory; see Listing 15.3. The driver rejection rules are applied after the GPUSetting structure has been populated and a GPU has been selected. They can be used to show an error to the end user or even to prompt them to update their graphics driver. Note that such a message requires a comment on why this driver was rejected in the first place. This is useful for testing newer versions or just keeping track of a potential issue and its root cause. The main challenge is to successfully retrieve the version number on most of the platforms and graphics APIs. Internally, we use the NVIDIA API (NVAPI) and AMD GPU Services (AGS) libraries. The standard Vulkan structure does not adequately support vendor formats, especially those from AMD. Here are the format specifications we use for the main vendors:

- **NVIDIA:** <Major>.<Minor>, e.g., 537.13.

- **AMD:** <YEAR>.<MONTH>.<REVISION>, e.g., 23.10.23.03.

- **Intel:** We only use the <BUILD_NUMBER>. Normally it's supposed to look like <OS>.<BUILD_NUMBER>, but Vulkan only returns the last part: for instance, 31.0.101.5074 will become 101.5074. See [Intel 24].

15.4.3 Configuration Settings

As shown in Listing 15.4, most of the properties are accessible for reading and writing. This allows you to disable features on a certain set of devices. Note that you can also fine-tune this file for each of your deployment targets, e.g., to use a different file on mobile than PC. We are currently employing this system to turn off the dynamic rendering extension for a specific GPU vendor that provides insufficient support. Furthermore, this system was utilized to integrate a geometry shader to compensate for the GLSL `primitiveID`'s incomplete support on the Steam Deck.

```
BEGIN_GPU_SETTINGS;
# nvidia
maxRootSignatureDWORDS; vendorID == 0x10DE; 64;
# amd
maxRootSignatureDWORDS; vendorID == 0x1002; 13;
# disable tesselation support on arm system
tessellationsupported; vendorID == 0x13B5; 0;
# disable ray tracing if not enough memory
raytracingsupported; vram < 2147483648: 0;
END_GPU_SETTINGS;
```

Listing 15.4. GPU configuration, gpu.cfg.

Listing 15.5 demonstrates that we also support application-defined settings, which offer a quick way to dynamically configure a program. However, note that this should not be used as a complete configuration panel.

```
BEGIN_USER_SETTINGS;
# Office = 1, Low = 2, Medium = 3, High = 4, Ultra = 5
MyApplicationSetting; GpuPerformanceIndex >= 5; 42;
MSAASampleCount; GpuPerformanceIndex >= 2; 4;
DisableGodRays; GpuPerformanceIndex <= 2; 1;
DisableGodRays; GpuPerformanceIndex > 2; 0;
BindlessSupported; MaxBoundTextures < 4610; 0;
EnableAOIT; RasterOrderViewSupport == 1; 1;
END_USER_SETTINGS;
```

Listing 15.5. User setting, gpu.cfg.

15.5 Available Properties

The available properties are listed in Table 15.1.

15.6 Further Ideas and Improvements

In the future we will provide more rules on how to pick one GPU with its model ID over the other and incorporate tracking in a central place of the cross-platform app. Developers must proactively verify certain features, such as ray tracing support, before its actually use. We are working on raising notifications automatically if the feature is used on an incompatible hardware, such as signaling an error during the pipeline creation process. We also plan to add the option to use custom rules for enabling or disabling specific texture formats. We are

Property	Readable	Writable
BuiltinDrawid	✓	✓
CubemapTextureArraySupported	✓	✓
IndirectDrawSupported	✓	✓
DeviceId	✓	×
DirectxFeaturelevel	✓	✓
GeometryShaderSupported	✓	✓
GpuPerformanceIndex	✓	✓
GraphicQueueSupported	✓	✓
HdrSupported	✓	✓
DynamicRenderingEnabled	✓	✓
IndirectCommandbufferSupported	✓	✓
IndirectRootconstant	✓	✓
MaxBoundTextures	✓	✓
MaxVertexInputBindings	✓	✓
MultiDrawindirectSupported	✓	✓
OcclusionQueriesSupported	✓	✓
PrimitiveIdSupported	✓	✓
RasterOrderViewsupport	✓	✓
RaytracingSupported	✓	✓
RayquerySupported	✓	✓
SoftwareVRSSupported	✓	✓
TessellationSupported	✓	✓
TimestampQueriesSupported	✓	✓
UniformBufferAlignment	✓	✓
VendorId	✓	×
Vram	✓	✓
WaveLaneCount	✓	✓
WaveOpsSupport	✓	✓

Table 15.1. List of available properties.

consistently expanding our support to include new platforms, driven by the continuous introduction of new handheld consoles that have been inspired by the popularity of the Steam Deck.

15.7 Conclusion

In summary, we presented a flexible system that enables application developers to dynamically adjust their application's requirements according to the hardware it operates on. The system is based on the information provided by the manufacturer, which can be modified for your own experiment. Those properties can then guide the process of selecting the appropriate GPU and be used to change your renderer's configuration on the fly.

Bibliography

[Intel 24] Intel. "Understanding the Intel Graphics Driver Version Number." Intel Product Support, 2024. https://www.intel.com/content/www/us/en/support/articles/000005654/graphics.html.

The Forge Shader Language
Manas Kulkarni, and Wolfgang Engel

16.1 Introduction

Modern games are aiming to launch on as many platforms as possible at once to amortize the cost of art asset and gameplay development. To streamline the development of shaders, a cross-platform shader system is necessary that compiles and runs on a wide range of platforms originating from one shader source file. The Forge Shader Language (FSL) is a system that can generate shaders for PC, macOS, all Xbox, all PlayStation, Switch, iOS/Android, and Steam Deck platforms. The FSL translator is an external tool to existing compilers such as DXC and other platform compilers. Due to the on-going lack of reliability of DXC and SPIR-V code generation and translations, the complex compiler-based systems are lacking the practical ability to cross-compile or translate shaders. Even the basic compilation of native shaders with these shader compilers is error prone and quite often generates inefficient code. To be able to circumvent broken and inefficient compilers, the FSL translator can be extended quickly to other compilers and platforms. In other words, one important advantage of the system is that integrating a new platform with a new native shader compiler or newly released features, can be done with very little effort, compared to an approach of adding a new shader language to DXC and/or SPIR-V.

16.1.1 Manual Cross-Platform Shader Maintenance

When targeting multiple platforms for game development, it is crucial to share as much CPU and GPU code between platforms as possible. Shader code bases can quickly bloat into a sizeable number of source files. Maintaining separate shaders to target different languages can be achieved for toy projects to a small extent, but quickly the overhead of keeping separate implementations in sync is not justifiable.

16.1.2 Previous Work

The most widely used cross-platform shader systems come in two flavors: solutions based on Intermediate Representation (IR) or Standard Portable Intermediate Representation (SPIR-V) and on a preprocessor.

Preprocessor-Based Solutions The advantage of preprocessor-based cross-platform shader systems is their speed and simplicity. Preprocessors can efficiently process large amounts of code, due to their purely syntactical nature. Most programmers are familiar with the C preprocessor, therefore offering good maintenance and extensibility. Conversely, purely preprocessor-based solutions are too simplistic and restrictive to allow the use of advanced shader features, and cannot efficiently bridge the syntax gap between recent shading languages. The result is overly cumbersome macro-constructs that get in the way of expressiveness and flexibility. At that point, preprocessor-based solutions are not trivial to debug and difficult to reason about, which nullifies the prior advantages.

IR/SPIR-V–Based Solutions SPIR-V–based [Khronos Group 24] solutions are powerful but also inherently limited due to the necessary lowering to an intermediate representation. They are also difficult to maintain and extend. Most notably, platform-specific intrinsics cannot be used since they would get lost due to not having a representation in the intermediate language. In most cases the high-level semantics that would be necessary for translation have been eliminated. Translating from a high-level language to an IR, translating back to a high level and lowering again, may result in redundant instructions, sub-optimal register allocation, and loss of information. Customized control of code generation without recompiling a massive IR-translation code base is challenging—if not out of reach—for most teams. It is therefore desirable to limit its use as much as possible.

An existing system worth noting is Slang [NVIDIA 24]. While being an existing solution with a similar aim, we found its complexity and dependency on a custom LLVM fork to exhibit the same downsides mentioned above.

16.2   System Overview

The goal of FSL is to be a simple, efficient, cross-platform shader language and generation system. Extension and maintenance should be achievable by very small teams, while not requiring knowledge of compiler construction, abstract syntax trees (ASTs), etc.

Instead of creating yet another preprocessor or IR-based translator, we chose a combination of preprocessor logic and light-weight code modifications. The system is designed around two preprocessing steps, with a code replacement pass in between. By having full control over macro expansion in the intermediate generation steps, the system can make the necessary modifications without resorting to semantic analysis. A challenge of implementing this solution was the need to support a wide range of shaders for the most popular platforms from the start. All common shader features and some more recent ones needed to be directly supported.

FSL is intended to be used as a single tool that consumes *.fsl files and outputs compiled shader binaries. Additional metadata is embedded to avoid the need for costly runtime reflection. The invocation behavior of the tool is kept close to a regular language compiler and can therefore easily be integrated into existing build systems. It operates in three passes:

- binary collection and preprocessing,

- translation to target language,

- compilation using target SDKs.

FSL shaders generally do not map to a single platform binary. For example, on platforms that do not have built-in support for the SV_Primitive_ID semantic in the vertex shader (VS) stage, an additional geometry shader (GS) stage is generated and compiled alongside the VS. This feature was originally only necessary for the PlayStation 4, but it has also proven useful for certain combinations of Android devices and their drivers. We encountered cases where the driver would report support for the feature, but accessing the value would produce undefined results. For these cases, we automatically generate a GS stage and embed it alongside the VS. The runtime can then transparently link it into the full pipeline state object.

Shaders written in FSL are purposefully tailored to be executed within The Forge framework. For example, the custom binary headers directly integrate with the GPU capability system to choose the appropriate variant at runtime.

Since the code generation step is kept minimal (mostly emitting resource declarations and other constructs), native shader backend code can be used inline.

16.2.1 Binary Collection and Preprocessing

In the very first step, the FSL system parses top-level source files and collects binary declarations, which will later be used to compile shader binaries as outlined in Section 16.3.2. For the preprocessing step, we make use of mcpp [Kiyoshi MATSUI 24] on Windows and the built-in C compiler on macOS and Linux (Steam Deck). Any user-defined macros are evaluated in this stage, and we process a separate version per requested target platform. The evaluation of macros used internally by FSL is deferred to the actual compilation step with the target compiler. Source generation flags and compilation options are also collected in this stage.

16.2.2 Translation to Target Language

Once the source has been preprocessed, the system parses the source and collects resource declarations, shader inputs and outputs, and various other macros. Since, at this point, the FSL macros have not yet been expanded to their final platform-specific form, the logic can make a range of assumptions, making the syntax parsing very simple, efficient, and unified across the target languages.

HLSL: Direct3D 12 The code generation for Microsoft's High-Level Shading Language (HLSL) is the most straightforward since the base syntax is held most closely to it. Although, for the generation of root signature declarations, it is necessary to collect any global resources and assemble a target-specific definition of resource tables. For Direct3D 12, we generate a root signature string and for PlayStation Shader Language (PSSL) a shader resource table (SRT) struct declaration.

HLSL: Direct3D 11 For backwards compatibility, FSL also supports a limited subset of features targeting Direct3D 11.

PSSL The PSSL generation is handled mostly identically to HLSL, though the resource declarations are directly replaced by structs representing the different update frequencies per descriptor set. If necessary, we also generate pass-through geometry stages during this phase. Of special consideration is the handling of `BeginNonUniformResourceIndex`/`EndNonUniformResourceIndex` blocks. For older targets we unroll this to a loop over all potential indices and scalarize the resource access.

GLSL For OpenGL Shading Language (GLSL), the resource declarations are rewritten in the usual way. For the case of `BeginNonUniformResourceIndex`/`EndNonUniformResourceIndex` blocks, three variants are generated; at runtime the most efficient variant is chosen based on device capabilities and the stability of the feature implementation in the driver.

MSL Generating Metal Shading Language (MSL) is the most complex task for the FSL generator. In a previous iteration, we tried making use of the well-known shader struct paradigm where the whole user code is wrapped inside of a C++ struct. Using a constructor together with references, global variables can thus be emulated. We have found that on low-end iPhone devices these shaders lead to various crashes during pipeline state object (PSO) creation and other instabilities. We therefore chose to go the more-involved route and pass global variables down from the entry function via arguments. This step necessitates a more-involved parsing and generation step, since functions signatures and call sites need to be collected and modified.

16.2.3   Compilation Using Target SDKs

Eventually the platform-specific compilers are invoked on the resulting HLSL/ GLSL/PSSL/MSL files and the binary results collected. We currently support debug and release compilation modes. For analysis tool purposes, we also output intermediate results. These can be directly fed into platform and SDK tools. An interface for customized additional optimization steps is also provided. For certain features such as divergent resource accesses, we compile different variants to account for different hardware capabilities. The compilation results are now combined with a binary FSL header, which contains additional metadata that is used at runtime, such as the number of threads in a compute group, that is not part of the MSL binaries.

16.3 FSL Syntax

Due to its popularity, we chose to base the syntax on HLSL, with some modifications intended to make it simpler to expand the code as necessary. Supported are vertex, fragment, and compute shaders. Tessellation shaders are also supported, though their usage is discouraged. As mentioned, geometry shader stages are not exposed to the user. We define a range of macros to both ease code transformation and let the preprocessor handle the necessary modifications.

Generally, regular C syntax can be used everywhere. To ease the parsing and insertion of semantic attributes, any struct referenced inside a shader resource needs to be annotated using the STRUCT(MyStruct) macro and fields need to be annotated using DATA(float, position, SV_Position).

16.3.1 Shader Entry

The shader entry point is the main function that defines the input and output interface. It therefore requires special annotations and needs to be referenced at runtime during PSO creation. The first statement in the entry function should be

```
INIT_MAIN;
```

The translation step expands this statement to insert target language-specific initialization. A simple complete shader is shown in Listing 16.1.

```
STRUCT(VSOutput)
{
    DATA(float4, Position, SV_Position);
    DATA(float, TexCoord, TEXCOORD);
};

float4 PS_MAIN( VSOutput In )
{
    INIT_MAIN;
    float4 color = SampleTex2D(Get(uTexture0),
        Get(uSampler0), In.TexCoord);
    RETURN(color);
}
```

Listing 16.1. Basic FSL shader.

16.3.2 Binary Declarations

FSL is designed to be easily integrated into existing build systems. To further simplify the handling of variants, we offer functionality to declare inline binary variant artifacts. We allow a single "translation unit" to result in multiple binary shaders. To declare a single binary output named myshader.frag, we use the syntax shown in Listing 16.2. This file name will be used at runtime to load the correct FSL binary. It is independent of the original FSL source file name. In other words, it is possible to have a single FSL source file with appropriate binary declarations to emit all required shaders for a given project.

```
#frag myshader.frag
// Block only active for myshader.frag translation
#end
```

Listing 16.2. Binary declaration.

The `#frag` and `#end` keywords map to `#ifdef shadername` and `#endif`. For each such declaration the FSL translator will preprocess the code and enable a definition matching the output name. When declaring multiple such blocks, only one will be active per translation pass. With this we support a wide range of patterns, such as in Listing 16.3.

```
float4 PS_MAIN( )
{
#frag myshader_red.frag
    float4 color = float4(1,0,0,1);
#end
#frag myshader_green.frag
    float4 color = float4(0,1,0,1);
#end
    RETURN(color);
}
```

Listing 16.3. Multiple binary declarations in single FSL shader.

To simplify translation, we limit these to the top-level FSL source file. In practice we have not found this to be a limiting factor.

16.3.3 Feature Flags

To control features and binary compilation behavior, FSL offers a range of feature flags that can be added to binary declarations (Listing 16.4).

```
// SV_PrimitiveID and potentially generate pass-through GS
FT_PRIM_ID
// Ray-Query interface
FT_RAYTRACING
// Variable rate shading interface
FT_VRS
// Multiview rendering for VR
FT_MULTIVIEW
// Suppression of argument buffer generation for MSL
FT_NO_AB
// Indicating that this shader will be used by an indirect command
FT_ICB
// Vertex draw parameters, force SV_InstanceID and SV_DrawID
// register allocation on Sony platforms
FT_VDP
```

Listing 16.4. Feature flags.

FT_PRIM_ID is necessary when a shader makes use of the SV_PrimitiveID input. For platforms that do not have immediate support for the semantic in the vertex stage, we generate a geometry stage on the fly and load it transparently at runtime. FT_RAYTRACING enables the cross-platform ray query API used for ray tracing. To enable hardware variable-rate shading, FT_VRS needs to be declared. FT_MULTIVIEW enables a range of extensions and macros to allow stereo rendering for virtual reality (VR) platforms.

The FT_NO_AB and FT_ICB feature flags relate to the Metal generator. The former has the effect to prohibit the instantiation of argument buffers. We generally aim to limit their use as we encountered numerous issues on lower-end iPhone devices. The only difficulty with this approach is to handle arrays of buffer resources, since they are not supported as top-level arguments in MSL. As a workaround, we manually unroll the array on the descriptor level and assemble it to an array variable as part of the generated shader runtime setup code. The second flag, FT_ICB needs to be enabled whenever a shader is to be used in an indirect fashion. Only indirect arguments can be used for such indirect calls on Metal, we therefore force the generator to generate Argument Buffers in all cases.

Feature flags are added to any binary declaration and can also be enabled and disabled globally (Listing 16.5).

```
#pragma FT_ICB FT_VRS // Enable FT_ICB and FT_VRS flags
#pragma ~FT_VRS // Disable FT_VRS
#vert FT_PRIM_ID FT_MULTIVIEW out.vert
// out.vert will compiled using features
// FT_ICB, FT_PRIM_ID and FT_MULTIVIEW
#end
```

Listing 16.5. Feature flag usage.

16.3.4 Parameter Modifiers

FSL supports the usual in, out, and inout type modifiers, to allow pass-by reference semantics (Listing 16.6).

```
void fn(
    in(float) param_in,
    out(float) param_out,
    inout(float) param_inout
    ) {}
```

Listing 16.6. Parameter modifiers.

16.3.5 Vectors and Matrices

FSL matrices are column-major. Matrices declared inside constant buffers, push constants, or structure buffers are initialized from memory in column-major order. Due to the different matrix conventions across APIs, it is necessary to access matrix elements using the provided macros (Listing 16.7).

```
// Initialize a 3x2 matrix from three 2D row vectors
f3x2 M = f3x2Rows(r0, r1, r2);
// Sets the element at col 0, row 1 to 42
setElem(M, 0, 1, 42.0f);
float3 col0 = getCol0(M);
float2 row1 = getRow1(M);
```

Listing 16.7. Matrix initialization and element access.

16.3.6 Shader Resources

FSL shader resources come in three categories: constant buffers, push constants, and generic resources. Generic resources and constant buffers require the declaration of a descriptor set index or space in HLSL. We map these directly to the update frequencies found in The Forge (Listing 16.8).

```
UPDATE_FREQ_NONE
UPDATE_FREQ_PER_FRAME
UPDATE_FREQ_PER_BATCH
UPDATE_FREQ_PER_DRAW
```

Listing 16.8. Resource update frequencies.

Constant buffers use the syntax in Listing 16.9 and implicitly declare a structure.

```
CBUFFER(Uniforms, UPDATE_FRE_NONE, b0, binding=0)
{
    DATA(f4x4, mvp, None);
};
```

Listing 16.9. Constant buffer declaration.

We currently allow specifying both the HLSL virtual register as well as the GLSL binding point to allow maximum flexibility in the root signature layout. We hope to change this in the near future and unify the register declarations.

Push constants use a similar syntax, but do not require an updated frequency (Listing 16.10).

```
PUSH_CONSTANT(PushConstants, b0)
{
    DATA(uint, index, None);
};
```

Listing 16.10. Push constant declaration.

Accessing the constant buffer and push constant fields inside the shader code necessitates the use of the Get(X) macro syntax, where X is the name of the field.

Generic resources are composed of buffers and textures. Their declaration uses the syntax shown in Listing 16.11.

```
RES(Type, name, UPDATE_FREQ_NONE, b0, binding=0);
```

Listing 16.11. Generic resource declaration.

Buffers are sub-typed using any fundamental or user data types. Supported are `Buffer`, `RWBuffer` (read-write buffer), `WBuffer` (write-only buffer), `ByteBuffer`, and `RWByteBuffer`.

16.4 Example

In this section we present a basic shader that covers the most frequently used FSL features. A vertex shader is declared, which consumes two attributes, transforms the position, and passes the texture coordinates through to the pixel shader. The transform is controlled by a constant buffer containing view-projection and model matrices (Listing 16.12).

```
STRUCT(VSInput)
{
    DATA(float3, Position,   POSITION);
    DATA(float2, TexCoords, TEXCOORD);
};

STRUCT(VSOutput)
{
    DATA(float4, Position,   SV_Position);
    DATA(float2, texcoords, TEXCOORD);
};

CBUFFER(uniformBlock, UPDATE_FREQ_PER_FRAME, b0, binding = 0)
{
    DATA(float4x4, ProjectionViewMat, None);
    DATA(float4x4, ModelMatrix, None);
};

VSOutput VS_MAIN(VSInput In)
{
    INIT_MAIN;
    VSOutput Out;
    float4x4 mvp = mul(Get(ProjectionViewMat), Get(ModelMatrix));
    Out.Position = mul(mvp, float4(In.Position.xyz, 1.0f));
    Out.texcoords = In.TexCoords;
    RETURN(Out);
}
```

Listing 16.12. Vertex shader example.

In the corresponding pixel shader in Listing 16.13, the texture coordinates are used to sample a texture and the result is returned.

From this short sample, we can see that FSL macros allow using pre-existing knowledge of established syntax to write expressive and readable shader code. The best source for additional examples is the open-source repository, [The Forge Interactive 24], where a wide range of advanced rendering techniques are implemented using FSL.

```
STRUCT(VSOutput)
{
  DATA(float4, Position, SV_Position);
    DATA(float2, texcoords, TEXCOORD);
};

RES(SamplerState,  uSampler0,  UPDATE_FREQ_NONE, s8, binding = 8);
RES(Tex2D(float4), uTexture0, UPDATE_FREQ_NONE, t7, binding = 7);

float4 PS_MAIN(VSOutput In)
{
  INIT_MAIN;
  float4 Out;
  Out = SampleTex2D(Get(uTexture0), Get(uSampler0), In.texcoords);
  RETURN(Out);
}
```

Listing 16.13. Pixel shader example.

16.5   Further Ideas and Improvements

For the future, we have a range of improvements in mind:

- Syntax for inline declarations of root signatures and their consumption could be improved. Currently, we use shader reflection to generate root signatures that match a given set of shaders. While very user-friendly, it would be more beneficial to allow for maximum control of the signature layouts. This would allow the use of more shared root signatures and eventually less switching at runtime. In practical terms, the generator can directly validate whether a given set of resource declarations is compatible with a given root signature.

- A range of syntax improvements are planned for the near future. The syntax requirements around struct declarations, return statements, and shader initialization can be simplified by adopting C-like language semantics, which would result in smaller and simpler language to parse.

- Auto-completion and syntax highlighting are two features important to most users of a programming language. Instead of developing custom high-lighters or completion engines, the route via a lightweight C-like language redefinition can offer these features virtually for free.

- Improving support for GPU Work Graphs is an exciting development, and we cannot wait to add those to FSL. As can be seen by the recent addition of ray-query features, this work should be doable with very little effort.

- Extending the syntax for GPU-driven features to allow inline resource declarations that directly integrate with data-driven PSO and texture creation is another feature we look forward to adding.

16.6 Conclusion

The Forge Shading Language system has been developed in two phases. The core system was set in place over the course of a couple weeks, while two years of continuous improvements followed. The system has been heavily used internally for the development and maintenance of The Forge framework. It has also found use in major projects that have resulted in further mileage and testing. The resulting simplicity and efficiency have led us to conclude that its development was a success, and we look forward to further improving and extending its capabilities.

Many people have worked on this ongoing research project. Over the last couple of years, the following people have been contributing to and improving the architecture: Borja Portugal, Olaf Schalk, David Erler, and Manas Kulkarni. It is always a team effort at The Forge Interactive to sustain and push these projects forward. Thanks to everyone who contributed.

Bibliography

[Khronos Group 24] Khronos Group. "SPIRV Tools." GitHub, 2024. https:// github.com/KhronosGroup/SPIRV-Tools.

[Kiyoshi MATSUI 24] Kiyoshi MATSUI. "mcpp." sourceforge, 2024. https:// mcpp.sourceforge.net.

[NVIDIA 24] NVIDIA. "Slang." GitHub, 2024. https://github.com/shader-slang/slang.

[The Forge Interactive 24] The Forge Interactive. "The Forge." GitHub, 2024. https://github.com/ConfettiFX/The-Forge.

Simple Automatic Resource Synchronization Method for Vulkan Applications

Grigory Javadyan

17.1 Introduction

Older graphics APIs, such as OpenGL, provide a lot of implicit guarantees regarding the order of memory operations. For example, the use of an image as a color attachment for one draw call, followed by using the same image as a texture to sample from in the next draw call, works as expected intuitively. For the API user, this is rather simple and convenient, however modern GPUs do not function is such a simple way: they are massively parallel machines with nontrivial memory hierarchies. That means, for example, that certain stages of a draw call may be executed in parallel with other stages of another draw call, or that flushing a cache might be necessary for stage A to "see" the memory effects of some operations performed by stage B. Unless orchestrated properly, memory operations may conflict with each other: writes may "compete" with each other, reads may return partial or outdated data, etc. Legacy API implementations abstract away many details of memory access synchronization, so users generally don't have to worry about them.

By contrast, the Vulkan API leaves it up to the application developer to ensure that accesses to resource memory do not have conflicts among themselves. To that end, Vulkan provides a range of tools—memory barriers, events, semaphores, etc.—that the API user is expected to leverage in order to manage the synchronization of accesses explicitly.

The explicit approach to synchronization makes it feasible, in theory, to achieve a greater degree of parallelism on the GPU than legacy APIs allow for. However, taking on the burden of managing synchronization is no easy task—it could reasonably be considered one of the most complex and confusing aspects of Vulkan. To achieve acceptable performance while remaining correct and portable, applications require a systematic approach for dealing with the complexity of explicit synchronization.

A popular way of dealing with synchronization is often referred to as a *render graph* or *frame graph* [O'Donnell 17]. It has been used to great success in many shipping applications. By virtue of knowing what resources will be used within

399

a given frame, as well as the nature and order of the operations applied to the resources, a render graph can deduce the optimal way to synchronize the commands within the frame, allowing for the maximum degree of parallelism while not introducing any conflicts. In addition to that, render graphs can be used to automatically re-use the same backing memory for different resources at different points in the frame - a technique known as *resource aliasing*, which helps to reduce GPU memory usage.

For all its virtues, a render graph is not necessarily the ideal solution for everyone. It can have nontrivial implementation and maintenance costs, and force the renderer's code into patterns that might not have been chosen otherwise. Some applications would do well to trade off certain benefits of render graphs for more simplicity and more flexibility in how the rendering code can be written.

In this article, we present a comparatively simple alternative method for solving the synchronization problem. It trades off some of the parallelism achievable with render graphs for simplicity in implementation, maintenance, and usage. Similar approaches are known to have been used in the industry previously, so the author does not claim novelty. The article assumes the reader to have at least a basic level of familiarity with Vulkan.

The specific implementation of the method described in this article was developed for nicegraf [nicebyte 24], an open-source graphics API abstraction layer. nicegraf can be best described as a render hardware interface (RHI)—an interface that closely resembles existing GPU APIs, with specific implementations for each supported platform. As far as RHIs go, nicegraf aims to be at the "middle" abstraction level. To that end, nicegraf does not require the user to manually manage resource memory or synchronization. nicegraf's Vulkan backend automatically deduces and inserts the necessary memory barriers that are not overly restrictive.

17.1.1   Prior Work

Frame graphs/render graphs have been used extensively by several game engines, and their use is well documented [O'Donnell 17, Arntzen 17, Gaule 24].

The method presented in this article is more similar in spirit to how drivers for APIs without explicit synchronization manage hazard tracking. The particular implementation discussed here was first presented during the Vulkanised 2024 conference [Dzhavadyan 24], albeit with less implementation details. Similar approaches have been used in the Vulkan backend of Dawn (an implementation of the WebGPU API [Dawn 24, Bernhardsson 24]) and the NVIDIA Rendering Hardware Interface (NVRHI) [NVIDIA 24]. It is also somewhat similar to the approach taken by Synchronization Validation from the LunarG Vulkan SDK [Zulauf 24], issuing missing barriers rather than simply reporting them, although a significant difference is that the validation layer has to take the effects of user-issued synchronization commands into account.

17.1.2 Overview

Below we present a brief road map of the sections comprising the rest of this article:

- In Section 17.2, we provide a general overview of the technique. We state the problem that makes naive auto-synchronization untenable in the presence of multiple command buffers being recorded at a time, and propose a solution to it.

- Section 17.3 introduces the notions of a synchronization request and a resource's synchronization state. We describe both structures and discuss in detail how synchronization requests are issued and handled.

- Section 17.4 discusses how synchronization requests are translated into actual Vulkan synchronization commands in a manner that attempts to minimize the amount of calls to `vkCmdPipelineBarrier`.

- Section 17.5 describes what happens when a resource needs to be read or written by a command, thus showing how the concepts from the prior sections are used together in order to achieve correct synchronization within a single command buffer.

- Section 17.6 discusses the problem of synchronization across different command buffers.

- We conclude the article by discussing the limitations of the presented approach and examining the results of applying said approach in a practical setting.

17.2 The Technique

17.2.1 The Problem with Command Buffers

Vulkan, similar to some other GPU APIs, introduces the concept of command buffers. Command buffers give applications a lot of flexibility in terms of how GPU commands can be issued. However, command buffers also make the task of automating resource access synchronization harder.

To see why that is so, let us first consider the simple case where the application is only allowed to record a single command buffer at a time. Under that scenario, consider the following example (see Figure 17.1):

- We have two resources: an image A and a buffer B.

- A render pass uses A as a color attachment.

- A compute pass writes some data to the buffer B.

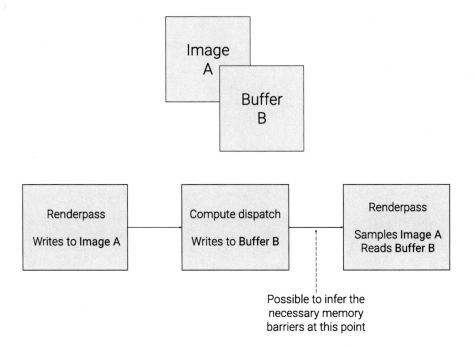

Figure 17.1. Simple case for automatic synchronization.

- Finally, another render pass samples the image A and reads from the buffer B.

The commands corresponding to these operations are recorded into our only command buffer in the order listed above. As long as we keep track of which resources have been touched by which operations, it is not too difficult to deduce and emit the correct memory barriers as we go about recording commands into our command buffer. Indeed, by the time we have to start recording commands for the final render pass in our example, we already have all the necessary context:

- We know that a render pass has written to A.

- We know that a compute dispatch has written to B.

We have that context because, by the time we're about to start recording the last render pass, we have seen the entire preceding history of the commands within our only command buffer. There is no way for us to have missed some command that needs to be synchronized with: all commands go into the same command buffer in a well-defined order.

However, once we introduce the possibility of having multiple command buffers actively being recorded at any given time, the problem becomes more

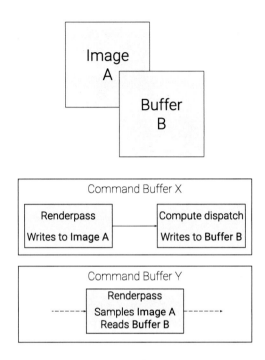

Figure 17.2. Multiple command buffers complicate automatic synchronization.

challenging. Consider an example similar to the one above, except the commands that write to A and B are recorded into command buffer X, while the commands that read from A and B are recorded into another command buffer, Y (see Figure 17.2).

Under these conditions, we no longer have the necessary context for emitting memory barriers while recording a command buffer. For example, when recording commands for the render pass in the command buffer Y, we don't know whether the command buffer X will be submitted before or after Y. In fact, the commands that modify A and B might not have even been recorded into X at all at the moment when we need to record our commands into Y.

The fundamental problem with the simultaneous presence of multiple active command buffer objects is that there isn't a single, well-ordered stream of commands to analyze. In the case with a single command buffer, we had access to the complete history of commands in submission order. However, we don't have it in the case that allows multiple command buffers: their order of submission is unknown a priori.

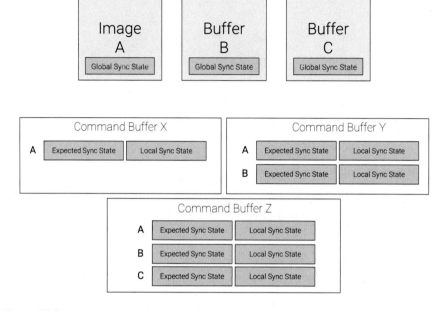

Figure 17.3. Each resource has a single global synchronization state corresponding to it. Each command buffer has an associated table of resources used within it that stores the resources' expected and local synchronization states for that command buffer.

17.2.2 Interim Barriers

The solution to the problem discussed above consists of two parts:

1. Making simplifying assumptions about synchronization at certain points when recording individual command buffers.

2. Revisiting those assumptions at a later point, and inserting any memory barriers that we might have missed.

Let's examine the first part.

We introduce the notion of a resource's *synchronization state*, which can be thought of as a piece of data used to track accesses by different pipeline stages to the resource. Each resource has a single *global* synchronization state. Additionally, each resource has one *local* synchronization state per each command buffer in which it is used (see Figure 17.3).

While recording individual command buffers, we shall make certain simplifying assumptions about whether synchronization is needed. To be more exact, we shall assume that the very first access to a resource by a pipeline stage within a given command buffer shall not require synchronization. For subsequent accesses by the same pipeline stage, the resource's *local* synchronization state is used as an input for an algorithm that decides whether synchronization is required for a given access (we'll describe the algorithm in detail later). For each pipeline stage accessing the resource, we shall keep track of its *first* access to the resource, as well as all the *subsequent* accesses up to the first one that does require synchronization. We shall collectively refer to that set of stage-access pairs as the *expected* synchronization state of the resource for the given command buffer. The expected synchronization state effectively specifies which accesses within which pipeline stages should require no synchronization with respect to the given resource before executing the command buffer. As long as the requirements expressed by each of the participating resources' expected synchronization states are satisfied, each individual command buffer that we record shall introduce no hazards.

The second part of the solution involves inserting missing synchronization once the content and the order of submission of all the command buffers within a frame have become known. Recall that in the previous step we had assumed that all initial accesses to a resource would require no synchronization. With all the commands for a given frame and their submission order available to us, these assumptions can be re-examined and, if proven wrong, rectified by patching in the missing memory barriers.

All command buffers for a frame are submitted on the same thread, forming an ordered timeline. For each submitted command buffer, we compare the *expected* synchronization states of the resources used within it to their respective *global* synchronization states. As a result of this comparison, it is straightforward to infer the memory barriers necessary to satisfy the expected synchronization states for the upcoming command buffer, thus maintaining a well-synchronized stream of commands. The inferred barriers are recorded into an auxiliary command buffer, which is submitted prior to the submission of the upcoming main command buffer, which is then followed by an update to all of the participating resources' *global* synchronization states.

17.3 Synchronization State and Synchronization Request

In this section, we describe the synchronization state data structure in more detail. We also introduce the concept of a *synchronization request*. Finally, we will describe the procedure that decides whether a memory barrier is necessary within a given context.

17.3.1 Synchronization State

Listing 17.1 contains the definition of the synchronization state data structure, as it is used in nicegraf.

The synchronization state comprises three main components:

- A field specifying which access in which pipeline stage has last modified the resource. It is named `last_writer_masks` in Listing 17.1.

```
typedef struct ngfvk_sync_barrier_masks {
  VkAccessFlags          access_mask;
  VkPipelineStageFlags stage_mask;
} ngfvk_sync_barrier_masks;
// ...
typedef struct ngfvk_sync_state {
  ngfvk_sync_barrier_masks last_writer_masks;
  uint32_t                 per_stage_readers_map;
  VkImageLayout            layout;
} ngfvk_sync_state;
```

Listing 17.1. The synchronization state data structure.

- A field specifying which accesses in which pipeline stages have had the results of the last write made visible and available to them via a memory barrier. It is named **per_stage_readers_map** in Listing 17.1. The field maps a stage-access pair to a binary value indicating whether the given access in the given stage has observed the results of the last write operation. In nicegraf, this mapping is implemented as a bitmap (see Figure 17.4) because less than 32 bits are enough to handle all the possible combinations

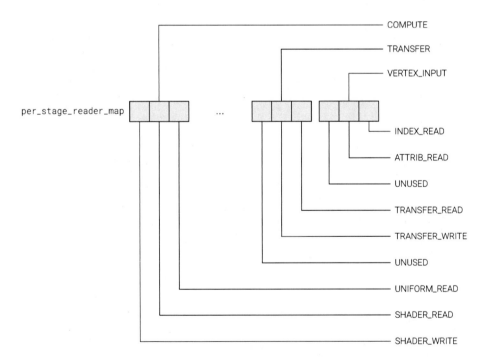

Figure 17.4. Correspondence of bits to stage-access pairs in the per-stage reader map field of the synchronization state. Not all stage-access pairs are shown. Each group of 3 bits corresponds to a pipeline stage, and each bit within the group corresponds to an access type.

of stages and accesses that we have to contend with. Each group of 3 bits within the field corresponds to a particular pipeline stage, and each bit within a 3-bit group either corresponds to a particular access within its stage or is unused.

- Finally, there is a field specifying the current layout of the resource (if the resource is an image), named `layout` in Listing 17.1.

17.3.2 Synchronization Request

A *synchronization request* (or sync request) describes the intent to access a resource. It comprises two parts:

1. bitmasks specifying the pipeline stages requesting access, as well as the types of accesses requested;

2. the layout that the resource has to be in while being accessed (relevant for images only).

Here is the definition of the corresponding `ngfvk_sync_req` structure, as it is used in nicegraf:

```
typedef struct ngfvk_sync_req {
  ngfvk_sync_barrier_masks  stage_and_access_masks;
  VkImageLayout             layout;
} ngfvk_sync_req;
```

Synchronization requests are issued at any point when we are about to record commands that might result in a resource being either read or modified. In nicegraf, synchronization requests are issued in the following cases:

- **Binding an attribute or index buffer:** When this happens, a sync request is issued for the buffer being bound. The request's pipeline stage mask is set to `VK_PIPELINE_STAGE_VERTEX_INPUT_BIT` and the access mask is set either to `VK_ACCESS_VERTEX_ATTRIBUTE_READ_BIT` (if an attribute buffer is being bound) or to `VK_ACCESS_INDEX_READ_BIT` (if an index buffer is being bound).

- **Initiating a transfer operation:** (For instance, buffer to buffer, buffer to image, image to buffer.) In this case, two synchronization requests are issued: one for the source resource and one for the target resource. The pipeline stage mask for both requests is set to `VK_PIPELINE_STAGE_TRANSFER_BIT`. The access mask for the request corresponding to the source resource is set to `VK_ACCESS_TRANSFER_READ_BIT`, while the access mask for the destination resource is set to `VK_ACCESS_TRANSFER_WRITE_BIT`. If the source resource is an image, its corresponding synchronization request sets the desired layout to `VK_LAYOUT_TRANSFER_SRC_OPTIMAL`. If the destination resource is an image, its corresponding synchronization request sets the desired layout to `VK_LAYOUT_TRANSFER_DST_OPTIMAL`.

- **Beginning a render pass:** When this happens, we issue a synchronization request for each of the attachments to which the render pass is about to write. For each of the color attachments, the sync request's pipeline stage mask is set to VK_PIPELINE_STAGE_COLOR_ATTACHMENT_OUTPUT_BIT, while both VK_ACCESS_COLOR_ATTACHMENT_READ_BIT and VK_ACCESS_COLOR_ATTACHMENT_WRITE_BIT are added to the access mask. The layout specified in sync requests for color attachments is VK_LAYOUT_COLOR_ATTACHMENT_OPTIMAL. For depth/stencil attachments, the sync request's pipeline stage mask is set to include both VK_PIPELINE_STAGE_EARLY_FRAGMENT_TESTS_BIT and VK_PIPELINE_STAGE_LATE_FRAGMENT_TESTS_BIT, and the access mask is set to include both VK_ACCESS_DEPTH_STENCIL_ATTACHMENT_READ_BIT and VK_ACCESS_DEPTH_STENCIL_ATTACHMENT_WRITE_BIT. The layout for depth/stencil attachments is set to VK_IMAGE_LAYOUT_DEPTH_STENCIL_ATTACHMENT_OPTIMAL.

- **Binding a resource to be used in a shader:** In this case, a sync request is issued for the resource being bound. The pipeline stage mask is set based on which shader stages actually use the descriptor to which the resource is bound. These stages can be determined by using the SPIRV-Reflect library to analyze the shader modules used in the currently bound pipeline state object (this analysis is done only once, during pipeline state object creation). The type of the descriptor determines the access mask:

  - VK_ACCESS_SHADER_READ_BIT for read-only textures, read-only storage buffers, and texel buffers;

  - VK_ACCESS_UNIFORM_READ_BIT for uniform buffers;

  - VK_ACCESS_SHADER_READ_BIT | VK_ACCESS_SHADER_WRITE_BIT for read-write storage images and storage buffers.

  Note that we make the distinction between read-only and read-write storage buffers, which allows the resulting memory barriers to be less restrictive.

Synchronization requests may or may not result in memory barriers being emitted: that decision is made by a special procedure that takes as input both the sync request and the current synchronization state of the resource for which the synchronization request is issued.

17.3.3   Rules for Handling Synchronization Requests

The procedure that decides whether a particular sync request merits a memory barrier has to follow a certain set of rules in order to provide the required correctness and performance guarantees. Here are these rules:

- Concurrent reads should almost always be allowed. This is a prerequisite for being able to run more things in parallel.

- A write cannot be concurrent with any other writes or reads to the same memory location. This is a prerequisite for avoiding conflicts. This means that any pipeline stage requesting write access gets *exclusive* access to the resource. Ideally, the exclusive access would be limited to exactly the subregion of the resource that is being affected by the write operation. However, nicegraf's implementation is suboptimal here because we apply the limitation to the entire resource. This limits the theoretically achievable parallelism of GPU operations, but makes synchronization state tracking easier. In general, there is a trade-off between how granular the state tracking is and how much CPU overhead it induces: more granular tracking may result in better-behaved GPU memory barriers, but comes with the cost of more spent CPU cycles.

- Once the results of a prior write to a resource have been made available and visible to an access within a pipeline stage, that access needs no further synchronization with respect to the resource until the resource is modified again. This is a prerequisite for avoiding superfluous synchronization.

- Image layout transitions are read-modify-write operations, and for the purposes of barrier emission, they are treated as writes. They are the only notable exception to the first rule: two reads from the same image cannot be made concurrent if they require the source image to use different layouts. For example, think of a transfer operation copying pixels from an image into a buffer, followed by a compute dispatch sampling the same image. Unless the image uses the layout VK_IMAGE_LAYOUT_GENERAL, these two read-only operations cannot be made concurrent because there needs to be a layout transition between them.

17.3.4 Algorithm for Handling Synchronization Requests

We shall now describe the procedure that nicegraf uses to determine whether a synchronization request merits a memory barrier, given the synchronization state of the resource for which the request is issued.

Synchronization requests can be categorized as either *modifying* or *non-modifying*. If a synchronization request specifies any accesses that imply writing to a resource (e.g., VK_ACCESS_COLOR_ATTACHMENT_WRITE, VK_ACCESS_SHADER_WRITE, etc.), then the request is categorized as modifying. Additionally, if the synchronization request implies an image layout transition, it is considered to be modifying as well (even if the requested accesses are read-only). We determine whether a layout transition is implied by comparing the synchronization request's layout field to the layout specified in the given synchronization state. If no layout transition is implied, and the requested access(es) are read-only, the request is considered non-modifying.

If the synchronization request is *non-modifying*, we first check whether the resource has seen a preceding write. This is done by simply comparing the current synchronization state's `last_writer_masks` against zero. If the resource hasn't seen any preceding writes, no memory barrier is necessary. However, we still need to update the bits of the `per_stage_readers_map` field that correspond to the stages and accesses specified in the synchronization request. This is done in order to be able to synchronize the reads with any future read or modify operations. If the resource has seen a preceding write, we need to check the bits of `per_stage_readers_map` corresponding the accesses and pipeline stages specified in the sync request, in order to determine whether those accesses have caught up to the preceding write. If any of the relevant bits are 0, a corresponding memory barrier needs to be emitted to avoid a read-after-write conflict, after which the bits need to be updated. Otherwise, no action needs to be taken.

If the synchronization request is a *modifying* one, and the resource has seen any preceding read or write operations, a relevant memory barrier needs to be emitted to avoid write-after-read and write-after-write conflicts. Following that, the `last_writer_masks` field of the synchronization state needs to be assigned the accesses and pipeline stages specified in the request, and the `per_stage_readers_map` field needs to be zeroed out. If a layout transition is being performed, the layout field of the synchronization state needs to be updated accordingly, and the bits corresponding to the requested access and stage in `per_stage_readers_map` need to be set, because the result of the layout transition is made available and visible to them automatically according to the Vulkan specification.

17.4   Emitting Barriers

17.4.1   Minimizing the Number of Calls to `vkCmdPipelineBarrier2`

For performance-related reasons, it is considered good practice in Vulkan to minimize the number of calls to `vkCmdPipelineBarrier2`, preferring to emit several barriers with a single call if possible. To achieve this, nicegraf handles synchronization requests in bulk: When a request is issued, its processing is delayed until the last possible moment. When that moment comes, we process the batch of pending sync requests all together, in the order they were issued. The previously described sync-request-handling algorithm is applied to each request in the batch, in order to determine whether a memory barrier is necessary. All the memory barriers generated as a result are emitted using a single call to `vkCmdPipelineBarrier2`.

We use the `VK_KHR_synchronization2` extension wherever possible. There is generally no good reason to not use this extension, as there is an SDK layer that emulates it on platforms that don't have native support. One of the reasons to prefer `VK_KHR_synchronization2` over the legacy synchronization API is that the legacy `vkCmdPipelineBarrier` function requires combining the source and destination pipeline stages of all memory barriers into two bitmasks (as opposed to `vkCmdPipelineBarrier2`, which allows individual barriers to specify their own stage masks). This may create false dependencies and thus less efficient synchronization.

17.4.2 Handling Sync Request Batches

For compute dispatches, all pending synchronization requests are processed and barriers are emitted immediately before the dispatch command is recorded.

For draw calls, the situation is a bit more complicated. The issue is that the Vulkan specification limits the synchronization scopes to just the current subpass for barriers emitted within a render pass instance. This means that if we need to synchronize some command inside a render pass instance with something outside of the render pass instance, we need to emit the corresponding memory barrier(s) outside of the render pass instance as well. However, in order to know with what exactly we might want to synchronize, we need to have seen all of the commands within the render pass. This means that we can't immediately record render pass commands when we encounter them. There are a few possible ways out of this situation:

- Do not use render passes at all, relying on `VK_KHR_dynamic_rendering` instead. Then, sync requests can be handled before each draw call, similar to how it's done for compute dispatches.

- If using `VK_KHR_dynamic_rendering` is off the table, another way would be to record the barrier commands into a secondary command buffer, to which the main command buffer should call out before beginning the render pass instance.

- Another possible approach is buffering up render pass commands, deferring their actual recording into the command buffer until after the user ends the render pass. Avoiding secondary command buffers does save on the potential small cost of indirection, but more importantly, this approach can be seen as a hedge against any potential implementation quirks, as secondary command buffers are a somewhat under-used feature of Vulkan. This is the approach chosen by nicegraf.

17.5 Synchronization in a Single Command Buffer

17.5.1 The Command Buffer Resource Table

In nicegraf, all command buffer objects have an associated table, containing a corresponding entry for each resource used within the command buffer. It is implemented as a simple flat hash table using open addressing and the `murmur3` hash function. Each entry within the table contains, among other things, the corresponding resource's local synchronization state, as well as its expected synchronization state:

```
typedef struct ngfvk_sync_res_data {
 // Latest synchronization state.
 ngfvk_sync_state local_sync_state;

 // Expected sync state.
 ngfvk_sync_req expected_sync_state;
 //...
} ngfvk_sync_res_data;
```

The *expected* synchronization state of the resource communicates which accesses within which pipeline stages should *not* require synchronization with respect to the resource before the command buffer is executed (as well as what layout the resource should be in, for images). This corresponds exactly to the information contained in a synchronization request, and that is why the expected synchronization state is expressed as a `ngfvk_sync_req`.

The *local* synchronization state is an instance of `ngfvk_sync_state`, which has been described in Listing 17.1. When a resource is first used within the command buffer, its local synchronization state is considered a "blank slate": no preceding readers or writers are assumed. That means that the last writer and per-stage readers map are all set to zero.

17.5.2   Using a Resource within a Command Buffer

Whenever we record a command that may result in a particular resource being either read or modified, a synchronization request is issued against the resource's current *local* synchronization state for the pipeline stage and access corresponding to the command. Because the local synchronization state initially assumes no prior writes or reads, the very first synchronization request will not result in any barriers being emitted. We shall simply set the corresponding access and pipeline stage bits in the resource's *expected* synchronization state.

It is possible that even the second, third, etc. synchronization requests issued for a resource might not result in memory barriers being emitted. This could happen, for example, in the case when the first access was a read and the second access was also a read that could be made concurrent with the first one. As long as all of the sync requests issued for the resource so far have not resulted in a barrier, we need to keep adding their corresponding access and stage bits to the resource's *expected* synchronization state, in order to keep track of what barrier(s) might potentially be needed for the resource before executing the command buffer in which the resource is being used. We can stop updating the expected synchronization state only after a synchronization request results in a barrier for the first time during the recording of the current command buffer.

17.6 Synchronization across Command Buffers

Applying the methods described so far, we should be able to obtain individual internally well-synchronized command buffers. Being *internally well-synchronized* means that, as long as the requirements expressed by all of the participating resources' expected synchronization states are satisfied, the command buffer does not result in any synchronization hazards when submitted. The requirements corresponding to a particular *main* command buffer can be satisfied by submitting an auxiliary command buffer containing the appropriate memory barrier operations, prior to submitting the main command buffer itself. This operation can be performed at submit time, because at that point the order of submission of the main command buffers is known, making the task of deducing the necessary memory barriers fairly straightforward.

In nicegraf, all command buffers are submitted by a single thread, and that thread is the only one that is allowed to read or write the resources' *global* synchronization states. We shall now cover what happens when a set of internally well-synchronized command buffers is submitted for execution.

For each main command buffer that is about to be submitted to the GPU queue for execution, the following procedure is performed:

- For each resource participating in the upcoming main command buffer, we generate a synchronization request against the resource's *global* synchronization state. The stages, accesses, and layout in the request are determined by the resource's *expected* synchronization state.

- We handle the synchronization requests generated during the preceding step in bulk, and record the memory barriers generated as a result into an auxiliary command buffer.

- The auxiliary command buffer is enqueued for execution. This is only done if there were any memory barriers generated during the preceding step.

- The upcoming main command buffer is enqueued for execution.

- For each resource participating in the last enqueued command buffer, we update the resource's global synchronization state. This is something that needs to be done regardless of whether we had to submit an auxiliary command buffer with interim barriers during the previous steps. This process is not exactly straightforward and depends on whether the last enqueued command buffer has any operations that write to the resource (keep in mind that layout transitions count as writes).

  – If the resource is written to by the last enqueued command buffer, its corresponding global synchronization state can be simply overwritten with the last known local synchronization state from the last enqueued command buffer.

    — Otherwise, only the per-stage readers mask of the resource's local synchronization state from the last enqueued command buffer should be merged into the per-stage readers mask of the resource's global synchronization state (i.e., the two masks need to be bit-wise OR-ed together and the result recorded into the global per-stage readers mask). Taking these measures is necessary because the last write to the resource might have been done by some older command buffer. The local synchronization state from the last enqueued command buffer would not contain information about writes done by preceding command buffers. Using that local synchronization state to overwrite the global synchronization state would make us lose track of which access within which pipeline stage had modified the resource last.

17.7   Limitations

In this section we shall cover the fundamental limitations of the described method, as well as the limitations of its particular implementation in nicegraf.

- **Poor synchronization granularity:** As mentioned before, nicegraf puts strict limitations on operations modifying the same resource: they cannot be concurrent even when touching completely disjoint parts of a resource (i.e., when allowing them to be concurrent would not actually result in a conflict). We'll discuss potential ways to address this in Section 17.9.

- **No support for bindless:** nicegraf currently does not support the concept of bindless resources. The automated tracking relies on every bind having to be executed using a command recorded on the CPU. Attempting to determine which of the descriptors from a (potentially huge) descriptor table are actually being used in a given shader is impractical, so a more explicit approach with some user cooperation would be needed for bindless support.

- **No split barriers:** Inherent to the presented method is the fact that the memory barriers are emitted at the very last possible moment. This precludes implementing a *split barrier* with VkEvents, where one could, e.g., initiate a layout transition earlier and overlap it with some other useful work before actually having to use the image with the new layout. Incidentally, this is something that could be achieved using a render graph.

- **No resource aliasing:** nicegraf does not expose memory management to the user, so aliasing resources does not really make sense in the first place. If resource aliasing is desired, render graphs would serve that use case better.

- **Single queue only:** nicegraf's particular implementation is designed to handle only a single GPU command queue. That being said, there isn't a fundamental reason the presented method could not be extended to support multiple queues.

- **No support for stores or atomics in vertex and fragment shaders:** nicegraf's particular implementation does not handle stores and atomics in vertex and fragment shaders at the moment. This isn't a fundamental limitation of the presented method and can be added in a fairly straightforward manner if desired.

17.8 Results

In this section, we will review the results of applying the automatic synchronization algorithm described above to a rendering workload representative of a high-quality indie game. We shall examine the GPU barriers produced by the algorithm, as well as investigate the CPU-side overhead of the algorithm.

At the time of this writing, nicegraf is being used by one studio as an RHI for their in-house game engine for an upcoming title. The renderer has several features, including compute-based character skinning and deformable meshes, real-time soft shadows, global illumination, and temporal antialiasing. This means there are several passes—both graphics and compute—working in concert, passing data to one another in order to construct a single frame. Writing synchronization manually for that setup would be possible, but quite tedious.

The specific algorithmic details of the renderer are out of scope for this article, but in Figure 17.5 we provide a schematic overview of all the passes involved in constructing the frame. The flow of data between passes is represented with arrows (going from producer to consumer).

Given this setup, nicegraf's synchronization automation produces one `vkCmdPipelineBarrier` call per pass, each including the resources involved in that pass (inputs and outputs). For example, the frame in Figure 17.6 involves 18 calls to `vkCmdPipelineBarrier`, which matches the number of individual passes involved. Note that the engine developers don't have to explicitly specify any "graph nodes" or their inputs or outputs: they just write their rendering code in a style similar to OpenGL, or Metal, without explicit synchronization.

The generated barriers themselves have precise stage and access masks, meaning that they do not introduce extra unnecessary restrictions. For example, the barrier generated before handing off the temporal antialiasing (TAA) output to the first downsampling pass has the following stage masks set:

- source stage mask, VK_PIPELINE_STAGE_COLOR_ATTACHMENT_OUTPUT_BIT;

- destination stage mask, VK_PIPELINE_STAGE_FRAGMENT_SHADER_BIT.

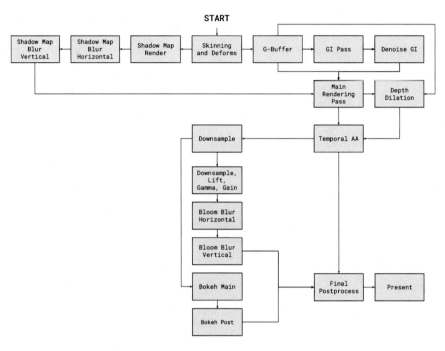

Figure 17.5. Schematic representation of all render and compute passes within a frame rendered by the engine.

Figure 17.6. Screenshot of a test scene demonstrating some of the engine's features.

Thanks to SPIR-V introspection, we know that the descriptor to which we're binding the TAA output texture is only accessed by the fragment stage of the downsample shader. This helps us keep the set bits in the destination stage mask to a minimum and avoid setting overbroad masks like `VK_PIPELINE_STAGE_FRAGMENT_SHADER_BIT | VK_PIPELINE_STAGE_VERTEX_SHADER_BIT` "just in case." Adding extra stage bits can harm performance on certain tile-based deferred rendering (TBDR)–style GPUs: to enhance performance, they rely on overlapping the vertex processing for the next frame with the fragment processing for the current frame, however having the vertex shader bit set in the destination stage mask of a memory barrier precludes this optimization. This shows why being precise with stage/access masks is important.

When measuring the impact on CPU performance, it was found that about 5% of the profiler samples ended up in functions related to automatic synchronization tracking. It is quite far from being the engine's bottleneck—at the time of this writing, CPU time is actually dominated by handling gameplay-related updates.

17.9 Future Work

The poor synchronization granularity exhibited by the method presented here is possible to address, for example, by tracking image mipmap levels individually, or asking the API user to specify predefined disjoint regions of a buffer to be tracked separately. However, all of these solutions come with a trade-off: increased overhead from hazard tracking due to the increased number of tracked subresources.

One observation that might help is that not all resources need to be tracked all the time. For example, it is very common for an image that is used as a texture to be written only once (during the texture upload), after which the image is only ever read. It's possible to add an API that marks resources as *immutable*. After being marked as immutable, resources can no longer be written to (or experience layout transitions). Such resources can be excluded from tracking entirely, thus reducing the CPU overhead.

As another point for future improvement, the presented method can be extended to handle commands being submitted to multiple GPU queues. For that, a queue-local resource synchronization state would need to be introduced (recall that we already have global and command-buffer-local resource synchronization states). Cross-queue hazard tracking would use an approach somewhat similar to what we have described for tracking hazards across command buffers submitted to the same queue; the emission of the necessary barriers would need to occur at queue submission boundaries.

17.10   Conclusion

In this article, we have presented a method for automatically synchronizing access to resources in Vulkan applications. Compared to the frame graph approach, our method waives most expectations from the client code, making it more similar in style to code for such APIs as WebGPU, Metal, or Direct3D 11. The increased flexibility comes at the cost of somewhat reduced GPU parallelism.

We have examined one case of applying our method in a practical setting—an indie game with a nontrivial rendering pipeline—and found both GPU and CPU performance to be well within acceptable bounds for the project in question. At the same time, developers were able to quickly iterate on their renderer without getting involved with the finer details of resource synchronization at all.

Finally, we have described the shortcomings of the presented method and showed how some of them could be potentially addressed in the future.

Overall, this approach to synchronization offers a decent result-to-effort ratio, and would be a good starting point for any application that is not necessarily concerned with taking advantage of every last bit of parallelism on the GPU.

Bibliography

[Arntzen 17] Hans-Kristian Arntzen. "Render Graphs and Vulkan—A Deep Dive." Maister's Graphics Adventures, August 15, 2017. https://themaister. net/blog/2017/08/15/render-graphs-and-vulkan-a-deep-dive/.

[Bernhardsson 24] Albin Bernhardsson. "Vulkan Synchronization for WebGPU." Presented at Vulkanised Conference, 2024. https://vulkan.org/user/pages/ 09.events/vulkanised-2024/vulkanised-2024-albin-bernhardsson-arm.pdf.

[Dawn 24] Dawn. "Dawn WebGPU Implementation." Dawn Git Repository, 2024. https://dawn.googlesource.com/dawn/+/refs/heads/main/src/dawn/ native/vulkan/.

[Dzhavadyan 24] Grigory Dzhavadyan. "Vulkan Synchronization Made Easy." Presented at Vulkanised Conference, 2024. https://vulkan.org/user/pages/ 09.events/vulkanised-2024/vulkanised-2024-grigory-dzhavadyan.pdf.

[Gaule 24] Akio Gaule. "Mastering Chaos: Navigating Vulkan Synchronization on O3DE." Presented at Vulkanised Conference, 2024. https://vulkan.org/user/pages/09.events/vulkanised-2024/vulkanised- 2024-akio-gaule-o3de.pdf.

[nicebyte 24] nicebyte. "nicegraf." GitHub, 2024. http://nice.graphics/.

[NVIDIA 24] NVIDIA. "NVRHI." NVIDIA GameWorks, GitHub, 2024. https: //github.com/NVIDIAGameWorks/nvrhi.

[O'Donnell 17] Yuriy O'Donnell. "FrameGraph: Extensible Rendering Architecture in Frostbite." Presented at Game Developers Conference, 2017. https://www.gdcvault.com/play/1024612/FrameGraph-Extensible-Rendering-Architecture-in.

[Zulauf 24] John Zulauf. "Guide to Vulkan Synchronization Validation." LunarG Whitepaper, 2024. https://www.lunarg.com/wp-content/uploads/2024/01/Guide-to-Vulkan-Synchronization-Validation-FINAL-01-18-2024.pdf.

Tools of the Trade
Kirill Bazhenov and Anton Kaplanyan, Editors

Welcome to the Tools of the Trade section, where the focus is on leveraging the GPU to improve production workflows, improve performance, or use the GPU for unconventional tasks.

The first two articles focus on using differentiable programming and machine learning to improve artist productivity and automate boring non-creative tasks such as level of detail and texture mipmap creation. "Differentiable Graphics with Slang.D for Appearance-Based Optimization," by Bartlomiej Wronski, Sai Bangaru, Marco Salvi, Yong He, Lifan Wu, and Jacob Munkberg, addresses the fundamental concepts and BRDF-aware texture minification in particular, while "DRToolkit: Boosting Rendering Performance Using Differentiable Rendering," by Chen Qiao, Xiang Lan, Yijie Shi, Xueqiang Wang, Xilei Wei, and Jiang Qin, further explores differentiable programming for optimizing complete assets, shader effects, and practical production pipelines integrated into the game engine.

The next two articles—"Flowmap Baking with LBM-SWE" and "Animating Water Using Profile Buffer" by Haozhe Su, Wei Li, Zherong Pan, Xifeng Gao, Zhenyu Mao, and Kui Wu—present several novel water rendering methods that solve various issues that conventional flowmaps have, as well as an efficient authoring pipeline for water assets.

"Advanced Techniques for Radix Sort," by Atsushi Yoshimura and Chih-Chen Kao, introduces a high-performance and memory-efficient radix sort implementation on the GPU. Efficient GPU sorting opens up a possibility to use the GPU for many tasks that rely on sorting data.

"Two-Pass HZB Occlusion Culling," by Miloš Kruškonja, discusses a GPU occlusion culling system and production workflows that improve the rendering performance of dense geometry.

Last but not least, the "Shader Server System" article by Djordje Pepic focuses on graphics programmer productivity and reducing iteration times when working with shaders on multiple platforms.

Due to the raising expectations for titles, development costs have increased across the board, raising the bar for artist and programmer productivity. We hope that you will find the ideas presented here useful and practical for amplifying the productivity of the development team.

Differentiable Graphics with Slang.D for Appearance-Based Optimization

Bartlomiej Wronski, Sai Bangaru, Marco Salvi, Yong He, Lifan Wu, and Jacob Munkberg

18.1 Introduction

In computer graphics, we want to create images that faithfully match reality or the artistic vision. To achieve this, we formulate models that are implemented as renderers and driven by various controllable parameters, such as meshes or material textures. While creating those manually allows for substantial artistic control, it requires much effort. To keep artists working creatively and their effort well spent, we aim to automate any task required because of our models' limitations.

Consider the problem of specular antialiasing. When artists create detailed meshes, high-resolution normal maps, and roughness textures, those look great and as authored up close, but when zoomed out, they show either significant aliasing (when not using mipmaps) or an appearance change when naively mipmapping the textures. This problem has been studied before, and many solutions were proposed [Olano and Baker 10, Toksvig 05, Han et al. 07, Neubelt and Pettineo 13, Karis 18]. Those solutions add new models that approximate the desired behavior through analytical or statistical fitting based on the used BRDF and adjust the material property texture mipmaps accordingly. While the results can be satisfactory and are used in virtually all shipping games, those models are limited, not a perfect match, and must be re-derived for every new BRDF.

Furthermore, while specular aliasing or appearance change problems are immediately visible and properly recognized in research and practice, other effects related to minification and the use of trilinear filtering include sharpness and texture detail loss. The artist sees and intuitively feels that the result can be improved, and they work around this issue with some ad hoc practices, such as sharpening mipmaps. This can lead to additional errors if not done correctly and further wastes artists' time and productivity on a non-creative process.

Given a material rendered with any arbitrary BRDF at any distance, it would be great if we could get the material mipmaps that reproduce that exact look as closely as possible without creating any additional approximations or assumptions. This data-driven approach could fit the appearance more accurately than a statistical model and save time building those. Unfortunately, rendering is highly nonlinear, and there are no simple closed-form solutions to this problem—given an existing renderer and an image of the scene, we cannot task it with reproducing the inputs, such as textures—but this is where numerical optimization and differentiable programming can help.

In this article, we will introduce the reader to numerical mathematical optimization. In this process, we formulate a goal (such as maximizing the appearance fit of a material at different resolutions) and augment an existing renderer with *differentiable programming* capabilities that iteratively improve this goal using gradient descent. We will also describe a convenient tool for this task: Slang.D shading language [Bangaru et al. 23], a new addition to Slang [He et al. 18], which is a modern, actively developed, open-source shading language, widely used inside of NVIDIA and with external partners. The biggest advantage of Slang for this task is that it is fully backward compatible with HLSL and can be cross-compiled to multiple other shading languages, backends, and platforms, facilitating its and differentiable programming's immediate use in existing, traditional renderers.

We will show how the theory of optimization and gradient descent and the new Slang capabilities allow for efficient, minimal implementation of the appearance-preserving specular antialiasing task and other applications, such as texture compression, automatic Jacobian computation for Monte Carlo rendering, or physically based shading.

18.2   What Is Differentiable Programming?

The name *differentiable programming* is associated with a programming paradigm where derivatives of functions (together with higher-order constructs, such as Jacobian or Hessian matrices) are first-class citizens of a programming language. This concept typically appears in machine learning, but we will demonstrate how it applies to many common graphics tasks, such as appearance-based material minification. In this section, we will briefly introduce how it is typically used and why it is a handy tool essential for the explosive growth of machine learning and beyond.

18.2.1   Data-Driven Techniques and Optimization

Typically, when real-time programmers discuss *optimization*, this means performance, power, or memory usage improvements. Conversely, the scientific community typically understands *optimization* as a subdomain of applied mathematics. Throughout this article, we will use both meanings of those terms and try to specify which one we discuss.

Mathematical optimization defines a *cost function*, often called a *loss function*. The optimization process aims to reduce the loss function's value as much as possible by adjusting the variable values. This cost can be literal (mathematical optimization used in business modeling) or correspond to the degree of deviation from desirable outcomes—for example, how much a rendered image differs from a reference photo. In the example of material minification, our loss function will be defined as the average per-pixel difference between rendering an asset at a high resolution using original materials and the coarser-resolution mipmaps. The loss function typically involves multiple variables (in the case of neural networks, up to over a trillion different parameters and variables!). Similarly, in graphics, we have to optimize over a million parameters for a single-channel 1K texture!

How can optimization be used in computer graphics? Even if we ignore the most popular new application—neural networks—finding optimal parameters can automate many tasks: from function fitting and simplification through optimizing scene parameters for a given appearance to finally adjusting textures or materials for desirable outcomes.

While some linear optimization problems can be solved algebraically and in closed form, most interesting problems in graphics are not linear. The solution cannot be expressed as a linear regression of a set of parameters multiplying certain predefined inputs. Nonlinear optimization problems, in general, do not have closed-form solutions.

18.2.2 Gradient Descent

To make the optimization goals more concrete, we start with a simple example— we are looking for a minimum value of a single-valued function of two parameters:

$$f(x, y) = \frac{1}{2}\sin(3x)x + x^2 + xy + y^2 + \frac{x}{4}. \tag{18.1}$$

How do we find a minimum value of this function in a domain of $x \in [-1, 1]$ and $y \in [-1, 1]$? Since this is a two-dimensional function, we can look at its values enumerated over the domain (Figure 18.1(a)) and manually find the approximate minimum and the corresponding parameter. In optimization, this approach is often called an *exhaustive* or *brute-force* search.

It works well on small problems and low-dimensional functions with just a few variables. Unfortunately, it suffers from the so-called *curse of dimensionality*. When the number of parameters grows to D and we want to evaluate each parameter at N locations, we must take N^D samples. Even with a small parameter count like 20, this becomes prohibitive, while optimizing all texels of a 1K texture requires optimizing over a million texels. The parameter counts in modern neural networks exceed hundreds of billions! We need an approach that scales better with the dimensions.

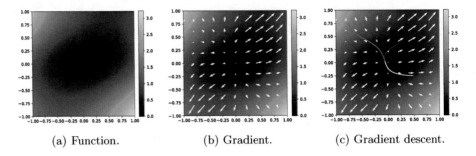

(a) Function.   (b) Gradient.   (c) Gradient descent.

Figure 18.1. (a) A simple 2D function, (b) its gradient, and (c) examples of gradient descent from three different starting points.

There are many possible solutions to the problem, but one of the most popular and successful ones is *gradient descent*. First, we compute the gradient—a multidimensional vector representing derivatives of the scalar loss function—and take a step in its opposite direction. Intuitively, the gradient at each point shows the direction in which the function grows the most, and the magnitude of the gradient describes how quickly it grows. For Equation 18.1, the gradient is given by

$$\nabla f = \begin{bmatrix} \dfrac{\partial f}{\partial x} \\[2mm] \dfrac{\partial f}{\partial y} \end{bmatrix} = \begin{bmatrix} \dfrac{3\cos(3x)x + \sin(3x)}{2} + 2x + y + \dfrac{1}{4} \\[2mm] x + 2y \end{bmatrix}. \tag{18.2}$$

Computing gradients of functions or combinations of functions is generally easy in calculus, and we will see in Section 18.3.3 how Slang can do it automatically in shaders. We plot the gradient as arrows in Figure 18.1(b). The function changes its value fastest in regions with the largest gradient, and its minimum is in the region where the gradient is close to zero.

The idea of gradient descent is simple: having access to the gradient of a function, we start from a *reasonable* starting point and always go in the direction opposite to the gradient. We subtract the current parameter values by the product of the gradient and a small value called the *learning rate* (Section 18.2.3). We repeat this process until we perform enough steps—exceeding our computational budget or reaching a region with a very small gradient so that it is most likely a local minimum. We demonstrate gradient descent from three different starting points in Figure 18.1(c).

Before discussing the limitations of gradient descent, we can already see why it is an appealing solution. Taking only small steps is guaranteed not to make the results worse than the starting point. Gradient descent steps through all dimensions simultaneously, therefore its ability to reach the function minimum does not directly depend on the problem's dimensionality, as in brute-force search.

18.2.3 Gradient Descent Common Pitfalls

Gradient descent is extremely useful and large-scale neural network training cannot be performed without it, but it is not a silver bullet for every optimization problem. In particular, when differentiable programming is used for non-neural tasks, such as optimizing parameters of models, meshes, or textures in computer graphics, gradient descent can fail to converge, result in not-a-number (NaN) values, or find a suboptimal solution. We describe some possible limitations that one may encounter in traditional graphics applications and potential solutions to work around them.

We start with the problem of local minima. Gradient descent is not guaranteed to find the optimal solution (i.e., the global minimum); in some cases, it can find a poor solution. The main reason for general optimization problems is that they have many local minima—many suboptimal solutions can have gradient values close to zero. Starting gradient descent at any point not close to the real global minimum will fail to find the optimal solution. Gradient descent is theoretically not guaranteed to find solutions in the presence of so-called saddle points—regions where a function temporarily "flattens out." Gradient descent is guaranteed to find the global minimum only on *convex functions* with nonnegative second-order derivatives over the whole evaluation domain. Unfortunately, most *interesting* optimized loss functions (including the ones used in neural networks!) are not convex.

While using momentum methods (discussed later in this section) typically reduces the optimization problem of getting stuck in areas with a small magnitude of a gradient, local minima can still be found instead of the globally optimal solution. Luckily, many strategies can help it work well in practice (even if we don't have a formal and mathematical guarantee of optimality). We will list some of those practical solutions.

Good Initialization The easiest solution to the local minimum problem is using domain knowledge to choose a starting point that is expected to be reasonably close to the desirable solution. For example, an upsampled version of images or textures is a reasonable initialization for the super-resolution problem. In Section 18.4.2, we will use a color bounding box to initialize block compression endpoints. Similarly, in Section 18.4.3, we will show that using downsampled BRDF properties gives a reasonable starting point for finding correct, appearance-preserving properties.

Neither of those initializations is the correct or optimal solution. However, after the gradient descent refinement, we are guaranteed to end up with a better solution than the starting point.

Combining with Other Optimization Methods Gradient descent scales favorably with the dimension count, while global optimization solutions like brute-force search do not. We can, however, combine gradient descent with some of the ideas from those optimization methods. For instance, one can run multiple gradient descent processes from multiple initialization points in parallel and pick the best solution. This approach is called *ensembling*. Finally, one can randomly interrupt the gradient descent process and accept worse solutions with a predefined probability that typically decreases as the training progresses. This approach is called *simulated annealing gradient descent*.

Stochastic Gradient Descent Traditional gradient descent computed the gradient of the loss function over all the available data. In practice, training neural networks with full gradient descent scales poorly, as training dataset sizes can be measured in terabytes. Instead, neural networks are trained with *stochastic gradient descent*, where only some randomly selected dataset points are used for evaluating the gradient. The same idea applies to graphics problems, like the appearance-preserving minification. Instead of computing the loss function over all possible view and light directions, we can pick random ones in each step. Alternatively, for problems where optimized parameters contribute to the whole image, one can randomly select a subset of pixels (such as crops) instead of computing the loss value and gradient for all of them.

This can accelerate the gradient descent but also makes the gradient estimates noisier. This might seem a disadvantage, but it has been shown to "blur" the loss function and, together with momentum methods, can jump over local minima, improving the final solution and generalization.

In practice, for graphics problems, when evaluating the loss over a domain such as a hemisphere of all possible densely sampled lighting directions, it can be beneficial to sample randomly different directions at each iteration. Alternatively, when working with loss over a whole image, one can randomly select a subset of pixels.

Over-Parameterization One counterintuitive solution to improving gradient descent and the found local minima is to over-parameterize the problem. What does this mean? Imagine that we optimize a variable a. Over-parameterization would be writing the same variable as $a_1 + a_2$ or $a_1 * a_2$. It might seem counterintuitive why over-parameterization would help here, as we need to find not just one but two variables, making the problem more difficult. The problem's dimensionality is as large as before. However, instead of a single solution and a single optimal value of a, we have infinitely many combinations of a_1 and a_2 that produce the same result. In a more practical example related to computer graphics, rotation can be minimally expressed as Euler angles or a normalized quaternion. Over-parameterized rotation is expressed as an orthonormal matrix or a product of multiple orthonormal matrices and optimizes significantly easier, avoiding discontinuities and the optimization getting stuck.

Over-parameterization is one of the secrets of why neural networks train so well with gradient descent—they have infinitely many combinations of parameters that produce reasonable solutions. Multiple research papers have shown

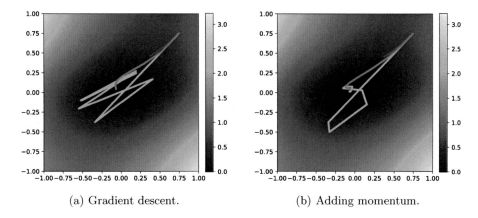

(a) Gradient descent.   (b) Adding momentum.

Figure 18.2. (a) Sixteen steps of gradient descent, with red indicating where the too-low learning rate 0.01 never converges, orange where the too-high learning rate 0.4 diverges, and green where the close-to-optimal learning rate 0.1 gets close to the minimum. (b) The same learning rates but additionally using momentum, with red indicating where momentum does not help much, as sixteen steps are insufficient to accumulate it and orange and green where adding momentum helps to converge to the minimum.

that parameterizing a computer graphics problem as a neural network aids the optimization process—with NeRF [Mildenhall et al. 21] being the most famous example. Instead of optimizing the density field directly, NeRF optimizes the parameters of a neural network that predicts the density parameters. NeRF has been demonstrated to work significantly better than earlier approaches. After optimization, one can eliminate the over-parameterization and collapse it (in our simple example, adding $a_1 + a_2 = a$) or even "bake" to a different solution, for example, converting a NeRF to a density field or a mesh.

Selecting the Learning Rate and Different Optimizers One of the practical challenges when using gradient descent to solve problems is finding a suitable learning rate. There are no universal guidelines on how to select one. If we select a learning rate that is too small, we need to take prohibitively many gradient descent steps, and the optimization process can take many hours and never reach the desired solution. Conversely, selecting a too-high learning rate can result in "jumping" around the solutions and, in the worst case, missing it entirely or causing the optimization to diverge. We demonstrate those cases in Figure 18.2(a). Intuitively, we want to select a learning rate that is as high as possible but without causing those problems.

Luckily, we do not need pure trial-and-error and guessing to find a suitable learning rate—many *adaptive* methods exist. The most successful ones are variations of gradient descent using *momentum*. The name comes from physics and physical momentum; we pretend that parameters have some mass and momentum, and the gradient computed at each iteration updates the speed:

$$v_n = mv_{n-1} + (1-m)\frac{\partial f}{\partial x_n}, \qquad x_n = x_{n-1} - \lambda v_n. \tag{18.3}$$

This has the effect of dampening fast gradient changes and accumulating them slowly over time. Alternative formulation interpolates the momentum and the learning rate, resulting in exponential decay. We present how adding such simple momentum aids the optimization in Figure 18.2(b). It is especially beneficial with higher learning rates, dampening the oscillations and overshoots. Using momentum is sufficient in practice to avoid getting stuck in the saddle points, and it can even help the process progress over poor local minima.

Discussing various optimizers is beyond the scope of this article. However, we recommend Adam [Kingma and Ba 14], which adds a second moment and is one of the most commonly used ones in neural networks while being very simple to implement. It requires additional memory cost to store the moments but otherwise has almost no computational performance penalty. In our experience, it also helps all graphics optimization tasks we experimented with.

Another common practice is to start with a high learning rate and reduce it throughout the training. This helps to explore the parameter space quickly, possibly jumping over poor local minima and fine-tuning the solution in the regions of interest.

Non-differentiable Functions One challenge in using gradient descent to optimize functions and workloads that were not designed for it is that they might be non-differentiable or contain non-differentiable steps and components. Some ubiquitous examples are binary selection, quantization, and rounding. All of those operations have the same problem—their gradient is zero everywhere, except for points of discontinuity, where it's not defined. We encounter this problem in Section 18.4.2 when we use optimization for texture compression. If we tried to optimize a function that gets rounded, we would get no gradient of any parameter, and the gradient descent would not progress. There are many possible solutions to this problem. We will demonstrate them using the rounding example.

The first solution is to replace the hard rounding with an approximate solution during the optimization. For example, we can replace rounding of x by $x - \sin(2\pi x)/2\pi$. One can also use piecewise polynomial approximations or other functions for approximation. (See Figure 18.3.)

A second solution is to use a "fake" gradient. In the case of rounding, we can pretend that no rounding is happening and return the derivative of rounding to be the same as the derivative of the function inside. This is commonly called a *pass-through operator*. Note that we still compute the loss functions and the results in the same way but differentiate them differently.

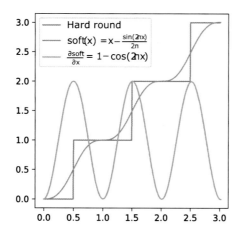

Figure 18.3. Comparing hard rounding and other approximate solutions.

Unfortunately, when working with gradient descent, one must analyze functions to identify the non-differentiable components and solve them individually. Some pipelines are so complicated that addressing non-differentiable functions would be cumbersome. The solution for those cases can be similar to the over-parameterization technique for the local minima problem—optimizing a *proxy* problem that is differentiable. For example, one can train a neural network to simulate the system's operations [Tseng et al. 19] or optimize a neural network that predicts those parameters [Wronski 21].

Careful handling of non-differentiable components is crucial when considering geometry parameters since rendering procedures for classical geometry, such as meshes and signed distance fields, are inherently discontinuous during rendering due to occlusion and silhouettes. Efficiently handling such discontinuities is still an active research area with approaches ranging from using novel "blurred" geometry [Liu et al. 19], differentiable antialiasing [Laine et al. 20], boundary sampling [Li et al. 18, Zhang et al. 20], and domain reparameterizations [Loubet et al. 19, Bangaru et al. 20].

Exploding Gradients Even differentiable and smooth functions can pose significant issues during gradient descent. Graphics programmers are very well aware of NaN values caused by certain operations, including division by zero, operations on infinities, or taking a power of a negative value. Seeing a raw division in code often looks suspicious to an experienced programmer, who can use their experience to debug a potential numerical issue. Unfortunately, differentiable programming expands those potential "traps" to more functions. We care about not only how well a function behaves over its domain but also how well its gradient behaves over the same domain.

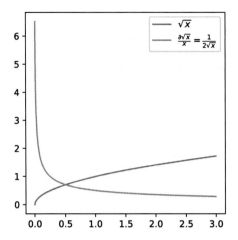

Figure 18.4. The square root function and its derivative.

A simple example is the square root function, ubiquitous in graphics. (See Figure 18.4.) Some code uses it even as a fast approximation to the sRG-B/gamma function. The square root function is defined and valid in $[0, \infty)$ and is differentiable in $(0, \infty)$. The derivative of $\sqrt{x}$ is $\frac{1}{2\sqrt{x}}$. When it approaches zero, it goes toward infinity. This can be a massive problem in the optimization process. Imagine using the square root to approximate the sRGB function after the tone mapping to compute the loss function in a perceptually aligned space. Anytime we get brightness values around zero, the gradient values will be huge and numerically unstable, which causes the optimization to diverge and is called *exploding gradients*.

This can be solved in a few ways. The solution for using a square root to approximate the gamma function is to use real, piecewise sRGB or Rec709 functions. This function was designed piecewise precisely to limit its slope and prevent an infinite gain around zero! The slope of the linear segment is 12.92 and should not cause problems during gradient descent.

While using a proper display transfer function solves the problem of the square root or power gamma, exploding gradients can appear in many other places, including components inside BRDF functions or whole graphics pipelines. Unfortunately, there are no ideal and universal solutions there. Solving them involves debugging the differentiable pipelines, overriding the problematic functions, or replacing them with approximations.

However, one pragmatic approach is to *clip* gradients and limit them to some predefined values. Gradients can be bounded in the implementations of differentiable functions and their derivatives, when they are used for optimizing functions or updating the momentum in the optimizer. Most machine learning frameworks, such as PyTorch, offer functions to clip gradients and automatically discard any infinite or NaN values in the optimizer code behind the programmer's back.

18.3 Differentiable Shader Programming with Slang

Differentiation by hand is possible but cumbersome. It does not scale to large and complex pipelines and requires re-deriving the gradient code each time the forward model is changed. *Automatic differentiation* (auto-diff) is therefore a critical compiler feature for rapid prototyping, but most existing frameworks (e.g., PyTorch), over-specialize to machine learning workloads and are poorly suited to generate derivatives for graphics pipelines.

Slang [He et al. 18] is a modern shading language designed specifically to enable high-performance differentiable graphics workloads.

18.3.1 Slang Language Overview

Slang is a fast-innovating, cross-platform shading language that brings modern programming language features to shader programming. Slang supports modules, visibility control, generics, interfaces, and many other convenience features, allowing developers to build complex rendering systems with modular and maintainable code without compromising runtime performance. Slang can cross-compile shader code for Direct3D 12, Vulkan, CUDA, Optix, and CPU; it has been adopted by several commercial rendering products such as NVIDIA Omniverse. One of the biggest advantages of using Slang for differentiable programming in shaders is that it is backward compatible with HLSL. It is possible to convert existing rendering workloads to be differentiable without duplicating or rewriting the code in another language or framework, such as PyTorch.

With the recent support of automatic differentiation, Slang bridges the world of real-time graphics and machine learning by enabling graphics developers to adopt machine learning techniques with automatically generated derivative functions. Most existing machine learning and differentiable programming research is done in PyTorch. To allow for easy experimentation with existing ML packages, the `slangpy` Python package allows direct integration of differentiable functions written in Slang as PyTorch kernels, granting machine learning applications easy access to graphics code.

18.3.2 Automatic Differentiation Basics

Section 18.2.2 showed how to use derivatives of some function f with gradient descent. Here, we discuss how to obtain these derivatives of a function f in a programming language. In general, such a function can have multiple inputs and outputs. Therefore, its derivative is a complete *Jacobian* matrix $\mathbf{J}$ where each element $J_{i,j}$ represents the derivative of the ith output with regards to (w.r.t.) the jth input.

Auto-diff tools typically *do not* compute the full matrix $\mathbf{J}$, as doing so is wasteful when most (if not all) use cases require only the multiplication of a gradient vector $\mathbf{v}$ with $\mathbf{J}$: the main reason is that the derivative of a chain of composed functions is simply a series of vector-matrix products.

For example, if we have a pipeline built of the composition of multiple functions $L = f \circ g \circ h(x, y, z)$, the derivatives of an objective function $\mathcal{L}$, w.r.t. the input variables (x, y, z), can be computed by a composition of vector-matrix products, thanks to the chain rule of differentiation:

$$\left(\frac{\partial \mathcal{L}}{\partial x}, \frac{\partial \mathcal{L}}{\partial y}, \frac{\partial \mathcal{L}}{\partial z} \right) = \left(\frac{\partial \mathcal{L}}{\partial L} \right)^{\mathrm{T}} \cdot J_f \cdot J_g \cdot J_h. \tag{18.4}$$

This chain of products can be computed from left to right to avoid ever materializing a full Jacobian matrix; that is, we only need to compute the product of an arbitrary vector $\mathbf{v}$ with the Jacobian $\mathbf{J}$ of a given function.

Since there are actually two ways to compute this product, auto-diff tools are categorized into two modes:

1. *Forward-mode* accepts a (column) derivative vector w.r.t. inputs $\frac{\partial L}{\partial \mathbf{x}}$ and computes derivatives w.r.t. the outputs $\frac{\partial L}{\partial \mathbf{y}}$ by right product with the Jacobian (i.e., $\mathbf{J} \cdot \mathbf{v}$). Forward-mode derivatives are cheap to compute and are useful for operations such as computing PDFs from sampling procedures and visualizing the gradient of a single variable (e.g., the x-translation of the camera) on all pixels of an image at once.

2. *Reverse-mode* accepts a (row) derivative vector w.r.t. outputs $\frac{\partial L}{\partial \mathbf{y}}$ and computes the derivatives w.r.t. the inputs through left product with the Jacobian (i.e., $\mathbf{v}^T \cdot \mathbf{J}$). Reverse-mode derivatives are more expensive to compute, but are the predominant approach used throughout learning-based approaches, most commonly to propagate derivatives of a scalar loss function to all the input parameters (of which there can be thousands or even millions), in a single pass.

18.3.3   Using Slang to Differentiate a Function

In Slang, the differentiation of a function is expressed as a high-order operator on functions. Given a function f, developers can use the `fwd_diff(f)` and `bwd_diff(f)` operators to obtain the forward-mode and backward-mode derivative functions of f. For example, here is a simple function that computes the sum of squares of input x and y:

```
[Differentiable]
float square(float x, float y)
{
    return x * x + y * y;
}
```

The code is mostly standard HLSL, with the addition of the `[Differentiable]` attribute, which tells the Slang compiler that the `square` function should be treated as a differentiable function.

The forward derivative function of `square` will take the derivatives of some latent value L regarding inputs x and y to compute the derivative of L regarding the `square`'s return value, i.e., it computes $\frac{\partial L}{\partial f}$ from $\frac{\partial L}{\partial x}$ and $\frac{\partial L}{\partial y}$, where $f =$ `square`(x, y). The following code illustrates how to call the forward derivative function:

```
void test()
{
    // x = px.p = 3.0
    // dL/dx = px.d = 1.0
    DifferentialPair<float> px = diffPair(3.0, 1.0);

    // y = py.p = 4.0
    // dL/dy = py.d = 1.0
    DifferentialPair<float> py = diffPair(4.0, 1.0);

    DifferentailPair<float> pf = fwd_diff(square)(px, py);
    // f = pf.p == 25.0
    // dL/df = pf.d == 14.0
}
```

In this example, `fwd_diff(square)` evaluates to a function of the following signature:

```
DifferentialPair<float> fwd_diff_square(
    DifferentialPair<float> px,
    DifferentialPair<float> py);
```

Here, `DifferentialPair` is a generic pair type that holds both the primal (original) and the differential value. The forward derivative function of `square` takes in both the primal and derivative values of x and y and uses them to compute the primal and derivative values of the output. In this example, the automatically generated forward derivative function is equivalent to the following code:

```
DifferentialPair<float> fwd_diff_square(
    DifferentialPair<float> px,
    DifferentialPair<float> py)
{
    float r = px.p * px.p + py.p * py.p;
    float dr = 2.0 * px.p * px.d + 2.0 * py.p * py.d;
    return diffPair(r, dr);
}
```

Forward derivatives are nice and simple, but backward derivative functions are more frequently used in machine learning. In contrast to forward derivatives, a backward derivative computes the derivatives of some latent value L w.r.t. the input parameters from the derivative of L w.r.t. the output value of the function. In the `square` example, its backward derivative will compute $\frac{\partial L}{\partial x}$ and $\frac{\partial L}{\partial y}$ from $\frac{\partial L}{\partial f}$.

To obtain the backward derivative, developers can use Slang's `bwd_diff` operator, as in the following code:

```
void test()
{
    DifferentialPair<float> px = diffPair(3.0, 0.0);
    DifferentialPair<float> py = diffPair(4.0, 0.0);
    bwd_diff(square)(px, py, 1.0);
    // px.d == 6.0
    // py.d == 8.0
}
```

The signature of `bwd_diff(square)` is:

```
void bwd_diff_square(
    inout DifferentialPair<float> px,
    inout DifferentialPair<float> py,
    float resultDerivative);
```

This backward derivative function takes as input the primal values of x and y stored in `px.p` and `py.p`, as well as the result derivative $\frac{\partial L}{\partial f}$ (which equals 1.0 in this example), and stores the output $\frac{\partial L}{\partial x}$ and $\frac{\partial L}{\partial y}$ in `px.d` and `py.d`.

18.3.4   Differentiating Memory Accesses

So far, we covered how to automatically differentiate code that is purely functional, i.e., all inputs and outputs are represented as function parameters or return values. In practice, most shader code involves complex memory access patterns, such as reads and writes at dynamic locations in global memory or textures. Often, these buffers represent important scene data (vertex buffers, material textures, etc.) for which derivatives need to be computed.

Unfortunately, automatically generating derivative code to handle global memory accesses is fraught with complications. For example, allocating/binding new global buffers within shader code is not a standard feature of shading languages. Further, under reverse-mode auto-diff, memory reads become memory writes, which causes race conditions and thread contention, both of which are difficult for a compiler to optimally handle.

Slang's solution to this is to treat all global memory accesses such as texture I/O as non-differentiable operations (i.e., derivative code will not be automatically generated for these operations). Instead, Slang allows users to define custom derivative functions for explicitly specifying how derivatives are propagated through these non-auto-differentiable operations.

Consider the following code example that applies a 3×3 box filter to an image:

```
uniform int width;
uniform int height;
uniform Texture2D<float> inputTexture;
uniform RWTexture2D<float> outputTexture;

float computePixel(int2 pixelLoc)
{
    // Track the sum of neighboring pixels and the number
    // of pixels currently accumulated.
    int count = 0;
    float sumValue = 0.0;
```

```
    // Iterate through the surrounding area.
    for (int offsetX = -1; offsetX <= 1; offsetX++)
    {
        // Skip out-of-bounds pixels.
        int x = pixelLoc.x + offsetX;
        if (x < 0 || x >= width) continue;

        for (int offsetY = -1; offsetY <= 1; offsetY++)
        {
            int y = pixelLoc.y + offsetY;
            if (y < 0 || y >= height) continue;
            sumValue += inputTexture[uint2(x, y)];
            count++;
        }
    }

    // Comptue the average value.
    sumValue /= count;

    return sumValue;
}

[numthreads(16,16,1]
void computeMain(uint2 tid : SV_DispatchThreadID)
{
    outputTexture[tid] = computePixel(tid);
}
```

How do we apply automatic differentiation to `computePixel` to compute the derivative of some latent term L w.r.t. to each input texel value?

Note that the texture access function `inputTexture[...]` is a non-differentiable operation, so the derivatives cannot be propagated into the corresponding texels. However, we can wrap this texture fetch operation in a function and provide a custom derivative implementation of this wrapper function:

```
float readInputTexture(uint2 loc)
{
    return inputTexture[loc];
}

uniform RWTexture2D<float> inputDerivativeTexture;

[BackwardDerivativeOf(readInputTexture)]
void readInputTexture_bwd_diff(uint2 loc, float dResult)
{
    inputDerivativeTexture.InterlockedAddF32(loc, dResult);
}
```

Here, we explicitly provided the backward derivative function implementation for our texture read wrapper `readInputTexture`, which simply writes the derivatives propagated to the texel into a separate texture resource at the same texel location. Note that the the backward derivative function takes a `uint2` as the type for parameter `loc` instead of a `DifferentialPair<uint2>`, because the `uint2` type (for the `loc` parameter) is not a differentiable type. Function parameters that have non-differentiable types are passed to derivative functions as is without any type changes.

With this wrapper, we can rewrite our `computePixel` function to call the `readInputTexture` wrapper instead of doing texture loads directly:

```
[Differentiable]
float computePixel(int2 pixelLoc)
{
    // Track the sum of neighboring pixels and the number
    // of pixels currently accumulated.
    int count = 0;
    float sumValue = 0.0;

    // Iterate through the surrounding area.
    for (int offsetX = -1; offsetX <= 1; offsetX++)
    {
        // Skip out-of-bounds pixels.
        int x = pixelLoc.x + offsetX;
        if (x < 0 || x >= width) continue;

        for (int offsetY = -1; offsetY <= 1; offsetY++)
        {
            int y = pixelLoc.y + offsetY;
            if (y < 0 || y >= height) continue;
            sumValue += readInputTexture(uint2(x, y));
            count++;
        }
    }

    // Comptue the average value.
    sumValue /= count;

    return sumValue;
}
```

Now when we differentiate `computePixel`, the automatically generated backward derivative function of `computePixel` will call `readInputTexture_bwd_diff` with the derivative value $\frac{\partial L}{\partial T}$ whenever the derivative propagates to an input texel `T`. Inside the custom derivative function, we simply accumulate the derivative to the corresponding texel location in a separate texture resource used to store the propagated derivatives.

With that, we can write a new compute shader entry point to propagate the derivative into input texels:

```
uniform int width;
uniform int height;
uniform Texture2D<float> inputTexture;
uniform RWTexture2D<float> outputTexture;
uniform RWTexture2D<float> inputDerivativeTexture;

float readInputTexture(uint2 loc){...}

[BackwardDerivativeOf(readInputTexture)]
void readInputTexture_bwd_diff(uint2 loc, float resultDerivative)
{...}

[Differentiable]
float computePixel(int2 pixelLoc) {...}

uniform float dLoss;

[numthreads(16,16,1)]
void comptueMain(uint2 tid: SV_DispatchThreadId)
```

```
{
    bwd_diff(computePixel)(tid, dLoss);
    // Results will be stored into inputDerivativeTexture.
}
```

18.3.5   Sharp Edges of Automatic Differentiation

Here we will quickly go over some sharp edges when using automatic differentiation and some tools Slang provides to work around them.

A common problem with the reverse-mode auto-diff technique is that it can result in a large amount of (often unnecessary) memory overhead. Fundamentally, this is because the process involves (1) running the program normally, while (2) caching any necessary intermediate results, and finally (3) calculating the derivatives of the program starting from the last instruction (i.e., the returned values) backward until we reach the first instruction (i.e., the inputs). The Slang compiler automatically handles step (1) by inserting new static variable declarations wherever necessary.

This can lead to three distinct problems:

1. Caching too many intermediate values can result in a large amount of static memory requirements for each thread. This further leads to variables spilling over to global memory, which sharply reduces the performance of the resulting derivative program.

   SOLUTION: Slang employs a heuristic to attempt to recompute variables whenever possible. However, doing this *optimally* is still an open problem, so Slang provides a way for users to control the caching behavior through two function decorators [PreferRecompute] and [PreferCheckpoint], which hint to the compiler whether to recompute or store the results of a specific function.

2. The compiler is sometimes unable to determine the maximum number of iterations in loop constructs such as `for` or `while` blocks. This upper bound is necessary for Slang to allocate space to cache intermediate values within the loop body (i.e., if the loop executes five times, every variable in the loop needs a size-5 array to remember the results for the derivative pass).

   SOLUTION: For simple loops of the form `for (i=0; i<N; i++)`, Slang can infer the upper bound automatically. For complex loops, we require users to provide a manual upper bound through a decoration [MaxIters(n)]. Note that `n` can be treated as a specialization parameter and multiple versions with different cache sizes can be compiled, if necessary, to maximize memory utilization.

   This restriction is a known drawback of reverse-mode auto-diff, and truly unbounded/dynamic loops require special handling. Such loops may need to be partially unrolled (e.g., unroll every 10 iterations to improve compute-memory trade-off) or provided with a manually differentiated loop through Slang's custom derivative mechanism. (See Section 18.3.4.)

3. In-place modifications on local arrays can lead to the compiler having to store the entire array multiple times and cause the same memory-spilling problem as described in problem 1. A common instance of this pattern is when each element of an array is processed individually and sequentially in a loop: `for (i=0; i<N; i++) { arr[i] = f(arr[i]); }`. This in-place mutation causes the compiler to cache the state of the array at each step of the loop.

SOLUTION: There are a few ways to avoid this: (a) If the array has a bound known at compile time, the `[ForceUnroll]` attribute can be used to unroll the loop. (b) If the array is not static, try to use thread-parallel computation instead of a local array (distribute the array over a dynamic number of threads). (c) If both (a) and (b) are not possible, allocate a global read-write buffer `RWStructuredBuffer` to hold the array data for every thread, and use a differentiable accessor method to index into the appropriate location. See Section 18.3.4 for more information on this approach.

18.4   Applications

In this section, we present three graphics applications using Slang's automatic differentiation features. First, we show how to use Slang's forward-mode auto-diff to compute the Jacobian matrix of a function (Section 18.4.1), which is a common use case in computer graphics. Next, we demonstrate the usage of Slang's reverse-mode auto-diff to optimize texture compression (Section 18.4.2). Last, we present a data-driven approach for appearance-preserving minification (Section 18.4.3). This example is more complicated and is discussed in detail; we hope to show an end-to-end pipeline built in Slang and shed light on how to use Slang to solve real-world problems in practice.

18.4.1   Jacobian of a Projection Transformation

The use of Jacobian matrices is ubiquitous in graphics and physics [Anderson et al. 17], and Slang's forward-mode auto-diff can be used to automatically compute the Jacobian of an arbitrary function. In this example, we illustrate how to calculate the Jacobian of a projective transformation, which is useful in a number of scenarios, including splatting 3D Gaussian blobs on the image plane. First, we define our projection matrix and the projection function:

```
[Differentiable]
float4x4 genProjMat(float z_near, float2 fov)
{
    // Reverse Z projection matrix
```

```
      let cotan_half_fov = rcp(tan(fov / 2));
      float4x4 m = { { cotan_half_fov[0], 0, 0, 0 },
                     { 0, cotan_half_fov[1], 0, 0 },
                     { 0, 0, 0, z_near },
                     { 0, 0, 1, 0 } };
      return m;
}

[Differentiable]
float3 projectPoint(float3 pos)
{
      let projMat = genProjMat(0.1, float2(1, 0.5));
      let projPos = mul(projMat, float4(pos, 1));
      return projPos.xyz / projPos.w;
}
```

Next, we construct the Jacobian matrix corresponding to our projection transformation. This is accomplished by applying the `fwd_diff()` operator to each row of the transformation matrix. By manipulating the input gradient, we isolate and differentiate against each component (i.e., x, y, and z) of the input position vector in turn:

```
[Differentiable]
float3x3 projectionJacobian(float3 pos)
{
      float3x3 J = { fwd_diff(projectPoint)(diffPair(pos, float3(1,
                         0, 0))).d,
                     fwd_diff(projectPoint)(diffPair(pos, float3(0,
                         1, 0))).d,
                     fwd_diff(projectPoint)(diffPair(pos, float3(0,
                         0, 1))).d};
      return J;
}
```

Since differentiation is done at compile time, it incurs no additional performance cost compared to manually computing the Jacobian matrix. If the projection matrix structure ever changes, the Jacobian will change correspondingly without the need for re-deriving it and without potential errors due to the code getting out of sync.

18.4.2 Texture compression

Texture compression is essentially an optimization problem, aiming to find a balance between file size and perceived image quality. To achieve this, we will leverage Slang's automatic differentiation capabilities to compress BC7 textures through gradient descent.

The BC7 texture compression format includes eight distinct modes, with our emphasis on Mode 6. This mode encodes RGBA values of a 128-bit 4×4 texel block by linearly interpolating between 7-bit RGBA endpoints for each block, using 4-bit scalar weights for each texel. The decoding process for a single texel is straightforward:

```
struct BCTile : IDifferentiable
{
      // BC7 Mode 6 tile data
```

```
    float   weights[16];
    float4 minEndPoints;
    float4 maxEndPoints;

    [Differentiable]
    float4 decodeTexel(int i)
    {
        return (1 - weights[i]) * minEndPoints + weights[i] *
        maxEndPoints;
    }
}
```

Our goal is to minimize the difference between the original, uncompressed texture and its compressed BC7 Mode 6 version. We start this process with a simple initial guess: endpoints are set to the min and max corners of the axis-aligned bounding box enveloping all texel values in a block, while interpolation weights are uniformly set to 0.5 for midpoint interpolation.

```
// Initialize tile weights for midpoint interpolation.
BCTile tile = {{0.5}, {1} , {0}};

// Loop over texels in a 4x4 tile and init endpoints with
// colorspace AABB.
for (int i = 0; i < 16; i++)
{
    let texel = gInputTex[texelBlockCoords + int2(i % 4, i / 4)];
    tile.minEndPoints = min(tile.minEndPoints, texel);
    tile.maxEndPoints = max(tile.maxEndPoints, texel);
}
```

The next phase involves jointly optimizing interpolation weights and endpoints for each tile, via gradient descent. Each step is guided by the error measured using the L2 norm between the target (uncompressed) texels and the BC7 texels:

```
[Differentiable]
void L2(BCTile tile, no_diff float4 target[16], out float 12[16])
{
    for (int i = 0; i < 16; i++)
    {
        let error = target[i] - tile.decode(i);
        12[i] = dot(error, error);
    }
}
```

The gradient of the error with respect to the BC tile weights and endpoints is used to perform a gradient descent step:

```
// Compute gradient via backpropagation.
var dp_tile = diffPair(tile);
bwd_diff(L2)(dp_tile, target, {1});

// Take a step along the gradient to update the BC tile weights
// and endpoints.
let gradient = dp_tile.d;
tile = tile - 0.1 * gradient;
```

In practice, we also use the Adam optimizer [Kingma and Ba 14] to enhance convergence and improve the quality of our compressed textures.

Figure 18.5. Progression of texture compression. From left to right: the initial state, the state after 5 optimization steps, and the state after 20 steps, showcasing rapid convergence toward high-quality compression.

Initially, all optimization steps are performed using floating point arithmetic to accurately calculate gradients without considering quantization. After this first phase, weights are quantized to 4 bits and then frozen. Additional gradient descent steps are employed to fine-tune the endpoints before their final quantization to 7 bits, resulting in the final BC7 Mode 6 block data. Note how by employing gradient descent, we eliminate the need to explicitly write the compression code, as Slang automatically generates the gradients of BC7 block color interpolation through backward differentiation of the Mode 6 decoder.

To achieve high processing speeds, we fuse the forward (BC7 decoding) and backward (gradient descent) passes in a single compute shader, where each thread compresses a single BC7 block. This configuration improves performance in two ways. First, it eliminates the need to offload gradient storage to memory, keeping all data in registers. Second, it removes the need for atomic operations during gradient accumulation, since BC7 blocks are independent, and one block maps to one thread.

This approach ensures high-quality compressed textures. While we don't claim it can compete with the best manually derived compressors on metrics like the peak signal-to-noise ratio (PSNR), unlike them, it can be guided end-to-end by user-defined error metrics. For instance, one can use a different loss function for normal maps or, alternatively, emphasize not producing discolorations or discontinuities. As long as the error function used is differentiable, no changes in the compressor code are needed other than writing it in Slang! By comparison, it might be impossible to incorporate such metrics in many traditional compression algorithms that use, for example, principal component analysis (PCA).

As illustrated in Figure 18.5, only a limited number of optimization steps are needed to achieve rapid convergence. Typically, optimal compression is reached after approximately 50 to 100 gradient descent iterations, yet the process is highly efficient on modern GPUs. On an NVIDIA RTX 4090, this method can compress 400 4K textures every second, achieving a compression speed of 6.5

gigatexels per second. On a laptop (low-power) NVIDIA RTX A2000 GPU, we observe a compression speed of approximately 0.7 gigatexels per second. Furthermore, Slang's automatic differentiation capabilities make the implementation both extremely simple and intuitive (see [Kallweit 23]).

18.4.3 Appearance-Based Minification

One of the basic building blocks in computer graphics is BRDF texture maps representing multiple properties of materials and describing how the light interacts with the rendered surfaces. Artists author and preview textures, but then rendering algorithms transform them automatically, for instance, filtering, by blending the BRDF properties, or creating mipmaps.

Rendering is highly nonlinear, so linear operations on texture maps do not produce the correct linearly changing appearance. Various models have been proposed to preserve appearance in applications, such as building a mipmap pyramid. We describe how a data-driven approach can be used to preserve the appearance.

Problem Statement When normal-mapped specular surfaces are minified, the normal map details and variations are lost, and surfaces become flat, resulting in too glossy, flat specular reflections. We want to filter not the BRDF properties but the rendered appearance. Olano [Olano and Baker 10] and Toksvig [Toksvig 05] proposed the most commonly used approaches for preserving appearance under the minification of normal-mapped surfaces using analytical models. The variance of normal directions is computed during minification to increase the roughness values locally. This approach translates the normal map variation into BRDF microfacet surface variation. Models and approaches like this are approximate and are produced by curve fitting under strong assumptions, such as a specific microfacet distribution. They are created only for a specific BRDF and must be redesigned when a BRDF changes or a new one is added to the rendering engine.

Subsequent work [Han et al. 07, Neubelt and Pettineo 13, Karis 18] proposed alternative formulations using spherical convolutions and spherical basis functions, expanded the mipmap roughness modifications to more BRDFs, and mentioned the necessity of adjusting the normals as well. Those approaches assume that minified surface microfacet directions follow the same statistical distribution as the used BRDF model. This assumption introduces error. For example, a strong correlation of orientation surface normal directions requires an anisotropic distribution. A simple isotropic BRDF does not capture its directional appearance variation properly. Additionally, while those models better preserve the specular appearance and reduce specular aliasing, they don't include other minification and filtering appearance effects, such as visual loss of perceived sharpness and acuity. Many artists work around those issues manually, for example, by ad hoc sharpening the albedo mipmaps. This can produce

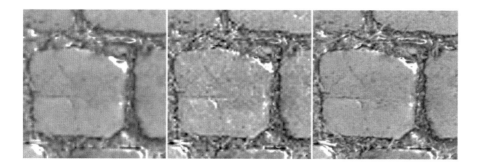

Figure 18.6. Inverse rendering enables appearance-preserving minification of a material: naively downsampled material (left), low-resolution material optimized with Slang (middle), and the reference (right).

better-looking assets at a distance, but if done inaccurately, it introduces errors and requires manual tuning.

Instead of refining those models, we propose to use differentiable rendering and a data-driven approach to build appearance-preserving mipmaps for each material separately. Before describing the proposed approach, we present results in Figure 18.6. The surface is rendered with a naively downsampled material, then the same surface is rendered with a low-resolution material obtained from an optimization algorithm implemented using Slang's automatic differentiation feature. Compare these to the rendering result using the reference material without downsampling. The optimized material's rendering preserves more details than the naively downsampled material and much more closely matches the reference material.

Appearance-Based Minification Overview Our approach involves rendering the optimized material as a flat surface using the original and lower-resolution textures under multiple lighting directions and optimizing the properties to match the appearance as closely as possible. We do it by computing the difference between the rendered images, calculating its gradient, and backpropagating the gradient to the mipmap texture parameters.

In Python-like pseudocode, it can be expressed as:

```
material_mip_map = downsample(orginal_material)
for iteration in range(ITERATION_COUNT):
    random_light_direction = sample_hemisphere()
    reference_render = render(orginal_material, random_light_direction)
    optimized_render = render(material_mip_map, random_light_direction)
    # Simplest L2 loss. Other loss functions might be more
    # suitable.
    difference = average(square(optimized_render - reference_render))
    # Compute the gradient w.r.t. material_mip_map parameters.
    gradient = compute_gradient(difference, material_mip_map)
    # Simple SGD; in practice, Adam optimizer works much better.
    material_mip_map -= LEARNING_RATE * gradient
```

In practice, we will combine producing the optimized render and its gradient in a single shader to improve the performance substantially. The choice of rendered resolution impacts the optimization target. We always render the reference material at full resolution, but then can do either of the following:

- Render the optimized material at its (smaller) resolution and compute the difference between it and the downsampled reference rendered image.

- Render the optimized material at the reference resolution and use bilinear upsampling of the parameters. Optimization will learn to compensate for bilinear upsampling of the material parameters in an optimal, data-driven way.

Both approaches are valid for different applications and produce different results. In this example, we use the second one, as it demonstrates how gradient descent can automatically learn to *sharpen* the material parameters to compensate for blurry bilinear upsampling.

We will describe now how to achieve this in Slang. All source code is available at [Wronski 24].

Setting up the Forward Rendering We need a BRDF for the parameters we want to optimize. While we could try to optimize BRDF parameters placed on a mesh, rendering it as a full-screen quad with a specific fixed lighting direction and a view vector is significantly easier to implement. We note, however, that using real meshes with mesh levels of detail (LODs) can be beneficial and automatically bake geometric normals lost during geometry simplification into normal maps.

We implement a Disney BRDF in Slang and the forward rendering in Slang's CUDA binding to avoid adding a dependency on any specific rendering engine and allow for easy result presentation. For a minimal implementation and to use rich Python and PyTorch ecosystems, we represent the material texture as a PyTorch 3D tensor, $w \times h \times c$, where c represents all material channels. Slang integrates well with both real-time renderers and Python frameworks.

Making BRDF functions differentiable is as easy as marking them as, for example, `Differentiable`:

```
[Differentiable]
float smithG_GGX(float NdotV, float alphaG)
{
    float a = alphaG * alphaG;
    float b = NdotV * NdotV;
    return 1 / (NdotV + sqrt(a + b - a * b));
}
```

The biggest complication in implementing the proposed pipeline as differentiable functions is that we must backpropagate the parameter derivatives to the textures. We follow the guidelines described in Section 18.3.4, with one additional change: we implement software bilinear filtering. This is necessary as a single forward rendering look-up has to write the gradient for four original texels (weighted by bilinear weights).

```
[Differentiable]
float bilin_weight(float t)
{
    if (abs(t) > 1.0f)
        return 0.0f;
    return 1.0f - abs(t);
}

[Differentiable]
float sampleBilinear(DiffTensorView<float> input,
                     no_diff float2 uv,
                     no_diff int z_slice)
{
    float2 accum = 0.0f;
    float2 pixel_coord = uv * float2(input.size(0), input.size(1)) -
    0.5;
    int2 pixel_coord_int = int2(floor(pixel_coord));
    float2 frac_offset = no_diff float2(pixel_coord_int) - pixel_coord;
    for (int dy = 0; dy <= 1; dy++)
    {
        for (int dx = 0; dx <= 1; dx++)
        {
            int2 finalCoordFloat = pixel_coord_int + int2(dx, dy);
            float2 relativeDiff = frac_offset + float2(dx, dy);
            float w = bilin_weight(relativeDiff.x) *
            bilin_weight(relativeDiff.y);

            accum += float2(getInputElement(input,
            int3(finalCoordFloat, z_slice)), 1.0f) * w;
        }
    }
    return accum.x;
}
```

This function can be reused and ensures the gradient is correctly passed to all texels, contributing to the interpolated result.

Differentiating the Loss Function   We define a loss function as a so-called *L2* loss function, meaning the average squared difference between all channels and pixels of a reference image and an image rendered with the optimized parameters. Machine learning literature proposes many alternative and better loss functions, but a squared difference is typically a reasonable starting point in any data-driven optimization experiments. We operate on tone-mapped/gamma-corrected results. In Slang, computing the loss is as simple as follows:

```
[Differentiable]
float loss(DiffTensorView<float> input,
           no_diff float2 uv,
           no_diff float3 reference,
           no_diff Params params)
{
    float3 lighting = computeLighting(input, uv, params);
    // Use an epsilon to avoid exploding gradient.
    float3 gamma_corrected = sqrt(max(lighting, float3(EPSILON)));
    // Reference is already gamma-corrected.
    float3 diff = gamma_corrected - reference;
    // Squared difference summed in R,G,B.
    return dot(diff, diff);
}
```

We can write Slang code automatically translated to a CUDA kernel that can be called directly from Python. Note that in the same kernel, we both compute the loss *image* (for debugging and visualization) and backpropagate the parameters.

```
[AutoPyBindCUDA]
[CudaKernel]
[Differentiable]
void brdf_loss(DiffTensorView<float> input, DiffTensorView<float> output
    , TensorView<float> reference, InputParams input_params)
{
    uint3 globalIdx = cudaBlockIdx() * cudaBlockDim() + cudaThreadIdx();

    if (globalIdx.x >= output.size(0) ||
        globalIdx.y >= output.size(1))
        return;

    float2 uv = (globalIdx.xy+0.5) / float2(output.size(0), output.size
        (1));
    float3 referenceVal = float3(reference[int3(globalIdx.xy, 0)],
        reference[int3(globalIdx.xy, 1)], reference[int3(globalIdx.xy, 2)]);
    float loss = loss(input, uv, referenceVal, input_params);

    output.store(globalIdx, loss);
}
```

Optimization Procedure We initialize textures to the naively downsampled BRDF maps to start the optimization procedure. While such initialization is not optimal, it provides a reasonable starting point. We do not have a rigorous mathematical guarantee of convergence to a global optimum, but gradient descent with a low learning rate guarantees that the result will not be any worse than the initialization.

Now that we can compute gradients of the BRDF properties, we do the following:

- Generate a random light direction vector.

- Render the reference full-resolution image.

- Render the image using current mipmapped properties.

- Compute the loss as the squared difference of those renderings.

- Perform a stochastic gradient descent step on the BRDF properties.

We repeat these steps until convergence. We note that for complete appearance preservation from all viewing angles, randomization of the view vector would be desirable. To simplify the demo application and the training loop, we omit this step, but encourage its inclusion in the practical application.

The whole optimization loop in Python becomes the following:

```
for i in range(ITER_COUNT):
    L = random_hemi_vector()
    V = (0.0, 0.0, 1.0)
    input_params = (*L, *V)
    loss_output = torch.zeros((tex_size[0], tex_size[1], 1)).cuda()
    output_grad = torch.ones_like(loss_output).cuda()
    m.brdf(input=full_res_brdf,
           output=lighting_from_full_res_brdf,
           input_params=input_params).launchRaw(blockSize=
           block_size, gridSize=grid_size)

    m.brdf_loss.bwd(input=(half_res_brdf, gradient_output),
                    output=(loss_output, output_grad),
                    reference=lighting_from_full_res_brdf,
                    input_params=input_params).launchRaw(blockSize=
                    block_size, gridSize=grid_size)
    # Clip gradients and prevent possible not-a-number (NaN) gradient
    values.
    gradient_output = torch.nan_to_num(gradient_output, 0.0)
    gradient_output = torch.clamp(gradient_output, -1.0, 1.0)
    half_res_brdf = torch.clip(half_res_brdf - LR
    * gradient_output, LR, 1.0)
```

In practice, we observe significantly improved results with stochastic gradient descent (SGD) in just 10K iterations. The optimization converges in under a minute on a desktop and a laptop NVIDIA GPU. Similar timing suggests that the largest bottleneck is caused by using PyTorch as the demonstration framework and the multiple unnecessary copies and synchronization points it creates. With proper, per-pixel random lighting directions, the Adam optimizer, and a C++ implementation in a real renderer, this can be further reduced by an order of magnitude.

Optimization Results We demonstrate the optimized BRDF properties and look at the behavior of the optimization process in Figure 18.7.

Figure 18.7. Top: Naively downsampled BRDF property maps. Bottom: Optimized BRDF property maps. From left to right: albedo, normal, and roughness textures.

The behavior matches some well-known analytical approximate models, such as LEAN [Olano and Baker 10] and Toksvig [Toksvig 05] mapping—roughness increases in areas with a large normal map variation. On top of it, the optimization process *sharpens* the BRDF maps to compensate for upsampling with a bilinear kernel. Interestingly, this is a common "ad hoc" practice of video game artists (sharpening the mipmaps), but data-driven methods can achieve it automatically and guarantee appearance-preserving visual outcomes.

Both behaviors are automatically inferred from the data and gradients of the BRDF function. Data-driven texture optimization does not approximate the results with best-fit formulas or any assumptions about the normal direction distribution. The prior approaches use limited parameters (variance or covariance matrix of the normal distribution), while our method matches the appearance closely for the input normals and other BRDF properties. Unlike analytical models created for specific BRDFs, our method can work as a drop-in for many BRDFs or even BRDF mixtures.

Next Steps The method, as presented, is a proof of concept, demonstrating how easy it is to set up a data-driven, appearance-preserving pipeline for material minification using Slang. We recommend some additional steps for production renderers to improve their performance and appearance preservation. First, we recommend using a better optimizer, such as Adam. Second, generating per-pixel random lighting directions will provide faster convergence. In the example, we assume the view direction to be perpendicular to the surface, which might not yield the best appearance-preserving results for highly view-dependent materials. Some experiments with different loss functions can yield results more suitable for rendering; similarly, different spaces where the loss function is computed (tone mapped or log space). Finally, materials can be simplified together with geometry for mesh LODs. Hasselgren et al. [Hasselgren et al. 21] have demonstrated how differentiable rendering can simplify meshes and materials jointly. To reduce the cost of their approach, we can keep the mesh LODs as created by other tools and only optimize mipmaps and materials to recover the appearance effects of the lost normal variation from mesh simplification. Finally, a fused C++ implementation without unnecessary CPU-GPU copies and GPU allocations inherent to using PyTorch as a convenient wrapper would be significantly faster.

18.5   Conclusion

In this article, we described a new useful tool for real-time computer graphics—differentiable programming. Differentiable programming is a powerful tool for computer graphics, computer vision, and image synthesis, and we have demonstrated its use in three neural-network–free applications.

In particular, we hope optimization techniques can be utilized further to reduce the time spent on many uncreative, time-consuming tasks performed today by programmers, artists, designers, or animators. Differentiable programming has many uses beyond the performance-oriented tasks that we described. Gradient descent refinement can improve the quality of UV mapping to reduce distortions, fit the parameters of a sky model to a reference sky photograph or painting, tune the color correction and post-processing to resemble an art mood board, or reconstruct materials and objects from photographs in inverse rendering applications. As long as the pipeline and a loss function can be differentiable, almost any task that requires tuning can be automated or improved with optimization.

Now, with Slang, real-time renderers can be made differentiable without significant changes to existing large code bases. With that, we look forward to the future of bridging real-time graphics and machine learning with innovations in photorealistic neural and data-driven techniques.

Acknowledgements

We are grateful for the help, support, and leadership of our colleagues, in particular Aaron Lefohn for allowing this research to happen and Theresa Foley for her leadership on the Slang language development. We also want to acknowledge Benedikt Bitterli, who came up with the idea and initial implementation of using automatic differentiation to automatically compute Jacobians used in Monte Carlo and other rendering techniques.

Bibliography

[Anderson et al. 17] Luke Anderson, Tzu-Mao Li, Jaakko Lehtinen, and Fr'edo Durand. "Aether: An Embedded Domain Specific Sampling Language for Monte Carlo Rendering." *ACM Transactions on Graphics (Proceedings of SIGGRAPH 2017)* 36:4 (2017), 99:1–99:16.

[Bangaru et al. 20] Sai Bangaru, Tzu-Mao Li, and Frédo Durand. "Unbiased Warped-Area Sampling for Differentiable Rendering." *ACM Transactions on Graphics* 39:6 (2020), 245:1–245:18.

[Bangaru et al. 23] Sai Praveen Bangaru, Lifan Wu, Tzu-Mao Li, Jacob Munkberg, Gilbert Bernstein, Jonathan Ragan-Kelley, Frédo Durand, Aaron Lefohn, and Yong He. "SLANG.D: Fast, Modular and Differentiable Shader Programming." *ACM Transactions on Graphics* 42:6 (2023), 1–28.

[Han et al. 07] Charles Han, Bo Sun, Ravi Ramamoorthi, and Eitan Grinspun. "Frequency Domain Normal Map Filtering." *ACM Transactions on Graphics (Proceedings of SIGGRAPH 2007)* 26:3 (2007), 28:1–28:12.

[Hasselgren et al. 21] Jon Hasselgren, Jacob Munkberg, Jaakko Lehtinen, Miika Aittala, and Samuli Laine. "Appearance-Driven Automatic 3D Model Simplification." In *32nd Eurographics Symposium on Rendering, EGSR 2021—Digital Library Only Track*, pp. 85–97. Eurographics Association, 2021.

[He et al. 18] Yong He, Kayvon Fatahalian, and Tim Foley. "Slang: Language Mechanisms for Extensible Real-Time Shading Systems." *ACM Transactions on Graphics* 37:4 (2018), 1–13.

[Kallweit 23] Simon Kallweit. "TinyBC." NVIDIA GameWorks Falcor GitHub, 2023. https://github.com/NVIDIAGameWorks/Falcor/tree/master/scripts/python/TinyBC.

[Karis 18] Brian Karis. "Normal Map Filtering Using vMF (Part 3)." Graphic Rants, May 12, 2018. https://graphicrants.blogspot.com/2018/05/normal-map-filtering-using-vmf-part-3.html.

[Kingma and Ba 14] Diederik P. Kingma and Jimmy Ba. "Adam: A method for Stochastic Optimization." Preprint, arXiv:1412.6980, 2014. https://arxiv.org/abs/1412.6980.

[Laine et al. 20] Samuli Laine, Janne Hellsten, Tero Karras, Yeongho Seol, Jaakko Lehtinen, and Timo Aila. "Modular Primitives for High-Performance Differentiable Rendering." *ACM Transactions on Graphics* 39:6 (2020), 194:1–194:14.

[Li et al. 18] Tzu-Mao Li, Miika Aittala, Frédo Durand, and Jaakko Lehtinen. "Differentiable Monte Carlo Ray Tracing through Edge Sampling." *ACM Transactions on Graphics (Proceedings of SIGGRAPH Asia 2018)* 37:6 (2018), 222:1–222:11.

[Liu et al. 19] Shichen Liu, Tianye Li, Weikai Chen, and Hao Li. "Soft Rasterizer: A Differentiable Renderer for Image-based 3D Reasoning." In *2019 IEEE/CVF International Conference on Computer Vision (ICCV)*, pp. 7707–7716. IEEE, 2019.

[Loubet et al. 19] Guillaume Loubet, Nicolas Holzschuch, and Wenzel Jakob. "Reparameterizing Discontinuous Integrands for Differentiable Rendering." *ACM Transactions on Graphics (Proceedings of SIGGRAPH Asia 2019)* 38:6 (2019), 228:1–228:14.

[Mildenhall et al. 21] Ben Mildenhall, Pratul P. Srinivasan, Matthew Tancik, Jonathan T Barron, Ravi Ramamoorthi, and Ren Ng. "NeRF: Representing Scenes as Neural Radiance Fields for View Synthesis." *Communications of the ACM* 65:1 (2021), 99–106.

[Neubelt and Pettineo 13] David Neubelt and Matt Pettineo. "Crafting a Next-Gen Material Pipeline for The Order: 1886." ACM SIGGRAPH Course: Physically Based Shading in Theory and Practice, 2013.

[Olano and Baker 10] Marc Olano and Dan Baker. "LEAN Mapping." In *Proceedings of the 2010 ACM SIGGRAPH Symposium on Interactive 3D Graphics and Games*, pp. 181–188. Association for Computing Machinery, 2010.

[Toksvig 05] Michael Toksvig. "Mipmapping Normal Maps." *Journal of Graphics Tools* 10:3 (2005), 65–71.

[Tseng et al. 19] Ethan Tseng, Felix Yu, Yuting Yang, Fahim Mannan, Karl St. Arnaud, Derek Nowrouzezahrai, Jean-Francois Lalonde, and Felix Heide. "Hyperparameter Optimization in Black-Box Image Processing Using Differentiable Proxies." *ACM Transactions on Graphics* 38:4 (2019), 27:1–27:14.

[Wronski 21] Bartlomiej Wronski. "Procedural Kernel Networks." Preprint, arXiv:2112.09318, 2021. https://arxiv.org/abs/2112.09318.

[Wronski 24] Bartlomiej Wronski. "slangpy.ipynb." Slang Python GitHub, 2024. https://github.com/shader-slang/slang-python/blob/main/examples/brdf-appearance-optimize-example/slangpy.ipynb.

[Zhang et al. 20] Cheng Zhang, Bailey Miller, Kai Yan, Ioannis Gkioulekas, and Shuang Zhao. "Path-Space Differentiable Rendering." *ACM Transactions on Graphics (Proceedings of SIGGRAPH 2020)* 39:6 (2020), 143:1–143:19.

DRToolkit: Boosting Rendering Performance Using Differentiable Rendering

Chen Qiao, Xiang Lan, Yijie Shi,
Xueqiang Wang, Xilei Wei, and Jiang Qin

19.1 Introduction

In the development of cross-platform games or console-to-mobile ported games, differences in computational capabilities and energy consumption across various platforms ultimately lead to differences in game asset specifications. If we can quickly generate corresponding game assets for various platforms based on the exact visual appearances of artistic design, it would greatly help reduce development costs and improve project development efficiency. Furthermore, optimizing the game performance on low-end devices and minimizing the requirements for entry-level devices as much as possible can make the game more competitive in the emerging market. For such issues, the emerging differentiable rendering technology can provide significant assistance.

Differentiable rendering is a groundbreaking technology in computer graphics that integrates the rendering process with the backpropagation algorithm. This technology can produce consistent visual outputs across diverse rendering systems. Consider two scenarios: First, we have a set of physically based rendering (PBR) materials that contain gameplay logic. In this case, differentiable rendering can automatically convert them into diffuse textures with minimal visual differences. Second, we have a set of parameters used in complex post-processing algorithms. Differentiable rendering can generate corresponding parameters for simpler post-processing algorithms, achieving the same appearances. All of these can help enhance performance on low-end devices from the asset aspect.

In this article, we will introduce some attempts in the application aspect. In the previous article, He et al. present a more in-depth theoretical discussion about differentiable rendering and introduce SLANG.D, which significantly impacts the entire field [He et al. 24]. Meanwhile, our tools are also transitioning to the SLANG.D version.

Differentiable renderers have limitations when it comes to adapting to game asset scenarios. For instance, renderers that are primarily designed for recon-

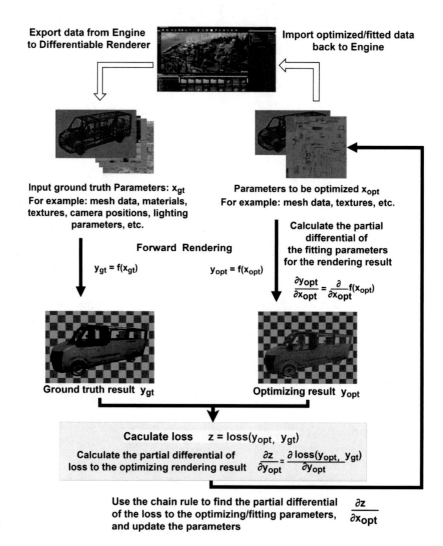

Figure 19.1. A general framework for optimization using differentiable rendering.

struction purposes can process only a single mesh with 0–1 texture coordinate, which is insufficient for game development.

To address the gap between differentiable rendering and game asset scenarios, we developed DRToolkit, a differentiable rendering-based optimization solution. (See Figure 19.1.) This toolkit has been implemented and is currently being used by NExT Studios in their game *SYNCED: Off-Plane* to optimize resources and achieve near-identical visual appearances with less consumption. MoreFun Studios is also using it for their procedural content generation (PCG) pipeline Falcon.

19.2 Overview of Differentiable Rendering

19.2.1 What Is Differentiable Rendering?

Traditional rendering produces a 2D image from information about the scene's geometry, material, lighting, and camera. This process cannot directly compute derivatives, thus hindering the use of gradient-based optimization algorithms. Differentiable rendering is a novel computer graphics technology that combines the rendering process with the backpropagation algorithm. This technology enables neural networks to learn and optimize rendering parameters directly. It makes handling tasks in computer vision and machine learning (such as image synthesis, mesh reconstruction, and scene understanding) more intuitive and efficient.

Differentiable rendering faces two primary challenges: (1) the efficient calculation of derivatives and (2) rendering discontinuities. The community addresses these challenges by creating rendering-dedicated automatic differentiation frameworks and redesigning rendering algorithms.

In the realm of rendering-dedicated automatic differentiation frameworks, two standout works are Dr.Jit [Jakob et al. 22] and SLANG.D [Bangaru et al. 23, Foley 24, He et al. 24]. Dr.Jit is a just-in-time (JIT) compiler for differentiable computation, originally developed for Mitsuba 3. It's a versatile tool that can also help with other forms of parallel computation. SLANG.D, a derivative of the Slang language, is a shading language with integrated automatic differentiation. It fosters a shared ecosystem between machine learning and graphics hardware rendering systems, encouraging cross-domain component and idea exchange. For detailed information about SLANG.D, please refer to the corresponding article in this book [He et al. 24].

In those redesigned approaches to differentiable rendering, methods based on Monte Carlo and rasterization are employed, just like traditional rendering. Monte Carlo–based methods include strategies such as edge sampling [Li et al. 18], path-space differential rendering [Zhang et al. 20], reparameterization [Loubet et al. 19], and unbiased warped-area sampling [Bangaru et al. 20]. Alternatively, rasterization-based methods include SoftRas [Liu et al. 19], Neural Mesh Render [Kato et al. 18], and nvdiffrast [Laine et al. 20].

The two mainstream implementations of rasterization-based differentiable renderers are SoftRas and nvdiffrast. SoftRas introduces soft rasterization and aggregation functions to solve the discontinuity problems in the XY screen space and the Z depth direction. PyTorch3D adopts this scheme. Nvdiffrast implements a highly efficient differentiable rendering system based on deferred shading through custom basic operations in the graphics pipeline: rasterization, attribute interpolation, texture filtering, and antialiasing. A series of projects has been developed based on nvdiffrast. Nvdiffmodeling [Hasselgren et al. 21] enhances nvdiffrast with shader-like operations, vertex transformations, and supports for

PBR material and light sources. Nvdiffrec [Munkberg et al. 22], focusing on reconstruction, uses differentiable marching tetrahedra and multilayer perceptron (MLP) with position encoding to generate new triangle mesh models and corresponding PBR textures. Lastly, nvdiffrecmc [Hasselgren et al. 22] improves upon nvdiffrec by combining ray tracing and Monte Carlo integration for better shape, material, and lighting decomposition, with multiple importance sampling and denoising for improved convergence. Additionally, Dressi [Takimoto et al. 22] proposed an extension of HardSoftRas, a cross-platform implementation of Vulkan, and the corresponding automatic differentiation implementation, Dressi-AD.

19.2.2 Applications in the Gaming Industry

As previously described, differentiating rendering bridges the gap between 2D and 3D processing methods, enabling the optimization of 3D scene parameters through backpropagation. As shown below, the gaming industry has already begun to adopt differentiable rendering for tasks such as character model reconstruction and game asset conversion, although it has yet to be directly integrated into existing commercial game engines.

Developers can extract geometric, material, and lighting information from real-world photos or videos through reconstruction technology based on differentiable rendering to generate game art assets. For example, in 2020, the PokerFace-GAN method was proposed for automatically creating expressionless facial data for game characters [Shi et al. 20]. This method can generate expressionless facial models that are highly similar to the input photos, achieving the automatic creation of game characters using a single image. Proposed in 2022, a convolutional neural network–based framework can obtain facial model data (including mesh, head pose, expression, diffuse and specular reflection textures, and lighting environment) from a single face image [Deng et al. 22]. This framework incorporates a differentiable renderer to measure the discrepancy between the input and the learning outcome to facilitate the self-supervised training process.

Regarding resource conversion, the *Honor of Kings* project applied differentiable rendering for resource auxiliary production, greatly accelerating the production of level of detail (LOD) assets [Ling and Zhang 23]. The visual appearance is comparable to high-precision assets, helping the project comfortably tackle the dual challenges of stringent performance and quality requirements.

Furthermore, although SLANG.D, introduced in the previous article [He et al. 24], has not yet been fully integrated into commercial engines due to its recent release, it is being adopted by Valve's Source 2 Engine through Slang [Foley 24]. It is certain to impact the gaming industry significantly. RenderDoc has also added support for Slang in the 1.32 update [Karlsson 24].

19.3   System Overview

Like the typical neural network training process, differentiable rendering–based art asset optimization involves similar or identical steps such as data preparation, model definition, loss function and optimization algorithm selection, training/-fitting loop, and model evaluation and deployment. In the current usage, fitting data like textures is equivalent to training a single-layer network. Hence, this article prefers "fitting" or "optimization" rather than "training." Figure 19.2 illustrates the basic process of fitting resources through differentiable rendering.

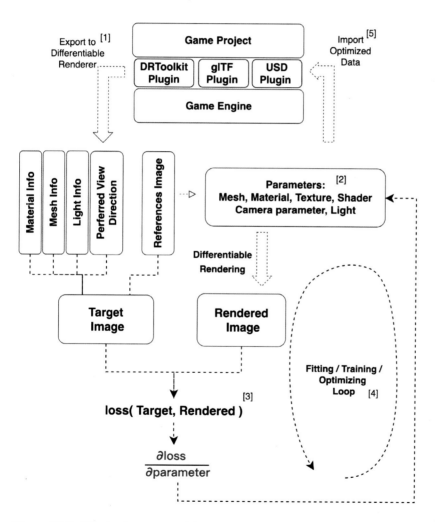

Figure 19.2. The basic process of fitting resources via differentiable rendering.

19.3.1   Data Preparation

Export the data that requires processing from the game engine:

- the object's mesh data (including vertex position, normal direction, and UV coordinates);

- the specific materials and textures the object uses;

- the object's transformation matrix in the game scene (position, rotation, and scaling);

- the object's environmental illumination information in the current game environment;

- the expected observation position group of the gameplay camera;

- the current position's scene color (SceneColor) or the render target texture (G-buffer/cached data saved as render target) in the rendering process, if necessary.

Using the exported data, we can achieve the same visual appearance by re-rendering it outside the engine.

19.3.2   Define and Initialize the Data that Needs to be Fitted

Different data parameters have different initialization methods. The initial data can be sourced either from traditional algorithms or from algorithms based on neural networks. Here are some methods we use.

For PBR material textures:

- **Texture 0:** Half gray sRGB albedo color and opaque alpha value with default value $(187, 187, 187, 255)$.

- **Texture 1:** Ambient occlusion (default 1), roughness (default 0.5), metallic (default 0), and displacement (default 1) in RGBA channels.

- **Texture 2:** Tangent-space normal map with Z-up convention.

For mesh data:

- **Approximate LOD mesh:** Used for tuning or optimization tasks; subsequent processes will make minor modifications to the mesh data.

- **Icosphere mesh:** Used with the desired number of vertices for remesh tasks; subsequent processes will shape an approximate mesh from the sphere, which looks like sculpting clay.

19.3.3 Define the Loss Function and Optimization Algorithm

The loss function may include image-space loss, contour loss, and others. Different fitting tasks can use different loss functions and loss weights. Additionally, in a fitting batch with multiple cameras, different cameras can have different loss weights. The optimization algorithms may include stochastic gradient descent (SGD), Adam, RMSprop, IsotropicAdam, and others. These algorithms are all based on gradient descent, but have different optimization strategies and update rules. Different tasks can choose different loss functions and optimization algorithms.

19.3.4 Training/Fitting Loop

The training/fitting loop generally consists of forward propagation, loss calculation, backpropagation, parameter updates, validation, and early stopping. The forward propagation process renders intermediate resources during the fitting process using the differentiable renderer. The loss function calculates the loss value of the intermediate fitting result and the fitting target result. The fitting target result can be obtained by rendering the target data in the same differentiable renderer or using the exported scene color or G-buffer. The backpropagation process calculates the gradient of the loss function for the fitting parameters. The specific optimization algorithm updates the parameters in the fitting according to the gradient value. Evaluate the current status of the fitting parameters. If there is no significant improvement within a certain number of consecutive training/fitting rounds, the process will be stopped early to avoid over-fitting.

19.3.5 Evaluation of Results and Import to the Engine

After completing the fitting process, we observe the fitting result and determine whether it meets our quality expectations. If it does, we import the fitted data back into the engine and finish setting up the engine's internal parameters according to the project's needs.

The following sections will detail the integration of this process framework.

19.4 Renderer Implementation

To be compatible with game assets, supporting the rendering of multiple meshes is necessary. Figure 19.3 shows the refactoring and extension of the differentiable renderer. The light red sections mark the basic steps of the differentiable renderer, similar to the steps in SoftRas and nvdiffrast.

Based on traditional differentiable rendering's single draw call, this method encapsulates mesh, material, and location information according to mesh parts to complete the rendering. It also adds operations to merge multiple draw call results and antialiasing operations, thus supporting the rendering of multiple mesh parts. The light purple sections in Figure 19.3 mark this part.

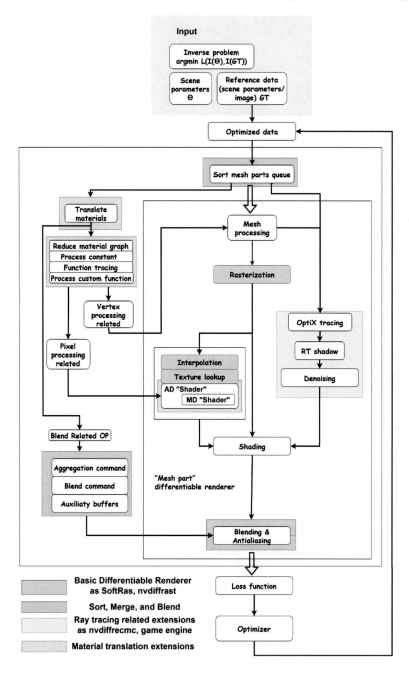

Figure 19.3. Extension of the differentiable renderer.

As the yellow part in Figure 19.3 indicates, we add the calculation of light source shadows using ray tracing to deal with lighting and shadow.

Furthermore, we perform a conversion operation on all material instances. In material conversion, for common computational nodes and standard built-in material functions in the Unreal Engine, such as the `MaterialLayerBlend`-related nodes, `WorldPositionUV`-related nodes, `WorldNormal`-related nodes, and others, our method adds a manual differentiation CUDA implementation to accelerate the calculation for complex materials and reduce memory usage. This part is marked in light blue in Figure 19.3 and will be detailed later.

The process begins at the exporting phase. When exporting the list of objects, we gather all tuples (mesh, material, coordinate list) related to them. Here, we also establish a bounding volume hierarchy (BVH) for the exported opaque object data with OptiX for later shadowing and shading stages.

After gathering all the tuples, we move to the sorting phase. We divide these tuples into `RenderItems` with and without optimization/fitting content. We treat the `RenderItems` with optimization as "a sort of transparent" content, equivalent to adding a type of "transparent" object that needs to be processed in the queue.

First, all opaque `RenderItems` without optimization content are sorted by distance and rendered in order from near to far. The primary purpose of rendering from near to far is to use depth for culling during the rendering stage to reduce the drawing of unnecessary objects/pixels. Then, render the opaque `RenderItems` with optimization content. Next, all transparent `RenderItems` (both those involved in optimization and those not involved) are sorted and drawn in order from far to near to ensure the correctness of the alpha blending. There may be overlaps between items that participate in optimization and those that do not. In this case, we merge the meshes of the `RenderItems` not participating in the optimization into those of the `RenderItems` to be optimized and add the non-optimization mark to the extra vertex attributes. The corresponding calculations are selected based on the vertex attributes in the shading stage.

The next phase involves rendering each object in the list. In each object's shading stage, we use ray tracing to obtain the shadow of the primary light source. It ensures the transmission of gradients while improving the appearance effect through differentiable noise reduction and then overlays the effect of ambient light to complete the final rendering. We adopt a method similar to nvdiffrecmc and the existing game engine. It performs mixed ray tracing integration, as shown in Figure 19.4.

We need to apply depth peeling to render transparent objects. Once the rendering is complete, we merge and blend the rendering results of each render item.

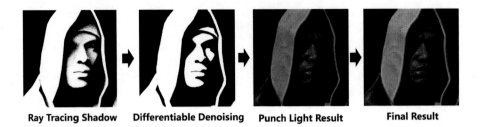

Figure 19.4. Hybrid ray tracing shadow calculation.

19.5 Handling Materials

19.5.1 Selection of Observation Cameras

Reconstruction tasks often capture scenes according to camera positions distributed uniformly in an approximate hemisphere. This camera distribution method is unsuitable for games. For example, in third-person shooter games, the distribution probability of the player's camera is unequal. Moreover, due to the camera collision logic, the radius of this observation hemisphere also changes. Therefore, we must determine the observation camera's position and direction based on the player's possible positions. Due to differences in the model's shape, the expected observation position and direction may also vary for each model. For example, some cameras' positions and directions are better suited to capture the intricate details of a model's features, making them particularly useful for processing materials and meshes. In addition, camera rails in games and position information of automated testing script points are also of great reference value. Therefore, we classify the observation cameras into three types: CV_{manual}, CV_{nav}, and CV_{mesh}. Table 19.1 shows the classification method, and Figure 19.5 displays the gizmos of observation cameras.

Observation Camera Type	Description
CV_{manual}	The specific positions and directions are generated through information developers provide (e.g., manually specified positions, camera rail curves).
CV_{nav}	The positions and directions of observation cameras are generated through the player's ground navigation mesh (navmesh) and the aerial area's sparse voxel octree (SVO).
CV_{mesh}	The positions and directions of the observation cameras are generated based on the features of the current mesh model.

Table 19.1. Classification of observation camera types.

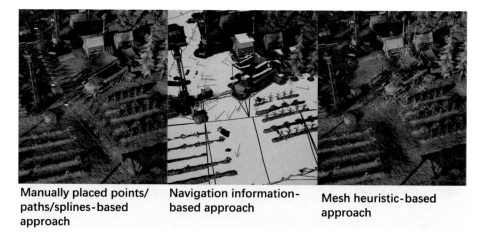

Manually placed points/ paths/splines-based approach   **Navigation information-based approach**   **Mesh heuristic-based approach**

Figure 19.5. Generated observation cameras for assets processing.

The purpose of the observation also needs to be considered. For instance, we primarily use camera observations that are closer to or cover only part of the object for material and mesh processing corresponding to LOD0 or LOD1. On the contrary, we use distant cameras for asset processing at higher LOD levels, even generating hierarchical LOD. Mixing these cameras could lead to errors or undesired effects.

As shown in Figure 19.6, based on the previously generated observation cameras, this method has fitted the truck materials in the scene. Compared with the

Figure 19.6. Original standard PBR material and fitted material (see Section 19.5.4).

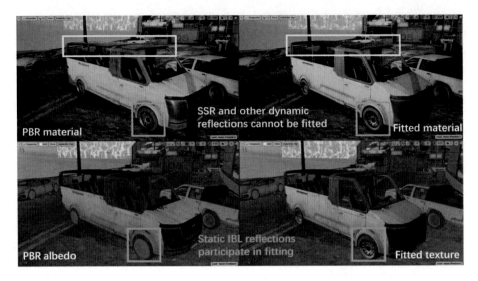

Figure 19.7. Reflections in standard PBR material and fitted material.

original PBR material, the fitted material retains the details and overlays the roughness, ambient occlusion, and other information in PBR with the current fitted texture as a reasonable "lighting" result. We can achieve a similar visual appearance using only Lambert diffuse light. For example, the fitted appearance on the upper part of the truck includes the normals and corresponding reflection effects.

Figure 19.7 shows the fitted results of the reflection lights in the scene. The reflection light from the screen-space reflection (SSR) on the vehicle's surface will not be fitted, as real-time reflection light does not participate in the fitting, so this part of the effect is missing. Of course, such effects would also be turned off on low-end devices. However, static image-based lighting (IBL) can participate in the fitting, and a similar visual appearance is also achieved.

19.5.2 Translation of Materials

The materials in actual projects are often quite complex. Take the monsters in *SYNCED: Off-Plane* as an example. As shown in Figure 19.8, a monster is rendered with only one draw call to support the rendering of massive numbers of monsters. For this, it uses vertex color control `TextureArray` to implement material blending, while gameplay-controlled dynamic effects are also overlaid on the monster's body. These contents cannot be pre-baked into a set of fixed PBR textures and thus cannot directly use the previous fitting process. Therefore, we split the character's material into static and dynamic layers. Static layers, such as primary PBR material layers, must be fitted. Dynamic layers, such as

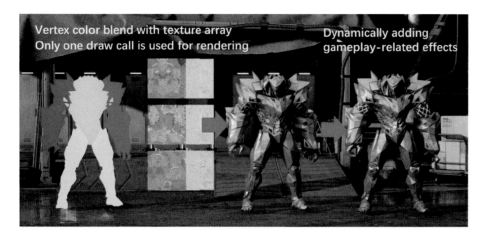

Figure 19.8. Complex materials in game scenario.

gameplay dynamic layers, do not participate in the fitting and overlay the static layers at runtime.

The material in the material editor of actual game projects is complex. Technical artists connect many material nodes to express the desired artistic effect, quality level–related switching controls, gameplay logic-related overlay effects, and others. Besides links between nodes, some of these effects are implemented through custom nodes with HLSL code. We must translate the project's existing materials to the external differentiable renderer, achieving exact computations and visual results.

In Unreal Engine, the HLSL material translator inserts the material node graph into the shader code template and generates many shader variants depending on the material's use in different scenarios. However, these codes are enormous and highly related to the engine's rendering pipeline. We aim to retain only the necessary material information for the differentiable renderer and enable static layer separation. The basic process for translating Unreal Engine's internal materials to materials used in differentiable renderer is as follows (see also Figure 19.9):

1. Find the base material and record the parameters changed by the current material instance.

2. Perform a depth-first traversal for each input of the `MaterialProperty` node, recording the current node traversal order and connection relationships.

3. Unfold the material function nodes.

4. Remove branch nodes that need not be processed, such as unsupported feature/quality/platform branches and unused if/switch/lerp branches. If

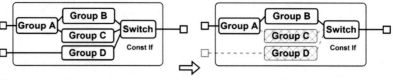

Remove unnecessary branch from switch (and const if)

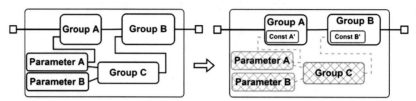

Treat parameters that can be processed statically as constants for substitution

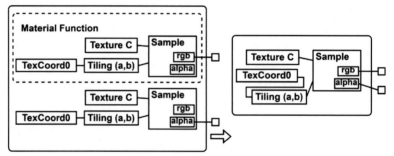

Expand material function and merge the same sample nodes

Figure 19.9. Simplification operations in material graph translation.

certain if-branch conditions can be determined to be constants during the phase, then branch optimization processing (const if) will be performed based on these constants.

5. For parameters not controlled by gameplay, such as material instance variation values, translate these nodes into previous recorded constant values.

6. For parameters controlled by gameplay, such as gameplay effect values, translate these nodes into constants. The constants should turn off dynamic layer effects.

7. Check and remove any repeated texture sampling.

8. Re-perform depth-first traversal on the pruned property nodes; check and obtain the simplified material node tree.

9. Translate the material node tree into PyTorch/PTX for shading part calculations in the differentiable renderer. If it includes a custom node, refer to the next section for processing.

19.5.3 Translation of HLSL Code in Custom Node

In Unreal Engine's material editor, developers can utilize custom HLSL code in custom nodes for complex material outputs. This code requires extra steps because the previous node translation cannot handle it. For other engines like Unity, ShaderToy, or those based on DirectX and OpenGL, shaders are typically text-based. So, we need to convert these text-based shaders into vectorized Python. Our primary focus is on vectorized implementations based on NumPy and PyTorch.

As the HLSL language advances, the HLSL team offers the open-source DXC project for translating HLSL into DXIL or SPIR-V for diverse rendering platforms. Therefore, we adapt DXC for HLSL syntax parsing. However, considering the ongoing updates of the DXC project, we need to limit our changes to prevent conflicts with future updates. We adjust the DXC project's DirectX Raytracing tool's Rewrite function to convert HLSL into our MetaDSL syntax. Then, we can independently translate to Python and vectorize without the DXC tool. We built this translation tool using C#.

The C# implementation includes translating to Python syntax, single-exit function transformation, establishing lexical scope and data flow structures, loop unrolling, and the most crucial vectorization derivation. Figure 19.10 shows the process.

Translating to Python language generally involves three parts of work. The first part is similar to the usual work based on abstract syntax tree (AST) code generation. This step can generate a scalar version of the function. Considering that some functions may not be able to derive a vectorized version, a vector-adapted version will also be generated for all functions with branches. The vector-adapted version is a function that accepts tensor parameters, iterates through the tensor, calls the scalar version function, and then combines the results into a tensor to return.

The second part involves performing a complex vectorization transformation on the program and generating a vector version for functions that can be vectorized. We will introduce further details on this transformation separately.

The third part is to write Python library functions to implement HLSL internal functions. The internal functions need to be implemented as strong-type functions; that is, a library function needs to be written for each combination of parameter types (similar to the renaming of overloaded functions in C++, different overloads correspond to different functions). We implement one set for the NumPy version and one set for the PyTorch version.

The specific work of the second part, vectorization transformation, is as follows:

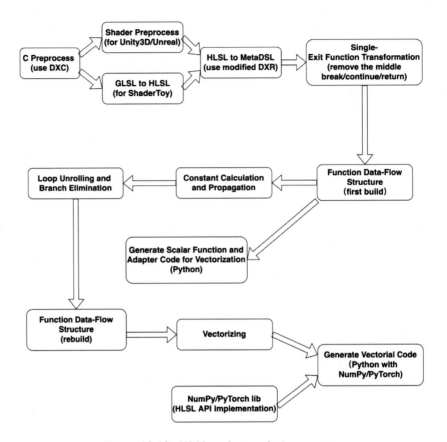

Figure 19.10. HLSL code translation process.

Single Exit Function Transformation Transform break/continue/return statements in the function body into if statements.

Vectorized Python execution and the original shader execution can be considered orthogonal. A shader is a form of multi-threaded parallelism, while vectorized execution is similar to SIMD instruction execution applied to the first line of shader code. Since the code used to process a single data set now has to process the entire tensor data set at the same time, the original code that interrupted the execution flow may not necessarily be the original behavior (unless the execution results of the entire tensor data are the same).

In this way, vectorized execution cannot skip the code within the function, so it is necessary to transform the statements interrupting the execution flow. The primary processing method is to introduce a control flag for each statement that interrupts the flow (which will become a tensor after vectorization) and then add a judgment on the control flag to all subsequent code to determine whether to execute.

Function Data Flow Analysis Data flow analysis mainly identifies variables defined outside the block and used inside the block and assigns them to external variables inside the block. We use this information for branch elimination, which includes variable renaming and branch result selection.

Constant Calculation and Propagation We mainly use constant calculation and propagation to calculate the number of loops for loop unrolling.

Loop Unrolling and Branch Elimination Perform loop unrolling for code with a calculable number of loops. Loop unrolling is necessary for the vectorization we implemented. Because vectorization actually changes the function parameter type to tensor type and then performs type derivation and type adjustment on the function, Python language variables are dynamically typed and allow inconsistent types before and after. Our current implementation uses a one-time forward derivation using Python's variable type inconsistency feature. However, a runtime type conflict may occur if there is a loop in the program flow.

Loop unrolling may require constant calculation to calculate the number of loops. If we cannot calculate the number of loops for specific loops, we cannot perform unrolling and, consequently, cannot vectorize the function. The translated Python code will use the vector-adapted version of this function. The performance of the vector-adapted version is relatively low, so we generally modify the shader code to make all loops expandable, typically by estimating the maximum number of loops that can be achieved.

After vectorization, the code is a tensor operation. In the case of tensor data, the original shader branch statement generally does not still execute the same branch. We adopt an execution method similar to GPU warp; all branch codes are executed, but only the actual branches that should be executed are selected (or the results that do not need to be executed are masked).

Branch elimination includes three steps: renaming external variables in branch blocks, executing all branch codes, and selecting valid branch results (assigning values to the original external variables after renaming). (This requires using data flow analysis to identify external variables referenced in the block.)

Vectorized Version of Shader Functions Based on type derivation, this step mainly changes the function parameters from scalar type to tensor type. It performs type derivation on the operations inside the function, modifying the result variable type to the corresponding tensor type.

A scalar function may need to be translated into different vector versions depending on the actual shader call situation (because when calling a function, not all parameters may need to be changed to tensors. According to the actual call requirements, each combination of actual parameter types corresponds to a vector version). The original shader function acts as a template function, instantiating different vectorized functions based on the combination of actual parameter types.

Figure 19.11. Tested shaders from Shadertoy [Quilez and Jeremias 24].

Now, we can process the materials created by connecting material nodes in the Unreal Engine material editor.

The source code for this C# tool is on GitHub [Dreamanlan 24b], as well as the modified version of DXC source code [Dreamanlan 24a] and the MetaDSL source code [Dreamanlan 24c].

We implemented tests on Shadertoy using approximately 50 shaders. The subsequent four images in Figure 19.11 are the results of translating these specific shaders into PyTorch. The illustrative examples of these translated effects feature "Green Field Diorama" by David Gallardo [Gallardo 21], "Raymarching—Primitives" by Inigo Quilez [Quilez 13], "Textured Ellipsoids" by Fabrice Neyret [Neyret 14], and "Procedural Walk Animation" by Shadertoy User TLC123 [TLC123 19]. All image copyrights belong to the original authors.

19.5.4 Visual Appearances after Material Optimization

During the material translation phase, because this method separates the dynamic layer controlled by gameplay logic and the primary material fitted layer, the fitting and conversion do not affect the effects related to gameplay logic. For example, in Figure 19.12, the fitted monster texture does not contain dynamic content like fluorescence, and the gameplay control logic here is unaffected. As shown in Figure 19.13, the fitted texture includes the fitted lighting effect, com-

Figure 19.12. Final fitted visual appearance: fitted visual appearance (left), fitted visual appearance with dynamic gameplay effect (middle), and target visual appearance (right).

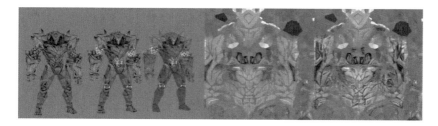

Figure 19.13. Final fitted texture (base color/albedo only). From left to right: fitted texture, fitted texture plus gameplay layer, original albedo plus gameplay layer, albedo texture in PBR material, and fitted material texture.

pared to the original albedo color. We can use the same processing method to fit terrain and objects like cliffs in the scene; our method supports multilayer material blending operations.

We experimented on the overall scene material conversion. Figure 19.14 shows the results: the top-row images represent the standard mode, while the bottom-row images represent the lite mode. In *lite mode*, we only use vertex normals for Lambert diffuse lighting calculations and fitted textures. As with the scene objects mentioned earlier, the metal or metal-like parts are brighter after being fitted. Non-metal parts can also overlay some effects of ambient occlusion and normals onto the fitted texture.

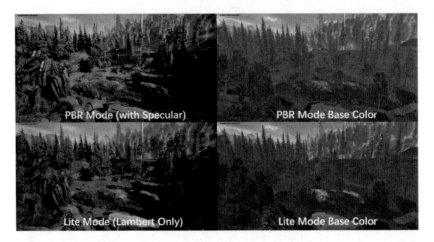

Figure 19.14. Scene result.

In the fitting process, we use a method similar to normalized IBL to overlay the reflection lights onto the albedo/diffuse texture. Therefore, we avoid runtime specular calculations when using the fitted texture. In addition, because the lite mode uses vertex normals to calculate lighting, it does not need to maintain the content of the tangent space used for pixel normals. Hence, it omits the calculations related to tangents and bitangents, only retaining the calculation of vertex normals. When lighting is a computational bottleneck, this optimization yields significant results by reducing computation. For the forward rendering pipeline, this optimization is straightforward and does not require significant modifications to the engine. For the deferred rendering pipeline, we may need to make slightly complicated modifications; if we pursue accuracy, we may need to store additional data for fitted albedo color. For low-end devices, using fitted resources can be a global switch. When switched to lite mode globally, it offers significant performance and memory benefits.

19.6   Processing of Meshes

Although differentiable rendering has achieved great success in scene reconstruction, some problems still need to be solved when using it solely for mesh processing. For instance, independently optimizing vertex positions may lead to triangle normal flipping or self-intersection. Once these defects occur, the optimization usually falls into a local minimum, resulting in folds and collapses.

From a practical standpoint in the project, the current Unreal Engine and digital content creation (DCC) pipelines include many mature LOD solutions for specific usage scenarios. These LOD solutions are based on quadratic error

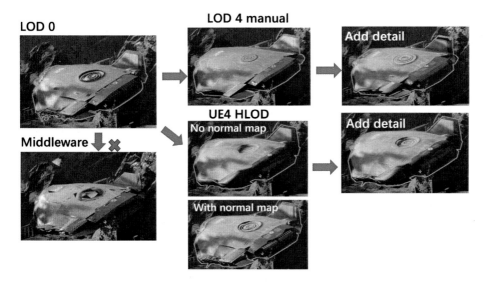

Figure 19.15. Add details to the mesh's LOD resources.

metrics (QEM), voxelization, and other methods. These solutions often reduce faces first and then generate textures by baking, but they do not optimize for the final joint visual appearance of objects' meshes and materials in the game.

In our project, we experimented with different methods to generate distant LOD4-level resources. The mesh reduction middleware, due to its algorithmic limitations, produced faulty LOD4 resources. Both manual and Unreal Engine–generated HLOD resources yielded good results, but the latter required normal textures, incurring additional usage costs. Thus, we used differentiable rendering to enhance existing resources' vertex normals and base-color textures, improving the appearance effect without using normal textures.

Figure 19.15 illustrates the comparison of LOD generation results for test assets. We first export the current model's LOD observation cameras and break the smooth group of vertices for the HLOD model to optimize. Using a differentiable renderer, we render the original and optimized model's 0–1 encoded normal effects. Then, we optimize vertex normals via differentiable rendering. Since two different LOD-level models have inconsistent detailed outlines, we reduce the weight of the loss function for the outline. The same method can be applied to process manually created LOD resources. Moreover, this method can also handle the vertex normal correction of LOD meshes for toon shading, which heavily relies on tuned normal directions.

For non-traditional methods of mesh processing, we attempt to modify the continuous remesh solution to simplify the mesh. *Continuous remesh* [Palfinger 22] is a method that optimizes and remeshes simultaneously. It proposes a coarse-to-fine optimization method that constantly adaptively meshes the sur-

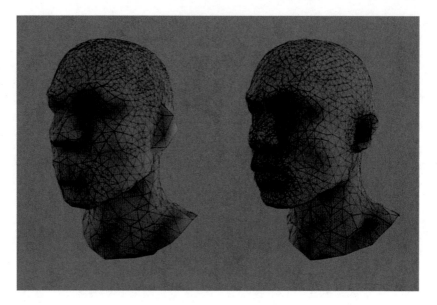

Figure 19.16. Distribute more triangles to detail-rich areas: original continuous remesh result (left) and the addition of area control through vertex color, distributing more triangles in the areas of interest (right).

face, avoiding problems such as triangle inversion and self-intersection. Compared with other methods, this method can generate more refined meshes faster, with fewer defects and parameter adjustments, and reconstruct more complex mesh objects.

This method considers the model's spatial consistency and upgrades Adam optimization to isotropic Adam optimization, simplifying calculations and slowing the update rate when nearing the target plane. This method modifies update rules and redefines α to avoid excessive triangle flipping to obtain a scale-invariant learning rate. Continuous remesh also introduces an edge length controller to manage the subdivision of triangles.

Based on continuous remesh, we added region control using the vertex colors of the original model. We "bake" the vertex colors onto the mesh during the iteration process, and these vertex colors adjust the subdivision coefficients. Figure 19.16 demonstrates that this method effectively allocates more triangles to detail-rich areas. Contrary to the original mesh splitting that led to uneven density distribution (high vertex density at the top of the head, as in the left of Figure 19.16), our area-controlled splitting technique allows for focused distribution to detail-needed locations like facial features (more vertices on facial features, as in the right of Figure 19.16).

19.7   Processing of Global Parameters

Using a differentiable rendering approach, we can also fit global parameters across rendering systems. However, fitting such parameters is more independent, possibly not requiring rasterization-related operations, and can be performed using exported G-buffers.

Atmospheric scattering is a good example. The effect of atmospheric scattering can generally be considered the sky's color superimposed by the aerial/atmospheric perspective.

Among them, sky color is relatively easy to achieve. However, calculating aerial perspective is relatively slow and challenging to implement on mobile devices. Some games use non-physically accurate algorithms, while most simply forgo the aerial perspective effect for performance reasons. The mainstream solutions for atmospheric scattering are as follows:

- **Non-physically accurate algorithms:** Use simplified algorithms [Hoffman and Preetham 03], which are easier to implement but difficult to determine the parameters for a specified effect.

- **Precomputation:** Exhaust all possible scenarios and precompute possible colors, but the sampling logic is complex and time-consuming.

- **Physically based and scalable methods** Render sky color and aerial perspective separately to low-resolution render targets using a simplified multiple scattering algorithm, and then sample the render targets during sky sphere rendering and scene object rendering to get the effect. Aerial perspective is rendered to a 3D volume texture and sampled using vertex texture fetch (VTF); however, sampling 3D volume textures using VTF is time-consuming on mobile tile-based deferred rendering (TBDR) GPUs [Hillaire 20].

We use differentiable rendering to find parameters on non-physically accurate algorithms to approximate the visual appearance of physically accurate algorithms.

First, this method uses the physically accurate algorithm as a benchmark, and the calculation formula is

$$L^{(\lambda)}(x) = L_0^{(\lambda)} e^{-\int_0^x \beta_{cx}^{(\lambda)}(x')dx'}$$
$$+ \int_0^x \left(e^{-\int_{x'}^x \beta_{cx}^\lambda(x'')dx''} \int_\Omega L_i^{(\lambda)}(\theta'\phi)\beta_{cx}^{(\lambda)}(\theta)d\omega \right) dx'.$$

Next, we fit the parameters corresponding to the physically accurate effects in the previous text within a non-physically accurate simplified algorithm. Based on the scheme proposed by [Hoffman and Preetham 03], the simplified calculation formula we used is

$$L_{\text{in}}(s, \theta) = \frac{\beta_R(\theta) + \beta_M(\theta)}{\beta_R + \beta_M} E_{\text{sun}},$$

Fitting process

Figure 19.17. Practice of fitting global atmospheric scattering parameters.

which can fit the most apparent features of atmospheric scattering. Our method's primary aim is to obtain atmospheric color parameters, such as the red of sunrise/sunset and the blue of daytime atmosphere, and to provide a complete set of color parameters for systems like exponential height fog.

This method simplifies the fitting process by removing the exponential term from the original scheme. This can be approximately interpreted as eliminating the calculation of atmospheric transparency during the fitting process.

This method uses the effects of the physically based and scalable methods in the aforementioned mainstream schemes as its target. It fits the corresponding effect parameters under the non-physically accurate algorithm through differentiable rendering and uses the non-physically accurate simplified algorithm and corresponding parameters at runtime to achieve a similar effect. Figure 19.17 shows the training process and fitting effect in the current framework. The final parameter values obtained through fitting are

$$\beta_R = [-0.1394, 0.8931, 1.5011], \quad \beta_M = [1.5033, 1.1154, -0.4261],$$
$$E_{\text{sun}} = [2.2874, 1.5177, 1.3635].$$

To compare the fitting results applied to the game engine, we have cropped the middle area of the screenshot showing atmospheric scattering for a unified comparison (see Figure 19.18). This method is close to the effect of PC atmospheric scattering and achieves a good balance between performance and realism on mobile devices.

19.8 Workflow Integration

Differentiable rendering can be performed through Jupyter notebooks, local projects, standalone applications, server-side computation, integrated plugins

Figure 19.18. LOD of global atmospheric scattering effects: target effect (top), fitted effect on mobile device (middle), and no effect (bottom).

in the game engine, and so on. We borrow the Houdini PCG pipeline's deployment, which lets us complete calculations on a remote server and then transfer them back for local use.

We divide this pipeline into two parts (as in Figure 19.19): a local plugin and a cloud service. We have deployed all the calculations outside of the engine on the cloud for several reasons:

- **Standardized computing environment:** This resolves inconsistent issues in the user environment.

- **Local lightweight deployment:** Our users do not need to install these DCCs and libraries.

- **Improved computational efficiency:** The cloud server we applied for has far superior specifications compared to our office computers, resulting in much higher computational efficiency.

We deploy the pipeline tool and computing capabilities on the server. The pipeline can hot-update tools within the engine, pull the latest tools from the server, and generate tool panels. It can perform computation-heavy tasks on the cloud server, such as differentiable rendering–based asset optimization, and complete asset setups automatically within the engine, eliminating the need for manual export and import operations.

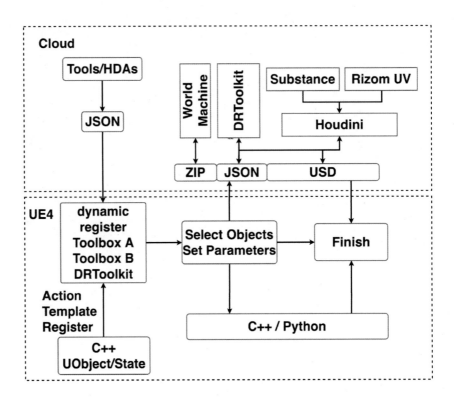

Figure 19.19. DRToolkit integrated in PCG pipeline Falcon.

19.9   Conclusion and Future Work

We apply differentiable rendering technology to optimize game assets and have achieved specific effects in various aspects.

We have modified and restructured the differentiable renderer to better suit game resource usage habits. We have also experimented with a combination of rasterization and ray tracing modes. In the next step, we will expand on ray tracing and global illumination, and explore more efficient automatic differentiation methods, such as adapting with SLANG.D.

For the project's complex materials and texture assets, we have created a "translation" framework for differentiable rendering material assets. The framework can handle complex assets in the existing Unreal Engine, separate materials by layer, and fit them layer by layer to achieve complex blending effects. We will conduct further experiments on more complex shading models and material systems, such as adapting to Unreal Engine's Substrate material system.

For the scene's mesh assets, we have adopted the existing LOD generation and usage rules of the Unreal Engine. We then apply differentiable rendering to generate and correct the mesh's LOD resources. Since LOD application scenarios are all specific, it is difficult to cover all scenarios with one algorithm. We plan to cover more LOD application scenarios in the future according to the project's needs, incorporating various methods.

For global effects, we have applied differentiable rendering to mimic atmospheric scattering effects. In the future, we will conduct experiments on volumetric fog, complex post-processing contents, and light parameters.

Acknowledgements

We would like to thank all DRToolkit team members and Falcon team members. In particular, we are grateful to the developers of prior technologies (such as SoftRas, nvdiffrast, nvdiffrec, nvdiffrecmc, etc.), whose contributions have laid a crucial foundation for our work. We also thank Kirill Bazhenov, the editor of this section, for smooth cooperation and, of course, Wolfgang Engel, the editor of the entire book, for his editorial work starting with the early ShaderX books up to this one.

Bibliography

[Bangaru et al. 20] Sai Bangaru, Tzu-Mao Li, and Frédo Durand. "Unbiased Warped-Area Sampling for Differentiable Rendering." *ACM Transactions on Graphics* 39:6 (2020), 245:1–245:18.

[Bangaru et al. 23] Sai Bangaru, Lifan Wu, Tzu-Mao Li, Jacob Munkberg, Gilbert Bernstein, Jonathan Ragan-Kelley, Fredo Durand, Aaron Lefohn, and Yong He. "SLANG.D: Fast, Modular and Differentiable Shader Programming." *ACM Transactions on Graphics (SIGGRAPH Asia)* 42:6 (2023), 1–28.

[Deng et al. 22] Qixin Deng, Binh H. Le, Aobo Jin, and Zhigang Deng. "End-to-End 3D Face Reconstruction with Expressions and Specular Albedos from Single In-the-Wild Images." In *MM '22: Proceedings of the 30th ACM International Conference on Multimedia*, p. 4694–4703. Association for Computing Machinery, 2022. https://doi.org/10.1145/3503161.3547800.

[Dreamanlan 24a] Dreamanlan. "DirectX Shader Compiler." GitHub, 2024. https://github.com/dreamanlan/DirectXShaderCompiler.

[Dreamanlan 24b] Dreamanlan. "Hlsl2Python." GitHub, 2024. https://github.com/dreamanlan/Hlsl2Python.

[Dreamanlan 24c] Dreamanlan. "MetaDSL." GitHub, 2024. https://github.com/dreamanlan/MetaDSL.

[Foley 24] Theresa Foley. "Toward a Next-Gen Vulkan Shading Language: Perspectives from Our Journey with Slang." Presented at Vulkanised Conference, 2024. https://vulkan.org/user/pages/09.events/vulkanised-2024/vulkanised-2024-thereas-foley-nvidia.pdf.

[Gallardo 21] David Gallardo. "Green Field Diorama." Shadertoy, 2021. https://www.shadertoy.com/view/7dSGW1.

[Hasselgren et al. 21] Jon Hasselgren, Jacob Munkberg, Jaakko Lehtinen, Miika Aittala, and Samuli Laine. "Appearance-Driven Automatic 3D Model Simplification." In *32nd Eurographics Symposium on Rendering*, pp. 85–97. Eurographics Association, 2021.

[Hasselgren et al. 22] Jon Hasselgren, Nikolai Hofmann, and Jacob Munkberg. "Shape, Light, and Material Decomposition from Images using Monte Carlo Rendering and Denoising." Preprint, arXiv:2206.03380, 2022. https://arxiv.org/abs/2206.03380.

[He et al. 24] Yong He, Bartlomiej Wronski, Sai Bangaru, Marco Salvi, Yong He, Lifan Wu, and Jacob Munkberg. "Differentiable Graphics with Slang.D for Appearance-Based Optimization." In *GPU Zen 3*, edited by Wolfgang Engel, Chapter 18. Black Cat Publishing, 2024.

[Hillaire 20] Sébastien Hillaire. "A Scalable and Production Ready Sky and Atmosphere Rendering Technique." *Computer Graphics Forum* 39:4 (2020), 13–22. https://onlinelibrary.wiley.com/doi/abs/10.1111/cgf.14050.

[Hoffman and Preetham 03] Naty Hoffman and Arcot J. Preetham. "Real-Time Light-Atmosphere Interactions for Outdoor Scenes." In *Graphics Programming Methods*, edited by Jeff Lander, p. 337–352. Charles River Media, 2003.

[Jakob et al. 22] Wenzel Jakob, Sébastien Speierer, Nicolas Roussel, and Delio Vicini. "Dr.Jit: A Just-In-Time Compiler for Differentiable Rendering." *Transactions on Graphics (Proceedings of SIGGRAPH)* 41:4.

[Karlsson 24] Baldur Karlsson. "RenderDoc Releases Version v1.32." GitHub, 2024. https://github.com/baldurk/renderdoc/releases/tag/v1.32.

[Kato et al. 18] Hiroharu Kato, Yoshitaka Ushiku, and Tatsuya Harada. "Neural 3D Mesh Renderer." In *2018 IEEE/CVF Conference on Computer Vision and Pattern Recognition*, pp. 3907–3916. IEEE, 2018.

[Laine et al. 20] Samuli Laine, Janne Hellsten, Tero Karras, Yeongho Seol, Jaakko Lehtinen, and Timo Aila. "Modular Primitives for High-Performance Differentiable Rendering." *ACM Transactions on Graphics* 39:6 (2020), 194:1–194:14.

[Li et al. 18] Tzu-Mao Li, Miika Aittala, Frédo Durand, and Jaakko Lehtinen. "Differentiable Monte Carlo Ray Tracing through Edge Sampling." *ACM Transactions on Graphics (Proceedings of SIGGRAPH Asia)* 37:6 (2018), 222:1–222:11.

[Ling and Zhang 23] Fei Ling and Frei Zhang. "Differentiable Rendering for Scalable Asset Pipeline in 'Honor of Kings'." Presented at Machine Learning Summit, Game Developers Conference, 2023. https://gdcvault.com/play/1028758/Machine-Learning-Summit-Differentiable-Rendering.

[Liu et al. 19] Shichen Liu, Tianye Li, Weikai Chen, and Hao Li. "Soft Rasterizer: A Differentiable Renderer for Image-based 3D Reasoning." In *2019 IEEE/CVF International Conference on Computer Vision (ICCV)*, pp. 7707–7716. IEEE, 2019.

[Loubet et al. 19] Guillaume Loubet, Nicolas Holzschuch, and Wenzel Jakob. "Reparameterizing Discontinuous Integrands for Differentiable Rendering." *ACM Transactions on Graphics (Proceedings of SIGGRAPH Asia)* 38:6 (2019), 228:1–228:14.

[Munkberg et al. 22] Jacob Munkberg, Jon Hasselgren, Tianchang Shen, Jun Gao, Wenzheng Chen, Alex Evans, Thomas Müller, and Sanja Fidler. "Extracting Triangular 3D Models, Materials, and Lighting from Images." In *2022 IEEE/CVF Conference on Computer Vision and Pattern Recognition (CVPR)*, pp. 8280–8290. IEEE, 2022.

[Neyret 14] Fabrice Neyret. "Textured Ellipsoids." Shadertoy, 2014. https://www.shadertoy.com/view/XsfXW8.

[Palfinger 22] Werner Palfinger. "Continuous Remeshing for Inverse Rendering." *Computer Animation and Virtual Worlds* 33:5 (2022), e2101. https://onlinelibrary.wiley.com/doi/abs/10.1002/cav.2101.

[Quilez and Jeremias 24] Inigo Quilez and Pol Jeremias. "Shadertoy." Homepage, 2024. https://www.shadertoy.com/.

[Quilez 13] Inigo Quilez. "Raymarching—Primitives." Shadertoy, 2013. https://www.shadertoy.com/view/Xds3zN.

[Shi et al. 20] Tianyang Shi, Zhengxia Zou, Xinhui Song, Zheng Song, Changjian Gu, Changjie Fan, and Yi Yuan. "Neutral Face Game Character Auto-Creation via PokerFace-GAN." In *MM '20: Proceedings of the 28th ACM International Conference on Multimedia*, pp. 3201–3209. Association for Computing Machinery, 2020. https://doi.org/10.1145/3394171.3413806.

[Takimoto et al. 22] Yusuke Takimoto, Hiroyuki Sato, Hikari Takehara, Keishiro Uragaki, Takehiro Tawara, Xiao Liang, Kentaro Oku, Wataru Kishimoto, and Bo Zheng. "Dressi: A Hardware-Agnostic Differentiable Renderer with Reactive Shader Packing and Soft Rasterization." Preprint, arXiv:2204.01386, 2022. https://arxiv.org/abs/2204.01386.

[TLC123 19] TLC123. "Procedural Walk Animation." Shadertoy, 2019. https://www.shadertoy.com/view/WlsSWS.

[Zhang et al. 20] Cheng Zhang, Bailey Miller, Kai Yan, Ioannis Gkioulekas, and Shuang Zhao. "Path-Space Differentiable Rendering." *ACM Transactions on Graphics* 39:4 (2020), 143:1–143:19.

Flowmap Baking
with LBM-SWE

Wei Li, Haozhe Su, Zherong Pan, Xifeng Gao, Zhenyu Mao, and Kui Wu

20.1   Introduction

The real-time simulation of water dynamics holds paramount importance across various industries, particularly in gaming and virtual reality applications. The integration of realistic water rendering significantly enhances user experiences, fostering immersive and visually captivating virtual landscapes. The ability to achieve dynamic and responsive water surfaces encompassing oceans, rivers, and lakes contributes to the creation of a more authentic and engaging virtual environment. While numerous research directions, including position-based fluids (PBF) [Macklin and Müller 13], smoothed particle hydrodynamics (SPH) [Koschier et al. 22], and shallow water equations (SWE) [Su et al. 23, Chentanez and Müller 10], have advanced the field of real-time water simulation, these methods encounter challenges when addressing large-scale simulation domains with the demand for high-fidelity outcomes.

An alternative approach employed in the gaming industry involves precomputing a 2D velocity field texture, known as a *flowmap*. This flowmap is utilized to animate water movement by displacing the water surface texture in UV space. Further details on flowmaps can be found in [Vlachos 10]. Leveraging a flowmap enables game developers to achieve realistic and dynamic water movement while significantly reducing computational costs during gameplay. Unfortunately, the current flowmap creation pipeline heavily relies on manual craftsmanship by artists, leading to time-consuming processes. Although conventional 2D Navier—Stokes simulation methods can generate flowmaps, these approaches typically neglect underwater terrain considerations, thereby impacting the fidelity of simulation results. The lattice Boltzmann model for shallow water equations (LBM-SWE) [Zhou 02] presents an approach for simulating large bodies of water, including oceans, seas, and large lakes, under the shallow water assumption. This model has been employed [Grenier 18] to compute flowmaps, benefiting from its high computational efficiency and effective handling of underwater terrain. However, a significant drawback emerges in its susceptibility to instability issues when simulating turbulent cases. These challenges frequently lead to failures in generating accurate flowmaps, particularly in complex scenarios.

In the following sections, we present an enhanced LBM-SWE formulation incorporating a new force model to bolster stability and robustness in turbulent flow, particularly at high Reynolds numbers. Our approach yields an accurate and stable LBM solver capable of addressing both laminar and turbulent flow problems. Experimental results demonstrate the efficacy of our model, showcasing its ability to produce accurate simulations. Additionally, our model supports a wide range of Reynolds numbers in complex geometries, further substantiating its versatility and applicability.

20.2   Related Work

The shallow water equations are employed to simulate the behavior of water in environments where the water depth is significantly smaller than the horizontal dimensions, particularly in large-scale scenarios, such as oceans, seas, or large lakes. Derived from the full Navier–Stokes equations for fluid dynamics, SWE makes specific assumptions that enable more computationally efficient simulations. This approach has found widespread use in diverse applications, including ocean engineering [Salmon 99], hydraulic engineering [Valiani et al. 02], and coastal engineering [Tubbs and Tsai 19]. Traditional methods for solving SWE include the finite difference method [Su et al. 23, Chentanez and Müller 10], finite volume method [Brodtkorb et al. 12], and finite element method [Ricchiuto and Bollermann 09]. However, these conventional techniques introduce notable numerical dispersion, resulting in pronounced viscosity in the output results. They often encounter difficulties in accurately simulating bed slope and friction forces due to inherent numerical errors [García-Navarro et al. 19]. Moreover, these methods face challenges in handling complex geometries and are computationally expensive.

The lattice Boltzmann method (LBM) [Chen and Doolen 98] is a mesoscopic method based on statistical theory and has gained prominence as an effective alternative for simulating turbulent, incompressible flow, grounded in the Boltzmann equation and kinetic theory. A key advantage of LBM lies in its utilization of local streaming and collision operators, endowing it with high parallelizability [Li et al. 20, Lyu et al. 21, Li et al. 21, Li et al. 22, Li and Desbrun 23, Li et al. 23]. The Bhatnagar–Gross–Krook lattice Boltzmann method (BGK-LBM) has been extensively applied to solve shallow water equations with appropriate equilibrium distribution functions [Zhou 02]. In the pursuit of enhanced accuracy and stability, multiple-relaxation time (MRT) collision models have been proposed in various works [García-Navarro et al. 19]. Among these MRT methods, the non-orthogonal central-moment (NO-CMR) based lattice Boltzmann scheme has demonstrated superior performance [De Rosis 17].

The lattice Boltzmann model for shallow water equations, as introduced in [Zhou 02], offers an effective approach for simulating large bodies of water due to its computational efficiency, derived from the LBM scheme. However, a limitation arises from its reliance on the BGK collision model, which, due to its first-order nature, is constrained in handling low Reynolds numbers. To address this limitation, the non-orthogonal central moment (NO-CMR) was introduced into LBM-SWE [De Rosis 17]. This method transforms the distribution function into a central-moment space, where each component relaxes toward its equilibrium with an individual rate before being converted back. Despite this improvement, the force term in [De Rosis 17] still employs the low-order expression from [Zhou 02], which may not be accurate enough for turbulent flows. In our new LBM-SWE solver, we propose a high-order forcing model in moment space and a second-order weighted estimation for force calculation to obtain accurate force evaluation. To obtain stable boundary treatment in complex geometries, we also propose a hybrid bounce-back method for turbulent flowmaps.

20.3 Background

In this section, we first review the shallow water equations and then their corresponding lattice Boltzmann model.

20.3.1 Shallow Water Equations

The 2D shallow water equations are derived according to the continuity and momentum conservation, which can be written in a tensor form as

$$\frac{\partial h}{\partial t} + \frac{\partial h\mathbf{u}}{\partial \mathbf{x}} = 0, \tag{20.1}$$

$$\frac{\partial h\mathbf{u}}{\partial t} + \nabla \cdot (h\mathbf{u}\mathbf{u}) = -\frac{g}{2}\nabla^2 h + \nu\nabla \cdot \left(h\left(\nabla\mathbf{u} + (\nabla\mathbf{u})^T\right)\right) + F, \tag{20.2}$$

where $\mathbf{x}$ is the the Cartesian coordinate, h is the water height, $\mathbf{u}$ is the depth-averaged velocity component, $g = 9.81$ m/s^2 is the gravitational acceleration, ν is the kinematic viscosity, and F is the external force term. In particular, the external force term is defined as the sum of the hydrostatic pressure and bed shear stress:

$$\mathbf{F} = -gh\nabla z - \frac{\boldsymbol{\tau}_b}{\rho}, \tag{20.3}$$

where z is terrain height and $\boldsymbol{\tau}_b$ is the bed shear stress.

20.3.2 BGK-LBM for Shallow Water Equations

With the BGK approximation, Zhou [Zhou 02] first formulated SWE into the following lattice Boltzmann equation:

$$f_i(\mathbf{x} + \Delta t\mathbf{c}_i, t + \Delta t) - f_i(\mathbf{x}, t) = \frac{1}{\tau}\left[f_i^{\text{eq}}(\mathbf{x}, t) - f_i(\mathbf{x}, t)\right] + \Delta t\mathcal{F}_i(\mathbf{x}, t), \tag{20.4}$$

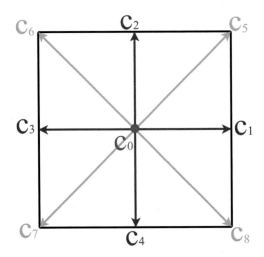

Figure 20.1. Two-dimensional nine-speed (D2Q9) lattice structure.

where $\mathcal{F}_i(\mathbf{x}, t)$ is the force term, f_i and f_i^{eq} are the current distribution function and local equilibrium distribution function along ith direction on the nine-speed square lattice, as shown in Figure 20.1. The lattice velocity vector $\mathbf{c}_i$ is defined as

$$\mathbf{c}_i = \begin{cases} [0,0], & i = 0; \\ [1,0], [0,1], [-1,0], [0,-1], & i = 1, 2, 3, 4; \\ [1,1], [-1,1], [-1,-1], [1,-1], & i = 5, 6, 7, 8. \end{cases} \tag{20.5}$$

The relaxation factor τ is based on the fluid kinematic viscosity ν as $\tau = 3\nu + 0.5$, and the time step $\Delta t = 1$ is the convention as LBM space is dimensionless space.

Equation (20.4) can be solved using the splitting method with two steps:

Step 1: Streaming First, note that

$$f_i^*(\mathbf{x} + \Delta t \mathbf{c}_i, t + \Delta t) = f_i(\mathbf{x}, t). \tag{20.6}$$

Then, the macroscopic variables h and $\mathbf{u}$ can be updated as

$$h = \sum_{i=0}^{8} f_i, \tag{20.7}$$

$$\mathbf{u}^* = \sum_{i=0}^{8} \frac{f_i^* \mathbf{c}_i}{h}. \tag{20.8}$$

Step 2: Collision For the second step,

$$f_i(\mathbf{x}, t) = f_i^*(\mathbf{x}, t) + \frac{1}{\tau} \left[f_i^{eq}(\mathbf{x}, t) - f_i^*(\mathbf{x}, t) \right] + \Delta t \mathcal{F}_i(\mathbf{x}, t), \qquad (20.9)$$

where the local equilibrium distribution function f_i^{eq} is defined as

$$f_i^{eq} = \begin{cases} h - \frac{5gh^2}{6} - \frac{2h}{3}\mathbf{u} \cdot \mathbf{u}, & i = 0; \\ \frac{gh^2}{6} + \frac{h}{3}\mathbf{c}_i \cdot \mathbf{u} + \frac{h^2}{2}(\mathbf{c}_i \cdot \mathbf{u})^2 - \frac{h}{6}\mathbf{c}_i \cdot \mathbf{u}, & i = 1, 2, 3, 4; \\ \frac{gh^2}{24} + \frac{h}{12}\mathbf{c}_i \cdot \mathbf{u} + \frac{h^2}{8}(\mathbf{c}_i \cdot \mathbf{u})^2 - \frac{h}{24}\mathbf{c}_i \cdot \mathbf{u}, & i = 5, 6, 7, 8. \end{cases} \qquad (20.10)$$

The force term $\mathcal{F}_i(\mathbf{x}, t)$ can be computed by accounting for the external force $\mathbf{F} = (F_x, F_y)$:

$$\mathcal{F}_i(\mathbf{x}, t) = \frac{1}{6}\mathbf{c}_i \cdot \mathbf{F}(\mathbf{x}, t), \qquad (20.11)$$

where the external force $\mathbf{F} = [F_x, F_y]$ is defined in Equation (20.3).

20.4 Our Method

In this section, we first review the central-moment MRT model for LBM, then introduce our high-order forcing formula, followed by our hybrid bounce-back method for stable boundary treatment.

20.4.1 NO-CMR LBM-SWE

The central-moment MRT model was first introduced to significantly improve LBM accuracy [De Rosis 17]. In 2D, this model uses non-orthogonal central moments $\mathbf{m}$ derived from distribution functions $\mathbf{f} = [f_0, ..., f_8]$ via a linear transform $\mathbf{m} = \mathbf{M}\mathbf{f}$, where $\mathbf{M}$ is a matrix known in closed form as a function of the macroscopic velocity $\mathbf{u}$. In particular, $\mathbf{M} = [m_0, ..., m_8]^T$ is a 9×9 moment-space projection matrix in which each row is defined as

$$m_0 = [1, 1, 1, 1, 1, 1, 1, 1, 1], \qquad (20.12)$$

$$m_1 = [\bar{\mathbf{c}}_{0,x}, ..., \bar{\mathbf{c}}_{8,x}], \qquad (20.13)$$

$$m_2 = [\bar{\mathbf{c}}_{0,y}, ..., \bar{\mathbf{c}}_{8,y}], \qquad (20.14)$$

$$m_3 = [\bar{\mathbf{c}}_{0,x}^2 + \bar{\mathbf{c}}_{0,y}^2, ..., \bar{\mathbf{c}}_{8,x}^2 + \bar{\mathbf{c}}_{8,y}^2], \qquad (20.15)$$

$$m_4 = [\bar{\mathbf{c}}_{0,x}^2 - \bar{\mathbf{c}}_{0,y}^2, ..., \bar{\mathbf{c}}_{8,x}^2 - \bar{\mathbf{c}}_{8,y}^2], \qquad (20.16)$$

$$m_5 = [\bar{\mathbf{c}}_{0,x}\bar{\mathbf{c}}_{0,y}, ..., \bar{\mathbf{c}}_{8,x}\bar{\mathbf{c}}_{8,y}], \qquad (20.17)$$

$$m_6 = [\bar{\mathbf{c}}_{0,x}^2\bar{\mathbf{c}}_{0,y}, ..., \bar{\mathbf{c}}_{8,x}^2\bar{\mathbf{c}}_{8,y}], \qquad (20.18)$$

$$m_7 = [\bar{\mathbf{c}}_{0,x}\bar{\mathbf{c}}_{0,y}^2, ..., \bar{\mathbf{c}}_{8,x}\bar{\mathbf{c}}_{8,y}^2], \qquad (20.19)$$

$$m_8 = [\bar{\mathbf{c}}_{0,x}^2\bar{\mathbf{c}}_{0,y}^2, ..., \bar{\mathbf{c}}_{8,x}^2\bar{\mathbf{c}}_{8,y}^2], \qquad (20.20)$$

where $\bar{\mathbf{c}}_i = [\bar{c}_{i,x}, \bar{c}_{i,y}]$ is the shifted lattice velocities by the local fluid velocity $\mathbf{u}^*$, with $\bar{c}_{i,x} = c_{i,x} - \mathbf{u}_x^*$ and $\bar{c}_{i,y} = c_{i,y} - \mathbf{u}_y^*$. Row m_0 is simply the zeroth-order moment (equal to density), m_1 and m_2 are the components of the vector representing the first-order moment, $m_3, \ldots, m_5$ are the components of the symmetric second-order moment, and the others are high-order moments.

Then, Equation (20.4) can be rewritten in the moment format as

$$\mathbf{f}^{t+1} - \mathbf{f}^t = \mathbf{M}^{-1}\big(\mathbf{R}(\mathbf{m}^{\mathrm{eq}} - \mathbf{m}) - \mathbf{M}\mathcal{F}\big), \tag{20.21}$$

where $\mathbf{R} = \mathrm{diag}\{r_0, ..., r_1\}$ is the diagonal matrix containing the relaxation rates $r_i = \frac{1}{\tau}$ for $i = 4, 5$ and otherwise set to 1 [De Rosis 17].

20.4.2 High-Order Forcing for NO-CMR

We can divide the force terms into two parts according to the trapezoidal rule or Crank–Nicolson discretization. First, add one-half force into macro velocity after the streaming step:

$$h\mathbf{u}^* = \sum_i f_i^* c_i + \frac{\mathbf{F}}{2} = h\mathbf{u}^t + \frac{\mathbf{F}}{2}. \tag{20.22}$$

Then, the NO-CMR collision model from Equation (20.21) becomes

$$\mathbf{f}^{t+1} = \mathbf{f}^t - \mathbf{M}^{-1}\big(\mathbf{R}(\mathbf{m} - \mathbf{m}^{\mathrm{eq}}) + (\mathbf{I} - \tfrac{1}{2}\mathbf{R})\mathbf{K}\big), \tag{20.23}$$

where $\mathbf{K}$ represents the force terms projected into central-moment space,

$$\mathbf{K} = \left[0, F_x, F_y, 0, 0, 0, \frac{1}{3}F_y, \frac{1}{3}F_x, 0\right]^T. \tag{20.24}$$

It is easy to verify the forcing model's accuracy by taking the first-order moment of Equation (20.23) as

$$\mathbf{u}^{t+1} = \frac{\sum_i f_i^* c_i}{h} + \frac{\mathbf{F}}{2h} = \mathbf{u}^* + \frac{\mathbf{F}}{2h} = \mathbf{u}^t + \frac{\mathbf{F}}{h}. \tag{20.25}$$

For $\mathbf{R}$, we introduce the high-order relaxation times $\nu_6 = \nu_7 = 0.1$ and $\nu_8 = 0.1$ for corresponding to relaxation rate $r_i = 1/(3 * \nu_i + 0.5)$ for a lower dissipation error [Li et al. 20].

Instead of approximating the first term ∇z in Equation (20.3) by the central difference method [Zhou 02], We use the second-order weighted estimation used in [Li et al. 21]:

$$\nabla z(\mathbf{x}) = \sum_i w_i \mathbf{c}_i z(\mathbf{x} + \mathbf{c}_i). \tag{20.26}$$

It is a rotationally symmetric gradient approximation, which is more accurate and stable than the traditional central difference method.

20.4.3 Hybrid Bounce-Back

Zhou [Zhou 02] proposed the bounced-back method for the boundary treatment, as illustrated in Figure 20.2 (left), which can be written as

$$\mathbf{f}_i(\mathbf{x}, t+1) = \mathbf{f}_{i'}(\mathbf{x}, t). \tag{20.27}$$

It means that the function $\mathbf{f}_{i'}$ at node $\mathbf{x}$ along the i' direction that collides with the solid boundary will bounce back to the ith direction to update $\mathbf{f}_i(\mathbf{x}, t+1)$. Unfortunately, it is too unstable to handle complex terrain geometries as it brings high-frequency ghost modes into low-order velocity moments, which ruins the simulation.

Motivated by the single-node boundary treatment [Li et al. 22, Filippova and Hänel 98], we proposed the stable hybrid bounce-back method in the LBM-SWE framework. In particular, the incoming distribution function coming from the boundary toward a fluid node along a boundary-crossing link l (dotted blue line in Figure 20.2, left) can be partially approximated by the equilibrium distribution function of a point at the intersection of the link and the boundary. In the context of shallow water fluid simulation with static obstacles, we impose the zero-velocity boundary condition (see Figure 20.2, right) on the obstacle to evaluate the local values of $\mathbf{f}^{\mathrm{eq}}(\mathbf{x})$ and blend the bounce-back distribution $\mathbf{f}_{i'}(\mathbf{x})$ and the equilibrium $\mathbf{f}_{i'}^{\mathrm{eq}}(\mathbf{x})$ on the fluid node $\mathbf{x}$ near the solid:

$$\mathbf{f}_i(\mathbf{x}, t+1) = (1 - \alpha)\mathbf{f}_{i'}(\mathbf{x}, t) + \alpha\mathbf{f}_{i'}^{\mathrm{eq}}(\mathbf{x}, t), \tag{20.28}$$

where we set $\alpha = 0.1$ in practice. By adding the equilibrium function, we can filter out non-physical oscillations in the distribution function $\mathbf{f}_i$ after boundary treatment, which shows better stability in turbulent flow simulations.

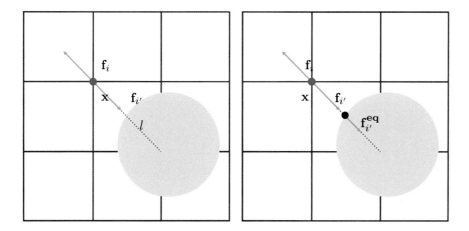

Figure 20.2. Boundary treatment: bounce-back method used in [Zhou 02] (left), and our hybrid bounce-back method (right).

20.4.4   Inlet/Outlet Boundary Conditions

We use the Dirichlet boundary condition for macroscopic variables, the water height h and the velocity $\mathbf{u}$. Based on the assumption that the distribution function $\mathbf{f}$ deviates only slightly from the equilibrium state $\mathbf{f}^{eq}$, we use $\mathbf{f}^{eq}$ to approximate $\mathbf{f}$ based on Equation (20.10).

20.4.5   Implementation Details

We implemented our approach in CUDA, using a structure-of-arrays (SOA) data structure [Chen et al. 22], storing 24 variables per grid node, in which nine variables store the distribution functions $\mathbf{f}$, with two copies to facilitate the time update, two variables for velocity, two variables for force terms, one variable for z, and one variable for h. Listing 20.1 provides the pseudocode of one iteration of our LBM-SWE update scheme. For specific implementations, please refer to the *GPU Zen 3* source code distribution, which contains an example application.

```
for each node at x
{
    for each direction i
    {
        if (Node x − cᵢ is not water or h(x − cᵢ) < z(x − cᵢ))
        {
            Hybrid bounce-back              // Section 20.4.3
        }
        else
        {
            Streaming                       // Equation (20.6)
        }
    }
    Evaluate h and u*                       // Equation (20.7)
    Calculate force terms                   // Section 20.4.2
    Update u                                // Equation (20.22)
    Collision                               // Equation (20.23)
    Boundary treatment                      // Section 20.4.4
}
```

Listing 20.1. Pseudocode of our LBM-SWE solver.

20.5   Results

In this section, we test our LBM-SWE solver on one benchmark case for verification and two examples with complex terrains to showcase the effectiveness of our method.

20.5.1   Circular Dam Break

We test our method in a circular dam break scene (proposed in [Peng et al. 16]) with a square periodic domain with length $L = 40$ m. In the center of this domain is a cylindrical water column with the following initial settings:

$$\mathbf{u}(\mathbf{x},0) = 0; \tag{20.29}$$

$$h(\mathbf{x},0) = \begin{cases} 2.5, & (\mathbf{x} - \mathbf{x}_c)^2 \le R^2; \\ 0.5, & (\mathbf{x} - \mathbf{x}_c)^2 > R^2; \end{cases} \tag{20.30}$$

where $\mathbf{x}_c = [\frac{L}{2}, \frac{L}{2}]$ and the radius $R = 2.5$ m.

We use 100×100 grid nodes to discretize the domain with world-space $dt = 0.05$ s for each time step. Figure 20.3 visualizes the height profile at $t = 3.5$ s at the cross-section of $\mathbf{x} = x_c$, where circles indicate our result and dots the reference data from [Peng et al. 16]. The graph shows that our method demonstrates the same accuracy and robustness as the raw moment-based collision model does, but our central-moment model also has the ability to handle turbulent flow with complex terrain situations.

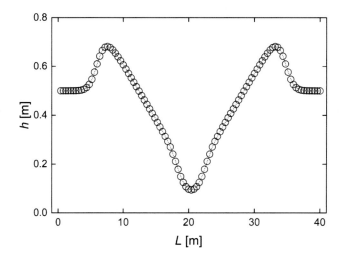

Figure 20.3. The height profile of a circular dam break generated by our solver (black circles) and reference data from [Peng et al. 16] (red dots).

20.5.2   Flow through a Canyon

To highlight our handling of complex geometries, we run our LBM-SWE in a canyon in which the terrain height h is normalized in a range of $[0.02, 8]$. The simulation resolution is 512×512. Figure 20.4 demonstrates the result of the velocity magnitude with different Reynolds numbers settings: Re $= 4000$, Re $= 80000$, and Re $= 800,000$. With a lower Reynolds number, the resulting flowmap demonstrates the smooth behavior of laminar flow with high viscous forces. In contrast, with a high Reynolds number, we can get a turbulent flow with eddies,

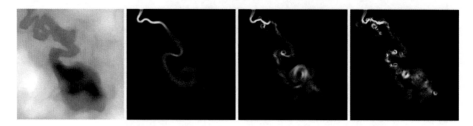

Figure 20.4. Given the height map of the terrain (left), the flowmaps are generated by our LBM-SWE with different Reynolds numbers: Re = 4000, Re = 80000, and Re = 800,000. The brighter the color, the larger the velocity magnitude.

vortices, and turbulent structures throughout the flow field, which highlights the advantage of our method over previous techniques.

We further evaluate the performance over three different resolutions, 256^2, 512^2, and 1024^2, on NVIDIA GeForce RTX 2070 Super (laptop GPU). We only need one frame of the velocity field as the flowmap to drive the water animation in real time. We run our LBM-SWE simulator for 18,000 steps to get a relatively stable velocity, the total times of which are 9 s, 27 s, and 126 s, respectively.

20.5.3   Flow in a River

We further test our solver by simulating the flow through a river. The simulation domain is discretized into a 502×502 grid, and the terrain height z is normalized to the range of $[0.01, 8]$. In this case, we set an inlet to the left of the river terrain and set a circle outlet at the end (Figure 20.5). In practice, we add the force term after 4000 steps to dampen the pressure wave from distribution functions in the initialization stage. Figure 20.6 demonstrates an example of foam and water displacement driven by the flowmap generated by our LBM-SWE solver.

Figure 20.5. Given the height map (left), flowmaps are generated by our LBM-SWE solver with a fixed inlet and a constant outlet boundary (the pale yellow circle). With different Reynolds numbers (Re = 400, Re = 6000, and Re = 60,000), our LBM-SWE solver can capture different vortex details as shown in flowmaps. The brighter the color, the larger the velocity magnitude.

Figure 20.6. The foam and water displacement driven by the flowmap generated by our LBM-SWE.

20.6 Conclusion

In this article, we proposed a new LBM-SWE solver with high-order force evaluation in moment space and symmetric gradient approximation for bed gradient, based on the central-moment collision model [De Rosis 17]. A new hybrid bounce-back was formulated to handle complex terrain for turbulent flow.

Leveraging the highly parallel nature of our solver, we achieved the efficient generation of all flowmaps, even at 2K × 2K resolution, within a matter of minutes. This practical and efficient computational performance renders our method well-suited for gaming applications.

Bibliography

[Brodtkorb et al. 12] André R. Brodtkorb, Martin L. Sætra, and Mustafa Altinakar. "Efficient Shallow Water Simulations on GPUs: Implementation, Visualization, Verification, and Validation." *Computers & Fluids* 55 (2012), 1–12.

[Chen and Doolen 98] Shiyi Chen and Gary D. Doolen. "Lattice Boltzmann Method for Fluid Flows." *Annual Review of Fluid Mechanics* 30:1 (1998), 329–364.

[Chen et al. 22] Yixin Chen, Wei Li, Rui Fan, and Xiaopei Liu. "GPU Optimization for High-Quality Kinetic Fluid Simulation." *IEEE Transactions on Visualization and Computer Graphics* 28:9 (2022), 3235–3251.

[Chentanez and Müller 10] Nuttapong Chentanez and Matthias Müller. "Real-Time Simulation of Large Bodies of Water with Small Scale Details." In *Proceedings of the 2010 ACM SIGGRAPH/Eurographics Symposium on Computer Animation*, p. 197–206. Eurographics Association, 2010.

[De Rosis 17] Alessandro De Rosis. "A Central Moments-Based Lattice Boltzmann Scheme for Shallow Water Equations." *Computer Methods in Applied Mechanics and Engineering* 319 (2017), 379–392.

[Filippova and Hänel 98] Olga Filippova and Dieter Hänel. "Grid Refinement for Lattice-BGK Models." *Journal of Computational Physics* 147:1 (1998), 219–228.

[García-Navarro et al. 19] Pilar García-Navarro, J Murillo, J Fernández-Pato, Isabel Echeverribar, and Mario Morales-Hernández. "The Shallow Water Equations and Their Application to Realistic Cases." *Environmental Fluid Mechanics* 19 (2019), 1235–1252.

[Grenier 18] Jean-Philippe Grenier. "River Editor: Water Simulation in Real-Time." Interview by Kirill Tokarev, 80 Level, October 24, 2018. https://80.lv/articles/river-editor-water-simulation-in-real-time/.

[Koschier et al. 22] Dan Koschier, Jan Bender, Barbara Solenthaler, and Matthias Teschner. "A Survey on SPH Methods in Computer Graphics." *Computer Graphics Forum* 41:2 (2022), 737–760.

[Li and Desbrun 23] Wei Li and Mathieu Desbrun. "Fluid-Solid Coupling in Kinetic Two-Phase Flow Simulation." *ACM Transactions on Graphics* 42:4 (2023), 123:1–123:14.

[Li et al. 20] Wei Li, Yixin Chen, Mathieu Desbrun, Changxi Zheng, and Xiaopei Liu. "Fast and Scalable Turbulent Flow Simulation with Two-Way Coupling." *ACM Transactions on Graphics* 39:4 (2020), 47:1–47:20.

[Li et al. 21] Wei Li, Daoming Liu, Mathieu Desbrun, Jin Huang, and Xiaopei Liu. "Kinetic-Based Multiphase Flow Simulation." *IEEE Transactions on Visualization and Computer Graphics* 27:7 (2021), 3318–3334.

[Li et al. 22] Wei Li, Yihui Ma, Xiaopei Liu, and Mathieu Desbrun. "Efficient Kinetic Simulation of Two-Phase Flows." *ACM Transactions on Graphics* 41:4 (2022), 114:1–114:17.

[Li et al. 23] Wei Li, Tongtong Wang, Zherong Pan, Xifeng Gao, Kui Wu, and Mathieu Desbrun. "High-Order Moment-Encoded Kinetic Simulation of Turbulent Flows." *ACM Transactions on Graphics* 42:6 (2023), 1–13.

[Lyu et al. 21] Chaoyang Lyu, Wei Li, Mathieu Desbrun, and Xiaopei Liu. "Fast and Versatile Fluid-Solid Coupling for Turbulent Flow Simulation." *ACM Transactions on Graphics* 40:6 (2021), 201:1–201:18.

[Macklin and Müller 13] Miles Macklin and Matthias Müller. "Position Based Fluids." *ACM Transactions on Graphics* 32:4 (2013), 104:1–104:12.

[Peng et al. 16] Y. Peng, J. M. Zhang, and J. G. Zhou. "Lattice Boltzmann Model Using Two Relaxation Times for Shallow-Water Equations." *Journal of Hydraulic Engineering* 142:2 (2016), 06015017.

[Ricchiuto and Bollermann 09] Mario Ricchiuto and Andreas Bollermann. "Stabilized Residual Distribution for Shallow Water Simulations." *Journal of Computational Physics* 228:4 (2009), 1071–1115.

[Salmon 99] Rick Salmon. "The Lattice Boltzmann Method as a Basis for Ocean Circulation Modeling." *Journal of Marine Research* 57:3 (1999), 503–535.

[Su et al. 23] Haozhe Su, Siyu Zhang, Zherong Pan, Mridul Aanjaneya, Xifeng Gao, and Kui Wu. "Real-Time Height-Field Simulation of Sand and Water Mixtures." In *SIGGRAPH Asia 2023 Conference Papers, SA '23*, pp. 65:1–65:10. Association for Computing Machinery, 2023.

[Tubbs and Tsai 19] Kevin R. Tubbs and Frank T.-C. Tsai. "MRT-Lattice Boltzmann Model for Multilayer Shallow Water Flow." *Water* 11:8 (2019), 1623.

[Valiani et al. 02] Alessandro Valiani, Valerio Caleffi, and Andrea Zanni. "Case Study: Malpasset Dam-Break Simulation Using a Two-Dimensional Finite Volume Method." *Journal of Hydraulic Engineering* 128:5 (2002), 460–472.

[Vlachos 10] Alex Vlachos. "Water Flow in Portal 2.", 2010. Advances in Real-Time Rendering in 3D Graphics and Games, SIGGRAPH Course.

[Zhou 02] Jian Guo Zhou. "A Lattice Boltzmann Model for the Shallow Water Equations." *Computer Methods in Applied Mechanics and Engineering* 191:32 (2002), 3527–3539.

Animating Water Using Profile Buffer

Haozhe Su, Wei Li, Zherong Pan, Xifeng Gao, Zhenyu Mao, and Kui Wu

21.1 Introduction

Water plays a crucial role in video games, contributing to both the visual and interactive aspects of the gaming experience. One technique to create a realistic water surface animation is via a flowmap, a 2D velocity field texture, to advect the water displacement and normal textures at runtime. More details about flowmaps can be found in [Vlachos 10]. While the flowmap technique stands out for its computational efficiency in animating water within video games, it is not without limitations. One notable drawback is the potential for large distortion and stretching artifacts, particularly in regions where the velocity magnitude is substantial. This article introduces a novel approach to real-time water animation, leveraging a wavelet-based methodology enhanced by a precomputed profile buffer technique for optimal performance. The proposed technique aims to create water waves dynamically based on factors such as world position, time, and velocity present in the flowmap.

21.2 Background

In this section, we delve into the nuances of spectrum-based methods for simulating water waves, initially introduced in [Jeschke et al. 18]. Unlike partial differential equation (PDE)–based methods that rely on precise spatial discretization, linear wave theory [Johnson 97] describes the wave height dynamics $\eta(\mathbf{x}, t)$ at the position $\mathbf{x}$ in the 2D simulation domain with time t that can be articulated in terms of frequencies as

$$\eta(\mathbf{x}, t) = \int_{\mathrm{R}^2} \mathcal{A}(\mathbf{x}, \mathbf{k}, t) \cos{(\mathbf{k} \cdot \mathbf{x} - \omega(k)t)} d\mathbf{k}, \qquad (21.1)$$

where $\mathcal{A}$ is the amplitude function that depends on $\mathbf{k}$, $\mathbf{x}$, and t and the term $\cos{(\mathbf{k} \cdot \mathbf{x} - \omega(k)t)}$ represents a traveling wave. The wave vector $\mathbf{k}$ is a two-dimensional frequency function such that $k = |\mathbf{k}|$ is the wave number and $\hat{\mathbf{k}} = \mathbf{k}/k$ is the wave direction. The angular frequency $\omega(k) = \sqrt{gk}$ represents the dispersion relation for deep water waves by encoding the speed of each wave based on its wave number k and gravity g. To further elaborate on the formula by employing the polar representation of the wave vector $\mathbf{k}$, we have

$$\eta(\mathbf{x}, t) = \int_0^{2\pi} \int_0^\infty \mathcal{A}(\mathbf{x}, \mathbf{k}, t) \cos\left(\mathbf{k} \cdot \mathbf{x} - \omega(k)t\right) k \, dk \, d\theta. \qquad (21.2)$$

For more information, please refer to [Jeschke et al. 18].

21.3   Our Method

In this section, we first introduce our decomposition of the amplitude field $\mathcal{A}$ and then describe the discretization of each decomposed component.

21.3.1   Amplitude Field Decomposition

Unlike the previous work [Jeschke et al. 18] that evolves the amplitude field $\mathcal{A}(\mathbf{x}, \mathbf{k}, t)$ in each time step to accurately depict wave movements, our input water flow remains static and is specified by a precomputed flowmap, such that the amplitude field $\mathcal{A}$ is only affected by the position and wave vector. Furthermore, we introduce the following novel decomposition of the amplitude field:

$$\mathcal{A}(\mathbf{x}, \mathbf{k}) = A \, W(\mathbf{x}, \theta) \, \psi(k), \qquad (21.3)$$

where A serves as a constant factor for adjusting the wave strength, $W(\mathbf{x}, \theta)$ represents the weight associated with the wave direction θ at spatial position $\mathbf{x}$, and $\psi(k)$ denotes the basis function of the wave. In the remainder of this section, we aim to provide insight into this simplified wave model by offering detailed explanations of each component.

Direction Weight $W(\mathbf{x}, \theta)$ We denote the time-independent direction at the location $\mathbf{x}$ from the flowmap as the primary wave direction θ_p:

$$\theta_p(\mathbf{x}) = \arctan\left(\frac{v_x}{v_z}\right), \qquad (21.4)$$

where v_x and v_z are the velocity components along the x- and z-axis, respectively. By assuming that the wave direction is in the vicinity of the primary wave direction, the corresponding weight $W(\mathbf{x}, \theta)$ can be computed as

$$W(\mathbf{x}, \theta) = \begin{cases} 1 - \dfrac{|\theta - \theta_p(\mathbf{x})|}{C}, & \text{if } |\theta - \theta_p(\mathbf{x})| \le C; \\ 0, & \text{otherwise}; \end{cases} \qquad (21.5)$$

where C is the half-width of the angle range with nonzero weight, which will be addressed in Section 21.4.3. The farther the angle deviates from the primary angle, the smaller the weight becomes. Figure 21.1 illustrates comparisons between utilizing smaller and larger angle ranges with nonzero weights.

Figure 21.1. Top: Uniform water flow from left to right with consistent strength. Bottom: Circular water flow. For both, the left result uses a small relative angle range $[-\frac{\pi}{8}, \frac{\pi}{8}]$, whereas the right uses a large relative angle range $[-\frac{\pi}{2}, \frac{\pi}{2}]$.

```
// Wave basis
float phillips_spectrum(float waveNumber)
{
    float windSpeed = 10.f;
    float A = 2.f * PI / waveNumber;
    float B = expf(-1.8038f * A * A / powf(windSpeed, 4));
    return 0.1391f * sqrtf(A * B);
}
```

Listing 21.1. The Phillips spectrum.

Wave Basis $\psi(k)$ In the frequency space, $\psi(k)$ symbolizes the wave shape with a representative wave number k. Although any wave spectrum can be used as the wave basis, we choose to adopt the Phillips spectrum (Listing 21.1) as the basis for our waves.

Substituting Equation (21.3) into Equation (21.2) yields

$$
\begin{aligned}
\eta(\mathbf{x}, t) &= \int_0^{2\pi} \int_0^\infty AW(\mathbf{x}, \theta)\psi(k) \cos\left(\mathbf{k} \cdot \mathbf{x} - \omega(k)t\right) k dk d\theta \\
&= \int_0^{2\pi} AW(\mathbf{x}, \theta) \left(\int_0^\infty \psi(k) \cos\left(\mathbf{k} \cdot \mathbf{x} - \omega(k)t\right) k dk\right) d\theta.
\end{aligned}
\tag{21.6}
$$

Profile Buffer $\bar{\Psi}(p, t)$ Performing a double integral to calculate $\eta(\mathbf{x}, t)$ via Equation (21.6) for each pixel in the domain can be time-consuming, especially for high-resolution animations. Following the idea proposed by [Jeschke et al. 18], we define the profile buffer $\bar{\Psi}(p,t)$:

$$\bar{\Psi}(p,t) = \int_0^\infty \psi(k)\cos\left(kp - \omega(k)t\right)kdk, \tag{21.7}$$

where $p = \hat{\mathbf{k}} \cdot \mathbf{x}$ is the projected position. By precomputing the integral of $\bar{\Psi}(p,t)$, the original double integral in Equation (21.6) can be converted into a single integral:

$$\eta(\mathbf{x},t) = \int_0^{2\pi} AW(\mathbf{x},\theta)\bar{\Psi}(p,t)d\theta. \tag{21.8}$$

It is important to note that the profile buffer $\bar{\Psi}(p,t)$ is a function of both p and t, requiring updates in every time step.

21.3.2   Discretization

Discretization of $\bar{\Psi}(p,t)$ In theory, the integral of the profile buffer involves an infinite number of calculations when converted to the summation form. In practice, we approximate Equation (21.8) with a finite number of summations as

$$\bar{\Psi}(p,t) = \sum_{i=0}^{N_k-1} \psi(k_i)\cos\left(k_i p - \omega(k_i)t\right)k_i\Delta k, \tag{21.9}$$

where N_k represents the total number of sampled wave number values taken into account.

The profile buffer is designed to be periodic, ensuring seamless tiling across all of space. We introduce a spatial periodicity parameter L and define the normalized projected position $\bar{p} \in [0,1)$ as

$$\bar{p} = \frac{p - \lfloor p/L \rfloor L}{L}. \tag{21.10}$$

With this normalization, we can express the profile buffer in a reformulated manner:

$$\bar{\Psi}(p,t) = \bar{\Psi}(\bar{p},t) = \sum_{i=0}^{N_k-1} \psi(k_i)\cos\left(k_i L\bar{p} - \omega(k_i)t\right)k_i\Delta k. \tag{21.11}$$

We can store the profile buffer result in this 1D array by uniformly sampling N_k points in the interval $[0,1]$ as $\bar{p}_i$. The computation of the jth entry can be achieved via

$$\bar{\Psi}(\bar{p}_j,t) = \sum_{i=0}^{N_k-1} \psi(k_i)\cos\left(k_i L\bar{p}_j - \omega(k_i)t\right)k_i\Delta k, \tag{21.12}$$

where $\bar{p}_j = (j + 0.5)/N_k$ and $j = 0,1,2,\ldots,N_k - 1$. With lower and upper limits of the wave number, $k_{\min}$ and $k_{\max}$, we have $\Delta k = (k_{\max} - k_{\min})/N_k$ and $k_i = k_{\min} + (i + 0.5)\Delta k$.

Discretization of $\eta(\mathbf{x}, t)$ Similarly, we discretize the wave direction θ into N_θ samples and rewrite Equation (21.8) as

$$\eta(\mathbf{x}, t) = \frac{2\pi A}{N_\theta} \sum_{i=0}^{N_\theta - 1} W(\mathbf{x}, \theta_i) \bar{\Psi}(\hat{\mathbf{k}}_i \cdot \mathbf{x}, t), \qquad (21.13)$$

where $\theta_i = 2\pi i / N_\theta$, $\mathbf{x} = (z, x)$, and $\hat{\mathbf{k}}_i = (\cos\theta_i, \sin\theta_i)$.

21.4 Implementation Details

In this section, we delineate the numerical algorithm for solving Equation (21.8), along with specific code implementations. At each time step, two primary tasks must be executed: computing the profile buffer and performing height integration. Refer to Listing 21.2 for an overview of the algorithm pipeline. In our implementation, we use a CUDA kernel to compute the profile buffer at the beginning of each frame and send it to OpenGL as a 1D texture via CUDA OpenGL `interop`.

```
t ← 0
Initialization                                   // Section 21.4.1
while t < T
{
    Precompute profile buffers                   // Section 21.4.2
    Integrate water height in vertex shader      // Section 21.4.3
    Integrate water normal in fragment shader    // Section 21.4.4
    t ← t + Δt
}
```

Listing 21.2. Pseudocode of our water wave animation.

21.4.1 Initialization

We initialize the simulation through the following steps. Firstly, as both the terrain and water are represented by height maps, we import these height maps to construct the scene. Secondly, a flowmap, which records the fluid velocity field at a stable state, is imported to indicate the wave propagation direction and strength within the simulation domain. Lastly, we define several macros to control the simulation details, as depicted in Listing 21.3.

```
// Physical constants
#define PI                  3.14159265359f
#define TAU                 6.28318530718f
#define GRAVITY             9.81f

// Profile buffer constants
#define DIR_NUM             32
#define SEG_PER_DIR         8
#define PB_RESOLUTION       4096
#define WAVE_DIM            4
#define FINE_DIR_NUM        (DIR_NUM * SEG_PER_DIR)
```

Listing 21.3. Constants for our simulation.

21.4.2   Precomputing the Profile Buffer

Profile buffer computation stands as a crucial element in achieving real-time wave animation. Rather than performing intensive summations at all pixels/vertices in the domain at every time step, we calculate the profile buffer at the onset of each time step. We use the Phillips spectrum as the wave basis $\psi(k)$ mentioned in Section 21.1.

A 1×4096 texture with four channels (WAVE_DIM=4) is used as the profile buffer, in which displacement and spatial derivatives along vertical and horizontal directions are stored at four channels, respectively. Note that the cosine term in Equation (21.9) indicates the vertical displacement of the Gerstner wave, while displacement and spatial derivatives can be computed as demonstrated in Listing 21.4.

```
void gerstner_wave(float* gw, float phase, float k)
{
  float s = sin(phase);
  float c = cos(phase);

  gw[0] = -s;        // Horizontal displacement
  gw[1] =  c;        // Vertical displacement
  gw[2] = -k * c;    // Derivative of gw[0]
  gw[3] = -k * s;    // Derivative of gw[1]
}
```

Listing 21.4. The Gerstner wave.

To simulate water waves across large open worlds, we construct the profile buffers to be periodic for seamless extension in the world space. This configuration could lead to potential discontinuities near the borders of neighboring profile buffers, as illustrated in Figure 21.2. To resolve this, we introduce cubic bumps:

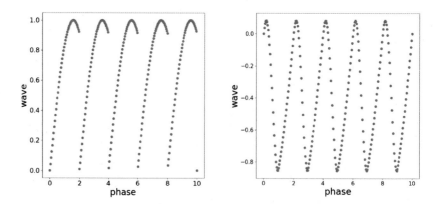

Figure 21.2. Left: Simplified wave without interpolation. Discontinuities arise at the boundary between adjacent profile buffers. Right: Interpolated wave.

$$\mathtt{cubic\_bump}\,(x) = \begin{cases} x^2(2|x| - 3) + 1, & \text{if } |x| < 1; \\ 0, & \text{otherwise}; \end{cases} \qquad (21.14)$$

with which we can interpolate the Gerstner wave without concern for discontinuity, as shown in Listing 21.5.

```
void interpolate_gerstner_wave(
    real* gw, real k, real p, real L, real scale, real t)
{
    real phase1 = k * p - disper_relation(k, scale) * t;
    real phase2 = k * (p - L) - disper_relation(k, scale) * t;

    real gw1[WAVE_DIM];
    real gw2[WAVE_DIM];

    gerstner_wave(gw1, phase1, k);
    gerstner_wave(gw2, phase2, k);

    real weight1 = p / L;
    real weight2 = 1 - weight1;

    real cb1 = cubic_bump(weight1);
    real cb2 = cubic_bump(weight2);

    for (int i = 0; i < WAVE_DIM; ++i)
    {
        gw[i] = cb1 * gw1[i] + cb2 * gw2[i];
    }
}
```

Listing 21.5. Gerstner wave interpolation.

Equation (21.9) can now be computed straightforwardly, as shown in Listing 21.6.

```
void compute_profile_buffer(
    real* result, real k, real p, real L, real scale, real t)
{
    real waveLength = TAU / k;

    real gw[WAVE_DIM];
    interpolate_gerstner_wave(gw, k, p, L, scale, t);

    real ps = phillips_spectrum(k);
    for (int i = 0; i < WAVE_DIM; ++i)
    {
        result[i] += waveLength * ps * gw[i];
    }
}
```

Listing 21.6. Profile buffer computation.

Fast/Slow Profile Tuning To gain finer control over wave behavior, we introduce the profile scale s to adjust the wave propagation speed. The modified dispersion relation $\omega(k)$ can then be expressed as

$$\omega(k) = s\sqrt{gk}. \qquad (21.15)$$

A larger $\omega(k)$ corresponds to faster wave propagation. In practice, we utilize two distinct values, s_fast and s_slow, to represent fast and slow wave propagation, respectively. The profile buffers are then stored in two separate textures: d_PBf_ field_ and d_PBs_field_.

21.4.3 Height Integration

Given the computed profile buffer, we integrate the displacement of the water surface vertex via Gaussian quadrature on the fly in the vertex shader. In particular, given a vertex position inPosition at its rest state, we integrate its world position based on the precomputed profile buffers pbOFieldTex and flowmap layerDataTex.

Integration with Gaussian Quadrature Equation (21.13) represents the classical Riemann sum method designed for numerical integration. However, it necessitates a greater number of summations to attain high precision.

We introduce Gaussian quadrature to provide an exact result for polynomials of degree $2N_{\mathrm{int}} - 1$ or lower through a suitable selection of nodes P_i and weights α_i for $i = 0, \ldots, N_{\mathrm{int}} - 1$. It's important to note that Gaussian quadrature can be applied without modification when the original limits of integration are $[-1, 1]$. In this scenario, the positions of integration points $P_0, P_1, \ldots, P_{N_{\mathrm{int}}-1}$ as well as their associated weights $\alpha_0, \alpha_1, \ldots, \alpha_{N_{\mathrm{int}}-1}$ can be precomputed, without requiring knowledge of the specific expression of the integrand. With this, we can transform the original Riemann sum into a new form:

$$\eta(\mathbf{x}, t) = s_G A \sum_{i=0}^{N_{\mathrm{int}}-1} \alpha_i W(\mathbf{x}, \theta_i) \bar{\Psi}(z \cos \theta_i + x \sin \theta_i, t), \qquad (21.16)$$

where $\theta_i = \pi P_i + \pi$ and $s_G = \frac{2\pi}{2} = \pi$ is a scaling factor. When the limits of integration change to a custom range, the integration requires scaling, and the scaling factor is simply the ratio of the actual limit length to the original limit length, which is 2 for the range $[-1, 1]$. In the experiment, we utilize 32 points of integration. The precomputed Gaussian quadrature point positions and their associated weights are provided in Listing 21.7.

Next, we provide a detailed implementation for computing each entry in the summation in Equation (21.16) at the vertex position inPosition. Assuming we have computed the primary angle $\theta_p = \arctan(v_x/v_z)$, we can calculate the weight $W(\mathbf{x}, \theta_i)$ as follows:

```
float diffa = abs(theta_p - theta_i);
float W = 1 - min(C, min(diffa, TAU-diffa))/C;
```

In our experiments, blending two profiles enhances the portrayal of wave propagation details. Depending on the strength of velocity, we define a weight function $w = \min(1, |\mathbf{v}|)$, ensuring that the fast profile buffer occupies a larger

```
int nnodes = 32;
float nodes[32] = {
    -0.9972638618494816f,    -0.9856115115452684f,
    -0.9647622555875064f,    -0.9349060759377397f,
    -0.8963211557660522f,    -0.84936761373257f,
    -0.7944837959679424f,    -0.7321821187402897f,
    -0.6630442669302152f,    -0.5877157572407623f,
    -0.5068999089322294f,    -0.4213512761306353f,
    -0.3318686022821276f,    -0.2392873622521370f,
    -0.1444719615827965f,    -0.04830766568773831f,
    0.04830766568773831f,     0.1444719615827965f,
    0.2392873622521370f,      0.3318686022821276f,
    0.4213512761306353f,      0.5068999089322294f,
    0.5877157572407623f,      0.6630442669302152f,
    0.7321821187402897f,      0.7944837959679424f,
    0.84936761373257f,        0.8963211557660522f,
    0.9349060759377397f,      0.9647622555875064f,
    0.9856115115452684f,      0.9972638618494816f};
float weights[32] = {
    0.007018610009469298f,    0.016274394730905965f,
    0.025392065309262427f,    0.034273862913021626f,
    0.042835898022226426f,    0.050998059262376244f,
    0.058684093478535704f,    0.06582222277636175f,
    0.07234579410884845f,     0.07819389578707031f,
    0.08331192422694685f,     0.08765209300440391f,
    0.09117387869576386f,     0.09384439908080457f,
    0.09563872007927483f,     0.09654008851472781f,
    0.09654008851472781f,     0.09563872007927483f,
    0.09384439908080457f,     0.09117387869576386f,
    0.08765209300440391f,     0.08331192422694685f,
    0.07819389578707031f,     0.07234579410884845f,
    0.06582222277636175f,     0.058684093478535704f,
    0.050998059262376244f,    0.042835898022226426f,
    0.034273862913021626f,    0.025392065309262427f,
    0.016274394730905965f,    0.007018610009469298f};
```

Listing 21.7. Gaussian quadrature points and weights.

proportion as the magnitude of the current velocity increases. Readers may have observed that the retrieved profile buffer comprises four components, which are arranged in their original order as the horizontal and vertical displacements of both the slow and fast profile buffers. The blended profile buffer can be represented as:

```
vec2 pbb = (1.f - scale) * pb.xy + scale * pb.wz;
```

Here, `pb.xy` and `pb.wz` represent the displacement parts of the slow and fast profile buffer, respectively.

Adaptive Limits of Integration   We assume that the wave only propagates within a range near the primary angle, as defined in Equation (21.4). Expanding this range results in more waves in different directions blending together, whereas narrowing it makes the wave appear to move predominantly in one direction. We have demonstrated in Figure 21.1 that a narrow range can lead to artificial constructive patterns. Conversely, an excessively wide range can obscure the recognition of wave direction, resulting in smoothed-out wave propagation. To dynamically adjust the angle range of wave propagation, we calculate the maximum difference in velocity direction at each cell center with its neighboring cells, which serves as an indicator of local velocity variation. (See Listing 21.8.)

```
for each cell i in simulation domain
{
    M_i ← Neighboring cells of cell i
    θ_i ← arctan(v_i/u_i)
    Δθ_max ← 0
    for each cell j ∈ M_i
    {
        θ_j ← arctan(v_j/u_j)
        Δθ ← ‖θ_j − θ_i‖
        Δθ ← min(Δθ, 2π − Δθ)
        if Δθ > Δθ_max
        {
            Δθ_max ← Δθ
        }
    }
}
```

Listing 21.8. Pseudocode for local velocity variation computation.

With primary angles calculated and the maximum difference in velocity direction precomputed, the subsequent step involves determining the limits of integration associated with nonzero weights. We operate under the assumption that within a given area, if the local velocity variation is significant, we require a larger range of integration angles to accurately represent the varying wave propagation directions. (See Figure 21.3.) As previously mentioned, we partition all possible propagation directions within the range $[0, 2\pi]$ into DIR_NUM segments. Each segment is further subdivided into SEG_PER_DIR pieces, resulting in a total of DIR_NUM * SEG_PER_DIR subdivisions across the full 2π range. Subsequently, we determine which subdivisions correspond to nonzero weights. We calculate the half-width of the nonzero weight area, denoted as C in Listing 21.9.

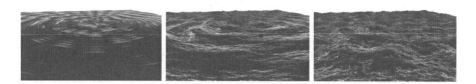

Figure 21.3. Adaptive limits of integration: A flowmap characterized by uniform strength and a radial outward direction from a central point is evaluated. From left to right, we employ a fixed small integration range, an adaptive integration range, and a fixed large integration range. Prominent artificial patterns are discernible on the left, while the wave propagation appears excessively smooth, hindering clear recognition on the right. Our model in the middle exemplifies the outward movement of waves with realistic turbulence.

```
int INT_NUM = min(16,4+int(500*delta_mag/TAU));
int SEG_HW = SEG_PER_DIR*INT_NUM;
float C = float(SEG_HW)/float(FINE_DIR_NUM)*TAU;
```

Listing 21.9. Compute adaptive limits of integration.

21.4.4 Normal Integration

Surface normal calculation is indispensable for visually representing the surface shape of waves in rendering. Theoretically, the surface normal of a height map can be computed via $\mathbf{n} = \mathbf{T}_z \times \mathbf{T}_x / \|\mathbf{T}_z \times \mathbf{T}_x\|$, where $\mathbf{T}_z$ and $\mathbf{T}_x$ are the gradient vectors in the z- and x-directions (in other words, the horizontal directions in OpenGL), respectively. Given the integration process for wave height from Equation (21.8), we can calculate the gradient of the height map concerning the horizontal position:

$$
\begin{aligned}
\nabla_{\mathbf{x}} \eta(\mathbf{x}, t) &= \nabla_{\mathbf{x}} \int_0^{2\pi} AW(\mathbf{x}, \theta) \bar{\Psi}(p, t) d\theta \\
&= \int_0^{2\pi} \nabla_{\mathbf{x}} \left(AW(\mathbf{x}, \theta) \right) \bar{\Psi}(p, t) d\theta + \int_0^{2\pi} AW(\mathbf{x}, \theta) \nabla_{\mathbf{x}} \left(\bar{\Psi}(p, t) \right) d\theta.
\end{aligned}
\tag{21.17}
$$

We adopt the approach suggested in [Jeschke et al. 18], wherein we omit the first term. This decision is supported by the observation that the flowmap maintains continuity in space, indicating that the derivative $\nabla_{\mathbf{x}} \left(A\omega(\mathbf{x}, \theta) \right)$ tends to be close to 0. We can now finalize the formula for calculating height gradients as follows:

$$
\nabla_{\mathbf{x}} \eta(\mathbf{x}, t) = \int_0^{2\pi} AW(\mathbf{x}, \theta) \nabla_{\mathbf{x}} \bar{\Psi}(p, t) d\theta.
\tag{21.18}
$$

The calculation of the gradient vectors $\mathbf{T}_z$ and $\mathbf{T}_x$ can be executed as

$$
\mathbf{T}_z = (1, 0, \nabla_{\mathbf{x}} \eta_z) \Rightarrow \mathbf{T}_z = \frac{\mathbf{T}_z}{\|\mathbf{T}_z\|},
\tag{21.19}
$$

$$
\mathbf{T}_x = (0, 1, \nabla_{\mathbf{x}} \eta_x) \Rightarrow \mathbf{T}_x = \frac{\mathbf{T}_x}{\|\mathbf{T}_x\|}.
\tag{21.20}
$$

Note that we have not taken into account the horizontal displacement, but only the vertical displacement. Normal integration procedure is executed within the fragment shader, and the pipeline closely resembles that of height integration, albeit with the additional step of integrating $\mathbf{T}_z$ and $\mathbf{T}_x$ and subsequently employing the cross-product operation to derive the normal vector, as in Listing 21.10.

```
... // Initial setup
vec3 tz = vec3(0.f, 0.f, 1.f);
vec3 tx = vec3(1.f, 0.f, 0.f);
for(int sid = 0; sid < nnodes; ++sid)
{
    ... // Normal integration
}
vec3 newNormal = cross(tz, tx);
newNormal = normalize(newNormal);
```

Listing 21.10. Normal integration.

21.5 Results

In this section, we demonstrate the effectiveness of our method. In particular, we showcase how the profiling time is significantly reduced through the implementation of Gaussian quadrature. Additionally, we elucidate how adaptive limits of integration contribute to overall quality improvement and highlight how blending two profile buffers enhances the depiction of wave movements. We utilize a custom-designed map featuring a river scene for all demonstrations and comparisons, as shown in Figure 21.4. All tests have been conducted using a 4.0 GHz AMD Ryzen Threadripper PRO 5955WX 16-Cores processor paired with an NVIDIA GeForce RTX 4080 GPU with 16 GB of memory.

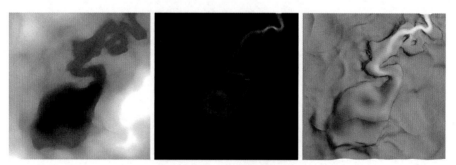

Figure 21.4. Left: Terrain height map; the whiter areas indicate higher elevations. Middle: Flowmap; the dark purple shades represent lower velocity magnitudes, while the bright yellow shades represent higher velocity magnitudes. Right: Top view of the rendered scene.

21.5.1 Riemann Sum vs. Gaussian Quadrature

We first demonstrate the performance improvement by comparing Riemann sum with various integration points, ranging from 32 to 192, and Gaussian quadrature with 32 integration points. We observe that Gaussian quadrature with 32 integration points achieves visual results comparable to those of Riemann

Integration Method	# Integration Points	Runtime (ms)
Riemann sum	32	3.01
	64	4.65
	96	4.91
	144	6.46
	192	8.26
Gaussian quadrature	32	3.03

Table 21.1. Performance comparison between the Riemann sum with different numbers of integration points and the Gaussian quadrature.

sum with 192 integration points. Notably, this achievement is accompanied by a significant reduction in profiling time by 63%, highlighting the efficiency of our proposed method. (See Table 21.1.) Moreover, to achieve a similar profiling time, Riemann sum is constrained to using only 32 points, resulting in a compromised visual appearance. This trade-off underscores the superiority of Gaussian quadrature in balancing computational efficiency with visual quality. Please refer to the results depicted in Figure 21.5.

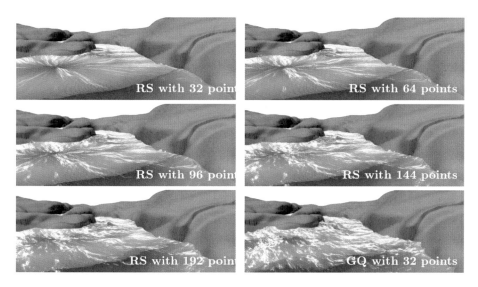

Figure 21.5. Comparison between Riemann sum (RS) with different numbers of integration points (32, 64, 96, 144, 192) and Gaussian quadrature (GQ). The Riemann sum exhibits noticeable unnatural patterns with an insufficient number of integration points (32). Furthermore, the Riemann sum method requires approximately six times the number of integration points to attain comparable results in visual fidelity and detail.

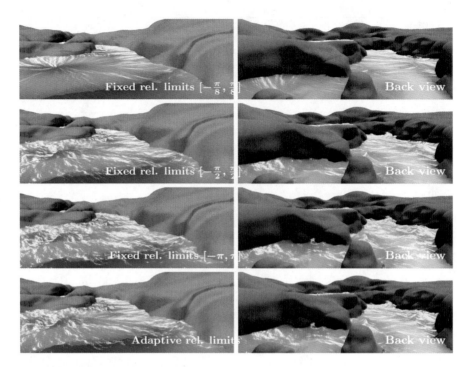

Figure 21.6. Adaptive integration limits are examined in comparison to fixed limits of integration (relative ranges include $[-\frac{\pi}{8}, \frac{\pi}{8}]$, $[-\frac{\pi}{2}, \frac{\pi}{2}]$, and $[-\pi, \pi]$). With a small integration range, anomalous constructive patterns emerge, while a large range results in overly smoothed wave movement and vague wave propagation direction. Adaptive integration limits effectively mitigate observable constructive structures and enhance the clarity of wave propagation direction.

21.5.2   Adaptive Limits of Integration

Next, we delve into the adaptive limits of integration, showcasing its impact on visual appearance. During per-pixel normal integration and per-vertex height integration, the flowmap indicates the local flow orientation, and we set the maximum amplitude strength to appear along this direction. The amplitude strength linearly diminishes as the direction deviates further from the central orientation. The proposed adaptive strategy decides the maximum nonzero amplitude range, based on variation in the local flowmap. See the results in Figure 21.6.

21.5.3   Fast/Slow Wave Propagation Blending

Next, we compare wave behaviors characterized by fast propagation speed, slow propagation speed, and the blending of the two, illustrated in Figure 21.7.

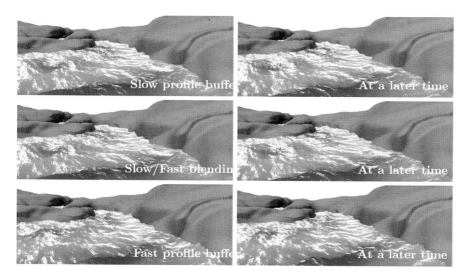

Figure 21.7. We compare the visual appearance of using a slow profile buffer (top), a fast profile buffer (bottom), and a blend of the slow/fast profile buffers (middle).

21.6 Conclusion

We have introduced a real-time framework for simulating waves in open-world scenarios. Central to our approach is the profile buffer, which efficiently transforms computationally intensive integration tasks into reusable texture fetching operations. By incorporating Gaussian quadrature, we achieve significant speed improvements while maintaining visual quality. Furthermore, the adaptive limits of integration enable us to achieve diverse visual effects, while the blending of profile buffers enriches wave propagation details.

Acknowledgements

The authors would like to specially thank Stefan Jeschke and Chris Wojtan for their support and guidance.

Bibliography

[Jeschke et al. 18] Stefan Jeschke, Tomáš Skřivan, Matthias Müller-Fischer, Nuttapong Chentanez, Miles Macklin, and Chris Wojtan. "Water Surface Wavelets." *ACM Transactions on Graphics* 37:4 (2018), 94:1–94:13.

[Johnson 97] R. S. Johnson. *A Modern Introduction to the Mathematical Theory of Water Waves.* Cambridge Texts in Applied Mathematics, Cambridge University Press, 1997.

[Vlachos 10] Alex Vlachos. "Water Flow in Portal 2." Advances in Real-Time Rendering in 3D Graphics and Games, SIGGRAPH Course, 2010.

Advanced Techniques
for Radix Sort

Atsushi Yoshimura and Chih-Chen Kao

22.1 Introduction

Radix sort is an efficient non-compare-based algorithm that can efficiently sort many discrete keys such as integers, strings, and even floating point values. Usually, radix sort is significantly faster than compare-based algorithms when the number of sort elements is large. It distributes keys into buckets based on their individual digits and reorders them accordingly. Being a stable algorithm, this process can be repeated from the least-significant digit to the most significant digit. Radix sort is also one of the most popular choices for sorting on the GPU since it can leverage compute units by splitting the input keys into GPU groups to compute them in parallel [Harada and Howes 11]. Because of the efficiency, several applications such as spatial data structure constructions use radix sort. Thus, they can benefit from an optimized sort implementation [Karras 12].

Generally, GPU radix sort can be structured as follows: *counting* keys to build a histogram, *prefix scanning* to compute offsets, and *reordering* keys. A potential inefficiency arises when both counting and reordering read exactly the same values from the global memory multiple times, which creates redundant memory access operations. Combining kernels may resolve the redundancy, but it is not straightforward.

To address the issue, Adinets and Merrill [Adinets and Merrill 22] proposed the *Onesweep* radix sort algorithm to reduce the number of global memory operations by combining the prefix scan and reordering stages, while minimizing the latency with the decoupled look-back method [Merrill and Garland 16]. However, since Onesweep requires a temporal buffer whose size is proportional to the number of elements to be sorted, there is still room for optimizing memory allocation.

In this article, we introduce another high-performance and memory-efficient radix sort implementation on the GPU that further improves Onesweep. Specifically, we propose an extension to reduce the allocation of temporal memory for prefix scans by using a constant-sized circular buffer. We also introduce general optimization techniques. The article is summarized as follows:

1. A brief introduction to a classic radix sort implementation on the GPU.

2. Details of the state-of-the-art Onesweep radix sort.

3. Our circular buffer extension for fast and memory-efficient radix sort.

4. Optimization techniques used in our implementation such as parallel local sorting.

The performance of our radix sort implementation reaches approximately 16 GKey/s on the AMD Radeon 7900 XTX GPU, 5 GKey/s on AMD Radeon RX 6600 XT, and 3.4 GKey/s on AMD Radeon RX 5500.[1] The implementation utilizes AMD Orochi [Harada 22], a library that loads HIP and CUDA driver APIs dynamically at runtime, making it platform-independent.

22.2   Conventional Radix Sort

Before diving into Onesweep radix sort, we introduce the classic radix sort and move to Onesweep later since the algorithm is extended from the core concept. The process of the radix sort algorithm can be summarized as the following three steps: *counting*, *prefix scan*, and *reordering*. At the beginning of the algorithm, we count the occurrence of the elements from the given partition of input data and store the results in a bucket. Next, in order to compute the address offset of each element in the input data, we perform a prefix scan on the count result from the previous step. Since the prefix scan gives the total count of all elements that are less than an element value, the result marks the starting offset for the value. Finally, we reorder the given input data based on the calculated offset. An overview of each iteration of the sorting process is illustrated in Figure 22.1. Note that the bucket size used in the counting stage grows proportionally to the number of bits for sorting. For example, 32 bits for counting requires 2^{32} for the bucket size. However, since radix sort is a stable sorting algorithm, which means the relative order remains the same after being sorted for any two elements that are considered equivalent, we could partition the entire sorting process into multiple passes and start from the least-significant bit to avoid having a single gigantic bucket.

22.3   Classic Radix Sort on the GPU

In practice, the aforementioned three steps of classic radix sort can be implemented as individual kernels to run on GPUs. Initially, the input elements are divided into smaller chunks and assigned to GPU blocks. The output offset of each digit and each GPU block is determined in a prefix scan stage. To conduct a parallel prefix scan, the data to be processed (in this instance, the occurrences of elements stored in tables from the count) is first partitioned into chunks and

---

[1]The performance is measured with 32-bit randomized integer keys.

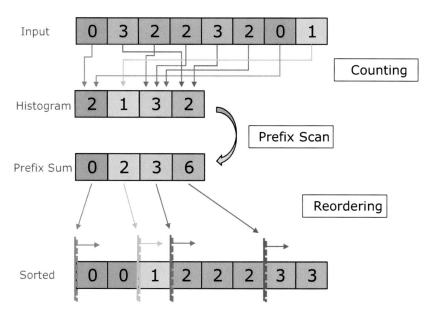

Figure 22.1. An overview of each iteration of the standard count-scan-reorder radix sort. This example demonstrates 2-bit sorting. In counting, the bucket for each number is created to record the occurrences. The result is passed to the prefix scan to compute the global offset for each number. Finally, in reordering, those numbers are reordered based on the calculated offset and sorted accordingly.

allocated to individual GPU blocks. A straightforward but inefficient implementation would necessitate each GPU block to output its partial prefix sums to the global memory, followed by the launch of another kernel to merge the final result. Multi-kernel dispatches issue global barriers for synchronizing the kernels, and propagation of the partial prefix requires additional memory transfer. Consequently, this incurs a performance penalty, since kernel launch and memory transfers typically entail high latency and overhead.

One optimization method involves restructuring the prefix scan computation pattern into a single-pass kernel launch. In this pattern, the local prefix sum for each GPU block is calculated in parallel, and the global offset of each block is resolved by waiting for the preceding block to complete the local sum. Thus, this method effectively reduces the memory accesses for an input of n elements from $3n$ (with $2n$ reads and n writes) to $2n$ (with n reads and n writes) since all calculations can be done in a single kernel dispatch. This approach is known as *chained-scan*, from a way to resolve global offsets among GPU blocks [Yan et al. 13, Meister et al. 23].

A performance bottleneck in classic radix sort arises from the fact that the inputs are accessed twice, once in counting and once in reordering. There is a lot of room for optimization since memory access to the global memory bears a huge latency and the read values are the same between the two kernels. Additionally, the performance of chained-scan is hindered by the latency of data propagation, as each GPU block must wait for the prefix sum of its direct predecessor to become available.

22.4   Decoupled Look-Back and Onesweep

In a recent development, Merrill et al. introduced a work-efficient, single-pass method for the parallel computation of prefix scan called *decoupled look-back*, which dramatically reduces prefix propagation latency [Merrill and Garland 16]. The key concept is to decouple the singular dependence of each GPU block on its immediate predecessor by letting the blocks access the local sums. The decoupled look-back method allows GPU blocks to inspect the status of predecessors by accumulating the local sum that is increasingly further way. On decoupled look-back, a prefix scan completion of only one of the predecessors is enough to finish looking back, while the chained-scan approach is required to wait for the direct predecessor's prefix scan completion.

Later, Adinets and Merrill further adopted and extended this concept into the so-called *Onesweep* algorithm [Adinets and Merrill 22], a least-significant digit (LSD) radix sorting algorithm, which further reduces the number of memory operations since it combines separated kernels into one and thus eliminates the need of accessing the same input from the global memory multiple times. Figure 22.2 illustrates the reordering for one particular digit in Onesweep. The

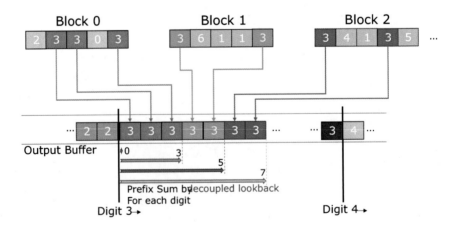

Figure 22.2. An illustration of reordering for a digit (3 in this example) in Onesweep. Each block first calculates a local histogram for each digit. The prefix sum for each digit is calculated by decoupled look-back and used to determine the global output location.

prefix sum used for indicating the head of the output location for digit elements in the block is calculated on the fly by decoupled look-back. Although the re-ordering kernel has to pay the cost of decoupled look-back, the GPU stall is small enough compared to the chained-scan approach. Note that the output location for each digit can be calculated in advance, unlike classic radix sort, since the global histogram for each digit is invariant during the sorting process.

22.4.1   Decoupled Look-Back and Its Implementation Details

In decoupled look-back, each GPU block has to expose its local sum and its prefix sum later for the subsequent blocks. The status of each GPU block is initially updated through block-wise local sum computation (aggregation). Since each block's local sum can be independently computed, the subsequent blocks can freely access the local sum of preceding blocks as soon as it becomes available. This allows them to progressively accumulate results until the complete inclusive scan (prefix sum) is achieved. Subsequently, each block's status is further updated with its prefix sum. Practically, implementing decoupled look-back involves adding an extra status flag as a variable for each GPU block, indicating whether the local sum or prefix sum is currently available. When a block observes its predecessors, it can simply reference this status flag to determine whether it needs to accumulate the local sum or utilize the prefix sum and conclude the process. Even if the direct predecessor has not completed the calculation of the prefix scan, the local sum can be utilized instead, then the execution will attempt to read the prefix from the preceding predecessors.

Figure 22.3 demonstrates how decoupled look-back is performed to calculate prefix sum for the offsets. In the figure, the state transition for each block is shown in chronological order from top to bottom. Although the local sum calculation itself cannot be avoided in the looking-back process, it reduces the latency dramatically since the local sum does not have any dependency on the other blocks.

In the actual implementation, this extra status flag is packed together with the local sum and the prefix sum in a 32-bit or 64-bit structure. Customized with bitfields, the size of this structure is designed to match that of primitive types, ensuring it is treated as a primitive type when updated. This guarantees that both the content (the sum and the flag) are modified atomically in one in-struction. Furthermore, we use the *volatile* qualifier to ensure that any reference to this variable compiles to an actual memory read or write instruction. This ensures that its effect is immediately visible to other GPU blocks and will not be cached.

22.4.2   Temporal Memory Allocation

Onesweep outperforms traditional radix sort by minimizing memory bandwidth, performing an efficient prefix scan, and haiving fewer kernel dispatches. Never-

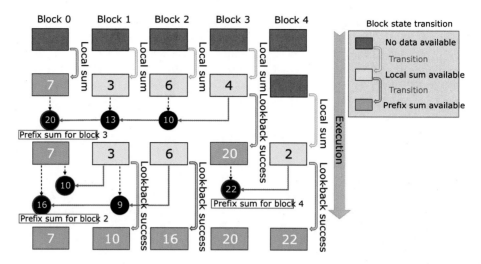

Figure 22.3. An example of the decoupled look-back process for prefix scan in chronological order from top to bottom. Each block checks the lower indexed blocks until the prefix sum is available (red circles) without performing spinning waits. With this look-back scheme, the prefix sum is calculated without a singular dependence and thus increases the overall efficiency.

theless, a drawback of the standard Onesweep lies in its requirement of temporal memory to store the status of the prefix scan for decoupled look-back, which increases proportionally with the number of elements to be sorted. This is attributed to the necessity of maintaining memory access locality and sequentiality, restricting the granularity of the chunk size per GPU block. Hence, we propose to use a circular buffer for the temporal buffer to make the allocation fixed-size regardless of input elements.

22.4.3 Circular Buffer

Since the standard decoupled look-back does not have a length limit for looking back, even the very last element could access the very first element theoretically. It makes the reuse of the buffer difficult. Thus, we limit the number of blocks $L_{\text{look-back}}$ for looking back from the target element to make a disposable data range of the GPU blocks. Under this constraint, it is guaranteed that data in the GPU blocks that are indexed as $[0, i_{\text{tail}} - L_{\text{look-back}})$ are not read and can be safely overwritten in the circular buffer, where i_{tail} is a count of the elements that have consecutively finished processing from the first element. We call this counter a *tail iterator*. Figure 22.4 shows how the tail iterator defines the boundary of free range on a circular buffer. Note that since looking back can go beyond the tail iterator location, the boundary where we can safely overwrite is offset by $L_{\text{look-back}}$.

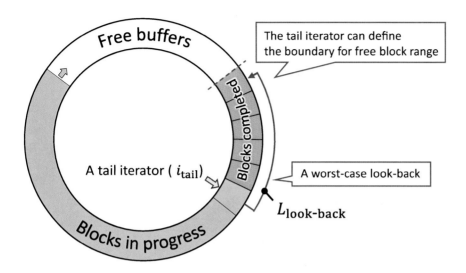

Figure 22.4. A circular buffer can be used for decoupled look-back. We use a tail iterator to avoid overwriting the buffers that are currently in use for looking back.

Listing 22.1 shows a naïve tail iterator increment implementation by atomic operations with sequential increments among GPU blocks. This is a serial execution of the blocks, which results in inefficient execution. Thus, we allow multiple blocks to run simultaneously to increment the iterator. This can be implemented by allowing out-of-order increments in the lowest bits to alleviate the stall. Listing 22.2 is the optimized tail iterator implementation. Since the higher bits are incremented sequentially, the conservative value of the tail iterator can be obtained by discarding the lower bits, where "conservative" means a buffer region of GPU blocks that is still in use is not reused. We utilise the

```
... // Finished the use of the temporal buffer in a block.

__syncthreads();

if( threadIdx.x == 0 )
{
   while( atomicAdd( i_tail, 0 ) != blockIdx.x )
      ;

   atomicInc( i_tail, 0xFFFFFFFF );
}

...
```

Listing 22.1. A naïve tail iterator increment. The tail iterator is incremented sequentially among GPU blocks in the exact order of the index of the block.

```
... // Finished the use of the temporal buffer on a decoupled
    // lookback in a block.

__syncthreads();

if( threadIdx.x == 0 )
{
    constexpr u32 TAIL_MASK = 0xFFFFFFFFu << TAIL_BITS;
    while( ( atomicAdd( i_tail, 0 ) & TAIL_MASK ) != ( blockIdx.x &
    TAIL_MASK ) )
        ;

    atomicInc( i_tail, 0xFFFFFFFF );
}
```

Listing 22.2. Optimized tail iterator increment. The lower bits of the tail iterator are incremented out of order to reduce spin waiting.

tail iterator to wait for previous GPU blocks to avoid conflicted use of the circular buffer. The range of the GPU blocks that can use the circular buffer is $[i_{\text{tail}} - L_{\text{look-back}}, i_{\text{tail}} - L_{\text{look-back}} + N_{table})$, where N_{table} is the size of the circular buffer, because the data in $[0, i_{\text{tail}} - L_{\text{look-back}})$ are not read by any GPU blocks. We let decoupled look-back wait with a spin to avoid conflicts, as shown in Listing 22.3. Considering that the length of a look-back cannot exceed the circular buffer size, $L_{\text{look-back}}$ must be smaller than N_{table}. As N_{table} has to be large enough to utilize all of the GPU processors, $L_{\text{look-back}} < N_{\text{table}}$ is easily met.

```
if( threadIdx.x == 0 && N_table <= blockIdx.x )
{
    // Wait until blockIdx.x < tail - L_look-back + N_table
    constexpr u32 TAIL_MASK = 0xFFFFFFFFu << TAIL_BITS;
    while( ( atomicAdd( i_tail, 0 ) & TAIL_MASK ) - L_look-back + N_table <=
    blockIdx.x )
        ;
}
__syncthreads();

... // Decoupled look-back with a circular buffer

... // Increment tail iterator as shown in Listing 22.2
```

Listing 22.3. A spin-waiting implementation to avoid conflicts of circular buffer use.

Since the circular buffer elements are reused by multiple GPU blocks, each element has to be distinguished whether it is written by the block that is needed for the look-back. Thus, we use a 64-bit variable for each element in the table to include the block index in addition to the status flag. Despite this doubling of the allocation and that we use a conservatively large number to avoid spin waiting due to running out of the circular buffer, only 2 MB are allocated for the circular buffer in our implementation, which is negligible in practice.

22.5 Optimizations

The Onesweep algorithm consists of two GPU kernels: *counting* and *reordering*. In this section, we introduce optimization techniques and strategies adopted in our implementation.

22.5.1 Count in Onesweep

We calculate the prefix sum of the global histogram for each digit in a single kernel such that the input elements are read only once. We split the input and distribute the histogram calculation to the GPU blocks. Since the bucket size of the global histogram is small (k bits are processed in each iteration and we use $k = 8$), we calculate the prefix sum of the histogram in shared memory for each GPU block and merge them by `atomicAdd()` operations. We use *persistent thread* [Gupta et al. 12] to minimize the number of `atomicAdd()` calls. The number of GPU blocks to be launched is calculated to fully utilize all the processors on the GPU.

22.5.2 Reorder in Onesweep

Local Sorting Elements in a GPU block are moved to the target location. Since sequential memory access from consecutive threads in a block is coalesced into a single transaction to reduce the memory operation cost, we perform a local sorting for each GPU block as an optimization.

Parallel Local Sorting We perform a classic radix sort utilizing threads in the GPU block. Elements assigned to the GPU block are further split into smaller groups to distribute the sorting workload among warps in the GPU block. The histogram of assigned elements and local offsets in the same digit for sorting can be calculated easily in a single thread. However, due to the serial execution pattern, we cannot utilize all threads in a warp. Therefore, we use *GPU Multisplit* to let every thread participate in the calculation [Ashkiani et al. 17]. Figure 22.5 illustrates the core idea of parallel radix sort on a warp. To obtain the output locations in the GPU block from the local offsets, we calculate the prefix sum of the histograms from the warps and apply them to the local offset. Listing 22.4 shows an implementation of GPU Multisplit. Each thread broadcasts a bit from the input value and extracts threads that have the same bit as a bitmask. This process repeats until all input bits are broadcasted. The histogram value is then calculated by counting the set bits of the bitmask. Similarly, the local offset is obtained by masking out the bits equal to or greater than the bit location of the thread.

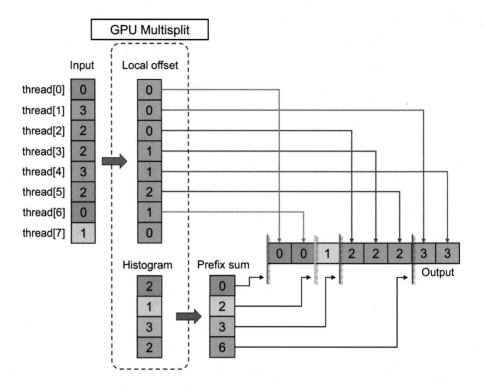

Figure 22.5. Illustration of a parallel radix sort on a warp with eight threads and eight inputs. The local offset and histogram are calculated by GPU Multisplit cooperatively among the threads.

```
u32 lane = threadIdx.x % 32;
u32 input = ... // Load an element for each thread
u32 broThreads = 0xFFFFFFFF;

for( int i = 0; i < k; i++ )
{
    u32 bit = ( input >> i ) & 0x1;
    u32 diff = ( 0xFFFFFFFF * bit ) ^ __ballot( bit != 0 );
    broThreads &= ~diff;
}

u32 histogramValue = __popc( broThreads );
u32 lowerMask = ( 1u << lane ) - 1;
u32 localOffset  = __popc( broThreads & lowerMask );
```

Listing 22.4. An implementation of GPU Multisplit with k-bit inputs in a warp.

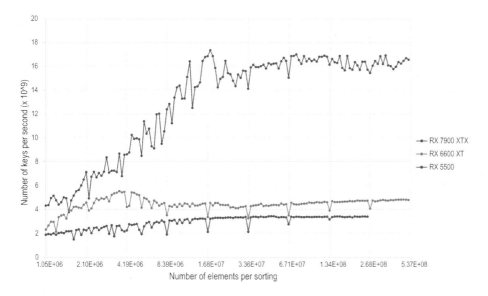

Figure 22.6. Throughput of our Onesweep implementation for 32-bit randomized integer keys on RX 7900 XTX, RX 6600 XT, and RX 5500.

22.6   Performance

We measured the performance of our Onesweep implementation for 32-bit uniformly distributed random integer keys with varying numbers of elements for sorting on AMD Radeon RX 7900 XTX, RX 6600 XT, and RX 5500. Figure 22.6 illustrates the throughput of our implementation across various input sizes, ranging from 2^{16} to 2^{29}, per sort. Our implementation achieves a throughput of 16 GKey/s when the number of elements per sort exceeds 2^{24} on the RX 7900 XTX, while the throughput of the RX 6600 XT saturates to 5 GKey/s when processing around 2^{21} elements. The throughput of RX 5500 saturates to 3.4 GKey/s gently for the number of elements. The maximum number of elements on RX 5500 is limited by the device's physical memory. All exhibit lower throughput when sorting a small number of elements. This could be attributed to GPU stalls and overhead caused by GPU block scheduling and synchronization for each kernel.

Although reordering takes longer due to the overhead of decoupled look-back compared to classic radix sort, the total execution time of each iteration is faster than classic radix sort. This is because Onesweep does not require performing the counting and prefix scan stages for each iteration, but only once at the beginning. Figure 22.7 compares the kernel execution between classic radix sort and Onesweep with 32-bit integer key sorting.

Figure 22.8 illustrates the throughput of Onesweep radix sort and the classic radix sort. As shown in the figure, our implementation outperforms the classic

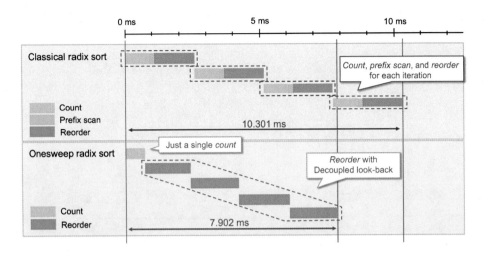

Figure 22.7. Comparison of kernel executions between classic radix sort and Onesweep with 32-bit integer key sorting. The measurement is on AMD Radeon RX 7900 XTX GPU, with 2^{27} randomized integer keys.

one among all input sizes on AMD RX 7900 XTX. (Specifically, the Onesweep implementation can handle approximately 2×2^9 more keys per second compared to that of the classic method.)

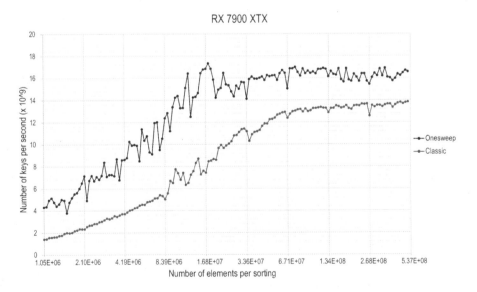

Figure 22.8. The comparison of the throughput between our Onesweep radix sort and classic radix sort for 32-bit randomized integer keys on RX 7900 XTX

22.7 Conclusion

In this article, we introduced advanced techniques for radix sort. We began
with an overview of the classic radix sort algorithm, delved into the specifics
of Onesweep radix sort, and later explored our extension aimed at optimizing
temporal memory allocation and a specific look-back scheme to decouple its
required size from the number of input elements. Additionally, we outlined
general optimization strategies employed in our implementations. Finally, we
showcased the performance in terms of maximum throughput across various
AMD GPU architectures and input sizes. Further exploration into optimizing
the sorting of smaller arrays of elements presents an intriguing avenue for future
research.

Acknowledgements

We extend our sincere appreciation to Takahiro Harada and Daniel Meister for
their diligent proofreading and constructive suggestions. We firmly believe that
their invaluable advice has elevated the quality of this article, making it comprehensive. Furthermore, we express our gratitude to Gautham Moily for facilitating access to machines equipped with various GPUs for our benchmarks. This
assistance has greatly enhanced the depth and accuracy of our work.

Bibliography

[Adinets and Merrill 22] Andy Adinets and Duane Merrill. "Onesweep: A Faster
    Least Significant Digit Radix Sort for GPUs." Preprint, arXiv:2206.01784,
    2022. https://arxiv.org/abs/2206.01784.

[Ashkiani et al. 17] Saman Ashkiani, Andrew Davidson, Ulrich Meyer, and
    John D. Owens. "GPU Multisplit: An Extended Study of a Parallel Al-
    gorithm." *ACM Transaction on Parallel Computing* 4:1 (2017), 2:1–2:44.
    https://doi.org/10.1145/3108139.

[Gupta et al. 12] Kshitij Gupta, Jeff A. Stuart, and John D. Owens. "A Study
    of Persistent Threads Style GPU Programming for GPGPU Workloads." In
    2012 Innovative Parallel Computing (InPar), pp. 1–14. IEEE, 2012.

[Harada and Howes 11] Takahiro Harada and Lee W. Howes. "Introduction
    to GPU Radix Sort." Preprint, 2011. https://gpuopen.com/download/
    publications/Introduction_to_GPU_Radix_Sort.pdf.

[Harada 22] Takahiro Harada. "Orochi: Dynamic Loading of HIP/CUDA
    from a Single Binary." GitHub, 2022. https://github.com/GPUOpen-
    LibrariesAndSDKs/Orochi.

[Karras 12] Tero Karras. "Maximizing Parallelism in the Construction of BVHs, Octrees, and k-d Trees." In *Proceedings of the Fourth ACM SIGGRAPH / Eurographics Conference on High-Performance Graphics, EGGH-HPG'12*, pp. 33–37. Eurographics Association, 2012.

[Meister et al. 23] Daniel Meister, Atsushi Yoshimura, and Chih-Chen Kao. "GPU Programming Primitives for Computer Graphics." In *ACM SIGGRAPH Asia 2023 Courses, SIGGRAPH Asia 2023*, pp. 9:1–9:81. Association for Computing Machinery, 2023.

[Merrill and Garland 16] Duane Merrill and Michael Garland. "Single-Pass Parallel Prefix Scan with Decoupled Look-Back." Technical Report NVR-2016-002, NVIDIA, 2016.

[Yan et al. 13] Shengen Yan, Guoping Long, and Yunquan Zhang. "StreamScan: Fast Scan Algorithms for GPUs without Global Barrier Synchronization." In *Proceedings of the 18th ACM SIGPLAN Symposium on Principles and Practice of Parallel Programming, PPoPP '13*, pp. 229–238. Association for Computing Machinery, 2013. https://doi.org/10.1145/2442516.2442539.

Two-Pass HZB Occlusion Culling

Miloš Kruškonja

23.1 Introduction

Occlusion Culling is an optimization technique used to improve performance by skipping the rendering of objects that are hidden by some other objects in the scene. There are various occlusion culling techniques, each presenting different sets of problems such as visible popping, data authoring, performance issues, etc. A popular approach in modern real-time rendering is a form of a GPU-driven culling technique called hierarchical Z-buffer (HZB) occlusion culling [Anagnostou 17]. However, this method also has major flaws, which two-pass HZB occlusion culling attempts to improve.

23.2 Brief Overview of HZB Culling

Generally, an HZB (Figure 23.1) is essentially a mipmap chain generated by downsampling a depth buffer using the min or max depth value of sets of four texels to create each new texel for the next mipmap level. Whether the min or max is used is dependent on whether the reversed-Z method [Reed 21] is used. Then, objects can be culled against the HZB using its bounding volumes. Beyond occlusion culling, an HZB can be utilized in the rendering of volumetric fog, screen-space reflections, etc.

There are a few ways to optimize the process of building an HZB. Two such methods are texture gathering and sampler reduction modes, both of which allow reducing the number of texture samples, resulting in improved performance.

Testing against an HZB is typically done in a compute shader using axis-aligned bounding boxes (AABBs). The result of this shader dispatch is usually a set of indirect draw call arguments representing only visible objects, which are then used to perform an indirect draw call.

An HZB occlusion test is performed by first choosing the correct mipmap level. The goal here is to find a right mipmap where an AABB covers four neighboring texels. This is typically done by some logarithmic equation that factors in sides of an AABB (Listing 23.1). Mipmap level selection is slightly more complex if the lengths of the sides of the HZB are not the same.

Figure 23.1. An example of HZB built from a depth buffer with reversed-Z. Pixel colors are normalized in order to appear more visible.

```
int mipLevel = floor(log2(max(AABB.width, AABB.height)));
```

Listing 23.1. Example of mipmap level selection logic for occlusion culling.

After the sufficient mipmap level is chosen, the depth value of mentioned four texels is then compared to the depth of the object's closest point to the camera. The result of this comparison tells whether the object is culled or not. After the occlusion test is finished for the entire scene, objects that passed the occlusion test can be rendered (Figure 23.2).

23.3 Problem

As already stated, a depth buffer is required to build an HZB. The question is, how is this depth buffer formed in the first place? One might presume that rendering all objects is necessary to fill the depth buffer, but this would defeat the purpose of culling in general.

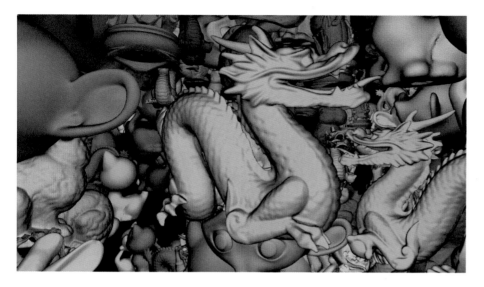

Figure 23.2. An example of a rendered frame that utilizes HZB occlusion culling.

23.4   Potential Solutions

23.4.1   Depth Pre-pass

One common approach involves rendering a small subset of objects, which would serve as occluders. These occluders are typically handpicked and authored by artists. They are usually large objects such as buildings, walls, and terrain. The rendering of occluder objects is typically done only to the depth buffer, without fragment shader invocations, a process known as a *depth pre-pass*. Using the resulting depth buffer enables the construction of an incomplete yet conservative HZB. This HZB is then used in the occlusion culling process. Although effective, this technique demands a significant amount of manual effort to maintain its usefulness.

23.4.2   Occluder Simplification

To reduce the number of rendered triangles in the pre-pass, one can use simplified mesh versions. This can be achieved by repurposing regular level of detail (LOD) meshes. However, for further triangle count reduction, specialized techniques can be used. One such technique is occluder simplification using planar sections [Silvennoinen et al. 14], which is capable of extreme error-bounded simplification due to its volumetric nature.

The process of generating these occluders involves several steps. First, the mesh is voxelized, with the voxel size determined by a specified error. Next, this voxelized mesh is used to create multiple omnidirectional mesh slices. Each slice is rendered into a texture using a custom rasterization pipeline and then extracted into a polygonal mesh from this texture. Only a few slices are selected based on how much of the interior mesh space each slice occupies. These selected slices are then merged to resemble a mesh. This process can be repeated with different specified errors to generate different occluder LODs. This entire process can be performed offline, and depending on a screen-space error, an occluder LOD can be selected at runtime.

Although effective, this technique can be challenging to implement.

23.4.3   Depth Reprojection

In many scenarios, it would be reasonable to assume that visible objects from the previous frame will mostly remain visible in the current frame as well. One way to make use of this insight is to recycle the previous frame's depth buffer in order to generate an approximation of the new depth buffer for the current frame. This technique, known as *depth buffer reprojection* [Haar and Aaltonen 15], involves taking into account the new camera transform and velocity vector buffer from the previous frame. Depth reprojection can also be useful for building shadow map HZBs. A notable advantage of depth reprojection is its ability to reduce the necessity for manual occluder selection. However, combining both depth reprojection and manual occluder selection can yield even better results.

Despite its numerous advantages, depth reprojection is not without significant limitations. One major problem is precision. Since an HZB construction relies on a depth buffer approximation, the culling process may become non-conservative in some cases. This can lead to issues like visible popping, where objects may abruptly appear while moving relative to the camera.

23.5   Two-Pass Solution

Combining insights from the two previously mentioned solutions, it should be possible to achieve the best of both worlds: the precision from depth pre-pass and the absence of data authoring from depth reprojection. The presented approach shares similarities with depth reprojection in a sense of reusing data from a previous frame. However, instead of reprojection depth, only visible objects from the previous frame are "reprojected." Essentially, this involves rendering these previously visible objects in some sort of a pre-pass at the beginning of a frame. These objects make excellent candidates for occluders in the current frame, assuming non-drastic camera movements. This pre-pass is going to be referred to as the first pass from now on. In comparison to the depth pre-pass, the first pass usually doesn't store only depth, but rather some additional information, depending on which rendering pipeline is used: G-buffers in the case of deferred rendering, for example. After finishing the first pass, the remaining culling process should closely resemble the standard HZB occlusion culling, where only the objects not rendered in the first pass are considered for drawing.

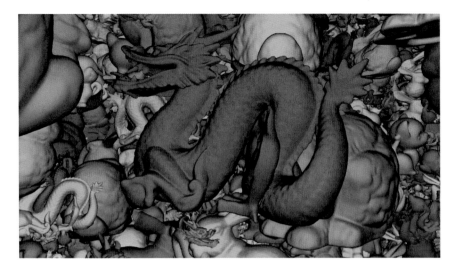

Figure 23.3. An example of a rendered frame that utilizes two-pass HZB occlusion culling and frustum culling.

This technique is called *two-pass occlusion culling* (Figure 23.3) and is currently getting more popular due to its appearance in Unreal Engine 5's Nanite [Karis et al. 21]. This technique can reduce the number of rendered triangles drastically in some scenes (Figure 23.4).

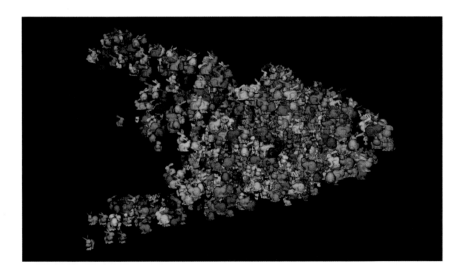

Figure 23.4. A debug view of a scene that utilizes two-pass HZB occlusion culling and frustum culling.

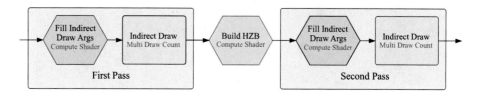

Figure 23.5. Two-pass occlusion culling pipeline.

As the name suggests, two-pass occlusion culling involves dividing scene objects into two groups and then rendering each group in a single pass (Figure 23.5). Each pass consists of a singular compute shader dispatch, whose purpose is to fill indirect draw call arguments. Subsequently, an indirect draw call is executed, preferably by utilizing `MultiDrawCountIndirect` if supported by the hardware. This technique fits the GPU-driven approach very well.

23.5.1 First Pass

As previously stated, the first pass is only responsible for processing objects that were visible in the previous frame. To achieve this, a compute shader is dispatched with the same number of threads as the total number of objects in the scene. Each thread in addition can perform optional frustum culling and LOD selection on objects that were previously visible, while skipping previously non-visible objects entirely. The result of this compute shader is stored in a GPU buffer as indirect draw call arguments.

After the indirect draw call arguments are gathered, they are executed with an indirect draw call. To track the visibility of objects from the previous frame, another GPU buffer is used, known as the visibility buffer. Each element in this buffer corresponds to a single object in the scene, where 0 indicates that an object is not visible and 1 that an object is visible (Listing 23.2). The visibility buffer should be initialized with either 0s or 1s. Also, multiple visibility bits can be packed in a single buffer element in order to save memory.

After the first pass is finished, an HZB can be generated from the resulting depth buffer. This is a completely conservative approach compared to the approximated depth buffer from the reprojection technique.

23.5.2 Second Pass

In the second pass, once again, a compute shader is dispatched with the same number of threads as the total number of objects in the scene. However, this time, each thread performs occlusion culling in addition to potential frustum culling and LOD selection, regardless of whether the object was previously visible or not. The result of this dispatch is again a set of indirect draw call arguments representing objects found to be visible in this pass, but were not drawn in the

```
...

// Read object's visibility from the previous frame.
bool visible = visibilityBuffer[drawIndex];

// [Optional] Check if previously visible object is frustum culled
// in the current frame.
if (visible)
{
  bool frustumCulled = isFrustumCulled(...);
  visible &&= !frustumCulled;
}

// Only objects that were visible in the previous frame should be
// drawn in the first pass.
bool shouldDraw = visible;
if (shouldDraw)
{
  // [Optional] Select LOD.
  ...

  // Fill indirect draw call arguments.
  IndirectDrawArgs drawArgs;
  ...

  drawArgs[drawArgsIndex] = drawArgs;
}
```

Listing 23.2. First pass compute shader code snippet.

first pass. These draw arguments are stored in a GPU buffer and later executed
as an indirect draw call, similar to the first pass.

To prevent the redrawing of objects that were already drawn in the first
pass, it is necessary to skip objects that had a visibility of 1 in the previous
frame. Additionally, the visibility buffer should be updated for each object in
preparation for the next frame, based on the results from frustum and occlusion
culling, regardless of whether they are drawn in the second pass (Listing 23.3).

```
...

// [Optional] Check if object is frustum culled in the current
// frame.
bool frustumCulled = isFrustumCulled(...);

bool visible = !frustumCulled;

// Check if object is occlusion culled in the current frame.
if (visible)
{
  bool occlusionCulled = isOcclusionCulled(...);
  visible &&= !occlusionCulled;
}

// Only object that is visible in the current frame and was not
// drawn in the first pass should be drawn in the second pass.
bool shouldDraw = visible && !visibilityBuffer[drawIndex];
if (shouldDraw)
{
  // [Optional] Select LOD.
```

```
    ...

  // Fill indirect draw call arguments.
  IndirectDrawArgs drawArgs;
  ...

  drawArgs[drawArgsIndex] = drawArgs;
}

// Fill visibility buffer for the next frame.
visibilityBuffer[drawIndex] = visible;
```

Listing 23.3. Second pass compute shader code snippet.

23.5.3 Example

As an illustration, consider a scene featuring five static objects and a moving camera (Figure 23.6), observing the two-pass occlusion culling process for a single frame.

In the first pass, all five objects are getting processed. If an object had a visibility of 0 in the previous frame, it's skipped. For objects that had a visibility of 1, optional frustum culling and LOD selection can be performed. Say that only three objects were visible in the previous frame, but since the camera is moving to the left, one of the objects is no longer visible due to it being outside the camera's frustum (Figure 23.7). Assuming that the frustum culling is enabled, as a result only two objects that are still visible are rendered and the third one is skipped (Figure 23.8).

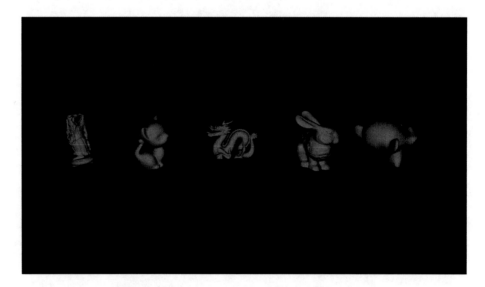

Figure 23.6. Example test scene with five objects.

Figure 23.7. Previous frame where the object colored in red is about to leave the camera view.

0	1	1	1	1
0	1	2	3	4

Figure 23.8. Visibility buffer from a previous frame during the first pass, where green indicates objects that are going to be drawn in this pass, which are still visible in the current frame.

In the second pass, all five objects in the scene are processed again regardless of their previous visibility. Then optional frustum culling, optional LOD selection, and occlusion culling are performed on all five objects. Say that compared to the previous frame, one previously non-visible object enters the camera frustum and becomes visible in the current frame (Figure 23.9). This means that, in this pass, only this additional object is drawn on top of the two already drawn objects from the first pass, resulting in a total of three rendered objects. Also, the visibility buffer is appropriately updated for the next frame (Figure 23.10).

23.5.4   Meshlet Culling

In recent years, GPU manufacturers have introduced a new programmable geometric shading pipeline known as the *mesh shading pipeline* [Kubisch 18]. It consists of two new shading stages with new types of shaders: task shaders and mesh shaders. These shader stages are designed to replace the vertex, tessellation, and geometry shader stages while leaving the fragment shader stage unaffected. Task

Figure 23.9. Current frame where the object colored in green has entered the camera view.

0	1	1	1	0
0	1	2	3	4

Figure 23.10. Updated visibility buffer after the second pass, where green indicates objects that are drawn in the second pass and not in the first pass.

shaders operate on a meshlet basis, where *meshlets*, or clusters, are typically very small mesh segments from which the entire mesh is constructed. Meshlets are usually generated in an offline process using various techniques [Jensen et al. 23]. Mesh shaders, on the other hand, operate on a per-primitive basis and are emitted by a task shader directly from a GPU. The purpose of mesh shaders is to emit primitives directly into the rasterizer. These two shader stages provide full control over each meshlet and primitive, enabling efficient culling, LOD techniques, and procedural generation. Currently, task shaders are in a bad state due to their performance limitations and their strong dependency on specific vendors. Many developers today opt to replace them with custom compute shaders, which directly feed task data to mesh shaders.

Since task shaders operate per meshlet, various meshlet culling techniques can be implemented in this shader stage. For culling purposes, each mesh should have some sort of bounds, most likely a bounding sphere. Two of the simplest meshlet culling techniques are frustum culling and backface cone culling. If

Figure 23.11. An example of a rendered frame that utilizes two-pass meshlet HZB occlusion culling, frustum culling, and cone culling.

the mesh shading pipeline is used in the previously presented two-pass solution, these two culling techniques can easily be implemented in both passes. The meshlet occlusion culling process closely resembles the object-based approach (Figure 23.11). An additional meshlet visibility buffer is required to track which meshlets were visible in the previous frame. Similarly to object occlusion culling, in the first pass only the visible meshlets of visible objects are rendered, followed by the generation of an HZB. In the second pass, all meshlets are appropriately culled, updating the meshlet visibility buffer and rendering the remaining meshlets that were not rendered in the first pass. This technique significantly reduces the number of rendered triangles on the screen (Figure 23.12). Additionally, in the mesh shaders, individual primitives can be culled, where backface primitive culling and small primitive culling are likely to be the most effective.

As the mesh shading pipeline is currently supported by only a handful of GPUs, this entire pipeline can be emulated using compute shaders, which is also a good fallback technique in practice.

23.6   Conclusion

Two-pass occlusion culling is generally a very effective optimization technique, but it may show its limits in situations with very radical movements relative to the camera. These types of object movements are uncommon and are often

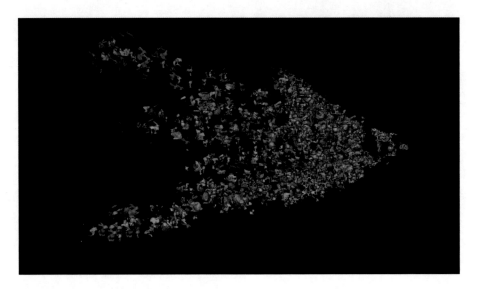

Figure 23.12. A debug view of a scene that utilizes two-pass meshlet HZB occlusion culling, frustum culling, and cone culling.

seen in cut-scene transitions. If they do occur, they may impact performance for a single frame after the cut was made. To address these issues, one potential solution would be to introduce an additional depth pre-pass.

As previously stated, this technique can also be used for meshlet and triangle occlusion culling, although triangle culling usually doesn't have performance gains. It can be used in forward rendering, deferred rendering, deferred materials, visibility buffering, and more. For highly dense geometry, deferred materials and visibility buffering (not to be confused with the visibility buffer mentioned previously) are likely to work the best. Considering that the majority of modern game engines are adopting the GPU-driven approach, it is reasonable to assume that most of them will incorporate some form of the presented occlusion culling solution, given its performance gains and simplicity.

Bibliography

[Anagnostou 17] Kostas Anagnostou. "Experiments in GPU-Based Occlusion Culling." Interplay of Light, November 15, 2017. https://interplayoflight. wordpress.com/2017/11/15/experiments-in-gpu-based-occlusion-culling/.

[Haar and Aaltonen 15] Ulrich Haar and Sebastian Aaltonen. "GPU-Driven Rendering Pipelines." Advances in Real-Time Rendering in Games,

SIGGRAPH Course, 2015. https://advances.realtimerendering.com/s2015/aaltonenhaar_siggraph2015_combined_final_footer_220dpi.pdf.

[Jensen et al. 23] Mark Bo Jensen, Jeppe Revall Frisvad, and J. Andreas Bærentzen. "Performance Comparison of Meshlet Generation Strategies." *Journal of Computer Graphics Techniques* 12:2 (2023), 1–27.

[Karis et al. 21] Brian Karis, Rune Stubbe, and Graham Wihlidal. "Nanite: A Deep Dive." Advances in Real-Time Rendering in Games, SIGGRAPH Course, 2021. https://advances.realtimerendering.com/s2021/Karis_Nanite_SIGGRAPH_Advances_2021_final.pdf.

[Kubisch 18] Christoph Kubisch. "Introduction to Turing Mesh Shaders." NVIDIA Developer, Technical Blog, 2018. https://developer.nvidia.com/blog/introduction-turing-mesh-shaders/.

[Reed 21] Nathan Reed. "Depth Precision Visualized." NVIDIA Developer, 2021. https://developer.nvidia.com/content/depth-precision-visualized.

[Silvennoinen et al. 14] Ari Silvennoinen, Hannu Saransaari, Samuli Laine, and Jaakko Lehtinen. "Occluder Simplification Using Planar Sections." *Computer Graphics Forum* 33:1 (2014), 235–245.

Shader Server System

Djordje Pepic

24.1 Introduction

To decrease development times of games, it is important that the graphics programming team can iterate as quickly as possible. This article covers a client server recompilation system for all platforms (PC, macOS, all Xbox, all PlayStation, Switch, iOS, Android, and Steam Deck) that allows the programming team to recompile shaders while the game is running with the press of a button. In other words, they do not need to reboot the whole game to see changes in shaders, which can take in some games during development 30–90 minutes.

While there might not be much that can be done to improve the iteration speed of C/C++ code, improving the iteration speed of shader code can be done easily with a simple and robust dynamic runtime recompilation system.

Since shader compilation is typically much faster than the compilation/linking of C++ executables, shaders can often be recompiled at interactive speeds (less than 0.1 seconds). If your graphics engine supports runtime shader binary reloading (which The Forge [The Forge Interactive 24] and many others do), then it can be combined with runtime recompilation to provide an interactive development experience where changes in shader code are visible almost instantaneously in the application at the click of a button—dramatically improving shader iteration time. Many AAA game engines implement some version of this approach, since improving iteration time can save millions of dollars in development time wasted on waiting for builds.

In the article, we will provide a detailed description of the requirements and implementation of the runtime shader recompilation system in The Forge, including the cross-platform networking implementation used by the system. We will also explain how such a system could be implemented or improved upon in other projects that may have different requirements.

24.2 Typical Features of a Shader Compiler

Before delving into dynamic shader recompilation, we need to first explain what is meant by *shader compilation*.

For the purposes of this article, shader compilation refers to the process of turning shader source code into binary bytecode representation that is consumed by the graphics API at shader load time. This can be done using a native shader compiler, such as `glslangValidator` or `dxc`.

543

However, using only the native shader compilers to create shader binaries has several drawbacks, so most game engines usually implement several other features in order to improve performance and developer experience. The most common features will be discussed here.

24.2.1   High-Level Cross-Platform Shader Language

If you try to compile your shaders for a different platform, you might find that you get compilation errors even if the source code is technically correct, or that the shader does not work as intended. This is due to the various differences between platforms when it comes to shader compilation—even when using the same language. This makes it problematic to write a single shader source file that can be used by all of the different supported platforms.

To address the platform differences, a common approach is to create a higher-level *generic* shader language that has a common syntax for all platforms. Then, a tool is used to convert this higher-level generic source code into lower-level platform-specific source code that can be used correctly by the corresponding native shader compiler. This conversion step is usually done at shader build time, right before the native platform compilers are invoked so that shaders can be compiled from generic source code to bytecode in a single step. The Forge implements such a system, and its design is outlined in Article 16.

This might sound like a lot of effort at first, but in most cases the platform differences are minor and can be implemented using basic macros, so the *conversion tool* would just prepend platform-specific implementations of these macros to the generic shader source code, which can then be compiled normally using native shader compilers.

24.2.2   Shader/Asset Definition Files

Imagine you want to add an optional feature to your shader. You could do this using runtime variables, but this has a performance impact. Ideally you would compile multiple optimized shader binaries and switch between them at runtime. You can do this manually for each shader/feature, but doing this quickly becomes tedious, time-consuming, and error-prone.

To address these issues, most game engines use some kind of unified shader/asset definition file that is parsed before shader compilation and used to generate all of the required permutations of the shader source code. These optimized sources can then be passed to the shader compiler directly. The exact performance trade-off for using runtime variables in shader source code will depend on the game and its specific rendering techniques, but this issue is common enough that larger game engines usually implement a generic system that handles compiling all versions at build time and then loading the necessary version of shaders automatically at runtime.

A common use case of this approach is implementing materials. A basic material file might look like Listing 24.1.

```
textures = ["albedo0.tex", "normal0.tex", "roughness0.tex"]
shaders  = ["material.vert", "material.frag"]
defines  = ["MATERIAL_KIND=0"]
```

Listing 24.1. A basic material file.

In this case you could implement all all material code inside of `material.vert`/ `material.frag` and use the `MATERIAL_KIND` define to turn on features based on what kind of rendering techniques the material requires.

24.2.3 Shader Reflection and Auto-binding

Shader resources (such as textures, buffers, etc.) cannot be directly manipulated outside of shader code. Instead, graphics APIs (such as Vulkan) are used to bind shader resources to specific hardware locations, which can then be manipulated on the GPU in shader source code using named variables. While this approach allows maximum flexibility, it has an inherent problem: shader resource definitions might be duplicated inside and outside of shader source code.

Modern engines that target high-end devices can mitigate this issue through the use of bindless resources. The idea is to bind a global array of resources once during initialization, and to extract the required resources from this global array in shader source code at runtime (either using hard-coded indices or dynamic indices on modern devices that support non-dynamically uniform resource indices). However, on low-end devices with small hardware limits (i.e., cheap Android phones), these limits might make using bindless unfeasible, so the explicit binding method is still required to support these devices.

A common technique to address the duplication is to generate information for binding shader resources from the shader bytecode by using shader compiler reflection APIs. These APIs are tightly integrated with the native platform shader compiler and provide extensive information about every variable and definition in the source code. The generated reflection information is then read on startup by the game, and can be used to set up/bind all required shader resources automatically.

Aside from auto-binding, shader reflection can also help to optimize the rendering pipeline by allowing for the creation of more optimal descriptor sets and pipeline layouts, since all of the required information is generated in the reflections ahead of time. While the details of this and the techniques used are quite interesting, they are not directly relevant to this article. However, it serves to demonstrate that there could be several steps related to shader compilation that happen after the bytecode has been compiled, and that the output might have complicated dependencies. These are things we will need to consider when designing a dynamic recompilation system.

24.2.4   Offline Compilation and Build System Integration

Shader compilation is slow, especially with optimizations enabled. It becomes even more slow as you keep adding various features. Since games should be fast, we would like to avoid compiling shaders at runtime of possible. Not compiling shaders at runtime also prevents the game from needing to ship shader sources in the final package, reducing its size and reducing the possibility of reverse engineering.

Due to this, shader compilation systems are designed with the goal of compiling shader bytecode ahead of time so that the shipping game only ever consumes already-compiled shader bytecode, to avoid the performance penalties that are associated with compiling shader bytecode at runtime. This is usually done by integrating the shader compiler into the build system, so that shaders are built at the same time as the executable and respond to changes made in the editor.

Another common approach is to separate assets/shader/script compilation into a different application that is used to generate the final assets used by the game. Some AAA games (such as *Call of Duty*) use this approach as it allows for maximum flexibility for artists (who get to use an intuitive GUI to manage assets) and maximum optimization for developers (who get complete control over the entire asset/shader compilation/packaging/compression process). However, this approach typically involves a significant amount of work for it to be worthwhile, so it is only employed by larger companies.

If we want our dynamic shader recompilation system to integrate seamlessly with the rest of the engine, then we will need to consider the build process in our design. Most importantly, we need a way to communicate the state of the shader compilation between the build process and our recompilation system. This can be done in a generic, cross-platform manner using files or sockets to communicate between processes, but the exact setup will depend on the build process. A common approach is to generate a file during the build process into a well-known location that contains the required information, which is later read and processed by the application or recompilation system at an arbitrary time after the build has completed.

24.3   Designing a Dynamic Shader Recompilation System

24.3.1   Definition of Terms

Before proceeding, there are some terms we need to define for the sake of consistency. The *host PC* is the PC used for development. The *device* is used to run the *app* being developed on the host PC. The shader source code lives on the host PC, and the app loads shader bytecode compiled on the host PC.

24.3.2 How to Communicate between the Host PC and the Device

When developing on PC (Win32/macOS/Linux), the host PC *is* the device, but when developing on mobile or console, then the host PC *is not* the device (which might be an iPhone or Xbox, for example). For this reason, our recompilation system should be based on sockets, so that communication between the host PC and the device happens using the network, and will work regardless of whether the host PC is the device or not. The host PC will run a *server*, and the device runs the *app*, which uses a socket client to receive shader bytecode from the server running on the host PC.

24.3.3 Loading Updated Shaders

When it comes to loading shaders that have been recompiled more recently than the app has been compiled, there are two main approaches with different trade-offs.

Loading Once on Startup When the app is started, it asks the server which shaders were compiled more recently than the app, and downloads the bytecode for those shaders from the server, which are then loaded by the app normally during initialization. This approach is only relevant if shader compilation occurs separately from the app and is not integrated into the app's build process.

The main benefit of this approach is simplicity. Since the updated shaders are downloaded before initialization, the app does not need to worry about destroying/recreating any graphics resources associated to the shaders. As mentioned in Section 24.2, larger engines might have many preprocessing and post-processing steps associated with shaders and their resources, so solving the problem of recreating resources dynamically at runtime in an efficient way might not be worth the effort. In this case it might be beneficial to optimize the app's startup time instead, so that the difference between restarting the entire app and only reloading shaders is minimized. This is the approach taken by the engine in *Call of Duty*, for example. However, the main drawback of this approach is that if you cannot optimize the app's startup time, then shader development iteration time will likely not see an improvement from implementing this approach.

Dynamically Reloading On-Demand Here, the app can request a shader recompile from the server at any time. Upon receiving a request, the server recompiles the requested shaders and sends back the updated shader bytecode. The app receives the updated shaders from the server and recreates all associated graphics API resources using the updated shader bytecode.

The main benefits of this approach are speed and flexibility. Since recompiling a few shaders and recreating the associated resources is orders of magnitude faster than starting up the app for any nontrivial game, this means that recompiling shaders using this approach will be *fast*. In fact, in most cases when this approach is implemented well, recompiling shaders is almost instantaneous and feels incredibly responsive in comparison to restarting the entire app. This is the approach that we will implement in this article.

24.3.4 Triggering a Shader Recompile

Before we delve into a full implementation of the dynamic reloading approach, it might be helpful to outline the details of the problem we are trying to solve.

We want to run a server on the host PC that can recompile shaders for any arbitrary app. This has several implications.

First, the server needs to know how to compile shaders for a given app. As mentioned previously, compiling shaders with all of the preprocessing and post-processing steps might be a nontrivial process, and replicating this process in a separate application might be difficult for a number of different reasons. Due to this, the recompilation process should aim to reuse existing shader compilation architecture as much as possible, to prevent having to duplicate code or shader definitions and introduce unnecessary complexity into the server.

Second, to handle recompiling shaders for multiple apps correctly, the app must send identifying information to the server, which uses this information to recompile shaders for that specific app. This also solves the problem of recompiling the same shader for different apps since we organize the information required to recompile a shader on a per-app basis. The code for this might look something like Listing 24.2.

```
send_to_server(application_id)
response = receive_from_server()
if is_success(response):
    reload_shaders(response)
else:
    print_error(response)
```

Listing 24.2. Pseudocode for a recompile request.

A simple solution to the first problem is to cache the arguments used to invoke the shader compiler when shaders are first compiled, and to reuse those arguments when recompiling shaders. This approach will work regardless of whether native a platform shader compiler or a high-level cross-platform shader compiler is used, which allows us to maximize the usage of existing shader compilation architecture. So, how do we cache the arguments, and where do we store them?

Caching the arguments is fairly straightforward, all you need to do is create a wrapper script that forwards command line arguments to the actual shader compiler, and use that in your project instead of the actual shader compiler. These arguments can then be saved to disk right before the compiler is invoked.

Before discussing where the cached arguments will be stored, we should discuss how the app receives shader bytecode compiled on the host PC normally without considering dynamic recompilation. For this, there are two possibilities: either the shader compiler outputs the bytecode directly into the app's resource folder, or the shader compiler outputs the bytecode into a directory that is later copied into the app's resource folder. Since this is required to just load shaders normally, it is likely that such a system has already been implemented into the build process, so we can leverage it to communicate between the shader compiler and the app.

Consider this, if we cache arguments to some per-app directory A, and we write directory A to a file that is stored next to the shader bytecode, then this file can be read by the app like any other shader/asset, allowing the app to know where the cached arguments are stored. Also, since the directory is per-app, it should be unique for every app. The app can then use this directory as the ID in the recompile request. This allows the server to know exactly how to recompile all shaders for each app and to be able to uniquely identify each app based on the recompile request. The revised pseudocode would look something like Listing 24.3.

```
intermediate_dir = read_contents_of_file("ShaderServer.txt")
send_to_server(intermediate_dir)
response = receive_from_server()
if is_success(response):
    reload_shaders(response)
else:
    print_error(response)
```

Listing 24.3. Pseudocode for a recompile request using the directory as ID.

24.3.5 Detecting Updated Shaders Using File-Modification Times

Another question that must be answered before we can describe the complete implementation is: how do we detect when a shader has been modified and needs to be recompiled? While there are several ways that this problem can be solved, the fastest method is to compare file-modification times to determine if a shader has been modified since it was last compiled. Using file-modification times is preferable due to the vast performance improvement over other methods, such as comparing content hashes, and offers a similar level of robustness. Also, if shader recompilation is not triggered due to file-modification time conflicts, then the user can simply try again, and incorrect results that originate from invalid file-modification times will not have serious consequences.

One simple way of using file-modification times to check if a shader has been updated is to check whether the modification time of the input shader source code file is greater than the modification time of the output shader bytecode file. If the answer is yes, then the shader has been modified since the last time it was built and needs to be recompiled.

Depending on how your shader compiler works, then a different approach of detecting updated shaders might be more straightforward. It might be the case (and is for many large game engines, including The Forge) that your shader compiler already implements some level of build-caching in order to speed up shader compilation. In this case, compiling a shader that has not been modified would not modify the output shader bytecode. If this is the case for your shader compiler, then you can simply check file-modification times of shader bytecode files before and after recompiling all related shaders, and only the shader bytecode that was actually compiled will have a new file-modification time and can therefore be uploaded to the app for reloading. Since this is how The Forge's shader compiler works, this is the approach that we will use in the article. It also simplifies the code, as we do not need to keep track of how each shader source file maps to its binary source code file; we only check file-modification times of shader bytecode files.

24.3.6   Reloading Shaders on the Device

There is only one more question that needs to be answered: how do we reload shaders on the device? You might be tempted to answer that we should just iterate over every shader in the updated list of shaders uploaded from the server, but as mentioned before there may be complex dependencies between shaders that cannot easily be represented in the shader source code. Due to this, many engines have a concept of *global reload*, where all resources of a specific type are reloaded based on certain events in the app. You might want to recreate all render targets that depend on the window size when the user resizes the window, for example. Another example is reloading all shaders of a certain type when there are modifications. This allows all differences in structure offsets, resource bindings, etc. to be properly recreated in the most straightforward way possible. Also, since these engines usually also optimize startup/loading time heavily, reloading everything might not be much slower than reloading only certain parts, especially if complex calculations need to be done in order to determine exactly what needs to be recreated based on a possibly massive resource dependency graph. For this article we will implement the global reload approach, where a successful shader upload triggers a global reload, and updated shaders are queried by path in the regular shader bytecode loading function and are returned instead of loading the original shader bytecode from disk.

24.3.7   Final Workflow for a Dynamic Shader Recompile

Now that we have discussed all of the considerations for implementing dynamic shader recompilation, we can finally create a general algorithm outline that we will implement step by step in the following section.

1. The user runs the server script on the host PC.

2. When shaders are compiled (at build time), the arguments used are cached and the directory where these cached arguments are stored is written to a file that will be read by the app.

3. On initialization, the app reads the directory where arguments are cached from the file generated at build time.

4. The user triggers a shader recompile (by pressing a hotkey, UI button, etc.).

5. The app connects to the server on the host PC and sends the cached argument directory to identify itself when triggering a recompile.

6. The server receives the directory from the app and uses it to load the cached arguments.

7. The server recompiles shaders using the loaded cached arguments and creates a list of updated shader paths.

8. The server loads the updated shader binaries using the updated shader paths and encodes them all into a binary blob that will be sent to the app to be used for reloading shaders.

9. The app receives the updated shaders from the server, stores them in memory, and triggers a shader reload on the device.

10. When shaders are reloaded, the updated shaders are queried by path and used instead of the original shaders on disk.

11. The shader changes are now visible in the app.

24.4 Considerations when Implementing the Shader Server

Several implementation details are important to consider when creating a dynamic shader reload system. Since the example code for this article is written in Python, as well as the Shader Server implementation in The Forge, this section assumes that Python is used to create the server application on the host PC. However, most of the arguments are equally applicable to other languages (including statically compiled ones like C, C++, and Rust).

24.4.1 Caching Shader Compiler Arguments

When caching the arguments used to invoke the shader compiler, there are several performance considerations to be made to ensure reloads can happen as quickly as possible, as well as some quality of life considerations that will make using/debugging the system easier.

- Cached arguments are stored in a subdirectory inside the intermediate folder (e.g., a subdirectory called `cached_args`).

  - If we plan on generating files as part of the build process, placing them in a subdirectory helps keep the intermediate directory clean.

- When we recompile all shaders for an application, we can just iterate over the files in this directory without needing to worry about filtering files, which should make the code much faster and more concise.

- The input path should be hashed to generate the output filename.

  - We need a unique filename for every input path that includes information about nested subdirectories.

  - We do not want to create nested subdirectories in the cached arguments directory to speed up iterating over all files in this directory.

- Python's `pickle` library is used to serialize the arguments to disk.

  - We need to store/load the shader compiler arguments without any conversions or loss of information so invocations using the cached arguments will be identical to the original invocation without needing to escape/transform the arguments in any way (as this can lead to difficult-to-diagnose errors). Python's `pickle` library allows us to do exactly this.

24.4.2 Server/Client Networking

One of the first steps when it comes to writing software that uses networking is creating a basic server and client that communicate over the network. If the server application is written using Python or Rust, then setting up a socket and writing networking code is made much easier by the cross-platform networking libraries that are provided in the standard libraries of those languages. However in C/C++, networking involves using OS-specific networking functions.

If you wish to implement your own custom networking code in C, then there are a few things that you might be interested to know. First, aside from some minor caveats, the standard BSD socket API is supported by every modern gaming platform (PC, all consoles, and mobile). Many of these platforms implement standard UNIX/Windows APIs to some extent, but the BSD socket API is by far the most widely supported standard API. This means that if you write a fully compliant Win32/POSIX socket implementation that only uses the standard BSD socket API features and avoids all extensions and platform-specific features, then that code should compile and run correctly on all gaming platforms. If you are curious, you can read the source code of the networking implementation found in The Forge, located at `The-Forge/Common_3/Tools/Network/Network.c`. This single implementation is used and tested on every platform that The Forge supports and is the foundation for The Forge's implementation of Shader Server.

Finally, here are a few tips to make developing network code easier:

- When setting up the server, set the `SO_REUSEADDR` socket option before binding the server to an address. This prevents frustrating "Address already in use" errors when restarting the server application multiple times in quick succession during development.

- In the server application, listen on address `0.0.0.0`. This allows both connections on `localhost` and connections on the host PC's local network address (e.g., 192.168.0.12) to be accepted by the server.

24.4.3 Recompiling Shaders on the Host PC

In order for shaders to be recompiled on the host PC, there are several things that need to happen:

- The client must send the cached arguments directory to the server.

- The server loads cached arguments from files in the directory sent by the client.

- The server recompiles the shaders using the cached arguments that were loaded from disk.

- The server detects which shader binaries have been modified after recompiling.

- The server loads the modified shader binaries from disk.

- The server encodes the shader binaries into a network message and sends it to the client.

While most of this is fairly straightforward to achieve, there are a few things to keep in mind when implementing:

- Shaders can be recompiled in parallel by spawning multiple processes that invoke the shader compiler.

- Loading modified shader binaries from disk can be done in parallel using multiple threads.

- You want to reduce the size of the data sent over the network, so variable-length encodings are preferred. In the next section, we will describe a basic, extensible encoding for the server-client messages.

24.4.4 Message Protocol for Server-Client Communication

When writing networking code, it is important to design a protocol that is simple (to avoid bugs), but also efficient (to avoid sending unnecessary data over the network). A common approach is to create variable-length types that are prefixed with the data length. This allows the code receiving the data to read a fixed-size number, followed by a variable number of bytes that is specified by the number.

This is useful as it allows the receiving code to only perform a single allocation in order to read all data, which is good for performance.

Another common technique is to prefix the message with a *type* byte. This allows many different message types to be implemented, and the cost of reading this extra byte is often negligible compared to the rest of the message. Combining this with the technique to encode variable-length types, you can create a generic protocol that is efficient and flexible, and can be extended in the future.

One final consideration is *endianness*. Since the host PC and the device might be running on CPUs with different endianness, we need to be careful when encoding/decoding our network messages to avoid reading numbers with the wrong byte order. One simple way of doing this is to just encode all numbers as little-endian. Since little-endian is the most popular architecture, this results in the fastest code as it will avoid the cost of byte-swapping in most cases.

Here is a pseudo-implementation of the protocol that we will be using for our implementation of Shader Server:

```
enum MessageKind: uint8_t {
    Success = 0,
    Error = 1,
};
struct Header {
    MessageKind kind;
    uint32_t size; // Little-endian
};
struct Message {
    Header header;
    union {
        UpdatedShaders update;
        char error[]; // Variable-length (Header.size)
    };
};
struct UpdatedShaders {
    uint32_t shaderCount;        // Little-endian
    struct {
        uint32_t pathSize;       // Little-endian, includes null
                                 // byte
        uint32_t bytecodeSize;   // Little-endian
        char path[];             // Variable-length (pathSize)
        uint8_t bytecode[];      // Variable-length (bytecodeSize)

    } shaders[];                 // Variable-length (shaderCount)
};
```

In this protocol, there are two types of message: success (contains updated shaders) and error (contains an error message). To distinguish the type of message, we have a header that contains a *tag* byte, as well as the total message size. This allows us to always receive 5 bytes for the header, and to use the size information to receive the rest of the message using a single allocation and call to `recv`. In practice, you might need to call `recv` several times to receive the entire message, but it can happen using a single `recv` call with this approach.

The error message is simple; it just contains an array of bytes that is the error message. Also, since we already have the message size in the header, we can just use this size to represent the length of the error message (including the null byte, for consistency with the other fields).

The updated shaders message is just an array of shader (path, bytecode) pairs, encoded using the variable-length approach described previously. For the sake of consistency, we include the null byte (if present), in the `length` field of all variable-length encoded members.

24.4.5 Detecting the IP Address of the Host PC

While just using `localhost` in the client code will work on PC, in order to get Shader Server working on multiple platforms, you will need to communicate the address of the host PC to the client, so that it can make a request over the local network. This can be done quite easily, though: we can just append the IP address of the host PC to the file that is used to communicate the cached arguments directory to the app. Then during the app's startup, we can read this address after reading the directory and store it to be used for recompile requests, instead of `localhost`.

24.5 Considerations for a Production-Ready Implementation

24.5.1 Using `localhost` for Recompile Requests when Possible

When using the IP address of the host PC, the recompile request must first travel to the network router before it eventually is forwarded to the host PC. This introduces additional latency and points of failure, so we would prefer to avoid doing this if possible and to use `localhost` for the requests instead.

On some platforms (like iOS), we need to use the IP of the host PC for recompile requests in order for everything to work. On other platforms, using `localhost` will work identically to using the IP of the host PC. On Win32/Linux/macOS, this is because the host PC is equal to the device, so we can avoid the local network round trip by directly using `localhost`.

On some platforms it is also possible to redirect socket connections on a specific port to `localhost` on the development PC. For example, on Android you can use `adb reverse tcp:PORT tcp:PORT` to forward requests from `PORT` on the device to `localhost:PORT` on the development PC.

24.5.2 Recompiling in a Separate Thread

To simplify the code in this article, we avoid discussing threads, but considering them is important for a production implementation. A naive function that requests a shader recompile might block until it receives the updated shaders, but this could take a very long time. Since this function would be mostly blocking inside of networking system calls, it is a good candidate for moving to a separate thread. Then, the function that requests a shader recompile can simply launch a thread that does the actual recompile request, and return almost instantly. You will need to do extra bookkeeping to keep track of when a shader compilation is finished, but it is well worth the performance improvement.

24.5.3 Ensuring Only One Recompile Can Be in Flight at a Time in the App

If we launch threads that request recompilations, then we also need to ensure that only one recompile can be running at a time. Since a shader recompile is very fast using the approach presented in this article, we don't need to worry about dealing with multiple concurrent recompile requests, a single recompile at a time will suffice for a system that is primarily driven by user input.

To implement this, all that is needed is a variable to represent whether a shader recompilation is currently happening. Before launching a recompile thread, you check this variable, and if it is true then you skip the recompile (return early); otherwise you set the variable to true and launch the recompile thread. If the shader recompile request function will be called from multiple threads, then the "shader recompilation is currently happening" variable should be implemented using an atomic type, so that it will work correctly when used from multiple threads.

24.5.4 Multi-process Safety when Running Code on the Host PC

All explanations so far have assumed a single application being built and a single reload server running on the same PC as the application. In a production implementation, the shader compiler and reload server might be called from multiple processes for a number of reasons (build automation, continuous integration scripts, multiple devices connecting to a single development PC, etc.). To ensure our code works correctly when used from multiple processes, we can use operating system *file locking* APIs in order to create a system-wide lock that will allow coordination between multiple processes. Then, the unsafe code can be guarded using these locks, and that will prevent multiple processes from running on multiple servers or writing to the same files concurrently.

On Windows, create a *global mutex* by calling `CreateMutex` with a `name` argument that has the prefix `Global`. This mutex can then be used as any other Win32 mutex, but it will be synchronized between multiple processes. On Linux/macOS, the `flock` system calls implement a system-level lock that can be used to synchronize multiple processes.

24.5.5 Using Timeouts to Improve the Responsiveness of a Failed Recompilation

When a shader recompile fails on the app due to networking issues, there is a chance that the code might block indefinitely as it waits for a failed connection that will never return. When using `localhost`, this should never happen, so that is not a concern for platforms that support using `localhost` for shader recompile requests. However, for the other platforms it may be beneficial to set timeouts on the sockets used for connecting to the server. All platforms support the `SO_SNDTIMEO` and `SO_RCVTIMEO` socket options, but some platforms (such as Sony) additionally support setting timeouts for `connect` and `accept` socket calls, which can also be useful for improving responsiveness, as `connect` is called earlier than `send` and `recv`, and also may fail in the manner described.

24.6 Conclusion

While a production-ready runtime shader reloading implementation might have many considerations, a basic implementation can be created quickly and easily with minimal code, and will improve graphics developer iteration time without investing too much time to create such a system. Hopefully, with the ideas presented in this article, you will have a better understanding of the various ideas, trade-offs and requirements involved in writing a robust, reliable, runtime shader reloading system.

Bibliography

[The Forge Interactive 24] The Forge Interactive. "The Forge." GitHub repository, 2024. https://github.com/ConfettiFX/The-Forge.

About the Editors

Wessam Bahnassi is a 20-year veteran in 3D engine design and optimization. He has published many AAA games, as well as his own native 120-FPS PSVR space shooter game *Hyper Void*. He is a loyal contributor to the best GPU programming book series: *ShaderX*, *GPU Pro*, *GPU Zen*, and others series as well. He is currently a distinguished engineer at NVIDIA, implementing rendering optimizations and contributing to a few cool research projects.

Kirill Bazhenov is a seasoned game developer with a long history of working in various game companies and shipping a considerable amount of PC and console games across different genres, from smaller third-person action games to large MMORPGs.

Wolfgang Engel is the CEO of The Forge Interactive, a think tank for advanced real-time graphics research and a service provider for the video game and movie industry. The Forge Interactive worked in the last 15 years on many AAA IPs like *Tomb Raider*, *Battlefield 4*, *Murdered Soul Suspect*, *Star Citizen*, *Dirt 4*, *Vainglory*, *Transistor*, *Call of Duty Black Ops 3*, *Battlefield 1*, *Mafia 3*, and others. Wolfgang is the founder and editor of the *ShaderX*, *GPU Pro*, and *GPU Zen* book series, a former Microsoft MVP, the author of several books and articles on real-time rendering, and a regular contributor to websites and the Game Developers Conference. One of the books he edited, *ShaderX4*, won the Game Developer Front Line Award in 2006. Wolfgang is on the advisory boards of several companies. He is an active contributor to several future standards that drive the game industry.

Anton Kaplanyan leads graphics research at Intel, bringing a wealth of experience and knowledge in the field of computer graphics. His expertise spans various aspects of real-time computer graphics, including realistic rendering, light transport simulation, denoising of Monte Carlo rendering, neural graphics, as well as augmented and virtual reality with a PhD in Computer Graphics from Karlsruhe Institute of Technology. Anton has been instrumental in inventing and contributing to several groundbreaking technologies, such as Light Propagation Volumes in CryEngine, NVIDIA RTX hardware, and LightRig light editing technology licensed by Pixar and used in RenderMan since 2017, as well as working on perceptual and neural graphics for Meta's upcoming products and lately on shaping the new line of discrete GPU products at Intel, yielding over 57 patents. Anton has chaired multiple graphics conferences and published more than 30 papers in prestigious computer graphics conferences and journals, including ACM SIGGRAPH, *ACM Transactions on Graphics*, and Eurographics, which have garnered over 3,200 citations.

Nicolas Lopez is a technical architect on the *Assassin's Creed* brand and the Anvil Engine at Ubisoft Montreal. He has a passion for game engine architecture, global illumination, and large-scale rendering. He has contributed to several AAA titles such as *Neverdead, Star Wars Battlefront 2* or *Assassin's Creed Shadows*. He's also contributed to various high profile engines such as Frostbite and Anvil.

Laura Reznikov is an engineering manager at Meta focused on advancing avatar visuals and performance. Previously, she was a senior engineering manager responsible for Intel's award-winning render kernel libraries and a staff graphics engineer for Intel's game developer relations team. During her time at Intel, she made contributions to Variable Rate Shading and ray tracing hardware and APIs. She's passionate about graphics community building, founding the Graphics Programming community on Twitter, speaking at Game Developers Conference, jurying for SIGGRAPH, chairing for I3D, and creating RenderThreads.com. Laura holds a BFA degree in Film and Animation and received her MS in Computer Science, focused on physically based rendering, both from Rochester Institute of Technology.

Peter Sikachev has been messing with pixel shaders in AAA video games for over a decade. He has contributed to a few small titles, such as *Deus Ex: Mankind Divided, Red Dead Redemption 2*, and *Cyberpunk 2077*. Peter enjoys bragging about what he has done at SIGGRAPH and other venues. He is currently a Technical Director at Virtuos Warsaw and still allegedly writes code occasionally.

About the Authors

Russel Arbore is a graduate student studying computer science at the University of Illinois Urbana-Champaign, where he researches heterogeneous compiler implementation and sparse voxel representations for ray traced rendering applications. Previously, he developed deep learning compiler testing infrastructure at NVIDIA and volumetric cloud rendering software at Aechelon Technology.

Sai Bangaru is a Research Scientist at NVIDIA working on algorithms and compilers for differentiable programming, with applications in graphics and vision. His current research focuses on incorporating scalable, high-performance automatic differentiation into the Slang shading language. Sai received a PhD from MIT CSAIL in April 2024, advised by Prof. Frédo Durand.

Kirill Bazhenov is a seasoned game developer with a long history of working in various game companies and shipping a considerable amount of PC and console games across different genres, from smaller third-person action games to large MMORPGs.

Malte Bennewitz is a lead rendering software engineer at Electronic Arts, working on the *Madden NFL* series. Before that, he was a gameplay and later graphics programmer at Ubisoft Berlin, collaborating with studios around the world on games like *Far Cry 6* and *Skull and Bones*, where he was in charge of implementing a new texture streaming technique. His career began with a game mechanics programming position at Traveller's Tales, contributing to several LEGO video games. His focus is now on photorealistic rendering techniques and performance optimizations.

Darius Bouma is a Rendering Engineer at Traverse Research, where he is responsible for designing and implementing advanced rendering systems. Initially, he started by specializing in rendering architecture, primarily focusing on building a cross-API bindless renderer. Over time his focus shifted more toward real-time light transport, which led up to him leading the real-time path tracing for the Evolve benchmark. Prior to joining Traverse, Darius worked at the rendering

561

team at Lumion. He is highly driven to push rendering forward to new levels, on all platforms.

William Bussière is a rendering programmer at Ubisoft Montréal, where he is developing a ray traced global illumination solution for the Anvil engine. He modernized various post effects and designed a high-throughput rendering pipeline for distant vegetation on *Assassin's Creed Valhalla*.

Tim Cheblokov joined NVIDIA Corporation in 2004 and is currently a Distinguished Developer Technology Engineer. He focuses on GPU performance optimizations and real-time simulation and rendering techniques, including ray tracing and denoising.

Wolfgang Engel is the CEO of The Forge Interactive, a think tank for advanced real-time graphics research and a service provider for the video game and movie industry. The Forge Interactive worked in the last 15 years on many AAA IPs like *Tomb Raider*, *Battlefield 4*, *Murdered Soul Suspect*, *Star Citizen*, *Dirt 4*, *Vainglory*, *Transistor*, *Call of Duty Black Ops 3*, *Battlefield 1*, *Mafia 3*, and others. Wolfgang is the founder and editor of the *ShaderX*, *GPU Pro*, and *GPU Zen* book series, a former Microsoft MVP, the author of several books and articles on real-time rendering, and a regular contributor to websites and the Game Developers Conference. One of the books he edited, *ShaderX4*, won the Game Developer Front Line Award in 2006. Wolfgang is on the advisory boards of several companies. He is an active contributor to several future standards that drive the game industry.

Giovanni De Francesco is a Technical Lighting Artist with fifteen years of professional experience in computer graphics. In his position at CD PROJEKT RED, he started curating lighting art and ensuring world-class aesthetics for *Cyberpunk 2077*. Subsequently, he took on a technical role, designing and testing tools for the Red Engine and working as a link between lighting and rendering groups. He supported the implementation of third-party technology and helped NVIDIA developers implement cutting-edge rendering technology, such as ray tracing and path tracing. Before joining CD PROJEKT RED, he worked as a freelancer for various companies in the Italian territory, in both the fields of real-time and offline rendering.

Steven Gao is an undergraduate student majoring in Computer Science at the University of Illinois Urbana-Champaign. His research interests include efficient system algorithms for extended reality (XR) and machine learning workloads.

Xifeng Gao is a principal researcher at LightSpeed Studios, leading the R&D of 3D asset optimization and processing. His main expertise lies in geometry computing, with applications in computer graphics, computer-aided design and analysis, and robotics. He has more than 60 peer-reviewed papers published in top-ranked journals and conferences.

Justin Hall has a master's degree in Computer Science. His past interests have included parallel/distributed systems and GPU programming.

Yong He is a researcher at NVIDIA working on programming languages for real-time graphics applications. He leads the development of the Slang shading language. Yong received his PhD in computer science from Carnegie Mellon University in September 2018.

Nathan Hoobler began his computer graphics career at a young age, teaching gorillas to hurl bananas at one another in QBasic and moving on to becoming deeply fascinated by what all the text scrolling by meant as *DooM* loaded on his 386. Professionally he has worked in the gaming industry for nearly two decades, the majority of which have been spent working as an engineer in NVIDIA's Developer Technology Group.

Grigory Javadyan spent his past life working on an array of various projects ranging from trading software to search ads, practicing computer graphics as a hobby in the meanwhile. Currently, he is a rendering engineer on the RealityKit team. Prior to that, he worked virtual reality and augmented reality related projects at Google, and programmed GPUs at Waymo.

Wangziwei Jiang specialized in GPGPU and stylized rendering during his master's program at the South China University of Technology. His contribution to this book elaborates on the content of his paper at Eurographics Symposium on Rendering (EGSR) 2022. Upon completing his studies in 2022, he took on the role of a graphics programmer. In this capacity, he provides rendering features and GPU performance optimization for several well-known titles. Outside work, he dedicates his time to exploring innovative non-photorealistic rendering algorithms.

Chih-Chen Kao is a researcher and software engineer at AMD. Before that, he worked on autonomous driving. He earned his PhD in Computer Science from National Taiwan University in Taipei, Taiwan, in 2017. His research interests encompass real-time ray tracing, physically based rendering, heterogeneous computing, and the application of deep learning in computer graphics.

Kaori Kato is an expert rendering programmer at Ubisoft Singapore. In *Skull and Bones*, she was in charge of various features such as terrain, procedural asset pipeline, volumetric fog, and clouds. The biggest task in the project was implementing a new resource streaming system. Previously, she worked at KOEI, a Japanese developer, and contributed to *GPU Pro* on screen-space cloud lighting.

Jon Kennedy is a Principal Developer Technology Engineer at NVIDIA, leveraging his expertise in games and graphics cultivated over the past 25+ years. Throughout his career, Jon has delved into various facets of the industry, from virtual reality software and CAD to GPU drivers and game development, encompassing software design, performance analysis, and optimization. Presently, his focus lies on CPU performance analysis and enhancing gaming experiences by collaborating closely with developers to integrate cutting-edge technologies into applications running on NVIDIA GeForce graphics cards.

سفيان خياط (Soufiane KHIAT) is a Lead Rendering Software Engineer at EA Criterion, where he works for the *Battlefield* franchise. Before joining EA Criterion, he was a Senior Graphics Engineer at Unity (High Definition Render Pipeline). Prior to that he was at Ubisoft Montréal at LaForge R&D department, working on *Watch Dogs 2* and *Assassin's Creed Unity*.

Jakub Knapik is VP of Art and Global Art Director at CD PROJEKT RED. He is a VFX Supervisor, Art Director, and CG Artist with over 22 years of experience working in the film and commercial industry. In his position, he oversees art in all of the projects the studio is developing. Before becoming the Global Art Director, Jakub worked as a Lighting and FX Art Director on *Cyberpunk 2077* and finally as an Art Director on *Cyberpunk 2077 Phantom Liberty*. He also has broad experience from before joining game development: as a generalist, compositing artist, lighting artist, and visual effects supervisor, both directly with clients but also on set with film crews. He had an opportunity to explore a vast world of projects and video clips, starting with deeply art-driven films like Lars Von Trier's *Melancholia*, through special projects for European Space Agency's mission Rosetta, sophisticated commercials for BMW, and "ARES" for *The Martian* movie, but also music video clips for rock legends like Radiohead. A few years ago, he decided to dive into the vivid world of game development with its fast-growing technology and visual language. He is deeply fascinated by both beautiful and intelligent visual storytelling and the complex technical side of computer graphics.

Pawel Kozlowski is a Principal Developer Technology Engineer in the Developer and Performance Technology group at NVIDIA. With over a decade of experience in real-time computer graphics, Pawel has contributed to significant advancements in the gaming industry. He was among the first to integrate real-time ray tracing into AAA games, with his work on *Battlefield V* marking a notable achievement. Since then, Pawel has contributed to many other games and engines in the real-time ray tracing space such as *Cyberpunk 2077*, the *Call of Duty* series, *Minecraft*, and Unreal Engine. Pawel values the transformative power of technology and advocates for the future of real-time graphics through real-time path tracing powered by AI and ReSTIR-like sampling algorithms. His academic background includes a PhD from the University of Oslo, Norway, and a BS and MSc from the University of Warsaw, Poland.

Milos Kruskonja is a Senior Rendering Engineer at The Multiplayer Group, where he is responsible for helping game studios by developing the latest rendering techniques. Prior to that, Milos began his rendering career with the rendering team at Ubisoft. Computer graphics have been his passion since university and are a central theme in his hobby projects. Recently, his main focus has been on real-time large-scale geometry rendering.

Manas Kulkarni is a software architect at The Forge Interactive for the last seven years. He helped to develop The Forge Framework (TM) and contributed to projects like Warzone Mobile, Starfield, Spiderman and many others. In his spare time he enjoys Martial Arts and playing the drums.

Xiang Lan is an expert engineer at Tencent IEG. He has more than 20 years of software development experience. He has been engaged in front-line research and development for a long time. He has rich experience in game clients and servers. He is currently mainly engaged in the development and support of game engines.

Wei Li is a senior research scientist at LightSpeed Studios, Tencent Shanghai. Previously, he was a postdoc at Inria Saclay, worked with Prof. Mathieu Desbrun. He obtained his doctorate from ShanghaiTech University in China, supervised by Prof. Xiaopei Liu, and majoring in computer graphics. Differing from traditional fluid simulation, his research is multi-disciplinary, covering many aspects in computer science and computational physics, as well as applying artificial intelligence in physical simulation.

Shiqiu (Edward) Liu is a Principal Research Scientist and Senior Research Manager at NVIDIA. His teams spearhead the research of integrating cutting-edge AI with traditional computer graphics, advancing the Pareto curve of rendering quality and performance. This research has been instrumental in the development of renowned products like DLSS. Prior to this, Shiqiu was a core contributor to the advancements of real-time ray tracing in games at NVIDIA.

Jeffrey Liu is an undergraduate student studying mathematics and computer science at the University of Illinois Urbana-Champaign, where he researches topics in extended reality with the ILLIXR group. Previously, he contributed to light tree importance sampling in Blender's Cycles path-tracer and also interned at Epic Games to develop extended reality features in Unreal Engine. His current research interests include real-time ray tracing, human perception, and optics.

Nicolas Lopez is a technical architect on the *Assassin's Creed* brand and the *Anvil Engine* at Ubisoft Montréal. He has a passion for game engine architecture, global illumination, and large-scale rendering. He has contributed to several AAA titles such as *Neverdead, Star Wars Battlefront 2*, and *Assassin's Creed Shadows*. He's also contributed to various high-profile engines such as Frostbite and Anvil.

Alessio Lustri is an undergraduate student studying computer science and mathematics at the University of Florence. His current interests and personal projects include real-time ray tracing and rasterization, as well as AI research.

Evgeny Makarov has been working as a developer technology engineer at NVIDIA since 2006, supporting game developers to improve visuals and performance in PC games.

Zhenyu Mao is a principal game engineer at LightSpeed Studios and has over 20 years of experience in game development. He focuses on 3D rendering, engine architecture, and optimization. He worked as a 3D tech lead in *Far Cry 5, Far Cry 6*, and other AAA titles such as *Rainbow Six, Splinter Cell 5*, and *End War*.

Juho Marttila is a Senior Research Scientist at NVIDIA, specializing in the development of advanced AI techniques to enhance real-time graphics quality and performance. Prior to his current role, Juho worked on large-scale 3D reconstruction, level-of-detail optimization, and streaming technologies.

Jacob Munkberg is a Principal Research Scientist in NVIDIA's real-time rendering research group. Prior to joining NVIDIA Research in 2016, Jacob worked as a senior research scientist in Intel's Advanced Rendering Technology team. He joined Intel in 2008 via Intel's acquisition of the startup, Swiftfoot Graphics, specializing in culling technology and efficient multi-view graphics. Jacob received his PhD in computer science from Lund University and his MS in engineering physics from Chalmers University of Technology. Jacob is currently working on 3D reconstruction through differentiable rendering and machine learning for real-time graphics applications.

Michael Murphy is a Senior Developer Technology Engineer at NVIDIA, where he focuses on optimization, path tracing, game engine integration, and graphics research projects.

Thibault Ober is a graphic engineer working at The Forge Interactive developing cutting-edge graphics middleware for the game and movie industries. He has experience working on different platforms ranging from Steam Deck and PC to console and mobile. Over the years, He worked on various in-house engines including some AAA game developers.

Nicola Palomba is a graphics programmer at The Forge Interactive. He has always been interested in any creative applications of computer science and software engineering, so game development was a natural fit. Before starting his career at The Forge, he was an intern at the Italian National Council of Researches (CNR), where he worked on compression algorithms for depth data and image enhancement techniques.

Zherong Pan is a senior researcher at Tencent America. He was a postdoctoral researcher at the Intelligent Motion Lab of the University of Illinois Urbana-Champaign. He obtained a PhD from the University of North Carolina at Chapel Hill. His research is focused on numerical analysis, motion planning, and physics-based modeling for high-dimensional dynamic systems.

Djordje Pepic is a graphics programmer at The Forge Interactive. During his time at The Forge, he has worked on the game engines for *Call of Duty Warzone Mobile* and *Hytale* on mobile and PC platforms. His passion is optimizing shaders, and in his free time he enjoys developing high-performance GPU-driven voxel simulations. He is also the author of the Shader Server system found in The Forge.

Chen Qiao is a senior engineer at Tencent Games. During his time at Tencent, he has worked on developing numerous projects. His primary focus is on illumination, material rendering, optimization tasks, and the application of artificial intelligence technology.

Jiang Qin is a principal technical artist at Tencent MoreFun Studios, leading the R&D of the PCG pipeline Falcon. He has more than 15 years of game development experience. His main expertise lies in the field of technical art, which includes materials, shading, visual effects (VFX), procedural content generation (PCG), and the pipeline of art tools.

Randall Rauwendaal is a Principal Architect on the Graphics Research Team at Qualcomm. He leads investigations spanning rendering, compression, and machine learning with the ultimate goal of optimizing Qualcomm's power efficient GPUs. Previously, he architected and designed graphics features for Apple GPUs, including the Tessellator, Variable Rasterization Rate, and many more.

Jake Ryan is a developer technology engineer at AMD, where he works with game studios to optimize application performance and integrate AMD middleware. He received his bachelor's degree from DigiPen Institute of Technology in 2021. In his free time, Jake likes to study real-time rendering techniques with his hobby renderer.

Matej Sakmary is a graduate student at Czech Technical University in Prague, where he pursues a master's degree in Computer Graphics. In his free time, he focuses on implementing, improving, and developing a variety of rendering techniques that he adds to his ongoing research and hobby sandbox project.

Marco Salvi is a Principal Research Scientist at NVIDIA, where he works on rendering algorithms for the post-Moore's law era. His research interests span a broad range of topics, from antialiasing and order-independent transparency to ray tracing hardware, texture compression, and neural rendering. Marco has made numerous contributions to rendering APIs, and his early work on real-time neural image reconstruction has led to the development of NVIDIA DLSS. Prior to becoming a researcher, Marco worked at Ninja Theory and LucasArts architecting advanced graphics engines, performing low-level optimizations, and developing new rendering techniques for games on two generations of PlayStation and Xbox consoles.

Dr. Eric Shaffer is an Associate Teaching Professor in the Department of Computer Science at the University of Illinois Urbana-Champaign. He teaches courses on and pursues research in the areas of computer graphics, visualization, and game development.

Yijie Shi is an engine programmer with a passion for pushing performance boundaries. Her early experience developing an in-house engine for desktop games honed her ability to identify performance bottlenecks in C++ and Gameplay code. She excels at implementing simple yet effective optimizations, enabling games to run smoothly even on low-end mobile devices. In recent years, she's been focusing on using GPU-driven techniques to reduce CPU load, alongside optimizing performance for volumetric rendering effects.

Haozhe Su is a senior researcher at LightSpeed Studios, Tencent America. He received his PhD degree in Computer Science from Rutgers University, under the supervision of Prof. Mridul Aanjaneya. His research interests lie in numerical computation/algorithms and their applications in physics-based simulation.

Xueqiang Wang is an expert engine programmer at Tencent Games. He has worked on the rendering and tools for various games, and has optimized many titles on PC, console, virtual reality, and mobile platforms.

Aidan Wefel has a degree in physics from the University of Illinois Urbana-Champaign and is currently studying computer science there as a graduate student. He works on virtual reality and augmented reality applications.

Xilei Wei is a principal game engineer at Tencent MoreFun Studios, leading R&D of the action game product line. He primarily focuses on action gameplay, engine architecture, and performance optimization. He has developed several mobile action games from scratch, all of which have been well received in the market.

Tomer Weiss is an assistant professor with the Department of Informatics at the New Jersey Institute of Technology. Before that, he was a research scientist with Wayfair, Boston. In 2018, he completed his PhD at the University of California, Los Angeles. He received the Best Paper Award from the ACM SIGGRAPH conference on Motion in Games, for his work on virtual crowd simulation. He was a finalist presenter in both ACM SIGGRAPH Thesis Fast Forward and the ACM SIGGRAPH Asia Doctoral Symposium in 2018. His research interests include crowd simulation and interactive visual computing.

Bartlomiej Wronski started his career in 2010 and initially worked as a game developer on franchises such as *The Witcher, Assassin's Creed, Far Cry*, and *God of War*. He took an almost five-year break from rendering at Google Research, working on computational photography, image processing, and machine learning. Some product applications of his research include Super Res Zoom and Night Sight on Google Pixel phones. Not able to resist coming back to computer graphics, Bart joined NVIDIA as a Principal Research Scientist in 2022 with a mission to bridge real-time rendering, machine learning, and signal processing.

Kui Wu is a principal research scientist at LightSpeed Studios, Tencent America. Previously, he was a postdoctoral associate at MIT CSAIL. He received a PhD in Computer Science from the University of Utah in 2019. His research interests are computer graphics, especially mesh processing, computational fabrication, real-time rendering, and physical-based simulation.

Lifan Wu is a Research Scientist at NVIDIA's real-time rendering research group. Lifan received his PhD from the University of California, San Diego in 2020, advised by Prof. Ravi Ramamoorthi. Before that, Lifan obtained his bachelor degree from Tsinghua University in 2015. Lifan is currently working on algorithms and systems for efficient differential light transport and inverse rendering. He is also interested in simulating and modeling complex visual appearance.

Yuwen Wu is a senior technical expert at NetEase Games, mainly working on graphics and engine programming. He has been developing NetEase's in-house game engine, the Messiah Engine, for over 10 years. In addition, he also enjoys algorithms and has won two Knuth Reward Checks.

Atsushi Yoshimura is a software engineer and also a researcher at AMD. His career started as a software engineer in the field of installation and art. Although his bachelor's education was in welfare taking advantage of computer science, his current interest is toward computer graphics, especially ray-traced global illumination even including machine learning–based techniques for graphics. Currently, he develops Radeon ProRender and conducts related research. He also helped organize and co-presented a GPU programming course, "GPU Programming Primitives for Computer Graphics," at SIGGRAPH Asia 2023 with his colleagues.

Dmitrii Zhdan is a developer technology engineer at NVIDIA, where he works with various game studios to bring best rendering techniques into modern games. This role also includes research and development, and the results of this work often push rendering in games to a new level.

Made in the USA
Las Vegas, NV
28 November 2024

12834258R00340